Beginning
Access 2000
VBA

Robert Smith & David Sussman

Wrox Press Ltd. ®

Beginning Access 2000 VBA

© 1999 Wrox Press

First Published   1999
Latest Reprint   June 2001

Published by Wrox Press Ltd.
Arden House, 1102 Warwick Road, Acocks Green, Birmingham, B27 6BH, UK
Printed in USA
ISBN 1-861001-76-2

Trademark Acknowledgements

Credits

Authors
Robert Smith
David Sussman

Managing Editor
Dominic Shakeshaft

Editors
Dev Lunsford
Peter Morgan

Technical Reviewers
Jody Baty
Max Dahl
Steve Danielson
Pamela Grimm
John Harris
Brian Johnson
Ron Landers
David Liske
Arnie Rowland
Dave Rowlands
Elizabeth Seifert
Richard Ward

Cover
Andrew Guillaume
Concept by Third Wave

Design/Layout
Tony Berry
Noel Donnelly

Index
Catherine Alexander
Andrew Criddle

About the Authors

Rob Smith is Senior Consultant in charge of database and Internet development for Amethyst Group Ltd, an independent IT services and training company in Edinburgh. He has been developing with Microsoft Access since time began (i.e. November 1992). The few hours he spends away from the office are made more bearable by dreams of owning a vineyard in South Australia or watching Crystal Palace winning the F.A. Cup. (Yes, he is quite, quite mad).

David Sussman is a developer, trainer and author, living in a quiet country village in Oxfordshire, surrounded by nothing but fields and trees. One day soon he intends to stop working so hard and get some sort of social life.

Acknowledgements

Rob would like to thank a number of people who all contributed in one way or another to keeping him sane during the writing of this book. Firstly, Stephen Rice, Margaret Owen and Rob Lowe for all their hard work looking after Amethyst when I was too busy writing this book. Secondly, John de Robeck, for doing the same but also keeping my plate and, more importantly, my glass full whenever I asked (and often when I didn't). Colin Rippey, for being a tireless worker, for putting up with my musical tastes and for sharing with me his expertise in stress management. And finally, as always, Valerie, for just being Valerie (which is all I could ever want and more than I really deserve).

Dave would like to thank Anthea, who keeps trying to explain to me what deadlines are, but it never quite sinks in. Dom S, for never being fazed by anything. The editors (and everyone) at Wrox for making this such an enjoyable job. Rob also deserves huge amounts of praise, for managing to write this book as well as having a proper job - thanks mate.

Pour Jan. Un petit livre de chevet pour les froides nuits parisiennes.

Table of Contents

Table of Contents

Appendix E: Microsoft DAO 3.6 Object Library Reference   771

Introduction

Who is This Book For?

You can achieve a great deal in Access without ever knowing anything about programming at all. As Access matures it becomes easier and easier to do complex tasks, as more and more wizards take control for you. However, if you're serious about database development, you'll want to endow your application with that added professional feel and functionality, and for this you really need to know how to use code. That is what Beginning Access 2000 VBA Programming will teach you.

The focus of the book is the programming language that underlies Access 2000 – Visual Basic for Applications, or VBA for short. This is the language that is now standard across the Office suite of applications, and if you learn to program in VBA in Access, you'll find you have an easy ride when it comes to working with the other Office products and, of course, Microsoft's popular programming language – Visual Basic.

There are two types of user in particular that will benefit from this book:

❑   You have some experience of Access, but have not begun to learn Visual Basic for Applications. You have spent a bit of time familiarizing yourself with the different Access objects – tables, forms, queries, reports (and, perhaps, Data Pages) – and may have used macros to achieve a little automation. You have not really programmed before, but are keen to learn how to tap the power that VBA offers.

❑   You have programmed a little with another language, perhaps Visual Basic or some of the Scripting languages (such as VBScript or JScript), and need a primer into VBA and its use within Access. Even if you know a little VBA you'll find plenty in the book to keep you occupied.

What's Covered in This Book

Beginning Access 2000 VBA Programming covers everything that you need to gain the confidence to go away and experiment on your own. Programming is an art and cannot simply be taught – like anything worth doing in life, it's a question of 'practice makes perfect'. This book will provide the necessary information to get you up and running and will show you enough interesting and practical examples to whet your appetite and ensure that your experiences of VBA don't end with the last page of the book.

We'll start by looking at some of the major changes in Access 2000 that affect you as a programmer. This will help to explain some of the directions we've taken in the book. Chapter 2 will then take off to introduce application design, and then explain the sample databases included on the CD-ROM that comes with the book, posing some problems that need solving to turn your application from adequate to great. As you'll see, the only way to get what you want from the database is to use VBA.

We'll move on to explain about **event-driven** programming, and show how Access fits into that, and what it really means in programming terms. We'll look at the events that Access responds to, and look at the fundamentals of programming, introducing you to the coding environment and basic principles such as variables, controls structures, data types, and procedures. We'll also look at objects within Access, which will help you to get the best from your code.

Once we have some solid foundations to build on, we'll start to look at how to use VBA in a more practical sense, looking at how to create recordsets and other objects at run-time, how to import and export data, and how to work with reports. We'll also look at some issues that you must bear in mind when programming any application – one of which is errors, including what they are, how to find them, how to correct them, and most importantly, how to prevent them.

In the later part of the book, we'll take a look at some more advanced topics, such as object orientation, working in a multi-user environment, using libraries and add-ins, and using automation with other applications. Finally, we'll look at applying the finishing touches, to add that final polish to your application.

What's Not Covered in This Book

ActiveX Data Objects (ADO) is the new data access strategy from Microsoft, and despite it being the default for Access 2000 databases, we are not covering it in detail in this book. This is primarily a book about Visual Basic for Applications, and there are some technical reasons why ADO doesn't achieve what we need it to for this book. So, while we do mention ADO in a few places, we are using the existing Data Access Objects (DAO) that have been a part of Access for many years. There are a few examples comparing DAO and ADO in Appendix B.

What You Need To Use This Book

Apart from a bit of time and dedication to learn, you'll need access to a PC running Windows 95, Windows 98, or Windows NT, and a copy of Access 2000. For some of the chapters a copy of Microsoft Excel, Microsoft Word, and Microsoft Outlook are required for some of the samples.

The CD-ROM

The CD-ROM that accompanies this book contains all of the sample databases from the book, as well as worked solutions for the exercises we pose at the end of each chapter. You'll need approximately 20Mb to copy all of the sample databases, although to complete the exercises throughout the book, you'll generally only be working in one database.

The Ice Cream Shop

The sample database for this book is built around a fictitious wholesale supplier of ice cream. All of the samples will be built around this sample database, showing you how to create new objects, as well as extend existing ones.

There is a database for each chapter, which contains all of the cumulative code up to the end of that chapter. So, the database `IceCream5.mdb`, contains all of the code and samples for Chapters 1 to 5. If you worked through the samples in Chapter 6, the database would then be the same as `IceCream6.mdb`. There is nothing in the samples that isn't included in the chapters. There is a single database called `IceCream.mdb`, which should be your starting point, and you should use this database for all of your work. As you reach the end of a chapter your database will be the same as the database for that chapter.

Chapter 18 doesn't change the Ice Cream database at all, as all changes are put in a new database, `Performance.mdb`. This is because they don't explicitly relate to the Ice Cream database and it keeps things nice and tidy.

There is also a database called `Solutions.mdb`, which contains the solutions to the end of chapter exercises. These solutions are documented in Exercise Solutions.

Conventions

We use a number of different styles of text and layout in the book to help differentiate between the various styles of information. Here are examples of the styles we use along with explanations of what they mean:

Try It Out – Conventions

The Try It Out is an exercise you should work through, following the text in the book.

1. They usually consist of a set of steps.

2. Each step has a number.

3. Follow the steps through with your copy of the database.

Introduction

How it Works

After each Try It Out, the code you've typed in will be explained in detail.

Background information will look like this

> **Not-to-be missed information looks like this.**

Bulleted information is shown like this:

- ❑ **Important Words** have a special font.
- ❑ Words that appear on the screen (such as menu options) are a similar font to the one used on the screen, e.g. the File menu
- ❑ Keys that you press on the keyboard, like *Ctrl* and *Enter*, are in italics.
- ❑ All file names are in this style: IceCream.mdb.
- ❑ Any code fragments within normal text are highlighted in a special font.

Code shown for the first time, or other relevant code, is in the following format:

```
Dim intVariable As Integer

intVariable = 10
Debug.Print intVariable
```

while less important code, or code that you have seen before, looks like this:

```
intVariable = 10
```

Tell Us What You Think

We have tried to make this book accurate, enjoyable and worthwhile. But what really matters is whether or not you find it useful, and we would appreciate your views and comments. You can return the reply paid card at the back of the book, or contact us at:

feedback@wrox.com
http://www.wrox.com
or
http://www.wrox.co.uk

Access 2000 – A Long Journey

Access 2000 has a great deal of importance for Microsoft. There have been some major changes made to the product that might make you think more about how you develop your Access applications, and the introduction of some new technologies could confuse many people.

In this short introductory chapter, we're going to look at the following topics:

- ❑ The structure of the book, especially with regard to the data access methods we opted for.
- ❑ New features of Access 2000 and the future of the product.

This will give you a clear picture of the features of Access 2000, and why we've written the book in the way we have. We want you to understand the reasons behind our decision not to just dive straight into all the new features Access has to offer. We also want to reinforce the point that the book is designed to help you learn how to use VBA, and for that reason we're not interested in anything that would complicate matters.

The Book Structure

We had a quandary while planning this book, because we were initially unsure as to which direction we should take. Should we stick with the older features of Access, or radically change our ideas to implement the new features? After all, this is a VBA book, and VBA hasn't fundamentally changed since the previous version. But VBA is just the tool used to perform more complex tasks, such as making decisions within the application and accessing data in Access tables.

We found the decision of which data access method to use caused the big problem, because Access 2000 comes with a new method (ADO), although the old method (DAO) is still available for use. Should we switch to this new method, or stick with the old one? You might think that the obvious solution would be to use the new method, but this is not necessarily the case because of the way that Access 2000 can be used. The two main ways to use Access 2000 are

- ❑ As a stand-alone database. This is probably the most common usage, and in most ways remains unchanged from the previous version of Access. The new data access method can be used here, but the old one works better.

❑   As the front-end to a client/server database. Although this was possible in previous versions of Access, it's been taken a step further with Access 2000, to provide a better client/server environment. Only the new data access method works in this situation.

If we went for the second of these options, we'd have to open up a huge area that really would take too much time to study. The design of specialized client/server applications takes whole books in itself. And then there's the back-end database to think of.... We'd have to teach you how to use that, and that would really take a while! We'd be looking at a huge text, even before we started showing you how to use VBA.

So we agreed that to teach you what you really need to know, we would concentrate on using Access as a stand-alone database, and that means using the older technology (**Data Access Objects**, or **DAO**). Now don't get us wrong – this technology isn't suddenly redundant, and won't disappear from view, but it's not what Microsoft are pushing as the latest and greatest (**ActiveX Data Objects**, or **ADO**). The trouble with ADO is that it doesn't sit too well using Access in a stand-alone mode. Sure, it works, but it's not particularly well integrated, and doesn't fit together comfortably. That means that we'd be teaching you ways to get around problems with the technology, rather than teaching you how to use it.

So what we've decided is to stick with the tried and tested DAO methods, which is how Access has been used for years. Even though it's not using the latest technology, everything you learn in this book will stand you in good stead for the future, so that switching to the new way of working can be achieved with a minimum of effort. A discussion of these two data access technologies can be found at the start of Chapter 7.

We're not going to explain these data access technologies here, as they are covered in detail in Chapter 7, but it's important to explain something early on, so you understand *exactly* what we are covering in this book. It's important to make this clear – this book does not cover ActiveX Data Objects (ADO) in any detail. In this book, we are trying to teach Visual Basic for Applications (VBA), and for that reason we've kept the database design simple. This means using MDB files (as in previous versions of Access) rather than any of the new client/server design features, which really pose too many problems for a beginner trying to learn a new language. Since we are using MDB files, the use of Data Access Objects (DAO) is much more efficient than ADO.

Access 2000

The current release of Access has seen huge changes and suggests that the positioning of Access as being only a desktop database is no longer true. Let's briefly look at some of the new features, so you can see what's happening to Access as a product.

Data Stores

A data store is... well, um, a store of data. Since we're talking about Access, you'll probably realize that Access is itself a data store. After all, that's what databases are for.

Previous versions of Access gave us the MDB file, which contains all of the items that make up an Access database. We could also use other sources of data in addition to the MDB file, such as text files, spreadsheets, or larger databases such as SQL Server, but this was never really part of the original design goals for Access. It was more a feature allowing access to this other data.

Access 2000 has the ability to use not only its own MDB file, but also an external database as its main data store, opening up the world of client/server. The three types of external data store you can use are:

❑ The Integrated Store, which ships with Office 2000

❑ SQL Server 6.5

❑ SQL Server 7.0

It's important to note that the Integrated Store is not the same as JET, the format used by an MDB file. It's called MSDE (Microsoft Database Engine), and is in fact a version of SQL Server 7.0 that will run on Windows 9x as well as Windows NT. This is not a full version of SQL Server 7.0, so you don't get the Enterprise Manager, but just the database engine (as well as a few utilities to help with connectivity and data transformation).

Now the important thing is not to panic when reading this. Access still exists as a stand-alone product, using JET, and you can still do the front-end/back-end split with JET that you did in the past. The existing MDB file is the default database format, and the one we will be covering in this book.

Access Projects

In previous versions of Access, everything was usually held within a single MDB file, because that was its main data store. You could split the database apart, storing the data in one file, and the forms, queries, reports, code, and so on in another, but they were both still Access databases (MDB files) in their own right.

Access 2000 introduces the concept of Projects, which allows you to use Access as the front-end interface to one of the data stores discussed above. In this case there is an Access Project file (with an extension of ADP), which contains the forms, reports, macros, modules, and data access pages. This file contains no data, and is designed specifically for client/server environments. The data, along with stored procedures and views, is stored in the data store. We won't be covering Access Projects in this book.

Data Access Pages

A Data Access Page is a Web page specifically designed for publishing Access data to the Internet. The previous version of Access allowed only HTML, IDC, or ASP files, but Data Access Pages are Internet Explorer 5-specific pages with embedded DHTML and ActiveX controls.

This technique makes it suitable for intranet situations where you control a database and want users without Access to view the data. Previously you would have had to install Access on the client machine, or let the users use MSQuery or some other query tool. Now you can simply create a Web page using the same design environment as Access forms.

Data Access Pages are covered in Chapter 17.

Name Auto-Correct

This is a great feature for developers, as it allows you to change the names of objects, and let Access correct all other occurrences of that object name. This is particularly useful during the development cycle, when the database design might change after you have written some code.

Sub Datasheets

This is a really cool feature that acts a bit like automatic sub-forms, but for datasheets. So, when you open a table and the table has related records, you can see the related records too. This is easy to imagine if you think of a set of customers and their orders. Opening the Customers table would allow you to view the orders for any customer within the same view, just by a clicking an icon. This makes browsing sets of related data much simpler.

Programmability

This will be one feature that confuses many existing programmers, as the built-in code editor has been scrapped and replaced with the Office-wide Visual Basic Editor, the same one that is found in Word, Excel and PowerPoint. Despite the slight culture shock of moving out of the Access environment when programming, it provides a more consistent view across all applications, and allows much more interoperability within the products. You'll be using this new editor a lot as you go through the book.

For Data Access Pages, there is a Script Editor, allowing you to add VBScript or JScript to your web pages. These are programming languages specially designed for use in Web pages. This Script Editor is effectively the Visual Studio 6 code editor, and contains a superb environment for editing HTML script. We won't be covering the Script Editor, as it's really outside the scope of the book.

JET 4.0

Some time ago there were rumors that JET was not going to be enhanced at all, and that only bug fixes would be performed. This clearly isn't the case, as significant changes have happened to JET. We won't be explicitly covering all of these JET 4.0 features in the book, so we've included a brief list below:

Unicode

The first change is the implementation of full Unicode support, allowing the storage of character sets that require two bytes for each character, such as Japanese and Chinese. In previous versions of Access only one byte was used to store each character. The main reason for this is to allow Access to store foreign characters more easily.

Data Types

To ease the introduction of the MSDE and to aid compatibility with Microsoft SQL Server, the data types have been aligned with those of Microsoft SQL Server. This will make it less confusing when upsizing a database.

SQL 92

As with data types, the introduction of more SQL 92 functionality has been partly to aid the process of migrating applications to SQL Server. SQL 92 is an ANSI standard defining the SQL language, and previous versions of Access have not adhered to this closely. JET 4.0 has been enhanced to conform more closely to this standard. This is a good feature, because most databases conform to the ANSI standard, thus making it easier to transfer SQL code between databases.

The American National Standards Institute (ANSI) is a body that produces, and controls, many different standards across the world.

Locking

To avoid the possibility that two users could modify the same data in different ways at the same time, Access locks data while it is being edited. Data in Access is stored in pages, where each page now contains 4K (that's 4096 bytes). Previous versions of Access could only lock, at minimum, a single page (then 2K) of data at a time. With the increase in page size, it was decided that this might cause too much of an inconvenience, so row-level locking has been (optionally) introduced. By default, when you modify a record, only that record will be locked.

In addition, automatic lock promotion allows Access to automatically escalate page locks (if in use) to table locks if it deems necessary. This should improve performance when a large number of rows are being updated.

Users

With the introduction of ADO it is now possible to obtain a list of users currently connected to the database. This is particularly useful for maintenance situations where you need to ask users to disconnect before updating the database. ADO is briefly covered in Chapter 7, and this particular feature is covered in Chapter 14.

Replication

Another feature introduced to ease the interoperability with SQL is that of replication. Previous versions of Access have allowed bi-directional replication with other Access databases, but now this is possible with SQL Server 7.0. Only data can be replicated (not stored procedures, etc), and SQL Server must be the central replication hub, but this still allows a great deal of flexibility.

The Future

The introduction of Access Projects, using a back-end database, has moved Access from the small workgroup database into the big league of client/server development. Although JET has had some new features added, none of these are really huge reasons to switch from previous versions of Access. After all, the existing data access method hasn't changed at all, and we've already said that we are using the older methods here.

So is there any point in upgrading? Well, yes, there is, because Access has had a lot of work done on it. Admittedly, most of this is in the client/server area, but you might well find that this is the direction your projects will take in the long term. Even if your company isn't expanding, you can guarantee that the amount of data you are storing is getting bigger every day.

This release has changed the way many people perceive Access. It's not just a small, desktop database, but is now a design tool for client/server databases. And that's the way its development is probably going to go in the future. Although Microsoft have said that no more development of JET will take place, support for JET will still exist, purely because of the huge amount of code already in existence. The way forward, however, seems to be client/server, using the new data access technologies.

Summary

Hopefully this short introduction has helped you to understand why we structured the book in the way we did. We're going to be looking at programming with VBA, and to do that it's just a lot less complicated to use tried and tested technologies than it would be to go into detail about the new features Access has. The next chapter is going to introduce you to project design, and then show us why we need VBA in the first place.

Designing Applications

Access 2000 is mostly a very intuitive and easy to use application. From the early days of Access 1.0, usability has been one of the primary development focuses behind Access. In fact it was this ease of use that was a major factor in the incredible speed with which Access came to be accepted as the definitive desktop database development tool.

But Access has always appealed to a wider audience than simply end users and inexperienced developers. Behind its ease of use, Access has always provided a very powerful database and application development tool – and the latest release of Access has extended this power even further with the introduction of features such as Access Database Projects (ADPs), Data Access Pages (DAPs) and the integration of VBA 6 as its programming language.

In this chapter, we introduce the application we will be developing throughout the course of this book. After that we'll contrast the differences between macros and VBA, and highlight one of the limitations you will encounter using macros.

But before any of this, let's begin by defining an Access Application, and take you through the design processes you ought to consider before you even begin coding.

What Is An Access Application?

One way of defining an Access application is to describe it as...

A collection of database and code objects that co-operate to perform a common task or set of related tasks to achieve a specific objective (typically business-related)

When you create a new database file (.mdb file) in Microsoft Access 2000, the first thing that you see is the database window. This is a container that will eventually hold a wide variety of different objects. Tables will be used to store data; queries will be designed to retrieve data in meaningful ways; forms, reports and data access pages will all be used to display the results of those queries in ways that users can understand; and macros and VBA modules will provide the logic which 'glues' the whole application together.

If you use Access 2000 to create a project (.adp file) instead, then the database window will also expose additional server-side objects (such as database diagrams and stored procedures), which also go to make up the application.

All of these objects can play an important role in providing the functionality of the end product – whether it is hosted solely in an Access database or uses a client-server database project.

The aim of this book is to illustrate the important role played by Visual Basic for Applications in orchestrating these objects; in binding them together through the use of logic to control workflow and to implement specific business rules; and in turning a collection of individual objects into a coherent and effective application. Yes, we want to teach you how to use VBA, but to do that without first telling you how to design an application would be irresponsible.

The Development Process

There are many skills involved in the development and delivery of successful Microsoft Access 2000 applications. The database designers need to be able to understand the principles of relational database design, so that they can design the tables that will hold the data and the relationships between those tables. The application developers need to have a feel for visual design, so that the forms they design for users of the application to interact with will be intuitive and easy to use. They will also need to understand both SQL (Structured Query Language) and VBA so that they can write queries and procedures that not only return the correct data or perform the required task, but also do so quickly and efficiently.

There are other less technical (but no less complex) skills to master. Analysts need to be able to understand the business requirements of the users for whom the application is being designed, and to translate these requirements into a design specification from which the developers can work. Technical documenters need to be able to articulate how the application works, to anticipate confusions that users might experience and to clearly express their thoughts in documentation that is both accessible and informative. And project managers need to know how to monitor progress and track resource usage to ensure that the application is delivered on time and within budget.

Sometimes, if the application being developed is large-scale or complex, then there will be many different people involved in the application development lifecycle. Some will be responsible purely for analysis or design, others will work solely on designing queries or developing forms, and yet others will be responsible for other tasks such as migrating legacy data into the Access database or producing user documentation. But at other times, particularly if the application is less complex, or if resources (such as money or people) are scarcer, then it is not uncommon for many of these tasks to be undertaken by individuals. Indeed, in many situations, a single person can be responsible for the entire analysis and development process.

Irrespective of the number of people involved, or the development methodology employed, the development lifecycle for an Access application will typically involve the following steps:

Analysis ➔ Design ➔ Coding ➔ Testing ➔ Documentation ➔ Acceptance ➔ Review

In practice, however, these steps do not rigidly follow one after another. It is beyond the scope of this book to enter into a detailed discussion of different project lifecycle plans. However, it is undoubtedly true that the speed with which Access forms and reports can be produced makes Access an excellent tool for using in a more iterative lifecycle model. In such a situation, the lifecycle would look more like this.

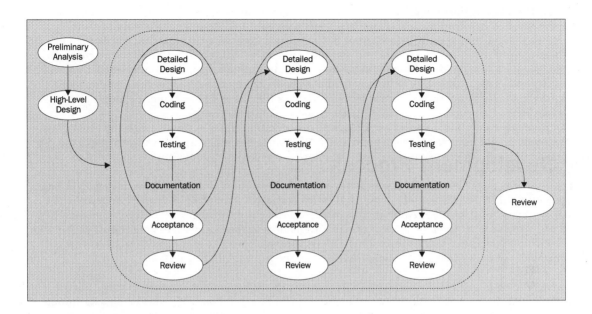

The Analysis Phase

Irrespective of the type of project lifecycle mode, the first stage is inevitably one of analysis. Without adequate analysis you will not be able to determine what the user wants from the application, the technical infrastructure within which the application will be implemented and the constraints imposed by the data with which you will be working.

Requirements Analysis

The starting point for creating any successful Access application is to have a clear understanding of what the users of an application want out of it. You need to know this before you can even start to think about how to design any solution. The kind of questions you will need to ask in this stage include, among others:

- ❑ What is the business process we are trying to automate?
- ❑ What benefit is the new application designed to achieve? How will we measure the benefit?
- ❑ Do we simply want to automate the existing process, or restructure the process and automate it?
- ❑ Will the application have to interoperate with other existing or planned systems or processes?
- ❑ What volume of data will the application be expected to handle?
- ❑ How many users will use the system concurrently/in total?
- ❑ What is the anticipated mix of insert and update activity compared to query and reporting activity?

The problem is that the only people who can answer these questions are the customers who will use the finished application, and sometimes it can prove difficult to get answers out of them. It might be that the demands of their current business are so pressing that they have little time to answer questions about some future application. It might be that the sensitivities of internal office politics will make them unwilling to be too helpful in designing an application in which they feel they have too little ownership. Or it may be that they are trying to be helpful but just don't know the answers to these questions, because it is something they have never thought about.

Requirements analysis is a skilled art and many organizations fail to appreciate the fact that good developers do not necessarily make good analysts. In fact, in many ways, developers make the worst analysts. By their very nature, good developers are constantly looking for solutions to problems. Someone mentions a business requirement and you can almost hear the cogs whirring in their brains as their eyes glaze over and they start working out how they will produce a solution to that requirement. That is not what you want from an analyst. You want an analyst to be able to take an objective look at the requirement expressed by the user, to check that they understand it correctly, to ask what the relevance of this requirement is to the business, to determine benchmarks by which the successful implementation of the requirement can be judged and to express that requirement in a way that other parties involved in the project will understand.

A variety of tools and methods are available to assist the requirements analysis process. For example, JAD (Joint Application Development) is a technique that assists requirements definition by bringing all of the various parties who are interested in the development together in intense off-site meetings to focus on the business problem to be solved rather than worrying about specific technical issues.

Whether you use such techniques is up to you. What is important is that you value the requirements analysis process. This phase of a project is so important because it is the fundamental mechanism for defining both the scope of the project and the critical success factors that show when the project has been achieved its requirements. It forms the basis for the contract between the users and the developers and is the touchstone to be used when resolving conflict or confusion later on in the project lifecycle.

Ironically, the importance of sound requirements analysis is most clearly seen in its absence. When requirements are not properly defined or documented, one of two consequences almost inevitably follow. Either the requirements remain unmodified, with the result that the application fails to achieve its intended objectives; or the requirements are modified later in the development cycle. Late changes such as these can have a huge impact on project costs as their effects 'ripple' out and affect other areas such as documentation, design, coding, testing, personnel assignments, sub-contractor requirements etc. Indeed, some studies indicate that such changes can be 50 to 200 times more expensive than they would have been if they had been made at the appropriate time!

Technical Analysis

As well as determining the nature of the solution required by the users of the application, it is also necessary to determine the technical infrastructure that will support this solution. The types of questions posed are ones such as these:

❑ What operating system will the application run on?

❑ Are 16-bit and 32-bit versions of the application required?

    ❑   What is the specification (i.e. in terms of processor, memory, disk space) of the machines that the application will run on?

    ❑   What type of network will connect the computers? Will lack of available bandwidth prove a problem?

    ❑   What security policy will the application need to operate?

    ❑   What type of fault-tolerance or recovery issues will need to be considered?

The purpose of the technical analysis should be to produce an application architecture and implementation framework within which the resultant application will nestle. Again, it may well turn out that developers are not the best people to undertake this type of analysis. Technical analysis requires a good understanding of networking, security, and technical issues and these skills may not be present in all of your developers.

Data Analysis

By this stage, you should have a contract in place that defines what the application is meant to provide and you will probably have a good idea of the technical infrastructure within which the design will be implemented. The next stage is to analyze the data that you will be working with. Now, I must confess that I frequently find this task less than stimulating, but I know that it is imperative if I am to achieve a sound database design. As tedious as data analysis is, it sure beats the pants off rewriting an application because a fundamental misunderstanding of the underlying data only comes to light two weeks before the project is due to be delivered.

Now this is not a primer on data analysis. Although simple enough in theory, data analysis can be quite complex in practice and if you are new to the subject, you would do well to get some training in this discipline. If nothing else, you should make sure that you understand the basics of **normalization**, as this is fundamental to the data analysis and design process for systems that will use relational databases such as Access. The purpose of normalization is the elimination of dependencies in our data. This, in turn, should realize the twin benefits of reducing redundancy and minimizing opportunities for inconsistency being introduced into our data.

> *One of the most authoritative discussions of the theory of normalization can be found in 'An Introduction to Database Systems' by CJ Date (Addison-Wesley, 1995, ISBN 0-201-54329-X). A less theoretical (and thus much more accessible) approach can be found in Database Design for Mere Mortals: A Hands-On Guide to Database Design by Michael J. Hernandez (Addison-Wesley, 1997, ISBN 0-201-69471-9).*

The principles behind sound data analysis are straightforward enough:

    ❑   Identify all of the data entities you will be dealing with

    ❑   Establish the attributes of these entities

    ❑   Define the relationships between these entities

    ❑   Document, document, document…

As with the requirements analysis and the technical analysis, a variety of methods and tools can be employed to assist in the task of data analysis. Whichever you choose to employ, I would encourage you to bear the following two principles in mind.

First, when selecting a tool, it is paramount that you choose one that allows you to clearly document the results of the analysis in a format that everyone involved can understand. Use diagrams to illustrate the relationships between your entities, by all means, but don't forget the detail (however boring it might be to gather!). Complex entity relationship diagrams may look very impressive and have a professional look about them, but if you can't use your documentation to tell you whether Widget Part Codes are 8 or 9 characters long, then you are going to struggle.

Second, it is very seldom that I have come across data analysis that has suffered from being **too** detailed. Document everything – datatypes, field lengths, allowable values, calculated values – get it all down on paper and do so while it is fresh in your mind. If there is something you are not sure about, don't guess. Go back, check it out and write it down. The temptation is always there to wrap up the data analysis early and get on with the fun part of the project (design and development). Resist the temptation. You'll thank yourself for it later on.

Design and Coding

So then, now that the analysis is out of the way, it's time to get on with coding. Right? Wrong!!! As tempting as it might be to just plunge in and start coding straight away, you first need to spend some time deciding on an appropriate design for the application. One of the chief aims of the design process is to establish the blueprints from which the application can be built. A few of the issues that you will need to consider when designing the solution are:

- Data Storage / Location
- Import / Export Mechanisms
- Error Handling
- Portability Issues
- Performance Considerations
- Calculation Methods

But design is not just about establishing an immutable set of blueprints. Successful applications are normally those where the application designers have designed for change.

Designing for Change

The concept of "Designing for Change" was first discussed by David Parnas in the early 1970's. It is a principle that recognizes the fact that, however good the analysis has been, there will frequently occur during the lifetime of a project a number of influences that will necessitate change to occur after the initial design has been completed. It might be a change in the legal or business environment in which the customers operate, a change in available technology, or simply a change in understanding on the part of either the customer or the developer. The purpose of designing for change is to ensure that these changes can be accommodated into the project with the minimum possible disruption or delay.

Three of the most important techniques involved in designing for change are described below:

Identify Volatile Areas

Some issues are more liable to change than others during a development project. These include business rules, file formats, sequences in which items will be processed and any number of other difficult design areas. The first step is to identify all such volatile areas and document them.

Use Information Hiding

Once these issues have been listed, you can employ information hiding. The principle here is to wrap up these volatile issues in a module or procedure that hides the complexity or volatility of the processes involved. These modules or procedures should have an interface that can remain the same, irrespective of any changes that may occur within the module or procedure as a result of any of the influences we identified earlier. If a change occurs, it should only affect that module or procedure. Other modules that interact with it should not need to be aware of the fact that anything has changed.

For example, you might be designing an application that is used for sending out pre-renewal reminder notices to customers prior to the expiry of their insurance policies. Perhaps a business rule states that pre-renewal notices are to be sent out 2 months before expiry. This is just the type of rule that could easily change and a good design will account for this. Accordingly, a procedure could be written which encapsulated that rule and which was invoked whenever various parts of the application needed to know when the reminder should be sent. Changes to the business rule would only need to be incorporated in a single procedure, the procedure would still be invoked in the same way and yet the effects of the change would be available throughout the application. We will look at this subject in more detail when we examine the use of classes in Access in Chapter 13.

Employ a Change Plan

As well as information hiding, there are other techniques that can assist in reducing the impact of change and these should be prescribed in a change plan. For example, the change plan might specify that:

- ❑ Named constants should be used wherever possible in place of hard coded values

- ❑ Settings and configuration options should be stored in the Registry rather than hard-coded within the application itself

- ❑ Generic and widely used processes should be identified and grouped together in modules, separate from code with specialized functionality only called by specific parts of an application

One of the best ways to determine which elements to incorporate into a change plan is to perform post-implementation reviews just after a project has been delivered (or post-mortems if they don't get that far!). Identify what changed during the project lifecycle, what impact that change had and how the impact of that change could have been lessened. Then put that knowledge into your next change plan and make sure you don't make the same mistake twice!

Coding

Once your design is complete, you can start to code. That's the part of the process that we will be examining in most detail throughout the rest of this book. We will start by looking at the specifics of the VBA language and the structure of VBA procedures and modules. Then we will look at the Access object model and how this can be manipulated in code. After a short look at some more advanced programming techniques, we will look at how to handle errors that might occur in our application, how to make the best use of class modules, libraries and add-ins, and how to optimize the performance of our application. We will also look at some of the issues we need to be aware of if our application is being used in a multi-user environment and how we can bring some of the power of the Internet to our Access application. Finally, we will look at the finishing touches we can apply to round out our application and give it a more professional look and feel.

Testing

There are a number of quality assurance practices that you can apply to your project, but by far the most basic is testing. This involves unit testing (or component testing) where the developer verifies that the code he or she has written works correctly; system testing where someone checks that the entire application works together as expected; and acceptance testing, where the users of the application check that the results that the application produces are those they desire (or, at least, that they are those they asked for in the first place!).

The purpose of testing is to break code; to determine ways of making an application misbehave; to expose flaws in either the design or execution of the development process. For this reason, many developers dislike the testing phase (in the same way that many authors dislike the editing phase). If you have spent endless weeks working late to get a tough reporting module finished, if you have missed the ball game for the last four weeks in a row trying to get that import routine to work, if you couldn't make the Christmas party because you were wrestling with a suite of reports that you had to finish, then it is unlikely that you will approach the testing phase with anything other than fear and loathing.

The problem is that testing has a propensity for delivering bad news at the wrong time. The solution is to allow plenty of time for testing, to test early in the development cycle and to build plenty of time for re-working code after the testing has completed. Being told that a routine you have written does not produce the right results is seldom welcome news to any developer, but it is a lot easier to bear if the developer is told this early on and knows that there is plenty of time to correct the offending code. Test early and allow for re-writes!

It also bears mentioning that a proper test plan is essential for both system testing and user acceptance testing and the basis for this test plan should be the documentation that was produced during the requirements analysis stage. In particular, the test plan should define not just what is to be tested, but also what results the application should generate in response to that testing.

> *One particularly effective technique that is growing more and more popular is the use of "Use Cases". These provide a method for describing the behavior of the application from a user's standpoint by identifying actions and reactions. For more information on how to produce Use Cases, you might want to have a look at Jake Sturm's VB6 UML Design and Development, ISBN 1-861002-51-3, from Wrox Press.*

Documentation

Documentation is a bit like ironing. It's one of those things you have to do, but I have yet to meet anyone who enjoys doing it. It's one of those things that we all know we should do, but we all find boring. It's not surprising. I enjoy playing soccer, but I would soon get bored if I had to write a detailed game report every time I played, explaining what tactics we employed, why we employed them, when we scored, and so on. It's the same with documenting development projects. For most developers, the fun is in creating the solution and putting it into action. Writing it up is major-league boredom…

Yes, I know it is important. I know that I am as likely to benefit from it as any one else when I revisit my code later. I know that the users have paid for it! I know it makes the difference between a good application and a great application. That's why I do it and why I make sure that everyone working with me does it and does it well. But I am not going to pretend for a moment that I enjoy it!

Acceptance

Ah, the bliss! It's all over and the users love the application you have written for them. Great! If you have any sense, you will seize the moment and make sure that three things happen.

First, get the users to sign off the project. If you have drawn up a comprehensive requirements definition and have met all of the success factors identified by the users at the start of the project, this should be a formality. But it is no less an important step for all that.

Second, get the users to tell their colleagues about the new application they are using. Many users have very short memories, and it won't be long before the users forget just how bad the manual processes they relied on were before you wrote this application for them and just what a difference this application makes. Get them to sing your praises while they are still hooked. That's when you will get the best recommendations, whether you are collecting them for your company's marketing brochure or for your own personnel review (and, hopefully, pay rise) in three months' time.

Finally, get the users to start thinking about the next release. Some features might have been axed because there wasn't time to implement them; others might have been identified too late to make it into this release; and others might have always been destined for future releases. Once you are convinced that the users love the product you have given them, remind them about what it doesn't do… yet!

Review

The final stage is the post-implementation review. This is the point where you look back at the project and decide what worked and what didn't, what caused problems and how those problems could have been avoided or their impacts minimized. Did you hit all of your deadlines? Did all of the intended functionality make it into the final product? How are relations with the customer at the end of it all? What state are your developers in at the end of it all? Given the opportunity, would you do it all again?

The purpose of the post-implementation review is not just to give everyone a chance to whine and moan about what went wrong. Instead, the purpose is to identify the changes that need to be made to your project methodology and practices to make sure that the same problems don't happen again next time. At the same time, it is an opportunity to identify the successes and to make sure that the benefits of these can be reaped by future projects.

A final benefit of conducting post-implementation reviews is that it gives an appropriate opportunity for recognizing the efforts and contributions of everyone who worked on the project. Sincere praise in response to specific achievements is essential to the self-respect of individual developers and the continued morale of the team as a whole.

Further Reading

OK, that's enough for now on the theory behind designing and delivering software projects. If you want to learn some more about this subject there is ample reading material available, but perhaps one of the most interesting books on this subject is "Clouds to Code" (Wrox Press, 1998, ISBN 1-861000-95-2) in which Jesse Liberty documents the design and delivery of a real project with no holds barred. But this is where we leave behind the theory. From now on, this book will be a hands-on guide with real code examples for you to try out yourself and as we go through the book, we will rapidly find that we are building up a fully functional Access application.

The Ice Cream Shop Application

Once we have completed the design phase of our project, we should be in a position to answer the two following questions:

❑   What data items (or entities) and application objects will we need?

❑   How should these entities and objects fit together?

This book is not about how to design the data items and other application objects that make up the application. We are assuming that you know enough about tables, forms, reports and queries from your previous exploration of Access. This book is about how you use Visual Basic for Applications (VBA) to control the way that these objects interoperate as part of a larger system. In one sense, VBA can be thought of as the 'glue' that holds the whole application together.

The best way to understand how VBA fits in is, of course, not through theory but through practice. In the rest of this chapter, we will run the process of starting to create an application – the Ice Cream Shop database that accompanies this book. At a certain point we will hit a brick wall, when we try to automate our application and get it to display some intelligence. We'll then look at the two options available to us for solving the problem: VBA or macros. And we will look at why VBA is often the best and sometimes the only satisfactory choice.

You may find that this section covers a lot of familiar territory. However, if you do take the time to read it, it will acquaint you with the structure of the Ice Cream Shop database so that, when the crunch comes, and we have to use VBA, we will have a familiar database structure to work with.

Designing the Ice Cream Shop Database

As its name suggests, the Ice Cream Shop database is an application that has been designed to track stock and sales for an ice cream wholesaler called Dave and Rob's Ice Cream Shop. The requirements analysis we conducted indicated to us that the primary purpose of the database is to store information about the following things:

- ❑ Stock carried by the Ice Cream Shop
- ❑ Orders placed by companies
- ❑ Customer and supplier details

Our analysis has also indicated that ease of data entry and maintenance is a key requirement for the application and that the forms used by the staff at the shop must be intuitive and simple to use. In fact, it is this ease of use issue that will provide our first requirement for using VBA.

We have also conducted the appropriate technical analysis, which indicates that Access 2000 is an appropriate application development tool for the delivery of this database solution (which is just as well, otherwise this would be a very short book!).

Our data analysis has indicated that there are five primary entities:

- ❑ Suppliers
- ❑ Customer Companies
- ❑ Ice Creams
- ❑ Ingredients
- ❑ Sales

The four key processes that indicate the relationships between the entities are as follows:

- ❑ Ice Creams are sold to Customer Companies
- ❑ Each Ice Cream is composed of one or more Ingredients
- ❑ Each Ingredient can be used in one or more Ice Creams
- ❑ Ingredients are purchased from Suppliers

A more detailed analysis has revealed the attributes of the five entities that we need to record and our preliminary database design looks like this:

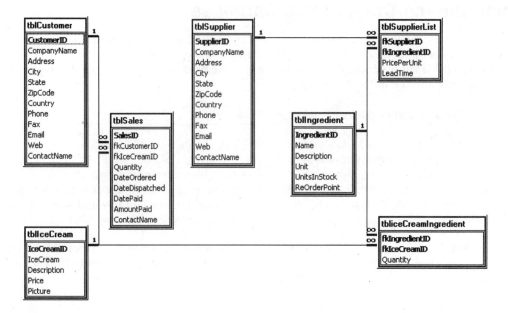

As you can see from the database diagram above, five tables have been created to represent the five basic entities identified in the data analysis:

tblSupplier	*represents*	the Suppliers entity
tblCustomer	*represents*	the Customers entity
tblIceCream	*represents*	the Ice Creams entity
tblIngredient	*represents*	the Ingredients entity
tblSales	*represents*	the Sales entity

One-to-many relationships between the entities have been denoted by creating straightforward one-to-many relationships between the tables.

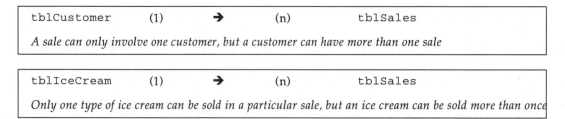

tblCustomer   (1)   →   (n)   tblSales

A sale can only involve one customer, but a customer can have more than one sale

tblIceCream   (1)   →   (n)   tblSales

Only one type of ice cream can be sold in a particular sale, but an ice cream can be sold more than once

Many-to-many relationships have been handled by creating two intermediate tables (tblIceCreamIngredient and tblSupplierList) and placing one-to-many relationships on either side of the intermediate table.

tblIceCream (1) ➔ (n) tblIceCreamIngredient (n) ⬅ (1) tblIngredient

An ice cream is composed of many ingredients and the same ingredient can be used in many ice creams

---

tblSupplier (1) ➔ (n) tblSupplierList   (n) ⬅ (1) tblIngredient

A supplier can provide many ingredients and the same ingredient could be provided by many suppliers

> *This use of intermediate tables is the standard way in which we join two tables together when the two tables have a many-to-many relationship. It's part of a process called normalization, which is a series of steps you go through to make sure your database is designed correctly. This process is really beyond the scope of this book, but there are plenty of books specializing in it. One such book is (as we've mentioned earlier) 'Database Design for Mere Mortals', Michael J. Hernandez, Addison-Wesley, ISBN 0-201-69471-9.*

Typical Dilemmas Regarding Data Storage

A few features of this database structure are worthy of note. Firstly, note the duplication of the ContactName attribute in the tblSupplier, tblCustomer and tblSales tables. This is deliberate and caters for the fact that although there is one primary contact for each supplier and for each customer; the Ice Cream Shop also wants to be able to assign separate contacts to individual sales.

Secondly, note the fact that the tblSupplier and tblCustomer tables have identical structures. Whenever we see this in a database structure it should alert us to the fact that what we have represented as two discrete entities might instead be represented as a single entity. So what is it that differentiates a supplier from a customer? Obviously, we buy from suppliers and customers buy from us. But is that sufficient reason for treating them as separate entities? After all, what happens if a supplier is also a customer? If this were to occur, and we were maintaining separate tblSupplier and tblCustomer tables, then changes to, say, the address of the company involved would necessitate a change to both the tblSupplier and tblCustomer tables.

A better alternative might be to combine the two tables into a generic tblCompany table.

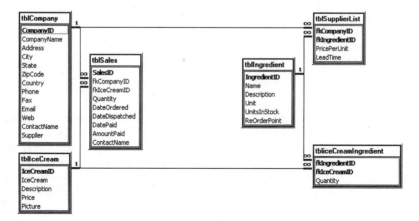

This is actually the database design that has been employed in the Ice Cream Shop database that accompanies this book. The `tblCompany` table now holds details of both suppliers and customers. In order to distinguish between those companies that appear in the `tblCompany` table because they are either customers or suppliers, we have added a new `Supplier` field to the table. This field has a Yes/No datatype and we will use to indicate whether the company should appear in supplier lists.

This is not the only way that we could have chosen to implement the physical design of the database. There is often no one correct database design. A fully normalized design might please the relational database theorists, but they are not the ones who will have to maintain the database or account for its performance in a production environment. Database design, as with most aspects of system design and development, is all about achieving the best compromise. There is nothing inherently wrong with denormalizing a database and it can be an excellent tool for increasing query performance. However, before you decide to denormalize a database, you should ensure that it doesn't introduce any significant data anomalies and that either:

❑   it will allow you to achieve a measurable improvement in performance, with a minimal increase in administrative overhead, or

❑   it will allow you to achieve a measurable reduction in administrative overhead, with a minimal degradation of performance.

Another aspect of the `tblCompany` table that required careful consideration was the question of how to hold address information. Look at the structure of the table. The address information has been broken down into five fields (`Address`, `City`, `State`, `ZipCode`, `Country`). Why do you think this has been done, instead of holding the address in a single field? The answer is that by breaking it into five fields, we make it easier for our users to analyze their orders by city, state, zip code and country individually. This would be difficult, if not impossible, if the address were stored in a single field.

Note however, that only one field is used for the first part of the address (i.e. the lines that precede the city, state, zip code and country.)

Address:	37 Walnut Grove
City:	Nutbush
State:	Tennessee
Postcode/Zip Code:	38053
Country:	USA

Even though this first part of the address might contain more than one line (especially if the address contains a building name) we can store it in a single field, because Access allows us to store and display multi-line values in one field. We store these in one field because they logically belong together and you shouldn't need to split them up at all. Sometimes you will see databases with tables that store this part of the address in multiple fields, because the database cannot easily handle carriage returns as part of the data in a field. That's not a problem with Access though.

The other advantage with storing the first part of the address in a single field is that it makes it a lot easier to amend the address. Just imagine if you had stored the above address with a separate field for every line of the address and then had to change it to:

Address:	**Unit 17**
	37 Walnut Grove
City:	Nutbush
State:	Tennessee
Postcode/Zip Code:	38053
Country:	USA

Choosing a Storage Engine

Another choice which developers of Access 2000 applications will now need to make is which database engine will they use to store the applications data in. Traditionally, Microsoft Access has always used JET as its native database engine and, in fact, Access 2000 comes with a new version of the JET engine called JET 4.0. For the first time, however, Access developers are offered the choice of using a second desktop database engine, the Microsoft Data Engine (MSDE), derived from SQL Server 7.0.

To keep this chapter concise and to the point, we have placed the discussion of which storage engine to use in Appendix A. It is also worth reiterating at this point, that the purpose of this book is to teach how to use VBA in Access and for that reason all of the data access examples will be against JET databases.

Entering and Viewing Data

So far, we've considered the need for careful analysis and table design. But that's only the start. Now we have to consider how the users of our system are going to enter information into the tables. Of course, they could type information straight into the tables in datasheet mode, but that would be inelegant and inefficient and would make it difficult to check data entry properly. We need to put an acceptable face on our application and shield the users from the complexity of the table structure.

Designing a Form

The simplest way to create a quick-and-easy form is to use one of the Form Wizards. Using a wizard to produce a form will give you all the fields you require from one or more tables. This is great, but sometimes you'll need to add extra functionality to the form, in which case you'll have to make any additional modifications for yourself. We're going to use a Form Wizard to create one of the key forms in the application – the form for maintaining company information.

Try It Out – Creating a Form Using the AutoForm Wizard

> As we explained in the Introduction, your starting point for the Try It Out
> sections in this book is the IceCream.mdb database, found on the CD-ROM. We
> have also included on the CD partially completed databases that reflect each
> chapter's development, in case you lose your own copy, or want to jump in at a
> later chapter. The databases are numbered such that they correspond to the state
> at the end of a chapter – in other words, IceCream4 is the database you'd get when
> you'd worked through to the end of Chapter 3. We think it's better if you work
> through all the Try It Outs, though, so you can really get a feel for how
> everything works and fits together.

OK. Let's get started!

1. Load up the database file `IceCream.mdb`. In the Database window, select the Tables tab
and then the tblCompany table.

2. Select AutoF<u>o</u>rm from the <u>I</u>nsert menu, or click the down arrow next to the New Object
button on the toolbar and select AutoF<u>o</u>rm from the drop-down menu.

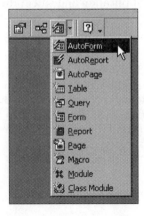

3. Access will now generate a form with all the fields from the **tblCompany** table and display the first record.

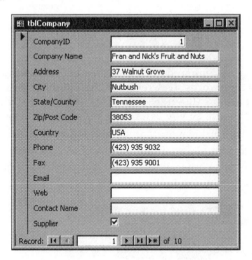

This is OK, but it's not perfect. There are several things that we can improve:

❑ The form caption is **tblCompany**, which isn't very instructive to the user.

❑ We will probably want to hide the **CompanyID** field, as it's of little relevance to the user.

❑ Some of the fields are the wrong shape. For example, we will want to make the Address text box taller, to accommodate larger addresses.

❑ The navigation buttons at the bottom of the form are a bit small and fiddly – this is a key form and must be as easy to use as possible.

So let's change the form so that it looks a little more professional.

Try It Out – Changing a Form's Appearance in Design View

1. Save the form you've just created by choosing **S**ave from the **F**ile menu or by hitting *Ctrl + S*. A dialog box will appear allowing you to type in a name for the form. Call it **frmCompany**:

2. Now switch to Design view for the newly saved form by selecting **Design View** from the **View** menu or by clicking the **Design View** button.

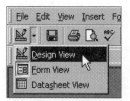

3. We can now attempt to make the changes that we highlighted earlier. To change the form's caption, you bring up the form's property sheet by double-clicking the Form Selector (the small gray box in the upper left corner of the form where the rulers meet), or by clicking the **Properties** button on the toolbar.

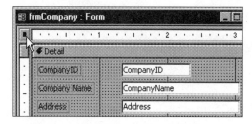

4. When the Properties window appears, make sure that the **Format** tab is selected and then change the text of the **Caption** property to **Company Details**.

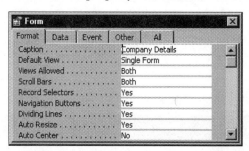

5. Next we must delete the **CompanyID** text box and its label. To do this, we must select the text box on the form by clicking it once, then hit the *Delete* key. The **CompanyID** text box and its label will be deleted:

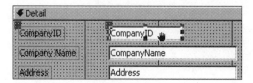

6. Next we'll change the size of the **Address** text box. To do this, first select all of the controls on the form below the **Address** text box. You can do this by dragging a rectangle around them with the primary mouse button held down or by clicking them in turn with the *Shift* key held down. Once the controls have been selected, place the mouse over one of the selected controls. The mouse pointer will turn into a small hand, indicating that the controls can be moved.

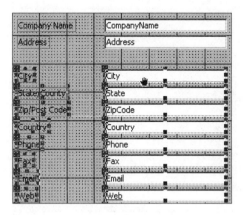

7. Hold down the primary mouse button and drag the controls down the form to leave some space for the **Address** text box, which we are going to resize.

You may have noticed that the wizard initially generated the form with just enough room for the controls. Don't worry about it, the form will automatically extend when you move the controls down.

8. Once you have created some space, resize the **Address** text box. To do this, we select the **Address** text box by clicking it and then click the resizing handle (it looks like a black square) at the bottom center of the text box. Dragging the resizing handle down will give us a taller shape for the text box.

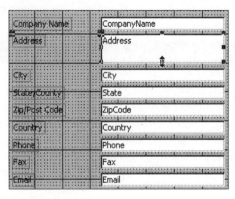

9. Finally, change the form back to Form View to see the changes you've made. You can do this by selecting Form View from the View menu or by clicking the button that has replaced the Design View button.

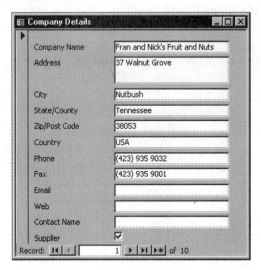

We've now made the first three of the changes we decided on and our form certainly looks a little more professional. But what about the other change? We still need to put more manageable navigation buttons on the screen. This is where things get a little more advanced!

Creating Navigation Buttons

To make the form easier to use, we can place some command buttons on the screen to replace the present navigation buttons. We can then use macros to move through the records behind the form. A macro, to remind you, is simply a stored collection of instructions that correspond to the actions that a user might carry out. So, in this case, our macro would contain the instructions to move to the next, previous, first or last records.

Of course, this book is about VBA, not macros. However, using them here will help show you their limitations.

Try It Out – Adding Simple Navigation Buttons to a Form

1. Switch back to Design view. We're going to use headers and footers, so go to the View menu and select the Form Header/Footer option. A header section and footer section will then appear on the form. We don't have to add the buttons to the footer of the form. We could add them onto the Detail section of the form instead. However, putting them on the footer keeps them in one place and we don't have to worry about them getting in the way if we decide to change around the other controls in the Detail section.

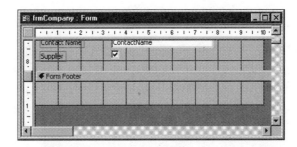

2. Next, we must remove the navigation buttons that Access supplies by default. So, click the Form Selector to bring up the form's property sheet and on the property sheet's **Format** tab, change the value of the **Navigation Buttons** property from **Yes** to **No**. You can do this by double-clicking the property value or by clicking on the arrow and selecting **No** from the drop-down list that appears.

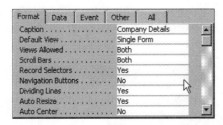

Once you have done this, you can also set the following form properties:

Scroll Bars	Neither
Record Selectors	No
Dividing Lines	No

Now you can add the first of your own navigation buttons. We'll start by creating a **Next Record** button.

3. Make sure that the toolbox is visible by clicking the **Toolbox** button on the toolbar:

4. Then, make sure the **Control Wizards** button isn't depressed (that's the one with the magic wand on it), and select the **Command Button** tool from the toolbox. This will allow us to place a command button on the form.

5. Draw the button a suitable size on the footer.

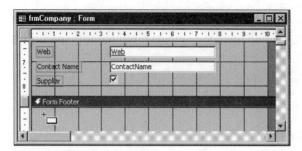

6. Now go to the property sheet and change the Name property of the button (found under the Other tab) to cmdNext and its Caption property (found under the Format tab) to Next.

7. Now we must instruct the button to display the next record whenever it is clicked. To do this, you right-click on the button and select Build Event... from the pop-up menu which appears.

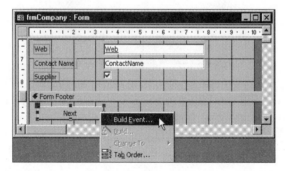

8. This will, in turn, bring up the Choose Builder dialog. For the moment, we want to use a macro, so select Macro Builder and hit the OK button.

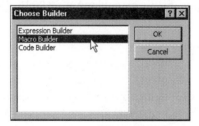

9. We've said that we want a macro behind the button, so Access now helps us to build it. It displays the macro design window and prompts us for the name that we want to give the macro. We will call it macNextButton so you should type in macNextButton and then press OK.

10. Now we get to specify the macro commands that will be carried out when we hit the command button. We want the button to make the form go to the next record. To get it to do this, you must click the down arrow in the Action column and select GoToRecord from the drop-down list that appears.

11. We then need to specify which record we want the command button to move us to. Click in the Record box in the lower pane of the screen, click the down arrow and select which record you want to go to from the drop-down list. We want to go to the next record, so make sure Next is selected. In fact, Next is the default selection in the drop-down list.

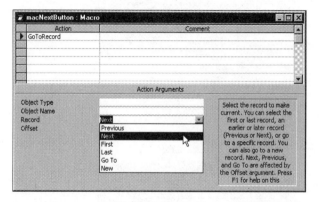

12. Now close the macro window and choose Yes when prompted to save the macro you have just created. Then change the frmCompany form to Form view and save the changes you made to it. When you open the form in form view, there should be a navigation button on it that allows you to move forward through the records in the form.

If you look at the button's properties, you will see that the name of the macro is listed in the On Click property on the Event tab. This is how Access knows to run the macro when the button is clicked. The macro name was inserted automatically into the event property because you right-clicked the button to select Build Event... and the click *event is the default event for buttons. If you had built the macro yourself, you could still make Access use it whenever you click the* cmdNext *button, but you would have to insert the macro's name manually into the On Click event property before it would work. We'll look at this whole area in a lot more detail in the next chapter.*

13. Finally, complete the form by adding navigation buttons to enable you to move to the previous, first, last and new records. You should be able to work out how to do this simply enough by referring to the steps described above.

The Finished Product

So there we have it! Your own handcrafted navigation buttons! You can customize these further if you wish – you may want to change the caption on the Next button to add a 'greater than' sign (>). You may even want to add a tooltip by modifying the ControlTipText property of each button.

You can also provide a hotkey for each of the buttons. This allows the user to activate the button from the keyboard by pressing *Alt* and a particular letter. To set this up, you simply type an ampersand (&) in the button's Caption property, before the letter that you want to activate the button. So, for example, if you typed &Next the user could select the button by pressing *Alt-N*. The hot key (in this case N) will appear underlined on the button.

Once you have added the other buttons, your form should look something similar to the one shown below.

The form looks better, but it's still not perfect. If you haven't already done so, try clicking the First button to move to the first record. Now try clicking the Previous button to move to the previous record. Obviously, there's no record previous to the first record, so an error occurs and an error message box appears.

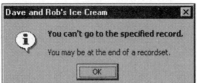

Wouldn't it be better if the buttons were intelligent and only allowed you to click them if they represented a valid choice? In other words, if you were already at the first record, the Previous button should appear grayed out or **disabled**.

Sure, you may say, but how? There doesn't appear to be any way to determine where you are in the recordset when you're using macros. So how is it done? You have just come across one of the shortcomings of macros. Macros are good at automating simple tasks, but they're less useful when the task (or the logic behind the task) becomes more complex. The only way to make these buttons intelligent is to use VBA, and we'll show you how to do this in the next chapter.

Macros Or VBA?

Obviously, there are some simple tasks that can be performed happily by macros, but the example above should have highlighted one of their limitations. We could create navigation buttons using macros, but we could not disable or enable them according to where we were in the records behind the form. That may not be a problem for some people, but if you want a slick interface that will win over your end-users, you'll probably want to enable and disable buttons. Our users will be sitting in front of this screen a lot, so we want to get it right.

Why You Should Use VBA

The advantages that VBA has over macros can be summarized as follows:

VBA enables you to provide complex functionality.
You'll remember that when we tried to move back from the first record we encountered an error and Access displayed an error message. What if we wanted to display our own error message instead? This type of intelligence isn't possible with macros.

You can trap (i.e. intercept) and handle errors using VBA.
Handling errors is impossible with macros but simple enough with VBA. Also, in some circumstances, you *have* to handle errors yourself. If you don't, your application could easily crash! We look in detail at error handling in Chapter 12.

VBA is faster to execute than macros.
Code is executed faster than macros. Although you may not notice the difference in a one-line macro, the difference in speed becomes more noticeable the longer and more complex the macro you are creating. Since speed is normally a critical factor in impressing end-users, we have another notch in favor of VBA.

Using VBA makes your database easier to maintain.
Macros are completely separate from the objects that call them. Although we created the navigation button macro from within the form, the macro is actually stored as a separate object in the database window. Click the Macros tab and you'll see it's there. In contrast, you can save VBA code with the form itself. This means that if you want to move the form into another database, the code automatically goes with it. With macros, you would have to find out for yourself which macros you needed to take as well.

Using VBA allows you to interact with other applications.
With VBA you are able to make full use of Automation. This facility allows you to access the functionality of applications like Excel and Word from within your Access application. It also allows you to control Access programmatically from applications like Excel and Word. More on this in Chapter 15.

Using VBA gives you more programmatic control.
Macros are good at performing set tasks where there's little need for flexibility. They can't pass variables from one macro to another in the form of parameters, are unable to ask for and receive input from the user, and they have extremely limited methods for controlling the sequence in which actions are performed.

VBA is easier to read.

Because you can only view one set of Action arguments at a time in the lower pane of the macro window, it is difficult to see the details of a macro. You have to select each action one after the other and look at its arguments in turn. In contrast, VBA with its color-coded text and Full Module View is very easy to read.

VBA is common to all Microsoft applications (well, almost!)

And, finally, VBA is the language on which all Microsoft applications are now standardizing. VBA code written in Access is easily portable to Excel, Word, and any other applications that use VBA (we shall be showing you more about this in chapter 15). In contrast, macros are highly specific to their native application.

When to Use Macros

By this stage, you may be wondering why you should ever bother to use macros if VBA has so much in its favor! Well, there are still a couple of things that you can't do in VBA that you need macros for, and we'll look at these below. They are:

- ❑ Trapping certain keystrokes throughout the application
- ❑ Carrying out a series of actions whenever a database is opened (this is done via the Autoexec macro)

But, these apart, you'll find that with VBA you can do all you could with macros and lots more besides.

In early versions of Access, you also had to use macros if you wanted to create custom menu bars or attach custom functionality to buttons on toolbars. However, from Access 97 onwards, both of these tasks are now achieved from the Customize... *dialog box available from* Toolbars *on the* View *menu.*

Before we move on to the next chapter and completely discard macros in favor of VBA, let's just take a look at the two things mentioned above where we still need macros.

Trapping Keystrokes Throughout an Application

Something you may want to do to make your application more user-friendly is to assign frequently used actions to certain keystrokes. For example, you may want your application to print the current record when your users hit *Ctrl+P*.

We have already seen that on a specific form you can implement a hotkey by using an ampersand (&) in the caption for a control. That's what we did with the navigation button on the Company Details form. However, if you want to implement a global keyboard shortcut – one that is available throughout your application – you can do so by creating a special macro.

First create a new macro (click the down arrow next to the New Object button on the toolbar and select Macro from the drop-down menu). You will need to save the macro with the name Autokeys, as this is the name of the macro in which Access looks for keyboard shortcuts. To display the Macro Name column, click on the Macro Names button on the toolbar. This button toggles the column between visible and invisible. You can also do this by selecting Macro Names from the View menu.

Then you specify the keystroke that you wish to instigate the required action in the Macro Name column and the action itself in the Action column. For example, the following macro will cause the currently selected records to be printed whenever *Ctrl+P* is pressed.

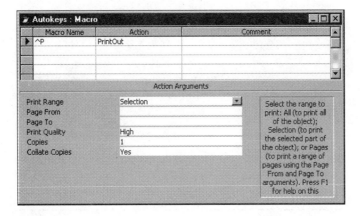

The lower pane of the macro window lists the arguments that you can pass to the PrintOut action to define exactly how it should operate. For example, we've specified Selection as the Print Range argument. This causes Access to only print out those records that were selected when the key combination *Ctrl+P* was pressed. If we had only wanted to print out the first two pages of the currently selected object, we could have chosen Pages as the Print Range argument and then typed 1 as the Page From argument and 2 as the Page To argument.

The caret sign (^) is used to indicate that the Ctrl *key is held down at the same time as the* P *key. For more information on these key codes, search Microsoft Access Help using the phrase "Autokeys Key Combinations"*

Carrying Out Actions when a Database is Opened – the Autoexec Macro

When you open up an existing database, the first thing that Access does is to set any options that have been specified in the Tools/Startup... dialog. After this it checks to see if a macro called Autoexec is present. If it is, then Access executes it immediately. This handy feature allows you to carry out actions such as writing a record to a log file to indicate that your application has started up.

Users of versions of Access 2.x and earlier should note that many of the conventional uses of the Autoexec *macro have now been replaced by the* Startup... *option on the* Tools *menu. If you're converting an application from a version 2.x or earlier, you may want to remove the functionality from the* Autoexec *macro and use the* Startup... *dialog instead.*

If you want to perform an action whenever the database is opened, but want to get the benefits of using VBA, rather than macros, then you should write a procedure in VBA and call the procedure from the Autoexec macro. You can do this by using the RunCode action in your Autoexec macro:

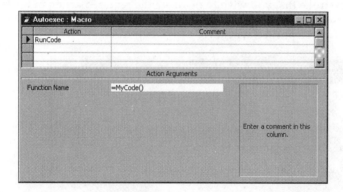

In this situation, when the database opens, the Autoexec macro is executed and this causes the MyCode() procedure – written in VBA – to be executed.

> Be aware, however, that a user can prevent the Tools/Startup... options or the Autoexec macro from running by holding down the *Shift* key when the database is being opened.

You can prevent a user from bypassing the Tools/Startup... options and the Autoexec macro by setting the database's AllowBypassKey property to False. However, the AllowBypassKey property isn't available normally and so can't be set in the usual way. We'll look at how to set this property from VBA later on.

Moving to VBA

Macros have their purposes then, but, while undoubtedly useful for some things, they don't offer the power of VBA. We've just demonstrated in a few pages how and where you should apply macros. We'll now use the rest of the book describing how and where you can use VBA.

Summary

In this chapter, we've worked our way through the process of creating part of an Access application with one aim in mind – to deliberately hit a brick wall. That brick wall is the implementation of the intelligent navigation buttons. We just can't implement them properly using macros. Instead, we need VBA...

So, in brief, we have covered:

- How to go about designing an application
- An introduction to the application that forms the basis of this book – `IceCream.mdb`
- Creating the main form for the application and adding custom navigation buttons
- Why macros aren't sufficient for our needs
- When to use VBA and when to use macros

In the next chapter, we'll look at how you can polish up the Company Details form using VBA. If this chapter has been a success, you'll hunger for the power to solve the problems we've come up against – so let's get on with it.

Exercises

1. With Office applications you have the Customize dialog (available from Toolbars on the View menu) to allow you to create custom menus, toolbars and shortcut menus – something that was only possible with macros in previous versions of Access. Make sure that you know how to take advantage of this powerful new dialog. Try adding a menu bar to the Company Details form (frmCompany) that allows the user to navigate through the records in the same way as the buttons in the form footer without using macros.

2. The Autokeys macro is used to associate macro actions with keyboard shortcuts. Try using the Autokeys macro to display the property window whenever you hit *F4*. When does this shortcut not work? What happens if you try to associate this action with *Alt+F4* and why?

   For a hint, use the Access Help and search for Autokeys using the Answer Wizard.

Introduction to Event Driven Programming

This chapter introduces a key concept in VBA programming. Indeed, the concept of event-driven programming is one which is central to all Windows programming, whether it is in low level languages such as Visual C++ or higher level languages such as Visual Basic for Applications (VBA) or Visual Basic Scripting Edition (VBScript). In essence, when we say that Access is an event-driven application, what we mean is that nothing happens in Access unless it is in response to some event that Access has detected.

In itself, that should not be a very difficult concept to grasp. After all, most of us are event-driven in the way that we behave. The phone rings, so we answer it. It gets dark, so we switch the lights on. We feel hungry, so we buy a burger. That's event-driven behavior at its simplest.

These three examples all have something in common, which characterizes the way that event-driven programming works.

❑ **An event occurs**
The events that occurred in the three examples above are the phone ringing, it getting dark, and us feeling hungry. Events are sometimes triggered by external forces (such as a visitor ringing the doorbell), and sometimes they are triggered by an internal change of state (we start to feel hungry).

❑ **The event is detected by the system**
We are only concerned about events that can be detected. For example, if a phone three blocks away rings we are not bothered, either because we cannot hear it or because we know that it is someone else's responsibility to handle the phone call. It is like that in Windows programming. Windows applications can only respond to events if they can detect them, and they will only handle events that they know it is their responsibility to handle.

❑   **The system responds to the event**
The response can take the forms of various explicit actions, such as
turning on the light or buying a burger. Alternatively, the system can
respond to the event in a less dramatic fashion, by incrementing a
counter which keeps tally of how many times the event has occurred. In
fact, the system can acknowledge the event and choose to do nothing.
The important thing to note is that once the system has carried out its
pre-defined response to the event, the event is said to have been
handled and the system can go back to its dormant state, waiting for the
next event to occur.

Now that's fine as far as we are concerned, but how does that help us with Windows programming
in general and Access VBA programming in particular? What are the events that arise in Windows
and in Access? And what actions do Windows and Access come up with in response to those
actions?

Examples of Events

Here is an item that should be familiar to all of us. It is the Windows Desktop.

Whenever we start one of the Windows family of operating systems we will see something similar
to this. So what do we do next? Well, that depends on what we want to achieve. Let us suggest that
we want to delete the documents in our Recycle Bin. So we right-click the icon representing the
Recycle Bin and choose Empty Recycle Bin – a seemingly simple enough event. Only it is not quite
as simple as all that. When we look more closely we will see that there are a number of events and
responses underlying this seemingly simple action.

❑ **Move the mouse button**
This event is detected by Windows, which responds by repainting the mouse pointer at the new location on the screen. In fact, this event occurs repeatedly and Windows responds repeatedly until the mouse comes to rest over the Recycle Bin.

❑ **Right-click the mouse button over the Recycle Bin**
This event is also detected by Windows and the response is two-fold. First, the Recycle Bin icon is shaded to indicate that it has been selected. Second, a popup menu specific to the Recycle Bin is displayed at the location of the mouse pointer.

❑ **Move the mouse to the Empty Recycle Bin menu item**
Notice how Windows again detects the mouse moving and responds by repainting the mouse pointer. This time, however, because the mouse is over a menu, the menu is repainted to highlight the menu items over which the mouse passes.

❑ **Click the Empty Recycle Bin menu item**
The menu item detects that the menu item has been selected, and in response displays a dialog box asking whether we really want to delete the items in the Recycle Bin. At the same time, it hides the popup menu.

❑ **Move the mouse to the dialog box**
Again, Windows detects the mouse movement and repaints the cursor.

❑ **Click the Yes button**
The message box determines that we have clicked the mouse button over the Yes button and responds by causing the Recycle Bin to delete all items within it. In addition, the Recycle Bin icon is changed to an image of an empty trashcan.

Notice that in every case, the same three steps occur.

❑ An event occurs

❑ The event is detected by the system

❑ The system responds to the event

How Windows Handles Events

So far, we have looked at what events are and we have seen an example of a typical series of events and responses. But, before we go any further, let's have a look in a little more detail at what was happening when we emptied the Recycle Bin. Just who or what was detecting the events? And what is it that determines which action is carried out in response to the event?

Whenever Windows detects that an event has occurred – the mouse may have been moved or a mouse button clicked – Windows generates a message and directs it to the specific window to which the event relates. So, when the user clicks the mouse over the Yes button on the Confirm File Delete dialog box, Windows generates a message and directs it to the Yes button.

Windows can direct messages to windows or controls either by sending them directly or by placing the message in a message queue and marking it with the handle (identifier) of the window or control the message is destined for.

The type of message generated will be different for every type of event that Windows detects. For example, when Windows detects that the mouse has been moved, it generates one type of message. And when it detects that the user has clicked a mouse button, it generates a different message. All of these messages, irrespective of their type, are automatically generated by Windows and directed to the window to which the event relates. It is then up to the window that receives the message to decide how to handle the event indicated by the message it received.

When the window receives the message it can carry out some particular action in response to the message – such as displaying a dialog box. Alternatively, the window can decide that it does not need to take any specific action. In this case it can elect for the default action for that event to be carried out – the default action is what Windows does if we haven't told it to do anything different. In fact, most windows will only process a few messages specifically and will pass the rest of the messages back for the system to handle with the default action.

So how does this help us? Well, a few more things should have become apparent:

- ❑ The Windows operating system automatically detects when events occur.

- ❑ The operating system automatically notifies windows or controls as events arise which relate to them.

- ❑ If the window decides it does not want to do anything special, it can simply pass the message back to allow the default response to occur.

The implication of all this is that as programmers, we can limit ourselves to writing code that handles specific events in a specific manner. We don't need to bother with the hassle of detecting events – Windows does that for us. And we don't need to write code to handle events where we want our windows or controls to react in the default manner.

We can see this if we take a look at the form that we created in the previous chapter.

Try It Out: Examining Event Properties

1. Open the IceCream database and, if necessary hit *F11* to display the database window.

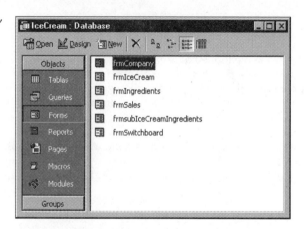

2. Now open the `frmCompany` form in design view by right-clicking it and selecting Design View.

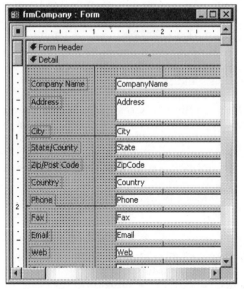

3. Select the `cmdFirst` button (First) at the bottom of the form and display the Properties window. You can do this by choosing Properties from the View menu, by right-clicking the command button and choosing Properties or by selecting the command button and depressing the Properties toolbar button.

4. Select the Event tab on the Properties sheet. This will display all of the events that can occur for the selected command button. There are quite a few, aren't there?

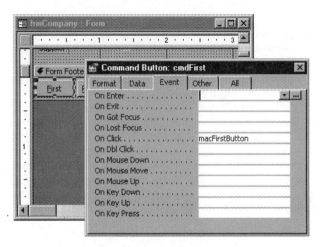

Twelve different events that we can handle for a single command button! As it happens there is only one event that we are concerned with. We want to carry out a specific action when the user **clicks** the button. We don't care what happens when the mouse moves over the button; we don't care what happens when the user presses a key when the button is selected; all we care about is what happens when the button is clicked. That is why we have specified a macro (macFirstButton) to be run when the Click event occurs. If we had wanted an action to occur whenever the user moved the mouse pointer across the button, we would have specified a macro to be run when the MouseMove event occurs and so on.

Two important characteristics of event handling in Access that we examined a little earlier – characteristics that are major contributing factors in making Access such an excellent tool for rapid design and prototyping – are worth repeating here. The first is that the programmer does not need to determine when a particular event happens. We don't have to work out when the user clicks one of our buttons or when the user moves the mouse pointer over it. Windows automatically detects the event and the operating system notifies Access, which in turn causes the specific event to be raised, so executing the code or macro that the programmer has specified in the property sheet for that particular event.

The second noteworthy characteristic of this method of event handling is that the programmer need only supply macros or code for those events that the programmer wants to be handled in a 'non-default' manner. For example, clicking on a button causes the appearance of the button to change to reflect the fact that it has been depressed, whether or not we supply our own event handling macro or code. We don't need to worry about that because it is a type of default behavior common to all buttons. So for the cmdFirst button, all we need to worry about is the code or macro that is required to move the form to the first record.

Some Definitions

We have introduced a few new terms in this chapter and it is probably worthwhile clarifying just what they mean. They are terms that we will be using throughout the rest of the book, so it is as well to make sure that we all know what we are talking about!

An **event handler** is any VBA code (or macro) that the programmer constructs to be executed when a specific event occurs for a specific object. In the example above, we specified that the macFirstButton macro should be the event handler for the Click event of the cmdFirst button.

An **event property** is the mechanism that Access provides to allow us to attach an event handler to a specific event for a specific object. These event properties are exposed on the Event tab of an object's property sheet (kind of logical, huh!). In the example above, we can see that our command button has 12 event properties. That means that there are 12 different events that we can choose to handle through VBA code or macros. It is worth noting that the same event handler can, in fact, be assigned to many different event properties on many different objects.

The same types of object will always have the same number and type of event properties. So, every command button that you place on a form in Access will have the same 12 event properties that are listed in our example above. Event properties often start with the word On and their names reflect the event they allow the programmer to handle. So, the On Click event property is where we specify the VBA code or macro that we will use to handle the Click event. The On Mouse Move property is used to handle the MouseMove event and so on.

So, to recap terminology, in our earlier example we can see that the cmdFirst button has a Click event. We can write a macro or piece of VBA code to act as an event handler for that event. And we specify that the macro or VBA code is the event handler for the Click event, by entering its name in the On Click event property for the button.

So Many Events...

Reading through the previous paragraphs, you might well have thought "Whaaaat? 12 events for a measly little button!" VBA gurus call this a rich programmatic interface. Most other folk call it downright scary... It can be daunting when you start programming and are faced with a vast number of events to choose between. Sometimes it is obvious which to use. We want our form to move to the first record when the user clicks the button so we use the Click event. But it is not always that straightforward. For example, report sections have an On Retreat event property. What's that all about? And what is the On No Data event property of a report used for?

Well, you don't have to worry. In the first place, there are excellent reference materials online in the shape of Access Help. And secondly, you'll find that there are a few core events that you will use time and time again, and you will soon become familiar with what these are. For example, let's look at command buttons again. Although there are 12 possible events, you will soon discover that for (at least) 99% of the time, you will only ever need to handle the Click event. Why? Because that's what people are used to. Sure, you could write an elegant and highly inventive handler that makes use of one or more of the other events. But bear in mind that users, like horses, scare easily. They are not used to things happening when they move their mouse over buttons. They are used to things happening when they click buttons. Buttons are to be clicked – no more, no less. Please don't misinterpret this as either an attack on the intelligence of users or an attempt to limit the creativity of developers. It is just that people are used to interacting with the Windows interface in a certain manner. They expect buttons just to sit there and wait to be clicked; they don't expect strange things to happen when you move the mouse over them. A user's expectation of how your application will behave is a very powerful force. Use it to your advantage, make your application conform to the standards of Windows interface behavior and you will find that the task of getting users to feel comfortable with your application will be ten times easier than if you attempt to surprise them with cool new methods of interaction.

> *That is (more than) enough on interface design considerations. If you want to know more about this subject, an excellent reference is About Face by Alan Cooper (IDG, ISBN: 1568843224). Alternatively, you could consult the Windows Interface Guidelines for Software Design, which is available online on the Microsoft Developer Network (MSDN) web site.*

Default Events

One of the helpful things about the way that Access exposes events to programmers is that each object has a **default** event. The default event is the event that Microsoft believes programmers are most likely to want to use when handling events for that type of object. For example, the default event for command buttons is the Click event. That is obviously because the event we are most likely to want to handle when using command buttons is the Click event. By way of contrast, for a text box the default event is the BeforeUpdate event. This is because Microsoft believes that, as programmers, we are more likely to want to write a piece of VBA code or macro to handle the BeforeUpdate event than any other event that occurs with text boxes.

In fact, we have come across default events before. In the previous chapter, when we wanted to attach a macro to the cmdNext button, we did so by right-clicking the button in design view and selecting Build Event... from the popup menu.

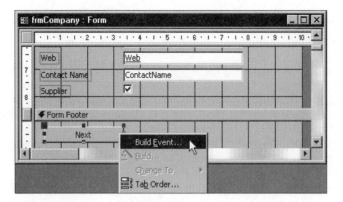

This brought up the Choose Builder dialog that allowed us to select the technique we wanted to use to write the logic that would handle the button's behavior. We selected Macro Builder, built a macro and when we closed the macro window, Access entered the name of the macro into the On Click event property.

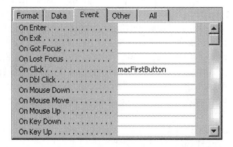

Right-clicking an object and selecting Build Event... will always create an event handler for the object's default event. If, instead, we want to create an event handler for a non-default event we have to do it through the object's property window. For example, if we wanted to create a macro to handle the MouseMove event of the cmdFirstButton command button, we could type the name of a saved macro directly into the property sheet for the button's On Mouse Move event.

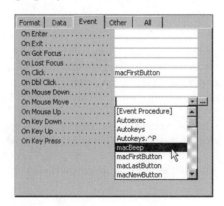

Alternatively, we could click the builder button (the one with the ellipsis or three dots) to the right of the **On Mouse Move** event in the buttons **Property** window. This would allow us to invoke the Macro Builder to build a macro to handle the `MouseMove` event.

One Action, Many Events...

Something else to bear in mind when deciding which event to handle is the fact that what seems like a single action may actually result in a number of different events being triggered. For example, let's consider what happens when a user has changed the text in a text box (`txtFirst`) and then hits the TAB key to move to a new text box (`txtSecond`). The single action of hitting the TAB key will trigger the following events in order:

Which event you decide to handle depends very much on just what you want to do. For example, the `BeforeUpdate` event occurs after the text in the text box has been changed on screen but before the value is actually saved. As such it is an excellent candidate for holding validation rules that can check the validity of what has been entered in the control before the value actually gets saved.

> For a fuller listing of the order in which events happen as a result of common actions, type "Find out when events occur" in the Answer Wizard of the Access online help.

Handling Events in Access with VBA

So far then, we have looked at what events are and how we can use macros to perform certain tasks as those events occur. The example we have used is the `frmCompany` form that we created in the previous chapter. That form has five buttons on it, whose purpose is to allow the user to navigate through all of the records in the underlying table. Each of the buttons has a macro attached to its **On Click** property that determines which record the form will move to when the button is clicked.

You should also recall that this solution is not perfect. If we click the Eirst button (cmdFirst) to move to the first record in the form and then click the Previous button (cmdPrevious), a dialog box tells us that an error has occurred, because Access tried to move to the record before the first record (and obviously there isn't one).

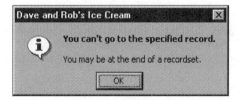

What we decided we needed was some intelligent navigation buttons – buttons which knew what record the form was on and therefore buttons which could enable and disable themselves depending on whether the actions they represented were valid at that point in time. That degree of intelligence simply isn't possible with macros. Macros are great for automating very simple tasks, but they just don't have the flexibility to allow us to use them for anything too sophisticated.

The alternative to using macros is to write your event handlers in VBA. In fact, you will find that in almost all professional Access applications VBA is used for event handlers. Some of the reasons for this were mentioned in the previous chapter but, to recap, the most important are as follows:

- ❑   VBA allows you to add more complex logic to your event handlers
- ❑   VBA allows you to execute a more varied selection of actions than are available through macros
- ❑   VBA allows you to extend the functionality of Access by making use of other components or applications, such as Excel or Word, through automation
- ❑   VBA code executes faster than the equivalent macro actions

❑ VBA code is portable between any applications that support VBA, whereas macros are proprietary to Access

❑ VBA allows you to trap errors and handle them gracefully

❑ VBA code is easier to read and print out than macros

Put simply, VBA gives you more control. So, let's waste no more time and rewrite our event handlers in VBA code.

Try It Out: Writing VBA Event Handlers

1. If you haven't done so already, open the `IceCream` database and, if necessary hit *F11* to display the database window.

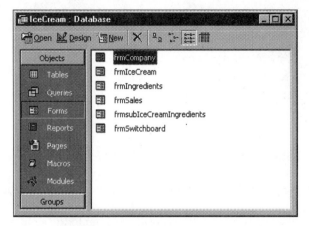

2. Now open the `frmCompany` form in design view by right-clicking it and selecting Design View.

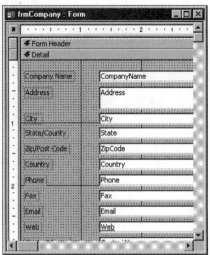

3. Select the `cmdFirst` button at the base of the form and display the Properties window. You can do this by choosing Properties from the View menu, by right-clicking the command button and choosing Properties or by selecting the command button and depressing the Properties toolbar button.

4. Select the Event tab on the Properties sheet. Notice that the event handler for the `Click` event is the `macFirstButton` macro.

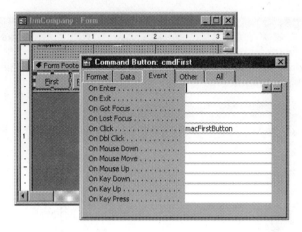

5. Select the On Click event property and delete the text `macFirstButton`. Note that by doing this we are not deleting the actual macro. We are simply instructing Access that the macro is no longer to be used as the handler for the `Click` event of this button.

6. Click the Builder button (the one with the ellipsis or three dots) to the right of the On Click event property. This will display a dialog box asking us how we want to build your event handler. We want to use VBA code rather than macros, so select Code Builder and hit the OK button.

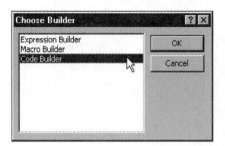

7. Clicking **OK** opens up the VBA integrated development environment (IDE). A new window should appear looking something like this.

The last two lines of code shown in the window above form the VBA event handler for the Click event of the cmdFirst button. These are automatically entered by VBA when you decide to use the Click event of cmdFirst. The event procedure (that's another term for an event handler written in VBA) starts with the line

```
Private Sub cmdFirst_Click()
```

and ends with the line

```
End Sub
```

Everything that goes between these two lines will be executed whenever the cmdFirst button is clicked. At the moment there is nothing there, so nothing beyond the default action (the button appears to be pressed-down) will happen when the button is clicked.

8. Type the following line of code in the event procedure, making sure that you type it exactly as it appears below, including the two commas.

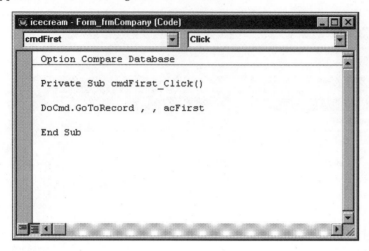

Don't worry if some strange popups (looking a bit like tooltips) appear while you are typing the line of code. These two features – Auto List Members and Auto Quick Info – are discussed a little later in this chapter.

9. Now switch back to Access by hitting *ALT + F11*. The words [Event Procedure] should now appear against the On Click property of the cmdFirst button. This indicates that the Click event for this button is now being handled by VBA code.

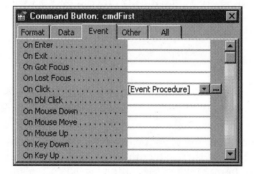

10. Close the Properties window, switch to Form View and move to the second record by hitting the <u>N</u>ext button. Then click the <u>F</u>irst button. If you've done everything correctly, you will be able to use the button to navigate back to the first record on the form. Congratulations! You have written your first VBA procedure!

How It Works

OK, so let's have a look in more detail at the code you typed in:

```
DoCmd.GoToRecord , , acFirst
```

It's really quite simple. We'll look at each part in turn.

The DoCmd at the start of the line indicates that we want Access to carry out an **action**. In other words, we want Access to do something that we could have performed using either the keyboard (or mouse) or a macro. The action that we want to carry out is the GoToRecord action. This is what would happen if we selected G̲o To from the Edit menu when the form's open in Form view. You may remember from the last chapter that this is also the name of the action we selected in the macro that was originally behind this button.

Once we've specified the action, we need to tell Access which record we want to go to. This is the purpose of the constant acFirst – the record we want is the first record. (We'll be looking at constants in the next chapter.)

The two commas before acFirst indicate that there are additional optional arguments we could have supplied to make our code more specific. In this case, we could have specified the type of object we want to move within (in our case a form) and the name of the object, frmCompany. So, we could have written the code like this:

```
DoCmd.GoToRecord acForm, "frmCompany", acFirst
```

If we omit these two arguments, Access will assume that we mean the current object. This is fine in our case, so we can leave the optional arguments out. However, we still have to insert a comma to indicate where arguments have been omitted. So that's how we end up with the line of code:

```
DoCmd.GoToRecord , , acFirst
```

> *If arguments are still a mystery to you, don't worry, as we will be covering them in more depth in the next chapter.*

What are Actions and Methods?

At this stage you might be getting a little confused over just what the difference is between actions and methods. After all, there is a GoToRecord action (which we used in the original macro) and a GoToRecord method (which we used in VBA) and they both do the same thing. What's the difference?

Actions are the building blocks of **macros**. Many of them correspond to tasks carried out by the user by selecting items from a menu. Others allow you to perform different tasks that a user can't, such as displaying a message box or making the computer beep. The main thing to remember, however is that actions occur in macros.

Methods, however, occur in **VBA**. A method is used to make an object behave in a certain way and we'll look at the idea of objects and methods in more detail in Chapter 6. Because you cannot use actions outside of macros, you use methods to achieve the same ends in VBA. There are two objects whose methods you use to perform almost all of the macro actions in VBA. These are the Application object and the DoCmd object.

So, if we want to write a VBA statement that performs the same action as the `Quit` action in a macro, we would use the `Quit` method of the `Application` object.

```
Application.Quit
```

In fact, the `Application` object is the default object, and refers to Access itself, so we can omit it and simply type this as our line of code.

```
Quit
```

Almost all of the macro actions, however, correspond to methods of the `DoCmd` object. So if we want to write a line of VBA that does the same as the `Beep` macro action, we would write this:

```
DoCmd.Beep
```

> *To find out the VBA equivalent of a macro action, simply look up the action in Access online help. If there is an equivalent VBA method, it will be described on the help page for the action.*

Why is the Code in Different Colors?

One of the nice things about VBA is colored code. This is not just a pretty device. The different colors are used to distinguish the different components of code and can make your code easier to read. You can set these colors yourself on the **Editor Format** tab of the **Options...** dialog on the **Tools** menu in the VBA IDE.

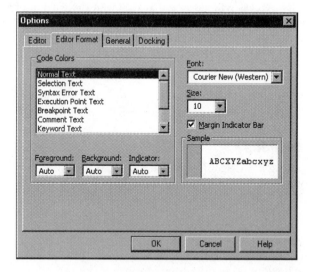

The colors really can make it easier for you to read and understand the code. For example, you can alter the color of the line of code that is due to be executed next. This makes it easier to see what is happening when you step through your code one line at a time. Or you can choose to have all your comments in gray so that they don't appear too intrusive.

> *Stepping through the code by running it line by line is useful for debugging the code. This is covered later in the book, in Chapter 12, "Error Handling and Debugging".*

You can also use different colors to distinguish between the different types of word you use in your code. **Keywords** – reserved words, such as DoCmd, which always have a special meaning to Access – can be in one color, and **identifiers** – such as the names of forms you have created or messages you want to display – can be in another color. This can make it easier to understand what your code (or someone else's code!) is doing.

What were all those Popup Thingies?

Good question! Before you have finished typing even half a word you may find VBA trying to butt in and finish the job for you. It all looks a bit disconcerting at first but, once you get used to the way it works, it can make your code both easier to write and less prone to errors. The proper terms for these popups are Auto List Members and Auto Quick Info. We'll look at them now in more detail. As we go through this over the next few pages, it would be worth your while to keep the VBA IDE open, and just have a play around to become accustomed to how these pop-ups operate.

> *The Auto List Members and Auto Quick Info features can be turned on and off via*
> *Tools/Options.../Editor on the menu of the VBA IDE. Make sure that these options are*
> *checked if you want to observe the behavior described below.*

The Auto List Members feature of the VBA IDE suggests a list of all the valid words that can come next in your VBA code. (More specifically, it lists the relevant methods, properties, events, members or constants. We'll be looking at what these words mean in the next few chapters). You can see this at work if you type the phrase DoCmd. in VBA. As soon as you have done so, VBA suggests a list of possible methods that could come next.

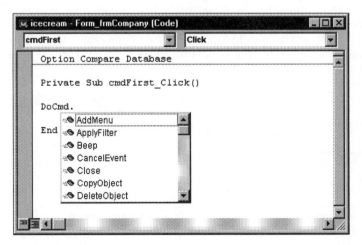

All of the words in the popup list box are valid methods that can follow the DoCmd object. We saw earlier how the DoCmd object allows us to carry out the same actions we can perform in macros. Well, once we have decided that we want to use the DoCmd object, the popup lists all of those actions for you.

You can either select an item from the list by double-clicking it or by hitting the *Tab* key, or the space bar. Or if you want you can carry on typing your code. If you do carry on typing your code, VBA will highlight the word that matches most closely what you are typing.

The other popup you may have seen is displayed by the Auto Quick Info feature. This one helps you to remember the syntax of difficult-to-remember commands. You'll see it whenever you type the name of a recognized function or subprocedure in VBA. So, in our example above, once you had typed DoCmd.GotoRecord, VBA displayed the Auto Quick Info popup to help you with the rest of the command.

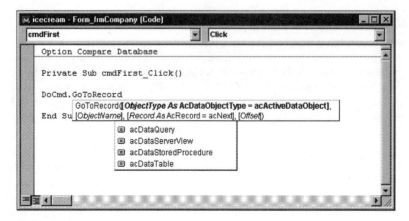

The popup window acts as a memory aid, to remind you what arguments you need to type in after DoCmd.GoToRecord. The next argument you need to type in is always highlighted in bold, and any optional arguments are displayed inside square brackets.

In the example above, the next argument we should type in is the ObjectType argument. There is even an Auto List Members popup behind the Auto Quick Info popup to list the possible values you can type in for the ObjectType argument! Since the ObjectType argument is shown in square brackets, we can ignore it, as it is an optional argument. However, we still need to type a comma to acknowledge the fact that we have omitted the optional argument.

Typing the comma causes VBA to highlight the next argument in the Auto Quick Info popup.

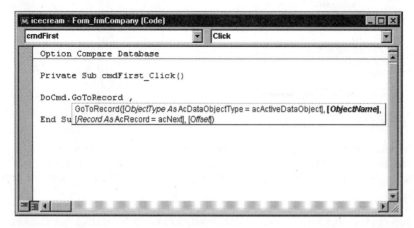

Again the argument is optional, so we can ignore it and simply type a comma in its place. The highlight then moves to the third argument.

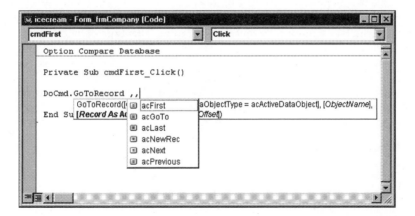

Even though the Record argument is optional, we want to use it, as this is the one that tells VBA which record we want to move to. And what's cool is that VBA displays an Auto List Members popup that lists the possible values we can supply for this argument. We can click acFirst and VBA inserts that argument in our line of code. The last argument, Offset, is also optional, so we can ignore it and just hit the *Enter* key to complete our line of code.

Auto List Members and Auto Quick Info aren't just gimmicks. They really help you to get your VBA code right the first time without needing to spend time looking in Online Help or other manuals. As such they are a great aid to productivity.

What if I still Get It Wrong?

So none of us are perfect! Even with Auto List Members and Auto Quick Info looking over our shoulder and telling us what to write we still make mistakes. Another way in which VBA makes the job of writing code a bit easier is that it will inform you if you have made a mistake in a line of code. For example, you might have mistyped the line of code as:

```
Do Cmd GoToRecord , , acLast
```

Then, when you tried to move off the line, VBA would have highlighted the line of code (and the word Cmd) and displayed this dialog box:

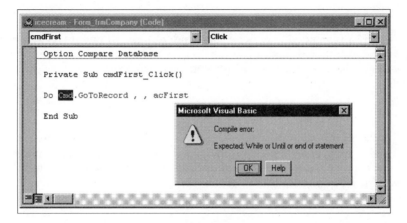

This indicates that the word `Do` must always be followed by the words `While` or `Until` (we'll cover this in Chapter 5), or else it must appear on its own. Of course, we don't want the word `Do` – we want to use `DoCmd`, which is something altogether different. This type of error is called a **syntax error**.

However, if the error is less obvious, VBA may only be able to recognize the fact that it's an error when you try to run the code (i.e. when you click the button). This is called a **run-time error** and will result in a rather unfriendly dialog box being presented to the user when they click the button. For example, if you had missed out a comma and typed:

```
DoCmd.GoToRecord , acFirst
```

VBA wouldn't have generated a syntax error when you moved off the line but, when the `cmdFirst` button was clicked at run-time, it would have interpreted `acFirst` as the second argument (rather than the third) and would have displayed the following dialog box:

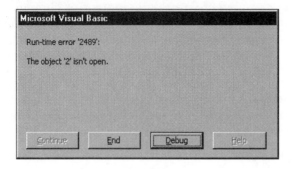

Here, the constant `acFirst` has the value 2 within VBA, a value that the missing optional parameter should not have. Later in the book we shall be looking at how to prevent these run-time errors and how to handle them more gracefully.

The third type of error that you can create when writing code occurs when the code that you type in is syntactically correct, but does not produce the desired effect. In this situation, the program appears to function normally, but in fact doesn't perform as you intended. For example, you may have accidentally typed:

```
DoCmd.GoToRecord , , acLast
```

This is a **logic error** - you had intended to type `acFirst` not `acLast`. It might take some time for you or the users of your application to notice that the `cmdFirst` button was moving the current record pointer to the last rather than the first record. You may also hear this type of error referred to as a **semantic error**.

Compiling Code

You've seen how VBA checks for the more obvious errors as you type. However, there is another method that can be used to prevent errors. This is the process known as **compiling**, and is used to trap the less obvious errors that might crop up in your code. When your code is compiled, routine checks are performed – such as checking that variables have been declared (if `Option Explicit` has been set) and that procedures you call are named in your application.

Compiling involves assembling the code in preparation for execution, but doesn't actually execute the code. Compiling can't catch all errors, but it will pick up general consistency problems in your code. If compiling doesn't produce any errors, then control is returned to you. You don't need to worry about this now, as we look at the issue of compiling code in more detail in Chapter 18, and variables and Option Explicit are covered in more detail in the next chapter.

Other Events

So where are we now? We have looked at what events are, and how fundamental they are to the operation of Windows and Access. We have also looked at how we can use macros and VBA to write event handlers. But so far we have only mentioned one or two events. We'll take a quick look at some of the more common events that can be handled within Access, what triggers them and how they can be useful to us. You can find a comprehensive list of all of the events that Access handles in Appendix F. It should give you an idea of just how much you can achieve in Access through the careful use of event handlers.

Event Property	Belongs to...	Occurs...	Used for...
On Change	Controls on a form	after the contents of a control change (e.g. by typing a character).	triggering the update of related controls on the form.
On Click	Forms, Controls and sections on a form	when the user clicks the mouse button over a form or control; when the user takes some action which has the same effect as clicking (e.g. pressing the spacebar to check a checkbox).	just about anything – this is one of the most used of all events, and is about the only event used with command buttons.
On Close	Forms, Reports	after a form or report has been closed and removed from the screen.	triggering the opening of the next form, and for "cleaning up" the current form.
On Current	Forms	when the form is opened or re-queried; after the focus moves to a different record, but before the new record is displayed.	implementing intelligent navigation buttons (see example below).
On Dirty	Forms	after the user has updated any data in the current record but before the record has been saved.	determining whether you need to ask the user if any changes should be saved.

Table Continued on Following Page

Event Property	Belongs to...	Occurs...	Used for...
On Dbl Click	Forms; Controls and sections on a form	when the user depresses and releases the left mouse button twice over the same object.	selecting an item in a list and carrying out the actions of the OK button in one go.
On Delete	Forms	when the user attempts to delete a record.	preventing the user from deleting records.
On Error	Forms; Reports	when a run-time database engine error occurs (but not a VBA error). We look at this in more detail in Chapter 13.	intercepting errors and displaying your own custom error messages.
On Mouse Move	Forms; Controls and sections on a form	when the mouse pointer moves over objects.	displaying X and Y coordinates of the mouse pointer.
On Mouse Up	Forms; Controls and sections on a form	when the user releases a mouse button.	detecting whether the user has a mouse button depressed when clicking an object.

The final column of the table is only intended to give an indication of the type of action that you can perform in the event handler. It isn't meant to be an exhaustive or comprehensive list of the uses of each event handler.

Also, the table above only lists the more commonly used event properties. For a fuller listing, refer to Appendix F.

You will notice that the table lists event properties rather than events. Remember, an event property is a property that appears in the property sheet and allows you to handle a specific event. Therefore, the event handler for the Click event of a command button is exposed via the button's On Click event property.

The VBA IDE

Now that we have written our first procedure, it is probably as good a time as any to take a look at the VBA integrated development environment (IDE). The VBA IDE is the place where you will type all of your VBA code, and if you have not seen it before it can appear quite daunting.

You will sometimes see the VBA IDE referred to simply as the VBE or Visual Basic Editor. Don't be confused; they are just two different names for the same thing.

If you have used Access before, one of the first things that you may have noticed is that the VBA IDE is now in a separate window to Access itself. So, even though the code we are writing relates to Access objects, we enter the code in the VBA IDE window rather than within Access itself. Actually, the VBA IDE is now common to all of the VBA-enabled applications that make up Microsoft Office 2000, as well as to Visual Basic itself. So, whichever Office 2000 application you are in, if it supports VBA you will be able to use the VBA IDE to write VBA code.

> *In previous versions of Access, the code editor was integrated within Access itself. It might seem a little counter-intuitive to abstract the code development environment into a separate window, rather than retaining it within the application itself. However, the benefits – in terms of ease of learning and portability of code – of sharing a common, **integrated** development environment between all of the Office 2000 applications is, in the author's opinion, well worth the effort of occasionally having to ALT+TAB (or ALT+F11) between windows.*

OK, so let's have a look in a little more detail at the VBA IDE.

Components of the VBA IDE

When we wrote our first event procedure in VBA earlier in this chapter, we concentrated on just one window, the code window. In fact, the VBA IDE is comprised of 7 different windows, each of which can be hidden or displayed according to the user's preferences. The screenshot below shows what the VBA IDE looks like with all seven windows displayed:

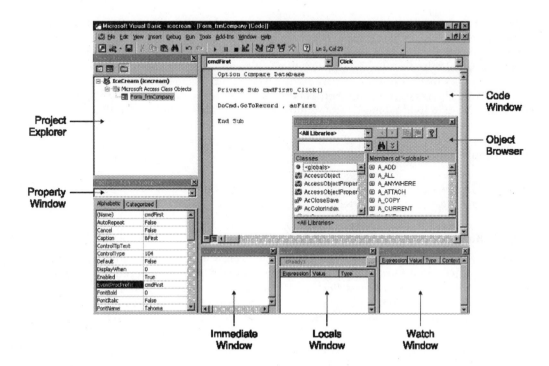

Remember, if the VBA IDE isn't displayed, press Alt+F11, *or select* **Code** *from the* **View** *menu when you're in Design view. Note also that when you call it up, it may not show all seven windows.*

We will look at how all of these windows can be used throughout this book, but before we go much further, it probably makes sense to familiarize ourselves with two of them in particular, the Project Explorer and the Code Window.

Project Explorer

All code within VBA must be stored within a **project**. As far as we are concerned, all of the code that we use within an Access database is stored within a single project. By default the name of the VBA project that holds our code is given the same name as the Access database to which the code relates. So, when we created our first event procedure in the `IceCream.mdb` database, Access created a new VBA project and called it `IceCream`.

> Be careful not to confuse a VBA project with an Access project. A VBA project is the mechanism used by VBA to store all of the code that is associated with a specific database. By contrast, an Access Data Project (or `.adp` file) is a special type of lightweight database front-end, introduced in Access 2000 to facilitate client-server development against databases such as SQL Server or Oracle.

Within a VBA project, code is arranged within a series of **modules**. These are simply a method of grouping together related chunks of code. If it makes it any easier, think of a filing cabinet at the office – you might use the top drawer for product detail files, the second for customer files and the third for invoices and sales details. The drawers of a filing cabinet allow you to store similar files together, but in a way that keeps them separate from each other. In the same way, a module allows you to store related chunks of code together. The Project Explorer window allows us to navigate our project and locate individual modules and individual chunks of code (we call them **procedures,** and will explain more about them in the next chapter) within those modules. The three types of module that are displayed in the Project Explorer window are class modules, form and report modules, and standard modules.

If the Project Explorer window is not immediately visible in the VBA IDE, it might be hidden. To make it visible, just hit Ctrl+R.

Form and Report Modules

Every form and report can have a built-in module, called a **class module**, associated with it that contains all the code for that form or report. This code includes both event procedures – such as the `cmdFirst_Click()` event we wrote earlier – and other general procedures. The class module is tightly bound to the form or report object – so if you copy a form or report into another database and the form or report has a class module, the class module is automatically copied as well.

Note that new forms and reports do not automatically have a module associated with them. Instead, the module is only created if you decide to use VBA code in your form.

Standalone Class Modules

Class modules can also exist without an associated form or report. When created without an associated form or report, they are used to create custom objects. We will look at this use of class modules in more detail in Chapter 13.

Standard Modules

Standard modules always exist outside of forms or reports as objects in their own right, and are used for grouping together procedures that aren't associated with any one form or report in particular. These procedures can then be used by any form or report in the database. For example, you may have a standard module that contains specific functions that your company uses. These may carry out complex calculations such as wind loading in a construction company, or they may format and check the text of a site-visit report in line with your company's safety policy. These can also be included in code libraries. We discuss these in Chapter 14.

Working with Modules

The three types of module (class modules associated with Access forms or reports, standalone class modules and standard modules) are all displayed hierarchically in the Project Explorer window in the VBA IDE. In the example below, we can see how VBA groups together.

❑ Class modules associated with forms or reports (referred to as Microsoft Access Class Objects)

❑ Standard modules (referred to just as Modules)

❑ Standalone class modules (referred to as Class Modules)

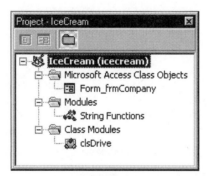

In this example, Form_frmCompany is the class module associated with the frmCompany form, String Functions is a standard module and clsDrive is a standalone class module.

The last two modules – String Functions and clsDrive – will not appear in IceCream.mdb, the database accompanying this book, but are shown here for illustrative purposes only.

To open a module from within the VBA IDE, simply select the module in the Project Explorer window, and then either double-click it or right-click it and select View Code from the popup menu. Alternatively, you could hit the View Code button on the toolbar.

If we were to select the **Modules** tab in the Database window in Access, we would see the standalone class module and the standard module displayed like this:

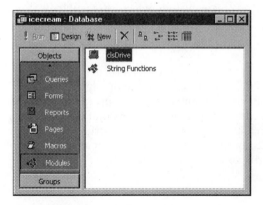

You can open one of these modules in number of ways. For example, you can select it and hit the **Code** button on the toolbar, or you can simply double click it. Other ways of opening the module include right-clicking it and selecting <u>D</u>esign View or selecting it and choosing <u>C</u>ode from the <u>V</u>iew menu.

Note that the class module associated with the `frmCompany` form is not displayed in the Database window. To open that class module from within Access, you should select the form in the Database window or open it in design view and then either hit the **Code** button or choose <u>C</u>ode from the <u>V</u>iew menu.

If you want to toggle between the Access window and the Visual Basic IDE, you can just hit
`ALT+F11`

Code Window

When we open up a module, whether it's a class module associated with a form or report, a standalone class module or a standard modules, the Code Window is displayed. As its name suggests, the code window is where we type our VBA code.

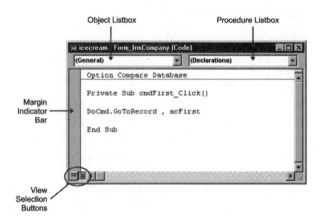

Each separate code window contains all of the code within a module, so opening a new module will open a new code window. You can view the code in a module one procedure at a time or you can decide that the procedures should be shown continuously. To toggle between full module view and single procedure view, simply click the appropriate View selection button in the lower left corner of the code window.

> *You can determine whether the code window will default to full module view or single procedure view by checking or unchecking the* **Default to Full Module View** *checkbox on the* **Editor** *tab of the dialog displayed when you select* **Options...** *from the* **Tools** *menu.*

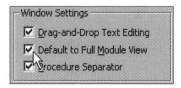

> *If you do decide to use Full Module View, you can use the* **Procedure Separator** *checkbox to determine whether or not procedure separators (thin gray lines) should be displayed in the code window to demarcate where one procedure ends and another starts.*

At the top of the code window you will notice two dropdown lists, referred to as the **object listbox** and the **procedure listbox**. The object listbox is used to select the object whose code you want to look at. For standard modules, the only option listed is (General) as standard modules do not contain objects, only procedures. For class modules associated with forms or reports (also called form or report modules), the object listbox will also contain in alphabetical order a list of all of the objects (such as command buttons) contained on the form or report.

The procedure listbox details the events associated with the specific object selected in the object listbox. For example, if we opened the form module for our frmCompany form and selected the cmdFirst button in the object listbox, the procedure listbox would display all of the event procedures that we could write for that object. If we have actually chosen to handle one of these events by entering code in the event handler, the name of the event will appear in bold in the procedure listbox.

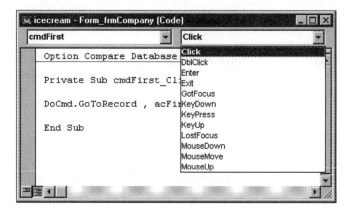

The (General) Object

The (General) object isn't really an object at all, but it's where everything goes that relates to the module as a whole. So, in a form or report module, you could put procedures here that aren't necessarily event procedures tied to a particular object, but are procedures that are general to the form. In standard modules, all procedures go in this section.

Options

You also set Options in the (General) section of a module. Every module has certain options that can be set using statements commencing with the Option keyword:

Option Explicit

This is the most widely used of the options. If it's set, it means that all variables have to be declared before being used. You will see why this is a good idea in later chapters. You can turn on Option Explicit by default in new modules by selecting Options from the Tools menu (in the VBA IDE) and checking Require Variable Declaration on the Editor page.

Option Base

This statement allows you to set the default lower limit for arrays. This is normally 0. Arrays are explained later on in the book, so you don't need to worry about this at the moment.

Option Compare

This is one statement that you will frequently see. It determines how VBA compares strings (i.e. text values). Normally, this is set to Database, but it can be Binary or Text as well.

When Option Compare Binary is set, VBA will use the internal binary representation of characters when comparing them in that module. This means that it will regard lower and upper case versions of the same letter as different. It also means that when VBA sorts values it will place all upper-case letters before all lower-case letters, so whereas a word beginning with a upper-case Z is placed after one starting with an uppercase Y, a word beginning with a lower-case a is placed after both of these.

Option Compare Database, which is the default setting, causes VBA to use the Access database's sort order when comparing strings in that module. The sort order of the database is determined by what the setting of the New Database Sort Order option on the General tab of the Tools/Options... dialog (in Access) was when the database was created.

If the value in the New Database Sort Order drop-down box is General, then the database will be created with a sort order defined by the system locale. We can change the system locale by using the Regional Settings utility in the Control Panel. As well as defining the sort order, the system locale also affects other features such as the way that dates are formatted or how currency values are displayed. Alternatively, if we want to use a sort order different from that specified by the system locale, we can select a different sort order in the New Database Sort Order drop-down box.

Changes we make to the New Database Sort Order drop-down box are only reflected in new databases that are created after we change the setting. Note, however, that when we tell Access to compact a database, it physically creates a new database into which it compacts the old. This means that the new database that is created will have the new sort order. In fact, this is the recommended way of changing the sort order of a database. Option Compare Text uses the system locale to determine the sort order, but is always case insensitive.

Option Private

This makes the whole module private, so that none of the code within it can be accessed from another module. This saves you having to use the `Private` keyword on each procedure. Again, we'll explain these concepts in more detail in later chapters, so don't worry too much about them for now.

You will not normally need to modify any of these `Option` *settings in day-to-day use. The only one to keep an eye on is* `Option Explicit`. *We'll look at the reasons for that in the next chapter.*

Declarations

As well as setting options, the `(General)` section can also be used to declare external functions, variables and constants that apply to the whole module. We'll look at this subject in more detail in the next chapter.

Converting Macros to VBA

So far, we have looked at events and event handlers and we have begun to familiarize ourselves with the VBA IDE. In particular, we have looked at how to execute a procedure when the user clicks a button. "Well," you may say, "that's great but so what? It's not exactly an earth-shattering example of the power of VBA. After all, the VBA procedure does exactly what the macro did!" True, but the purpose of this example was to show you how easy it is to write VBA. One simple line of code is all it takes. There will be plenty of time later on to look at some of the more complex things you can do with VBA. For the moment, we are just trying to familiarize ourselves with how to write VBA procedures.

Of course, if this is your first foray into VBA programming, it might well be the case that your application already contains a large amount of application logic contained in macros. Fortunately, Access provides a simple mechanism to convert existing macros into VBA code. We'll use this feature to convert the event handlers behind the other four buttons to VBA.

*You will only be able to carry out this next exercise if you selected **Additional Wizards** to be installed as part of the Access setup. The additional wizards are not included with the typical setup, but are available either by choosing custom setup when you first install Access or by selecting the **Add or Remove Features** option if you re-run setup after Access has been installed.*

Try It Out – Converting Macros to VBA

1. Make sure the `frmCompany` form is open in design view and then click the Code button to view the code module for this form in the VBA IDE. This should contain the event handler for the `Click` event of the `cmdFirst` button.

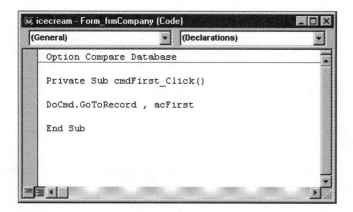

2. Check that the event handlers for the `Click` event of the other four buttons use the macros created in the earlier chapter, by returning to the form in design view, clicking each button in turn and inspecting the **On Click** property on the **Event** tab of the property window. This should contain the name of the macro that handles the `Click` event.

3. Now select **Macro** from the **Tools** menu and from the submenu that appears click **Convert Form's Macros to Visual Basic**.

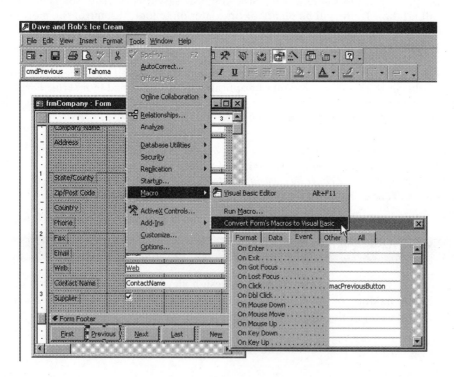

4. A dialog box will appear asking whether you want to add error handling and whether you want to include macro comments in the generated code. Make sure that both of these boxes are checked and then hit the <u>C</u>onvert button.

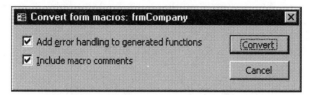

5. Access will then convert the macro-based event handlers behind the four remaining buttons into VBA and display a message box when it has succeeded in doing so. Hit ALT+F11 to view the code module for the form and you will be able to view the newly generated event handlers. The code for the Click event of the cmdPrevious button is shown below.

```
'------------------------------------------------------------
' cmdPrevious_Click
'
'------------------------------------------------------------
Private Sub cmdPrevious_Click()
On Error GoTo cmdPrevious_Click_Err

    DoCmd.GoToRecord , "", acPrevious


cmdPrevious_Click_Exit:
    Exit Sub

cmdPrevious_Click_Err:
    MsgBox Error$
    Resume cmdPrevious_Click_Exit

End Sub
```

How It Works

If you look at the code that Access creates when it converts the event-handling macro into VBA, you will see a familiar statement using the DoCmd object that we encountered earlier when writing the event handler for the cmdFirst button:

```
DoCmd.GoToRecord , "", acPrevious
```

So what is the rest of the code that Access has inserted? Well, the first four lines are comments. These are remarks inserted, normally by the programmer, to explain the purpose of the code that follows them.

```
'------------------------------------------------------------
' cmdPrevious_Click
'
'------------------------------------------------------------
```

Comments are denoted by an apostrophe, which prevents Access from trying to run these lines as if they were executable code. (By default, Access displays comments in green). If our macro had contained any comments, the Access Macro to VBA converter would have placed these before the appropriate line of code in the VBA procedure.

With the exception of the comments and the statement that uses the DoCmd object, the rest of the code generated by the converter is for error handling purposes. You may remember that one of the reasons for implementing VBA instead of macros was 'VBA allows you to trap errors and handle them gracefully'. We'll be looking at error handling in more detail in Chapter 12.

Completing the Company Contacts Form

So how does all this help us? If you remember, our original mission in this chapter was to produce intelligent navigation buttons. That is to say, we need to create navigation buttons that disable themselves when they are unavailable. How can we do this? Well, first of all we'll show you the answer, and then we'll explain how it works.

Try It Out – Creating An 'Intelligent' Navigation Button

1. Open the frmCompany form in Design view.

2. Make sure that the form's properties are visible by double-clicking on the form selector at the top left, where the rulers meet.

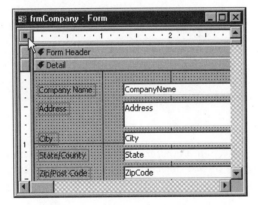

3. Open the form's `Current` event procedure by clicking on the builder button to the right of the **On Current** property and selecting **Code Builder**.

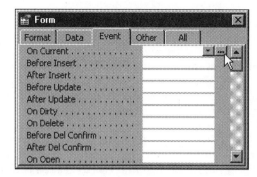

4. Add the following code to the form's `Current` event procedure:

```
Private Sub Form_Current()
```

```
'If the form is on a new record, we should disable the Next button.

'To do this we have to shift the focus first. If there is
'a value in CompanyID, we must enable the button.

If Me.NewRecord = True Then
    cmdPrevious.SetFocus
    cmdNext.Enabled = False
Else
    cmdNext.Enabled = True
End If
```

```
End Sub
```

5. Switch back to Access by hitting *ALT+F11*. Close the `frmCompany` form and save it when prompted. When you open the form again, what do you know! You've got an 'intelligent' **Next** button! When you get to the end of the records (by hitting the **New** button, for example), the **Next** button becomes disabled. However, clicking the **Previous** button enables the **Next** button again.

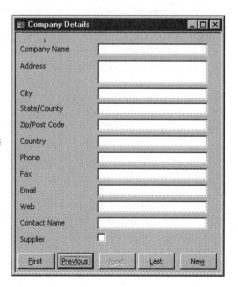

How It Works

Well, it looks simple enough, but bear in mind that we are only dealing with one button here – and in fact it's the easiest one to handle! The first thing to note is that we have used the On Current event property. We need to enable or disable the button as soon as the form is opened, and then whenever the user moves from one record to another. Looking through the list of events, there is only one that fits the bill, and that is the On Current event. This event occurs whenever a form is opened and then when moving between records on that form – the very times that we need to check whether the button should be enabled or disabled.

After deciding which event handler to use, we must determine what rules we will use for enabling and disabling the Next button. Well, we want the Next button disabled only when the user cannot move any further forward through the records. That means that the Next button should be disabled when the user is in a new (blank) record.

> Bear in mind that Access provides a new blank record at the end of every updateable table or form. For now, we will allow the user to move to this record so that they can enter details of a new company. We will modify this behavior a little in Chapter 7 to cater for situations where the user cannot add new records.

If we are on a new record, the Next button should be disabled. If not a new record, the button should be enabled. We can determine whether or not the form is currently on a new record by inspecting the value of the form's `NewRecord` property. This property returns `True` if the form is on a new record and `False` otherwise.

```
If Me.NewRecord = True Then
```

The `Me` keyword simply indicates to Access that we want to use the current object (which is our `frmCompany` form).

However, it's not quite that easy – we can't just disable the Next button directly because it has the focus – it has just been clicked. Access does not allow us to disable an item that has the focus, and if we try to do so we'll get a run-time error. So first we must move the focus somewhere else, and where better than to the Previous button. This is likely to be the one you want to use next anyway. To set the focus to a control, we just call its `SetFocus` method.

```
If Me.NewRecord = True Then
    cmdPrevious.SetFocus
    cmdNext.Enabled = False
```

You'll notice that to enable or disable a control, we just set its `Enabled` property to `True` or `False`.

As it stands, the button will be disabled when we find ourselves in a new record (or if there are no records in the form when it opens) but it will also remain grayed out when we scroll back to an existing record. We must re-enable it each time the current record is *not* a new one...

```
Else
    cmdNext.Enabled = True
End If
```

This code uses the If...Then...Else *construct which may be new to you. This is pretty intuitive, but in case you aren't familiar with branching statements, they are explained in more detail in Chapter 5.*

Summary

So, there we are. In this chapter we have had our first taste of VBA code. The chapter should also have given you some idea of how an application is built. As a developer, you build your forms and reports and then write code that causes the objects you have created to respond to events in a particular way. In an event-driven environment like Access, you can let the users decide the order in which your code modules are executed.

We have spent some time looking at the different events that can occur in Access and how these can be put to use. You have seen, for example, how the **On Current** event can be used to solve one of the tasks we set ourselves at the start of the chapter – enabling and disabling navigation buttons depending on our position in the recordset. We shall complete this feature for all the buttons in later chapters, once we have a few more programming concepts under our belt.

We have also spent some time looking at the VBA IDE, and by now you should feel comfortable with:

- ❑ What events are.
- ❑ How to make an Access object respond to an event.
- ❑ The VBA IDE.
- ❑ What modules are and how they are used to store code.
- ❑ How to use the **On Current** event to make a navigation button intelligent.

In the next couple of chapters, we will be looking at the nuts and bolts of VBA so that you will be able to write your own event handlers more easily.

Exercises

1. One of the most important things to remember when working with events in VBA is the order in which events occur. For example, when you save a record on a form, several events occur, one after another. By looking at the list of events on the property sheet, try to work out the order in which they happen.

2. Take some time to read through the list of events and their uses. You will find that some events are more useful that others – in other words, you will find yourself writing custom even handlers for some events more often than for other events. Look at the list and try to think about which events you would most commonly handle with custom event handlers.

Creating Code

Well, we really should start looking more deeply at some code. After all, this is a VBA book! The next two chapters are going to lay the foundations of programming and VBA. So far we've looked at the programming environment, and seen how event-driven programming works, so now it's time to start putting this into practice.

In this chapter we will be dealing with what code is, and how you can build up code in small segments to make programming easier. In particular we shall look at:

- ❑ What procedures are and how you use them
- ❑ How to pass information into procedures
- ❑ What variables are and how they store data
- ❑ The different types of data you can store
- ❑ How to make decisions in your code

This is the heart of the VBA language, and will lay the foundations for all programming you do later.

Procedures

You use procedures in life every day, even if you don't think about it. From making breakfast to requesting that brand new PC at work you've always wanted, there's a procedure to follow. A specific set of actions you take to get it done. The whole idea of a procedure is to break down a task into smaller, more manageable tasks. Let's look at making some ice cream. What are the tasks you would need to perform?

1. Beat egg yolks lightly.

2. Beat in sugar.

3. Heat the cream/milk on the stove.

4. Beat in cocoa powder.

5. Heat cream/milk/cocoa mix until steaming.

6. Stir into egg/sugar mix.

7. Add vanilla extract.

8. Cool.

9. Freeze in ice cream maker.

This is the procedure we would follow to make a basic ice cream.

Now we have defined this set of instructions, we don't need to write them out again. We can just refer to the recipe by its name. So what's this got to do with programming? Well, in programming you can do the same sort of thing. You can group together a set of instructions under a single name, and then use this name when you want to run those instructions. And is that a good thing? Yes it is, for several reasons:

- ❑ It allows us to break complex problems into smaller, more discrete tasks. This can often make the problem easier to solve.
- ❑ It makes your code smaller, because you only need the instructions entered once.
- ❑ It makes your code easier to maintain, because if there is an error in the instructions, you only need to correct it in one place.
- ❑ It makes it easy to use the instructions in other applications.
- ❑ You can change the inner workings of your procedure without worrying about others who use it. As long as it has the same result no one will know the difference.

You may not think this is a big issue, but as your programs start to get larger you'll find that dealing with procedures is much easier than having a single large chunk of code. That last point is one you'll see mentioned again later in the book, as it means you can change the internal workings of a procedure, perhaps to improve performance, without changing the end result of the procedure. Think about our 'making ice cream' example. If you make ice cream by hand, you don't use step 9 above. There may be two or three steps here instead, describing how long you should place the ice cream in the freezer for, and how often you should stir it. If you suddenly buy an ice cream making machine, you could replace these steps with step 9, and the end result would be the same.

Modules

One term that you've already seen is **modules**. From the pictures in the previous chapter you saw that the Visual Basic IDE can have many modules. But what exactly are they? A module is really just a place to store procedures. It's a bit like a filing cabinet in a way. A filing cabinet can have many files in it, and each file can have many documents. A database can have many modules, each with many procedures.

We generally group procedures into logical units. So, if we created a set of string handling procedures, we could put them all together in a single module, and call the module String Handling. As you go through the book you'll see this in practice. Each chapter has its own code module where the code for the chapter goes. This makes them easy to find.

Subroutines and Functions

In VBA programming terms there are two types of procedures: **subroutines** and **functions**. They really only have one difference, which is that a function returns a value to you. Let's say you ask someone to make some ice cream for you. They wander off to the kitchen and make the ice cream, and then come back, but they don't tell you anything about how the process went, or whether it's ready or not. That's a subroutine. On the other hand, if they come back and bring you a dish of chocolate chip ice cream, then that's a function.

Let's make this a bit clearer by turning the steps involved in making ice cream into a subroutine, and then into a function. The first thing we have to do is give the procedure a name – MakeIceCream seems sensible (it's squashed together because procedure names can't have spaces in them). We then use a special keyword called Sub, to tell Access that we are starting a new subroutine, and then we put our steps after that, followed by more keywords to tell Access that we've reached the end of the subroutine. Here's how it looks:

```
Sub MakeIceCream()
    Beat egg yolks lightly
    Beat in sugar
    Heat the cream/milk on the stove
    Beat in cocoa powder
    Heat cream/milk/cocoa mix until steaming
    Stir into egg/sugar mix
    Add vanilla extract
    Cool
    Freeze in ice cream maker
End Sub
```

Now, anywhere in our program, we can just say MakeIceCream, and this subroutine is run. Access starts at the first line in the subroutine, and runs each line in turn until it gets to the end. You can see how much easier this is than typing in all of the lines again. So, the actual details of the procedure are just typed once, and to run it you don't type the details again, just the procedure name.

For a function, we need the procedure to tell us something – perhaps whether vanilla extract was added or not. The way it is used is slightly different:

```
Function MakeIceCream()
    Beat egg yolks lightly
    Beat in sugar
    Heat the cream/milk on the stove
    Beat in cocoa powder.
    Heat cream/milk/cocoa mix until steaming
    Stir into egg/sugar mix
    Add vanilla extract (if there is any)
    Cool
    Freeze in ice cream maker.

    If vanilla extract added Then
        MakeIceCream = "Vanilla"
    Else
        MakeIceCream = "No Vanilla"
    End If
End Function
```

Notice that instead of Sub we use Function. At the end of the function we determine whether or not vanilla extract was added, and we set the function name to a value to indicate this.

When calling a function from within our code we can now see what happened – its return value tells us what kind of ice cream was made. For example:

```
If MakeIceCream = "Vanilla" Then
    Chocolate vanilla ice cream was made
Else
    Plain chocolate ice cream was made
End If
```

Don't worry too much if you don't understand some of the things here. The important thing is to remember that we are making little blocks of code, and then we'll use these blocks to build bigger blocks and programs.

Procedure Declaration

The act of telling Access what a procedure is named is called the **declaration**. When you declare a procedure you must follow some special rules. For a subroutine, the syntax (just like sentence structure in English) is like this:

```
Sub SubroutineName (Arguments)
```

For a function it's like this:

```
Function FunctionName (Arguments) As Type
```

There are two new things you haven't seen here, the Arguments and the Type, but we'll be covering those in the next section. For the name there are some special rules that apply:

- ❑ It must start with a letter.
- ❑ After the first letter, it can contain letters, numbers or the underscore character (_).

❑   It cannot be more than 255 characters long.

❑   It shouldn't be the same name as an existing VBA keyword.

Apart from that, you can name procedures as you like, although it's always best to keep the names meaningful, and descriptive of the task they perform. For example, calling our ice cream making routine `CalculatePayRise` would be perfectly legal, but it doesn't make any sense because that's not what the procedure does.

Function Types

For the function syntax shown above you saw `As Type` added to the end of the declaration. This allows us to tell Access what sort of value the function is going to return (e.g. a number, a date, etc.), and allows Access to perform checking on the values. This can stop errors later on in the code.

For our making ice cream function we return a character string, either "Vanilla" or "No Vanilla", so our type would have been `String`. So our function should really be declared like this:

```
Function MakeIceCream() As String
```

You can actually leave the function type out and you won't get an error, but it's best to explicitly state the type. Leaving the type out means you get a generic catch-all type, which may not be what you really want. One of the reasons why we have these special types is so that VBA can try to understand what we are trying to do, and so that it can store information in a more intelligent way.

The value being sent back by the function is called the **return value**, and always involves using the function name. Its format is:

```
FunctionName = ReturnValue
```

In the example above this was:

```
MakeIceCream = "Vanilla"
```

Since we've talked about functions, let's create a simple ice cream-making function to see how they work.

Try It Out – The MakeIceCream Function

1.   Open your working database (`IceCream.mdb`), press *F11* to view the main Access window, and select **Modules** from the database window.

2.   From the **Insert** menu, select **Module** to insert a new VBA module. If you can't see the **Module** option, just click the double chevron at the bottom of the menu to see all of the menu options. (This is one of those new Office 2000 'intelligent features' that hides options you don't use so often).

3.   In the new module, type the following code:

```
Function MakeIceCream() As String

    Debug.Print "Making ice cream"

    Debug.Print "Adding Vanilla"

    MakeIceCream = "Vanilla"

End Function
```

4. From the <u>V</u>iew menu, select <u>I</u>mmediate Window (or hit *Ctrl-G*).

The Immediate window is where we print values to with Debug.Print *and what we use to test procedures. We'll be looking at it in depth in Chapter 13, when we look at error handling and debugging.*

5. In the Immediate window type the following, followed by the *Return* key:

?MakeIceCream

You'll see the function being run, and its result:

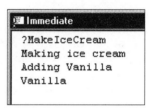

How It Works

You've seen how a function is declared, but what about the code we put in it? The statement Debug.Print just prints things out to the Immediate window. It's often used for debugging and tracing functions. In the last line we set the return value to Vanilla.

In the Immediate window we used a question mark before the function name. This tells VBA to print out the return value. You can try typing in just the function name without the question mark. The function will still run, but the return value isn't printed.

Try It Out – Calling Functions from Functions

Let's add another procedure to call the first one.

1. In the module window, move the cursor to below the End Function line, and type the following:

```
Sub Hungry()

    MakeIceCream

End Sub
```

2. Back in the Immediate window, type the following:

```
Hungry
```

Notice that the return value isn't printed out this time.

3. Try typing this:

```
?Hungry
```

Uh-oh. An error. But don't worry, this is meant to happen. You can press **OK** to clear the error box. Remember that in the Immediate window the question mark prints out the return value of a function. Well `Hungry` isn't a function, but a subroutine, so it doesn't have a return value. So how do we see the return value?

4. Switch back to the code window and place a `Debug.Print` statement in front of the function call:

```
Sub Hungry()

Debug.Print MakeIceCream

End Sub
```

Now try the immediate window procedure again, without the question mark. This time the return value is printed, because `MakeIceCream` returned its return value to the procedure that called it. Confused? Have a look at this diagram:

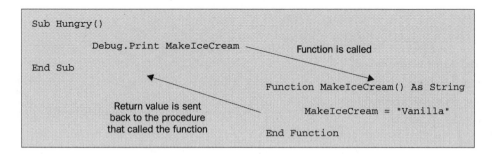

This means that the calling procedure has the return value, and it has to do something with it. In this case it prints it to the Immediate window, but it could also store it for later use.

Parameters or Arguments

The one limit our procedure now has is that there is no way for us to pass any information into it – no way to tell it anything. In some situations that's fine, all we might want to say is `MakeIceCream`. But, what if we want to make some ice cream that's not chocolate based (hard to imagine, I know!)? You could have another procedure, `MakePlainIceCream`, that just skips this step, but then you have two pieces of very similar code. Wouldn't it be better if we could have just one procedure which we can tell whether or not cocoa powder is to be added? This is where **arguments** (often called **parameters**) come in.

The argument is our way of passing a value into the procedure. Let's look at an example:

```
Function MakeIceCream (CocoaToBeAdded As Boolean) As String
```

Here we have added the argument within the parentheses of the function. The syntax of an argument is:

```
Name As Type
```

The `Name` follows the same rules as a procedure name, and is the variable that will hold the value of the argument. The `As Type` part is the same as in the function – it tells Access what type of data is to be held in the variable. We'll be looking at variables and data types later on.

Within the procedure you can use this variable to make choices. For example, our function would now look like this:

```
Function MakeIceCream (CocoaToBeAdded As Boolean) As String
    Beat egg yolks lightly
    Beat in sugar
    Heat the cream/milk on the stove

    If CocoaToBeAdded = True Then
        Beat in cocoa powder.
    End If

    Heat cream/milk/cocoa mix until steaming
    Stir into egg/sugar mix
    Add vanilla extract (if there is any)
    Cool
    Freeze in ice cream maker.

    If vanilla extract added Then
        MakeIceCream = "Vanilla"
    Else
        MakeIceCream = "No Vanilla"
    End If
End Function
```

If we wanted to make chocolate ice cream we could then call this function with the following line:

```
MakeIceCream (True)
```

To make plain ice cream, we'd use this:

```
MakeIceCream (False)
```

Remember, don't worry about the values. We'll explain those in a minute. The term we use is to **pass in** a value. So in the latter example, we are **passing in** a value of `False`.

You aren't limited to just one argument – there can be as many as you need. There is a physical limit, but if you reach it you really need to consider rewriting your procedure! You separate multiple arguments with a comma. For example:

```
Function MakeIceCream (CocoaToBeAdded As Boolean, _
                      VanillaToBeAdded As Boolean) As String
```

> *The underscore character, when it's the last character on a line and preceded by a space, tells Access that the statement isn't finished, and it continues onto the next line. This allows you to split long lines into easily readable chunks.*

To call this you would use this type of command:

```
MakeIceCream (True, False)
```

Here we are passing in two values. The first is `True`, and would be passed into the first argument, `CocoaToBeAdded`. The second is `False`, and would be passed into the second argument, `VanillaToBeAdded`.

Try It Out – Arguments

Let's add some arguments to our existing function.

1. Modify the `MakeIceCream` function so it looks like this:

```
Function MakeIceCream (VanillaToBeAdded As Boolean) As String

   Debug.Print "Making ice cream"

   If VanillaToBeAdded = True Then
      MakeIceCream = "Vanilla"
   Else
      MakeIceCream = "No Vanilla"
   End If

End Function
```

2. Switch to the Immediate window and type the following:

```
?MakeIceCream (True)
```

Notice the return value.

3. Now type this:

```
?MakeIceCream (False)
```

See how the return value has changed?

This shows that arguments allow you to build procedures that can change their behavior depending upon how they are called.

Optional Arguments

If you have a procedure that accepts two arguments, then you have to pass in both arguments every time. We would get an error if we tried to call the procedure without both arguments. Wouldn't it be nice if we could make the procedure clever, so that it knew it could go ahead and make chocolate vanilla ice cream by default, if we don't tell it otherwise? Luckily we can make our arguments **optional**, allowing us to test whether they have been supplied or not. This is achieved by putting Optional in front of the arguments:

```
Function MakeIceCream (Optional CocoaToBeAdded As Boolean, _
        Optional VanillaToBeAdded As Boolean) As String
```

However, this leads to a problem. Since we've now said that these arguments don't have to be supplied, how do we know if they have been supplied or not? If we created a function like the one above, then if we didn't supply the arguments, they would have a default value of False. The program would have no way of telling the difference between the situation where the arguments were supplied with values of False, and that where the arguments were left out. The same problem occurs if our optional arguments are of other data types, although the default values differ depending upon the type – strings are empty, and numbers are 0.

To get around this problem, you can declare your optional arguments to be of a special type – Variant. This doesn't affect the data they can hold because a Variant can hold different types of data. We'll be looking at the Variant data type later. So what we have to do is this:

```
Function MakeIceCream (Optional CocoaToBeAdded As Variant, _
        Optional VanillaToBeAdded As Variant) As String
```

Now within the code we need to check whether those arguments have been supplied, since they are optional and might not have been supplied. For this we use the IsMissing function. This is a built in function, supplied by Access, which returns a value of True if the argument is missing, and False if it is present. So if wanted to make our default ice cream have chocolate and vanilla, we could modify our code to look like this:

```
Function MakeIceCream (Optional CocoaToBeAdded As Variant, _
        Optional VanillaToBeAdded As Variant) As String

    If IsMissing(CocoaToBeAdded) Then
        CocoaToBeAdded = True
    Else
        CocoaToBeAdded = False
    End If

    If IsMissing(VanillaToBeAdded) Then
        VanillaToBeAdded = True
    Else
        VanillaToBeAdded = False
    End If
```

```
    rest of code goes here
End Function
```

This shows that we test both of the arguments, and if they are missing we simply set their values to `True`. You can now call this procedure in a few ways:

`MakeIceCream (True, False)`	This is the original syntax, using both arguments.
`MakeIceCream`	This doesn't supply any arguments. In both cases the `IsMissing` test sets the value of `CocoaToBeAdded` and `VanillaToBeAdded` to `True`.
`MakeIceCream (True)`	This only supplies one argument, so this would be the first one (`CocoaToBeAdded`) The `IsMissing` test for the first argument fails, but the second sets the value of `VanillaToBeAdded` to `True`.
`MakeIceCream (, False)`	This only supplies one argument, but has supplied the comma, indicating that the first argument is skipped. Here `CocoaToBeAdded` would be missing, and therefore gets set to `True`, but `VanillaToBeAdded` wouldn't be. If you are skipping arguments, you must supply the comma.

As we'll see later on, a new Variant variable has a default value of Empty, which is why we can use the IsMissing function to check it.

One important point to note is that optional arguments must be the last arguments in the argument list. In our example, both of the arguments are optional, so that's OK. We could also make the first argument compulsory and the second optional – that would be fine too. What we can't do is make the first optional and the second compulsory.

Using Optional Arguments to Aid Maintenance

So, using optional arguments gives us flexibility. There's also one very important use of optional arguments, and that's in maintenance. Although it would be nice to think of everything before you start writing, you occasionally have an existing procedure that does <u>almost</u> what you want. However, changing it would mean you would have to change everywhere it is used. There are two things you can do here. The first is to write a new version of the procedure, and support both. This goes against the idea of reusing code and writing procedures. The second is to add an optional argument, and modify the code accordingly. This means that any existing use of the procedure can stay as it is, and only if you include the optional argument will the new functionality be available.

Default Values

Another way to get around the problem of missing optional arguments is to use default values. This allows us to tell VBA what the default value of the variable should be if the user does not supply a value. For example:

```
Function MakeIceCream (Optional CocoaToBeAdded As Boolean = True, _
          Optional VanillaToBeAdded As Boolean = True) _
             As String
```

Here, after the variable type, we put the equals sign followed by the default value. Now if the argument is not supplied, it will automatically supply the value `True`. The only problem with this method is that if you omit an argument that has a default value, VBA fills in the default. This means that `IsMissing` would never work correctly, because all it sees is a correctly supplied variable. The fact that VBA supplied the value, rather than the user, is immaterial.

If you are using optional arguments, and you need to supply default values, then use the method shown above, rather than using `IsMissing`. However, if you need to do more advanced processing, or you need to check whether the argument has been supplied (and not filled in by VBA), then you will need to use `IsMissing`, (and not supply default arguments).

Named Arguments

So far you've seen a simple procedure with two arguments, but what happens if you have a procedure with lots of arguments? For example, imagine our `MakeIceCream` procedure had an argument for every ingredient type, to indicate how much of that ingredient to use. When using this procedure it would get confusing as to which argument is which. To avoid this confusion you can name the arguments as you use them. For example, imagine our procedure was declared like this:

```
Function MakeIceCream (EggYolks As Integer, Sugar As Integer, _
          Cream As Integer, Milk As Integer, _
          Cocoa As Integer, Vanilla As Integer, _
          Optional CocoaToBeAdded As Boolean = True, _
          Optional VanillaToBeAdded As Boolean = True) _
             As String
```

If you came across a line of code that called this function you might be confused as to which of the arguments represented which ingredient:

```
MakeIceCream (3, 25, 1, 1, 2, 2, True, False)
```

Confusing, huh? To get around this you can use the name of the argument as it is used:

```
MakeIceCream (EggYolks:=3, Sugar:=25, _
   Cream:=1, Milk:=1, _
   Cocoa:=2, Vanilla:=2, _
   CocoaToBeAdded:=True, VanillaToBeAdded:=False)
```

Note the colon just before the equals sign. You can now easily see which argument is which. Since you are explicitly naming the arguments, you can also put them in any order.

Now imagine how useful this is if you have a procedure with lots of optional arguments. Remember how we said that to skip an argument you must supply the comma? Well, with named arguments you don't have to, because if you name them VBA knows which argument you are supplying. So, if all of our arguments to `MakeIceCream` were optional, we could call it like this:

```
MakeIceCream (CocoaToBeAdded:=True)
```

All of the other arguments are simply taken to be missing, or use their defaults if they have them. Note that even though you are using named arguments, you still have to follow the rules as to whether the arguments are optional or not. Using named arguments just means that you can explicitly name the argument, and put it in any order, but if it's a compulsory argument you still have to supply a value for it.

Built-In Functions

So far you've seen what procedures are and how they can be used. VBA has a whole host of functions built in to make things easy for you. You've already seen an example of one – IsMissing.

We're not going to give a full list of functions in the book because there are far too many of them, and anyway the Access documentation has a very good list. You can find it under the Visual Basic Help, under Visual Basic Language Reference: Functions.

You'll see some of these in use as we explain variables in the next section, and plenty of examples throughout the rest of the book.

Variables

A **variable** is what VBA uses to store pieces of data in while your code is running. Obviously, with Access being a database, data is stored in tables, but there is some information that you don't want to keep permanently. For example, if your user enters a date to search the database for, you obviously don't want to be storing that date in a table somewhere. Instead, you put the value into a variable so you can use it when you need it. When your application stops running, the variable is destroyed.

You've actually already seen variables in action, because arguments are variables. These are used to store the details of what information is to be passed into a procedure. Within the procedure itself we can have other variables, to store other information.

Let's look at a simple example. Looking back to our ice cream making from earlier, and how we set the return value of the function, we used IsMissing to determine if the argument was missing or not, and then used this to make a decision.

```
If IsMissing(VanillaToBeAdded) Then
    VanillaToBeAdded = True
Else
    VanillaToBeAdded = False
End If
```

Now what happens if we need to make this decision twice in the same procedure? We could do this:

```
If IsMissing(VanillaToBeAdded) Then
```

```
' some more code here

If IsMissing(VanillaToBeAdded) Then
```

This is a little wasteful because we are calling the same function twice with the same argument, so the result will be the same. What we can do is use a variable to store the result of the function, and then test the variable:

```
blnMissing = IsMissing (VanillaToBeAdded)
If blnMissing Then
    VanillaToBeAdded = True
Else
    VanillaToBeAdded = False
End If
```

Now if we need to see if the argument is missing more than once, we don't have the overhead of running the function every time. Remember how we said that using procedures allows us to call a set of instructions just by a single name? That saves us having to type out all of those lines again. Well, assigning a variable to the result of a function saves VBA from having to call the function more than once. In this case IsMissing is not a very complex function, and therefore runs very quickly, but if we were calling a long and complex function, then calling it more than once would be a little wasteful.

> *Don't worry too much about the If statement, as we'll be covering that in the next chapter.*

You can see that to set the value of a variable, we use the equals sign. The general rule is:

Variable = Value

In the above example we set our variable to hold the return value from a function, but you can set variables directly. For example:

```
blnMissing = True
strName = "Janine Lloyd"
intAge = 27
ccyPrice = 24.95
```

Declaring Variables

You've seen a few examples of variables but may not realize exactly what they are, or why we need them. The reason is that VBA is very ordered, and it can't put things just anywhere. If VBA is storing something, it needs a place to store it, and that place has to be suitable. Declaring a variable tells VBA to put aside some memory to store the variable in, and specifying the variable type tells VBA what sort of data will be stored. That way it knows how much memory to put aside, as different variable types take different amounts of memory.

We have variable types to store different types of information. Strings, for example, need to be stored in a different way to numbers, and the variable type tells VBA how to handle that variable as well as how to store it.

To declare a variable we use the `Dim` statement:

```
Dim VariableName As VariableType
```

VariableName is the name of the variable, and follows the same conventions as procedure names. We also often prefix the variable name with the type of data it is going to hold. For example, in the above example we used the variable `blnMissing`, using `bln` as the prefix to indicate a `Boolean` value (which can be either `True` or `False`). We look at naming conventions in more detail at the end of this chapter. Until we do, just keep in mind that wherever you see a variable used, the prefix indicates its data type.

VariableType indicates the type of data that this variable will hold, for example string, number, date, boolean, etc. We'll also look at data types in more detail later on.

For our boolean variable we would have used the following declaration:

```
Dim blnMissing As Boolean
```

Variable names are not case sensitive, and VBA will convert variables to the case they were declared in. There is no specific place where variables must be declared, but by convention they are generally put at the top of procedures. This makes them all easy to find.

There are many different data types all designed to hold specific kinds of data.

Manipulating Variables

Remember back to your math classes? Come on, it wasn't that long ago. Remember how you used to have all this stuff about x, y and z, and if x is 3, then z should be half of y...? And you used to write things like this:

$x = y^2 + z^2$

This is manipulating variables, and you can do it just the same in VBA. You can use any of the standard math operators just like you did back then:

intX = intY * intY + intZ * intZ

Addition, subtraction, it all works the same way, with all of the numeric data types.

When dealing with strings, though, you can't do some of this. But one thing you can (and will) do is join strings together. For this you use the `&` sign, as so:

```
Dim strFirstName As String
Dim strLastName As String
Dim strFullName As String

strFirstName = "Janine"
strLastName = "Lloyd"

strFullName = strFirstName & strLastName
```

This gives you:

JanineLloyd

But this doesn't look too good, since the first name and last name are right next to each other, which is perhaps not quite what you wanted. What would be better was if we could add a space in the middle of the two names. You might think that you'd need to create a new variable and assign it a string that just contains a space, but you can actually join strings without them being in a variable:

```
strFullName = strFirstName & " " & strLastName
```

This just adds a space in between the two strings. You're also not limited to just using strings in the middle of expressions, as the following lines show:

```
strFullName = "Janine " & strLastName
strFullName = strFirstName & " Lloyd"
```

So don't think that once you've stored a value in a variable it's untouchable. You can manipulate it to your heart's content.

Variable Types

The following table shows the standard variable types and how they are used:

Type	Used For
Boolean	True or False values only
Byte	Single values between 0 and 255
Currency	Numbers with 4 decimal places, ranging from −922,337,203,685,477.5808 to 922,337,203,685,477.5807
Date	Store dates in the range 1 January 100 to 31 December 9999, and times from 0:00:00 to 23:59:59
Double	Floating point numbers in the range $-1.79769313486231*10^{308}$ to $-4.94065645841247*10^{-324}$ for negative numbers and $4.94065645841247*10^{-324}$ to $1.79769313486232*10^{308}$ for positive numbers
Integer	Whole numbers in the range −32,768 to 32,767
Long	Whole numbers in the range −2,147,483,648 to 2,147,483,647
Object	Any type of Object
Single	Floating point numbers in the range $-3.402823*10^{38}$ to $-1.401298*10^{-45}$ for negative numbers and $1.401298*10^{-45}$ to $3.402823*10^{38}$ for positive numbers
String	Character data with up to 2 billion (2^{31}) characters for a variable length string, or 64,000 (2^{16}) for fixed length strings

Type	Used For
Variant	Different types of data (we'll go into detail later)
Hyperlink	Text that identifies a hyperlink address

You can also define your own, complex, types of data, and this will be covered later in the book, when we look at advanced programming topics.

> It is extremely important to declare your variables as the correct type, otherwise unpredictable results can occur, both during the writing and running of your code.

Boolean

Booleans are used to stored values that can only be one of two values – True or False. They allow us to store values that can be used to make decisions with.

When numbers are converted to Boolean, 0 becomes False and any other number becomes True. When converting from Boolean to a number, False becomes 0 and True becomes -1.

Byte

The Byte data type is probably one of the least used. Not because it's not useful, but because the type of data it holds is less used than other types of data. A Byte can hold a single value between 0 and 255. On its own this isn't great, but in an array it can be used to hold binary data, such as an image.

You can assign a value to a Byte like so:

```
bytChar = 243
```

Currency

The Currency type is specifically designed for dealing with numerical currency information, such as prices. It is often more accurate than Single or Double values because it doesn't suffer from rounding errors. This is due to the way the data is stored internally by VBA. A currency value can be assigned like this:

```
ccyPrice = 19.99
```

Double and Single

Double and Single values are for floating point numbers which aren't currency based. They have a greater range than Currency but can suffer from rounding problems if a particularly large number of decimal places are used. The reason we have both Single and Double is that they take up different amounts of memory – Single being the smaller. Therefore, if you know your number will not exceed the range of a Single, use a Single because it will take up less memory. However, you should always consider the largest possible value that the variable could store, because assigning a value that is outside the range of a variable will cause an error.

Singles or Doubles can be assigned like so:

```
sngNumber = 123.456
dblNumber = 789.012
```

Integer and Long

Integer and Long are for dealing with whole numbers. Like Single and Double they take up different amounts of memory, and Integer is the smaller. This of course means that the Integer has a smaller range, so remember not to assign a very large number to it, otherwise an error will be generated.

Integers and Longs can be assigned like this:

```
intNumber = 123
lngLongNumber = 123456
```

String

Strings are used to hold any form of character data, such as names, descriptions, etc. When assigning Strings you must use double quotes, like this:

```
strName = "Janine Lloyd"
strDescription = "Jan's favorite ice cream is Strawberry Cheesecake"
```

Object

The Object type is used to hold objects for which we don't know the exact object type. Usually we know what type of object we are dealing with (Recordset, Form, Word Document, etc), but there are times when the type of object is decided after the code has been written, (such as when the program is running, or if the user decides upon the object type). You'll see examples of this later in the book.

You use the Set statement to assign a value to an object:

```
Set objWordDocument = Word.ActiveDocument
```

Hyperlink

A Hyperlink allows us to store details about Internet hyperlinks, such as web addresses. The Hyperlink variable contains several pieces of information, and we discuss this more in Chapter 17, when we look at the Internet.

Variant

Since a Variant can hold different types of data, in fact any type shown in the table above, we'll examine it in more detail. If you read any of the documentation you might see that the Variant is the default variable type, which means that if you leave off the As Type clause from a Dim statement, you'll get a Variant. For example, both statements below declare the variable as a Variant:

```
Dim varAnyThing
Dim varAnyThing As Variant
```

However, it's a good idea to explicitly declare variants, as it makes your code easier to maintain if you can easily see where your variants are.

Since a `Variant` can hold any type of data, you can do things like this:

```
Dim varAnyThing As Variant

varAnyThing = 31
varAnyThing = "Any old thing"
```

This first assigns the variable to an integer value of 31, and then to a string. VBA doesn't care what type of data it is.

So far this isn't any advantage over an `Integer` or a `String`, but what about the following:

```
Dim varAnyThing As Variant

varAnyThing = 31
varAnyThing = varAnyThing & " is half of 62"
```

This firstly stores an integer in the `Variant`. We then try to append a string onto the end of the number, which doesn't really make any sense. But, since a `Variant` can hold different types of data, VBA realizes what is happening and treats the first number as though it was a string. The result of this is that we end up with a string containing:

```
31 is half of 62
```

Let's look at a converse example:

```
Dim varAnyThing As Variant

varAnyThing = "31"
varAnyThing = varAnyThing + 10
```

This time we start with a string (note the quotation marks), and add a number onto it. VBA recognizes that the string contains a number and converts it into a number, and adds 10, giving us a result of 41.

Where this can get confusing is under these circumstances:

```
Dim varAnyThing As Variant

varAnyThing = "31"
varAnyThing = varAnyThing + "10"
```

Does this convert both strings to numbers? Well, no, unfortunately it doesn't. You're used to the plus sign being used for addition, but it can also be used to join strings together, so the answer you get here is a string containing 3110. Remember that a number inside a string is treated as a string.

This illustrates an important point, in that VBA will convert variants into the appropriate type when they are used in expressions.

If you use the + operator on variants, remember the following:

- ❑ If both values are strings, but contain numbers, they are treated as strings, and joined together.
- ❑ If both values are numbers, then they are treated as numbers.
- ❑ If one of the values is a number and the other a string, VBA attempts to convert the string into a number. If successful, the two values are added together. If unsuccessful, an error occurs.

This latter case can be demonstrated with the following code:

```
Dim varAnyThing As Variant

varAnyThing = 31
varAnyThing = varAnyThing + "thirty four"
```

This gives a **Type Mismatch** error, indicating that we are trying to do addition with incompatible types.

Determining the Type of a Variant

You've seen that variants can hold different types of data, but what do you do if you need to find out the exact type of data held in a variant? VBA provides a function called `VarType` for this purpose, which returns a value to indicate the exact data type. The table below shows these values:

Value	Variant type
0	Empty (unitialized)
1	Null (no valid data)
2	Integer
3	Long Integer
4	Single
5	Double
6	Currency
7	Date
8	String
9	Object
10	Error value
11	Boolean
12	Variant (only used with arrays of variants)
13	Data access object

Value	Variant type
14	Decimal value
17	Byte
36	User Defined Type
8192	Array

There are a few things here that you haven't seen yet. The Empty and Null values are described a little later in this chapter. The Decimal value doesn't exist as a type on its own, and can only exist as sub-type of a variant. We won't be covering it here. The User Defined Type will be covered later in the book.

Try It Out – Examining a Variant

1. Open up IceCream.mdb, and select the **Modules**.

2. Add a new module by selecting **New** from the toolbar:

3. In the Visual Basic Editor, create a new subroutine called VariantExample:

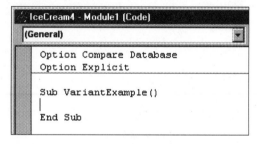

4. Add the following code:

```
Sub VariantExample()
Dim varAnyThing As Variant

varAnyThing = 12.345
Debug.Print VarType(varAnyThing)

varAnyThing = 12.345
varAnyThing = varAnyThing & " is a number"
Debug.Print VarType(varAnyThing)

varAnyThing = 12.345
varAnyThing = varAnyThing + "10"
Debug.Print VarType(varAnyThing)

varAnyThing = 12345
Debug.Print VarType(varAnyThing)

varAnyThing = 123456
Debug.Print VarType(varAnyThing)
End Sub
```

5. Switch to the Immediate window (remember *Ctrl-G* is a shortcut for this) and type
VariantExample, followed by the *Return* key.

How It Works

You can see that five values have been printed out, and that two are the same. Let's see what value
VarType was looking at:

Value	Is a ...	So VarType returns
12.345	Double	5
12.345 is a number	String	8
12.345 + "10"	Double	5
12345	Integer	2
123456	Long	3

Notice that the two numbers with decimal points are assigned to a Double. This is because VBA
picks the largest numeric type, rather than a Single. Also notice that when dealing with 123456 a
Long is automatically picked, as VBA realizes that this is too big a number to fit into an Integer.

The Empty Value

When numeric variables are declared they have an initial value of 0, and strings are initially a zero length string (i.e. ""). But when a variant data type is first declared it is **empty**, because VBA doesn't know what type of data it is going to hold, so an initial value cannot be assigned. The empty value is special in that it is not the same as 0, "", or the **null** value, which we'll look at a little later.

A variant has the empty value before it is assigned. When used in expressions, a variant that is empty is treated as 0 or "", depending upon the expression. For example:

```
Dim varAnyThing As Variant

varAnyThing = varAnyThing + 1.23
```

This leaves `varAnyThing` as 1.23, since it was initially treated as 0.

Assigning any value to a variant overwrites the empty value. You can use the `IsEmpty` function to determine whether a variant has been assigned or not.

```
If IsEmpty(varAnyThing) Then
```

The Null Value

The null value is another value special to the variant. In fact, a variant is the only data type that can hold this value – if you assign null to any other type of value an error will occur. You can use the `IsNull` function to test for the null value:

```
If IsNull(varAnyThing) Then
```

The null value behaves differently from the empty value, as it is said to **propagate** through expressions. That means that if you use a null value in an expression, the whole expression will become null. For example:

```
Dim varAnyThing As Variant

varAnyThing = Null
varAnyThing = varAnyThing + 1.23
```

Unlike the empty value, this doesn't result in 1.23, but `Null`.

Try It Out – How Null Propagates

1. Insert a new procedure called `VariantStringTest` into your existing module.

2. Add the following code:

```
Dim varFirstName   As Variant
Dim varLastName    As Variant
Dim varFullName    As Variant

varFirstName = "Janine"
varLastName = Null
```

```
varFullName = varFirstName & varLastName

Debug.Print varFullName
```

3. Run the procedure by typing `VariantStringTest` into the Immediate window. Notice that only the first name is printed.

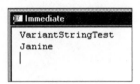

4. Now change the & into a + and run the procedure again.

How it Works

When you use &, and one of the expressions is null, it is treated as a zero length string. So in the first case we only see the first name. If both parts of the name had been null an empty string would have been returned. Using the + sign however, a null value is returned. This is because nulls propagate through expressions when the + sign is used, meaning that if any part of the expression is null, then the whole expression is null.

This shows one very important point:

Do not use the + sign to join strings together.

When to use Variants

There are some good reasons for using variants:

- ❑ They make coding very easy, since you don't have to worry about data types.
- ❑ They are the only data type that can hold a null value. Databases often use null values to show that data hasn't been assigned, so you often have to use a variant if you are unsure about the source of the data.
- ❑ They have to be used when dealing with Optional arguments to procedures if you want to use the IsMissing function.

But, remember that there are also some very good reasons for not using them:

❑ Variants slow your application because every time a variant is accessed, VBA must determine the type of data that is being stored.

❑ They can encourage bad programming. Assigning the correct data type to a variable allows VBA to automatically prevent certain errors from occurring.

In general you should always use the explicit data types, rather than variants.

Date

The date type is one that requires a little explanation, since it can often be confusing when using it in VBA. The first thing to remember is that when assigning a date variable to a specific date you need to enclose the date within # signs, to tell VBA that the value is a date (and not a numerical division):

```
datToday = #12/31/98#
```

You can type in dates in almost every recognizable format, and VBA will convert them into the standard US format of mm/dd/yyyy. This is partly to stop errors in code, but also to get around the year 2000 problem. Years from 00 to 29 are treated as 2000 to 2029, and 30 to 99 are treated as 1930 to 1999.

Date arithmetic is something that is quite common. We often want to find out the differences between two dates, or how many days ahead a certain date is. The great thing about dates is that you can use + and - just as you can with normal numbers. For example:

```
Dim datToday As Date
Dim datNextWeek As Date
Dim datLastWeek As Date
Dim datePaymentDate As Date

datToday = Date()
datNextWeek = datToday + 7
datLastWeek = datToday - 7
datPaymentDate = datToday + 30
```

Date() is a function that returns the current date. You can then just add or subtract days from a date variable and VBA works it all out for you, including the flipping over of months and years if necessary. If you want to work with values other than days, such as weeks or months, then there are some other functions you can use:

❑ DateAdd allows us to add dates together.

❑ DateDiff allows us to work out the difference between two dates.

❑ DatePart allows us to extract a specific part of a date.

Let's have a look and see how these can be used, and then we'll explain more about them.

1. Create a new procedure called `DateTest` in the module you're using for this chapter.

2. Add the following code:

```
Sub DateTest()
Dim datDec As Date
Dim datMay As Date

datMay = #5/1/1998#
datDec = #12/1/1998#

Debug.Print DatePart("m", datDec)

Debug.Print DateDiff("m", datMay, datDec)

Debug.Print "August is " & DateAdd("m", 3, datMay)
End Sub
```

3. Now switch to the Immediate window, and type in `DateTest` followed by the *Return* key to run the procedure.

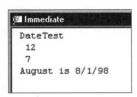

How it Works

Let's take this line by line, and look at each of these new functions in turn.

With the first statement we used `DatePart` to find out a specific part of the date:

```
Debug.Print DatePart("m", datDec)
```

`DatePart` takes four arguments, two of which are optional. (We'll look at the optional arguments when we discuss the `Format` function):

```
DatePart(Interval, Date [, FirstDayOfWeek [, FirstWeekOfYear]])
```

`Interval` identifies which part of the date to return. We used "m" which stands for month and it returned 12, for December. We could have used "yyyy" for the year, "d" for the day, or one of the others. We won't go into the other intervals here, but you can always look them up in the help file if you want.

With the second statement we used `DateDiff` to find the difference between dates:

```
Debug.Print DateDiff("m", datMay, datDec)
```

`DateDiff` takes five arguments, of which the latter two are again optional:

```
DateDiff(Interval, Date1, Date2 [, FirstDayOfWeek [, FirstWeekOfYear]])
```

The interval has the same settings as for `DatePart`, and we used "m" to return the difference in months. `Date1` and `Date2` are the two dates we want to find the difference between. In our case we wanted to find the number of months' difference between May and December.

For the third line we used `DateAdd` to add a number to a date:

```
Debug.Print "August is " & DateAdd("m", 3, datMay)
```

`DateAdd` takes three arguments

```
DateAdd (Interval, Number, Date)
```

`Interval` has the same settings as before. `Number` is the number of `Intervals` to be added to `Date`. We added 3 months to May, to get a date in August. You can use negative numbers to subtract numbers from a date. The date printed appears in the format as set in the Regional Settings in the Control Panel.

Times

The date type also stores times, either on their own, or as part of a date. You can assign a time to a date variable like so:

```
Dim datTime As Date
datTime = #3:20:15#
```

which sets it to twenty past three and fifteen seconds in the morning. As you type this in it will be converted by VBA to:

```
datTime = #3:20:15 AM#
```

If you type in a 24-hour date (e.g. 15:35) it is converted to 12-hour format and PM is added. Again this is only the internal storage, and not how times are shown on forms.

To assign both a date and a time you use this format:

```
datTime = #6/30/1998 3:20:15#
```

Other Useful Date and Time Fuctions

There are a few useful date and time functions that you haven't seen already:

- ❑ `Time()` returns the current time
- ❑ `Date()` returns the current date
- ❑ `Now()` returns the current date and time

You can use these quite effectively in your code to work out the difference between the current date and a user-supplied date, or for calculating a date a number of days in advance. For example, let's assume you are printing an invoice and want to give the payee 60 days; you could use this formula:

```
Dim datPayBy as Date

datPayBy = Date() + 60

Debug.Print "Payment is due by " & datPayBy
```

Try It Out – Using DatePart in a Query

You can see that although these date functions are quite simple functions, they give you quite a lot of power. For example, imagine you have sales data and you need to find out how many sales have taken place on a month-by-month basis. You can do a summary query quite easily, but how do you group by month? Well, using the DatePart function you could do this easily.

1. Create a new query based upon the sales data, from tblSales. You can do this from the main database window by selecting the **Queries**, and then double-clicking on **Create query in Design view**. When the **Show Table** dialog appears select tblSales, click **Add**, and then click **Close**.

2. Add the **DateOrdered** and **Quantity** fields to the query. You can do this by just double-clicking on these.

3. In the **DateOrdered** field, change the field so that it looks like this:

```
SalesMonth: DatePart ("m", [DateOrdered])
```

4. Add some sorting, so that we sort ascending by this new field. Also make sure the Show check box is still selected, so that the field appears in the query.

5. Make this a summary query, by selecting the totals button on the toolbar. For the **Quantity** column change the **Total** from **Group By** to **Sum**. The query should now look like this:

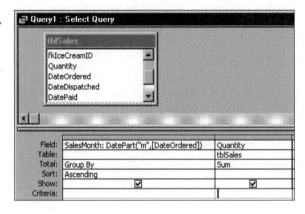

6. Now run the query:

So, not only can you use functions in code, you can use them in queries too. If you want to keep this query, don't forget to save it.

Formatting Variables

You've seen from the examples above that when used within VBA, dates and times are converted to the US format, but when they are printed out they use the local settings of the machine. This happens for numbers too. But what happens if you want to print out dates in a different format, or specify a format for a number? The solution to this is to use the formatting functions supplied with VBA.

Formatting Numbers

To format numbers you can use one of the formatting functions:

❑ `FormatCurrency` to format a number into a currency style.

❑ `FormatNumber` to format a number into a normal number style.

❑ `FormatPercent` to format a number into a percent style.

All of these functions have several arguments, most of which are optional. They allow us to change the number of digits after the decimal point, whether or not to include a leading 0 for fractions, whether or not to use parentheses for negative numbers, and whether or not a grouping separator is used. Have a look in the help file for the exact details of these arguments.

You can see the difference between these functions easily. Consider this code:

```
Dim dblNumber As Double

dblNumber = 1234.567

Debug.Print dblNumber
Debug.Print FormatCurrency(dblNumber)
Debug.Print FormatNumber(dblNumber)
Debug.Print FormatPercent(dblNumber)
```

This code gives the following output:

```
1234.567
$1,234.57
1,234.57
123,456.70%
```

You can see some interesting things here:

- ❑ All functions use the Regional Settings to determine the grouping of numbers and the number of decimal places

- ❑ `FormatCurrency` adds the local currency sign to the front of the number.

- ❑ `FormatNumber` adds no special formatting apart from grouping and rounding.

- ❑ `FormatPercent` multiplies the number by 100 and adds a percent sign to the end of the number. (Although this looks odd, it makes sense – 0.5 is 50%).

Formatting Dates

To format dates you can use the `FormatDateTime` function, which takes two arguments. This first is the date to be formatted, and the second (optionally) is the format. Have a look at the code below:

```
Dim datDateTime As Date

datDateTime = #11/30/1998 10:54:17#

Debug.Print datDateTime
Debug.Print FormatDateTime(datDateTime, vbGeneralDate)
Debug.Print FormatDateTime(datDateTime, vbLongDate)
Debug.Print FormatDateTime(datDateTime, vbLongTime)
Debug.Print FormatDateTime(datDateTime, vbShortDate)
Debug.Print FormatDateTime(datDateTime, vbShortTime)
```

The values used for the second argument are constants, pre-defined by VBA. We'll be looking at constants later in the chapter.

This code gives the following output:

```
11/30/1998 10:54:17 AM
11/30/1998 10:54:17 AM
Monday, November 30, 1998
10:54:17 AM
11/30/9
10:54
```

This shows that the general format is used by default when printing dates.

Custom Formats

The functions described above for formatting numbers and dates are all very well, but what if you want to specify the format yourself. For this you can use the `Format` function, which has the following syntax:

```
Format (Expression [, Format [, FirstDayOfWeek [, FirstWeekOfYear]]])
```

As you can see three of the arguments are optional. Let's look at them in turn.

❑ *Expression* is the item of data to be formatted.

❑ *Format* is the format we want the data to appear in. There are some predefined formats that allow quick formatting, but you can specify your own format too.

❑ *FirstDayOfWeek* allows us to specify which is the first day of the week. By default this is Sunday, but you could set this to Monday if you prefer to start your week on a Monday, as some countries do. This is quite important when converting dates into week numbers, as the day the week starts on could affect which week a date appears in. There are intrinsic constants for all days of the week – see the help file for a list.

❑ *FirstWeekOfYear* allows us to specify which week is defined as the first of the year. By default this is the week in which January 1ˢᵗ occurs, but it could be the first week with at least four full days, or the first full week. This is important when dealing with week numbers, especially as it allows you to set the starting week of a fiscal year.

We are only going to concern ourselves with the first two arguments. In fact, we're really going to look at the second argument – the format.

For dates you have a number of options for the format:

❑ Short Date, which is the same as FormatDateTime with vbShortDate

❑ Short Time, which is the same as FormatDateTime with vbShortTime

❑ Long Date, which is the same as FormatDateTime with vbLongDate

❑ Long Time, which is the same as FormatDateTime with vbLongTime

❑ A custom format.

For the custom format you can use, among others, a combination of:

❑ d or dd for the day number

❑ ddd for the shortened day name, e.g. Mon

❑ dddd for the full day name

❑ m or mm for the month number

❑ mmm for the shortened month name, e.g. Mar

❑ mmmm for the full month name

❑ yy for the two digit year

❑ yyyy for the four digit year

- ❏ h or hh for the hour
- ❏ m or mm for the minute
- ❏ s or ss for the seconds
- ❏ AMPM for an AM/PM indicator
- ❏ Any other text, which is printed out verbatim.

For example, with datDateTime set to 11/30/1998 10:54:17 AM:

Format	Results in
Format(datDateTime, "Long Date")	Monday, November 30, 1998
Format(datDateTime, "dd mmm yyyy")	30 Nov 1998
Format(datDateTime, "yyyy-mm-dd")	1998-11-30
Format(datDateTime, "mm dddd hh:mm")	11 Monday 10:54

You can see that although m and mm appear to be shared between months and minutes, their use is worked out depending upon the context.

Formatting numbers follows similar lines, where you can use:

- ❏ Currency (giving the same as FormatCurrency)
- ❏ Percent, (giving the same as FormatPercent)
- ❏ A custom format

For a custom format you can use a combination of:

- ❏ 0 to display a digit or a zero. This allows you to pad the string with zeros.
- ❏ # to display a digit. Nothing is displayed if no number is present.
- ❏ . for a decimal placeholder. You always use a decimal point here and not the placeholder specified in the regional settings.
- ❏ % for a percentage placeholder. Like FormatPercent the number is multiplied by 100.
- ❏ , for a thousands separator. You always use a comma here and not the separator in the regional settings.

For example, with dblNumber set to 12345.678:

Format	Results in
Format(dblNumber "0.00")	12345.68
Format(dblNumber "000000.00")	012345.68

Format	Results in
Format(dblNumber "#####0")	123456
Format(dblNumber "###,##0.00")	12,345.68

You can see that you can put any number of these placeholders in the format string to achieve exactly what you want.

Constants

Constants can be considered as read-only variables. They are declared while you are writing your code, and can be used anywhere in the code, but they can not be changed – that's why they are called constants. They are a great way to improve the readability and maintainability of your code because, like variables, they have a name, and you can therefore use the name instead of the actual value in your code.

You add constants to your code using the `Const` statement. For example:

```
Const clSpeedOfLight = 299792458
```

Once defined you can use the name in your code instead of the value. So what's the use of this? Well firstly it makes your code more readable. Seeing `299792458` in your, or someone else's, code might not be very meaningful (unless you're a rocket scientist), but seeing `clSpeedOfLight` instantly gives the game away. Another great reason is that should the value of a constant change, you only have to change it once, where it is defined, and not everywhere in the code. OK, it's unlikely the speed of light will ever change, but those quantum physicists get up to some pretty weird things, so you can never be too sure!

You can use constants anywhere in code, even in other constant definitions:

```
Const csMinute = 60
Const csHour = csMinute * 60
Const csDay = 24 * csHour
```

Constants also allow you to declare a type, which can improve the error checking that VBA can do:

```
Const clSpeedOfLight As Long = 299792458
Const csCleverPerson As String = "Albert Einstein"
```

Notice that there are also some naming standards applied to these constants – this is the `cs` and `cl` you see at the start of the constant name. We'll look at naming standards later.

Intrinsic Constants

Intrinsic constants are ones that are automatically defined by Access or VBA. You can find a full list of these in the Access help file, under the Visual Basic Language Reference section.

For example, earlier in the chapter we used the `VarType` function to determine the type of a variant. If you wanted to test a variant to see whether it contained a string you could do this:

```
If VarType(varAnyThing) = 8 Then
```

However, this has the immediate disadvantage in that you must know what the value 8 means. Luckily there is a set of intrinsic constants just for this purpose. Let's have another look at the table:

Value	Variant type	Constant
0	Empty (uninitialized)	vbEmpty
1	Null (no valid data)	vbNull
2	Integer	vbInteger
3	Long Integer	vbLong
4	Single	vbSingle
5	Double	vbDouble
6	Currency	vbCurrency
7	Date	vbDate
8	String	vbString
9	Object	vbObject
10	Error value	vbError
11	Boolean	vbBoolean
12	Variant (only used with arrays of variants)	vbVariant
13	Data access object	vbDataObject
14	Decimal value	vbDecimal
17	Byte	vbByte
36	User Defined Type	vbUserDefinedType
8192	Array	vbArray

Now our code becomes much more readable:

```
If VarType(varAnyThing) = vbString Then
```

You'll see plenty of uses of intrinsic and user-defined constants as we go through the book.

Variable Scope and Lifetime

Whether or not you can use a variable within a particular procedure depends on where and how the variable was declared, i.e. on the **scope** of a variable. Scope is the term given to the visibility of a variable, in other words, where it can be seen from. A variable that is created within a procedure can only be seen, and therefore can only be changed, from within that procedure. Its scope is **local** to the procedure. However, a variable can also be declared outside a procedure in the (General) (Declarations) section. In this case, it can be seen by all procedures in that module (and sometimes other modules as well). Thus, its scope is **public**.

The lifetime of a variable is defined as how long the variable can be seen for; in other words, how long it will contain the value assigned to it. Normally, local variables 'live' for as long as their procedure has the control – so when the procedure ends the variable ceases to exist. The next time the procedure is called, the local variables are recreated.

If you want local variables to exist even when the procedure exits, you can use the Static keyword. Making a variable Static ensures that its contents are not lost. You can also declare a procedure as Static, which makes all of the local variables within the procedure Static. However, Static variables still have the same scope as normal variables. They cannot be seen outside of their procedure, even though their lifetime is longer than the procedure.

A Public variable exists as long as the database is open and retains its contents throughout the life of the program.

> *With VBA, you can apply scope to the procedures themselves by using the **Public** and **Private** keywords. A **Private** procedure can only be called from within the module in which it is declared, whereas a **Public** procedure can be seen from everywhere.*

A procedure has to be Public for it to be called from the Immediate window. A Private procedure is only visible to other procedures in the same module. So if you are creating Private procedures and you need to test them from the Immediate window, you will have to change them to Public to test them. Don't forget to change them back though, once you've finished testing.

Let's look at these concepts in more detail.

Local Variables

You have already seen local variables in the VariantExample procedure and others that you created earlier. Remember that the variables are local to the procedure, no matter where the procedure can be seen from. So local variables in a Public procedure have the same scope as local variables in a Private procedure – it is just the procedure that can be seen from outside, not the variables. This means that you can have different procedures with local variables that have the same name.

Let's have a look at some simple examples that illustrate this.

Try It Out - Local Variables

1. Create a new subroutine and call it `Procedure1`. Make sure it's a Public procedure. Enter the following lines:

```
Public Sub Procedure1()



intVariable2 = 2

Debug.Print intVariable1
Debug.Print intVariable2
End Sub
```

2. Now create another subroutine, a Private one this time, called `Procedure2`, with these lines:

```
Private Sub Procedure2()
Dim intVariable1 As Integer

intVariable1 = 100

Debug.Print intVariable1
End Sub
```

3. Now you need a third subroutine called `TestLocal`, that calls the first two:

```
Public Sub TestLocal()
Procedure1
Procedure2
Procedure1
End Sub
```

4. Now open the Immediate window and run the `TestLocal` subroutine:

```
Debug.Print intVariable2
```

Before running the example again, think about what you expect to happen.

OK, that's long enough. Now try typing `TestLocal` in the Immediate window again. Were you surprised at receiving the error? Whether yes or no, the reason is simple. `Procedure1` declared `intVariable2` as local. Therefore, no other procedure can see the variable. Don't forget to remove this last line, otherwise it will cause error messages later.

Try It Out – Local Scope

Now let's look at another example to explain local scope.

1. Stop the module running by selecting the **Reset** button on the toolbar (the one that's a filled in square). Then create another Public subroutine, `TestLocal1`, and add the following lines:

```
Public Sub TestLocal1()
    Dim intVariable1 As Integer

    intVariable1 = intVariable1 + 1
    Debug.Print intVariable1
End Sub
```

Here, you are adding 1 to the variable even though it has not been used before. This is allowed, since an integer is set to 0 when first declared. This should give you a clue as to what happens when you run the program.

2. Now type `TestLocal1` in the Immediate window. Don't worry about the data that is already there - it won't affect what you are doing. Now type `TestLocal1` again. You should see:

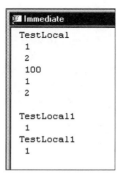

You can see that `intVariable1` is reset each time the procedure is called.

Local variables only exist while a procedure has the control. When the procedure ends, local variables 'die'. When the procedure is called again, local variables are reset.

Static Variables

To allow a variable to retain its value over multiple calls, you must declare it as Static. This means that the variable is only initialized once – the first time the procedure is called. To declare a variable in this manner, you replace the Dim with Static:

```
Static intVariable1 As Integer
```

Try It Out – Static Variables

1. Stop the module running by selecting the **Reset** button on the toolbar. Then create another subroutine called StaticScope. Add the same code as before, but this time change the variable declaration line from Dim to Static:

```
Static intVariable1 As Integer

intVariable1 = intVariable1 + 1
Debug.Print intVariable1
```

2. Run the subroutine several times from the Immediate window.

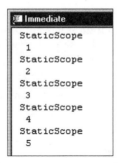

So, just by changing one word, you have dramatically altered the way the program works. You'll find this a useful feature; for example, you can use static variables to create a function that keeps a running total each time a new value is passed in, or one that keeps track of the number of times it has been called. This could be used, for instance, as a user name and password system for securing a system. You could limit the user to three tries before shutting the system down.

If you want all variables in a procedure to be static, just put Static before the procedure declaration:

```
Static Sub AllVariablesAreStatic ()
```

All variables will now be Static irrespective of whether they are declared with Static or Dim.

Global Variables

If you need other procedures to see your variables, you can use a global variable, defined in the (Declarations) section of a module. There are two types of global variables:

❑ Those that can be seen by every procedure in the module but can not be seen outside of the module. These are often called **Module** level variables. You declare these using the `Private` keyword.

❑ Those that can be seen everywhere in the program, even outside of the module. These are called **Public** variables. You declare these using the `Public` keyword.

Try It Out – Module Variables

We'll create two subroutines called `TestProc1` and `TestProc2` within the same module that you've been using throughout this chapter.

1. Move to the (Declarations) section of the module window and enter the following line under the `Option` statements:

```
Private intModuleVariable As Integer
```

2. Now create a subroutine, `TestProc1`, as follows:

```
Public Sub TestProc1
    intModuleVariable = intModuleVariable + 1
End Sub
```

3. Now create another subroutine, `TestProc2`, as follows:

```
Public Sub TestProc2
    Debug.Print intModuleVariable
End Sub
```

4. Try calling the two procedures from the Immediate window to see what happens:

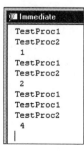

```
Immediate
TestProc1
TestProc2
 1
TestProc1
TestProc2
 2
TestProc1
TestProc1
TestProc2
 4
|
```

Here you can see that although neither procedure declared `intModuleVariable`, they can both access it. However, procedures in other modules or forms will not be able to access it.

> *A module- or form-level variable has the scope of the module or form. If, for example, you declare a variable in the* **(Declarations)** *section of a form, all procedures in that form will have access to it. When the form is unloaded, the variable and its contents will die and will be reset when the form is next loaded.*

5. Now add a third procedure, `TestProc3`, as follows:

```
Public Sub TestProc3
    Dim intModuleVariable As Integer
    intModuleVariable = 100
    Debug.Print intModuleVariable
End Sub
```

This declares `intModuleVariable` as a local variable when you already have it as a module-level variable.

6. Run through the procedure again to see what happens:

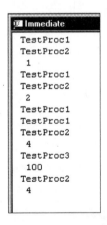

```
Immediate
TestProc1
TestProc2
1
TestProc1
TestProc2
2
TestProc1
TestProc1
TestProc2
4
TestProc3
100
TestProc2
4
```

The call to `TestProc3` does not change its own (separate) variable `intModuleVariable`, but also does not affect the public `intModuleVariable` variable. Only its own copy is in scope within the procedure.

So, not only can you have procedures with local variables of the same name, but you can also have local variables with the same names as public ones. In this case, the procedure with the local variable will always use its own variable, rather than the global one. You can probably see that it is not a very good idea to create local and public variables with the same name, as it can lead to confusion when looking at the code later. It is much better practice to use different names for your variables.

Public Variables

A public variable is one that can be accessed from all modules and forms. They can only be created in modules, not within the (Declarations) section of a form. To declare a public variable, replace the Private statement with Public:

```
Public intModuleVariable As Integer
```

This variable is now accessible to all modules and forms and has a lifetime until the database is closed.

You cannot declare Public variables within a procedure.

Public vs. Private

There are some general principles that you should bear in mind when deciding on the scope and lifetime of your variables:

❑ Unless you are writing a general routine, make procedures private. This is especially true if you are developing in teams or writing add-ins, as then there is no danger of your procedure clashing with another of the same name. However, you should never really have more than one procedure with the same name. The names of procedures should actually be decided at the design time, specifically to avoid this sort of confusion.

❑ Wherever possible, you should avoid manipulating variables that are declared outside a procedure. Instead, pass the value of the variable into the procedure using an argument. Inside the procedure, you can perform the calculations required and return the new value to the code that calls it. This not only protects you from errors that are difficult to find, but also makes your procedures far more generic and re-usable.

❑ Use public variables sparingly and with care. You will generally find that only a small number of public variables are used in most programs. It is sometimes much easier to use a public variable than to have the same variable declared in several procedures and passed as a parameter. However, do not always take the easy route. Think about how a variable is going to be used and try to plan ahead.

Naming Conventions

Naming conventions are one of the most important concepts in programming and yet are rarely taught. It's easy to ignore the importance of a systematic approach to naming variables, etc. – but believe me, once you start programming in earnest, you'll realize that not only does a set of conventions make thinking up new names easier, but it is a godsend when it comes to understanding the code you have written. For example, if you follow a set of conventions, you will be able to tell at a glance a variable's type and where it was declared (that is, whether it is local or public). This will save you having to look for the variable declaration to find this out – a process which can be especially tedious if you have several modules and public variables.

Naming conventions are, of course, a matter of personal taste and you should use whichever set of standards you prefer. There are no hard and fast rules (the ones shown here are fairly standard, although other people may use slightly different prefixes than the ones we've shown). All we can do is list our favorite set of conventions and let you make your own mind up...

Keep Names Meaningful

The first rule is to make variable names meaningful. They should describe what they hold. If you have a variable that holds someone's age, then call it Age. A birth date should be stored as DateOfBirth, or date_of_birth. We prefer the first method without the underscores, since we think it looks neater, but you can choose any style. The important point is to be consistent. If you have a system, then stick to it.

Prefix All Variables and Constants With Their Type

If you use a prefix, you can easily see what type the variable is. For example, if Age was stored as an integer, then you should use int as the prefix, giving intAge. The prefix is lower case to separate it from the variable name. The most commonly used prefixes are listed below:

Variable Type		Prefixes
Integer		int
Long		lng
Single		sng
Double		dbl
Currency		ccy
	or	cur
String		str
Variant		var
Date		dat
	or	dte
Boolean		bln
Byte		byt
Object		obj
Hyperlink		hyp

It's also a good idea to add a double prefix for the variant type. Use var to denote that a variant is in use, but add another prefix to denote the type of data the variant will store. For example, if the age was to be stored in this way, you could use intvarAge.

Prefix Global Variables with their Scope

Yet another prefix. Will it never stop? This is the last one and, in some ways, the most useful since it can be a great time saver. Use a prefix to denote the scope, i.e. whether it is a local, module or public variable. You can leave the prefix for local variables blank, since most will be local, but use m_ for module level, g_ for public (global) variables and s for static variables in procedures. Thus if Age was a public variant holding an integer value, it would become g_intvarAge.

OK, so in this case the prefixes are now larger than the variable name, but on the other hand you can see everything about this variable from its name. What could be clearer?

Naming Conventions for Controls

In the same way that you use conventions for variables, you should also consider using them for controls on forms and reports, especially if you are going to refer to these controls in your code.

Control	Prefix
Chart (graph)	cht
Check box	chk
Combo box	cbo
Command button	cmd
Frame	fra
Label	lbl
Line	lin
List box	lst
Option button	opt
Option group	grp
Page break	brk
Rectangle	rec
Subform/report	sub
Text box	txt
Toggle button	tgl
Hyperlink	hyp

The principle is exactly the same as for variables and, again, will make your code easier to read:

```
Function GetName () As String

    Dim strName As String
```

```
    strName = txtFirstName & " " & txtLastName
    GetName = strName

End Function
```

It immediately becomes obvious that the first and last names are stored on the form in text boxes.

Now that the use of ActiveX controls is becoming widespread, you may find you wish to use controls that do not fit into the above list. In this case just use a prefix that you find suitable. For example, we will be looking at the Calendar control later on, and for this you could use `cal`.

Naming Conventions for Objects

The same principle should be applied to objects, both in code and in the database window. So when you save your tables, queries, forms, etc., follow the same principle:

Object	Prefix
Table	tbl
Query	qry
Form	frm
Report	rpt
Macro	mac
Module	mod
Users	usr
Groups	grp
Containers	con
Documents	doc
Indexes	idx
Fields	fld
Property	pty
Pages	pag

You may not have come across many of these objects yet, but you will meet a few more as the book progresses.

Naming Conventions for Constants

For constants you follow a similar style to variables, although some people prefer to have their constants all in capitals. We recommend using a **c** at the front of the name, to indicate a constant, and then the prefix for the type, making sure that you always specify the type of the constant. For example:

```
Const clngSpeedOfLight As Long = 299792458
Const cstrCleverPerson As String = "Albert Einstein"
```

or a slightly shorter form:

```
Const clSpeedOfLight As Long = 299792458
Const csCleverPerson As String = "Albert Einstein"
```

Naming Conventions Summary

All of this may seem rather cumbersome and a waste of effort, but as your programs become larger, you will find it essential to be able to identify different variables/controls/objects. If you start using conventions as you learn the language, it will soon become second nature and, after a while, you won't even have to think about it!

One of the greatest advantages of naming conventions is in maintenance. You will inevitably spend a proportion of time maintaining code, and not necessarily your own code. If a standard set of conventions has been used, it makes your job so much easier. You will automatically know where global variables are stored, what type variables are, and what their scope is, and the chance of introducing errors is automatically reduced. If you follow this procedure, then it benefits others who have to maintain your code. No one likes maintenance, we all want to write cool new apps, so the quicker and more efficient you can make the process the better.

> The really important thing to remember is consistency. Whichever style you choose, you should be consistent with its use. Don't think that just because you are writing a small program or a single procedure that naming conventions have no place. If you are going to use a style, then use it everywhere.

Summary

This chapter has covered an awful lot of ground, but it's really important stuff. The techniques we've looked at are the building blocks of programming. Every program is made up from procedures, and these all use variables, other procedures, built in functions, and so on. Having a good understanding of this will make it easier to understand other code that you see, as well as making your own code better.

In this chapter, we looked at:

> ❑ What procedures and functions are. They are small groups of code that perform a task. Sometimes that task may be small, and other times it may be quite large, but the chunk of code is usually a logical unit, with a defined purpose. Making ice cream and making frozen yogurt are two separate tasks, although their procedures might be similar.

> ❑ What variables are, and how they can be used. Variables are where we store temporary information during a procedure. They allow us to store and manipulate different types of data.

> ❑ The scope (where the variable can be seen from) and lifetime (how long the variable keeps its value) of variables. It's important to always think about how great a scope you want for each variable, and how their lifetime will affect the code you're writing.

> ❑ Naming conventions, to show the importance of consistency. As you see more and more code, this can ease your understanding, as well as making it quicker to maintain.

Now that you've got a good understanding of these techniques, let's move on to look at how we can make decisions in our code, and use looping to help us with repetitive tasks.

Exercises

1. Create a function called Power with two integer arguments, the second of which is optional. The function should raise the first argument to the power of the second. If the second argument is omitted then raise the first number to the power of 2.

2. Spend some time looking through the help file, especially the list of VBA functions. You can find these under Visual Basic Language Reference, Functions.

Controlling the Program

Most of the procedures that you have seen so far have been fairly simple – they start at the first line, finish at the last, and execute the lines in between one after the other. However, there are times when you want to run only one section of code, or perhaps run a section of code more than once, depending on certain conditions. To do this, you have to introduce **control structures** into your code. These are what we'll look at in this chapter.

We'll cover:

- ❑ How to make decisions in a program
- ❑ How to perform repetitive tasks
- ❑ How to store variables in an array
- ❑ The difference between static and dynamic arrays

Programming Structures

There are three main structures that are used in programming. Firstly, **sequential**, where we need to do things one after the other, or in a certain order. We saw some of that in the previous chapter, and you'll see plenty more as we go through the book. Next comes **selection**, where we often need to make a choice based upon some piece of information, so we either do one thing or another. Lastly comes looping, or **repetition**, where we do the same thing over and over again.

Expressions

With VBA, you can check something and perform different operations depending on the results of the check. This check is usually called a **condition** or an **expression**. An expression always has a boolean result – that is, it's either True or False. The easy way to think about expressions is to just think about everyday decisions, like 'Do I want to open a large tub of ice cream?' That's probably going to be True (it is for me, anyway). You are not limited to just one statement – how about 'Do I want to stop work and open a large tub of ice cream?' Here, we've got two statements.

When dealing with multiple statements you generally join them together, either by an `And` or by an `Or`. In the above example we used `And`, which means that both statements have to be True for the whole expression to be True. If you want to stop work but don't feel like ice cream at the moment, then the expression is False. If we had used `Or`, then only one of the statements needed to have been True for the whole expression to be True. 'Do I want to stop work OR do I want to open a large tub of ice cream?'

When joining statements together in expressions, the rule is quite simple:

- ❑ If you use `Or` to join the statements, then only one statement has to be True for the expression to be True.

- ❑ If you use `And` to join the statements, then all statements have to be True for the expression to be True.

You can also mix the two types of statements. 'Do I want to stop work and open a large tub of ice cream, or do I want a cup of coffee?'

You'll see plenty of expressions as we go through this chapter, and we'll be revisiting them again in a little while, once we've looked at how we make decisions.

Selection Structures

We know that everyday life has many decisions, and VBA code often has plenty of them too. We use selection structures to make those decisions, and these structures are the VBA statements that mean we can perform one task or another.

If...Then...

We've already come across this statement back when we were creating an intelligent navigation button. We'll now take a look at the structure of the statement and then run through a couple of examples. You use `If...Then` when you want to execute a piece of code only when a certain statement is true. It has two formats; the single line format is as follows:

```
If expression Then statement
```

Its multi-line format runs like this:

```
If expression Then
  statement1
  statement2
End If
```

Both of the above perform the same operation. (The second example, however, allows more than one line as the *statement*). For example,

```
If strName = "" Then Exit Function
```

is the same as:

```
If strName = "" Then
   Exit Function
End If
```

Here, you test whether the argument `strName` is an empty string (denoted by the two double quotes together), and if so, exit the function directly.

The expression can also contain other functions:

```
Sub Test()

   Dim strNumber As String

   strNumber = "1234"

   If IsNumeric(strNumber) = True Then
       Debug.Print strNumber & " is a number"
   End If

   strNumber = "one two three four"

   If IsNumeric(strNumber) = True Then
       Debug.Print strNumber & " is a number"
   End If

End If
```

The function `IsNumeric` returns a value of True if the string passed in is a number. The above code would print out the following:

1234 is a number

There would be nothing printed for the second If statement because the string passed in does not contain a number.

If...Then...Else...

You can use the `If...Then...Else...` statement to decide which of two actions to perform. Let's revisit our number test, adding in a few lines:

```
Sub Test()

   Dim strNumber As String

   strNumber = "1234"

   If IsNumeric(strNumber) = True Then
       Debug.Print strNumber & " is a number"
   Else
       Debug.Print strNumber & " is not a number"
   End If

   strNumber = "one two three four"
```

```
    If IsNumeric(strNumber) = True Then
        Debug.Print strNumber & " is a number"
    Else
        Debug.Print strNumber & " is not a number"
    End If

End If
```

Here we test the string to see if it contains a number. If it does, we run the code as before. If the string is not a number, then we run some other code. This would produce:

1234 is a number
one two three four is not a number

You can include variables and numerical and relational operators in you expressions too:

```
Dim intAbc As Integer
Dim intDef As Integer
Dim strName As String

intAbc = 1
intDef = 2
strName = "Janine"

If intAbc = 1 Then Debug.Print "Abc is 1"
If intAbc = intDef Then Debug.Print "Two variables the same"
If intAbc > intDef Then Debug.Print "Abc is greater than Def"
If intAbc + 1 = intDef Then Debug.Print "Adding 1 to Abc gives Def"
if strName = "Janine" Then Debug.Print "Hello Jan"
```

Note that you can use any normal arithmetic operators within an If statement, such as +, -, *, /, or the relational operators <, >, = in conjunction with variables and values, to determine whether or not a condition is true.

ElseIf...

The ElseIf statement is used for joining a set of If conditions together. This is quite common when you need to check the results of several different conditions:

```
If intAbc = 1 Then
    Debug.Print "Abc is 1"
ElseIf intAbc = intDef Then
    Debug.Print "Two variables the same"
Else
    Debug.Print "Abc is not 1 and it is not the same as Def"
End If
```

If the first condition is true, then only the code between the Then statement and the ElseIf is executed and no more conditions are tested. If the first condition isn't true, the second is tried. If that isn't true, the Else statement is executed.

Logical Operators with the If statement

You can also make more complex queries with this statement by using logical operators. The three most common logical operators are AND, OR and NOT. You can use these to test a combination of expressions together to get a true or false answer. The answer is calculated via a set of truth tables which are applied for each operator:

AND	Expression 1	Expression 2	Result
	TRUE	TRUE	TRUE
	TRUE	FALSE	FALSE
	FALSE	TRUE	FALSE
	FALSE	FALSE	FALSE

OR	Expression 1	Expression 2	Result
	TRUE	TRUE	TRUE
	TRUE	FALSE	TRUE
	FALSE	TRUE	TRUE
	FALSE	FALSE	FALSE

NOT	Expression	Result
	TRUE	FALSE
	FALSE	TRUE

It's as easy, though, to use common sense to deduce what the answer should be. Think of it in terms of the English language; for example, if you break the speed limit OR you rob a bank, it's true that you've broken the law. Let's look at the earlier example to make the criteria slightly more complex.

```
Dim intAbc As Integer
Dim intDef As Integer
Dim strName As String

intAbc = 1
intDef = 2
strName = "Janine"

If intAbc = 1 And intDef = 2 Then Debug.Print "Abc is 1 and Def is 2"
If intAbc = 1 Or intDef = 2 Then Debug.Print "Either Abc is 1 or Def is 2"
```

Select Case

There's no limit to the number of ElseIf statements that you can have:

```
If datOrderDate >= #7/1/98# Then
.
.
.
ElseIf datOrderDate >= #6/1/98# And datOrderDate <= #6/30/98# Then
.
.
.
ElseIf datOrderDate < #6/1/98# Then
.
.
.
Else
.
.
.
End If
```

> *Remember that the # sign around the dates just tells VBA that this is a date value, otherwise VBA would take 6/1/98 as 6 divided by 1 divided by 98.*

You can see that the code is starting to look messy. There's a much better way – using the Select Case statement:

```
Select Case datOrderDate
Case Is >= #7/1/98#
.
.
.
Case #6/1/98# To #6/30/98#
.
.
.
Case Else
.
.
.
End Select
```

This is much clearer to read. If datOrderDate is equal to or after the 1st July then the section of code under this Case statement would be executed. The second Case statement checks for datOrderDate being from June 1st to June 30th, and the Case Else will get run if datOrderDate is any other date. Adding a Case Else statement is not compulsory, but it's always a good idea to include one, just in case the variable you are testing has an unexpected value. Even if you don't think you need a Case Else, it's best to put one in anyway, and put an error message there. That way, if some unexpected value appears you'll know about it, and be able to act accordingly.

You can also test for more than one value with Case:

```
Select Case intMainCount
Case 1, 2, 3
.
.
.
```

```
Case 4 To 6
  .
  .
  .
Case Else
  .
  .
  .
End Select
```

This shows two different ways of testing the condition. If `intMainCount` is 1, 2 or 3, the first section is executed. If it's between 4 and 6 inclusive, the second section is executed, and so on. You can achieve the same result using the `Is` keyword and an expression:

```
Select Case intMainCount
Case Is < 4
  .
  .
  .
Case Is < 7
  .
  .
  .
Case Else
  .
  .
  .
End Select
```

Here, if `intMainCount` is less than 4, the first section is executed, and so on.

Note that, as soon as a true expression is found in a `Select Case` statement, no more expressions are checked. An expression must fail one test to get to the next. This means that if you have an expression that matches two `Case` statements, only the first will be executed.

`Select Case` isn't limited to numeric tests – you can also use strings:

```
Select Case strSalutation
Case "Mrs", "Miss", "Ms"
  .
  .
  .
Case "Mr"
  .
  .
  .
Case Else
  .
  .
  .
End Select
```

You can also use the `To` form with strings:

```
Case "Alfred" To "Bertrand"
```

This would be executed if the condition matched any string within the range specified. Don't be put off by the fact the string has a range - strings are checked in alphabetical order, so Alfred comes before Bertrand. They can be tested alphabetically, so a value such as `"Basil"` would be accepted in such a condition, while `"Roy"` would be excluded.

As you can see, not only is the `Select Case` statement very flexible, but it can also greatly increase the clarity of your code. Let's give this a go:

Try It Out – Select Case

1. Create a new procedure called `Seat`, to find out where we are sitting on a plane. Add the following code:

```
Public Sub Seat(strSeatNumber As String)

    Dim intRow As Integer
    Dim strSeat As String

    intRow = Left$(strSeatNumber, 2)
    strSeat = Right$(strSeatNumber, 1)

    Select Case intRow
    Case 1
        Debug.Print "At the front eh? Must be the pilot"
    Case 2 To 5
        Debug.Print "First Class - a lottery winner"
    Case 6 To 10
        Debug.Print "Business Class - on a business trip"
    Case 11 To 54
        Debug.Print "Cattle Class - squeeze up now"
    Case Else
        Debug.Print "No seat - must be on the tail!"
    End Select

    Select Case strSeat
    Case "a" To "c"
        Debug.Print "To the left of the plane"
    Case "d" To "g"
        Debug.Print "In the middle"
    Case "h" To "j"
        Debug.Print "To the right of the plane"
    Case Else
        Debug.Print "In the aisle"
    End Select

End Sub
```

2. Switch to the Immediate window and try it out with a few seat numbers. These should have a two-digit row and a single character seat.

```
Immediate
Seat "14d"
Cattle Class - squeeze up now
In the middle

Seat "03a"
First Class - a lottery winner
To the left of the plane

Seat "99t"
No seat - must be on the tail!
In the aisle
```

How it Works

Firstly we have two variables, to store the row number and the seat letter.

```
Dim intRow As Integer
Dim strSeat As String
```

Before we can decide where you are sitting, we need to work out the row number. We use `Left$` for this, which extracts the leftmost characters from a string. Here, we are extracting the two characters at the left of the strings, as these will be the row number. We assign this to the integer variable, allowing VBA to automatically convert the string containing numbers into an integer number.

```
intRow = Left$(strSeatNumber, 2)
```

We then use `Right$` for a similar purpose, this time to extract the very rightmost character from the string. This will be the seat number.

```
strSeat = Right$(strSeatNumber, 1)
```

Now we can go ahead with our `Select` statement, first checking the row number. The first case will only happen if the row number is 1:

```
Select Case intRow
Case 1
    Debug.Print "At the front eh? Must be the pilot"
```

If the row is between 2 and 5 inclusive then the second case is run:

```
Case 2 To 5
    Debug.Print "First Class - a lottery winner"
```

For seats including 6 to 10 we have the third case:

```
Case 6 To 10
    Debug.Print "Business Class - on a business trip"
```

For the seats at the back of the plane, 11 through to 54, the fourth case is run:

```
Case 11 To 54
    Debug.Print "Cattle Class - squeeze up now"
```

If your row number is anything else then I hope you brought a coat, as it's quite windy on the tail!

```
Case Else
    Debug.Print "No seat - must be on the tail!"
End Select
```

Once the row number is decided, you can find out which side of the plane you are on. Seats a to c are on the left, d to g are in the middle, and h to j are on the right.

```
Select Case strSeat
Case "a" To "c"
   Debug.Print "To the left of the plane"
Case "d" To "g"
   Debug.Print "In the middle"
Case "h" To "j"
   Debug.Print "To the right of the plane"
Case Else
   Debug.Print "In the aisle"
End Select
```

You can easily see how much clearer this is than if we had used If statements.

IIf

There are certain places (such as in queries, but more on that later) where you need to be able to return one of two values, but you can't use the If statement. In these cases, you can use the **immediate if**, or IIf:

```
strName = "Janine"

strWhoAreYou = IIf (strName = "Janine", "Hi Jan", "Who are you?")
```

The IIf statement takes three arguments:

❑   The condition to test for

❑   The value to return if the condition was true

❑   The value to return if the condition was false

So, the statement below is exactly the same as the If statement above:

```
If strName = "Janine" Then
   strWhoAreYou = "Hi Jan"
Else
   strWhoAreYou = "Who are you?"
End If
```

Some people prefer using the IIf since it looks slightly neater, as it's all on one line, but it can be a cause of confusion, especially for new programmers. There is also a major drawback you have to be aware of. When using the IIf statement, all three arguments are evaluated by VBA. "So what?" you may ask. Consider the following examples, where we divide one number by another:

```
Function Divide (intNumber1 As Integer, intNumber2 As Integer) As Double

   If intNumber2 = 0 Then
      Divide = 0
   Else
      Divide = intNumber1 / intNumber2
   End If

End Function
```

```
Function Divide (intNumber1 As Integer, intNumber2 As Integer) As Double

   Divide = IIf (intNumber2 = 0, 0, intNumber1 / intNumber2)

End Function
```

The two functions look as though they should work the same, but this isn't the case. If intNumber2 is 0, the second version will give a Divide by Zero error because intNumber1 / intNumber2 is always evaluated. You must bear this in mind when you use IIf.

Because IIf evaluates all the arguments, it's slower to use than the normal If statement. Admittedly, you'll probably never notice this, but if you were to use IIf in a large loop, that small delay would gradually build up. You might not think that a small delay is a problem, but you can be sure that your users will think otherwise!

The real use for IIf is in queries and on forms and reports. You'll see examples of this later in the book.

Operator Precedence

When combining conditions and expressions, it's very important that you understand operator precedence. This defines the order in which parts of an expression are evaluated and is similar to the lessons that you learnt in mathematics when you were at school. The rules are recapped below and may, at first, seem complex, but do persevere. There are some examples later to make everything clear.

When operators from more than one category are combined in an expression, arithmetic operators are evaluated first, comparison operators next, and logical operators last. The order of operator evaluation is shown below, from top downwards:

Arithmetic	Arithmetic Symbol
Exponentiation	^
Negation	–
Multiplication and Division	* /
Integer division	\
Modulo arithmetic	Mod
Addition and Subtraction	+ –
String concatenation	&

Some miscellaneous points are:

- ❑ All comparison operators, such as =, < and Like, have equal precedence, the same level as addition and subtraction. This means that they are evaluated from left to right as they appear in expressions.
- ❑ Arithmetic operators with the same precedence are also evaluated from left to right.
- ❑ Operations within parentheses (brackets, like this) are always performed before those outside. This means that you can force the order in which evaluation takes place by using parentheses. However, normal precedence is maintained within the parentheses.

If that all sounds rather complex, don't worry. Here are some examples to help you.

You have four numbers: A, B, C and D, and you want to multiply the sum of A and B by the sum of C and D:

```
A = 1
B = 2
C = 3
D = 4

E = A + B * C + D
```

This doesn't produce 21, but 11, as multiplication has a higher precedence than addition. What happens is that B and C are multiplied, then A and D are added. To correct this, use:

```
E = (A + B) * (C + D)
```

This forces the additions to be performed first. In the example below, the parentheses have no effect (although, to some, they make the intention clearer):

```
E = A * B + C * D
```

```
E = (A * B) + (C * D)
```

With expressions in If statements, you have to follow a similar set of rules for using And and Or. You can liken And to * and Or to + in the previous examples, since And has a higher order of precedence. For example, consider the following, where A, B, C and D are all integers, all with the value of 1:

```
If A = 1 Or B = 1 And C = 1 Or D = 1 Then
```

This expression will be True if any of these conditions are True:

A is equal to 1

B is equal to 1 and C is equal to 1

D is equal to 1

However, consider the expression if we add parentheses:

```
If (A = 1 Or B = 1) And (C = 1 Or D = 1) Then
```

This expression will be `True` only if these conditions are `True`:

- ❑ Either A is equal to 1 or B is equal to 1
- ❑ Either C is equal to 1 or D is equal to 1

This is a fairly simplistic example, but you can clearly see the differences between the two sets of expressions. Most of the time, you will find that your expressions are much simpler, but it's important to know what happens when things get more complicated.

If you are at all unsure of the order of precedence of an expression, use parentheses to force your meaning. If the order was correct anyway, then you won't have lost anything, plus you will have made your code clearer.

Repetition

We've now considered how to deal with conditions but, sometimes, you need to go through a portion of code several times to arrive at a certain condition. Performing repetitive tasks that would otherwise drive the user crazy is one of the best programming tricks on offer. You don't want to know if your computer has to check a database with 10,000 entries, adding an extra 1 to every international phone number each time the codes are changed; you only want to know when it's finished.

Loops

VBA provides the `For...Next` and `Do...Loop` statements for this purpose. A loop is a piece of code that is executed repeatedly until a certain condition is met. We'll have a look at both these structures.

For...Next

The `For...Next` loop is useful when you know how many times you want to execute the statements within the loop:

```
For intLoop = 1 To 10
   .
   .
   .
Next
```

This starts the `intLoop` at 1 and then executes the code between the `For` and `Next` statements. When the `Next` is reached, VBA moves you back to the `For` statement and adds 1 to `intLoop`. This continues until `intLoop` is greater than 10.

The basic syntax is shown below:

```
For counter = start To end [Step increment]
   . . .
Next [counter]
```

where the terms are defined as:

counter	The variable you assign to the loop
start	The number with which you wish to start the loop
end	The number with which to stop the loop
increment	The number you add to start each time round the loop. (This is optional, and defaults to 1 if you omit the Step section.)

The argument increment can be either positive or negative, allowing loops to count both up and down. (If you leave out the Step and increment part of a For...Next loop, Access will assume that you just want to increment the value by one each time). For example, to get just the odd numbers you could do this:

```
For intLoop = 1 To 10 Step 2
```

Here, instead of adding 1 to intLoop every time the loop is run, VBA adds 2.

The counter after the Next statement is also optional and is usually left out. This isn't a bad thing but, if you have loops within loops, you may find that using the complete format is clearer, since you can easily see to which loop a Next statement refers. For example, imagine three loops within each other:

```
For intX = 1 To 10
   For intY = 1 To 10
      For intZ = 1 To 10
         . . .
      Next intZ
   Next intY
Next intX
```

Here you can see exactly which Next statement belongs to which For statement.

Do...Loop

The For...Next loop is ideal if you know how many times the loop is to be executed. There are occasions, however, when you want to perform loops until a certain condition is met. For those cases, you should use Do...Loop:

```
intSpeed = 0
intAcceleration = 5
Do Until intSpeed > 55
   intSpeed = intSpeed + intAcceleration
Loop
```

This executes until the variable intSpeed is greater than 55. If the variable is already greater than 55, the loop isn't entered and the code isn't executed. There is a second form of this loop, however, which allows you to test the condition at the end of the loop instead of at the beginning:

```
Do
    intSpeed = intSpeed + intAcceleration
Loop Until intSpeed > 55
```

This is basically the same as the previous example, but the code in the loop is always executed at least once. Even if intSpeed is greater than 55 when the loop is first started, the code in the loop is still executed. This may cause errors if intSpeed is being used in other expressions.

You can also replace the Until with While, which allows loops to be performed *while* a condition is True, rather than *until* it is True. For example:

```
Do
    intSpeed = intSpeed + intAcceleration
Loop While intSpeed < 55
```

This performs the same task as the Until version, but the condition is reversed, because now we want to continue the loop While the expression is True, not Until it is True. Which version you use is up to you, and may depend upon the expression and how easy it is to read.

> **You should always be careful about the conditions, because you can generate endless loops. This occurs when the loop test never becomes True (for Do...Until loops) or never stops being True (for Do...While loops). If you suspect that this is happening you can press *Ctrl-Break* to halt your code.**

Nested Control Structures

We have only looked at single control structures so far, but VBA does allow you to **nest** them (putting one structure inside another). Here is a trivial function that executes a loop ten times and uses the Mod function (which divides two numbers and returns the remainder) to determine whether the loop counter intLoop is odd or even:

```
Sub OddEven()

    Dim intLoop As Integer
    Dim intMainCount As Integer
    Dim strOutFinal As String

    intMainCount = 10

    For intLoop = 1 To intMainCount
        If (intLoop Mod 2 = 0) Then
            strOutFinal = "Even"
        Else
            strOutFinal = "Odd"
        End If
        Debug.Print intLoop, strOutFinal
    Next

End Sub
```

Here, the `If` structure is nested inside the `For...Next` loop. The code for both structures is indented to make it clear where they start and end. There's no limit to the amount of nesting that can be performed, but if you nest too many loops you'll find that your code becomes almost impossible to read (unless you've got a very wide monitor). If you need more than three or four levels of nesting, you should consider restructuring your code – perhaps by creating a new procedure, or maybe just by adjusting your tab width.

Exiting a Control Structure

The loops that we have looked at so far have all started and stopped at set places. Suppose, though, that because of some action that took place in a loop, you need to exit it straight away, without reaching the condition that normally terminates it. In this case, you can use the `Exit` *structure* statement. For example:

```
For intLoop = -1 To 10
    If (intLoop = 6) Then
        Exit For
    End If
    Debug.Print intLoop
Next
```

If the condition on the `If` line is true, (i.e. if `intLoop` equals 6), the `Exit For` statement immediately exits from the loop, rather than waiting until `intLoop` is larger than 10.

You can also use the `Exit Sub` or `Exit Function` statement to immediately exit a procedure:

```
If strInName = "" Then Exit Function
```

This will directly exit the function if `strInName` is an empty string.

You'll now have a good idea of the power and versatility that a loop can offer. However, loops can also serve another very useful purpose which we will look at now. They can be used to populate **arrays**.

Arrays

Your first question is probably, "What is an array?" Earlier, we said that variables are just temporary storage. If you think of a variable as a can of cola, then you can think of an array as a six-pack of cola. They are collections of variables, all with the same name and the same data type. Elements in an array are identified by their index – a number indicating their position in the array.

Arrays are used for collecting together a number of similar variables. Variables themselves are useful for holding specific information about a certain object, property or value. For example, if you want to store a number suggested by the user, you can create a variable to hold that value and then assign the value to the variable. These are the two lines of code that you might use to do that:

```
Dim intNum As Integer
intNum = InputBox("Please enter guess number 1", "Guess!")
```

The first line of code declares the variable as an integer. That is to say that the variable `intNum` will be able to hold any whole number between -32,768 and +32,767.

The second line of code assigns to the variable a number that has to be entered by the user. If you wanted the user to enter two numbers and you wanted to store the two values concurrently, you could create two variables as shown in the code below:

```
'Declare variables
Dim iNum As Integer
Dim iNum2 As Integer

'Assign values to variables
iNum = InputBox("Please enter guess number 1", "Guess!")
iNum2 = InputBox("Please enter guess number 2", "Guess!")
```

What if you want the user to be able to make five guesses...or twenty...or more? The answer is that your code could become very lengthy and repetitive. Given that the potential number of bugs in any program usually increases in proportion to the number of lines of code, you probably won't want to use the method shown above. What you need is a method for storing a collection of related variables together. That's just what an array provides.

The following are examples of items of data that you may want to collect in an array:

❑ The values of ten guesses made by the user

❑ Each individual letter making up a single string

❑ The enabled property of a number of different command buttons on a form

❑ The values of all the controls on a specific form

To show this at work, let's rewrite the code above to allow the user to make 10 initial guesses:

Try It Out – Declaring and Populating an Array

1. Open `IceCream.mdb` if it's not open already, and select the **Modules** tab from the database window. Create a new module and type in the following function procedure:

```
Public Sub ArrayExample()

    Dim i As Integer
    Dim iNum(1 To 10) As Integer

    For i = 1 To 10
        iNum(i) = InputBox("Please enter guess " & i, "Guess!")
    Next i

    For i = 1 To 10
        Debug.Print "Guess number " & i & " = " & iNum(i)
    Next i

End Sub
```

2. Run the `ArrayExample` procedure by typing `ArrayExample` in the Immediate window and hitting the *Enter* key. You'll be prompted to enter ten integers. Once you have entered the last of the ten integers, all ten will be displayed.

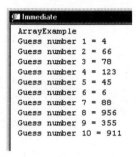

```
Immediate
ArrayExample
Guess number 1 = 4
Guess number 2 = 66
Guess number 3 = 78
Guess number 4 = 123
Guess number 5 = 45
Guess number 6 = 6
Guess number 7 = 88
Guess number 8 = 956
Guess number 9 = 355
Guess number 10 = 911
```

How It Works

Declaring an array is easy. We simply place parentheses indicating the array's dimensions after its name. So whereas this:

```
Dim intNum As Integer
```

declares an `Integer` type variable called `intNum`, this:

```
Dim intNum (1 To 10) As Integer
```

declares an array of ten `Integer` type variables called `intNum`. This tells VBA that `intNum` is to hold ten separate values, each of which will be a whole number between -32,768 and 32,767.

Note that an array need not hold `Integer` type variables. An array can hold any of the following data types:

❑ Integer

❑ Long

❑ Single

❑ Double

❑ Variant

❑ Currency

❑ String

❑ Boolean

❑ Byte

❑ Date

❑ Hyperlink

❑ Object

❑ User Defined Types

However, all elements of the array must be of the same data type. In other words, one array will not be able to store both strings and integers (although it could store `Variant` type variables with differing subtypes).

```
For i = 1 To 10
    iNum(i) = InputBox("Please enter guess" & i, "Guess!")
Next i
```

Now all that's needed is to populate the ten elements of the array with guesses from the user. Individual elements of the array are identified by their index (the number which appears in parentheses after the variable's name) so we create a simple `For...Next` loop and use the loop counter – in this case, the variable `i` – to refer to the elements of the array.

The ten elements of the `iNum` array are referred to as `iNum(1)`, `iNum(2)`, `iNum(3)`,...`iNum(10)`.

```
iNum(i) = InputBox("Please enter guess " & i, "Guess!")
```

To make this rather tedious task easier on the user, we have also used the loop counter, `i`, to indicate to the user how many guesses they have had:

```
For i = 1 To 10
    Debug.Print "Guess number " & i & " = " iNum(i)
Next i
```

Having stored the results of all the guesses in an array, we then loop through the elements of the array to display the results in the debug window.

Note that, if we wanted to allow the user to make twenty guesses instead of ten, we need only alter three lines of code. In fact, we could reduce this to one line by replacing the value `10` in the code above with the constant `ciNumberOfGuesses`. The procedure would then look like this:

```
Sub ArrayExampleWithConstant()

    Const ciNumberOfGuesses = 10
    Dim i As Integer
    Dim intNum(1 To ciNumberOfGuesses) As Integer

    For i = 1 To ciNumberOfGuesses
        intNum(i) = InputBox("Please enter guess " & i, "Guess!")
    Next i

    For i = 1 To ciNumberOfGuesses
        Debug.Print "Guess number " & i & " = " intNum(i)
    Next i

End Sub
```

To change the number of guesses that the user is allowed, we now need only to change the value of `ciNumberOfGuesses`.

Static Arrays

The examples above all made use of **static arrays**. That is to say, the number of elements in the array was fixed when the array was first declared. When you declare an array in this manner, the number of elements can't be changed.

Don't confuse static arrays with static variables. A static variable is one which has been declared with the Static statement and preserves its values between calls. A static array is one whose dimensions are fixed when it is declared.

Static (i.e. fixed-dimension) arrays can be declared with any of the following statements Dim, Static, Private or Public.

For example, typing the following in the Declarations section of a form's code module would declare an array with a fixed number of elements which would be visible to all procedures in that form:

```
Option Compare Database
Option Explicit

Private intNum(1 To 10) As Integer
```

whereas the following, if typed in the Declarations section of a standard code module, would declare an array with a fixed number of elements which was visible to all procedures throughout all code modules, forms and reports.

```
Option Compare Database
Option Explicit

Public intNum(1 To 10) As Integer
```

After you have created a static array, the elements of the array are initialized. All that means is that VBA gives these elements default values. The values with which they are initialized depend on the data type of the elements.

Data type	Initialization value
Any numeric	0
String (variable length)	Zero-length string (" ")
String (fixed length)	A fixed length string of Chr$(0) characters
Variant	Empty

Upper and Lower Bounds

The bounds of an array are its lowest and highest indexes. The lower bound of an array need not be 1. Had we wanted to, we could have typed:

```
Dim intNum(23 to 32) As Integer
```

This would also have given us an array which could hold a maximum of ten integers, but whose index would run from 23 to 32. To populate this array, we could use the following `For...Next` loop:

```
For i = 23 To 32
  intNum(i) = ...
Next i
```

Alternatively, if we had wished, we could have omitted the lower bound and typed instead:

```
Dim intNum(10) As Integer
```

However, you should note that, if you do not explicitly specify a lower bound, Access will use 0 as the lower bound. In other words, the line of code above is evaluated as:

```
Dim intNum(0 to 10) As Integer
```

This means that the array `intNum()` will be able to hold eleven values.

If you want Access to use 1 instead of 0 as the default lower bound for arrays, you should include the following line of code in the `Declarations` section of the code module:

```
Option Base 1
```

Dynamic Arrays

You may not know at the outset how many elements are required in your array. In this case, you should declare a **dynamic** array. You do this by placing **empty** parentheses after the array name; you can still use the `Dim`, `Static`, `Private` or `Public` keywords. The `ReDim` statement is then used later in the procedure to dynamically set the lower and upper bounds of the array.

For example, we could modify our original procedure to allow the user to specify how many guesses they want:

Try It Out – Dynamic Arrays

1. Create a new procedure called `DynamicArrayExample` with the following code:

```
Sub DynamicArrayExample()

    Dim i As Integer
    Dim intGuessCount As Integer
    Dim intNum() As Integer

    intGuessCount = InputBox("How many guesses do you want?")

    ReDim intNum(1 To intGuessCount)

    For i = 1 To intGuessCount
        intNum(i) = InputBox("Please enter guess " & i, _
              "Guess!")
```

```
    Next i

    For i = 1 To intGuessCount
        Debug.Print "Guess number " & i & " = "; intNum(i)
    Next i

End Sub
```

2. Switch to the Immediate window and run the procedure.

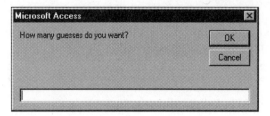

First, you're asked how many guesses you want.

3. Enter the number of tries you are going to have and press the OK button.

4. For each new dialog enter any integer (within reason!).

5. When you're finished you'll see the results in the Immediate window:

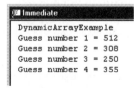

How it Works

You've seen some of the code before, so we'll just look at the new stuff here. The first thing to notice is that in the Dim statement we don't specify how many elements the array will contain:

```
Dim intNum() As Integer
```

The next thing to do is ask the user how many guesses they want – this will determine the number of array elements:

```
intGuessCount = InputBox("How many guesses do you want?")
```

Now we have the number of elements we can use ReDim to specify the size of the array:

```
ReDim intNum(1 To intGuessCount)
```

And finally, we use the number of guesses as the maximum in the loop.

```
For i = 1 To intGuessCount
```

This technique saves having to declare a large array just because you aren't sure how many elements it's going to have. In fact you can take this one step further, and increase the size of the array as you go along, and here, you only use as much memory as you need.

Try It Out – Very Dynamic Arrays

1. Create another procedure called `VeryDynamicArray`, like so:

```
Public Sub VeryDynamicArray()

    Dim i As Integer
    Dim intGuess As Integer
    Dim intNum() As Integer

    ReDim intNum(0)
    i = 1

    Do
        intGuess = InputBox("Please enter guess " & i & _
            vbCr & "Use -1 to exit", _
            "Guess!")
        If intGuess <> -1 Then
            ReDim Preserve intNum(i)
            intNum(i) = intGuess
            i = i + 1
        End If
    Loop Until intGuess = -1

    For i = 1 To UBound(intNum)
        Debug.Print "Guess number " & i & " = " & intNum(i)
    Next i

End Sub
```

2. Switch to the Immediate window and run this code by typing in `VeryDynamicArray` followed by the *Enter* key.

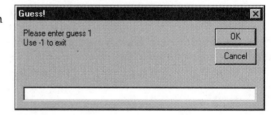

Notice that you haven't been asked how many guesses you want. You can just type in as many guesses as you like, and when you are finished you should enter −1.

3. Now switch back to the Immediate window to see the results:

```
Immediate
VeryDynamicArray
Guess number 1 = 980
Guess number 2 = 526
Guess number 3 = 399
```

How It Works

This is quite different from the previous two examples, so we'll look at this in more detail.

The first thing is defining the variables:

```
Dim i As Integer
Dim intGuess   As Integer
Dim intNum()   As Integer
```

Then we ReDim the array to make sure it's got at least one element in it and set the initial count number. We'll need these later.

```
ReDim intNum(0)
i = 1
```

Now we can start our loop. Notice that we are using a Do loop, so we can decide at run time when to end the loop.

```
Do
```

Now we are inside the loop so we ask for our guess. We've used a constant, vbCr (carriage return), to force the string to be split onto two lines. This just makes it easier for the user to read.

```
    intGuess = InputBox("Please enter guess " & i & _
        vbCr & "Use -1 to exit", _
        "Guess!")
```

Now we check to see if the user has entered –1, as we only want to add the number to the array if they haven't:

```
    If intGuess <> -1 Then
```

If they have entered a number other than –1, we do three things. First, we increase the size of the array. Notice the use of Preserve to make sure that any existing array elements are kept (we'll look at this a little later). Then we assign the new array element to the user guess, and then we increase the count number, before ending the If statement.

```
        ReDim Preserve intNum(i)
        intNum(i) = intGuess
        i = i + 1
    End If
```

Now we come to the end of the loop, and we only stop the loop if the user has entered –1.

```
Loop Until intGuess = -1
```

Now we need to print out the guesses. To find out how many times we should loop, we use UBound to find out the upper bound of the array.

```
For i = 1 To UBound(intNum)
    Debug.Print "Guess number " & i & " = " & intNum(i)
Next i
```

So, you can see that arrays are quite flexible, and you don't need to know in advance how many elements are required.

Redimensioning Existing Arrays

The ReDim statement can also be used to change the size of a dynamic array that already has a known number of elements set by a previous ReDim statement. For example, if you have an array of ten elements, declared with the following code:

```
Dim iNum() As Integer
...
...
ReDim iNum(1 To 10)
```

You can reduce the number of elements in the array later in the procedure to four, with the single line of code:

```
ReDim iNum(1 To 4)
```

You might want to do this if you had a large array but now only need a small one. Reducing the size of the array will save memory.

Normally, when you change the size of an array, you lose *all* the values that were in that array – it is re-initialized. However, you can avoid this by using the Preserve keyword. The following line of code would have the same effect as the previous one, except that the values stored in iNum(1), iNum(2), iNum(3) and iNum(4) would remain unchanged.

```
ReDim Preserve iNum(1 To 4)
```

The Dangers of ReDim

There's one important point to notice when using ReDim, which can be shown with a couple of lines of code:

```
Dim intNum() As Integer

ReDim intNun(10)
```

Notice that the variable in the second statement is different from that in the first. This can happen quite easily as a typing mistake. So what happens here? Usually when you use a variable that hasn't been declared, VBA gives you an error – but not with ReDim. This is because ReDim is effectively a declaration. In the above example this leads to two arrays, which can cause errors in your code. This actually happened to me while I was creating one of the above examples.

If you are getting errors telling you that an index is out of bounds, but you are sure you have dimensioned it correctly, then check your spelling – you might have given the wrong name to the variable in your ReDim statement.

Summary

In this chapter we've covered the important aspects of building code into useful sequences of statements. In the previous chapter we showed variables and their use – here we've looked at putting those variables into practice, and used them to help us control procedures.

In particular we've looked at:

❑ Using the `If` and `Select` statements to make decisions. These allow us to make our code change its behavior according to user input.

❑ Using loops to avoid unnecessarily repeating statements of code, and allowing actions to continue until user input decides otherwise.

❑ Using arrays to store several pieces of information of the same time. This allows the program to be flexible in allowing any number of user defined inputs.

Now that we've spent a while building these fundamentals it's time to start delving into Access, and the objects it controls.

Exercises

1. Using a control structure, create a procedure to print a number out as a string, such as those used on checks. For example, 120 should be printed as ONE TWO ZERO. Hint-Convert the number to a string first.

2. Convert the above function to use an array of strings for the words and replace one of the control structures. Now compare this version with the previous version and think about how this type of look-up can be used to improve the speed of functions within loops.

3. Create a user logon form that asks for a user name and a password and only lets the user carry on if the correct details have been entered. Think of two ways that you can use to make the user name case insensitive (so it ignores case)

Using Access Objects

While using Access you might get the impression that it's one big application. In reality, it consists of many smaller pieces, all working in harmony. These pieces are generally described as **Objects**. For example you have tables which store the data, queries which allow you to get at the data in a specific way, and forms to allow the data to be displayed in a user-friendly way. These objects can also contain other objects – forms, for example, contain controls, such as text boxes and command buttons. Access allows you to get at all of these objects.

In this chapter, we are going to look at the different objects within Access and how their structure provides the framework you can use to build better applications.

In particular we are going to look at:

- ❏   What objects are
- ❏   How they are used within Access 2000
- ❏   What collections are, and the different types in Access
- ❏   How to use properties and methods

Object-Oriented Programming

There is much talk these days about **object-oriented programming**, and many debates over what the term actually means. VBA has many object-oriented aspects to aid the programmer, some of which we will be considering in this chapter. There are several reasons why object-oriented aspects have been added to many languages, not just the VBA programming language. The main problem is that traditional languages (known as **procedural** languages) are failing to cope with contemporary trends such as:

- ❏   Efficient re-use of large portions of code in other applications
- ❏   Reduced turnover time for many programming projects, but the same expectancy of high quality
- ❏   Applications of ever-increasing complexity and size

❑   The demand for easier, more intuitive, graphical methods for users to communicate their actions to the system

❑   The need to access data stored on many different platforms and systems in many different ways

Of course, all of these problems also apply to Access (and VBA), and tackling them successfully will yield many benefits, but what puts many people off in the first place is the obscure and esoteric terminology in which object-oriented programming is often described. So let's start by defining our terms.

Objects

In the real world we use the word **object** to describe a whole number of things. A car, a computer, a house – they are all objects. An object can also be a collection of other objects: for example, a car is made up of a chassis, wheels, a transmission system and many other components which are objects in their own right.

The key thing about all these objects is that they know everything they need to know in order to do what they do. In other words, when the ignition key is turned, the battery, distributor and spark plugs know how to start the car; when the brake pedal is depressed, the braking mechanism knows how to slow the car down.

Likewise, in Access, a form is an object. It knows everything it needs to know in order to do what it does. When you hit the Close button, the form closes itself. When you hit the Minimize button, the form reduces itself to a minimized state.

Properties

All objects have **properties**. These are simply its characteristics. Just as a car has a size, weight and color, forms have their own properties. For example, forms have a Caption property, a Filter property, a DefaultView property, etc. QueryDefs have properties, too, for example an SQL property and an Updateable property. You can alter the value of an object's properties, either on the property sheet in design view, or with VBA code.

Methods

Methods are actions attached to objects. Our car might have a LightsOn method for turning on the headlights and a LightsOff method for extinguishing them. In Access, objects have methods for performing actions. For example, among the Database object's methods is the OpenRecordset method for creating a new recordset.

Classes

A **class** is a template, or blueprint, for an object. If we stick with our car analogy, then the class could be equated to the technical drawings for the car. At this stage we don't actually have a car, just the template, and to create the car we must build it. This gives us an **instance** of a car, and if we build more cars from the same template, we have multiple instances.

In the object world, we don't yet have an actual object, just a class. To create the object we **instantiate** the class, which creates an object based upon the class template – just like building our car. Also like the car, we can create multiple instances, so we could have several objects of the same type, all instantiated (created) from the same class template. It's important to note that although these objects are derived from the same class, they are not the same object – they each exist in their own right.

Generally, if you need multiple instances of an object you have a **collection**. If you've got lots of money you might have a collection of cars, all stored in a nice air-conditioned building. A collection of objects is similar – it's a way of grouping related objects together, and letting you work on them in a similar fashion.

Classes are examined in more detail later in the book.

The Advantages of Object-Orientation

There are several, related reasons why this class and object approach is good:

❑ Classes have their own self-contained properties and methods (this is called **encapsulation**), so they are generally self-sufficient. This makes your code neater, as everything to do with that class is stored within the class template.

❑ This encapsulation means that code re-use is easy, since you can just copy the class template and you know that you don't need anything else. This is useful when sharing code with others, or when re-using code from old projects, and should, over time, reduce development times and costs.

❑ Encapsulation also means that testing should be reduced, because if a class has been thoroughly tested, and it works, then it will work wherever it is used.

❑ Using the object idea means that you are often modeling real-life objects, such as orders or products. This means that your program design naturally maps onto the real world.

Object Models

If an application consists of many smaller objects, as Access does, then we use the term **Object Model** to show those objects and identify the relationship between them. This is generally shown in a diagrammatic form, and you'll see occurrences of these diagrams later in the book, for the data access object models.

The Access 2000 Object Model is quite large, so we won't be showing it here – to get it all on a page we'd have to make it too small to read! However, showing you a bit of the model and how the diagram looks can help to understand how some of the Access objects fit together:

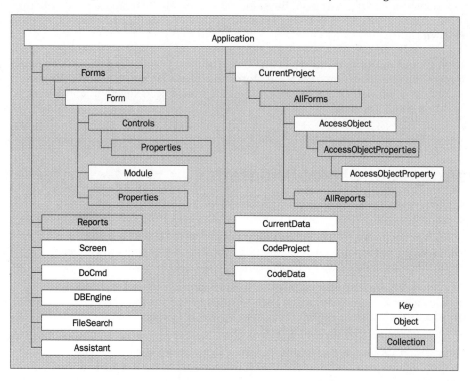

We'll be describing these objects in a minute, but you can see that at the top we have the Application, which is the main Access application. This contains several smaller objects and collections of objects, such as a Forms collection, which itself contains instances of Form objects, and each of these Form objects contains other objects. There are also some objects, such as the DoCmd object, which don't have any collections belonging to them.

Remember that this is just a portion of the object model - if you want to look at the full model, then you can find it in the Access Help File. It's under Programming Information, then Microsoft Access Visual Basic Reference, and then Microsoft Access Objects. As this is a help file it allows you to drill down into the objects for a more detailed look.

Using Object Models in VBA

Using object models in VBA is quite simple, because you can just use a period to separate the various objects and collections. For example, to get to the Forms collection you would do something like this:

```
Application.Forms
```

As the `Application` object is the main object it can generally be omitted when referencing sub-objects. For instance, the example above could be written as just:

```
Forms
```

To reference an individual item in an object you must either know its name, or its position in the collection. For example, if you have a form called `frmSwitchboard`, then you could do this:

```
Forms("frmSwitchboard")
```

Here we are using the name to find the object in the collection. This is a bit like the way we used a variable to index into a loop, and in fact, you can use that method too:

```
Forms(0)
```

This would give you the first object in the collection – it's the first object because collections start at 0.

To get further into the hierarchy of the model you just add the next item, separated by a period. For example:

```
Forms("frmSwitchboard").Controls(0)
```

This would get the first control on the form `frmSwitchboard`.

Don't worry too much about this now, because you'll be seeing lots of examples of using objects and collections as we go through this chapter.

Access 2000 Objects

There are several sets of objects that you might come across in Access, and they can be categorized quite simply:

- ❑ General Access Objects
- ❑ Data Access Objects
- ❑ ActiveX Data Objects

In this chapter we're only going to concern ourselves with the first of these – the Access objects. The Data Access Objects will be covered in the next two chapters, and ActiveX Data Objects are discussed in more detail in the appendices.

Access 2000 has brought a raft of new objects into play, allowing the programmer greater flexibility when dealing with Access. (The new ones are marked in italics). The complete list is shown below:

Access Object	Refers to	Used in
AccessObject	A particular Access object (see below)	This chapter

Table Continued on Following Page

Access Object	Refers to	Used in
AccessObjectProperty	A characteristic of an `AccessObject`	This chapter
Application	The active Access application	This chapter
CodeData	The objects stored by the data source	Chapter 14
CodeProject	The project for the code database	Chapter 14
ComAddIns	A collection of COM Add-Ins	Not applicable
Control	A control on a form or report, such as a text box or label	This chapter
CurrentData	The objects stored by the data source in the current database	Chapter 14
CurrentProject	The project for the current database	Chapter 14
DataAccessPage	A particular data access page	Chapter 17
DefaultWebOptions	Global options used when saving or opening a web page	Chapter 10
DoCmd	The actions that can be called from within Access	Various
FileSearch	A programmatic way to search for files without a dialog box	Not applicable
Form	An open Access form	This chapter
FormatCondition	The conditional format of a combo box or text box	Not applicable
Hyperlink	A hyperlink pointing to an internet URL or an Access object	Chapter 17
Module	A standard or class module	Not applicable
Page	An individual page on a tab control	Not applicable
Reference	A reference to another object's type library	Not applicable
Report	An open Access report	This chapter
Screen	A form, report or control that has the current focus	Various
VBE	The Visual Basic Editor functionality	Not applicable
WebOptions	Web options for data access pages	Chapter 17

Items marked Not applicable *are beyond the scope of this book, and are therefore not covered.*

The AccessObject Object

The AccessObject object (which is almost a tongue-twister) refers to one of the following:

- ❑ AllForms
- ❑ AllReports
- ❑ AllMacros
- ❑ AllTables
- ❑ AllDataAccessPages
- ❑ AllTables
- ❑ AllQueries
- ❑ AllViews
- ❑ AllStoredProcedures
- ❑ AllDatabaseDiagrams

You can probably guess what these are. AllForms for example, refers to all of the forms in a database or project. This allows us to easily get access to all of the objects stored. In previous versions of Access you would have had to use the Data Access Objects, and the Containers and Documents collections. This method is much easier. Let's have a look at a quick sample:

Try It Out – Viewing the Access Objects

1. Open IceCream.mdb and select Modules.

2. Insert a new module, and add the following procedure:

```
Public Sub ShowObjects()

    Dim objAO As AccessObject
    Dim objCP As Object

    Set objCP = Application.CurrentProject

    For Each objAO In objCP.AllForms
        Debug.Print objAO.Name
    Next

End Sub
```

3. Switch to the Immediate window and run the procedure:

```
Immediate
ShowObjects
frmCompany
frmIceCream
frmsubIceCreamIngredients
frmSwitchboard
frmReports
frmSales
frmIngredients
```

4. Now change `AllForms` to `AllReports` and run the procedure again:

How it Works

This code is quite simple, but there are a few things that need explaining. Let's start with the variable declarations.

```
Dim objAO As AccessObject
Dim objCP As Object
```

The first declares a variable to hold an Access object – this will be one of the `All` objects shown earlier. The second variable will hold the current project – this is the current database. We have to use a generic object type here, because, oddly enough, there isn't a specific type for an Access project.

Next we set this object to point to the current project. This will allow us access to all of the objects in the current database:

```
Set objCP = Application.CurrentProject
```

Once the current project is set we can loop through the `AllForms` collection, printing out the name.

```
For Each objAO In objCP.AllForms
    Debug.Print objAO.Name
Next
```

You'll be familiar with loops by now, but you might not have seen this particular version. The `For Each` statement is used with collections, allowing us to loop through the collection. The way this works is that you declare a variable that matches the type of the elements in the collection – in this case it's `AccessObject`, because we are looping through the `AllForms` collection. The general rule is:

```
Dim objObject As ObjectType

For Each objObject In Collection.Objects
```

This has the effect of running the loop for each object in the collection, and each time around, the loop variable (`objObject`, or `objAO` in the example above) is set to point to the individual collection member.

If this sounds confusing, just have a look at the diagram below:

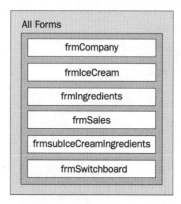

Each time around the loop `objAO` points to the next form. If you think of a collection as similar to an array then you'll get the general idea.

Dynamic List Boxes

So what we have is an easy way to find out what objects are within our database. Why is this useful? Given the way applications change, it's a good idea to build in some form of future proofing, to allow you to perform less maintenance as the application inevitably changes. Consider you have a form listing all of your reports. You've built this using a single form with hyperlinks, one hyperlink for each form. Something like this:

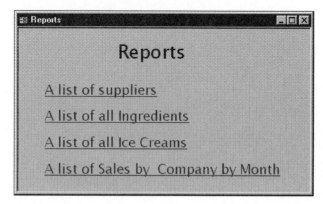

But what happens if you need to add another report? Or even two? You have to edit the form, squash things up so it fits on, etc. Wouldn't it be simpler to provide a dynamic list of reports? Maybe something like this:

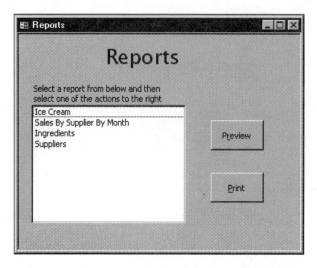

Now when you add a new report to the database it will automatically be added to the list box. Let's have a look and see how we can do this:

Try It Out – Using the AccessObject

1. Create a new form and add a list box onto it, calling the list box lstReports.

2. Press the **Code** button on the toolbar to create a code module, and add the following code to the Load event for the Form.

```
Private Sub Form_Load()

    Dim objAO As AccessObject
    Dim objCP As Object
    Dim strValues As String

    Set objCP = Application.CurrentProject

    For Each objAO In objCP.AllReports
        strValues = strValues & objAO.Name & ";"
    Next objAO

    lstReports.RowSourceType = "Value List"
    lstReports.RowSource = strValues

End Sub
```

3. Switch the form into form mode to see the results.

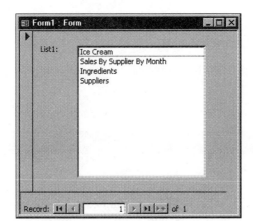

4. Switch the form back into design view, and set the **Record Selectors** and **Navigation Buttons** properties to **No**.

5. Save the form as frmReports.

How it Works

This method of filling a list box is really simple, and relies upon the fact that you can supply a list of values for a list box, just by separating the values by a semi-colon. So let's look at how this is done.

Firstly we have the variables, the first two of which you've seen before. This will be used to help us loop through the Report objects. The last variable, strValues, is a string that we will use to build up a list of report names.

```
Dim objAO As AccessObject
Dim objCP As Object
Dim strValues As String
```

Next we set a variable to point to the current project.

```
Set objCP = Application.CurrentProject
```

And then, we loop through the AllReports collection, adding the name of each report to a string. Notice how we add a semi-colon after the name of each report, as this is our list separator.

```
For Each objAO In objCP.AllReports
    strValues = strValues & objAO.Name & ";"
Next objAO
```

Finally we set the properties for the list box. The first is the `RowSourceType` property, which when set to `Value List` means that what's shown in the list box comes from a list of values. The second line actually sets those values, by setting the `RowSource` property to the contents of the string containing the report names.

```
lstReports.RowSourceType = "Value List"
lstReports.RowSource = strValues
```

That's it – a really simple way to use VBA to fill a list box. This isn't the only way to fill a list box with code, and you'll see another method a little later.

Now that we have a working list box, let's add those buttons so we can view or print the reports.

Try It Out – Adding the Print buttons

1. Switch the form back into design mode.

2. Add two command buttons. If you have the wizards enabled you can just cancel out of the screen it shows – we want to code these ourselves.

3. Name the buttons `cmdPreview` and `cmdPrint`, and set their captions accordingly.

4. Add a label at the top of the report, for a title, and change the label for the list box. Your form should now look something like this:

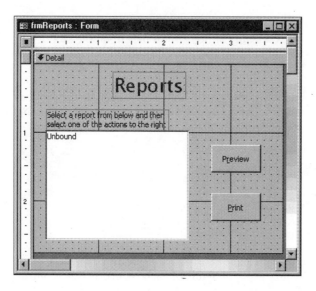

5. From the View menu, select Code, to create a code module for the form. This will switch us to the code editor.

6. Add the following subroutine:

```
Private Sub ProcessReport(intAction As Integer)

   If Not IsNull(lstReports) Then
      DoCmd.OpenReport lstReports, intAction
   End If

End Sub
```

7. Select cmdPreview from the object combo box (that's the one at the top left of the code window), and then select Click from the event combo box (the one on the right).

8. Enter the following line of code:

```
ProcessReport acViewPreview
```

9. Select cmdPrint from the object combo box, and Click from the event combo box.

10. Add the following line of code:

```
ProcessReport acNormal
```

11. Save the module and switch back to Access.

12. Switch the form from design view into form view and try out the buttons. Selecting Preview will open (in preview mode) whichever report is highlighted in the list box, and selecting Print will print it straight to the printer.

Pretty simple, eh? With just a few lines of code you have a couple of command buttons to preview and print any report.

How it Works – Previewing and Printing Reports

This code is really simple. The ProcessReport procedure first checks to see whether a report has been selected in the list box. The list box value will be Null if no report has been selected. So, if a report has been selected, we call the OpenReport method of the DoCmd object, passing in the report name (this name comes straight from the list box – if you refer to a list box in code, the value you get is whatever is selected). The second argument to OpenReport is the action – what we want to do. This is passed into ProcessReport as an argument.

```
   If Not IsNull(lstReports) Then
      DoCmd.OpenReport lstReports, intAction
   End If
```

Each of the command buttons calls `ProcessReport` passing in a different constant (pre-defined by Access). We either want to preview the report (`acViewPreview`) or we want to open the report normally (`acNormal`).

```
ProcessReport acViewPreview
ProcessReport acNormal
```

That's all there is to it.

Changing the Switchboard

Since we've just looked at opening reports, let's have a quick diversion into the switchboard, just to point out a couple of facts. If you've tried to use the switchboard to open other forms you'll notice that only two of the buttons are working – those for the Ice Creams and the Ingredients. You might also have noticed the method used to open these forms – using hyperlink addresses. Now we'll be covering these in more detail later in the book, but basically they give you a simple way to jump from form to form without any code.

There are a couple of problems with using hyperlinks for this though:

❑   The Web toolbar appears, which tends to be a bit confusing. After all, we're not dealing with web pages or any other Internet-related stuff, so why should this appear?

❑   It opens the form directly, without giving any ability to filter the records, so you can't show a subset of the form's records.

The best thing to do under these circumstances is to remove the hyperlinks and use VBA to open the forms.

Try It Out – Opening Forms

1.   Open the switchboard in design view.

2.   Select the Ice Cream button, and delete the contents of the Hyperlink Sub Address property.

3.   Now move to the On Click event and add an event procedure. You can do this by pressing the builder button to the right of the property (and selecting Code Builder from the next dialog if you don't default to always using event procedures).

4.   Add the following code:

```
DoCmd.OpenForm "frmIceCream"
```

5.   Now do the same for the Ingredients button, this time using `frmIngredients` as the form name.

6.   Do the same for the Reports button, using `frmReports` as the form name.

7. Now do the same for the Suppliers button, with `frmCompany` as the form name.

8. Switch back to Access, and view the form in form view to see the results. Notice that the forms open but that the Web toolbar doesn't appear. There's still a problem with the Suppliers button, though, because it shows all companies, and not just suppliers.

9. Switch back to the VBE and modify the code in the Suppliers event procedure so that it looks like this:

```
DoCmd.OpenForm "frmCompany", , , "Supplier = True"
```

10. Now switch back to Access and try again. Notice that only suppliers are shown.

This is the thing that hyperlinks just can't do. We are utilizing the `Where` argument of the `OpenForm` command, which allows us to specify a SQL `WHERE` clause as part of the open. This means that instead of `frmCompany` showing all records, it will only show records where the `Supplier` field is set to `True`. This means that we can have a single form that shows both suppliers and non-suppliers, without changing any code.

Dynamic List Boxes – The Return

Earlier in the chapter we showed you how to fill a list box using VBA code, and now it's time to look at another method for doing this. Why another method? Well, this new method has a lot more flexibility, allowing you to set various formatting options, and is the method that is documented in the help file. We've decided to include it here because you will invariably come across this function, either in the help file or in someone else's code, and it's quite a confusing piece of code. For that reason it warrants a good explanation.

Try It Out – Dynamic List Boxes

1. Create a new module in the Visual Basic Environment, and add the following function:

```
Function ListReports(fld As Control, id As Variant, _
        row As Variant, col As Variant, _
        code As Variant) As Variant

    Dim objAO As AccessObject
    Dim objCP As Object
    Static strReports() As String
    Static intEntries As Integer

    Select Case code
    Case acLBInitialize
        intEntries = 0
        Set objCP = Application.CurrentProject
```

```
        ReDim strReports(objCP.AllReports.Count)
        For Each objAO In objCP.AllReports
            strReports(intEntries) = objAO.Name
            intEntries = intEntries + 1
        Next objAO

        ListReports = intEntries

    Case acLBOpen
        ListReports = Timer

    Case acLBGetRowCount
        ListReports = intEntries

    Case acLBGetColumnCount
        ListReports = 1

    Case acLBGetColumnWidth
        ListReports = -1

    Case acLBGetValue
        ListReports = strReports(row)

    Case acLBGetFormat

    Case acLBEnd
        Erase strReports

    End Select

End Function
```

2. Save this module as `List Handling`.

3. Open up `frmReports` in design mode, and switch to the code behind the form.

4. Remove the code from the `Load` event for the `Form` object – we'll be using a different method to fill the list box.

5. Set the **Row Source Type** property of the list box to `ListReports`. Ignore the fact that this property appears to take three values supplied in a combo box – just type over what's already there.

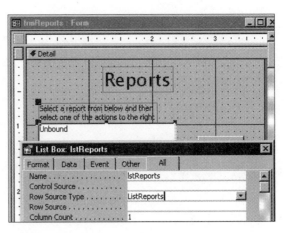

6. Save the report and switch back into form mode, just to see what happens. The result is exactly the same as our first method of filling the list box.

How it Works

The first thing to look at is the code. Where did this `ListReports` function come from? What are the arguments? How does it work?

The function can be any name you want, preferably a name that indicates what it does. We've called ours `ListReports`, but you could have named it something else if you wanted. The format, though, is laid down by Access. Access says that you can supply the details in a list box yourself from any function, as long as that function matches a certain format. What you do in the function is up to you, but the format is predefined. If you'd like to see what the help files say about this, look up 'RowSourceType Property(User-Defined Function) – Code Argument Values'.

Let's look at this function in detail:

```
Function ListReports(fld As Control, id As Variant, _
                     row As Variant, col As Variant, _
                     code As Variant) As Variant
```

There are five arguments that we have to include:

- ❑ `fld`, which identifies the control that this function is being called from. In our case this is the list box `lstReports`.

- ❑ `id`, which uniquely identifies the control being filled. This is in case you have the same function being used by two different controls.

- ❑ `row`, which identifies the current row in the list or combo box.

- ❑ `col`, which identifies the current column in the list or combo box.

- ❑ `code`, which identifies at which stage we are at in the processing. Access fills this in automatically, using some intrinsic constants.

So from this information we can identify the control we are trying to fill and the row and column in that control. Hmm, that's interesting. The row and column. But there could be several of these, so how does this work? Well Access calls this function several times, and what it passes in and what the function returns has an effect on what happens. Let's see the theory of when and why, and then we'll look at our code to see what we've done.

- ❑ Firstly it calls the function setting `code` to `acLBInitialize`. This indicates that the list box is being initialized. Access expects a non-zero value to tell it that it's OK to continue.

- ❑ Next it calls the function setting `code` to `acLBOpen`, telling us that the list box is being opened. Again we should return a non-zero value to indicate that the function can fill the list.

- ❑ It then calls the function setting `code` to `acLBGetRowCount`, asking us to supply how many rows there are going to be in the list.

❑   Next it calls the function setting `code` to `acLBGetColumnCount`, asking us to supply how many columns there are going to be in the list. This should match the number of columns set on the property sheet for the control.

❑   Now, for each column, it calls the function setting `code` to `acLBGetColumnWidth` and `col` to the column number, asking us to supply how wide this column is going to be. You should return a value in twips (one twip equals 1/20 of a point, or 1/1440 of an inch), or you should return −1 to let Access use the default width.

❑   Then, for every row, it calls the function setting `code` to `acLBGetValue`, `row` to the row number, and `col` to the column number. This is asking us to supply the value for that row and column.

❑   Next, for every row, it calls the function setting `code` to `acLBGetFormat`, `row` to the row number, and `col` to the column number. This is asking us to supply a format for the value for that row and column. You can use −1 to tell Access to use the default format.

❑   Finally, after all of the rows and columns have been processed, it calls the function setting `code` to `acLBEnd`, to indicate that the processing of the function is finished.

So what we end up with is a function that is called several times, under different conditions. Access tells us at what stage it is (via the `code`, `row` and `col` arguments), and we supply it with information as to what we want in the list box. Let's see exactly what we've done in our code.

At the top we have the function declaration, using the predefined format:

```
Function ListReports(fld As Control, id As Variant, _
                     row As Variant, col As Variant, _
                     code As Variant) As Variant
```

Next we have our variable declaration. The first two you've seen already, and will be used to access the reports. The next two will hold the report names and the number of reports. Notice that these are defined as `Static` variables. This is necessary because the function is called several times, and we need these two variables to retain their values over subsequent calls.

```
Dim objAO As AccessObject
Dim objCP As Object
Static strReports() As String
Static intEntries As Integer
```

Now we can find out what the value of the code argument is. Remember that Access will supply this value to us, and it will dictate what we are going to do:

```
Select Case code
```

If code indicates initialization, then we are going to get a list of reports, and put that list into our static array.

```
Case acLBInitialize
```

Firstly we set the count to 0. This is important because it is a static variable. Although this section of code will only be run once, as the form is opened, if the form is closed and reopened, then it will still have the value of the last time it was run (remember, static variables exist for the lifetime of the application). We then set our variable to point to the current project.

```
intEntries = 0
Set objCP = Application.CurrentProject
```

We now need to dimension our array so it's large enough to contain all of the reports. We use the `Count` property of the `AllReports` object to tell us how many reports there are:

```
ReDim strReports(objCP.AllReports.Count)
```

Once the array is dimensioned we can loop through the reports, putting each one into an element of the array. Remember that arrays start at 0, and since `intEntries` hasn't been set to a specific value, it will be 0:

```
For Each objAO In objCP.AllReports
    strReports(intEntries) = objAO.Name
    intEntries = intEntries + 1
Next objAO
```

And finally for the initialization we return the number of entries. This isn't used to calculate the row, but remember we have to return a non-zero result to tell Access it's OK to carry on. So we set the function return value to the number of entries:

```
ListReports = intEntries
```

The next time this function is called is when the list box is opened. Here we need to set a unique number for the ID of the list box. We use the `Timer` function, which returns the number of seconds elapsed since midnight. This is usually unique enough for a single instance of a running form.

```
Case acLBOpen
    ListReports = Timer
```

Next comes the count of rows. We've already set this back when we initialized the array, so we can just return this value:

```
Case acLBGetRowCount
    ListReports = intEntries
```

Now we set the number of columns. In this case we only want one column.

```
Case acLBGetColumnCount
    ListReports = 1
```

After the number of columns comes the width of the list box. We use –1 to indicate that the default width should be used:

```
Case acLBGetColumnWidth
    ListReports = -1
```

Next comes the value. Remember that this function will be called once for each row and column, and the `row` and `col` arguments will be set accordingly. In our case we have previously set the number of columns to 1 (that was the `acLBGetColumnCount` bit). What we need to return here is the value from the array (the report name) that corresponds to the row, so we use the row to index into our array of report names:

```
Case acLBGetValue
    ListReports = strReports(row)
```

Next comes any formatting for the value. We're not doing any special formatting, but it's a good idea to leave this in, even if it's not being used. That way you remember it's available.

```
Case acLBGetFormat
```

And finally, the end of the process. Here we `Erase` the array, which makes sure that all of the memory it used is freed up.

```
Case acLBEnd
    Erase strReports
```

So, although this function looks complex, it's really quite simple. All you have to remember is that Access defines what the arguments are, and what they mean. The function is called several times, so we just have to plug in our code where appropriate.

Custom List Box Summary

Let's just look at the two different methods of filling list boxes from VBA code, just to get a clear picture of which method you should use. Remember there are two methods:

❑ Creating a semicolon-separated list of values, and using the **Row Source Type** of **Value List**.

❑ Creating a custom function, which will be called from the **Row Source Type** property.

Of these two methods, the first is obviously the easier, but does it have any disadvantages? Not really, and in general you can probably use this method wherever you need to fill a list box from VBA. So what's the point of that long, complex function? Well not a great deal, to be honest. This complex method has been in Access for a long time, but I've always preferred the simple solution.

Forms and Reports

Two collections that we haven't discussed might seem a bit confusing. Remember how we said that `AllForms` and `AllReports` give us a list of forms and reports. Well, what about the `Forms` and `Reports` collections? What do they contain?

The `Forms` and `Reports` collections store details about the **open** forms and reports. So these are the ones that the user currently has open. This allows you to perform actions on the forms that the user is currently viewing, rather than the forms that are not being used. This is an important point, because you can use the `Forms` collection to change a visible form, but any changes you make are not saved when the form is closed.

The changes only exist while the form is open. If, however, the form is open in design view and you make changes, then these changes will be saved when you close the form, as long as you don't abandon the changes.

Let's just see this in action:

1. Close any open forms.

2. Create a new module, open the Immediate window, and type:

```
?forms(0).Name
```

3. Press *Enter* and you should see the following error message:

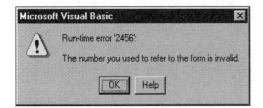

This is because there are no forms open, so the `Forms` collection is empty. The `Forms` collection, like an array, starts at 0, so trying to look at this entry when there are no forms in the collection causes an error.

4. Now open a form, perhaps `frmCompany`, and try this line again:

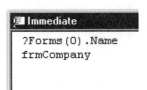

These two collections are very useful when you need to perform tasks on open forms. For example, changing the color scheme, or current font. This is really simple because each form has another collection, `Controls`. This contains an entry for each control on a form. So you could easily build a control that changes the current font for all controls, just by looping through this collection.

1. Create a new subroutine called `FormFonts`, like so:

```
Sub FormFonts (strFont As String)
```

```
   Dim frmCurrent As Form
   Dim ctlControl As Control

   For Each frmCurrent In Forms
      For each ctlControl In frmCurrent.Controls
         ctlControl.FontName = strFont
      Next
   Next

End Sub
```

2. Make sure that only the form frmCompany is open.

3. Run the new procedure from the Immediate window, passing in Rockwell as the font name, like so:

FormFonts "Rockwell"

If you don't have this font, substitute the name of one you do, preferably one that is obviously different. Why not try Wingdings (if you don't mind not being able to read it)? Or try Symbol for that Greek feel.

4. Press *Return* to run the procedure, and you should see another error message:

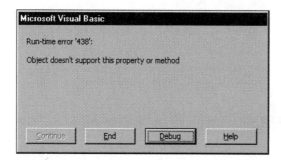

Now don't panic; this is expected. What we're doing is changing the font name for all of the controls. But what you may not realize is that not all controls have a font.

5. Switch back to Access and you'll see this:

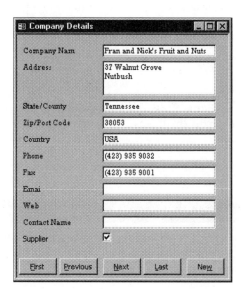

Notice that all of the text boxes have had their font changed, but we seemed to have stalled at the Supplier. That's because this is a check box field and it doesn't have a font, therefore it has no FontName property. Its associated label does, but the field itself doesn't. So we get the error. Notice that the command buttons haven't been changed either – they do have a FontName property, but since the Supplier field is before them in the collection they haven't been reached yet.

Control Types

So how do we get around this problem? How do we check for controls that don't have an associated font? Well, there are two ways to tackle this:

The first way is to check each control in the loop. Is it one of the controls that has a font? Something like this:

```
For Each frmCurrent In Forms
    For Each ctlControl In frmCurrent.Controls
        If ctlControl.Type <> acCheckBox Then
            ctlControl.Font = strFont
        End If
    Next
Next
```

This uses the ControlType property of each control to see if the control is a checkbox (acCheckBox is an intrinsic constant), and only changes the font if it isn't a check box. But again we run into a problem here, because there are several control types that don't have fonts: images, lines, etc. Should we check each one? Yes we could, but this would make our code hard to read and maintain.

The second way is to use the error handling of VBA and Access. We're going to discuss error handling in detail later on in the book, but you've already seen we've got an error – run-time error '438'. This is a fixed error number telling us the property is not supported. So what it's really saying is that the property we are trying to use doesn't exist. Now wouldn't it be nice if we could just say 'OK, I know it doesn't exist, so just skip trying to set the font for this control, and move onto the next control'? Well with error handling we can.

The Err Object

Whenever a VBA error is generated, a special object is used to hold the error details – this is the Err object. We'll look at this in more detail later in the book, but for the moment all you have to know is that one of the properties of the Err object is the Number property – this is the error number that we were shown in the error dialog.

Using error handling allows us to tell VBA that when an error occurs, it shouldn't just display an error message, but should run a special bit of code, which we can supply.

Try It Out – Objects, Controls and Errors

1. If you are in Access, switch back to the VBE, and press End on the error dialogWhenever.

2. Now change the code for the FormFonts procedure, so that it looks like this:

```
Sub FormFonts (strFont As String)

    On Error GoTo FormFonts_Err

    Dim frmCurrent As Form
    Dim ctlControl As Control

    For Each frmCurrent In Forms
        For Each ctlControl In frmCurrent.Controls
            ctlControl.FontName = strFont
        Next
    Next

FormFonts_Exit:
    Exit Sub

FormFonts_Err:
    If Err.Number = 438 Then
        Resume Next
    Else
        MsgBox Err.Description
        Resume FormFonts_Exit
    End If

End Sub
```

3. Switch back to Access, and close and re-open the form. This makes sure that the font is reset to its default – remember our changes aren't saved.

4. Switch back to the VBE and run the procedure again.

5. Now if you switch back to Access you'll see that all of the text has changed to our new font.

How it Works

As we've said, we won't go into detail about the error handling, as this is covered fully in the debugging chapter. But let's look at the collections a little more:

Every form has a collection of controls. This comprises everything on the form, and since it is held in a collection we can use the `For Each` method to iterate through it. This sets the variable `ctlControl` to point to successive controls, and then tries to set the `FontName` property of this control. If the control doesn't support this property, then an error is generated. However, we are using `On Error` to trap errors, so our special bit of code is run. This is the bit of code after `FormFonts_Err`. In this section of code we check to see if the error number is `438` – remember this error number identifies that the property doesn't exist. In this case we don't care, so we just tell the program to `Resume` at the `Next` statement. If the error number is anything other than `438`, then the error message is displayed, and the function exits.

Don't worry too much about this error handling code, as we will cover it in detail later. The thing to remember is that we now have a procedure that works on all open forms, irrespective of the controls they have on them.

One important thing to remember is that changes you make to an open form are not saved when you close the form. Later in the book we'll see ways of making permanent changes to forms and reports by opening the form in design mode and making changes there.

Referring to Objects

So far, you have only used an index into the collection to reference the required item, but there are other ways to find the object you require. The first method we'll look at is probably the most common. It allows you to refer to an object explicitly as a member of a collection. For example, to set an object variable to the form `frmCompany` you can use:

```
Dim frmP As Form
Set frmP = Forms!frmCompany
```

You use the exclamation mark to separate the collection from the object. If the object has spaces in its name, you have to enclose it within square brackets. For example, if the form were called `Company Details`, then you would do this:

```
Set frmP = Forms![Company Details]
```

The second method is similar to using an index, but instead of a number you use the name of the object or a string variable:

```
Set frmP = Forms("frmCompany")
```

Or, using a string containing the name:

```
strFormName = "frmCompany"
Set frmP = Forms(strFormName)
```

And, of course, you can use a number to refer to an object in a collection just like you would with an array:

```
Set frmP = Forms(3)
```

This would set `frmP` to point to the fourth form in the collection (collection numbers start at 0). So, you can access a form either from its name or its position in the `Forms` collection. If you use `For Each...` to cycle through the collection, you use the numeric position in the collection. Using the name allows you to access single objects directly.

Special Objects

There are some properties and objects in Access that we haven't covered yet, but which are quite useful. When changing the font earlier we used the `Forms` collection to look at all open forms, but what if we wanted this procedure to only work for the current form? Or what if we want to write a procedure where a form object is passed into it? Let's look at these special objects and properties, and see what they do:

Object	Property	Refers to...
Screen	ActiveControl	The control that has the focus.
Screen	ActiveDataAccess Page	The data access page that has the focus.
Screen	ActiveForm	The form that has the focus, or contains the control with the focus.
Screen	ActiveReport	The report that has the focus, or contains the control with the focus.
Screen	PreviousControl	The control that had the focus immediately before the control with the current focus.
Form or Report	Me	The current form or report.
Form or Report	Module	The form or report module.
Form or Report	RecordsetClone	A copy of the recordset that underlies a form or report. You'll see more of this in the next few chapters.
Subform, form, or the actual control	Form	For a subform control, this is the subform. For a form, it is the form itself. You'll see this in action later in the book.
Subreport, report, or the actual control	Report	For a subreport control, this is the subreport. For a report, it is the report itself.

Object	Property	Refers to...
Control	Parent	The form or report that contains the control.
Control	Section	The section of a form or a report upon which a control lies.

Some of these you might not use, but there are some, such as `ActiveForm`, `Me`, and `RecordsetClone`, that you'll use quite often.

Try It Out – The ActiveForm Property

1. Open the company form, `frmCompany`.

2. Switch to the VBE and show the Immediate window.

3. Type the following:

```
?Screen.ActiveForm.Name
```

4. Switch back to Access and open the Switchboard form, keeping the company form open too.

5. Switch back to the VBE and try it again.

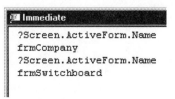

So you can see that the `ActiveForm` object changes, depending upon which form is the currently active one. This would be quite useful if you needed to write a procedure to act upon the current form. For example, in the `FormFonts` procedure we created earlier, we used the `Forms` collection to loop through all open forms, but if we only wanted to act upon the current form we could do this:

```
Dim frmCurrent As Form
Dim ctlControl As Control

For Each ctlControl In Screen.ActiveForm.Controls
   ctlControl.FontName = strFont
Next
```

The Me Property

You'll find the Me property extremely useful because it refers to the object currently being executed. So, if you use Me in a form module, it refers to the form, and if you use it in a report module, it refers to the report. This allows you write code that isn't dependent upon the form name, and that could be copied to another form module. For example, taking another look at the code to change the font of controls – it loops through the open forms. But what if we wanted to use this code in a single form – perhaps in response to a user request to change the font? One way would be to use the Forms collection, for example:

```
For Each ctlControl In Forms("frmCompany").Controls
```

One reason why this is bad is that you can't just copy the code – it would need changing if you pasted this into another form. Another reason is that it's wasteful – Access already knows what the active form is – Me:

```
Dim frmCurrent As Form
Dim ctlControl As Control

For Each ctlControl In Me.Controls
    ctlControl.FontName = strFont
Next
```

Now you might think that you could use ActiveForm, but Me and ActiveForm don't always refer to the same thing. For example, consider this diagram below:

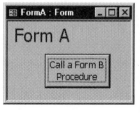
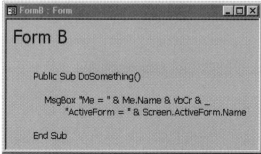

We have Form A, which is the active form. The button calls a public procedure in Form B, which displays the name of the form for Me and for the ActiveForm. Here's the result:

So this shows that even though DoSomething is executing in a different form, Me still points to the current form (i.e. the form under which the code is running), whereas ActiveForm is the form with the current focus.

The Object Browser

The Object Browser is part of the VBE, and it allows you to look up definitions of objects, methods, properties, and constants. You can easily call up the object browser by pressing *F2* (when you're in the VBE); it looks like this:

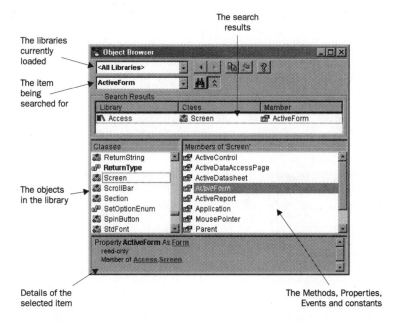

The search results

The libraries currently loaded

The item being searched for

The objects in the library

Details of the selected item

The Methods, Properties, Events and constants

There's a lot of information available in the object browser. The first combo box allows you to select a specific library:

In this example there are 6 libraries loaded:

❏ **Access** contains the objects for Access itself

❏ **DAO** contains the Data Access Objects

❏ **IceCream** contains the current database, so that includes forms, reports, etc.

❑ **Office** contains the standard Microsoft Office 2000 objects

❑ **stdole** contains some standard object features, which you'll never have to refer to

❑ **VBA** contains the objects for Visual Basic for Applications

In chapter 14 you'll see how to add more objects to this list.

The search window and results pane allows you to search for specific items. In the above diagram I searched for **ActiveForm**, and it only occurs once – in the Access library, belonging to the Screen object. This is extremely useful if you know the name of something (such as a method or property) but can't remember which object it belongs to.

In the above diagram you can see that we were looking at All Libraries, so every object is shown, in alphabetical order. To look at the objects within the current database, you can just change to the **IceCream** entry:

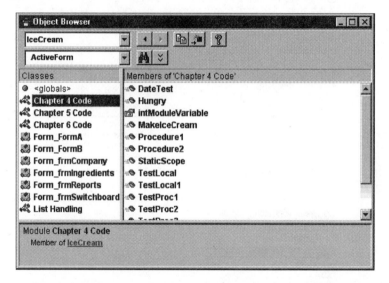

This shows a list of all of the objects in the **IceCream** database. The **Chapter 4 Code** module is selected, and the **Members** pane shows all of the items in that module. Notice that no reports appear here – this is because the reports in the database don't have any code behind them. Only objects with code appear in the object browser.

The Object Browser is your friend. Remember that it is there, use it, and your life will be easier. Trust me. You really can learn a lot from just browsing around in it. You'll be amazed at how many objects, properties and methods there are, and you're bound to find plenty that you didn't know existed.

Summary

In this chapter we've started to look into the object world, looking at the objects that Access has built in. This has concentrated on some of the main ones, such as forms, controls, etc, but you will be seeing more throughout the rest of the book.

An important thing to remember from this chapter is **collections**. If there is more than one of an object then there is a collection, with the collection name usually being the plural of the object. So to hold the form objects we have a `Forms` collection. Looping through these collections is easy with the `For Each` statement, so you can easily examine every item.

Once you have an object you can refer to its methods and properties, such as the `FontName` property for controls. So, from within your code, you have access to almost everything that you have access to when in design mode. This is a very powerful feature, and you'll see much more of it later. But for now, it's time you learned about data access.

Exercises

1. For the `FormsFonts` procedure, think about how you could make the changes to the font permanent. Remember that the `Forms` collection only shows the open forms, so you would have to use the `AllForms` collection. You should also remember that changes to a form opened in form view are never saved, so the form should be opened in design view. Have a look at the `OpenForm` and `Close` methods of the `DoCmd` object.

2. The above routine doesn't take into account controls that don't have a `FontName` property. You might like to amend it so that it does, in a similar fashion to the Try It Out – Objects, Controls and Errors.

Using DAO

Having read this far, you should now be familiar with some of the basics of VBA programming. We have looked at the nature of event-driven programming; we have written our first code in VBA and investigated some of the programming constructs we can use to add more complex logic to our application; and we have taken a look at the object model of the Access application.

That's all fine – and we need to make sure that we understand the basics before we move onto some of the more advanced concepts – but so far the ground that we have covered has been fairly generic. That is to say that the concepts we have looked at so far have dealt more with the basics of VBA programming as opposed to the specifics of database programming. That's all about to change now, as we get to grips with using VBA to manipulate tables, queries, and data that we keep in our databases.

DAO vs ADO

Anyone who has had dealings in the computer industry will know that use of the TLA (Three Letter Acronym) is rife. You will not be surprised to know that things are no different in the database world. Indeed, Microsoft have elevated the use of the TLA to new heights in recent years by not only repeatedly changing the TLAs that they use to describe their methods of database access, but by trying to devise as many TLAs as they can while using the fewest number of letters.

Try It Out: Invent a Data Access Method (DAM)

1. Take a photocopy of this page.

2. Cut out the following counters (Remember: scissors can be dangerous, so if you are not sure, ask an adult to do this for you).

3. Put all of the counters into an empty mug.

4. With your eyes closed, pull out three or four of the counters and lay them on the desk in front of you. Hey presto! You have your own Data Access Method. But we're not finished yet!

5. Wait for about a year until everybody has got used to using the new DAM you have invented. Now put all the counters back in the mug, pull out three or four more, and proclaim the resultant letters as your new (and even better!) Data Access Method.

They have been trying this for years in Redmond and in recent years we have had Microsoft espouse the following TLAs in their attempts to make database access as simple to understand as possible...

- ❏ DAO (Data Access Objects)
- ❏ RDO (Remote Data Objects)
- ❏ RDS (Remote Data Services)
- ❏ ADO (Active Data Objects, later ActiveX Data Objects)

So, before we plunge into looking at how we can use DAO from VBA, let's take a moment or two to look at what it is and how it has been developed.

For the latest information on Microsoft's data access strategy, check out the Universal Data Access section of Microsoft's web site at http://www.microsoft.com/data.

A Brief History Of DAO

The initial release of Microsoft Access in November 1992 was popular enough, but one of its few failings was the relatively limited programmatic access that it allowed to the database objects within it. The database engine it used was JET 1.0, and it was possible to access tables and queries in JET from code (which at the time was Access basic, not VBA) by using an interface known as Data Access Objects (DAO). But the number of operations that could be performed against JET objects through DAO 1.0 was very restrictive.

An interim release of Access in the following summer introduced JET 1.1 and DAO 1.1 which gave programmers the ability to perform more advanced operations against tables and queries, although again the feature set offered by DAO 1.1 still left significant room for improvement. The situation was not helped by the fact that the interim release of DAO was only available through Visual Basic 3 and not natively from within Access 1.1.

A little over a year later in the late spring of 1994, Microsoft released Access 2.0. Again, a new version of the database engine – JET 2.0 – accompanied the release along with a revised programmatic interface. DAO 2.0 was a significant improvement over its predecessors and exposed the objects within JET 2.0 as a complete hierarchical collection of objects with their own methods and properties with support for data definition (i.e. creating tables and queries) and security management as well as data manipulation.

A service pack released six months later introduced JET 2.5, but the next significant step forward came with Access 95, which provided the first full 32-bit implementation of JET. This not only offered significant performance improvements over its 16-bit predecessor, but also added support for replication.

With Access 97 came JET 3.5 and DAO 3.5. As the version numbering indicates, the changes from the previous version were fairly modest, with perhaps the most significant enhancement being the addition of **ODBCDirect**, a technology that allowed programmers to use the DAO interface to access data on remote enterprise servers (such as SQL Server or Sybase) efficiently.

JET 4.0, the version of the database engine that ships with Access 2000, shows a number of improvements over previous versions. This latest incarnation of JET supports Unicode and uses a SQL syntax which is not only ANSI compliant, but is also entirely compatible with SQL Server 7.0, making the task of upsizing a database from Access to SQL Server easier than ever. JET 4.0 also introduces row-level locking, improved replication functionality, and the ability to programmatically determine which users are currently accessing the database. As you would expect, the programmatic interface to JET 4.0 – DAO 3.6 – exposes all of this new functionality to the developer.

The Future of DAO

DAO has always been an excellent interface for working with native Access data, but companies keep data in a wide variety of databases other than Access. For example, a great number of companies keep their data in large client-server databases such as Microsoft SQL Server, Sybase or Oracle. What if you want to join data in SQL Server with data that resides in an Access database?

One approach – which has proved highly effective – is to attach the SQL Server tables to an Access database. The data remains in the SQL Server database but, to all intents and purposes, the attached tables appear just like Access tables and can be accessed programmatically using DAO in the same way that native Access tables can. The 'glue' that is used to attach tables from these client-server databases is a technology called ODBC or Open Database Connectivity. A vendor-independent technology, it was devised in the early 1990s as a method of connecting any client application to any relational database.

Although admirable for its simplicity, this approach had its limitations. For example, by accessing SQL Server tables as if they were Access tables, the developer was often prevented from taking advantage of SQL Server-specific functionality. The primary reason for this was that in order for an Access developer to programmatically fetch data from the base SQL Server table, the developer would have to use DAO, which would in turn call JET, which would in turn determine that the table wasn't actually an Access table but was a remote ODBC table and so (take a deep breath…) would in turn call ODBC, which would in turn load the appropriate database driver, which would in turn fetch the data from the base table in SQL Server (whew!). Although much of this chain of delegation was transparent to the developer, there was an impact – both in terms of response time and memory overhead – resulting from the number of DLLs that needed to be loaded for even simple operations against an ODBC database.

To get around this problem, Access 97 introduced ODBCDirect. This was a development of the RDO (Remote Data Objects) technology that had been in use in Visual Basic for a while. The advantage of ODBCDirect was that it used DAO to call ODBC, completely bypassing JET. Not only could this improve query response times against ODBC databases, but because JET was completely bypassed it meant that developers had more control over low-level connection and query configuration options.

The diagram below illustrates where each of the components we have described so far fits into the big picture as far as accessing data from Access or VBA is concerned.

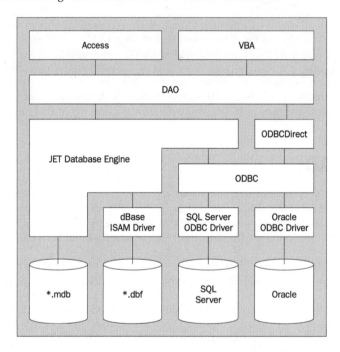

ODBCDirect was a big improvement, but there was still another problem. You see, ODBC was designed to work against relational databases like SQL Server and Oracle. At a pinch it could be made to work against non-relational tabular sets of data such as Microsoft Excel spreadsheets. But there was still an awful lot of data that ODBC wouldn't work with, simply because the data was not relational. For example, many companies have electronic mail systems such as Microsoft Exchange. Such a system holds a vast amount of information, both in the content of the messages and in the details of the senders themselves. If only we could get to this data...

OLEDB and ADO

Enter OLEDB, stage left... OLEDB is a new technology, developed by Microsoft, which provides access to both relational and non-relational data. So OLEDB can be used to extract data from Access databases and from SQL Server databases. But it can also be used to extract information from non-relational sources such as Microsoft Exchange, Microsoft Index Server, Active Directory Services in NT5, and decision support systems such as OLAP servers. It is the universality of the data that can be accessed through OLEDB – the underlying framework has been christened Universal Data Access (UDA) by Microsoft – that makes this technology so compelling. The diagram below shows the OLEDB architecture.

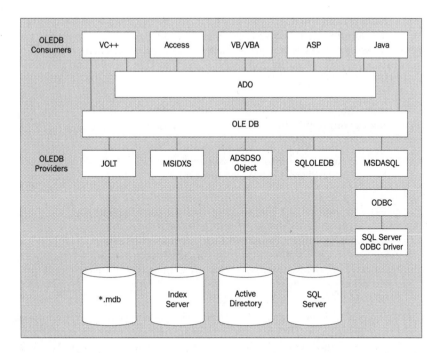

As you can see from this diagram OLEDB is able to communicate with these disparate data sources through drivers which are known as "Data Providers". A number of native providers have already been written – the provider for Access 2000 is nicknamed JOLT (well, it's easier to say than the Jet OLEDB 4.0 provider) and the native provider for SQL Server is SQLOLEDB. More native providers will be published in time, and it is even possible to connect to ODBC databases for which there is no native provider by using the MSDASQL provider which allows access via existing ODBC drivers.

So that is how OLEDB communicates with the different data sources. What is really cool, however, is how client applications communicate with OLEDB. OLEDB has a single programmatic interface called ADO (ActiveX Data Objects) and this is what client applications use irrespective of the type of provider. So you use the same syntax whether you are connecting to tables in SQL Server, tables in Access or data that is in an Exchange Server or in Index Server. That's a real big plus. So, where does that leave DAO?

Microsoft have made it clear that ADO is the way ahead and that DAO has a limited shelf-life. There will be no further development to DAO and Microsoft assert that the presence of DAO in Access 2000 is primarily intended to ease the migration path for developers whose Access 97 applications contain a large DAO codebase. That is the reason why – despite substantial changes between JET 3.x and JET 4.0 – the changes between DAO 3.5 (Access 97) and DAO 3.6 (Access 2000) are minimal.

However, it is not as simple as that (it never is!). You see, DAO really is very, very good for working with data in Access. And ADO? Well, like any newcomer it's got quite a lot to learn. The incarnation of ADO released with Access 2000 (ADO 2.1) and, more specifically, the native provider for JET (JOLT, or Jet OLEDB 4.0) just don't offer the same functionality.

True, there are some things you can do with ADO and JOLT that you can't do with DAO (such as viewing who is currently logged in to the database) but for a lot of the bread-and-butter tasks, DAO still has the edge. For example, if an Access form is based on an ADO recordset (i.e. the data in the form comes from Access tables via ADO rather than DAO) then the records are not updatable. Now that's quite a significant limitation. So, is it back to DAO then? The advice we would offer is this...

❑ If you will be working primarily with data in Access tables and you are unlikely to upsize your application to a client-server database such as SQL Server, then stick with DAO.

❑ If you will be using Access as a front-end to a client-server database, then use ADO instead (and create an Access project).

❑ If you are working primarily with data in Access but think that you might upsize the application to a client-server database like SQL Server, then it's your call... Using ADO from the start will make the migration to a client-server database much easier but, such are the limitations of the current version of JOLT, you will probably be counting down the days until you can upsize the database and use ADO in an environment which shows it off in its best light.

The decision over whether to base this book around DAO or ADO is one that has vexed the authors considerably. We would have loved ADO/JOLT to have been sufficiently mature to have allowed us to base the book around it with confidence. The problem is that for working with Access data – which is the primary focus of this book – DAO is still both faster and more feature rich. For the moment, it is a question of choosing the trusty old linebacker over the promising new draft pick. But ADO is an excellent technology and will surely one day soon become the data access method of choice from Access – until the next one comes along.

> If you want to know more about ADO, you will be glad to know that we will be using it (albeit briefly) in Chapter 13(Classes). In addition, there are two appendices at the back of this book with information about ADO. The first (Appendix B) goes into more detail about choosing between ADO and DAO. The second (Appendix C) details the ADO object model.

The DAO Hierarchy

So, DAO here we come... If we are to use DAO effectively, then we must start with an understanding of the DAO hierarchy. We saw in the previous chapter how we can interact programmatically with the Access application via the Access object model. This contained a number of objects, grouped together into collections, all arranged in a hierarchical manner.

For example, the `Forms` collection contains a number of `Form` objects representing every form that is currently open.

Each of these `Form` objects has a `Controls` collection that contains a `Control` object for every control appearing on that form.

Each `Control` object has a `Properties` collection that contains a `Property` object for every property of that control.

> **Make sure that you appreciate the difference between the Access object model and the DAO object model. The Access object model is what we use to interact programmatically with the Access user interface (e.g. forms and reports). The DAO hierarchy is what we use to programmatically interact with JET databases.**

The good news is that the DAO hierarchy is arranged in the same similar manner to the Access object model, with collections of objects, each of which has its own methods and properties. However, before we look at the DAO hierarchy, we need to make sure that we have a reference to DAO in our database.

Forms and reports in Access 2000 still use DAO rather than ADO to fetch the data that they display. Originally it was intended that they should use ADO, but Microsoft changed tack during the development cycle when it was clear that the limitations of ADO/JOLT would mean the loss of a great deal of functionality to which Access developers had grown accustomed.

However, despite the fact that DAO is the mechanism used for retrieving data in forms and reports, the default database access method from Visual Basic is now ADO. What do we mean by that? Well, if you open the `IceCream.mdb` database, switch to the VBA IDE by hitting *ALT+F11* and then look at the references that are set by default (by choosing References... from the Tools menu) you should see this:

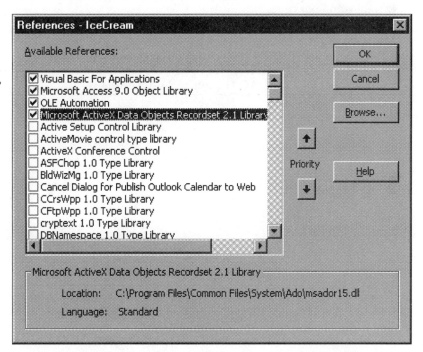

As you can see from the References dialog box, there are quite a number of libraries that we can reference from within VBA. We will look at libraries in more detail in Chapters 13 and 14, but for the moment you can think of them as collections of pre-built objects and functions that we can use in our code. Even though there might be many such libraries installed on our computer, it is unlikely that we will want to use them all in every database. So we can use the References dialog box to select those libraries that we want to be available from VBA within each database.

To make a library available from within VBA, we simply check the checkbox beside it. Unchecking the checkbox makes the library unavailable, which means that we will get an error if we try to refer to any of the objects or functions in that library.

The `IceCream.mdb` database has references to the four libraries that are available by default in new Access 2000 databases:

- ❑ Visual Basic for Applications
- ❑ Microsoft Access 9.0 Object Library
- ❑ OLE Automation
- ❑ Microsoft ActiveX Data Objects 2.1 Library (ADO)

Now we are not going to be using ADO in this chapter, but will be using DAO. So we need to remove the reference to ADO and add a reference to DAO. We do that by unchecking **Microsoft ActiveX Data Objects 2.1 Library** and checking **Microsoft DAO 3.6 Object Library**, which will be further down the list of references. Once we have done that and clicked OK, we will be able to use DAO 3.6 from within our code.

> Strictly speaking, we don't need to remove the reference to ADO. However, some of the objects in the ADO hierarchy have the same names as objects in the DAO hierarchy and retaining the reference to ADO could lead to confusion when writing code that uses the DAO version of those objects.

So let's have a look at the DAO 3.6 hierarchy:

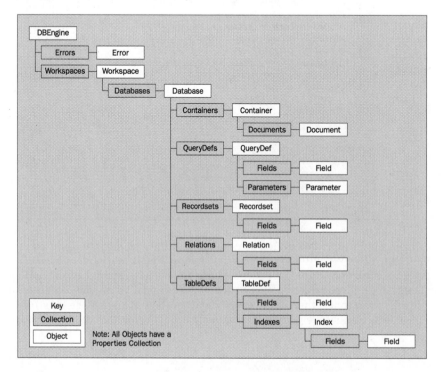

Two collections (Users and Groups) have been omitted from this diagram for the sake of simplicity. Don't worry; we'll be looking at these in a lot more detail when we deal with security in Chapter 16.

Hopefully, after reading the previous chapter, you should be familiar with the concept of object hierarchies. But probably the best way to learn how the DAO hierarchy works is to walk through the object model by using the Immediate window. And that's what we will do. So, pour yourself a nice strong cup of coffee, make sure you are sitting comfortably, open the Immediate window and get ready for a whistle-stop tour of the DAO hierarchy, starting from the top.

The DBEngine Object

In the Access object hierarchy, the topmost object was the Application object, representing the Access application. Well, as you can see from the diagram above, the topmost object in the DAO hierarchy is the DBEngine object. This represents the DAO interface into the JET engine – the database engine which Access uses for all of its native database management – and ODBCDirect, which is used for accessing remote ODBC databases. So what can we do with the DBEngine object? Well, we can start by determining what version of DAO we are using. To do this, type the following in the Immediate window and hit *ENTER*:

```
?DBEngine.Version
```

The result 3.6 should be displayed, indicating that we are using version 3.6 of DAO.

The DBEngine object contains two collections, the Errors collection and the Workspaces collection. The Errors collection is populated with Error objects every time a database-related error occurs, and we will look at this in more detail in Chapter 12 when we get to grips with error handling.

To be honest, there isn't that much else that you can do with the DBEngine object per se. In fact, you will probably find that most of the time you won't use the DBEngine object for anything other than as a way of getting to the Errors or Workspaces collections.

The Workspace Object

The other collection is the Workspaces collection, which we can think of as representing a single session or instance of a user interacting with the database engine.

For example, to find out the name of the currently logged-on user of Access, we could execute the following code in the Immediate window:

```
?DBEngine.Workspaces(0).UserName
```

If you are using an unsecured system database, and have not logged into Access, the name of the default user will be displayed:

```
admin
```

But if you have manually logged into Access, the user name you logged in with will be displayed instead. Notice that to get to this property we used the syntax DBEngine.Workspaces(0). This expression returns the first (and most of the time only) Workspace object in the Workspaces collection. This represents the currently logged on interactive session that you have with the database engine.

> *Earlier in this chapter we mentioned that Access 97 (or, more accurately, version 3.5 of DAO) saw the introduction of ODBCDirect, a technology that enables Access developers programmatic access to remote ODBC databases such as SQL Server or Oracle. In order to give developers tight control over the security and session management features of these databases, there is a special type of Workspace object that should be used when working with ODBCDirect. However, we don't need to worry about that because in this book we won't be dealing with ODBCDirect.*

The Workspace object used by JET contains a Users collection and a Groups collection that contain details of all users and groups defined in the current system database.

It also contains a Databases collection that holds a Database object representing every database that the current user for that Workspace object has open.

> *The Workspace object will be dealt with more fully in Chapter 17, when we consider multi-user and security issues.*

The Database Object

Normally, we will only have one database open at a time, so there will only be one Database object in the Databases collection for the current workspace. You can see this for yourself by typing this in the Immediate window and hitting *ENTER*:

```
?DBEngine.Workspaces(0).Databases.Count
```

which should return 1. To inspect this Database further, we could refer to it by its position in the Databases collection like this:

```
DBEngine.Workspaces(0).Databases(0)
```

So, to find the name of the currently open database we could type this in the Immediate window.

```
?DBEngine.Workspaces(0).Databases(0).Name
```

Alternatively, because the Workspaces collection is the default collection of the DBEngine object and the Databases collection is the default collection of the Workspace object, we could omit the collection names and use a shorthand notation like this:

```
?DBEngine(0)(0).Name
```

Or we could use this more friendly shortcut:

```
?CurrentDB.Name()
```

Although practically synonymous, the CurrentDB() *function and* DBEngine(0)(0) *are subtly different.* CurrentDB() *creates a new instance of the current database and returns a reference to it, whereas* DBEngine(0)(0) *returns a reference to the current instance of the open database. For subtle reasons, which we will not go into here, you should use* CurrentDB() *rather than* DBEngine(0)(0) *wherever possible. If you want to know more, take a look at Microsoft Knowledge Base article Q131881 (http://support.microsoft .com/support/kb/articles/q131/8/81.asp).*

To inspect the properties of the currently open database, we simply examine the properties of the object returned by CurrentDB(). For example:

```
?CurrentDB.Name
```

will return the file name and location of the currently open database, and

```
?CurrentDB.Version
```

will return the version of JET with which the current database was created. So, if we are in a database which was created with Access 2000, the value of CurrentDB.Version would be 4.0, because Access 2000 uses JET 4.0. However, if we were to use Access 2000 to open (not convert) a database created in Access 97, the value of CurrentDB.Version would be 3.0 instead, indicating that the database was created by JET 3.0.

So, what collections does the Database object contain? Well, if we look at the diagram, we can see that there are five of them.

This collection...	...contains these objects
Containers	One Container object for every collection of Documents.
QueryDefs	One QueryDef object for every saved query that exists within the database.
Recordsets	One Recordset object for every recordset that is currently open in the database.
Relations	One Relation object for every relationship defined between tables in the database.
TableDefs	One TableDef object for every table (including system tables, but excluding linked tables) which exists within the database.

We'll take a brief take look at the TableDefs and QueryDefs collections, just to make sure that we understand what they represent. Then we will focus on one collection in particular – the Recordsets collection – in a fair amount of detail. We shall not look at the Relations collection, as it is used so infrequently, and we shall leave our examination of the Containers collection to Chapter 17 when we discuss security.

The TableDefs Collection

First of all, let us use the `Tabledefs` collection to determine the number of tables in our database. Going back to the Immediate window in the `IceCream.mdb` database, if we type the following and hit the *ENTER* key:

```
?CurrentDB.TableDefs.Count
```

we should see that the current database has 11 tables in it. "Hold on!", you might say, as you switch to the Database window, "There are only six tables there!"

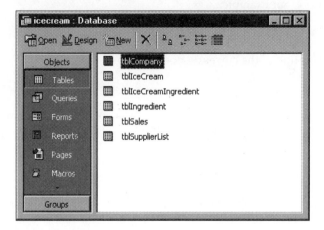

There certainly are six visible user-created tables, but the `TableDefs` collection also includes any hidden tables and system tables. If we view these, by checking the <u>H</u>idden Objects and S<u>y</u>stem Objects checkboxes on the View tab of the <u>T</u>ools/<u>O</u>ptions... dialog, we will see that there are indeed 11 tables in the database.

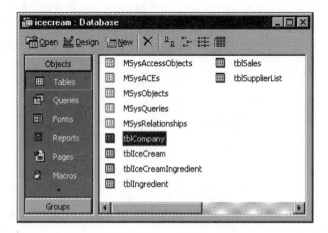

The QueryDefs Collection

If we examine the `QueryDefs` collection, then we would expect to see that the number of objects in the collection is equal to the number of queries in the database. So let's try it:

```
?CurrentDB.QueryDefs.Count
```

Now this is even more perplexing. If you evaluate this line of code in the Immediate window in `IceCream.mdb`, you will find that there are a great number of them! But if you go to the Query pane of the Database window, you will see that there are no saved queries. So where did these `QueryDef` objects come from?

The answer is that there are occasions when queries are stored in an Access database even though they may not be visible in the Database window. For example, if you create a form which contains a combo box, and then use a SQL statement as the **Rowsource** to populate that combo box, Access will compile the SQL and save the resulting query internally as a `QueryDef`. So the `QueryDefs` collection contains not just the queries that you explicitly created as queries and saved, but also any internal queries that exist within forms and reports.

The Recordsets Collection

The third collection contained within the `Database` object is the `Recordsets` collection. Recordsets are fundamental to data access through VBA and are something that you will really need to get to grips with. But don't worry, it's really not that tough! Now even if you don't know what a recordset is, you will almost certainly have used one already. Put simply, a `Recordset` is just what its name suggests – a set of records. When you open a table in Datasheet view, you are looking at a set of records. When you open a form, it will normally have a set of records behind it that supply the data for the form. Relational databases are all about sets of records (as opposed to flat-file databases which tend to deal with records on an individual basis) and you will find that the `Recordset` object will probably become the single most used of all of the Data Access Objects that you will come across in VBA. So, we will spend some time now looking in detail at the different types of `Recordset` and how we can use them in code.

Try It Out: Recordsets

1. Open up ICECREAM.MDB, create a new standard module and call it `Chapter 7 Code`. In the new module, add a subprocedure called `OpeningARecordset`.

2. Add the following code to the subprocedure:

```
Public Sub OpeningARecordset()

Dim db As Database
Dim rec As Recordset
Dim intRecords As Integer

Set db = CurrentDb()
Set rec = db.OpenRecordset("tblIceCream")
```

```
intRecords = rec.RecordCount
MsgBox "There are " & intRecords & " records in the tblIceCream table"
rec.Close

End Sub
```

3. Now run the procedure. Remember, there are four ways to do this: you can hit *F5*, select Run Sub/User Form from the <u>R</u>un menu, hit the Run Sub/User Form button on the toolbar or type `OpeningARecordset` in the Immediate window and hit the *Return* key. You will get a message box telling you how many records there are in the table `tblIceCream`.

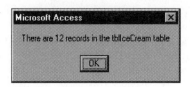

If you get a Compile Error when trying to run this code, go to References... *in the* Tools *menu of the VBE, and make sure* Microsoft DAO 3.6 Object Library *is checked, and not* Microsoft ActiveX Data Objects 2.1 Library.

4. You can check that this is correct by opening the table in Datasheet view and having a look.

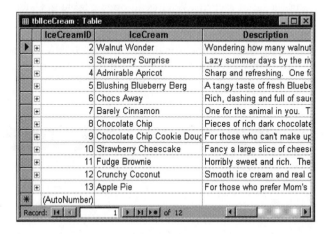

How It Works

You should be getting a feel for the VBA code by now, so we won't explain every line that we write. Instead, we'll concentrate on the new or interesting parts.

In this example, we fill a variable with the data from the table `tblIceCream`,

```
Set rec = db.OpenRecordset("tblIceCream")
```

and then use the `MsgBox` function to display the count of the records in the `Recordset`:

```
intRecords = rec.RecordCount
MsgBox "There are " & intRecords & " records in the tblIceCream table"
```

Notice also that we close the `Recordset` at the end of the procedure:

```
rec.Close
```

Once a `Recordset` has been closed, you can't do anything else with it. This allows VBA to free any resources associated with the `Recordset` and is particularly necessary in a multi-user environment or when you are dealing with linked tables. (These are tables that are stored in other currently open Access or non-Access databases, but which are linked and so can be manipulated as such if they were in the current Access database).

As we mentioned above, a `Recordset` is just that – a set of records. While a `Recordset` is open in your code (i.e. after it has been filled with records with the `OpenRecordset` method and before it is closed with the `Close` method), you can do what you like with the records in that `Recordset` – edit them, delete them or even add new records.

Different Types of Recordset

In VBA there are five different types of `Recordset` object that you can use. Which one you use depends on a combination of factors, such as:

- ❏ How many tables the underlying data comes from.
- ❏ Whether you want to update the records or just view them.
- ❏ Whether the tables are in Access or some other type of database.
- ❏ How many records there are in the recordset.

We'll look in detail at when to use each of the five types of `Recordset` a little later, but first let's have a look at what they are. The five types of `Recordset` object are:

- ❏ `Table`-type Recordset objects.
- ❏ `Dynaset`-type Recordset objects (normally just called dynasets).
- ❏ `Snapshot` type Recordset objects (or just snapshots).
- ❏ `Forward-only` type Recordset objects.
- ❏ `Dynamic` type Recordset objects.

Dynamic `Recordset` objects aren't actually part of JET and are instead part of ODBCDirect technology. They are used for accessing data in remote ODBC databases, rather than data in Access databases, so we need not concern ourselves with them here. Instead, we will concentrate on the four JET recordsets: table-type, dynaset-type, snapshot-type and forward-only-type recordsets.

We'll look at the differences between these four types in just a moment.

You open all four different types of `Recordset` object in the same way – using the `OpenRecordset` method against a `Database` object. Have another look at the portion of code that we used just now:

```
Dim db As Database
Dim rec As Recordset

Set db = CurrentDb()
Set rec = db.OpenRecordset("tblIceCream")
```

First we create a `Database` object that corresponds to the database we are currently in. Then we create a `Recordset` object within the current database and fill it with records from the table `tblIceCream`.

By default, this statement creates a table-type `Recordset` object because it is based on a single table. If we had wanted to be more explicit, we could have used the intrinsic constant, `dbOpenTable`, as a parameter to the `OpenRecordset` method just to make sure that the `Recordset` object would be a table-type `Recordset` object:

```
Set rec = db.OpenRecordset("tblIceCream", dbOpenTable)
```

If we had wanted a dynaset-type `Recordset` object instead, we would have used the `dbOpenDynaset` constant instead:

```
Set rec = db.OpenRecordset("tblIceCream ", dbOpenDynaset)
```

And, not surprisingly, if we had wanted a snapshot-type `Recordset` object or a forward-only-type `Recordset` object, we would have created them like this:

```
Set rec = db.OpenRecordset("tblIceCream ", dbOpenSnapshot)
```

```
Set rec = db.OpenRecordset("tblIceCream ", dbOpenForwardOnly)
```

We can see from the above statements, then, that there are three things we need to think about when we are creating a `Recordset` object:

- ❑ Which database are the records in?
- ❑ Whereabouts in that database are those records?
- ❑ What type of `Recordset` object do we want?

There are, in fact, further optional levels of control we can apply when we open `Recordset` objects, but we'll look at those a little later in Chapter 17 when we consider multi-user issues.

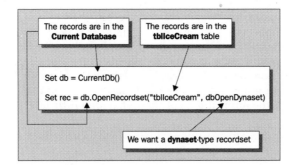

Access allows you to create a Recordset *object in a single line of code, without having to create a* Database *object. So you could say:*

```
Set rec = CurrentDB.OpenRecordset("tblIceCream", dbOpenDynaset)
```

However, the method we have used throughout this chapter, using an intermediate Database *object, is usually preferable, and is more efficient if you need to refer to the same database somewhere else in your procedure.*

Now we know how to create Recordset objects, which type should we use? Let's look at the different types in turn, and see which situations they are best suited to.

Table-type Recordset Objects

This is the default type for any Recordset objects where the records come from a single local or attached Access tables. In other words, if we try to create a Recordset object to retrieve records from a single Access table and we do not specify the type of Recordset object we want to open, Access will create a table-type Recordset object:

```
Set rec = db.OpenRecordset("tblIceCream")
```

Table-type Recordset objects are updateable (which means that we can make changes to the records in the Recordset and the changes will be reflected in the underlying table) objects. Another great advantage of using a table-type Recordset object is that you can use indexes on the table to speed up the process of searching for specific records. By contrast, you cannot use indexes against the other Recordset objects. In fact, we look at using indexes to locate records in a table-type Recordset later on in this chapter.

Dynaset-type Recordset Objects

A dynaset-type Recordset object can be based on either a local or attached table, or it can be based on the result of a query. There are two key features of dynaset-type Recordset objects:

❑ You can edit a dynaset and the results will be reflected in the underlying tables.

❑ While a dynaset is open, Access will update the records in your dynaset to reflect the changes that other people are making in the underlying tables.

To understand better the way that dynasets operate, it is probably helpful to see how they are created. Whenever a dynaset-type `Recordset` object is created, Access starts to build a copy of the **key values** from the result. That is, it copies the field or group of fields that uniquely identify each of the records in the result. The copy that it creates is, sensibly enough, called a keyset, because it is the set of key values. Then, whenever you want to view the records in the `Recordset` object, Access fetches the latest version of the non-key fields from the database based on the key values it has stored. Because of this behavior, you might sometimes see dynasets referred to as keyset-driven cursors. We will look at some of the implications of this behavior a little later.

Note that the keyset is not fully complete until the last record (key value) in the table has been accessed.

You should use dynaset-type `Recordset` objects if:

❑   You will need to update the records in the `Recordset` object.

❑   You want to see updates other users are making to those records.

❑   The `Recordset` object is very large.

❑   The `Recordset` object contains OLE objects such as bitmaps or Word documents.

Snapshot-type Recordset Objects

In contrast, snapshot-type `Recordset` objects are not updateable and do not reflect the changes that other users make to the records. In fact, just as the name suggests, you are taking a 'snapshot' of the data at a certain point in time. Whereas Access creates a copy of just the key values to create a dynaset, it takes a copy of the entire set of results to form a snapshot.

One of the advantages of snapshots is that with modestly-sized `Recordset` objects, snapshots are generally faster to create than dynasets. You would use a snapshot-type `Recordset` object in a situation where you don't wish to update the data and when the recordset won't contain more than about 500 records.

The terms dynaset and snapshot were introduced in early versions of Access, but Microsoft suggest that they should both be referred to just as recordsets. Throughout this chapter, if we mention dynasets and snapshots, we will be referring to dynaset-type `Recordset` *objects and snapshot-type* `Recordset` *objects respectively.*

Forward-Only-type Recordset Objects

Conceptually, forward-only-type recordsets are very similar to snapshots. They are read-only, do not reflect other users' changes, and are created by taking a copy of the entire qualifying set of results. Where they differ from snapshots is that they only allow you to move through them in one direction. In other words, with a forward-only recordset, you can read the records from it one after the other, but you can't then move back to previous records. Forward-only recordsets are sometimes referred to as firehose cursors.

What makes forward-only recordsets so attractive is the fact that they are very fast for moderately sized sets of results. So, if you are concerned about performance, if you can put up with the limited functionality and if there will not be more than about 500 records in the result, then forward-only recordsets are a good choice.

Building Recordsets Dynamically

We have already seen how `Recordset` objects can be created with the `OpenRecordset` method. The examples that we have looked at so far have all involved creating `Recordset` objects directly from tables. However, you can also create a `Recordset` object from a saved query or from a SQL `SELECT` statement. To do this, you simply substitute the query's name or the SQL `SELECT` statement for the table name. For example, if you had a query called `qryTotalOrders` in your database, you could create a dynaset-type `Recordset` object that contained the records from the query like this:

```
Set db = CurrentDb
Set rec = db.OpenRecordset("qryTotalOrders", dbOpenDynaset)
```

or by entering a SQL `SELECT` statement directly:

```
Set db = CurrentDb
Set rec = db.OpenRecordset("SELECT * FROM Order", dbOpenDynaset)
```

Using saved queries (as in the first of these two examples) will typically give slightly better performance, as the query will already be compiled and so JET will not have to go through the process of compiling the query before it is run. However, the second technique affords more flexibility and is often the only way out if you want to build up a query's definition dynamically in code (for example, in response to a user's selections on a form). There is an extended example of just this technique in the next chapter.

Default Types

If you do not specify the type of `Recordset` object that you want to open, Access will choose what is normally the best-performing type of `Recordset` object available:

- ❑ If the `Recordset` object is based on a single named table in the current database, Access will return a **table-type** `Recordset` object.

- ❑ If the `Recordset` object is based on a query or a SQL `SELECT` statement (or if it's from a table in a non-Access database), and if the underlying query or table can be updated, Access will return a **dynaset-type** `Recordset` object.

- ❑ In all other situations, Access will return a **snapshot-type** `Recordset` object.

However, there may be situations where you want to return a recordset of a different type than the one Access would normally return. For example, dynaset-type recordsets are generally quicker to open than snapshots, if the recordset contains more than a few hundred records. So in a situation where Access would otherwise have created the recordset as a snapshot, you might want to explicitly create a dynaset instead.

Requerying Data in Recordsets

If you want to make sure that the data in your `Recordset` is up-to-date, you can refresh it by executing the `Requery` method of the `Recordset` object:

```
rec.Requery
```

This re-executes the query that the `Recordset` object is based on, thus ensuring that the data is up-to-date. You can only do this, however, if the `Recordset` object supports requerying. In order to determine whether this is so, you should inspect the `Recordset` object's `Restartable` property. If the `Recordset` object's `Restartable` property is `True`, you can use the `Requery` method. You could test for this as follows:

```
If rec.Restartable = True Then rec.Requery
```

However, if the `Recordset` object's `Restartable` property is `False`, attempting to requery the recordset will generate an error. Table-type recordsets always have a `Restartable` property of `False` and so can never be requeried.

Working with Recordsets

So far, we have only really looked at how to create `Recordset` objects and ensure that the data in them is up-to-date. But, of course, what we normally want to do is to look at the data itself.

To refer to individual fields within a `Recordset` object, you can use a variety of different methods. We'll create a subprocedure that opens a dynaset-type `Recordset` object based on the `tblIceCream` table.

Try It Out – Looking at Values in a Recordset

1. In `IceCream.mdb`, in the same module you created earlier in this chapter, insert a procedure called `OpenIceCreamRecordset`:

```
Sub OpenIceCreamRecordset()

Dim db As Database
Dim rec As Recordset

Set db = CurrentDb()
Set rec = db.OpenRecordset("tblIceCream")

rec.Close

End Sub
```

2. Now place a `Stop` command after the `OpenRecordset` command. This has the effect of suspending execution of the code.

```
Set rec = db.OpenRecordset("tblIceCream")
```

```
Stop
```

```
rec.Close
```

3. Run the procedure, either by hitting *F5*, by selecting **Run Sub/User Form** from the <u>R</u>un menu, hitting the **Run Sub/User Form** button on the toolbar, or typing the name of the procedure in the Immediate window and hitting the Return key. When the line containing the Stop command is reached, execution of the code should pause and the line should be highlighted. We can now use the Immediate window to inspect the records in the recordset.

4. Make sure the Immediate window and Locals window are both visible. The Locals window should look like this. (If you have named your module differently, you will see a reference to the name you have given the module, rather than to Chapter 7 Code).

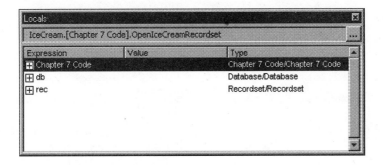

5. Now type the following in the Immediate window:

```
?rec(0), rec(1), rec(2)
```

6. Hit the *Enter* key and the value of the first three fields for the first record in the IceCream table should be displayed:

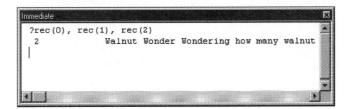

7. Now go to the Locals Window and find the variable called `rec`. If you click on the plus sign to the left of the variable's name, the tree will expand to display the properties of the `rec` variable. There are quite a few of them!

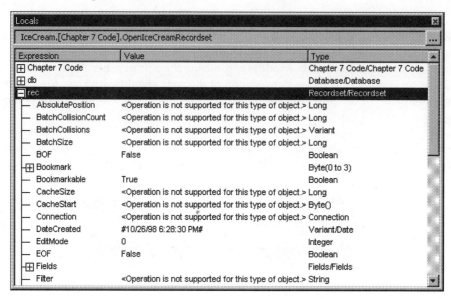

8. If you expand the entry for the `Fields` collection by clicking the plus button to its left, you will see it has 5 items (because there are 5 fields in the `Recordset` represented by the variable `rec`).

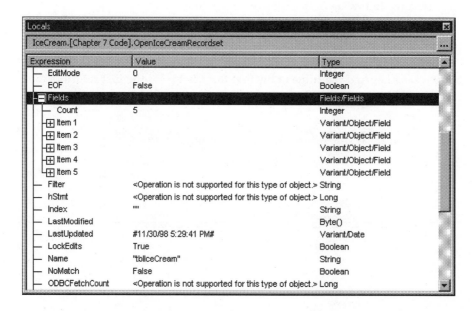

9. Expand Item 2, again by clicking the plus button to its left. You should see the properties of that particular `Field` object.

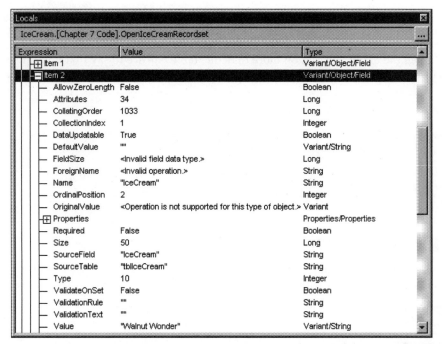

10. Note the values of the `CollectionIndex`, `Name`, `Size` and `Value` properties. From this you should be able to determine that the index of this field in the `Fields` collection of the `Recordset` is **1** (remember, these collections are zero-based); the name of the field is IceCream; the maximum length of values in this field is **50** characters; and the value of this field in the current record is `Walnut Wonder`.

11. Finally, return to the code window and hit either *F5* or the Run Sub/User Form button on the toolbar. This allows the procedure to run from where it is (at the `Stop` statement) to the end of the procedure and close the `Recordset` object.

How It Works

Whenever you create a `Recordset` object, the first row of the recordset becomes the current record. As we created a table-type `Recordset` object, the records are ordered according to the primary key (`IceCreamID`) and so the current row is the record containing data for the ice cream called `Walnut Wonder`. We can then examine the value of any of the fields in this record. In this example, we inspected the values of the first three fields of that record, the `IceCreamID`, `IceCream` and `Description` fields respectively.

At this point, you should note that the order of records in a query may not always be what you expect. If a query is based on a single table and you have not chosen to sort the records in some other way when you designed the query, then records in the query will normally be displayed in primary key order, or in their original insertion order if there is no primary key.

However, if your query contains a criterion for a field that is not the primary key, the records will usually be displayed in insertion order (that is, the order in which they were entered in the table). In fact, the rules for deciding in what order Access displays the records are even more complex, particularly when the query is based on more than one table. Suffice to say that you cannot rely on the records in a query being sorted in any particular order unless you have explicitly requested one.

> If you want the records in a query to be sorted, you should specify a sort criterion (or an ORDER BY clause) when you design the query.
>
> If you have not specified any sort criteria, you should not rely on the records in the result set being in any particular order.

Examining Field Values

To look at the values of individual fields within the current record, we can use one of the same three conventions that we could with other objects within collections. They are as follows:

General Syntax	Example
RecordsetName!FieldName	rec!IceCreamID
RecordsetName("FieldName")	rec("IceCreamID")
RecordsetName(FieldIndex)	rec(0)

When using the RecordsetName(FieldIndex) *syntax to refer to fields in a* Recordset *object, you should remember that Access will always give the first field an index of 0 rather than 1, irrespective of any* Option Base *setting you may have stated. So,* rec(2) *refers to the third field in the* Recordset *object,* rec, *not the second.*

Moving Through Recordsets

So far, however, things have been rather static. We are able to open a Recordset object and inspect all the values in the current record, but what if we want to move around the recordset? Suppose we wanted to move to the next record down and look at the values in that? Well, it's simple enough. If, after our Stop statement, we had applied the MoveNext method to the Recordset object in the last example by typing this in to the Immediate window,

```
rec.MoveNext
```

and then checked the value of the `IceCream` field, we would have found that it was `Strawberry Surprise`:

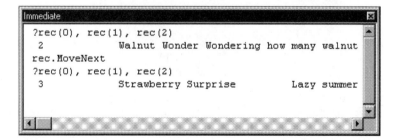

Moving around a recordset is really very simple. The methods that you can use are:

Method	Description
MoveNext	Makes the next record the current record.
MovePrevious	Makes the previous record the current record.
MoveFirst	Makes the first record the current record.
MoveLast	Makes the last record the current record.
Move n	Makes the record *n* records away from the current record (e.g. `rec.Move 3` or `rec.Move -2`).

This is all very well, but we are still faced with the problem that we encountered back in the first couple of chapters with our "unintelligent" navigation buttons. If we wanted to print the value of the `IceCream` field for every record in our recordset, we could keep on using the `MoveNext` method and then print the value of `IceCream`, but at some point we'll hit the last record. Access will let us try another `MoveNext`, but when we try to print the value of `IceCream`, we'll get a warning message telling us that there is no current record.

In Chapter 2, we had the same problem. We added logic to the buttons on the `frmCompany` form to enable us to move to the first, next, last or previous records or to the blank record at the end of the recordset that is used for inserting a new record, but there was nothing to stop us trying to move beyond this, in which case we also got an error message:

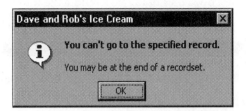

To make the form more user-friendly, we decided to disable certain buttons, depending on where we were in the recordset. In Chapter 3, we started to implement this feature and wrote code to disable the **Next** button when we were on the new blank record at the end of the table. Well, it's taken a while to get here, but now we can look at the code that looks after *all* the buttons.

We're in a position to deal with the problem for all of the buttons, because we have a set of methods at our disposal that allow us to test where we are in a recordset and actually move to the last record or first record in one straightforward action. Once we've executed these methods, we can then take appropriate action to disable the correct buttons. Before we move on to the actual code, however, let's make sure that we understand exactly when we want the navigation buttons to be enabled or disabled.

Position	First	Previous	Next	Last	New
First Record	Disabled	Disabled	Enabled	Enabled	Enabled
Intermediate Records	Enabled	Enabled	Enabled	Enabled	Enabled
Last Record	Enabled	Enabled	Disabled	Disabled	Enabled
New (Blank) Record	Enabled	Enabled	Disabled	Enabled	Enabled

Looking at the table above, we can see that when we are on the first record of the form we want the **Previous** button to be disabled, while the rest of the buttons will be enabled. On the last record and in the blank, new record at the end of the form we want the **Next** button to be disabled.

We also need to consider what will happen if the form does not allow new records to be added. By disabling the **Next** button on the last record, we prevent the user from using the **Next** button to try move from the last record into the blank, new record. So we are covered in that situation. However, we will also need to make sure that the **New** button is disabled if the form does not allow new records to be added.

Finally, we will need to make sure that all of the buttons except for the **New** button are disabled if there are no records at all in the form (or rather in the underlying recordset).

Now that we have sorted out the rules of engagement, we can go into battle...

1. If you haven't already done so, open up the IceCream.mdb database and switch to the VBA IDE by hitting *ALT + F11*.

2. Double-click the Form_frmCompany class module and locate the Current event. This should contain the code we wrote in Chapter 3.

3. Locate the Private Sub Form_Current() subprocedure, and replace it with the code given below:

```
Private Sub Form_Current()

Dim recClone As Recordset

'Make a clone of the recordset underlying the form so
'we can move around that without affecting the form's
'recordset

Set recClone = Me.RecordsetClone()

'If we are in a new record, disable the <Next> button
'and enable the rest of the buttons
If Me.NewRecord Then
    cmdFirst.Enabled = True
    cmdPrevious.Enabled = True
    cmdNext.Enabled = False
    cmdLast.Enabled = True
    cmdNew.Enabled = True
    Exit Sub
End If

'If we reach here, we know we are not in a new record
'so we can enable the <New> button if the form allows
'new records to be added
cmdNew.Enabled = Me.AllowAdditions

'But we need to check if there are no records. If so,
'we disable all buttons except for the <New> button
If recClone.RecordCount = 0 Then
    cmdFirst.Enabled = False
    cmdNext.Enabled = False
    cmdPrevious.Enabled = False
    cmdLast.Enabled = False
Else

    'If there are records, we know that the <First> and
    '<Last> buttons will always be enabled, irrespective
    'of where we are in the recordset
    cmdFirst.Enabled = True
    cmdLast.Enabled = True

    'Synchronise the current pointer in the two recordsets
    recClone.Bookmark = Me.Bookmark
```

```
      'Next, we must see if we are on the first record
      'If so, we should disable the <Previous> button
      recClone.MovePrevious
      cmdPrevious.Enabled = Not (recClone.BOF)
      recClone.MoveNext

      'And then check whether we are on the last record
      'If so, we should disable the <Next> button
      recClone.MoveNext
      cmdNext.Enabled = Not (recClone.EOF)
      recClone.MovePrevious
End If

'And finally close the cloned recordset
recClone.Close

End Sub
```

4. Now check that the code compiles by selecting Compile IceCream from the Debug menu.

5. Save the changes to the module and switch back to Access by hitting *ALT + F11*.

6. Close the frmCompany form (which should be in Design view) and open it up in Form view. Try moving through the records – you'll see that you now have intelligent navigation buttons.

Country	Scotland
Phone	+44 (131) 225 5999
Fax	+44 (131) 225 5999
Email	
Web	
Contact Name	
Supplier	☐

First	Previous	Next	Last	New

How It Works

The code is not complicated but there are a few new things, so let's have a look at it in detail.

```
Set recClone = Me.RecordsetClone()
```

The first thing we did was to create a duplicate copy of the form's Recordset object, using RecordsetClone(). This is an alternative to using the OpenRecordset method to create a Recordset object. Using the RecordsetClone() method against the form to create a **separate** copy of the recordset means that we can navigate or manipulate a form's records independently of the form itself. This is desirable, as we are going to want to move around the recordset behind the scenes and don't want our maneuvers to be reflected in the form itself. Instead, we are able to use a separate, cloned, read-only Recordset object that acts just as if it had been created using the OpenRecordset method.

```
If Me.NewRecord Then
```

The first condition that we check for is whether or not we are in a new record. The simplest way to do this is to check the `NewRecord` property of the form. If we are in a new record, we disable the <u>N</u>ext and Ne<u>w</u> buttons and then use the `Exit Sub` to exit the procedure without executing any more code.

```
cmdNew.Enabled = Me.AllowAdditions
```

We then need to work out whether the form allows new records to be added. Again we can determine this by inspecting a property of the form – in this case, the `AllowAdditions` property. If this returns `True` we want to enable the Ne<u>w</u> button, if it returns `False` we want to disable the Ne<u>w</u> button. In other words, the `Enabled` property of the Ne<u>w</u> button should be set to the same as the `AllowAdditions` property of the form.

```
If recClone.RecordCount = 0 Then
```

The next step is to check whether there are any records behind the form. It is often easy to forget to make this check but, if we try to move around a `Recordset` object with no records, Access will generate an error and cause our code to break. The easiest way to determine whether there are any records is to inspect the cloned `Recordset` object's `RecordCount` property. This will tell us the number of records in the recordset. If it is equal to zero, there are no records in the recordset and the only button that should be enabled is the Ne<u>w</u> button.

> *It's worth mentioning here that the `RecordCount` property of some types of `Recordset` object is not always immediately available. You might need to move to the last record in the recordset to update it. However, here the form is based on a single table and so the form's recordset is a table-type `Recordset` object that doesn't suffer from this problem. You'll see more of this in a moment.*

So, by now we have determined that we are not in a new record and that there is more than one record in the recordset. We can therefore enable the <u>F</u>irst and <u>L</u>ast buttons. Once we have done that, we need to work out where in the recordset we are – at the top, the bottom, or somewhere in the middle?

Before we can do this, we need to make sure that the current record in our cloned `Recordset` object is the same as the current record in the form. Whenever you create a `Recordset` object, the first record in that `Recordset` object becomes the current record. However, our procedure is called from the form's `Current` event (i.e. not only when the form is opened, but also whenever the user moves to a different record). When a clone is created, it doesn't have a current record. So, we need some sort of mechanism to set the current record in the cloned `Recordset` object to match that on the form. We can do this with a `Bookmark`.

```
recClone.Bookmark = Me.Bookmark
```

A `Bookmark` is simply way of identifying each individual row in a recordset. This is what Access uses in place of record numbers. A `Bookmark` consists of a `Byte` array. We shall be looking at them in a little more detail later on in this chapter when we discuss how we can find specific records in a recordset. For the moment, however, all we are concerned with is ensuring that the cloned `Recordset` object and the form are in sync. By assigning to the `Bookmark` property of the cloned `Recordset` object the same value as the `Bookmark` property of the form, we ensure that the clone has the same current record as the one the user can see displayed on the form.

So now it is time to work out where the current record is in the recordset. If the current record is the first record, we must disable the <u>P</u>revious button. If the current record is the last record, we must disable the <u>N</u>ext button. To determine whether the current record is at extremity of the recordset, we use the BOF and EOF properties. BOF stands for **Beginning Of File** and EOF stands for **End Of File**.

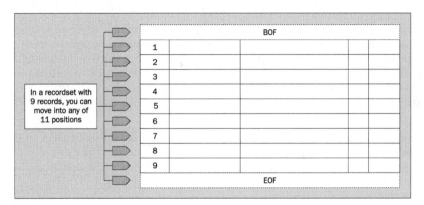

The BOF property of a `Recordset` object is `True` if the current record pointer is placed immediately before the first record, and the EOF property is `True` if the current record pointer is placed immediately after the last record. Consequently, if we attempt to move to the record previous to the current one and we find that the recordset's BOF property is `True`, we know that the current record is the first record in the recordset.

```
recClone.MovePrevious
cmdPrevious.Enabled = Not (recClone.BOF)
recClone.MoveNext
```

If this code seems a little hard to fathom at first, just remember that the BOF and EOF properties return a `True` or `False` value. If `recClone.BOF` returns `True`, we're at the beginning of a recordset and we need to disable the `cmdPrevious` button by setting its `Enabled` property to `False`. We use the NOT operator to simply reverse the Boolean value returned by the `recClone.BOF` expression. If `False` is returned, however, it means we're not at the beginning of a recordset, so we want the `cmdPrevious` button to be enabled by having a `True` value placed in its `Enabled` property.

If we had wanted to, we could also have expressed this with the following less succinct
If...Then structure.

```
recClone.MovePrevious
If recClone.BOF = True Then
    cmdPrevious.Enabled = False
Else
    cmdPrevious.Enabled = True
End If
recClone.MoveNext
```

Similarly, if we attempt to move to the record after the current record and we find that the EOF
property of the cloned Recordset object is True, we know that the current record is the last
record in the recordset.

```
recClone.MoveNext
cmdNext.Enabled = Not (recClone.EOF)
recClone.MovePrevious
```

And that's about it. We just close the cloned recordset and the code is complete.

Counting Records in a Recordset

In the last example, we used the RecordCount property of a Recordset object to determine how
many records it contained. The behavior of the RecordCount property is, in fact, a little more
complex than we let on, and depends on the type of recordset in question.

Table-Type Recordsets

When you open a table-type recordset, Access knows the number of records in the table, and so the
RecordCount property of the recordset is instantly set to that number.

Dynasets and Snapshots

In order to increase the performance of your code when creating dynaset-type Recordset objects
and snapshot-type Recordset objects, Access executes the next line after an OpenRecordset as
soon as the first row of data has been retrieved. Therefore, Access does not always immediately
know the number of records in these types of Recordset object. In order to force Access to
calculate the number of records in a dynaset-type Recordset object or in a snapshot-type
Recordset object, you have to use the MoveLast method of the Recordset object.

```
Set rec = db.OpenRecordset("qryTotalOrders", dbOpenDynaset)
rec.MoveLast
Debug.Print rec.RecordCount
```

This forces Access to fetch all the rows in the recordset before continuing, and so enables it to
determine the precise number of rows in the recordset.

If you only want to know whether there are any records in the recordset, as opposed to finding out how many, you do not need to use a MoveLast method. When you use the OpenRecordset method and the recordset is not empty, Access waits until the first record has been returned before executing the next line of code. In other words, if the RecordCount property of a recordset is equal to zero, there are definitely no more rows to be returned.

If you add or delete records in a dynaset-type Recordset object, the RecordCount property of the object increases or decreases accordingly. However, if other users add or delete records in the underlying tables, these changes are not reflected until the Recordset object is requeried (using the Requery method). Again, you will need to use the MoveLast method after the Recordset object has been requeried, to ensure that the RecordCount property is accurate.

AbsolutePosition and PercentPosition

The record counting behavior has implications for two other recordset properties. The AbsolutePosition property returns the position of the current record in the recordset relative to 0. When using the AbsolutePosition property, bear these factors in mind:

❑ If there is no current record, the AbsolutePosition property returns −1.

❑ It is by no means certain that records will always appear in the same order every time a recordset is opened unless a sort criterion (ORDER BY clause) has been specified.

❑ Remember that the AbsolutePosition of a record will change as records are inserted or deleted. For this reason, do not be tempted to use the AbsolutePosition property instead of a bookmark.

The PercentPosition property indicates the AbsolutePosition of the current record as a percentage of the total number of records that is returned by the RecordCount property. With regard to accuracy of the values returned, the same considerations apply to the PercentPosition property as to the RecordCount property. In order to ensure that the PercentPosition property returns an accurate figure, you should use the MoveLast method after opening or requerying Recordset objects, and before inspecting the PercentPosition property.

The AbsolutePosition and PercentPosition properties only apply to dynasets and snapshots. Trying to use them against table-type Recordset objects will result in a run-time error.

The following procedure can be used to display the record count and the absolute and percent positions returned by Access in the Ice Cream database.

```
Sub ShowPositions()

Dim db As Database
Dim rec As Recordset

Set db = CurrentDb()
Set rec = db.OpenRecordset("tblIceCream", dbOpenDynaset)

Debug.Print "Records", "Absolute", "Percent"

Do While Not rec.EOF
  Debug.Print rec.RecordCount, rec.AbsolutePosition, rec.PercentPosition
  rec.MoveNext
Loop

rec.Close

End Sub
```

If you run this procedure in the Ice Cream database, you will see that it creates a dynaset-type `Recordset` object based on the `tblIceCream` table and then loops through it, one record at a time. For each record, it displays the `RecordCount`, `AbsolutePosition` and `PercentPosition` properties of the recordset. The output it would print into the Immediate window would look like this:

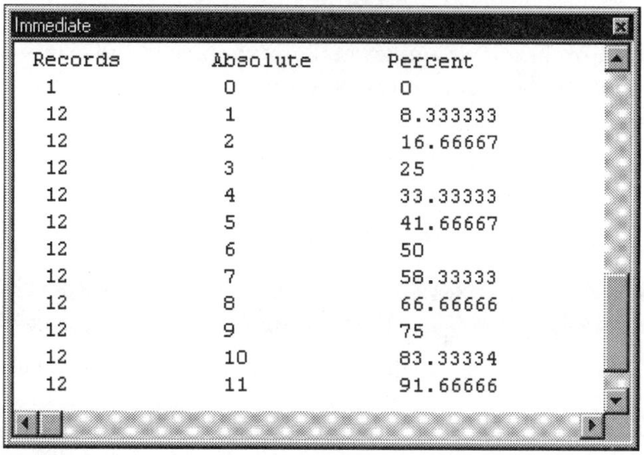

Records	Absolute	Percent
1	0	0
12	1	8.333333
12	2	16.66667
12	3	25
12	4	33.33333
12	5	41.66667
12	6	50
12	7	58.33333
12	8	66.66666
12	9	75
12	10	83.33334
12	11	91.66666

There are three things in particular that are worth noting in this procedure:

❑ Firstly, you can see that the `RecordCount` property returns the wrong value the first time round.

❑ Secondly, the `AbsolutePosition` property is zero-based and so returns 0 for the first record, 1 for the second record and so on.

❑ And finally, take a good look at the `Do While... Loop` structure seen here. This technique is commonly used in procedures that need to loop through every record in a recordset.

Looking for Specific Records

So far, we have only concerned ourselves with moving through a `Recordset` object using the various `Move` methods. But there may be occasions when you know exactly which record you wish to find. In that situation, you will find that the `Seek` and `Find` methods are more suited to your task.

Finding Records in Table-Type Recordsets

The quickest way to find a record in a table-type `Recordset` object is to use the `Seek` method.

One of the important processes involved in designing a database is to determine how the tables within the database are to be indexed. If you search on an indexed field, Access is able to find records much more quickly. Also, Access can perform operations, such as joins and sorts, much faster if the fields which are being joined or sorted are indexed. Bear in mind, however, that one down-side of indexes is that they add an overhead to the length of time it takes Access to update records (as the index needs to be updated in addition to the data) so they should only be used where they will provide a measurable improvement in performance.

As a programmer, you can take advantage of the extra speed provided by indexes if you use the `Seek` method. This allows you to perform a fast search on an indexed field. Using `Seek` is a two-step process:

- ❑ First select the indexed field that you wish to search on.
- ❑ Then specify the criteria for finding the record.

As an example, we'll search the `tblSales` table for sales that cost a certain amount.

Try It Out – Using the `Seek` Method

1. Open the `tblSales` table in design view and select the `AmountPaid` field.

2. If there is not one already, add a non-unique index to the field by changing its Indexed property to Yes (Duplicates OK).

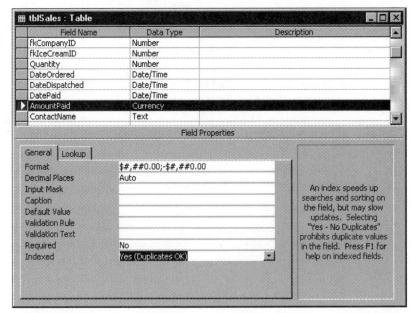

3. Now switch to Datasheet view, save the table design (if prompted), and sort the records by AmountPaid. This should be fast as the AmountPaid field is now indexed and, in any case, there are not too many records in the table.

4. Look for orders that cost the same amount, for instance, orders with a SalesID of 120 and 357 both cost $210.00. Make a note of the SalesID, DatePaid and AmountPaid values. We shall be using these in a moment.

5. Close down the table, saving your changes as you do so.

6. Now create a new procedure in the module you created earlier in the chapter and type in the following code:

```
Sub SeekByPrice(curPrice As Currency)

Dim db As Database
Dim rec As Recordset
Dim strSQL As String
Dim strMsg As String

strSQL = "tblSales"

Set db = CurrentDb()
Set rec = db.OpenRecordset(strSQL)

rec.Index = "AmountPaid"
rec.Seek "=", curPrice

strMsg = "Order No. " & rec("SalesID") & " placed on " & _
    FormatDateTime(rec("DateOrdered"), vbLongDate) & _
    " cost " & FormatCurrency(rec("AmountPaid"))

MsgBox strMsg
rec.Close

End Sub
```

7. Run the code by typing SeekByPrice 210 in the Immediate window and hitting the *Enter* key.

8. A message box appears telling you the first order it has found with the price of $210.00.

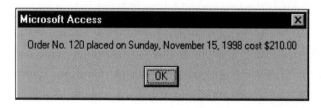

Microsoft Access

Order No. 120 placed on Sunday, November 15, 1998 cost $210.00

OK

Chapter 7

How Does It Work?

This example makes use of the `Index` property and `Seek` method to locate the required record in the table.

```
Set rec = db.OpenRecordset(strSQL)
```

The first thing we do is to create a table-type `Recordset` object. Note that we did not need to explicitly request that the `Recordset` object should be a table-type `Recordset` object as it is based on a single local Access table; table-type is the default type for `Recordset` objects created from local Access tables.

```
rec.Index = "AmountPaid"
```

The next step is to specify the index that we want to use when seeking the required record. When setting the `Index` property of the `Recordset` object, you should use the name of the index as it appears in the **Indexes** window of the table in Design view (you can view this by pressing the **Indexes** button on the toolbar). If you try to set the `Index` property of a `Recordset` object to an index that does not exist, Access will generate a run-time error.

```
rec.Seek "=", curPrice
```

Once we have chosen an index, we are ready to look for the record we require. We do this using the `Seek` method. When using `Seek`, we need to specify two arguments. The first indicates the type of comparison we want to carry out and the second indicates the value we want to compare against the index.

In our example, we want to find records for which the value of the indexed field is equal to 210, so the type of comparison is an equality comparison and the value we are comparing against the index is 210.

The following list shows the type of comparisons that can be carried out using the `Seek` method:

Comparison argument	Has this effect...
"="	Finds the first record whose indexed field is equal to the value specified.
">"	Finds the first record whose indexed field is greater than the value specified.
">="	Finds the first record whose indexed field is greater than or equal to the value specified.
"<"	Finds the first record whose indexed field is less than the value specified.
"<="	Finds the first record whose indexed field is less than or equal to the value specified.

Note that the comparison argument is enclosed in quotes. If you prefer, you can specify a string variable – or a variant variable of type vbString 8, – in place of the string literal. In other words, we could have written our code like this:

```
strComparison = "="
rec.Seek strComparison, curPrice
```

However, the important thing to remember is that the comparison argument must be a valid string expression.

```
strMsg = "Order No. " & rec("SalesID") & " placed on " & _
    FormatDateTime(rec("DateOrdered"), vbLongDate) & _
    " cost " & FormatCurrency(rec("AmountPaid"))
```

Once the Seek method has found a record matching the criterion we set, we display the result in a dialog box.

> *Remember that there was more than one record that matched our criterion; the Seek method returns the first match it finds.*

The above example assumes that Seek is going to be successful in finding a matching record. What happens, though, if this isn't the case?

Try It Out – Allowing for No Matches

1. Run the SeekByPrice procedure again, but this time pass it as an argument a value which you know will have no matching records, such as 3.64. The result of this is that the code breaks and Access displays a dialog box telling you that there is no current record.

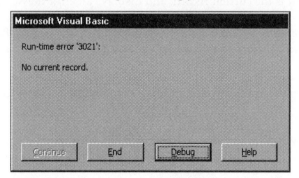

In order to work out how to solve this problem, we must first determine which line of our code caused the error to happen.

2. Hit the <u>D</u>ebug button. Access displays the code window with the offending line of code highlighted:

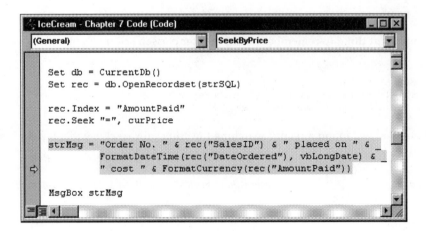

As you can see, the line that caused the error to occur was the one in which we attempted to display the dialog box informing the user of the matching record. The code did not break simply because there was no record which matched. In fact, it broke because when the Seek method fails to find a matching record, it doesn't know which record to make the current record and leaves the current record in an indeterminate state. So, when you subsequently try to perform an operation that requires the current record to be known, Access does not know which record is the current record, and displays an error message.

What we need, therefore, is some mechanism that allows us to determine whether or not the Seek method found a record, so that we only attempt to display the result if we know it was successful.

3. Stop the code from executing, by either hitting the Reset button or selecting Reset from the Run menu.

4. Modify the SeekByPrice procedure so that it now looks like this:

```
...
If rec.NoMatch = True Then
    strMsg = "No orders cost " & FormatCurrency(curPrice)
Else
    strMsg = "Order No. " & rec("SalesID") & " placed on " & _
            FormatDateTime(rec("DateOrdered"), vbLongDate) & _
            " cost " & FormatCurrency(rec("AmountPaid"))
End If
...
```

The NoMatch *property of a* Recordset *object is set to* True *when the* Seek *method (or any of the* Find *methods discussed below) fails to locate a record.*

5. Now run the procedure from the Immediate window, and pass 3.64 again. This time, you get a message box telling you what has happened:

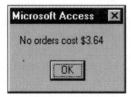

This is a much more friendly way of doing things!

As we've explained, one problem of failed Seek *or* Find *(see below) operations is that if no matching record is found, the current record is left in an indeterminate state. We will look at how to deal with this situation a little later in this chapter when we look at the* Bookmark *property.*

Finding Records in Dynasets and Snapshots

Using the Seek method is a very quick way of finding records, but it has a couple of notable limitations:

❑   It can only be used on indexed columns, which means that...

❑   It can only be used against table-type recordsets.

If we want to find records in dynaset- or snapshot-type Recordset objects, or in non-indexed fields of table-type Recordset objects, we must use one of the Find methods. There are four of these and their uses are described below:

This method...	Works like this...
FindFirst	Starts at the beginning of the recordset and searches downwards until it finds a record which matches the selected criteria and makes that record the current record.
FindLast	Starts at the end of the recordset and searches upwards until it finds a record which matches the selected criteria and makes that record the current record.
FindNext	Starts at the current record and searches downwards until it finds a record which matches the selected criteria and makes that record the current record.
FindPrevious	Starts at the current record and searches upwards until it finds a record which matches the selected criteria and makes that record the current record.

As with the Seek method, if any of the Find methods fail to find a record matching the specified criterion, the current record is left in an indeterminate state. This means that if you then try to perform any operation that requires the current record to be known, Access will generate a run-time error.

The syntax of the Find methods is somewhat different from that of the Seek method, as we need to specify the field we are searching on, as well as the value we are looking for. For example, if we had opened a snapshot-type Recordset object based on the tblSales table and wanted to use the FindFirst method to find the first with a DateOrdered after 10th July 1998, we would write this:

```
rec.FindFirst "DateOrdered > #07/10/1998#"
```

> *The argument we supply for a* Find *method is just the* WHERE *clause of a SQL statement, but without the* WHERE *in front.*

It's quite intuitive really – the only thing you need to remember is that the criteria must be enclosed in quotes.

As with the Seek method, we could use a string variable to specify the criteria:

```
strCriterion = "DateOrdered > #07/10/1998#"
rec.FindFirst strCriterion
```

Let's try rewriting the last example using the Find methods.

Try It Out – Using the Find Methods

1. Insert a new procedure and add the following code:

```
Sub FindByPrice(curPrice As Currency)

Dim db As Database
Dim rec As Recordset
Dim strSQL As String
Dim strMatches As String
Dim intCounter As Integer

strSQL = "tblSales"

Set db = CurrentDb()
Set rec = db.OpenRecordset(strSQL, dbOpenSnapshot)

rec.FindFirst "AmountPaid = " & curPrice
Do While rec.NoMatch = False
  intCounter = intCounter + 1
  strMatches = (strMatches & vbCrLf) & rec("SalesID")
  rec.FindNext "AmountPaid = " & curPrice
Loop

Select Case intCounter
  Case 0
    MsgBox "No orders cost " & FormatCurrency(curPrice)
  Case 1
```

```
  MsgBox "The following order cost " & _
    FormatCurrency(curPrice) & " : " & _
    vbCrLf & strMatches
 Case Else
   MsgBox "The following " & intCounter & " orders cost " & _
    FormatCurrency(curPrice) & " : " & _
    vbCrLf & strMatches
End Select

rec.Close

End Sub
```

2. Open the Immediate window and run the procedure, using the price 3.64. There are no matching records and the following dialog box is displayed:

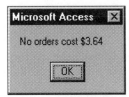

3. Now run it again, but this time pass as the argument 77, for which there is one match.

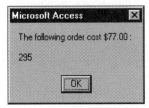

4. Finally, run the procedure again and pass a price for which there are several matches, e.g. 210.

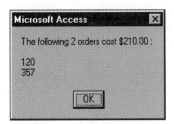

How It Works

The main difference in this portion of code is the method we use to find the matching records:

```
rec.FindFirst "AmountPaid = " & curPrice
```

We start by looking for the first record with a price matching the one entered.

```
Do While rec.NoMatch = False
  intCounter = intCounter + 1
  strMatches = strMatches & Chr$(10) & rec("SalesID")
  rec.FindNext "AmountPaid = " & curPrice
Loop
```

If there is no order with this price, rec.NoMatch is True and so the subsequent Do...Loop structure is not entered. However, if a matching order is found, rec.NoMatch is False and we enter the loop.

Once inside the loop, three things happen. First we increment a counter to indicate how many matches have been made; then we build up a string using the linefeed character Chr$(10) (which causes a new line to be created) and the SalesID of the matching record; and finally we have a look to see if there is another record which matches our criterion.

If there is, we return to the start of the loop and, as rec.NoMatch is False, we run through the whole process again.

When there are no more matches found, rec.NoMatch is True and the loop terminates. Then, all that is left is to display the results in a message box.

```
Select Case intCounter
  Case 0
    MsgBox "No orders cost " & FormatCurrency(curPrice)
  Case 1
    MsgBox "The following order cost " & _
      FormatCurrency(curPrice) & " : " & _
      Chr$(10) & strMatches
  Case Else
    MsgBox "The following " & intCounter & " orders cost " & _
      FormatCurrency(curPrice) & " : " & _
      Chr$(10) & strMatches
End Select
```

intCounter contains a count of the number of times we went through the loop, and, therefore, how many matches were found.

Notes on Formatting Dates and Currency Amounts in VBA

Among the most frequent types of data that you will search for in Recordset objects are dates and monetary amounts. For example, you may want to find orders placed on a certain day or worth a certain amount. If you do so, you need to be aware of how VBA handles date and currency formats, especially if you are working through this book somewhere other than in the United States.

VBA will format date and currency outputs according to the settings you make in the Regional Settings section of the Control Panel. No problem there.

You may, for example, have your computer set up to display dates in the British format (so that 10-Nov-94 is displayed as 10/11/94). This isn't a problem for VBA when formatting date or currency **output** – if VBA encounters a date of 10-Nov-94 and your Short Date Style is set to dd/mm/yy, VBA will display the date as 10/11/94. Just what you want.

However, VBA operates slightly differently when requesting date **input**. The locale of VBA is always English (United States) irrespective of the way that you have configured the Regional Settings in your Control Panel. As a result, if you enter a date in either a SQL statement or as in VBA, it will be interpreted as if it were in the format mm/dd/yy, i.e. in US format.

To ensure that all of the dates you enter will be interpreted correctly, it is best to explicitly convert all dates to US format before using them in SQL statements or in VBA. To convert a date to US format, you would replace a statement like this,

```
rec.FindFirst "OrderDate = " & dtOrder
```

with one like this:

```
rec.FindFirst "OrderDate = #" & Format(dtOrder, "mm/dd/yy") & "#"
```

When entering currency values, similar considerations apply. VBA expects currency values in 9.99 format – even if the currency separator defined in Control Panel is something other than a period.

> The problem of non-US date and currency formats only exists when you are dealing with dates and monetary amounts in VBA. In forms and in the query designer, you can enter dates and currency amounts in your own local format, and Access will convert them for you.

When to Use Find and Seek

So far, we have looked at how to use the Seek and Find methods to locate records in a recordset. However, in all of the examples, our task could have been completed more quickly by opening a Recordset object based on an SQL string which defined our search criteria. Don't worry if you don't know much about SQL, the SQL in this example is very simple and we will be looking at SQL in more detail in the next chapter few chapters.

```
strSQL = "SELECT * FROM tblSales WHERE AmountPaid = " & curPrice
```

It simply assigns to the string strSQL an SQL statement which selects every field (using the * symbol) for each record of the tblSales table where the AmountPaid is equal to the price held in the variable curPrice. So, if we add this to our code, the FindByPrice() procedure could be re-written like this:

```
Sub FindByPrice2(curPrice As Currency)

Dim db As Database
Dim rec As Recordset
Dim strSQL As String
Dim strMatches As String
Dim intCounter As Integer

strSQL = "SELECT * FROM tblSales WHERE AmountPaid = " & curPrice

Set db = CurrentDb()
Set rec = db.OpenRecordset(strSQL, dbOpenSnapshot)
Do Until rec.EOF
```

```
 strMatches = strMatches & Chr$(10) & rec!SalesID
 rec.MoveNext
Loop
intCounter = rec.RecordCount

Select Case intCounter
 Case 0
  MsgBox "No orders cost " & FormatCurrency(curPrice)
 Case 1
  MsgBox "The following order cost " & _
   FormatCurrency(curPrice) & " : " & _
   Chr$(10) & strMatches
 Case Else
  MsgBox "The following " & intCounter & " orders cost " & _
   FormatCurrency(curPrice) & " : " & _
   Chr$(10) & strMatches
End Select
rec.Close

End Sub
```

The difference in speed between executing FindByPrice() and FindByPrice2() could be particularly noticeable if you run the procedures against attached tables in a remote ODBC server such as SQL Server over a Local Area Network or particularly over a Wide Area Network.

The reason for this difference in speed is that, in the first example, we are opening a Recordset object that contains the entire contents of the tblSales table. All of these records would have to be read from disk on the remote computer, sent across the network and then read into cache locally – although, if it was a dynaset-type Recordset object, only the keys from each row are cached. Then we would have to search through all of the records for the few that meet our criteria.

In the second example, however, we are opening a Recordset object that contains only as many rows as there are matching records. This will be much more efficient and will result in considerably less network traffic, as only two or three rows will need to be retrieved.

Although the difference in speed might go unnoticed for relatively small tables, for other larger tables with many thousands of records the difference could be very great indeed.

For this reason, it is wiser to restrict the use of the Find methods to local tables, and to use SQL WHERE clauses in queries against attached tables in ODBC databases. If performance against local tables is still a problem, check whether the field you are searching on is (or can be) indexed, and use the Seek method instead.

Bookmarks

Earlier in the chapter, we used the Bookmark property to synchronize the current records in two Recordset objects that were clones of each other. The Bookmark property of a recordset is stored internally by Access as an array of bytes which uniquely identifies the current record. When you reference the Bookmark property in VBA code, however, you should always assign it to a String or Variant variable:

```
Dim strBookmark As String
strBookmark = rec.Bookmark
```

or:

```
Dim varBookmark As Variant
varBookmark = rec.Bookmark
```

Note that you can only use the Bookmark *property to synchronize current records in* Recordset *objects that are clones of each other. If the* Recordset *objects have been created separately – even if they are based on the same query or SQL – the bookmarks of individual records may not match.*

You can also use bookmarks to help you to return to records that you have already visited. This is done by storing the Bookmark property of the recordset in a variable when you are on a specific record, and then setting the Bookmark property of the recordset to that value when you want to return to that record. This is especially useful when used in conjunction with Seek or Find operations. Remember, if you are using Find or Seek and a matching record cannot be found, the current record will be left in an indeterminate state. So it makes sense to store the Bookmark property of the recordset before the operation and then reassigning this value to the Bookmark property of the recordset if the Find or Seek operation fails.
Our code would then look like this:

```
Dim strBookmark As String
strBookmark = rec.Bookmark

rec.FindFirst "DateOrdered > #07/10/1998#"

If rec.NoMatch = True Then
    strMsg = "No orders cost " & FormatCurrency(curPrice)
    rec.Bookmark = strBookmark
Else
    strMsg = "Order No. " & rec("SalesID") & " placed on " & _
             FormatDateTime(rec("DateOrdered"), vbLongDate) & _
             " cost " & FormatCurrency(rec("AmountPaid"))
End If
```

Comparing Bookmarks

Sometimes, you may wish to compare two Bookmark properties. For example, you may want to check whether the current record is one that you visited earlier and whose Bookmark you had saved.

Although you can store a Bookmark as a String variable, you need to remember that a Bookmark is stored internally as an array of Bytes. For this reason, you should use **binary comparison** when comparing two bookmarks with each other.

If the Option Compare Database statement is present in a module, which it is by default, comparisons will be made according to the sort order determined by the locale of the database. In other words, when you compare two strings together in Access, the default for US English is for the comparison to be case-insensitive. You can prove this by opening the Immediate window and evaluating the following expression:

```
?"aaa" = "AAA"
```

When you hit the *Enter* key, the result should be `True`, which means that string comparisons are not case-sensitive.

In contrast, when **binary comparison** is enabled, comparisons are made according to the internal binary representation of the characters, which is case-sensitive. Because lower case characters (for example "a") are represented differently internally than upper case characters ("A"), a binary comparison of `"aaa"` and `"AAA"` should return `False`.

When you compare `Bookmark` properties, you want to make sure that the comparison is case-sensitive, otherwise you may find that the comparison returns `True` when the `Bookmarks` are not completely identical. The safest way to do this is to compare string variables with the `StrComp` function, which returns 0 if the two variables that are being compared are identical. This has an argument that allows you to choose what type of comparison you wish to perform:

- ❑ If the comparison argument is set to `vbBinaryCompare` (0), it forces binary comparison of the two variables.
- ❑ If it is set to `vbTextCompare` (1), it forces textual comparison.
- ❑ And if it is set to `vbDatabaseCompare` (2), or is omitted, the comparison is performed based on the sort order that was in place when the database was created.

```
intResult=StrComp(strBkMk1, strBkMk2, 1vbTextCompare) 'Textual comparison

intResult=StrComp(strBkMk1, strBkMk2, 0vbBinaryCompare) 'Binary comparison
```

`Recordset` objects based on native Access tables should all support bookmarks. However, `Recordset` objects based on linked tables from some databases, such as Paradox tables with no primary key, may not support bookmarks. Before you attempt to use bookmarks, you can test whether the `Recordset` object supports them by inspecting its `Bookmarkable` property. This will be `True` if the `Recordset` object supports bookmarks.

Editing Records in Recordsets

You now know how to find particular records within a `Recordset` object, but what if you want to edit them once you've found them? There are five main methods that can be used for manipulating data in recordsets. These are listed here:

This method...	Has this effect...
`Edit`	Copies the current record to the copy buffer to allow editing.
`AddNew`	Creates a new record in the copy buffer with default values (if any).
`Update`	Saves any changes made to the record in the copy buffer.
`CancelUpdate`	Empties the copy buffer without saving any changes.
`Delete`	Deletes the current record.

From the table above you should be able to see that changes to records are made in the copy buffer rather than in the recordset itself. What this means in practice is that adding or amending a record is a three-part process:

- ❑ Copy the current record into the copy buffer with the Edit method, or place a new record in the copy buffer with the AddNew method.
- ❑ Make any required changes to the fields in that record.
- ❑ Save the changes from the copy buffer to disk with the Update method.

Note that if you try to make changes to a record without first copying it to the copy buffer (i.e. without using the Edit method), Access will generate a run-time error. And if you move to a new record without saving the changes to the current record in the copy buffer (using the Update method), those changes will be lost.

If you want to empty the copy buffer without moving to a new record, you can use the CancelUpdate method on the Recordset. This will undo any changes you may have made to the record in the copy buffer, but does not change the current record.

If you want to know whether any records have been copied into the copy buffer and not saved, you can inspect the EditMode property of the recordset. This can hold any of three values represented by the constants in the table below.

This constant...	Has this value...	And means this...
dbEditNone	0	There is no record in the copy buffer.
dbEditInProgress	1	The current record is in the copy buffer (the Edit method has been invoked).
dbEditAdd	2	The record in the copy buffer is a new record that hasn't been saved (the AddNew method has been invoked).

If you use the Delete method the deletion is immediate; you do not have to follow it with an Update method to make the deletion permanent. However, although the record is deleted, it is still regarded as the current record. You need to make a different record the current record before you perform any more operations that require a valid current record. Once you have moved away from a deleted record, you cannot make it current again.

We shall be looking at how Access locks records when editing and updating Recordset objects when we consider multi-user aspects of Access in Chapter 17.

1. Open the `tblCompany` table and have a look at the place-names in the `Country` field. They should be in mixed case.

		State/County	Zip/Post Code	Country	Phone
▶	⊞	Midlothian	EH3 7HA	Scotland	+44 (131) 225 5
	⊞	California	94056	USA	(650) 456 3298
	⊞	Massachusetts	02119	USA	(617) 540 3425
	⊞	Alabama	35210	USA	(205) 320 1908
	⊞	London	SW2 1SA	England	+44 (181) 676 2
	⊞	Tennessee	38053	USA	(423) 935 9032
	⊞	CO	80206	USA	303 322-1070
	⊞	London	E5 9JW	UK	+44 181 745 13
	⊞	Surrey	GU8 1AA	UK	+44 1428 1212'
	⊞		B27 2AA	UK	+44 121 789 45

tblCompany : Table — Record: 1 of 10

2. Close the table and then, in the code module you created earlier in this chapter, add the `Capitalize` procedure:

```
Function Capitalize(strTable As String, strFld As String)

Dim db As Database
Dim rec As Recordset

Set db = CurrentDB()
Set rec = db.OpenRecordset(strTable)

'Loop through all records until we go beyond the last record
Do While Not rec.EOF

    'Copy the current record to the copy buffer
    rec.Edit

    'Make changes to the record in the copy buffer
    rec(strFld) = UCase$(rec(strFld))

    'Save the contents of the copy buffer to disk
    rec.Update

    'Make the next record the current record
    rec.MoveNext


Loop

Capitalize = True

End Function
```

3. Now make sure that the Immediate window is visible and type the following line of code.

```
?Capitalize ("tblCompany", "Country")
```

4. When you hit the *Enter* key, if the Capitalize function executes correctly, it will convert all the names of the places in the Country field of the tblCompany table to upper case and then return True to indicate success.

5. Open the tblCompany table again and have a look at the names of the places in the Country field. They should now be in upper case.

	State/County	Zip/Post Code	Country	Phone
⊞	Midlothian	EH3 7HA	SCOTLAND	+44 (131) 225 5
⊞	California	94056	USA	(650) 456 3298
⊞	Massachusetts	02119	USA	(617) 540 3425
⊞	Alabama	35210	USA	(205) 320 1908
⊞	London	SW2 1SA	ENGLAND	+44 (181) 676 2
⊞	Tennessee	38053	USA	(423) 935 9032
⊞	CO	80206	USA	303 322-1070
⊞	London	E5 9JW	UK	+44 181 745 13
⊞	Surrey	GU8 1AA	UK	+44 1428 1212
⊞		B27 2AA	UK	+44 121 789 45

Record: 1 of 10

*Note that this example is simply an illustration of the sequence of events required when editing a record. In practice, using an **action query** would be considerably more efficient than stepping through all the records.*

When a Recordset can't be Updated

We started the chapter by pointing out the differences between the various types of recordset. One of the most obvious differences between snapshot-type Recordset objects and dynaset-type Recordset objects is that snapshots are static images of the data and are never editable. So, if you try to use the Edit, AddNew or Delete methods against a snapshot-type Recordset object, Access will generate a run-time error. However, there are also several occasions when a dynaset-type Recordset cannot be edited, such as:

- ❑ When it is based on a crosstab query
- ❑ When it is based on a union query
- ❑ When you have not been granted permission to update the records in the table on which the recordset is based

In order to be sure that your `Recordset` object can be edited, you can inspect its `Updatable` property. This will be `True` if the recordset can be updated, and `False` otherwise.

```
If rec.Updatable = True Then
  rec.Edit
  ...
  ...
  ...
  rec.Update
End If
```

Summary

In this chapter, we have looked at one of the key features that differentiates VBA from macros – the ability to work with sets of records at the record level. With macros, you can only see the big picture – you can deal with sets of records as a whole but there is no mechanism for manipulating individual records. With VBA, however, you can go down to the record level and then work on individual fields within each record. You will find that creating and manipulating `Recordset` objects is one of the most frequent and useful operations that you will perform if you choose to use DAO in VBA. If you can master the use of the `Recordset` object you have won most of the battle.

This chapter has covered:

- ❑ What the Data Access Object hierarchy is and how it has developed.
- ❑ What ActiveX Data Objects (ADO) is all about.
- ❑ The chief components of DAO.
- ❑ When to use the different types of `Recordset` objects – particularly tables, dynasets and snapshots.
- ❑ How to examine data in a `Recordset` using VBA.
- ❑ Creating intelligent navigation buttons using the `Move` methods.
- ❑ How to use `Find` and `Seek` to locate particular records.
- ❑ The `Bookmark` property and what it is used for.
- ❑ How to edit records in a `Recordset`.

However, that is just the beginning. In the next chapter we will look at some of the more advanced capabilities of the JET 4.0 engine and how we can access them through DAO.

Exercises

1. Earlier in this chapter we looked at the `AbsolutePosition` property of the recordset. See if you can use this to create a record indicator on the Company form (`frmCompany`). What are the limitations of this record indicator?

2. We mentioned earlier on that the `Relations` collection contains a `Relation` object for every relation defined between tables in a database. See whether you can write a procedure to document these relations in the Immediate window like this:

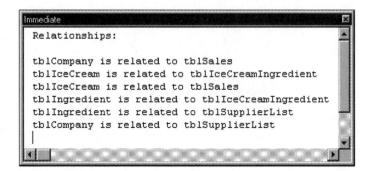

```
Immediate                                           ☒
  Relationships:

  tblCompany is related to tblSales
  tblIceCream is related to tblIceCreamIngredient
  tblIceCream is related to tblSales
  tblIngredient is related to tblIceCreamIngredient
  tblIngredient is related to tblSupplierList
  tblCompany is related to tblSupplierList
  |
```

Data Management Techniques

In the previous chapter, we looked at how recordsets are created and how we can move through records within a recordset one at a time, giving us a much finer degree of control than we have with macros. In this chapter, we will look at some of the other DAO objects – particularly the QueryDef and TableDef objects – and how, as developers, we are able to manipulate them to our best advantage.

Here, we will be concentrating on methods for creating queries and tables at run-time. This is a particularly handy way of allowing users to be as free as they like with the types of query they want to produce, without the developer having to relinquish too much control. The main topics that we will consider are:

- ❑ Creating queries at run-time
- ❑ Displaying records selected at run-time via one of three different methods
- ❑ Modifying the form's record source
- ❑ Using Structured Query Language (SQL)
- ❑ Creating a table of matching records
- ❑ How to create a table using the DAO hierarchy

The Challenge – Flexibility vs. Manageability

We have already seen how we can navigate around and modify the data in recordsets. The main theme running throughout this chapter, however, is the dynamic creation and modification of actual database objects such as tables and queries at run-time. In other words, we will see how it is possible to allow users of the application to modify the structure of the underlying database objects while they are using the application in a production environment.

You may wonder why anyone would want to create or modify a query – even less a table – at run-time. Why not just create the query correctly at design-time? Well, it's true that you should try to create as many of your queries at design-time as possible – this has definite performance benefits, as we will see later. However, sometimes you just don't have enough information at design-time to allow you to build all the queries that will be necessary for your application to run.

In the example we will be using, we have to enable the users to design queries while the application is running. In the Ice Cream database, `frmCriteria` is a simple form, which allows users to select sales based on a set of criteria that they specify themselves.

We'll start off by examining what our users want the application to be able to do. Once we have done that, we can work out how we are going to implement this functionality.

The Requirement – Ad Hoc Query Functionality

If you remember, one of the tables within the Ice Cream database is the `tblSales` table. This contains details of all of the sales (orders) that have been made for the ice creams that our shop produces. As well as detailing who ordered the ice cream, it also stores payment and delivery details. To remind you, here is the structure of the `tblSales` table.

Column	Data Type
SalesID	AutoNumber
fkCompanyID	Long Integer
fkIceCreamID	Long Integer
Quantity	Integer
DateOrdered	Date/Time
DateDispatched	Date/Time
DatePaid	Date/Time
AmountPaid	Currency
ContactName	Text

And here is a diagram of the relationships between the various tables:

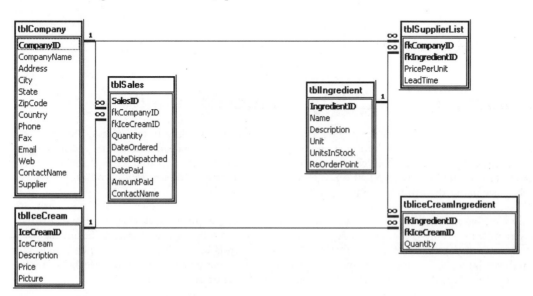

As you can see, relationships between the `tblSales`, `tblCompany`, `tblIceCream`, `tblIngredients` and `tblIceCreamIngredient` tables allow us to determine which companies ordered which ice creams and what ingredients were in those ice creams.

Now one of the requirements of our database is that it should allow users to look up previous sales that meet certain conditions or criteria. The criteria identified by the users are as follows:

❑   All sales made to a certain company

❑   All sales of a particular ice cream

❑   All sales of ice creams containing a particular ingredient

❑   All sales of ice creams ordered between certain dates

❑   All sales which it took longer than a certain period of time to fulfill

❑   All sales for which it took the customer longer than a certain period of time to pay

In itself, this might seem fairly daunting, but our users are even more demanding and want to be able to combine any or all of these criteria into a single query. For example, they might want to find out:

Which orders for ice creams were made by Jane's Diner in November 1998 where it took more than 7 days for us to fulfill the order?

When they run the query, the users want to know how many orders match the criteria that they have specified. They should then be presented with the opportunity of viewing those results in detail and printing a report containing the matching results.

Now this is not an uncommon type of request. In most database applications there is some type of requirement for flexible querying functionality. One of the characteristics of relational databases is that they decompose complex pieces of information into a number of smaller, related elements. That's what normalization is all about. And the consequence of this decomposition is that it allows us to view our data and analyze our data across multiple dimensions. For example, by decomposing our data into separate entities for sales, ice creams, companies and ingredients, we have made it a fairly simple task to allow a query to be created which finds the answer to the question posed above. In fact the query required to provide the answer is shown below:

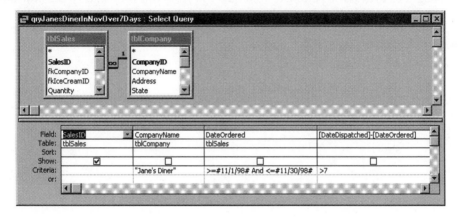

Alternatively, if we wanted to write the query in SQL, we would express it like this:

```
SELECT tblSales.SalesID
FROM tblCompany
   INNER JOIN tblSales
   ON tblCompany.CompanyID = tblSales.fkCompanyID
WHERE tblCompany.CompanyName = "Jane's Diner"
AND tblSales.DateOrdered >= #11/1/98#
AND tblSales.DateOrdered <= #11/30/98#
AND tblSales.[DateDispatched] - tblSales.[DateOrdered] > 7
```

> *Structured Query Language, or SQL, is the language that databases use for manipulating data. Later on in this chapter, we'll look at the basics of how SQL works. If you want to learn more about SQL, why not check out 'Instant SQL Programming', also by Wrox Press, ISBN 1874416508.*

Now writing that one query might not seem too complex in itself. But that is just one example of the queries that could have been requested. If you cast your mind back to the list of criteria that the users of the application want to search on, you can see that there are 6 of them, any of which can be combined to form a more complex query. Those of you with a mathematical inclination (and a knowledge of Pascal's triangle) will realize that this means that there are $2^6 = 64$ different ways in which these criteria can be combined (That's 1 combination involving no criteria, 6 combinations involving 1 criterion, 15 involving 2 criteria, 20 involving 3, 15 involving 4, 10 involving 5 and 1 combination involving all 6 criteria). Pascal's triangle or no Pascal's triangle, that is still a lot of combinations. In fact, when you add to this the fact that each of these criteria can accept different values, the number of combinations becomes truly daunting. So what are we to do?

> Our first reaction – and quite a tempting one – is simply to tell our users not to be so demanding. Apart from annoying our users, that solution would have the unwanted(?) side-effect of making this a much shorter chapter, so we will assume that we cannot offer this response and that this is the functionality we have to deliver!

Why Not Use Parameterised Queries?

One solution might be to devise a parameterized query to solve this problem. To see how this would work, let us assume that we are working with just three possible criteria: Quantity, AmountPaid and DatePaid. If we were to allow our users to select records based on these criteria, they could combine them in $2^3 = 8$ ways.

Now we could cater for all of these combinations with the following query:

The user will be prompted for values for the three different criteria and the query will return the correct values irrespective of which of the criteria the user chooses to fill in. But it is not the most intuitive of queries, especially if you see how the query looks in SQL.

```
SELECT tblSales.SalesID, tblSales.Quantity, tblSales.AmountPaid, tblSales.DatePaid
FROM tblSales
WHERE (((tblSales.Quantity)=[Amount Ordered:]) AND ((tblSales.AmountPaid)=[Money
Paid:]) AND ((tblSales.DatePaid)=[Payment Date:])) OR ((([Amount Ordered:]) Is Null)
AND (([Money Paid:]) Is Null) AND (([Payment Date:]) Is Null)) OR
(((tblSales.Quantity)=[Amount Ordered:]) AND ((tblSales.AmountPaid)=[Money Paid:])
AND (([Amount Ordered:]) Is Not Null) AND (([Money Paid:]) Is Not Null) AND
(([Payment Date:]) Is Null)) OR (((tblSales.Quantity)=[Amount Ordered:]) AND
((tblSales.DatePaid)=[Payment Date:]) AND (([Amount Ordered:]) Is Not Null) AND
(([Money Paid:]) Is Null) AND (([Payment Date:]) Is Null)) OR
(((tblSales.AmountPaid)=[Money Paid:]) AND ((tblSales.DatePaid)=[Payment Date:]) AND
(([Amount Ordered:]) Is Null) AND (([Money Paid:]) Is Not Null) AND (([Payment
Date:]) Is Not Null)) OR (((tblSales.DatePaid)=[Payment Date:]) AND (([Amount
Ordered:]) Is Null) AND (([Money Paid:]) Is Null) AND (([Payment Date:]) Is Not
Null)) OR (((tblSales.AmountPaid)=[Money Paid:]) AND (([Amount Ordered:]) Is Null)
AND (([Money Paid:]) Is Not Null) AND (([Payment Date:]) Is Null)) OR
(((tblSales.Quantity)=[Amount Ordered:]) AND (([Amount Ordered:]) Is Not Null) AND
(([Money Paid:]) Is Null) AND (([Payment Date:]) Is Null));
```

Now if you scale that up to 6 criteria, then you will find that the query needs 64 criteria rows, with various combinations of Is Null and Is Not Null – and the SQL doesn't even bear thinking about! I think that you will appreciate that this is not a prudent way of implementing the solution.

An alternative (and equally nightmarish) approach would be to create 64 queries and run whichever one corresponded to the particular combination of criteria selected by the user. Trust me, I wouldn't wish the implementation and administration of that solution on anyone…

The problem with the first approach, using the parameterized query, is that a very complex query is always run whenever the user asks a question, however simple the question is. Even if the user just wants to find the sales made on 1st November, the parameterized query approach will always require a behemoth of a query to be run.

The problem with the second approach is that you have to write and administer 64 separate queries, only one of which is ever used at any one time, irrespective of the questions the user asks. Both of these solutions, then, are very inefficient. What we really want is to have a single query, and for that query to be only as complex as the question posed by the user demands. And to do that we need to modify the query on the fly, in response to the user's selection of criteria. That's what we are going to do in this chapter.

> *By the way, the ability to view the SQL generated by the QBE grid in Access is very useful. Even experienced VBA database developers sometimes use the QBE grid to design a query. Then they switch to SQL view and copy the SQL it has generated into their VBA code. And it works just as well the other way. If you are using VBA to build a SQL string, then you can always copy and paste the SQL string into the Query Designer's SQL window. Then, when you switch to design view, you can see whether the query it produces is the one you intended.*

Building a Query by Form Interface

Our first challenge is working out how we are going to present the user with an intuitive way of selecting one of the 64 different combinations of criteria that are available. One of the best approaches to this problem is to use what is often referred to as a Query by Form, or QBF, interface.

A QBF interface is, at its simplest, just a form containing text boxes or combo boxes for each of the criteria that the user can specify. In our case, there are 6 criteria so the form would look something like this:

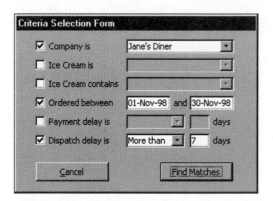

As you can see, the user clicks the check box to indicate that a particular criterion is to be used. The process of clicking this check box enables the text boxes or combo boxes in which the values for the criterion are then entered. The screen shot above illustrates how the form could be used to ask the question we highlighted earlier:

Which orders for ice creams were made by Jane's Diner in November 1998 where it took more than 7 days for us to fulfill the order?

In fact, the way the form has been designed, it actually allows substantially more than 64 queries to be produced as the user can specify either a lower or upper limit (or both) for the order date and can also select sales with a payment delay or dispatch delay either more than or less than a certain number of days. And yet this form uses only one query to answer all of those combinations of criteria, and it only takes a few dozen lines of code to make the whole thing work. We'll spend the rest of this chapter implementing this QBF functionality in the Ice Cream database. Once you have seen how it works in this situation you should be able to adapt the ideas that we will be covering to pretty much any situation that calls for QBF functionality. Here's what we are trying to do:

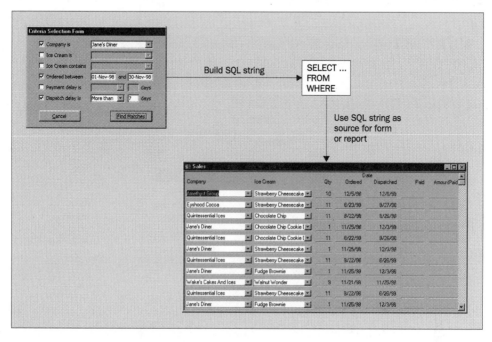

We are going to create the Criteria Form, which will allow us to select our criteria. This will build a SQL query, and this query will be used as the basis for a form or a report.

Before we start to modify any queries we first need to create the QBF form that is shown above. If you want to, you could try your hand at building it yourself, but to make life easier for you, there is a shell criteria form provided in the `IceCream7.mdb` database.

> If you have been building up the Ice Cream database by completing the exercises and Try It Outs as you have been working your way through the book, then you should import the form into the database you have been building. You can see how to do this in the next Try It Out. Alternatively, you can skip the Try It Out and use the copy of the database with all of the exercises and Try It Outs to date completed, which is `IceCream7.mdb` on the CD accompanying this book.

Try It Out – Importing the Criteria Form

1. Open the `IceCream.mdb` database that you have been building as you have been working through the book.

2. If the Database window is not displayed, make it visible by hitting *F11*.

3. From the File menu, select Get External Data and then Import.

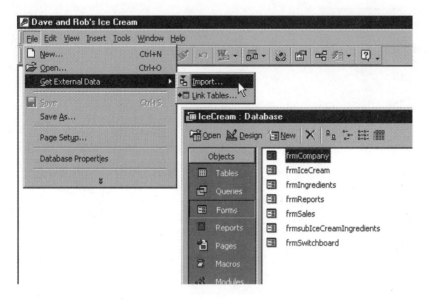

4. A dialog box will then appear and you will be asked to select the database from which you want to import objects. Select the `IceCream7.mdb` database and hit the *ENTER* key.

5. You will then be asked which objects you wish to import. Click the Forms tab and select `frmCriteria`.

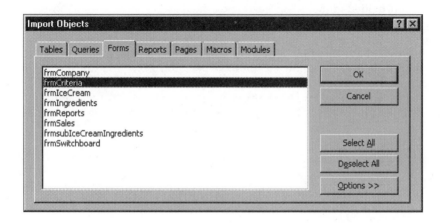

6. Hit the OK button and the `frmCriteria` form will be imported into the current database.

Now that we have a copy of the `frmCriteria` form in our database, we can take a look at what happens when the user selects values in it.

Try It Out – Using the Criteria Form

1. Open either the `IceCream.mdb` database that you have been building or the `IceCream7.mdb` database.

2. If the Database window is not displayed, make it visible by hitting *F11*.

3. Open the `frmCriteria` form.

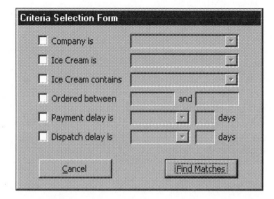

4. Check and uncheck the checkboxes on the left hand side of the form. Note how the associated text boxes and combo boxes are enabled and disabled as you check and uncheck the checkboxes.

5. Check the **Company**, **Ordered Between** and **Dispatch Delay** checkboxes and enter the following values into the text boxes on the form.

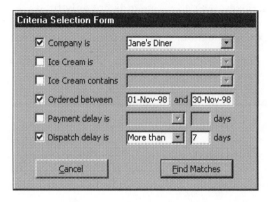

6. Now hit *CTRL+G* to open the VBA IDE and display the Immediate window.

7. In the Immediate window, we are going to look at the values held by some of the various combo boxes and text boxes on the form. To find the values they hold, evaluate the following expressions in the Immediate window. To do this, type each of the lines in turn into the Immediate window and hit the *Enter* key after each

```
?forms("frmCriteria")("chkCompanyID")
?forms("frmCriteria")("cboCompanyID")
?forms("frmCriteria")("chkDateOrdered")
?forms("frmCriteria")("txtDateFrom")
?forms("frmCriteria")("txtDateTo")
?forms("frmCriteria")("cboDispatchDelay")
?forms("frmCriteria")("txtDispatchDelay")
```

You should see the following values returned:

```
?forms("frmCriteria")("chkCompanyID")
-1
?forms("frmCriteria")("cboCompanyID")
10
?forms("frmCriteria")("chkDateOrdered")
-1
?forms("frmCriteria")("txtDateFrom")
11/1/98
?forms("frmCriteria")("txtDateTo")
11/30/98
?forms("frmCriteria")("cboDispatchDelay")
>
?forms("frmCriteria")("txtDispatchDelay")
7
```

So, although we have still quite a way to go, at least we have a good starting point. We have a form that we can use to gather all of the criteria required to run the various queries that our application needs to be able to cope with. But before we look at how to build the query, let's have a brief look at some of the other functionality in the frmCriteria form.

Firstly, if you want to know how the text boxes and combo boxes are enabled and disabled, just take a peek at the code module behind the form. Each of the check boxes has an event procedure handling its Click event. For check boxes, the Click event is not only fired when the user clicks the check box with the mouse; it is also fired when the user carries out any action which has the same effect as clicking the check box with the mouse, such as pressing the space bar while the check box is selected.

```
Private Sub chkCompanyID_Click()

cboCompanyID.Enabled = chkCompanyID

End Sub
```

So what the piece of code above does is to interrogate the value of chkCompanyID. If the check box has just been checked, its value will be True (-1); otherwise it will be False. All we then need to do is to assign this value to the Enabled property of any combo boxes or text boxes associated with the check box.

> The `Value` *property is the default property of a checkbox object, so evaluating*
> `chkCompanyID` *is equivalent to evaluating* `chkCompanyID.Value`*.*

Secondly, have a look at the values that the text boxes and combo boxes contain. Some of them are obvious, but others bear further investigation. For example, the top three combo boxes return numbers rather than the values that are selected. That is because the combo boxes are populated by a query with two columns. One of these columns is the one that is displayed on the form; the other is hidden (by having its `Width` set to 0) and contains the ID of the value being displayed. For example, the `cboCompanyID` combo box has been populated with this query, which is stored in the `Row Source` property of the combo box:

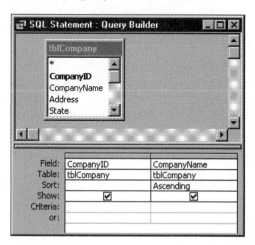
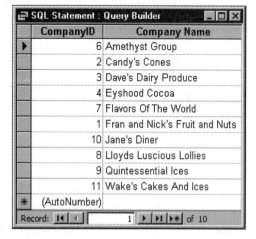

So, when `Jane's Diner` is selected in the combo box, the bound column contains the value 10, which is what is returned when we interrogate the value of `cboCompanyID`. Now that's all very interesting, but why bother? To answer that, let us have another look at the SQL that we used earlier in this chapter to evaluate this query:

```
SELECT tblSales.SalesID
FROM tblCompany
   INNER JOIN tblSales
   ON tblCompany.CompanyID = tblSales.fkCompanyID
WHERE tblCompany.CompanyName = "Jane's Diner"
AND tblSales.DateOrdered >= #11/1/98#
AND tblSales.DateOrdered <= #11/30/98#
AND tblSales.[DateDispatched] - tblSales.[DateOrdered] > 7
```

You see, the company name is the only part of this query which needs to be retrieved from a table other than the `tblSales` table. The `tblSales` table contains the `CompanyID`, not the `CompanyName` for the company that bought the ice cream. So, if we wanted to, we could re-write this query like this:

```
SELECT tblSales.SalesID
FROM tblSales
WHERE tblSales.fkCompanyID=10
AND tblSales.DateOrdered>=#11/1/98#
AND tblSales.DateOrdered<=#11/30/98#
AND [DateDispatched]-[DateOrdered]>7
```

Now rewriting the query in this fashion has two advantages. Firstly, the query should run slightly faster, because there is no need to create a join to a second table. But, more importantly for us, the query is much simpler to construct. Remember, we are going to need to be able to create a variety of different queries, depending on what the user selects. The more we can avoid joins, the easier that task will be for us.

The final thing to notice about this form is what happens when we hit the <u>F</u>ind Matches button. Have a look at the code in the event handler for the Click event of the cmdFind button and you will see this:

```
Private Sub cmdFind_Click()

Call EntriesValid

End Sub
```

So, when the Click event is fired, this line of code runs the EntriesValid procedure. As its name suggests, the EntriesValid procedure checks that each of the selections made by the user is valid. So if a user has, for example, checked the "**Company is**" check box, but has not selected a company, the EntriesValid function will display an error message warning the user of this inconsistency.

So, we have a convenient way of collecting input from the user, but how do we go about reflecting the user's selections in the query we will run. In order to do that, we need to know how to manipulate queries. Once we have done that, we will come back and implement that functionality in the frmCriteria form.

Creating and Modifying QueryDefs

You will probably remember from the previous chapter that a QueryDef is the name given to a query object variable in VBA. Just as we can create a String-type variable to hold a piece of text, so we can create a QueryDef object to hold a query definition. Note that a QueryDef object holds the **definition** of a query, not the results. Query results, as we saw in the previous chapter, are held in Recordset objects. If you want, you can think of the QueryDef as being like a query in design view and a Recordset as representing a query in datasheet view.

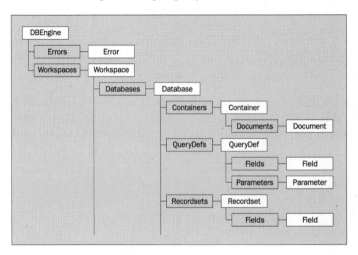

As you can see from the diagram above which shows a section of the DAO hierarchy, the `QueryDefs` collection belongs to the `Database` object. This is fairly logical really – after all, a database can have multiple queries in it, but a query can only exist in one database.

Try It Out – Creating and Modifying a QueryDef

1. Create a new standard code module and call it `Chapter 8 Code`.

2. Type in the procedure as it appears below.

```
Function MakeQueryDef(strSQL As String) As Boolean

Dim qdf As QueryDef

If strSQL = "" Then Exit Function

Set qdf = CurrentDb.CreateQueryDef("qryExample")
qdf.SQL = strSQL
qdf.Close
RefreshDatabaseWindow

MakeQueryDef = True

End Function
```

3. To run the procedure, open the Immediate window. Type in the following and hit *Enter*:

```
?MakeQueryDef("SELECT * FROM tblCompany WHERE CompanyID = 10")
```

4. The word `True` should appear in the Immediate window, indicating that the function completed successfully.

If you try to execute this procedure for a second time, Access will generate a run-time error, indicating that there is already a query called `qryExample` *in the database. We will look at how to handle this situation later on in the chapter.*

5. Press *ALT+F11* to view the Database window and change to the Queries tab. You should see a query there called `qryExample`.

6. Open `qryExample` in design view. The design of the query should match the criteria that you passed as an argument to the `MakeQueryDef` function.

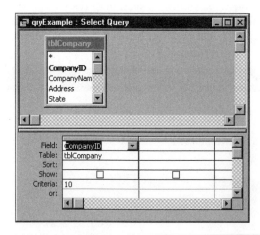

7. Now go back to the VBA IDE and type the following procedure in the code window for the `Chapter 8 Code` module:

```
Function ChangeQueryDef(strQuery As String, strSQL As String) As Boolean

If strQuery = "" Or strSQL = "" Then Exit Function

Dim qdf As QueryDef

Set qdf = CurrentDb.QueryDefs(strQuery)
qdf.SQL = strSQL
qdf.Close
RefreshDatabaseWindow

ChangeQueryDef = True

End Function
```

8. Run the procedure by typing the following in the Immediate window and hitting *Enter*:

```
?ChangeQueryDef("qryExample", "SELECT * FROM tblCompany ORDER BY CompanyName")
```

9. The word `True` should appear in the Immediate window, indicating that the function completed successfully.

10. Press *ALT+F11* to view the Database window and change to the **Queries** tab. Open `qryExample` in design view. The design of the query should now have changed to match the new SQL you passed to the `ChangeQueryDef` function.

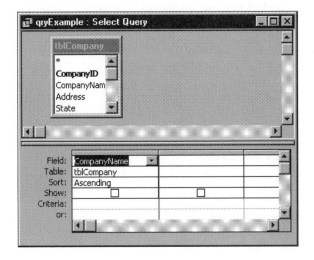

How It Works

Creating a `QueryDef` is very simple.

```
Dim qdf As QueryDef

Set qdf = CurrentDb.CreateQueryDef("qryExample")
```

First, we create an empty `QueryDef` object. The `CreateQueryDef` method both creates a `QueryDef` object and assigns it the name that it will have when it is saved. If you don't intend to save it and will only use it in the current procedure, you can give it an empty string (`""`) as its name and it won't be saved. However, we do want to save our `QueryDef`, and so we'll call it `qryExample`.

> If you try to create a `QueryDef` object with a name that is the same as a saved query that already exists in the database, Access will generate a run-time error.

```
qdf.SQL = strSQL
```

Next, we assign the `SQL` property of the `QueryDef` object. If you aren't too sure about how to write SQL, you can always try designing the query normally in the QBE grid and then switching the query to SQL view to see the SQL created. You can then copy the SQL to the clipboard and paste it into your procedure from there.

Finally, we close the `QueryDef`, with the following line:

```
qdf.Close
```

The act of closing the `QueryDef` saves changes to it in the database window. Then we refresh the database window:

```
RefreshDatabaseWindow
```

The `RefreshDatabaseWindow` method was new in Access 97. It causes any changes to database objects such as forms, reports and queries to be immediately reflected in the database window.

Modifying the `QueryDef` is just as simple as creating it. First you use a variable to reference the `QueryDef` called `qryExample` in the current database.

```
Dim qdf As QueryDef

Set qdf = CurrentDb.QueryDefs(strQuery)
```

And then you modify its `SQL` property, save it and refresh the database window like we did in the previous function.

Working with SQL

A `QueryDef` object has over a dozen different properties, but you will find that there is one property in particular that you will use more than any other; the `SQL` property. As we saw above, the `SQL` property is used to set the SQL statement that will be run when the `QueryDef` object is executed.

If the `frmCriteria` form is to be used to allow users to frame their queries in a manner of their own choosing, we will then need to convert the entries that the user makes on the form into an SQL statement and use that SQL statement to select the records that should be displayed.

SQL `SELECT` statements generally consist of three clauses:

```
SELECT fields
FROM source table
WHERE criteria
```

The `SELECT` clause indicates the columns or fields that will be displayed in the result set of the query. The `FROM` clause indicates the base tables from which the results are drawn and the `WHERE` clause indicates the criteria for determining which rows or records will be represented in the result set of the query.

Put another way, the `SELECT` clause is a form of vertical partitioning, and the `WHERE` clause a method of horizontal partitioning:

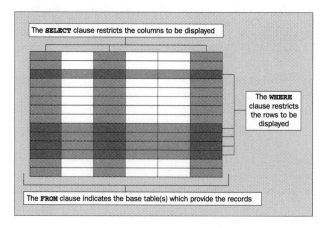

The **SELECT** clause restricts the columns to be displayed

The **WHERE** clause restricts the rows to be displayed

The **FROM** clause indicates the base table(s) which provide the records

So let's see how this works when we apply it to the `frmCriteria` form in the Ice Cream database.

Well, we know which fields we want displayed. We know that the user is to be shown details of each sale and so we will have to display all of the fields from the `tblSales` table. That will be fixed and won't change, irrespective of the criteria we select on `frmCriteria`. In other words, the `SELECT` clause will not change and will always be:

```
SELECT tblSales.*
```

which selects all of the fields from the `tblSales` table.

Things get slightly more complicated with the `FROM` clause. Most of the time we will only need to use the `tblSales` table. That is because most of the criteria on the `frmCriteria` form represent columns in the `tblSales` table. In fact, if we look at the following table, we can see which columns are represented by which criteria on the `frmCriteria` form.

This criterion...	...relates to this field
Company is	`tblSales.fkCompanyID`
Ice Cream is	`tblSales.fkIceCreamID`
Ice Cream contains	`tblIceCreamIngredient.fkIngredientID`
Ordered between	`tblSales.DateOrdered`
Payment delay is	`tblSales.DatePaid - tblSales.DateOrdered`
Dispatch delay	`tblSales.DateDispatched -` `tblSales.DateOrdered`

As you can see, however, one of these criteria is dependent on a field in a separate table. If we want to view sales of ice creams that contain specific ingredients, then we need to join the `tblSales` table with the `tblIceCreamIngredient` table and then search for records with an `fkIngredientID` matching the one selected on the criteria form.

> Remember, although the combo box on `frmCriteria` displays the ingredient's name, the bound column contains the ingredient's `fkIngredientID`. Without this `fkIngredientID`, we would have needed to join the `tblIngredient` table as well to search on the `Name` column.

So, we can see that most of the time our `FROM` clause will look like this:

```
FROM tblSales
```

The only variation is when the user chooses to restrict by ingredient, when the `FROM` clause will look like this:

```
FROM tblSales INNER JOIN tblIceCreamIngredient
   ON tblSales.fkIceCreamID = tblIceCreamIngredient.fkIceCreamID
```

This FROM clause implements the join between the two tables. The two tables to be joined are tblSales and tblIceCreamIgredients:

```
FROM tblSales INNER JOIN tblIceCreamIngredient
```

And the fields participating on either side of the join are both called fkIceCreamID:

```
ON tblSales.fkIceCreamID = tblIceCreamIngredient.fkIceCreamID
```

Now for the WHERE clause. This one is certainly going to change. What we are interested in is building up a SQL statement which will restrict the rows selected to those which meet our criteria and as we know, it is the WHERE clause which restricts the rows that are returned. Each of the criteria selected by the user will add at least one extra element to the WHERE clause. So, in the specific example we have been looking at so far, the following WHERE clause would be generated.

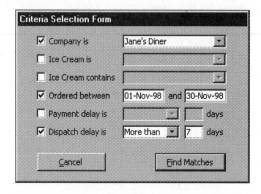

```
WHERE tblCompany.CompanyID=10
AND tblSales.DateOrdered>=#11/1/98#
AND tblSales.DateOrdered<=#11/30/98#
AND [DateDispatched]-[DateOrdered]>7
```

Anyway, enough of the theory; let's get on with writing a procedure which converts our criteria into a SQL string.

Try It Out – Building a SQL String

1. Open the IceCream.mdb database and open the code module for the frmCriteria form.

2. Now create a function called BuildSQLString and add the following code to it:

```
Function BuildSQLString(strSQL As String) As Boolean

Dim strSELECT As String
Dim strFROM As String
Dim strWHERE As String

strSELECT = "s.* "

strFROM = "tblSales s "
If chkIngredientID Then
    strFROM = strFROM & " INNER JOIN tblIceCreamIngredient i " & _
```

```
      "ON s.fkIceCreamID = i.fkIceCreamID "
   strWHERE = " AND i.fkIngredientID = " & cboIngredientID
End If

If chkCompanyID Then
   strWHERE = strWHERE & " AND s.fkCompanyID = " & cboCompanyID
End If

If chkIceCreamID Then
   strWHERE = strWHERE & " AND s.fkIceCreamID = " & cboIceCreamID
End If

If chkDateOrdered Then
   If Not IsNull(txtDateFrom) Then
      strWHERE = strWHERE & " AND s.DateOrdered >= " & _
      "#" & Format$(txtDateFrom, "mm/dd/yyyy") & "#"
   End If
   If Not IsNull(txtDateTo) Then
      strWHERE = strWHERE & " AND s.DateOrdered <= " & _
      "#" & Format$(txtDateTo, "mm/dd/yyyy") & "#"
   End If
End If

If chkPaymentDelay Then
   strWHERE = strWHERE & " AND (s.DatePaid - s.DateOrdered) " & _
   cboPaymentDelay & txtPaymentDelay
End If

If chkDispatchDelay Then
   strWHERE = strWHERE & " AND (s.DateDispatched - s.DateOrdered) " & _
   cboDispatchDelay & txtDispatchDelay
End If

strSQL = "SELECT " & strSELECT
strSQL = strSQL & "FROM " & strFROM
If strWHERE <> "" Then strSQL = strSQL & "WHERE " & Mid$(strWHERE, 6)

BuildSQLString = True

End Function
```

3. Next, amend the event handler for the Click event of the cmdFind button so that it looks like this:

```
Private Sub cmdFind_Click()

Dim strSQL As String

If Not EntriesValid Then Exit Sub

If Not BuildSQLString(strSQL) Then
   MsgBox "There was a problem building the SQL string"
   Exit Sub
End If

MsgBox strSQL

CurrentDb.QueryDefs("qryExample").SQL = strSQL

End Sub
```

4. Now save the changes you have made to the `Form_frmCriteria` module and switch back to Access by hitting *ALT+F11*.

5. Open the `frmCriteria` form and enter the following criteria.

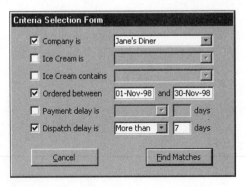

6. When you hit the <u>F</u>ind Matches button, a message box will appear displaying the SQL string that has been constructed.

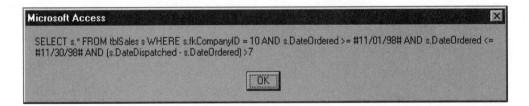

7. Hit the **OK** button and then open the `qryExample` query in design view. It should reflect the criteria that you entered.

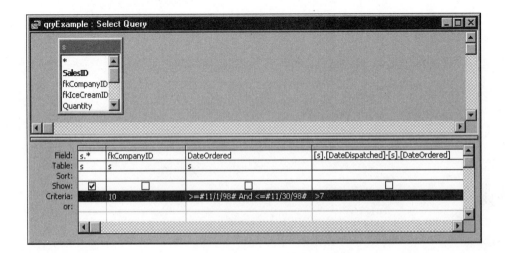

8. When you run the query it displays the records that meet your criteria.

How It Works

The principle behind this procedure is simple enough, although it may look a bit daunting at first! The general idea is that a `String`-type variable, `strSQL`, is passed into the procedure. The procedure eventually puts into that variable a SQL statement that reflects the choices entered by the user on `frmCriteria`.

In fact, there is nothing in this exercise that we have not already covered in this chapter. The first step was to create a procedure that generates a SQL string from the criteria that were selected. The heart of this procedure is three variables that correspond to the three parts of the SQL string.

```
Dim strSELECT As String
Dim strFROM As String
Dim strWHERE As String
```

As we said earlier, the `SELECT` clause is invariant, so we can populate that immediately.

```
strSELECT = "s.* "
```

The next step is to complete the `FROM` clause. Again, we looked at this earlier and decided that it should contain just the `tblSales` table unless the user chose to restrict by ingredient, in which case the `tblIceCreamIngredient` table should be joined to it.

```
strFROM = "tblSales s "
If chkIngredientID Then
    strFROM = strFROM & " INNER JOIN tblIceCreamIngredient i " & _
      "ON s.fkIceCreamID = i.fkIceCreamID "
    strWHERE = " AND i.fkIngredientID = " & cboIngredientID
End If
```

Next we construct the `WHERE` clause. To build the `WHERE` clause, we look at each of the text boxes in `frmCriteria` in turn. If the user has checked the check box for a criterion and has entered something in the relevant text box, we add that criterion to the `WHERE` clause.

For example:

```
If chkCompanyID Then
    strWHERE = strWHERE & " AND s.fkCompanyID = " & cboCompanyID
End If
```

Whenever we add a new section to the end of the WHERE clause, we also add an AND in front of it to link the sections together. Therefore, if the user has selected any criteria, at the end of the procedure we are left with a spare " AND " in front of the first criterion. We need to strip it off and replace it with " WHERE ". The string " AND " is 5 characters long, so we use the Mid$ function to return all the characters in strSQL from the 6th character onwards.

```
If chkCompanyID Then
    strWHERE = strWHERE & " AND s.fkCompanyID = " & cboCompanyID
End If

If chkIceCreamID Then
    strWHERE = strWHERE & " AND s.fkIceCreamID = " & cboIceCreamID
End If

If chkDateOrdered Then
    If Not IsNull(txtDateFrom) Then
        strWHERE = strWHERE & " AND str.DateOrdered >= " & _
        "#" & Format$(txtDateFrom, "mm/dd/yyyy") & "#"
    End If
    If Not IsNull(txtDateTo) Then
        strWHERE = strWHERE & " AND s.DateOrdered <= " & _
        "#" & Format$(txtDateTo, "mm/dd/yyyy") & "#"
    End If
End If

If chkPaymentDelay Then
    strWHERE = strWHERE & " AND (s.DatePaid - s.DateOrdered) " & _
    cboPaymentDelay & txtPaymentDelay
End If

If chkDispatchDelay Then
    strWHERE = strWHERE & " AND (s.DateDispatched - s.DateOrdered) " & _
    cboDispatchDelay & txtDispatchDelay
End If

strSQL = "SELECT " & strSELECT
strSQL = strSQL & "FROM " & strFROM
If strWHERE <> "" Then strSQL = strSQL & "WHERE " & Mid$(strWHERE, 6)
```

Note that the variable that is being populated with the SQL string is the one that was passed into the function at the start.

```
Function BuildSQLString(strSQL As String) As Boolean

    .
    .
    .

strSQL = "SELECT " & strSELECT
strSQL = strSQL & "FROM " & strFROM
If strWHERE <> "" Then strSQL = strSQL & "WHERE " & Mid$(strWHERE, 6)
```

This variable was passed in by reference (the default) which means that we can amend the contents of the variable and those changes will be seen when the procedure exits. We will look at the alternative – passing arguments by value – in Chapter 11.

All that is left in this procedure is to return `True` to indicate that the procedure completed successfully.

Having built the procedure, we then need to make sure that it is invoked when the user hits the <u>F</u>ind Matches button on the criteria form. So we modify the `cmdFind_Click` procedure by declaring a variable to hold the SQL string and then passing it into the `BuildSQLString` procedure.

```
Dim strSQL As String

If Not EntriesValid Then Exit Sub

If Not BuildSQLString(strSQL) Then
    MsgBox "There was a problem building the SQL string"
    Exit Sub
End If
```

Note how we check the return value of the `BuildSQLString` procedure and display an error message if it's `False`. If it is `True`, however, we display the string in a message box and then modify the `qryExample` query to contain the SQL string that we built.

```
MsgBox strSQL

CurrentDb.QueryDefs("qryExample").SQL = strSQL
```

That is fine as far as it goes and we are well on the way to achieving the functionality that we originally stated. If you remember, we stated earlier that when they run the query, the users want to know how many sales match the criteria that they have specified and should then be presented with the opportunity of viewing:

❑ the matching results in detail on screen, and

❑ a report containing the matching results.

Well, so far we have a way of determining the criteria that the user wants to use to restrict the sales records that he or she wants to view, and we have a method of programmatically modifying a query in Access to express the user's choice. So, where do we go from here?

Two Approaches to Displaying Results

It should be clear that the requirements expressed above would require a separate form and report to be written to satisfy them. We will need a form to display the matching results in detail, and if the user wants to print off the results, then we will also need a report showing the matching sales. Now we already have a form displaying details of sales (`frmSales`) and we will use this to display the results that match our criteria.

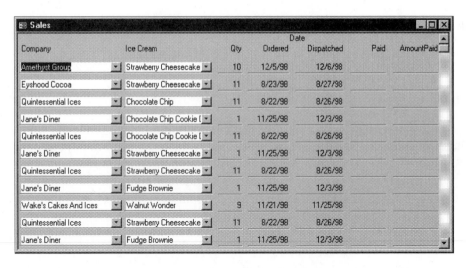

What we want to do now is to create a report that will display those results as well, so we can print them out. That is what we'll do now.

Try It Out – Saving a Form as a Report

1. Open the `IceCream.mdb` database and display the Database window if it is not already visible, by hitting *F11*.

2. Select the sales details form (`frmSales`) and right-click it. From the resultant popup menu, select **Save As...**

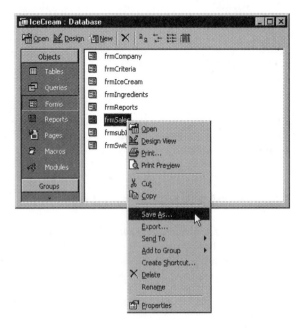

3. In the dialog that then appears, specify that you want to save the form as a report called rptSales.

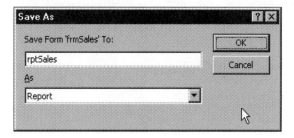

4. Now switch to the database window and open the report you have just created. It looks OK, but it could sure do with some tidying up.

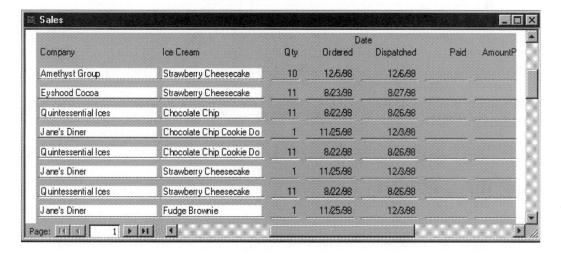

5. Switch to design view and make the following changes to the report. (You might also need to resize some of the controls to make sure that they all fit within the width of one page).

Object	Property	Setting
Report Header	Back Color	12632256 (Gray)
Detail	Back Color	16777215 (White)
fkCompanyID, fkIceCreamID, Quantity, DateOrdered, DateDispatched, DatePaid, AmountPaid	Special Effect	Flat
	Border Style	Transparent

6. Now switch back to report view. The report should now look like this:

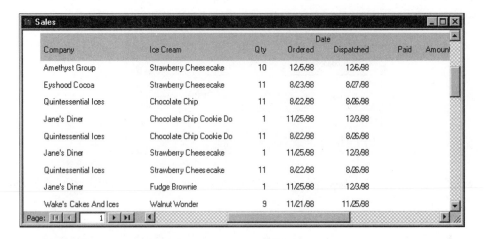

7. Close the report, saving the changes when prompted to do so.

Now we have a form (frmSales) and a report (rptSales) both based on the tblSales table. So, how do we go about ensuring that the form and the report display only the records that match the criteria selected by the user? In fact, there are two common methods that we can use to restrict the records displayed to those the user has selected. The first involves modifying the underlying QueryDef and the second involves creating a table of matching records. We will look at each of those in turn in some detail now.

Modifying the QueryDef

Perhaps the most intuitive way of restricting the records on a form or report is to modify the QueryDef object to which the form is bound. That is, after all, what we have been looking at so far. Why not simply bind the form and the report to the qryExample query that we modified above? That way, whenever the user hits the Find Matches button and the qryExample query is redesigned, the population of the form and report will be automatically be redefined to match the selected criteria.

This is a frequently used method and has the advantage of being fairly straightforward. In order to modify one form and one report, we simply modify one QueryDef object.

Try It Out

1. Open the rptSales report in design view and change its RecordSource property to be qryExample. Then close the report, saving changes when prompted to do so.

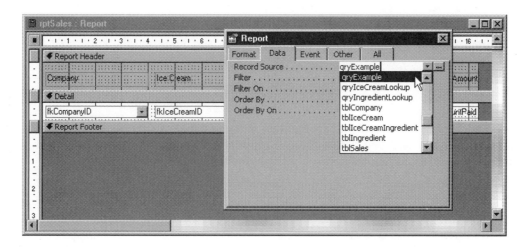

2. Now open the `frmSales` form in design view and change its `RecordSource` property to be `qryExample` as well. Instead of closing the form, place a command button in the footer of the form and call it `cmdPrint`.

3. Open the property window and select the button's `On Click` event property. Select [Event Procedure] and then hit the Builder button to the right of the property to create a VBA event handler for the `Click` event.

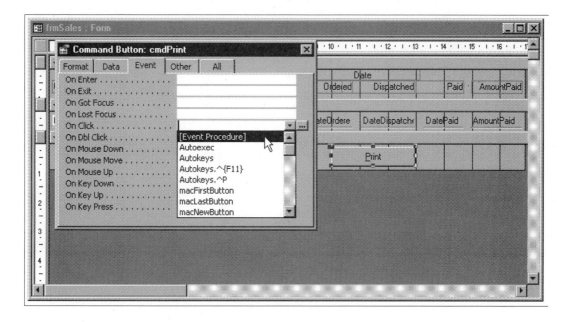

4. Add the following code to the `cmdPrint_Click` event.

```
Private Sub cmdPrint_Click()

DoCmd.OpenReport "rptSales", acViewPreview

End Sub
```

5. Now switch back to Access and add another button to the `frmSales` form and call it `cmdClose`. Add the following code to the event handler for the button's `Click` event and then close `frmSales`, saving changes when prompted to do so.

```
Private Sub cmdClose_Click()

DoCmd.Close acForm, Me.Name

End Sub
```

6. Next, switch back to the VBA IDE and open the `Form_frmCriteria` code module. Modify the code in the `cmdFind_Click` event procedure by adding a line to open the `frmSales` form. The procedure should now look like this.

```
Private Sub cmdFind_Click()

Dim strSQL As String

If Not EntriesValid Then Exit Sub

If Not BuildSQLString(strSQL) Then
    MsgBox "There was a problem building the SQL string"
    Exit Sub
End If

CurrentDb.QueryDefs("qryExample").SQL = strSQL

DoCmd.OpenForm "frmSales", acNormal

End Sub
```

7. Save the changes to this module and, after switching back to Access, save the changes to `frmCriteria`.

8. Finally, open `frmCriteria` and enter the following criteria.

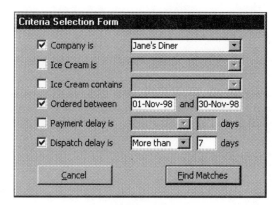

9. When you hit the <u>F</u>ind Matches button, the sales details form is displayed containing only the records that match the criteria you specified. When you hit the Print button, the report containing those records is previewed on screen.

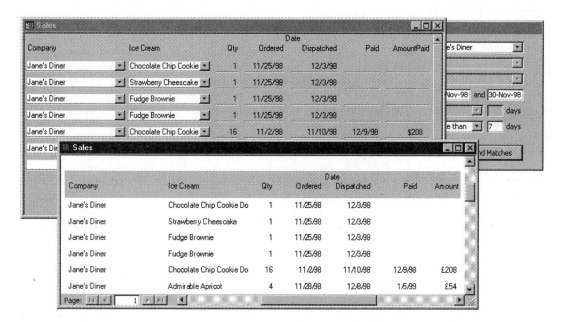

Now that really is something! We are well on our way to implementing the functionality that we set out to achieve at the start of this chapter. In fact the only thing that we haven't put in place is a message informing the user of the number of qualifying records. Don't worry about that, though; we'll look at that a little later. For the moment, let's consider in a little more detail the solution we have implemented.

To recap, then, the steps involved in producing this solution are as follows:

- ❑ The user selects various criteria
- ❑ The application modifies the query upon which `frmSales` and `rptSales` is based
- ❑ `frmSales` (and optionally `rptSales`) are then opened

In this particular situation this works fine. However, this method does have a drawback. It will only work if the form and the report can both use exactly the same query as their record source. What if we had wanted the report to contain two grouping levels such that the report was grouped first by company name and then by ice cream name? Not too difficult, you might think, until you try to implement it.

You see, if you have a look at the query on which the report is based, you will discover that it does not contain either the company name or the ice cream name. Just like the `frmSales` and `frmCriteria` forms, the `rptSales` report contains only the ID of the ice cream and the company. And, like the form, the report uses combo boxes to display the details of the ice cream and company. The combo box is populated by a query that displays the name of the ice cream or company, but stores its ID. What that means is that, as it stands, we could group on `fkIceCreamID` or `fkCompanyID` but not on the ice cream's name or the company's name, as they are not contained in the query.

Now in this situation we could get around this problem fairly easily by simply adding the ice cream name and company name into `qryExample` (although this would mean that the query now involves two join operations). In practice, however, once you have allowed your users to isolate the sales they are interested in, they might want to carry out a large number of operations on these results. They might want to use them in a mail merge; they might want to count how many of them there are; they might want to display the results in reports which have very different record sources, but use the same criteria to select from among those records. What we would like is to be able to run a complicated query once to determine the records we want to deal with and then achieve some kind of permanence or persistence to the results of that query. We might want to base all sorts of queries on the results that are returned to us, but we don't want to have to re-evaluate the criteria the user has selected. Let's do that once, save the results, and then we are free to do whatever we want with the results.

So the method that we have looked at so far – modifying `qryExample` every time we change our criteria – is good as far as it goes. But is there a better way?

Using a Matching Records table

We are now going to look at a slightly different way of tackling this problem and then we will look at some of the pros and cons of this new way of restricting records in a form and a report based on criteria selected by the user.

What we are going to do is to dynamically build a query – as before – but this time we are going to use it to generate a small table of matching key values rather than a table of matching rows. This table of key values (the values of `SalesID` for every record which matches the selected criteria) will be called `tblResults` and can be used in any query to restrict the results of that query to records that match the user's criteria.

It will probably become clearer once we have tried it out.

Try It Out – Building a Matching Results Table

1. Open the `IceCream.mdb` database (if it's not already open).

2. Now open `Form_frmCriteria`, the code module behind the `frmCriteria` form, and modify the `cmdFind_Click` procedure so that it now reads like this:

```
Private Sub cmdFind_Click()

Dim strSQL As String
Dim lngRecordsAffected As Long

If Not EntriesValid Then Exit Sub

If Not BuildSQLString(strSQL) Then
   MsgBox "There was a problem building the SQL string"
   Exit Sub
End If

If Not BuildResultsTable(strSQL, "tblResults", lngRecordsAffected) Then
   MsgBox "There was a problem building the results table"
   Exit Sub
End If

DoCmd.OpenForm "frmSales", acNormal

End Sub
```

3. Next, open the `BuildSQLString` function and change it so that it only returns the `SalesID` column.

```
Function BuildSQLString(strSQL As String) As Boolean

Dim strSELECT As String
Dim strFROM As String
Dim strWHERE As String

strSELECT = "s.SalesID "

strFROM = "tblSales s "
```

4. Now create a new function in `Form_frmCriteria` called `BuildResultsTable`. The function should look like this:

```
Function BuildResultsTable(strSQL As String, _
                     strTableName As String, _
                     lngRecordsAffected As Long)

Dim db As Database
Dim qdfAction As QueryDef

Set db = CurrentDb

On Error Resume Next
db.TableDefs.Delete strTableName
On Error GoTo 0
```

```
strSQL = Replace(strSQL, " FROM ", " INTO " & strTableName & " FROM ")
Set qdfAction = db.CreateQueryDef("", strSQL)
qdfAction.Execute dbFailOnError
lngRecordsAffected = qdfAction.RecordsAffected
qdfAction.Close

BuildResultsTable = True

End Function
```

5. Save the changes to this module and switch back to Access by hitting *ALT+F11*.

6. Now open the criteria form `frmCriteria` in form view and hit the <u>F</u>ind Matches button without entering any criteria.

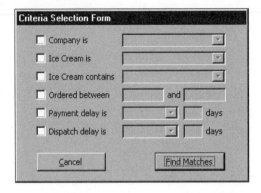

7. The `frmSales` form should now appear. Close it down and switch to the Tables tab of the database window. There should now be a table called `tblResults`.

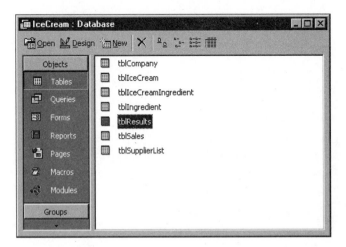

8. Next, create a new query with the following definition and save it as `qryResults`:

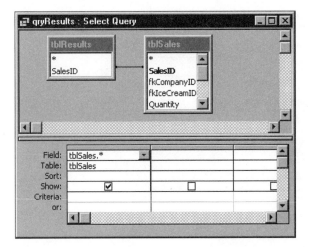

9. Now open the `frmSales` and `rptSales` forms and change their `RecordSource` property to be the name of the new query, `qryResults`. Close these objects, saving changes when prompted to do so.

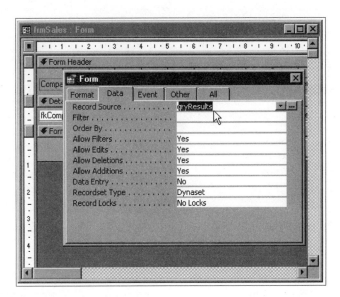

10. Finally open the criteria form `frmCriteria` in form view and enter the following criteria:

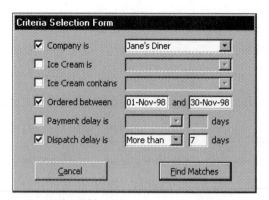

11. When you hit the <u>F</u>ind Matches button, the `frmSales` form should be displayed showing the results that match the criteria you have entered. When you hit the <u>P</u>rint button the `rptSales` report should appear with the same results displayed.

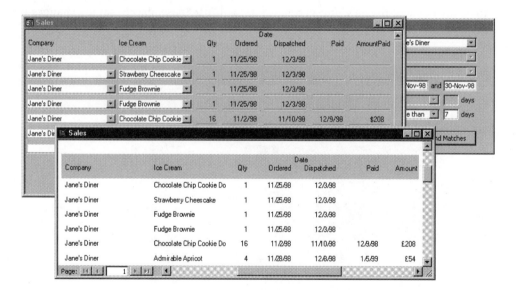

How It Works

There's quite a bit going on here, and it may seem that the end result is no different to what we had before. But bear with us, and you will see just what the benefits are of using this method of implementing the criteria functionality. To better understand what is happening, let's take a look at the query `qryResults` that now sits behind `frmSales` and `rptSales`.

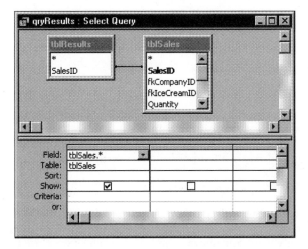

```
SELECT tblSales.*
FROM tblResults INNER JOIN tblSales ON tblResults.SalesID = tblSales.SalesID
```

This query joins the list of all sales with a list of the key values (`SalesID`) of those sales that meet the criteria we have specified. In order to implement this, we need to build a table containing those key values. Now obtaining the key values themselves is not too tricky – we simply modify the `BuildSQLString` procedure so that instead of returning all rows from `tblSales`:

```
strSELECT = "s.* "
```

it simply returns the key values:

```
strSELECT = "s.SalesID "
```

Now what we need to do is to somehow get those key values into a permanent table. The simplest way to do that is to change our **select** query into a **make-table** query.

Select queries always use this general syntax:

```
SELECT select-list
FROM table-list
WHERE criteria-list
```

Whereas make-table queries use this syntax:

```
SELECT select-list
INTO new-table
FROM table-list
WHERE criteria-list
```

So to turn our select query into a make-table query, we simply have to insert `INTO` and the name of the table we want to create between the `SELECT` and `FROM` clauses in our query. We can do that by using the `Replace` function, which replaces a number of characters in a string with other characters:

```
strSQL = Replace(strSQL, " FROM ", " INTO " & strTableName & " FROM ")
```

In this case we are replacing

```
" FROM "
```

with

```
" INTO " & strTableName & " FROM "
```

This has the effect of inserting the required INTO clause into our query string (strSQL). For more information on the Replace function consult the help file.

Then we take this SQL string and create a temporary query with strSQL as its SQL property.

```
Set qdfAction = db.CreateQueryDef("", strSQL)
```

Until now, we have only been dealing with permanently saved queries that are visible in the database window. However, if we create a QueryDef object and give it an empty string as its name, VBA knows that we only want a temporary query. As soon as we close the QueryDef object later in this procedure, the query will be deleted.

```
qdfAction.Execute dbFailOnError
```

Having created the query, we now execute it by calling the Execute method of the QueryDef object. Notice that we use the optional dbFailOnError argument with the Execute method. If we had not specified the dbFailOnError argument and our query could not be executed for some reason, VBA would have ignored the error and executed the next line of code without warning us. By specifying the dbFailOnError argument, we are instructing VBA to alert us if the query could not be run.

When we run the query, a new table is created and is called whatever we set the value of the argument strTableName to. In our example we set the value of this argument to tblResults so that is the name of the new table we created.

```
lngRecordsAffected = qdfAction.RecordsAffected
```

After running the query, we can then inspect the QueryDef object's RecordsAffected property. As its name suggests, this lets us know how many records were affected by the query. In this case it tells us how many records met the criteria we specified and were therefore inserted into the new tblResults table by our make-table query. If you remember, one of the demands made by our users was the ability to see how many records met the criteria they specified. The RecordsAffected property gives us just that ability.

```
qdfAction.Close
```

Finally, we close the QueryDef object. Because this was only a temporary query, the QueryDef is not saved as a query in the database window.

Of course, one potential problem is that the next time we run the BuildResultsTable, there will already be a table called tblResults. If we did not pre-empt this situation, then VBA would generate a run-time error telling us that the table already existed.

To get around this problem we delete the table before running the query:

```
On Error Resume Next
db.TableDefs.Delete strTableName
On Error GoTo 0
```

The first line (On Error Resume Next) instructs VBA to ignore any errors that may occur when we try to delete the table. This copes with the situation that arises the first time we run this function. In that case there will be no tblResults table to delete. The last line (On Error GoTo 0) instructs VBA not to ignore errors in any subsequent lines of code.

> You don't have to worry if you don't quite understand the error handling in this section of the code. We will be revisiting this code in more detail in Chapter 12 when we look at error handling. For the moment, you only need to understand that these lines of code delete the tblResults table if it already exists.

Now as you can see from the example above, the end result of rewriting this part of our application is that it yields exactly the same results as our previous attempt where we embedded the user's criteria directly within the query itself. So why bother? There are a couple of reasons for implementing this method of building a table of matching records as opposed to merely modifying a query to include the new criteria inline.

The first benefit of the 'matching-keys' method is that we only have to run the complicated query that evaluates which sales meet the user's criteria once, irrespective of the number of times that we want to use those results. By contrast, in the 'modify-query' method we used earlier, that complicated WHERE clause that was used to restrict the sales to those that met the user's criteria was run when both the frmSales form and the rptSales report were opened.

Now there is obviously going to be an overhead involved in creating the initial table of matching keys, and it is really the way that your application works that will determine whether this overhead is one that is worth bearing. In our example there is little difference between the overall time taken to open the form and report using either method. However, in many situations the user will want to select a number of records and then perform a large number of different operations against those records. If there were, for example, 2 forms and 10 reports that needed to be run against these records, we would see the following overheads:

Modify-Query Method	Matching-Keys Method
Build SQL string	Build SQL string
Modify query	Create make-table query
Run complex select query x 12	Run complex make-table query x 1
	Run simple select query x 12

Obviously, the more complex the initial query, the greater the benefits of the 'matching-keys' method will be. The initial query might be slow because it contains complex criteria or because the client PC has a modest processor or little RAM.

Because the 'matching-keys' method will only need to run the more complex query once, it will tend to give better performance than the 'modify-query' method which will have to run it whenever a form or report based on those results is to be opened.

Another benefit of the 'matching-keys' method comes from the fact that the results of the query are persisted (i.e. saved). This means that a user can exit the database and re-open it and the results of the last criteria search will still be there. We will look at the implications of this in more detail in Chapter 11 when we look at what we can do with custom properties.

A final and significant benefit of the 'matching keys' method is the flexibility that this method affords us. Using this technique, we no longer have to base a report and form on the same query. And once we have the key-set saved, we can use this in any subsequent queries without having to deal with the added complexity of redefining the selection of records in those queries.

Other Considerations

There are two normal methods of deploying Access database solutions in a networked environment:

❑ The first, most basic, solution employs a single database stored on a shared network drive. This one database contains all of the data as well as the other Access objects (i.e. forms, queries, reports and modules) that comprise the application.

❑ The second, and generally preferable, solution uses two databases. One is located on a shared network drive, and contains the base data in Access tables. The other database is located individually on each user's PC, and contains the other Access objects (i.e. forms, queries, reports and modules) that comprise the application. This local database contains links to the base data in the shared network database and the data appears, to all intents and purposes, to reside locally even though it is located elsewhere.

It is essential that you employ the second of these two architectures if you want to use either the 'modify-query' or 'matching-keys' method. That is because you want to ensure that the objects that the user is modifying (either `tblResults` or `qryExample`) are objects that belong solely to that user. If `tblResults` or `qryExample` existed in a central database that everyone shared, then one user's modifications would affect the result set that everyone else used.

Something else to beware of is the fact that constantly deleting and creating tables can lead to a condition that goes by the name of 'database bloat'. What that means is that Access allocates storage space when new objects are created, but does not reclaim that space when the object is deleted. The result is that frequent deletion and creation of tables will cause the database size to grow steadily, so causing a decrease in performance.

The good news is that this condition is easily cured. Either manually compact the database at frequent intervals or use the new Compact on Close option on the general tab of the Tools/Options… dialog, which causes the database to be automatically compacted whenever it is closed.

> 'Compact on Close' only causes the database to be compacted if doing so will reduce the size of the database by 256 Kb or more.

Building Tables

In the example above, we created a table by building a make-table query. We'll now see how to build a table using the Data Access Object hierarchy. One of the advantages of using DAO to create the table is that it gives us more control over the way the table is constructed. When you use a make-table query to create a table, Access determines the data types for the fields in the tables. Also tables created from make-table queries don't have any indexes. In contrast, however, if we create a table using DAO, we can specify the data types of the fields in the table and add whatever indexes we want.

> The judicious use of indexes can have a dramatic impact on the performance of queries, and indexing the `SalesID` column in the `tblResults` table can make the resulting `qryResults` query execute more quickly.

However, in order to do this, we must first understand exactly how tables are constructed. Aside from the data that is held in them, tables have two major constituents: `Fields` and `Indexes`.

❑ A `Field` is a column of data with a common data type and length. `Fields` may exhibit certain properties. For example, a `Field` has a `DefaultValue` property that, not surprisingly, indicates the default value that Access places there if the user doesn't supply one. Another property is the `Required` property that is `False` if a `Field` allows `Null` values and `True` if `Null` values aren't allowed.

❑ An `Index` is an object that holds information about the ordering and uniqueness of records in a field. Just as it is faster to look up a page in a large book if it has an index at the back, so it is faster for Access to retrieve records from a large table if the table is indexed. As well as containing `Fields` an `Index` object also has `Properties`. For example, the `Unique` property of an `Index` object indicates whether all values in the `Field` to which that `Index` applies should be unique.

We'll now take this opportunity to introduce another object that is very similar to the `QueryDef` object – the `TableDef` object. A `TableDef` object is an object that holds a complete table definition. Just as we saw with a `QueryDef` object, a `TableDef` object holds the definition of a table and not the actual data. If you want, you can think of the `TableDef` as being like a table in design view.

Access	VBA
Table (Design View)	`TableDef` object
Table (Datasheet View)	Table-type `Recordset` object
Query (Design View)	`QueryDef` object
Query (Datasheet View)	Dynaset-type, Snapshot-type or Forward-only-type `Recordset` object

The lower portion of the following diagram indicates how `TableDef` objects, `Field` objects and `Index` objects fit into the overall Data Access Object hierarchy.

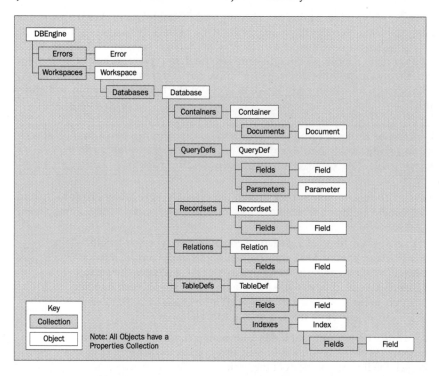

Once you understand the diagram above, creating tables in VBA is a relatively simple process. If you aren't sure you understand how objects and collections work, you should re-read the previous two chapters where they are described in detail. These are the fundamental building blocks of the Data Access Object hierarchy and you need to make sure that you are familiar with how they work.

The Ten Steps

To create an empty table using VBA, you will always carry out the following steps:

1. Create a `TableDef` object

2. Set any properties for the `TableDef`

3. Create one or more `Field` objects

4. Set any properties for the `Field` objects

5. Append the `Field` objects to the `Fields` collection of the `TableDef`

6. Create one or more `Index` objects

7. Set any properties for the `Index` objects

8. Append any `Field` objects to the `Fields` collection of the `Index`

9. Append the `Index` objects to the `Indexes` collection of the `TableDef`

10. Append the `TableDef` object to the `TableDefs` collection of the `Database`

Try It Out – Creating a Table Using the DAO

1. In the `IceCream.mdb` database, open the `Chapter 8 Code` module that you created earlier and type in the following subprocedure:

```
Sub MakeATable()

Dim db As Database
Dim tbl As TableDef
Dim fld As Field
Dim idx As Index

'Start by opening the database
Set db = CurrentDb()

'Create a TableDef object
Set tbl = db.CreateTableDef("tblCountries")

'Create a field; set its properties; add it to the TableDef
Set fld = tbl.CreateField("CountryID", dbLong)

fld.OrdinalPosition = 1
fld.Attributes = dbAutoIncrField

tbl.Fields.Append fld

'Create another; set its properties; add it to the TableDef
Set fld = tbl.CreateField("CountryName", dbText)

fld.OrdinalPosition = 2
fld.Size = 50
fld.Required = True
fld.AllowZeroLength = False

tbl.Fields.Append fld

'Create an index and set its properties
Set idx = tbl.CreateIndex("PrimaryKey")

idx.Primary = True
idx.Required = True
idx.Unique = True

'Add a field to the index
Set fld = idx.CreateField("CountryID")
idx.Fields.Append fld
```

```
'Add the index to the TableDef
tbl.Indexes.Append idx

'Finally add table to the database
db.TableDefs.Append tbl

'And refresh the database window
RefreshDatabaseWindow

'Indicate creation was successful
MsgBox "The " & tbl.Name & " table was successfully created"

End Sub
```

2. Now run the procedure, either by hitting *F5* or the Go/Continue button on the toolbar. You should see a message box informing you that the table has been successfully created. You will get an error message if this table already exists, so you might want to make sure the table doesn't exist before running this function.

3. Hit the OK button and then hit *ALT+F11* to switch to Access. If you go to the database window, the table that you have just created should be visible there. Open it in Design View and have a look at the two fields that you have created. Note the properties in the lower half of the window.

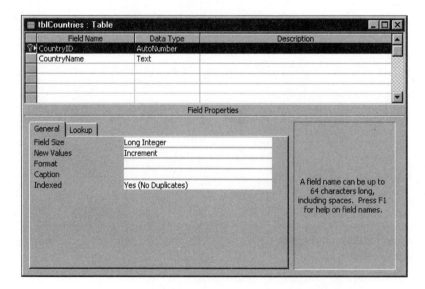

4. Now look at the indexes, either by clicking the Indexes button or by selecting Indexes from the View menu. Does everything look as you expected?

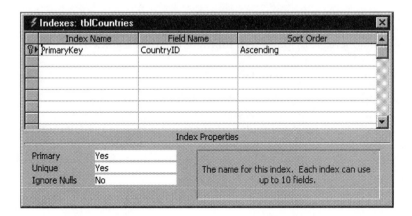

How It Works

Although the code may look a little tortuous, it's actually very easy to follow if you bear in mind the Data Access Object hierarchy and follow the steps listed above.

After opening the database, the first thing we must do is create a new `TableDef` object:

```
Set tbl = db.CreateTableDef("tblCountries")
```

Creating any Data Access Object is a simple task. All you need to do is use the `Create<Object>` method on the Data Access Object which is the next highest in the hierarchy. The `TableDefs` collection belongs to a `Database` object so, to create a `TableDef`, you use the `CreateTableDef` method on the `Database` object.

As with `QueryDefs`, when we create a `TableDef` object, we give it a name by which we can refer to it later and which will appear in the database window when it is saved.

We don't want to set any other properties for the `TableDef` (the next step in the process), and so we move on and create a `Field` object:

```
Set fld = tbl.CreateField("CountryID", dbLong)
```

`Fields` are a collection within the `TableDef` object, so we use the `CreateField` method on the `TableDef` object that will contain the `Field`, and give it a name by which we can refer to it later. We also need to specify the type of data that this `Field` will hold. We want the field to be an AutoNumber field, and as AutoNumber fields are long integers, we specify `dbLong` as the data type.

Next, we must set properties for the `Field`:

```
fld.OrdinalPosition = 1
fld.Attributes = dbAutoIncrField
```

The OrdinalPosition property indicates where a Field appears in a table. The leftmost Field in a table has an OrdinalPosition property of 1; the next has an OrdinalPosition property of 2, and so on. The OrdinalPosition property of the rightmost Field is equal to the number of Fields in the TableDef.

The Attributes property is used to specify how an object behaves. By setting the Attributes property of our Field to dbAutoIncrField, we are indicating that the field should behave like an AutoNumber field and increase by one every time a new record is added.

Now we must add the Field to the Fields collection of the TableDef using the Append method:

```
tbl.Fields.Append fld
```

We then repeat the process to create another Field and append it to our TableDef object.

Once all the Field objects have been added, we create an Index for the table and call it PrimaryKey:

```
Set idx = tbl.CreateIndex("PrimaryKey")
```

We then set its properties:

```
idx.Primary = True
idx.Required = True
idx.Unique = True
```

The Primary property indicates whether an Index is the primary key for the TableDef to which it is to be added. The Required property determines whether the Index can accept Null values – if it is True, Nulls will not be accepted. The Unique property determines whether duplicate values are allowed within the Index. We have set this to True, so duplicate values will not be allowed.

The next stage is to specify the Field that will be indexed:

```
Set fld = idx.CreateField("CountryID")
idx.Fields.Append fld
```

Here, we use the familiar Create<Object> syntax to create a Field object within the Index object. By setting the name of the Field object to CountryID, we are indicating that the Field called CountryID, which we created earlier in the procedure, is the one to be indexed. Next, we add the Index to the TableDef:

```
tbl.Indexes.Append idx
```

Finally, we add the TableDef to the Database:

```
db.TableDefs.Append tbl
```

And that's all there is to it!

If you cast your mind back to the `BuildResultsTable` function earlier in this chapter, you may remember that we created the `tblResults` table using a make-table query. It is left to you as an exercise at the end of this chapter to rewrite the procedure to allow the table to be created using the DAO hierarchy, but if you want to see how this is done, you can have a look at the `BuildResultsTable` function in the `IceCream8.mdb` database.

You need to be aware of the fact that the table might already exist in the database, in which case the `CreateTableDef` statement early on in this procedure would cause a run-time error to be generated. If this is a concern, you should insert some code to delete the table in the same way that we deleted the table earlier on when creating a table of matching keys. That would entail adding the following code to our procedure:

```
On Error Resume Next
Db.TableDefs.Delete "tblCountries"
On Error GoTo 0
Set tbl = db.CreateTableDef("tblCountries")
```

Summary

In this chapter, we have spent a good deal of time looking at the different methods that we can use to manipulate `TableDef` and `QueryDef` objects at run-time. The first part of the chapter was concerned with how to generate criteria to restrict the display of the records we needed. We used the user's input to create a SQL string using the `BuildSQLString` procedure.

Once we had created the SQL string, we had two choices for displaying the records we wanted to display:

- ❑ Base the `frmSales` and `rptSales` objects on a saved query and modify the query before we opened the form and report
- ❑ Create a table of matching records and use this in the record source for the sales form and report

You should have realized by this stage that the key to the whole thing is the Data Access Object hierarchy. If you have a sound knowledge of how this fits together, you should have little problem putting into practice any of the techniques we have used in this chapter.

Knowledge of SQL is also very important. It's a big subject, and we've only really scratched the surface. Hopefully, you've seen how useful it can be. It's definitely something that you should consider learning if you intend to use run-time queries at all.

If you work at these two areas, you will find that you become more and more inventive with the things you attempt and the results you achieve.

Exercises

1. You can use the Immediate window to inspect the properties of data access objects. What line would you have to type in the lower pane of the debug window to determine how many fields there are in the tblSales table?

2. See if you can use the Immediate window to determine how many properties each of the fields in the tblSales table have. Why do some have more properties than others?

3. In this chapter, we used the BuildResultsTable procedure to build up the tblResults table from a given SQL string. We built the table by running a make-table query. See if you can rewrite the BuildResultsTable procedure to build the table using the Data Access Object hierarchy instead. Once the table has been built using DAO, the procedure should populate it with an append query, for example:

```
INSERT INTO tblResults SELECT SalesID FROM …
```

4. Next (if you are feeling really brave) see if you can modify the BuildResultsTable function so that it has more flexibility. Change the function so that the declaration looks like this:

```
Function BuildResultsTable(sSQL As String, _
                    sTableName As String, _
                    lRecordsAffected As Long, _
                    Optional vIndexed As Variant, _
                    Optional vMethod As Variant)
```

The function arguments we want you to use are described below:

This argument...	does this...
SSQL	supplies the SQL statement which was built up from the selections made on the criteria selection form.
sTableName	supplies the name for the table to be created.
lRecordsAffected	is used to return a long integer signifying the number of records placed into the new table.
vIndexed	is used to indicate whether the new table should be indexed on the SalesID field. If this argument is not supplied, the field will not be indexed.
vMethod	is used to specify what method will be used to build the new table. If this argumentis not supplied, the table will be created using a make-table query. The alternative is to use DAO which you should have completed in the previous exercise.

5. Finally, see if you can modify the application so that it informs the user how many records met the criteria and asks whether the frmSales form should be displayed. Use this for the cmdFind_Click procedure on the criteria form and then put the required functionality into the DisplayResults procedure.

External Data

The main reason for owning a database is obviously to store data. So far, you've seen a lot about manipulating data within Access using VBA. But in business, you'll often have data in a variety of formats: text files, spreadsheets, and so on. When you're designing new business applications in Access you might need a way to get this data into and out of Access, so that you can incorporate it into your application.

Access has a very good wizard for importing data, but you might want data imports to be something that users can run, and you probably don't want them to have the (potentially dangerous) freedom of running the wizard. So what we're going to cover in this chapter is how to bypass that wizard (however nice it might be), and move data in and out of Access with code. That way it's you who are in control of the import and export process, and not the user.

In particular we shall be looking at:

- ❑ Importing and exporting data to other applications
- ❑ Importing and exporting data to text files, both in a fixed format, and a CSV (Comma Separated Values) format
- ❑ Sending data via electronic mail
- ❑ Using data that is stored in other databases

We're not going to be looking at exporting data to Web pages here, because we'll be covering that in a later chapter.

Other Applications

As mentioned briefly in chapter 1, the world today is full of data, and not all of it is stored in databases. Daily we have to deal with text files, spreadsheets, mail systems, and so on, and it never seems to stop. We as programmers would like it if our bosses (and every one else's too, come to think of it) just junked all those old machines and applications, and brought us heaving and groaning into the 21st century. However nice an idea that is, it seems unlikely to happen, especially considering that by the time you've upgraded the whole office, the first machine you bought is now out of date.

So we're stuck with our own old applications, and other people's, too. These applications may hold their data in a different format. This isn't a bad thing, as Access has built-in support for the most common data formats.

Databases

You've already seen that there are different versions of Access, and there are many more databases around than you'd realize. Transferring between databases and Access is pretty straight forward, because we can do it with one simple command – the TransferDatabase method of the DoCmd object:

DoCmd.TransferDatabase [*TransferType*], *DatabaseType*, *DatabaseName*,
**   [*ObjectType*], *Source*, *Destination*, [*StructureOnly*], [*SaveLoginID*]**

This is quite simple to use. For example, to export our ice cream details to a database called Prices, we could use this:

```
DoCmd.TransferDatabase acExport, "Microsoft Access", _
    "C:\IceCream\Prices.mdb", acTable, "tblIceCream", "tblIceCream"
```

This says the following:

- ❑ The TransferType is acExport, so we are exporting something.

- ❑ The DatabaseType is "Microsoft Access", because we are transferring to another Access database.

- ❑ The DatabaseName is "C:\IceCream\Prices.mdb", which is the database where the data is being transferred to.

- ❑ The ObjectType is acTable, to indicate we are exporting a table.

- ❑ The Source is "tblIceCream", which is the name of the table in our current database.

- ❑ The Destination is "tblIceCream", which is the name the table will take when it's in the new database. If this table already exists it will be overwritten.

When you use this method you need to make sure that both the directory and the target database exist, otherwise an error will be generated.

Importing some data would be just as simple:

```
DoCmd.TransferDatabase acImport, "Microsoft Access", _
    "C:\IceCream\Prices.mdb", acTable, "tblIceCream", "tblIceCream"
```

Here the difference is the TransferType argument, which in this case is acImport. This tells Access that we are going to import data. Notice that nothing else has changed. The DatabaseName stays the same, but since we are now importing, it becomes the source of the data, and the current database becomes the destination. That's an important point, because it shows that the DatabaseName argument changes its role depending on which way the data is going.

Since there are several options for these arguments, let's have a look at them in detail:

Argument	Description

TransferType	The action to be performed. It must be one of:
	      acImport, to import data
	      acExport, to export data
	      acLink, to link data
	 If you leave this blank, the default of acImport is used.

DatabaseType	The type of database that you wish to transfer from or to. It must be one of: Microsoft Access Jet 2.x Jet 3.x dBase III dBase IV dBase 5 Paradox 3.x Paradox 4.x Paradox 5.x Paradox 7.x ODBC Databases
DatabaseName	The full name of the database to import from or export to. This must include the path, and if exporting, this must already exist.
ObjectType	The type of object to be exported. it must be one of: acTable acQuery acForm acReport acMacro acModule acDataAccessPage acServerView acDiagram acStoredProcedure
Source	The name of the object that is supplying the data.
Destination	The name of the object once it is transferred.
StructureOnly	You should set this to True to indicate that only the structure of the object should be transferred, and set it to False (which is the default) to transfer the structure and the data. This allows you to just copy table details without copying the data.
SaveLoginID	You should set this to True if you are connecting to an ODBC database and wish the user details to be saved with the connection. That way if you connect to the same source, you won't have to enter the user details again. Setting this to False (which is the default) ensures that each time you connect to an ODBC database you have to supply the user details.

Try It Out – Exporting to a Database

1. Close any databases you have open and select <u>N</u>ew... from the <u>F</u>ile menu.

2. From the **General** tab pick **Database**. Name the new database `Sales` and place it in the same directory as your other databases from the book.

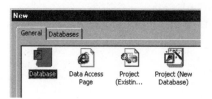

3. Now close this database and switch back to `IceCream.mdb`.

4. Create a new form, not based on a table or query, and put a command button on it. Call this button `cmdSales` and give it a suitable caption:

5. In the `Click` event for this button place the following code (remember you can create this event procedure by clicking the right mouse button and selecting the **Build Event** option from the menu that appears):

```
DoCmd.TransferDatabase acExport, "Microsoft Access", _
    "C:\BegVBA\Sales.mdb", acTable, "tblSales", "IceCreamSales"
MsgBox "Sales data exported"
```

Note that this assumes C:\BegVBA is your database directory. If your databases are elsewhere then change this directory name.

6. Switch back to Access, run the form, and press the button to export the data.

7. When the message box pops up, you can close this database. Don't forget to save your changes – save the form as `frmImportExport`.

8. Open up the Sales database (`Sales.mdb`) and have a look at the new table that you've just created. Notice that you get two errors when you open the table, both looking something like this:

This is because the fields `fkCompanyID` and `fkIceCreamID` are Lookup Fields, and get their values from other tables – the company table and the ice cream table. Since we've not transferred these tables we get an error when trying to open the table. You can get rid of the error by opening the table in design view, selecting the field, then deleting the contents of the Row Source property (on the Lookup tab).

9. Click on the OK button on the error dialogs and the table should open:

SalesID	fkCompanyID	fkIceCreamID	Quantity	Date
1	6	10	10	
2	4	10	11	
4	9	8	11	
5	10	9	1	
7	9	9	11	
8	10	10	1	
10	9	10	11	
11	10	11	1	
12	11	2	9	
13	9	10	11	

IceCreamSales : Table   Record: 1 of 509

There's one really important thing to notice here, and that's the lookup fields, `fkCompanyID` and `fkIceCreamID`. In our working database these show as combo boxes, with a list of values from other tables, but in this database these just appear as numbers. This is precisely because they are foreign key fields, which means that they link this table to other tables. When Access has all three tables in the database it knows what the links between them are, so it can show the names instead of the actual IDs. Since we've only transferred one table, only the IDs can be shown.

Exporting Foreign Keys

If you need to export the data from related tables, rather than their keys, you can use a Make Table query, and then specify the Sales database as the destination database:

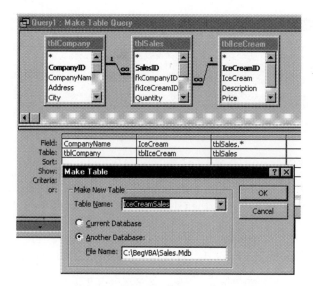

Spreadsheets

Transferring to spreadsheets is far more common than transferring to databases. Access is really good at reporting, but most people who need to analyze figures are more familiar with spreadsheets. Things like Pivot Tables and Charting are very simple in Excel, and although you can use them in Access, some people are more familiar with the Excel environment. You probably won't be surprised to learn that there's a TransferSpreadsheet command:

```
DoCmd.TransferSpreadsheet [TransferType], [SpreadsheetType],
    TableName, FileName, [HasFieldNames], [Range]
```

You can probably piece together how it works, but let's have a look at the arguments:

Argument	Description
TransferType	The action to be performed. It must be one of: acImport, to import data acExport, to export data acLink, to link data If you leave this blank, the default of acImport is used.
Spreadsheet Type	The type of spreadsheet you wish to transfer to, or import from. It must be one of: *acSpreadsheetTypeExcel3* *acSpreadsheetTypeExcel4* *acSpreadsheetTypeExcel5* *acSpreadsheetTypeExcel7* *acSpreadsheetTypeExcel8* *acSpreadsheetTypeExcel9* *acSpreadsheetTypeLotusWK1* *acSpreadsheetTypeLotusWK3* *acSpreadsheetTypeLotusWK4* *acSpreadsheetTypeLotusWJ2* If you leave this blank, the default is *acSpreadsheetTypeExcel8*.
TableName	The table name that the data should be imported into, or linked into; or a table name or query that is the source of the data to export from or link from.
FileName	The full name of the spreadsheet, including the path.
HasFieldNames	When importing or linking, you can set this to True if the source of the data has field names as the first row. The default of False is taken if you leave this argument empty, which assumes that the first row contains data.
Range	A valid range of cells, or the name of a range, in the spreadsheet. You cannot supply a range when exporting.

If you are exporting to an existing workbook, then the data is created in the next available worksheet.

Try It Out – Exporting to a Spreadsheet

1. Back in IceCream.mdb, open up frmImportExport in design mode.

2. Add another button, call it cmdSalesSheet, and give it a caption of **Sales Spreadsheet**.

3. In the `Click` event for this button, add the following code:

```
DoCmd.TransferSpreadsheet acExport, acSpreadsheetTypeExcel9, _
    "tblSales", "C:\BegVBA\Sales.xls"
MsgBox "Sales spreadsheet created"
```

4. Back in Access, switch the form into Form mode and click the new button. When the data has been exported you'll have a spreadsheet in the specified location. You'll have to open it up to see it, though.

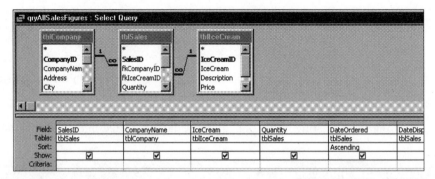

5. Notice this still suffers from the problem with the ID fields, but this time we **can** cure it with a query.

6. Back in Access create a new query, adding the `tblCompany`, `tblSales` and `tblIceCream` tables. You need to add all of the fields from the sales table to the query (except for `fkCompanyID` and `fkIceCreamID`, as these are just the ID numbers, and not the names). Instead of these two fields add `CompanyName` from `tblCompany` and `IceCream` from `tblIceCream`. Your query should now look like this:

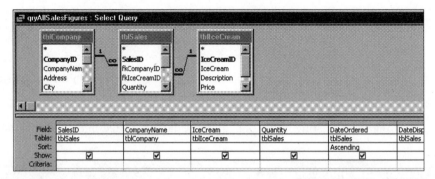

This just links the three tables together, and instead of outputting the company and ice cream ID fields, it outputs their names. You should also add a sort on the `DateOrdered` field. Save the query as `qryAllSalesFigures`.

7. Now in the code for the command button, change `tblSales` to `qryAllSalesFigures`. The code should now be:

```
DoCmd.TransferSpreadsheet acExport, acSpreadsheetTypeExcel9, _
    "qryAllSalesFigures", "C:\BegVBA\Sales.xls"
```

8. Now switch back to Access. Click that button again, and have another look at the spreadsheet:

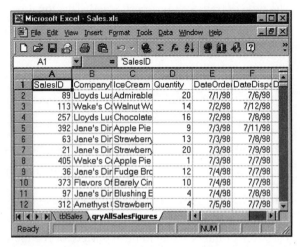

This is much better, as we can now see exactly which company and product each order relates to.

Later in the book we'll show you other ways of transferring data to Excel. Now, though, we're going to look at importing and exporting simple text files.

Text Files

Importing and exporting to text files is quite common, because this is really the one method that nearly all systems support. There are two types of text files that you might have to deal with:

- ❑ **Fixed width**, where the columns of data are aligned to a specific width. With this format you have to know in advance how wide each column is.

- ❑ **Comma Separated Values (CSV)**, (also known as **delimited** text files), where the columns are not aligned, but placed next to each other. Each column is separated from the next by a special character. Traditionally this separator character is a comma, so if you're using something else you'll need to tell Access what it is.

Whichever file type you use, you use the `TransferText` command:

```
DoCmd.TransferText [TransferType], [SpecificationName],
   TableName, FileName, [HasFieldNames],
   [HTMLTableName], [CodePage]
```

The arguments are fairly obvious, but let's look at them anyway:

Argument	Desciption
TransferType	The type of transfer to be performed. This must be one of: acExportDelim acExportFixed acExportHTML acExportMerge acImportDelim acImportFixed acImportHTML acLinkDelim acLinkFixed acLinkHTML If you leave this blank, the default of acImportDelim is used.
SpecificationName	The name of the specification. This is required for fixed-width transfers, but isn't always necessary for CSV files. If you are using a CSV file and leave this out then the default values are used. We'll look at specifications next.
TableName	The table or query name to be exported, or the table name to import or link.
FileName	The full name, including the path, of the file to export to or import or link from.
HasFieldNames	When importing or linking, you can set this to True if the source of the data has field names as the first row. The default of False is taken if you leave this argument empty, which assumes that the first row contains data.
HTMLTableName	The name of the table or list in the HTML document that you wish to import or link from. This is determined by the <CAPTION> tag, or by the <TITLE> tag. This argument is ignored unless acImportHTML or acLinkHTML are being used.
CodePage	A number that indicates the character set of the text file.

Specifications

When dealing with fixed-width files, or with CSV files with a separator other than a comma, you need to create a specification to tell Access how the text file is structured. This could have all been set by arguments in the `TransferText` method, but then it would have many more arguments and would be far harder to read. To make things easier, you can create a Specification including all of these details. In early versions of Access this had its own menu item, but now it's buried within the import/export area, in a very unfriendly manner. Here's how to do it:

Try It Out – Creating Specifications

1. Make sure you are in the Tables view of the database window, and select tblCompany.

2. From the File menu select Export....

3. On the Export dialog, select Text Files in the Save as type combo box at the bottom of the screen:

Don't worry about the file name, since you're not actually going to export anything, (although if the name in here already exists you will be asked if you want to overwrite it).

4. Click the Save button. This will start the Export Text Wizard. *Don't run through any of the wizard.*

5. Click the Advanced button. This will show the specification box:

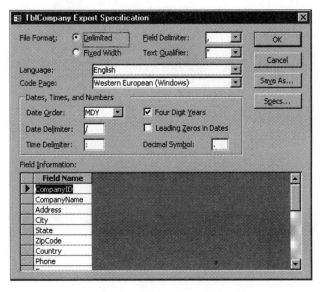

6. The above picture shows the view for CSV files. The two important items here are the Field Delimiter and Text Qualifier.

By way of explanation, look at this example text file:

```
1,"Fran and Nick's Fruit and Nuts","37 Walnut Grove
Nutbush","Tennessee","38053","USA","(423) 935 9032","(423) 935 9001",,,,1
2,"Candy's Cones","26 Wafer Street
Redwood City","California","94056","USA","(650) 456 3298","(650) 456 3201",,,,1
```

The Field Delimiter is what the fields will be separated by (it's usually a comma, as it is here). The Text Qualifier is what is placed around text fields, and is usually double quotation marks. Anything within these marks is treated as a single field. This means that a field can contain the field delimiter character without causing confusion. For example, if one of our address fields contained a comma, enclosing the field in quotes would mean that the comma in the field wasn't treated as the end of the field.

7. Save this specification by clicking the Save As... button. Give it a name of CompanyDelimited.

8. Now change from a delimited file format to a fixed width format, by selecting the appropriate radio button for the File Format at the top of the screen. Notice that the Field Information section has changed to show the start and width of each column:

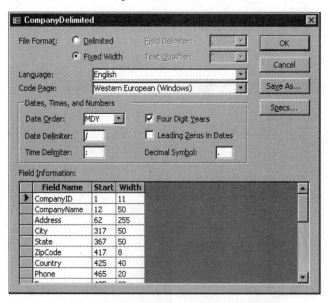

9. Click the Save As... button once more, and save this as CompanyFixed, in the BegVBA directory that you've previously used.

10. Press the OK button to return to the Export Text Wizard, and then click on Cancel to close it. This returns you to the database window.

So those are the two types of specification. Let's have a look and see what sort of results we get when importing and exporting data with them.

Try It Out – Export to a Fixed Width File

1. Open up `frmImportExport` in design view.

2. Add another button, calling it `cmdExportFixed`, and give it a caption of Export Company Fixed.

3. In the `Click` event of the button, add the following code:

```
DoCmd.TransferText acExportFixed, "CompanyFixed", "tblCompany", _
    "C:\BegVBA\CompanyFixed.txt", True
MsgBox "Company details exported"
```

4. Flip back to Access, switch the form into Form view, and click the Export Company Fixed button.

5. When the export has finished, take a look at the file it's created:

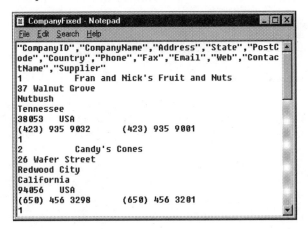

It doesn't look very nice, but that's only because it's wrapping over lines. Notice that the first column, CompanyID, is 11 characters wide, as laid out in the specification. Also note that the second column contains no quotes around it, even though it's a text field. That's because we've specified the length of the field, so there's no need to contain text fields in quotes.

You'll also notice something very odd here. Our line of code set the `HasFieldNames` argument to `True`, and you can see that the first line it has generated does indeed contain the field names. But (and this is the weird part), the fixed width format isn't used for these field names. We can only assume that the rationale behind this is that the field names themselves don't really fit as part of the specification, and so are output in the CSV default format.

Try It Out – Importing from a Fixed Width File

1. In Access, create a new button on our import and export form. Call this one `cmdImportFixed`, and caption it Import Company Fixed.

2. Add the following code to the `Click` event:

```
DoCmd.TransferText acImportFixed, "CompanyFixed", "tblCompanyFixed", _
     "C:\BegVBA\CompanyFixed.txt", True
MsgBox "Company details imported"
```

3. Flip back to Access, switch the form into Form mode and press the new import button. This will import the file you've just exported into a new table.

If you look at the list of Tables you'll see two new ones – tblCompanyFixed and CompanyFixed_ImportErrors. The first is the new table you imported, and the second is automatically created by Access because there were some import errors. If you open the errors table, you'll see what the problem is:

Error	Field	Row
Type Conversion Failure	CompanyID	7

Yeah, right. That's really useful. What this means is that Access has tried to add some data from the text file into the CompanyID field, but it was not the correct format. But hold on. Hasn't Access just exported this data – how can it be wrong? The answer lies in the record for Flavors Of The World:

7	Flavors Of The World	23 Eastcote Lane Clapham	London
8	Lloyds Luscious Lollies	18 20 Alverstan Road	London

Notice that the address field appears on two lines – it has a carriage return character in it. This isn't a problem in Access, but think about how the text file handles this – the carriage return indicates a new line. With fixed width text files, the import routine assumes that each new line is a new record. So when it imports this text file you get an error, as it is expecting a number (the CompanyID) at the beginning of the line, not part of the address. That's why we've got a Type Conversion Failure – Access is trying to convert a string into a number. If you open the newly imported table, tblCompanyFixed, you'll see what Access has done:

CompanyID	CompanyNam	Address	City	State	ZipCode	Country	
			S		+4	76 2232	
1	Fran and Nick's	37 Walnut Grov	Nutbush	Tennessee	38053	USA	(
2	Candy's Cones	26 Wafer Street	Redwood City	California	94056	USA	(
3	Dave's Dairy Pro	20 Milk Street	Boston	Massachusetts	02119	USA	(
4	Eyshood Cocoa	14 Bournville St	Birmingham	Alabama	35210	USA	(
6	Amethyst Group	42 Melville Stre	Edinburgh	Midlothian	EH3 7HA	SCOTLAND	+
7	Flavors Of The \	23 Eastcote Lar					
8	Lloyds Luscious	18-20 Alverston				Godalmin	
10	Jane's Diner	1827 East 1st A	Denver	CO	80206	USA	3
11	Wake's Cakes /	72 High Street	Birmingham		B27 2AA	UK	+

Notice that there is a record at the top without a `CompanyID` field – this is the extra record caused by the carriage return in the address field. The record for **Flavors Of The World** has incorrect information for its address fields, as does the record for **Lloyds Luscious Lollies**. That's because the record count is now incorrect and Access has difficulty catching up.

This is pretty disastrous, as it might mean a lot of data becomes corrupted. The way to solve this problem is to use delimited files with a text qualifier, as these import and export correctly. That's because the text qualifier marks the start and the end of a text field, so the carriage return is taken to be part of the field because it is within the quotes.

Try It Out – Export to a Comma Separated File

1. Add another button to your form. Call it `cmdExportSeparated` and caption it **Export Company Separated**.

2. Add the following code to the `Click` event for this button:

```
DoCmd.TransferText acExportDelim, "CompanyDelimited", "tblCompany", _
    "C:\BegVBA\CompanyDelimited.txt", True
MsgBox "Company details exported"
```

3. Back in Access, click this button.

4. When done, have a look at the file it's produced:

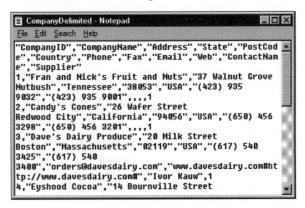

As you can see, now everything is in the same format as the header line. The comma is used to delimit the fields, and quotes are used around all text fields.

1. OK, add the last in our little line of buttons. This time call it `cmdImportDelimited` and caption it Import Company Delimited.

2. Add the following code to the `Click` event:

```
DoCmd.TransferText acImportDelim, "CompanyDelimited", "tblCompanyDelimited", _
      "C:\BegVBA\CompanyDelimited.txt", True
MsgBox "Company details imported"
```

3. Now, back in Access, click this button.

4. When it's done, have a look at the database window:

You now have a new table, containing exactly the same details as the company table. Although we used the standard layout with a comma, just changing the specification can let us easily use other characters. (In fact, because we used the default values, we could have quite easily omitted the specification).

Electronic Mail

Electronic mail is ubiquitous nowadays. Everyone has an email account. OK, that's a slight exaggeration. My Mom doesn't have email yet. Or even a computer, actually. My brother builds electrical things. I program them. And Mom looks on in that way that only parents can, saying 'Yes dear, very nice. Pour me another gin, would you please?'

Not only has email brought the world closer, it has opened up lines of communication. No longer do you have to print off a twenty-page report and fax it to your office in Outer Elbonia, only to find out they've run out of fax paper. You can simply pick names from an electronic address book, and with a single click your report is on its way. Having data quicker means decisions can be made in a more timely fashion. Let's face it, it's just less effort all around.

The email facilities in Access are not specific to any email software. I'll show you samples with Microsoft Outlook, because that's what I use, but other packages should work just as well.

To send email you use the SendObject method:

```
DoCmd.SendObject [ObjectType], [ObjectName], [OutputFormat],
    [To], [CC], [BCC], [Subject],
    [MessageText], [EditMessage], [TemplateFile]
```

You can probably guess what some of these arguments are, but let's look at them in more detail:

Argument	Description
ObjectType	The type of object you wish to send. It must be one of: acSendDataAccessPage acSendForm acSendModule acSendNoObject acSendQuery acSendReport acSendTable If this argument is omitted, acSendNoObject is used, which just sends mail, without attaching any objects.
ObjectName	The name of the object you wish to send.
OutputFormat	The format the object is to be sent in. It must be one of: acFormatDAP acFormatHTML acFormatRTF acFormatTXT acFormatXLS You will be prompted for a format if you leave this argument blank.
To	The recipient name, or list of recipient names, to whom the mail should be sent. You will be prompted for names if you leave this argument blank. To include multiple recipients, you just separate their names by a semi-colon. This name should be a valid address book entry, or the actual email address.
CC	The recipient name, or list of recipient names, to whom the mail should be CC'd.
BCC	The recipient name, or list of recipient names, to whom the mail should be BCC'd.
Subject	The text that comprises the Subject line of the message.
MessageText	The text that comprises the main body of the message.
EditMessage	Set this to True, which is the default, to open your mail application and allow editing of the message before it's sent. Set this to False to send the message straight away.
TemplateFile	The full name (including the path), of an HTML template file, to be used when sending HTML files.

Let's see this in action.

> It's important to note that the following code will only work if you have an email
> program installed on your computer. You don't actually have to have it connected
> to anything, as long as it is installed and setup to send mail. While writing this, I
> installed Outlook 2000 and set up a profile, even though I didn't have email on
> the test machine. Just follow the installation instructions for installing Outlook,
> and then follow the wizard to set up a service provider. It doesn't matter what
> you put into the wizard fields, because you're not actually going to be sending
> mail anyway.

Try It Out – Sending Mail

1. Open the import and export form in design view and add another button. Name this
    `cmdEmailPriceList`, and caption it **Email Price List**.

2. Add the following code to the `Click` event:

```
DoCmd.SendObject acSendTable, "tblIceCream", acFormatXLS, _
    "Janine Lloyd", "Karen Wake; Jane Donnelly", _
    "IceCreamLover@wrox.com", "Latest Prices", _
    "Hot off the press - our latest price list."
```

If you want to really send mail, you should change the names here to some of your own
contacts.

3. Back in Access, switch to Form view and press the email button. Since we left out the
    `EditMessage` argument, the default is to show the message before sending:

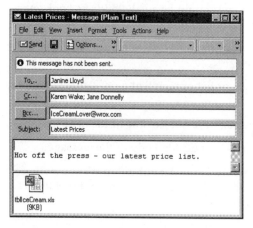

Notice how the names in the three address fields match those in our code. Also notice that because we specified `acFormatXLS` the table has been turned into an Excel spreadsheet before being attached to the mail message. If we had set the `EditMessage` argument to `False` the message would have been delivered without any user interaction. It's a simple as that. You'll be seeing other ways to send mail in a later chapter.

> **NOTE: It's important to realize that your application could actually send mail without the user being aware of it. You may consider this a security risk.**

Using External Data

So far in this chapter we've looked at how to get data into and out of Access, but we haven't addressed the point that imported data isn't live. In other words, when you import a set of data you'll be unaware of any subsequent changes that are made. In order to get access to live data, you have to **link** objects into Access as tables. They look like tables, they act like tables... heck, they even smell like tables. But in fact, they are really just a pointer back to the original data.

Let's assume you have two Access databases and a spreadsheet. One of the databases is yours, with the product descriptions stored in it. One is the Sales department's, with sales figures for the products. The spreadsheet comes from Accounts, and contains prices. You want to produce a query showing all three together. What you can do is link these external sources of data into Access, and once linked, they can be used as though they were normal tables. Have a look at this diagram:

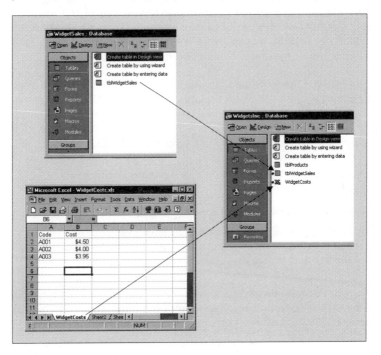

Here we see the sales database at the top and the costs spreadsheet at the bottom, both of which are linked into the main database. You can see that **WidgetCosts** is a spreadsheet because of its icon, and opening it makes it behave just like an Access table:

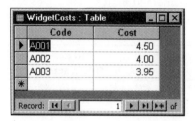

So this technique allows you to link into Access a variety of other objects. This is pretty important, because it allows you to use data that might not be yours to control. Other departments, for example, might not want you to control the data, even if they do let you access it.

The Database Splitter

One quite useful advantage of this linking is the ability to split your database into two without damaging it. There's actually an Add-In supplied called the Database Splitter. We're not going to run through this here, but it is worth mentioning why it's a good idea.

Let's take a typical business scenario. You've just developed a database for use in your department. You've spent months developing it, and have finally rolled it out. It's stored on your central server, so there's only one copy, and everyone has been using it – the data has started to accumulate quite rapidly. It's been a few weeks, and then your boss comes to you and says 'I want you to add this feature. By tomorrow.' Great. Now you've got to stop everyone from using the database, because you have to make the changes on the master, since it's the one with all of the data. They all complain, and you're now under pressure. Not a good way to work.

But, what if you've got two databases? One with all of the tables, and one with everything else – forms, queries, reports, and so on, with the actual data tables just linked from the other database. You can quite happily make changes to the forms database without affecting the data.

In fact, when redeveloping your front end, you can have three databases:

- ❑ The Data database. This is the one whose structure almost never changes.

- ❑ The Live forms database. This is the one the users use.

- ❑ A Test database, which is a copy of the Live database. You can make your changes to forms, etc., without affecting the users. You can test against the live data if necessary, just by linking in the tables.

In this situation, once you've made the changes to the test database, you can just copy it onto the server, overwriting the Live forms database. The tables are linked, so no data is lost. The users will only have a few moments delay while you perform the copy, and then they have the new changes.

This sort of scenario is used quite often. Many companies start using Access as their main development tool, and then grow beyond its capabilities. So they move their data into a bigger database, such as SQL Server, but leave the front end, the forms, in Access, and link the tables from SQL Server. This way the only cost, both in terms of time and resources, is the movement of the data, not the redevelopment of the whole application. This is one of the reasons why Access now has the ability to work with the MSDE and SQL Server in a much more integrated way.

Linked Tables

Since we've talked about linked tables, it's about time to give them a try. Let's use the `Sales.xls` spreadsheet we created earlier. If you've deleted it, you can simply recreate it from the import and export form.

Try It Out – Linking a Spreadsheet

1. Open `frmImportExport` in design view and add another button. Call it `cmdLink` and give it a caption of **Link Spreadsheet**.

2. In the `Click` event, add the following code:

```
DoCmd.TransferSpreadsheet acLink, acSpreadsheetTypeExcel9, _
      "SalesFigures", "C:\BegVBA\Sales.XLS", True
MsgBox "Spreadsheet linked"
```

3. Go back to the form and, in Form mode, click the new button.

4. Then, have a look at the database window:

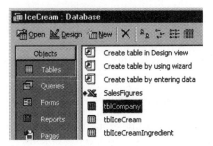

Notice the new table, the icon to indicate its source, and the arrow, to indicate it's a linked table. There are a few things you can't do (such as deleting data), but otherwise this behaves exactly like a normal table. If you change data, you are actually changing the spreadsheet. There's only one copy, and you've just got a link to it.

You can delete the link anytime you want, and it doesn't delete the original spreadsheet. All it does is delete the link. It's a bit like shortcuts in Windows – if you delete the shortcut, you don't delete the file it points to.

This technique is quite useful as it allows you to have a copy of the data on a central server, but it allows users to have a copy of the front-end database on their local machines. This would mean that it's quicker to open the database because it's stored locally. In fact, one often-used technique is to store some tables locally as well. These would be tables that change very rarely, or not at all. So the only data stored centrally is the data that changes frequently.

Differences between Linked and Local Tables

Linked tables have several advantages over local ones:

- ❑ You can store the data in its most appropriate location. For example, if the data is supplied by the finance department, and they are happier working in Excel than in Access, you can let them work in Excel. Linking the spreadsheet into Access lets you use the data as if it was an Access table.

- ❑ Linking tables allows you to access data you don't own, but need to use. This is especially true as companies start using data more for decision making.

- ❑ They allow you to separate your data from your user interface, allowing easier maintenance.

There are, however, certain drawbacks of linked tables:

- ❑ Linked tables aren't part of your database, so the records have to be retrieved from another file. This could lead to speed problems if the source of the data is on another machine on the network.

- ❑ Linked tables must be opened as dynaset or snapshot-type recordsets, and they therefore don't support the Seek method.

- ❑ You must be careful when joining tables from different places, such as one local table and one remote table, as the field type may not be completely compatible. Jet 4 has reduced the possibility of incompatibilities, but you should just be aware that this could be a problem.

- ❑ You should be careful when joining large remote tables to small local tables. If both tables are local Access can optimize the join, but if the large table is linked, all of the data must be brought across the link before the join can take place. This can lead to speed problems.

Don't let the above put you off linking tables, or even trying the database splitter with its back end/front end approach. This is the first step towards client/server systems, and can bring some big benefits.

Summary

In this chapter we've concerned ourselves purely with data from outside of the current database – what it is, where it is, and how to use it. We've looked at how we can use data from other sources, as well as supplying data to other sources. This is quite a common request, and you've seen that the programming required for this is fairly simple.

In particular we've looked at:

❑ How to import and export text files, spreadsheets, and database objects

❑ How to send electronic mail, incorporating data from Access

❑ How to use other data sources, whilst keeping the original source of the data

Now that we've got all of this data into Access, it's about time to see how reports can make it easier for us to view it.

Exercises

1. Use the Database Splitter to create a back-end and front-end database. Are there any changes you need to make to the front-end to make sure that it still works correctly?

2. If you are connected to a mail system, create a form to allow users to fill in Bug Reports and Enhancement Requests, and use the SendObject method to let the user send them to you.

Reports

The reporting facility is one of the best features of Access, and even though this is a VBA book, there are certain areas of reports that need covering. Reports, just like forms, can have code underneath them, and there are several events that you can use. You generally don't need much code on reports, but what little you do use can turn an ordinary report into a great report.

In particular we will be looking at:

- ❑ How to use expressions on reports
- ❑ Adding totals and summaries
- ❑ Events, and which ones to use

Starting Off

As we work through this chapter we're going to need a report to work on, so we're going to create a report that summarizes the sales data. We're not going to create this with the Report Wizard, because the wizard automatically does some of the things we want to do manually. That's not to say that you should never use the wizard, but if you work through some of the steps you'll understand what it does.

Try It Out – Creating the Query

1. This report is going to be based on a query, so create a new query, and add tblCompany and tblSales to it:

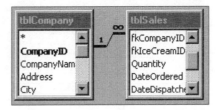

2. Click on the Totals button on the toolbar – that's the one that looks like this:

3. Select CompanyName from the company table and add it to the query. Now place the cursor in the empty Field box next to the CompanyName and type this:

```
MonthName: Format([DateOrdered], "mmmm")
```

4. Next, add Quantity to the query, as the third field. Place the cursor in the next empty Field box and type the following:

```
MonthNUmber: DatePart("m", [DateOrdered])
```

5. Now add some totaling and sorting. You need this setup:

Field	Total	Sort
CompanyName	Group By	Ascending
MonthName	Group By	
Quantity	Sum	
MonthNumber	Group By	Ascending

MonthName and Quantity should have empty Sort boxes.

6. Your query should now look like this:

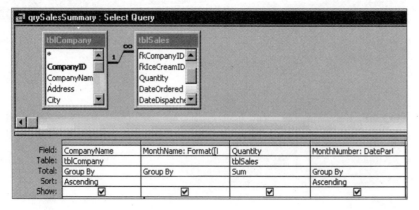

7. Save the query as `qrySalesSummary`.

8. Try out the query – you should have something that looks like this:

Company Name	MonthName	SumOfQuantity	MonthNumber
Amethyst Group	July	118	7
Amethyst Group	August	185	8
Amethyst Group	September	126	9
Amethyst Group	October	143	10
Amethyst Group	November	141	11
Amethyst Group	December	199	12
Eyshood Cocoa	August	11	8
Flavors Of The World	July	131	7
Flavors Of The World	August	163	8
Flavors Of The World	September	119	9
Flavors Of The World	October	132	10
Flavors Of The World	November	61	11
Flavors Of The World	December	162	12
Jane's Diner	July	148	7
Jane's Diner	August	100	8

Record: 1 of 37

How it Works

Let's just look at those bits of code we typed in, so you'll understand what's happening. In this report we want the company, the month of the order, and the total of the orders for that month, ordered by the company name and then the month. Ordering by the company name is not a problem since we can just sort on it, but the date is a bit of a problem. We want to show the full month name, but sort on the month number.

- ❑ So, the first field is the company name and we sort by that.

- ❑ The second field is the month name. We use the `Format` function to give us the full name of the month:

```
MonthName: Format([DateOrdered], "mmmm")
```

- ❑ The third field is the quantity, which will be the sum of sales for that month.

- ❑ The fourth field is the month number. Remember from an earlier chapter, where we looked at `DatePart` – using a format of `"m"` allows us to just get the month number of the order:

```
MonthNumber: DatePart("m", [DateOrdered])
```

Why do we need this? Well, what we want to show is the sum of the sales for each month, and we'd like the months to be shown in order. However, the month name is a string, and if we sort on the name we don't end up with the correct order, because strings are sorted in alphabetical order.

That means that February would come before January, which is not what we want. So we use another field, which is the number of the month, and we sort on that. This gives us the correct ordering.

So we end up with a correctly formatted query. OK, on to the report.

Try It Out – Creating the Report

1. Now we need to create a new report based on the above query. Don't use the Report Wizard, as we want to create this manually. Looking at the **Reports**, click the **New** button.

2. On the **New Report** dialog, select **Design View** from the list at the top, and select qrySalesSummary from the list at the bottom. This is the query the report will be based upon.

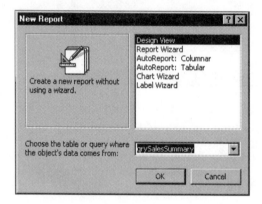

3. Press the **OK** button to create a blank report.

4. Click the **Sorting and Grouping** button. That's the one that looks like this:

5. Add CompanyName to the **Field/Expression** list, and set both the **Group Header** and **Group Footer** to Yes.

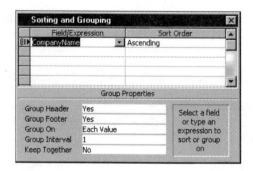

6. Add CompanyName and MonthNumber to the Field/Expression list. Close the Sorting and Grouping window once it looks the same as the one below:

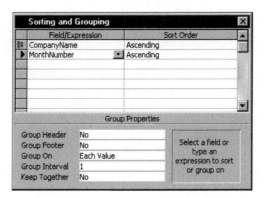

7. Now add the fields to the report. To see the fields select Field List from the View menu. You can just drag the fields from the list and drop them in the appropriate place on the report. You need the CompanyName in the CompanyName Header, and MonthName and SumOfQuantity in the Detail section. You can leave the CompanyName Footer and Page Footer blank for now. You might also like to remove the labels for the fields you've just added, so that the report doesn't look cluttered. You can also add a label in the Page Header to act as the report heading – the report should now look like this:

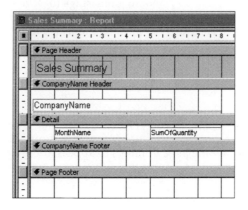

8. Save the report as Sales Summary. There's no need to close it, as we'll be using it straight away.

OK, that's the report set up. Let's look at what code we can now use on it.

Page Numbers

The report wizard automatically puts page numbers onto reports, and you can put them in yourself in design mode (you can simply add them from the Insert menu), but let's add them manually so you can see what these other methods actually do.

Try It Out – Page Numbers

1. In the page footer add a new text box. Place it at the right of the page.

2. Add the following code into the Control Source property for the new text box:

```
= "Page " & [Page] & " of " & [Pages]
```

3. Delete the label for this text box, as we won't need that.

4. Switch the report to Preview mode and have a look at the bottom of the page.

How it Works

This is really simple. You know that we use the & symbol to join strings together in expressions. Well, Page and Pages are predefined fields within any report, and identify the current page number and the total number of pages. We enclose them in square brackets to tell Access that these are fields and not strings.

IIf

We mentioned IIf earlier in the book, and warned you of its dangers (all of the arguments are run), but there are some times when it can be really useful. For example, suppose we want to print our report out double sided, and would like the page numbers to appear at the outer edge on both odd and even numbered pages. This means that for some pages it must be on the left, and for the others it must be on the right.

Let's give this a try.

Try It Out – The IIf Function

1. Switch the form back into design mode.

2. Move the page number field to the very left of the page, and set the text to be left aligned using the Align Left button on the toolbar.

3. Modify the **Control Source** property of the page number field, so it now looks like this:

```
=IIf([Page] Mod 2 = 0, "Page " & [Page] & " of " & [Pages], "")
```

4. Add another text box, this time at the right of the page. You can delete the label again.

5. Add the following code to this text box's **Control Source** property:

```
=IIf([Page] Mod 2 = 1, "Page " & [Page] & " of " & [Pages], "")
```

6. Now switch to preview mode to see what effect the changes have had. Step forward a few pages to see what happens for odd and even pages.

Notice that for the first page, and all odd numbered pages, the page numbers are on the right of the page. For all even numbers they are on the left.

How it Works

Let's look again at the arguments for the IIf function:

IIf (*Expression*, *TruePart*, *FalsePart*)

The arguments are:

- ❑ Expression, which is the expression to test.
- ❑ TruePart, which is the value to return if Expression is True.
- ❑ FalsePart, which is the value to return if Expression is False.

So, for the page numbers on the left we have this:

```
=IIf([Page] Mod 2 = 0, "Page " & [Page] & " of " & [Pages], "")
```

That means the Expression we are testing is:

```
[Page] Mod 2 = 0
```

This uses Mod to return the integer remainder of dividing the page number by two. This will be 0 if the page number is even, so the expression will only be True on even pages.

If Expression is True, then the TruePart of the IIf function:

```
"Page " & [Page] & " of " & [Pages]
```

is returned.

If Expression is False, then the FalsePart of the IIf function is returned, which is empty.

So this whole field will only show up on even numbered pages. The page number field for the odd numbered pages is pretty similar. The only difference is in the expression to test:

```
[Page] Mod 2 = 1
```

Here we check to see whether the page number is odd or not. If it is, then the same TruePart is returned.

This shows that with just one simple function you've made your report look much better than it did before.

You can find more about the Mod function in the help files.

Dates

You won't be surprised to learn that it's just as easy to put dates onto a report. This is particularly important, because there's no point in having a report if you're unsure as to how old it is. Ideally all reports should include the print date.

Try it Out – Adding the Print Date

1. Switch back into design view.

2. Add a new text box to the Page Header, at the right of the page. You can remove the label.

3. Make the background transparent by using the **Fill/Background Color** button on the toolbar, and align the text to the right.

4. Add the following to the **Control Source** property:

```
=Format(Now(), "Long Date")
```

5. Switch to Preview mode to see the result:

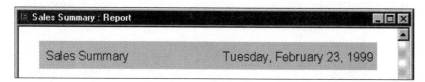

This simply uses one of the standard formatting functions shown earlier in the book. The function Now() just returns the current date and time.

Summarizing

One thing this report lacks is totals. Since we are showing sales figures on a month-by-month basis, we really ought to show totals for each company.

1. Switch the report back to design view.

2. Add a new field into the **CompanyName Footer**. Call it `txtCompanyTotal`.

3. Change the label of the new field to **Total**:

4. In the **Control Source** for the new field put the following:

```
=Sum([SumOfQuantity])
```

5. Switch to Preview mode:

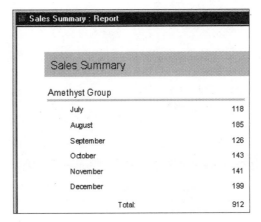

How it Works

You've seen the use of functions in fields, and `Sum` is just another function. When sum is used on a group footer, the argument you give it is the name of the field in the **Detail Section**. In our case this is `SumOfQuantity` – that's the field from the underlying query. All `Sum` does is sum up the values for the field in the **Detail Section**. It's as simple as that.

Expressions

You've already seen expressions in use in this chapter. Remember that an expression is just something that returns a value. So the following are all examples of expressions:

```
ccyTotal = ccyPrice * ccyQuantity
strName = strFirstName & " " & strLastName
strMonth = Format(datOrderDate, "mmmm")
```

So far you've seen expressions that use the page number, date, and the Sum function. With the latter this was placed in the section footer, and produced a total of records in the preceding detail section. You can also do this the other way round, by putting a field in the detail that references the total. For example, let's assume we'd like to see what percentage of a company's total sales occur in each month.

Try It Out – Expressions

1. Switch the form into design view.

2. Place a new text box on the form, in the detail section. Place it to the right of the SumOfQuantity field, and remove its label.

3. In the **Control Source** property put the following:

```
= [SumOfQuantity]/[txtCompanyTotal]
```

4. Change the **Format** property to Percent.

5. Now preview the form:

Sales Summary : Report

Sales Summary		11 December 1998
Amethyst Group		
July	118	12.94%
August	185	20.29%
September	126	13.82%
October	143	15.68%
November	141	15.46%
December	199	21.82%
Total:	912	

This just uses the total field we created earlier. So not only can you create new fields with expressions in them, but you can use those new fields in other expressions, too.

Events

The above examples simply illustrate using expressions and functions on your reports, but it's not really a large amount of VBA. What you might not realize is that reports also respond to events, just like forms. So opening and closing a report generates events, and you can add code to the events just as you would with a form. Just as forms have form modules behind them, reports have report modules. There's no real difference to the way the code is created or used. The only difference is the number of objects and events that are available in reports.

You can easily see which events are available by looking at the Events tab on the properties of the report:

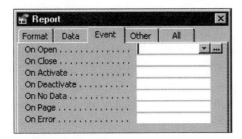

As you can see, the report has seven events. The header and footer sections have two events, as shown below:

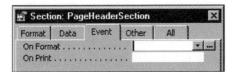

Group sections and the detail section have three events:

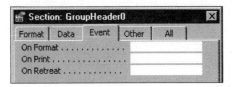

Let's look at all of these in a little more detail. We won't be building examples with these, but we're covering them in case you want to use them.

Open

The Open event is generated when a report is opened, before any printing takes place. There are several uses for this:

    ❑   On a report that takes a particularly long time to run, you could inform the user that they might have to wait a while, and offer them the option of not running it.

❏ In reports on sensitive information you could ask for a password before letting anyone run the report.

❏ You could open a form to allow filtering of the report data. You'll see an example of this later.

The Open event has one argument, Cancel, which is something you can set. It allows you to cancel the opening of the report from within code, and thus the report isn't previewed or printed. For example:

```
Private Sub Report_Open (Cancel As Integer)

        Dim blnResultintResult  As Integer
        Dim strWarning      As String

        strWarning = "This report may take some time." & _
              " I suggest you make a coffee, or perhaps do a little shopping!" & _
              " Or press Cancel to abort the operation."
        intResult = MsgBox (strWarning, vbOKCancel, "Warning")
        If intResult = vbCancel Then
              Cancel = True
        End If

End Sub
```

If you set the Cancel argument to true, then the report doesn't get opened.

Activate

The Activate event is generated when a report has been opened and becomes the active window. It will therefore occur after the Open event, and any time the report becomes the main window. You could use this to display a custom menu bar or toolbar:

```
Private Sub Report_Activate()

        DoCmd.ShowToolbar "AllOrders", acToolbarYes

End Sub
```

Deactivate

The Deactivate event is generated when a report stops being the active window, but before another Access window becomes active. This is an important point – it is not generated when another application becomes the active window, only when another Access window does. It can be used to reverse the actions of the Activate event. For example:

```
Private Sub Report_Deactivate()

        DoCmd.ShowToolbar "AllOrders", acToolbarNo

End Sub
```

Close

The Close event is generated when a report is closed and removed from the screen, and will occur after the Deactivate event. You could perhaps use this (or indeed the Open event) to log usage of reports, possibly for auditing purposes. Or if you've opened a filter form (which we'll be seeing shortly) during the Open event, you could close it here:

```
Private Sub Report_Close()

        DoCmd.Close acForm, "frmReportFilter", acSaveNo

End Sub
```

Error

The Error event is generated when an error occurs within the report. This includes database errors, but not VBA run-time errors. There are two arguments passed into this event:

- ❑ DataErr, which is the error number.
- ❑ Response, which is an output parameter which is used to determine how the error is reported.

Response can take one of two values:

- ❑ acDataErrContinue, which tells Access that the error should be ignored. This would be useful if you just want to log the error, and then continue silently without the user being aware of any problems.
- ❑ acDataErrDisplay, which tells Access to handle the error, so it shows the standard error details. This is the default value.

If you want to perform your own error logging, then some code like this would work:

```
Private Sub Report_Error(DataErr As Integer, Response As Integer)

        Response = acDataErrContinue
        LogError Me, DataErr

End Sub
```

This sets the response to indicate that Access should do nothing to handle the error, and then it calls a function called LogError (not included) to log the details.

Format

The Format event is generated when Access knows what data it is going to put in a section, but before the data is formatted. In previous versions of Access this tended to be used to display hidden fields. For example, at Rob and Dave's we try to flag these items:

- ❑ Those orders that were dispatched 6 or more days after the order date.

- ❑ Unpaid orders that are 35 or more days old.

There are two ways to highlight these orders:

Try It Out – Formatting with the Format Event

1. Open up the Sales By Supplier By Month report in design mode.

2. Add a new label to the detail section. Call it lblOverdue and give it a Caption of Payment Overdue. Place it over the Date Paid and Amount fields. It will only be visible for those orders where these fields are empty, so it will look OK.

3. Select the DateDispatched field and change the background color from Transparent to White.

4. Select on the gray Detail bar and view the properties.

5. Click the builder button for the On Format event.

6. In the event procedure add this code:

```
If IsNull(DatePaid) And (Date - DateOrdered) > 34 Then
        lblOverdue.Visible = True
Else
        lblOverdue.Visible = False
End If

If (DateDispatched - DateOrdered) > 5 Then
        DateDispatched.BackColor = vbRed
Else
        DateDispatched.BackColor = vbWhite
End If
```

7. Back in Access, switch the report into Preview mode:

Here you can see that the overdue warning only appears when the order is unpaid, and it is over 34 days old; also, the dispatched date is highlighted if we took more than 5 days to dispatch the order. It shows up gray on the printed page, but it's more visible on the screen.

How it Works

This code was added to the Format event for the Detail section, so it gets run for every row that appears in the detail section. Within this code we can refer to fields and set their properties just as we would on a form. So, in the first piece of code we check to see if the DatePaid is Null, meaning a payment hasn't been received. We also see if the difference between the current date (remember Date returns the current date) and the order date is greater than 34. If both of these are true, then we make the overdue label visible. If not true, then the label is hidden.

```
If IsNull(DatePaid) And (Date - DateOrdered) > 34 Then
        lblOverdue.Visible = True
Else
        lblOverdue.Visible = False
End If
```

In the second piece of code we work out the difference between the order date and dispatch date. If this difference is greater than 5 days we just make the background of the dispatch date red, and set it to white if the order was dispatched on time.

```
If (DateDispatched - DateOrdered) > 5 Then
        DateDispatched.BackColor = vbRed
Else
        DateDispatched.BackColor = vbWhite
End If
```

One thing to note about this is that you'll see the report running slower than it was without this code. That's simply because it runs this code for every line.

Conditional Formatting

Conditional formatting is a new feature of Access 2000 that allows you to apply formatting to a field depending upon certain conditions. Sounds very similar to what we've just done in code, doesn't it? However there are certain limitations, and it's not as flexible as the `Format` event. For example, you can't apply conditional formatting to a label, and you can only set the formatting of an object, not its visibility. However, white text on a white background is pretty hard to see, so you can get the same results.

Let's add some conditional formatting to the report to see how this works in comparison to the code method.

Try It Out – Conditional Formatting

1. Switch the form back into design view.

2. Add a new text box to the detail section, and remove its associated label. Place this field to the very left of the detail section, just to show it's different from our other overdue label. The name of the field isn't important.

3. Set the Control Source property of the text box to:

```
="Payment Overdue"
```

4. Set the Font/Fore Color to White.

5. With the text box selected, from the Format menu pick Conditional Formatting...

6. Set up the condition so that it looks like this:

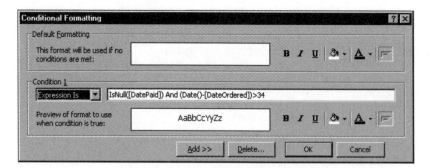

The important thing here is that the Font/Fore Color on this should be Black. So this field defaults to white text, and when the condition is true it becomes black. This emulates the visible/hidden idea we used earlier.

7. Press OK to close this dialog and switch the form into Preview mode:

Ordered		Sent	Ice Cream	Qty	Paid	AmountPaid
	8	7/7/98	Strawberry Cheescake	4	8/5/98	£60
Payment Overdue	8	7/10/98	Admirable Apricot	20		Payment Overdue
Payment Overdue	8	7/10/98	Strawberry Cheescake	6		Payment Overdue
	8	▮▮▮▮▮	Fudge Brownie	6	8/17/98	£60

Notice how the new overdue field follows the same rules as the old one. But notice how the Date Ordered field is being overwritten. That's because this new field is not transparent, but even if it were, the white text would still overwrite the field below it. This means you must make sure that this field is behind all other fields. You can do this from the Format menu, by selecting Send To Back.

8. Switch back to design view.

9. Select the DateOrdered field. We'll add the dispatched date formatting to this field just so you can see the difference between this method and the code method.

10. From the Format menu pick Conditional Formatting...

11. Set up the condition so that it looks like this:

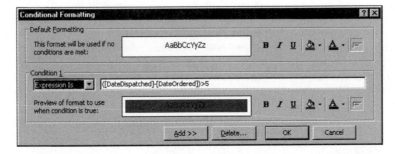

Here the back color is set to red if the condition is met.

12. Press OK to close this dialog and switch the form into Preview mode:

Ordered	Sent	Ice Cream	Qty	Paid	AmountPaid
7/5/98	7/7/98	Strawberry Cheescake	4	8/5/98	£60
Payment O 7/6/98	7/10/98	Admirable Apricot	20		Payment Overdue
Payment O 7/6/98	7/10/98	Strawberry Cheescake	6		Payment Overdue
▮▮▮▮ ▮▮▮▮		Fudge Brownie	6	8/17/98	£60

Of course, if we used this label instead of (and in the same place as) the VBA-formatted one, it would appear to behave similarly, as there wouldn't be any text for it to be masked by.

So there you have it. Two completely different ways to perform custom formatting on objects. Which is the best? It's really up to you. Use whichever method you feel more familiar with. The code method gives you more flexibility since you've got full control over the objects; the conditional formatting method is probably simpler, but here you've only got control of the formatting.

You might like to remove this new field and just stick with the coding method.

Cancel and FormatCount

When you were editing code for the format event you might have wondered about the arguments. The first, Cancel, you've seen before and works in the same way as the argument to the Open event. If you set this argument to True in the event procedure, then the section is not formatted. To be honest, I've never used this option.

FormatCount is a complex issue, and again one I've never used. But there might be conditions under which you need to use it. To understand this you must understand how formatting of report sections works. When Access formats a section it checks certain properties of the section, such as Force New Page, New Row or Col, or Keep Together. This last one is pretty important because if True, then the whole section should be kept together on a single page. This means that Access has to calculate how big the section will be, then see if that fits on the remainder of the current page. So, how does it know how big the section is going to be? Simple, it formats the section. If it doesn't fit on the remainder of the page, a new page is started, and the section is formatted again. So the FormatCount identifies how many times the formatting has been run.

This means that the code you put into the Format event could be run several times. Now if all you are doing is setting some formatting properties this doesn't matter too much, but this might be important if you are keeping totals from within code. For example, you might have declared a report-level variable, intTotalOrdersNDOT, and then be adding up some custom totals – perhaps keeping track of the number of orders that weren't delivered within the allocated time. If the format event were run twice, you'd end up counting some items twice. So you could do something like this:

```
If FormatCount = 1 Then
    If (DateDispatched - DateOrdered) > 5 Then
        intTotalOrdersNDOT = intTotalOrdersNDOT + 1
    End If
End If
```

This ensures that the totals are only calculated once.

Print

The Print event is generated after the section has been formatted, but before it is printed. You could use this to perform tasks that won't affect the layout of the report. In the above examples for the Format event we set properties on some fields, but these were contained within the section, and didn't cause the section to shrink or expand, so they could easily have been coded in the Print event.

The thing to watch out for in the Print event is that it is only executed for sections that are printed. So if you open a report in preview mode and then flip to the last page, the Print event is only generated for sections on the first and last pages. That means you should never use the Print event for calculating totals, since the calculations might not get run for the middle pages.

Like the Format event, the Print event has Cancel and PrintCount arguments, which behave in a similar fashion.

Retreat

The Retreat event is run in conjunction with the Format event. Remember how we said that formatting could occur several times? If a section doesn't fit on a page once it's been formatted, Access Retreats back through the section, and then formats the section on a new page. The Retreat event is triggered between the two formats, and allows you to undo anything, such as totals, that you might have performed while formatting.

NoData

The NoData event, as its name implies, is generated when there is no data on the report. This could happen perhaps if the report was generated according to some user defined selections, and indicates that there is no data in the underlying query. You could use this to display a custom error message rather than just displaying a blank report. For example:

```
Private Sub Report_NoData(Cancel As Integer)

        MsgBox ("No records matched your selection. Please try again.")
        Cancel = True

End Sub
```

The Cancel argument here behaves exactly like it does in the Open event, so setting it to True cancels the opening of the report. Setting it to False will open the report, but no records will be displayed.

The NoData event occurs after the Open event and before the Activate event.

Page

The Page event is triggered after a page is formatted, but before it is printed. You could use this to add graphics to a report as a whole, rather than just a section. For example, the following code draws a border around the whole report:

```
Me.Line(0,0) - (Me.ScaleWidth, Me.ScaleHeight),,B
```

This type of graphic is far more difficult to achieve by drawing it on the report in design view.

When To Use the Different Events

As the Format, Print and Retreat events are not used very often, deciding when to use which type of event can often be the hardest part of report design. Here are a few guidelines to help you:

Format

You should use this when your procedure could affect the layout of the page; for example, for making controls invisible. Access will actually lay out (format) the section after your procedure has run.

You could also use this in conjunction with a hidden section. If you need to perform some totaling for a section which is not visible, you can't use the Print event procedure since this will never be generated. In this case, you have to use the Format event procedure.

Print

This should be used when your procedure does not modify the layout of the report, or when the procedure depends upon the page the records are printed on. It only affects sections that print, so if you only print the last page of a report, the Print event is not generated for the other pages. This is particularly important if you are using the event to calculate running totals.

Retreat

This is best used in conjunction with the Format event. For example, if you have a Format event procedure that is calculating totals, you may wish to undo some of them if you are backing up (Retreating) over previously formatted sections.

The FormatCount and PrintCount Properties

You should use these to ensure that actions within the format and print event procedures are only executed once. These properties increment each time a record is formatted or printed, including occasions where a record does not fit on a page.

You will probably calculate most of your totals by using the Sum command in the footer sections of the report, but the Format and Print event procedures provide a flexible way of adding totals which are not based on a grouping. However, do bear in mind the problems you can experience if you don't remember to check these.

Filters

Reports are all very well, but their details are fixed at design time. What you really need to be able to do is allow users a little degree of customization, and this is where filtering comes in. A report has two properties to help with this:

- ❑ Filter, which holds the details of the filter, usually a SQL statement.
- ❑ FilterOn, which indicates whether the filter is on or off.

Obviously there is no way to allow a filter to be applied from the report itself – there's no visible way to interact with the report, so the easiest way to do this is to use a form.

What we are going to do next is create a form that gets shown when the report is opened. This will allow us to pick an order date, and whether to only show records that match, are greater than or less than this date. A couple of buttons on the form will apply and clear the filter.

We'll use the same report we've been using throughout this chapter, so you might like to remove the duplicate formatting we did earlier. I took off the ones we added later, using conditional formatting, and kept the code versions. This is quite a long Try It Out, but it's fairly easy.

Try It Out – Adding a Filter Form

1. Switch the form back into design view and add a new text box to the Report Header section, like so:

2. Name the text box `txtFilter`, and the label `lblFilter`. Set the Visible property for this text box and its label to No.

3. Switch to the VBE, and in the `NoData` event for the report add the following code:

```
MsgBox "There were no records for your selection."
Cancel = True
```

4. In the `Open` event for the report add the following code:

```
DoCmd.OpenForm "frmReportFilter"
```

5. In the `Close` event for the report add the following code:

```
DoCmd.Close acForm, "frmReportFilter", acSaveNo
```

6. Now switch back to Access and close the report, making sure you save your changes. Create a new form and lay it out like this:

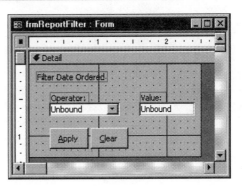

7. Name the combo box cboOperator, and set the **Row Source Type** property to **Value List**. In the **Row Source** property, type the following:

```
=;>;<;>=;<=
```

These are the operators which the user will use to search for dates.

8. Name the text box txtValue, and set the **Format** property to be **Short Date**. Now set the **Input Mask** property to the following:

```
99/99/00;0;_
```

9. Name the **Apply** button cmdApply, and the **Clear** button cmdClear.

10. Press the code button on the toolbar to create a code module for the form. This will switch you to the VBE. Now add the following variable declaration just after the Option Explicit statement:

```
Dim m_rptSales As Report
```

11. We're now going to code the various events for the filter form. Add the following line of code in the Form_Load event:

```
Set m_rptSales = Reports("Sales By Supplier By Month")
```

12. Next, add the following line to the Form_Unload event:

```
Set m_rptSales = Nothing
```

13. Now, in the cmdClear_Click event, add the following code:

```
txtValue = ""

With m_rptSales
    .Filter = ""
    .FilterOn = False
    .txtFilter.Visible = False
    .lblFilter.Visible = False
End With
```

14. Finally, in the `cmdApply_Click` event, add the following code:

```
Dim strWhere As String

strWhere = "[DateOrdered] " & _
    cboOperator & _
    " #" & txtValue & "#"

With m_rptSales
    .Filter = strWhere
    .FilterOn = True
    .txtFilter.Visible = True
    .txtFilter = strWhere
    .lblFilter.Visible = True
End With
```

15. Save all of your changes, and close the new form. Now open the report in Preview mode. Notice that the form is displayed too – it may be hidden by the report, so you might have to move it around on the screen.

16. Select the = sign from the operator combo box and add 7/20/98 to the text box. Now press the Apply button.

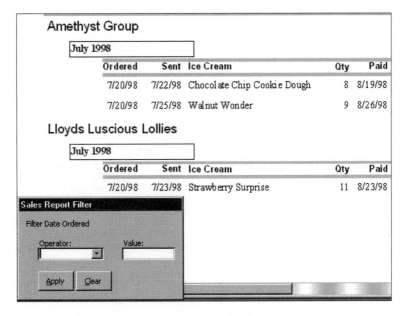

Notice how only those orders with an order date of 7/20/98 are shown.

17. Press the Clear button, and all of the records are restored.

How it Works

Let's start with the code in the report first.

In the NoData event we just want to inform the user that their selection didn't produce any records. We set Cancel to True to cancel the opening of the report.

```
MsgBox "There were no records for your selection." & _
    vbCr & "Please try again."
Cancel = True
```

When the report is opened, the Open event is generated, and here we just make sure the filter form is opened at the same time.

```
DoCmd.OpenForm "frmReportFilter"
```

When the report is closed the Close event is generated. There's no point keeping the filter form open once the report is closed, so we close the form.

```
DoCmd.Close acForm, "frmReportFilter", acSaveNo
```

That's all the code in the report. Now on to the filter form.

First, the variable declaration. Since we are going to be referring to an active report several times we declare a form level variable to hold a reference to the report.

```
Dim m_rptSales As Report
```

When the form is opened we want to set this variable to point to the currently active form, so we have some code in the Open event for the form. We know what the report is called so we use the report name to index into the Reports collection. Remember the Reports collection holds a list of all active reports. Once the variable is set we'll be able to use the variable to reference the report, rather than using the collection. This is not only easier to read, but faster too.

```
Set m_rptSales = Reports("Sales By Supplier By Month")
```

When the form is closing the Close event is triggered, so we just set the variable to Nothing to clear the memory associated with it.

```
Set m_rptSales = Nothing
```

Now we need to look at what happens when we click the **Apply** button. The first thing we do is declare a string variable to hold the filter. This is a standard SQL WHERE clause, but without the WHERE.

```
Dim strWhere As String
```

To build this filter we need the field we are filtering on, which is `DateOrdered`, followed by the operator, followed by the date. Notice that # signs have been put around `txtValue`, to tell VBA that the string is in fact a date:

```
strWhere = "[DateOrdered] " & _
   cboOperator & _
   " #" & txtValue & "#"
```

This gives us something like this:

```
[DateOrdered] = #7/20/98#
```

Now we have a filter statement, we need to set it on the report. We use the `With` construct here to save a bit of typing (it's more efficient, too).

```
With m_rptSales
```

We set the `Filter` property of the report to the filter statement we've constructed and then set the `FilterOn` property to `True`, indicating that a filter is in action.

```
   .Filter = strWhere
   .FilterOn = True
```

Since it's always a bad idea to show a filtered report without indicating that not all records are present, we set the text box and label to indicate what the filter is. Otherwise, you'd give the user the impression that all records were shown, and this could have implications if the report is used to satisfy customer queries, or contains financial information.

```
   .txtFilter.Visible = True
   .txtFilter = strWhere
   .lblFilter.Visible = True
End With
```

To clear the filter we almost do the opposite. We clear the `Filter` property and set the `FilterOn` to `False` to indicate that there is no filter in action.

```
txtValue = ""

With m_rptSales
   .Filter = ""
   .FilterOn = False
```

Since there is no filter in place anymore, we set the indicators to be hidden. So an unfiltered report has nothing extra on it, but a filtered one does.

```
   txtFilter.Visible = False
   lblFilter.Visible = False
End With
```

That's all there is to it. The steps are really quite simple:

- ❑ In the Report's Open event you open your filter form.
- ❑ On the filter form you construct the filter.
- ❑ To apply the filter you set the Filter property to point to the filter string, and set the FilterOn property to True.
- ❑ To clear the filter you can just turn the FilterOn property to False, set the Filter property to a blank string, or, as I did, do both.

Using this technique you can construct filter forms quite easily. To construct a generic filter form that could be used to apply to any filter is a little more difficult, since you have to find out the fields on the report, what type of data they hold, etc. It's something you might want to think about, but it's a little bit too involved to cover here.

Summary

In this chapter we've looked at how you use code in reports. This varies from just using functions in fields, to using events and larger sections of code in the code module behind the report. Even at its very simplest you can see that adding code to reports can make a difference.

The important things to consider are:

- ❑ You can use expressions as the ControlSource of a field, just by placing an = sign in front of the expression.
- ❑ You can use the Format event to allow you to change the layout of reports, such as making fields visible, or changing the formatting of a field.
- ❑ You can use the Open and Close events to trigger other actions, such as loading a form.

You probably won't use much code in your reports, just limiting it to the samples shown here. And now that you've seen code behind both forms and reports, it's time to look at a little advanced programming.

Exercise

1. How could you modify the filter form so that instead of being fixed to the date ordered, you can pick any of the fields on the form?

Advanced Programming Techniques

At this stage of the book, we have covered most of the fundamentals of programming with VBA, including the use of the objects in the Access object model and in the Data Access Object hierarchy. We will now take a look at some of the more sophisticated features of VBA. As such, this chapter is a mixed bag of ideas and techniques that have been either too complex to tackle until now, or that have required knowledge of other features before you could learn about them. We will also discuss in more detail a few items that we've already snuck into some of the earlier chapters. In effect, we are going to be looking at four separate subject areas under the broad umbrella of advanced programming.

First, we'll take another look at arrays, because there is a lot that we haven't yet considered, such as how VBA distinguishes arrays from variables. Then we'll have a look at some of the more interesting ways that we can pass arguments between VBA procedures. After that, we will be investigating how we can extend the functionality of VBA by using code from DLLs. And finally, we'll look at how we can extend Data Access Objects by adding our own properties to them.

So, then, the main topics of discussion are:

- ❑ Getting more out of arrays
- ❑ Passing parameters by reference and by value
- ❑ Using DLLs
- ❑ Creating custom properties for Data Access Objects

Arrays

We first encountered arrays in Chapter 5 where we looked at what an array is, and the difference between static and dynamic arrays. You will remember that an array is simply a group of variables, all with the same name and data type, differentiated by their index. We declare an array by placing parentheses after the variable name.

If we know how many elements the array will contain, we can specify this when we create the array:

```
Dim intArray(2) As Integer     'declares an array of 3 integers
```

In the example above, the bounds (0 To 2) indicate that the array will have three elements, intArray(0), intArray(1) and intArray(2).

> Remember, in VBA all arrays are indexed from 0 upwards by default. If you want to override this behavior and make the first element of your array have an index of 1, you would put an Option Base 1 statement in the Declarations section of the module.

We can declare what is known a **dynamic array** by omitting the bounds. We should do this if we do not know how many elements the array will contain, or if the array will need to be resized later:

```
Dim intArray() As Integer          'declares a dynamic array of integers
```

Before using a dynamic array we always need to tell VBA how many elements the array should contain by using a ReDim statement:

```
ReDim intArray(2)                  'resizes the array to hold 3 elements
```

Multi-dimensional Arrays

So far, all the arrays that we have been using have been one-dimensional. However, we might wish to store data that relates to a position on a grid, map or mathematical settings. Arrays can have two, three or even more dimensions and can store information in this way. For instance, we could store the SalesID and CompanyID of a number of sales in an array like this:

SalesID	CompanyID
1	6
2	4
4	9

To declare a multi-dimensional array, like the one above, simply specify the bounds of each dimension separated by commas. For example, to specify a array of 2 x 3 (i.e. 6) elements whose dimensions start at 1, use the following syntax:

```
Dim intNum(1 To 2, 1 To 3) As Integer
```

Alternatively, for an array of the same size, but whose dimensions start at 0, you could use:

```
Dim intNum(1, 2) As Integer
```

This would have the same effect as using this code:

```
Dim intNum(0 To 1, 0 To 2) As Integer
```

Dynamic Multi-dimensional Arrays

As with normal one-dimensional arrays, there is the option to make the arrays dynamic (i.e. resizable), according to our needs. To declare a dynamic, multi-dimensional array, we would use the following syntax:

```
Dim intNum() As Integer

ReDim intNum(1 To 2, 1 to 3)
```

Or, alternatively, for a dynamic array whose dimensions start at 0, we could use:

```
Dim intNum() As Integer

ReDim intNum(1, 2)
```

Referencing Elements in a Multi-dimensional Array

To reference elements in a multi-dimensional array, we simply specify the appropriate number of indexes to the array. The following code displays the results of raising the numbers 2 and 3 to the 3rd, 4th and 5th power in turn. In other words, it displays the values of 2^3, 2^4, 2^5, 3^3, 3^4 and 3^5. We do this by using the exponent operator, which looks like this: ^

```
Sub MultiDimArray()

    Dim i As Integer
    Dim j As Integer
    Dim intNum() As Integer                'Create a dynamic array

    ReDim intNum(2 To 3, 3 To 5)           'Resize the array

    For i = 2 To 3                         'Populate the array
        For j = 3 To 5
            intNum(i, j) = i ^ j
        Next j
    Next i

    For i = 2 To 3                          'Print the contents...
        For j = 3 To 5                      '...of the array
            Debug.Print i & "^" & j & "=" & intNum(i, j)
        Next j
    Next i

End Sub
```

This procedure produces the following results:

```
Immediate
MultiDimArray
2^3=8
2^4=16
2^5=32
3^3=27
3^4=81
3^5=243
```

As you can see, the procedure has two parts: the calculation and then printing the results. Each part has two loops, one nested inside the other. The inside loop is executed three times (For j = 3 to 5) for each value of i in the outer loop, which is executed twice (For i = 2 to 3).

The number of elements in a multi-dimensional array (i.e. the number of separate values that it can hold) is calculated by multiplying together the number of elements in each dimension of the array. For example, the array in the procedure above would be able to hold 2 x 3 = 6 values.

Similarly, the following declaration:

```
Dim intNum() As Integer

ReDim intNum(9, 19, 29)
```

would produce an array of 10 x 20 x 30 = 6,000 elements (assuming there is no Option Base 1 statement in the module).

Memory Considerations

We mentioned in Chapter 4 that it's important to select the right data type for your variables. This helps to avoid errors, but it's also important because the different data types take up different amounts of memory. For example, a long integer takes up more memory than an integer.

Arrays require twenty bytes of memory, plus four bytes for each array dimension, plus the number of bytes occupied by the data itself. The memory occupied by the data can be calculated by multiplying the number of data elements by the size of each element.

Therefore, to calculate the memory that the array intNum(9, 19, 29) would take up, we multiply the number of elements in the array by the size of each of the elements,

10 x 20 x 30 = 6,000 elements
6000 x 2 bytes for an integer = 12,000 bytes

and then add the overhead, which is always equal to 20 bytes + 4 bytes per dimension,

20 bytes + (3 x 4 bytes) = 32 bytes

giving a total of 12,032 bytes.

If we compare this to the amount of memory that the array would have taken up if it had been declared as a Variant, you'll see just why it is important to choose your data type carefully.

```
Dim varName As Variant

ReDim varName(9, 19, 29)
```

Variant type variables containing strings require (22 + the string length) bytes of memory per element. So, the memory requirements would have been,

10 x 20 x 30 = 6,000 elements
6000 x 22 bytes (minimum) for a Variant = 132,000 bytes

plus the overhead,

20 bytes + (3 x 4 bytes) = 32 bytes

giving a total of at least 132,032 bytes – around 128 K.

It is clear that the more dimensions you have in your array and the larger the data type, the easier it is to consume vast amounts of memory.

In theory, the maximum number of dimensions that you can declare in an array is 60. In practice, though, you will probably find it very hard to keep track of what is happening in arrays of more than three, or perhaps four, dimensions.

Erasing Arrays

When an array's lifetime expires, the memory that the array variable was taking up is automatically reclaimed by VBA. So, if you declare an array at the procedure level, then when the array is destroyed at the end of the procedure, VBA reclaims any memory that it was taking up.

However, you might want to explicitly free up the memory that an array was taking up without actually destroying the variable itself. For example, you might be using a module-level array variable (i.e. a variable declared in the Declaration section of a standard code module). Because standard code modules are always loaded in Access, the array variable will only be destroyed when Access is closed down.

If, in the meantime, you want to "empty" the array and free up the memory that its contents were taking up then you can use the Erase statement. If you use the Erase statement on a *dynamic* array, that's just what happens:

```
Erase intNum        'Empties contents of intNum array and reclaims its memory
```

However, this only works with dynamic arrays. Using the Erase statement on a *static* array will reinitialize the array, but will not reclaim the memory that it takes up. So, if you only need to use an array for part of the time – especially if it has a long lifetime – you should consider declaring it as a dynamic array.

> *When we say that an array is reinitialized, we mean that its elements are restored to their initial values. For numeric variables, the initial value is 0, for strings the initial value is an empty string ("") and for variants the initial value is the special* Empty *value.*

Parameter Arrays

VBA also allows you to pass parameter arrays to functions and subprocedures. A parameter array, as its name suggests, is an array of parameters. In other words, a parameter array allows you to pass a variable number of arguments to a procedure. This can be useful if, at design-time, you don't know how many arguments you will want to pass to a procedure.

Have a look at the following code:

```
Function Avge(ParamArray aValues() As Variant) As Double

    Dim varValue As Variant
    Dim dblTotal As Double

    For Each varValue In aValues
        dblTotal = dblTotal + varValue
    Next

    Avge = dblTotal / (UBound(aValues) + 1)

End Function
```

This function returns the average value of a series of numbers. If you add this procedure to a code module and use the Immediate window to determine the average of a series of numbers, you should see something like this when you hit the *Enter* key:

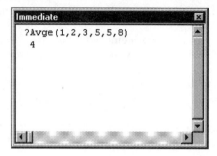

```
Immediate                        ☒
    ?Avge(1,2,3,5,5,8)
       4
```

In the above example, aValues() is a parameter array. To declare an argument as a parameter array, you just prefix it with the keyword ParamArray. There are two important things to remember when declaring parameter arrays:

- ❑ A ParamArray argument can only appear as the final argument passed to a Sub or Function
- ❑ ParamArray arguments are always of type Variant

In the Avge function, we loop through each of the elements in the aValues() array and add it to a running total, dblTotal.

```
For Each varValue In aValues
    dblTotal = dblTotal + varValue
Next
```

We then divide the total by the number of elements in the array.

```
Avge = dblTotal / (UBound(aValues) + 1)
```

We've used the UBound function which, if you remember from Chapter 4, returns the value of the highest index in the array. Note that, here, we calculate the number of elements as UBound(aValues) + 1. This is because parameter arrays always start at element 0 – *even* if you have specified Option Base 1 in the Declarations section of the module containing the procedure.

> That last sentence is important – if it didn't sink in just now, read it again. This is guaranteed to catch you out one day!

The Array Function

If we have a series of values that we want to insert into an array, we can do so with the Array function. Look at the following subprocedure:

```
Sub MonthNames()

    Dim varMonth As Variant

    varMonth = Array("Jan", "Feb", "Mar", "Apr")

    Debug.Print varMonth(1)
    Debug.Print varMonth(2)

End Sub
```

If you were to execute this procedure, the values Feb and Mar would be displayed in the Immediate window.

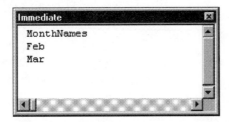

The Array function accepts a comma-delimited list of values which it then returns as a one-dimensional array. Two things in particular are worth remembering when you use the Array function. Firstly – and somewhat counter-intuitively given the way parameter arrays work – the index of the first element in the returned variant array is determined by the current Option Base statement if there is one. In the example above, the code module had no Option Base statement, so the index of the first element of the array was 0. Hence, varMonth(1) contains Feb, the second element of the array. The second thing to remember is that the array returned by the Array function must be stored in a variable of type Variant.

Although conceptually different, in practice there is no difference between an array of Variant variables and a Variant variable containing an array.

The GetRows Method

Another way to use a `Variant` array is to use the `GetRows` method of the `Recordset` object. This is used to copy a number of rows from a `Recordset` object into an array. The technique is very useful in a multi-user environment because it allows the `Recordset` object to be closed, minimizing potential locking conflicts, but still giving you access to the values in the records. In addition, it can be faster to perform repeated operations on the values stored in the array than continually re-reading the records from the `Recordset` object. That is because the array does not have the overhead of the sophisticated cursor functionality which Access provides via `Recordset` objects. Note, however, that because you will be working with a copy of the records, rather than the records themselves, any changes made to the values in the array will not be reflected in the recordset from which you copied them.

We'll now demonstrate with an example where we'll create an array which takes data from the first two rows of the `Sales` table.

Try It Out – GetRows

1. Create a new code module in `IceCream.mdb` and call it `Chapter 11 Code`. Then type in the following code:

```
Sub TestGetRows()

    Dim varValues As Variant
    Dim recSales As Recordset
    Dim intRowCount As Integer
    Dim intFieldCount As Integer
    Dim i As Integer
    Dim j As Integer

    Set recSales = CurrentDb().OpenRecordset("tblSales")
    varValues = recSales.GetRows(2)
    recSales.Close

    intFieldCount = UBound(varValues, 1)
    intRowCount = UBound(varValues, 2)

    For j = 0 To intRowCount
        For i = 0 To intFieldCount
            Debug.Print "Row " & j & ", Field " & i & ": ";
            Debug.Print varValues(i, j)
        Next i
    Next j

End Sub
```

2. Open the Immediate window and run `TestGetRows`. When you hit *Enter*, you should get a list of the contents of each field in each of the first two rows of the table `Order`.

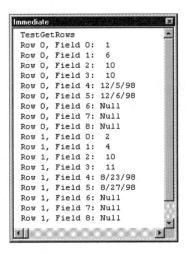

```
Immediate                                      [x]
TestGetRows
Row 0, Field 0:  1
Row 0, Field 1:  6
Row 0, Field 2:  10
Row 0, Field 3:  10
Row 0, Field 4: 12/5/98
Row 0, Field 5: 12/6/98
Row 0, Field 6: Null
Row 0, Field 7: Null
Row 0, Field 8: Null
Row 1, Field 0:  2
Row 1, Field 1:  4
Row 1, Field 2:  10
Row 1, Field 3:  11
Row 1, Field 4: 8/23/98
Row 1, Field 5: 8/27/98
Row 1, Field 6: Null
Row 1, Field 7: Null
Row 1, Field 8: Null
```

How It Works

The `GetRows` method takes as an argument the number of rows that we want to copy into the array:

```
varValues = recSales.GetRows(2)
```

Here, we copy the first two rows. The rows that are copied are relative to the current record. As the recordset has just been opened, the current record is the first row in the recordset, so the first two rows will be copied. If the number of rows requested is greater than the number of rows between the current record and the last record in the recordset, `GetRows` will return all the available rows.

After the `GetRows` method has been applied, the current row will be the one after those that have been copied. This is useful because it allows us to copy one block of records (say the first 50) into our array and process them. Then, when we have finished with them, we can read the next block.

Note that – as with the `Array` function – the rows are copied into a `Variant` variable, rather than into an array declared with the usual syntax.

```
Dim varValues As Variant
.
.
.
varValues = recSales.GetRows(2)
```

The array created by the `GetRows` method is always two-dimensional. The first element corresponds to the field index, the second to the row index. To inspect the index of the last field returned, inspect the value of the highest index in the first dimension of the array:

```
intFieldCount = UBound(varValues, 1)
```

When using UBound *with a multi-dimensional array, you should specify which dimension you want to find the highest index. Specify it as a number following the array name.*

To find the index of the last row returned, inspect the value of the highest index in the second dimension of the array returned:

```
intRowCount = UBound(varValues, 2)
```

Note that the array returned by GetRows *is zero-based. This means that the number of fields is* intFieldCount+1 *and the number of rows is* intRowCount+1.

Once we have determined the number of elements in each dimension of the array, we loop through each dimension, printing the results.

```
For j = 0 To intRowCount
   For i = 0 To intFieldCount
      Debug.Print "Row " & j & ", Field " & i & ": ";
      Debug.Print varValues(i, j)
   Next i
Next j
```

Using a semicolon as a separator in the Immediate window causes the two expressions to be printed next to each other without a carriage return. So placing a semicolon at the end of the first Debug.Print line means that there will be no carriage return before the next line is printed. In other words, in the Immediate window, the output of the two code lines will be printed together on one line.

You can also use a comma to separate expressions in the Immediate window. That causes the two expressions to be printed next to each other but separated by a tab (which sometimes makes the results easier to read).

Detecting Arrays

We have just seen two different uses of Variant variables to hold arrays. Of course, one of the problems with using Variant variables to hold arrays is that it isn't obvious whether the variable contains an array or just contains a single value. For example, in the TestGetRows procedure above, the variable varValues only contained an array after the GetRows method was used.

There are actually three different ways you can determine whether a variable contains a single value or an array. These involve using one of the following functions:

- ❏ IsArray
- ❏ VarType
- ❏ TypeName

The IsArray Function

This function returns `True` if the variable passed to it is an array, and `False` if it is not. Have a look at the following procedure:

```
Sub ArrayTest()

    Dim intNum1 As Integer
    Dim intNum(1 To 10) As Integer

    Debug.Print "intnum1: " & IsArray(intNum1)
    Debug.Print "intnum: " & IsArray(intNum)

End Sub
```

You can run this procedure by typing the above code into a module and then either hitting *F5*, or typing `ArrayTest` in the Immediate window and hitting *Enter*. Either way, you should see the words `False` and `True` appear in the Immediate window:

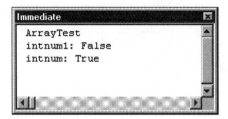

This is because `IsArray(intNum1)` is `False` and `IsArray(intNum)` is `True`. In other words, `intNum1` is not an array, whereas `intNum` is.

The VarType Function

Another method for determining whether or not a variable contains an array is to use the `VarType` function. We looked at this in Chapter 4 when we used it to determine the type of value being held within a variable of type `Variant`. In fact, we can also use this function to determine whether the variable holds an array. Have a look at this procedure:

```
Sub ArrayTest2()

    Dim intNum1 As Integer
    Dim intNum(1 To 10) As Integer

    Debug.Print "intnum1: " & VarType(intNum1)
    Debug.Print "intnum: " & VarType(intNum)

End Sub
```

If you run `ArrayTest2` by typing the above code into a code module and hitting *F5*, you should see the values 2 and 8194 in the Immediate window:

Now, you are probably asking yourself "What on earth does `8194` mean?" Well, if you cast your mind back to our discussion of the `VarType` function in Chapter 4, you will remember that the function returns a number indicating the type of data that the variable contains. The table below shows the values returned for each data type as well as the intrinsic constant that represents those numbers. For example, `2` or `vbInteger` indicates that the underlying data type of the variable is an integer.

Constant	Value	Variable type
vbEmpty	0	Empty (uninitialized)
vbNull	1	Null
vbInteger	2	Integer
vbLong	3	Long Integer
vbSingle	4	Single
vbDouble	5	Double
vbCurrency	6	Currency
vbDate	7	Date
vbString	8	String
vbObject	9	Object
vbError	10	Error value
vbBoolean	11	Boolean
vbVariant	12	Variant
vbDataObject	13	Data access object
vbDecimal	14	Decimal value
vbByte	17	Byte
vbArray	8192	Array

As you can see from the table, arrays are denoted by the value `8192` (`vbArray`). In fact, `vbArray` is never returned on its own. If the variable passed to `VarType` is an array, then the number that the `VarType` function returns is a combination of `vbArray` and the underlying data type.

So, in our example, both variables are of integer type (vbInteger, or 2), and the second one is an array (vbArray, or 8192) of integers, giving a total of vbArray + vbInteger = 8194.

Because the number 8192 can be represented by the intrinsic constant vbArray, we can modify the procedure to make the results a little more readable:

```
Sub ArrayTest3()

    Dim intNum1 As Integer
    Dim intNum(1 To 10) As Integer

    Debug.Print "Array: " & (VarType(intNum1) > vbArray),
    Debug.Print "Type: " & (VarType(intNum1) And Not vbArray)
    Debug.Print "Array: " & (VarType(intNum) > vbArray),
    Debug.Print "Type: " & (VarType(intNum) And Not vbArray)

End Sub
```

If you run this procedure, you should get the results shown below:

```
ArrayTest3
Array: False    Type: 2
Array: True     Type: 2
```

The code looks a little more complex, but isn't that hard to follow. The first thing to remember is that putting parentheses around an expression in VBA forces the expression to be evaluated first. So the parentheses around

```
(VarType(intNum) > vbArray)
```

force that expression to be evaluated first. The result of this expression is True because VarType(intNum) (which equals 8194) is indeed greater than vbArray (8192).

The next step is to determine the data type of each variable. We do that with this expression:

```
(VarType(intNum) And Not vbArray)
```

The parentheses again cause the expression to be evaluated. But what exactly is being evaluated? To understand the logical expression And Not we need to start thinking in binary again. If you remember, in Chapter 4 we looked at how an integer variable could be used as a set of flags. Well, that's how the vbArray constant is used.

To see how this works, let's look at what VarType(intNum) and vbArray look like in binary. We know from the previous procedure, ArrayTest2(), that the value of VarType(intNum) is 8194 and that vbArray is 8192. In binary those are 10000000000010 and 10000000000000 respectively.

		Array bit						
	16384	8192	4096	2048	1024	512	256	128
Data type	0	0	0	0	0	0	0	0
Array flag	0	1	0	0	0	0	0	0
Total	0	1	0	0	0	0	0	0

		Datatype bits						
64	32	16	8	4	2	1	Total	
0	0	0	0	0	1	0		2
0	0	0	0	0	0	0		8192
0	0	0	0	0	1	0		8194

The rightmost five binary digits are used to indicate the data type of the variable. The 14th binary digit from the right, whose value is 8192, is used to flag whether the variable is an array or not. If it is an array, this flag is set to 1, increasing the value of the VarType by 8192.

> *Don't worry about the other 10 bits. They are reserved for use in future versions of VBA and don't hold any meaningful information for us.*

What we want to do is to determine the value of the digits without the influence of the 14th digit, i.e. the vbArray digit. To do this we use the logical operator And against Not vbArray. Not vbArray is the reverse of vbArray. In other words, the 0s become 1s and the 1s become 0s. The result of an And operation is that bit flags in the result are set to 1 only if the bit was 1 in both the numbers being compared. So using an And with Not vbArray has the result of leaving 15 of the bits in the result the same as they were in the original number, while ensuring that the 14th bit is set to 0.

	32768	16384	Array bit 8192	4096	2048	1024	512
VarType (intNum1)	0	0	1	0	0	0	0
Not vbArray	1	1	0	1	1	1	1
Result	0	0	0	0	0	0	0

256	128	64	32	Datatype bits 16	8	4	2	1
0	0	0	0	0	0	0	1	0
1	1	1	1	1	1	1	1	1
0	0	0	0	0	0	0	1	0

As you can see, the result of this is 2, which is what we were expecting, indicating that the underlying data type is an integer.

The TypeName Function

The TypeName function does much the same as the VarType function, except that it returns its result in plainer terms.

For example, the following procedure:

```
Sub ArrayTest4()

    Dim intNum1 As Integer
    Dim intNum(1 To 10) As Integer

    Debug.Print "intnum1: " & TypeName(intNum1)
    Debug.Print "intnum: " & TypeName(intNum)

End Sub
```

will give these results:

```
ArrayTest4
intnum1: Integer
intnum: Integer()
```

As you can see, the return value of the `TypeName` function is a whole lot easier to understand. It returns the type of the variable in plainer terms, `Integer`, and adds a pair of empty parentheses if the variable is an array, `Integer()`. However, if you need to detect programmatically whether a variable contains an array, you will find it easier to use either the `IsArray` function or the `VarType` function (which has the advantage over `IsArray` in that it also returns the underlying data type.)

This concludes our look at arrays. Hopefully, splitting the discussion over two separate chapters hasn't confused you. This was necessary as we needed to discuss the fundamentals of what static and dynamic arrays were early in the book before we could move on to more unusual topics such as multi-dimensional arrays and using the `GetRows` method to create an array. The next topic is unrelated to arrays, but is a continuation of another concept learned earlier in the book: passing arguments.

Arguments

Normally, when an argument is passed to a function, it is passed by **reference**. In other words, the procedure receiving the argument is passed a reference, or pointer, which indicates where in memory the variable is stored. It *doesn't* receive the actual **value** of the variable.

Passing variables by reference has two effects. The advantage is that it's faster – Access doesn't need to make a copy of the value in another location ready for the procedure to read. However, because the procedure has access to the original variable (it knows where it is stored in memory), it can change the value of this variable. When the procedure ends, the code that called the procedure will see and work with the new value.

This is useful if you *want* the procedure to change the value, but it can create unexpected results if you don't expect it.

Passing Arguments By Value

The other alternative is to pass arguments by value. This is where VBA just makes a copy of the data and passes that copy to the procedure. In this way, if the value of the copy is changed, the original value remains the same.

Let's compare the two methods by using each of them to calculate the cube root of 8.

Try It Out – Passing Arguments By Reference and By Value

1. Open the `Chapter 11 Code` module and create the `CubeRoot` subprocedure by typing in the following code:

```
Sub CubeRoot(dblNumber As Double)

    dblNumber = dblNumber ^ (1 / 3)

End Sub
```

2. Now create a procedure which will call the CubeRoot procedure:

```
Sub CubeRootWrapper()

    Dim dblVariable As Double
    dblVariable = 8

    Debug.Print "Before: " & dblVariable
    CubeRoot dblVariable
    Debug.Print "After: " & dblVariable

End Sub
```

3. Run the CubeRootWrapper procedure either by hitting *F5* or by entering its name in the Immediate window and hitting *Enter*. You should then see the following in the Immediate window. If the Immediate window isn't already visible, you can display it by hitting *CTRL + G*:

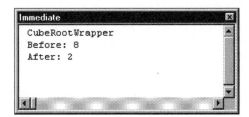

4. Now modify the CubeRoot subprocedure by inserting the keyword ByVal before the argument, like this:

```
Sub CubeRoot(ByVal dblNumber As Double)

    dblNumber = dblNumber ^ (1 / 3)

End Sub
```

5. Run the CubeRootWrapper procedure again. The output should now look like this:

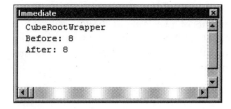

How It Works

The `CubeRoot` subprocedure simply calculates the cube root of a number (no surprises there). The main procedure then prints the number twice – once before the function is run and once after.

By default, VBA passes variables by reference. Therefore, the first time we run the `CubeRootWrapper` procedure, we pass the variable `dblVariable` to the `CubeRoot` procedure by reference. In other words, the `CubeRootWrapper` procedure passes a pointer to the place where `dblVariable` is stored in memory.

```
CubeRoot dblVariable
```

The `CubeRoot` procedure labels what it finds at this location as `dblNumber` and then modifies the contents of that memory location.

```
dblNumber = dblNumber ^ (1 / 3)
```

Consequently, when the `CubeRootWrapper` inspects what is at that location, it finds that its contents have changed.

```
Debug.Print "After: " & dblVariable
```

We then change the code in `CubeRoot`. Placing the `ByVal` keyword before the argument means that it will be passed by **value** instead of by reference – the actual value of the variable will be passed, as opposed to just a pointer to its memory address.

```
Sub CubeRoot(ByVal dblNumber As Double)
```

This time, the `CubeRoot` procedure has no idea where the original variable `dblVariable` in the calling procedure is located in memory – all it has got is its value. The variables `dblNumber` and `dblVariable` are now quite distinct from each other. It quite happily changes the value of `dblNumber`, but `dblVariable` is not modified.

> *Even if a procedure is expecting a variable to be passed by reference, you can pass a variable by value. To do this, you would simply enclose the variable in parentheses when passing it into a procedure, e.g.* `CubeRoot (dblVariable)`. *As we saw earlier, parentheses cause VBA to evaluate the expression within them. Consequently, what gets passed to* `CubeRoot` *is not* `dblVariable`, *but just the number which is the result of evaluating* `dblVariable`.

Passing arguments by reference is quicker than passing by value, as we noted earlier, but you should consider passing arguments by value in the following circumstances:

- ❑ When you do not want the contents of a variable to change, but you need to pass it to a procedure that someone else has written and you don't know how it works. After all, you've no idea what the procedure you are calling might do to your variable!

- ❑ When passing variables to procedures in DLLs.

If you have no idea what that last point means, don't worry. That's what we are going to look at now – how to extend the functionality of VBA through using DLLs.

Dynamic-Link Libraries (DLLs)

Even if you have not done any VBA or C coding before, you may well have come across DLLs. Just have a look in the System or System32 subdirectories of the Windows directory on your computer and you will find tens, if not hundreds or even thousands of them. But what exactly are DLLs?

Well, clearly they are files. In fact, they are code files, similar to the modules that you get in Access. DLL stands for **dynamic-link library** and if we look at what the name means, we begin to understand a little better how they work. They are called **libraries** because they contain a number of procedures that can be read and used. A library in real life is a place where lots of books have been collected. People can access the library and borrow a book whenever they want. This means that they don't need to buy their own copy of the book, saving them the expense and shelf-space.

So, in programming parlance, a library is a place where lots of procedures have been collected. Other programs can access (or **link** to) the library to use a procedure whenever they want. This means that the other programs don't need to contain their own copy of the procedure, saving the programmer's expense and the user's disk-space.

The **dynamic** part of the name comes from the fact that the DLL itself isn't loaded into memory until an application needs it. It's the same as saying that a book is only borrowed from a real library when someone wants to read it. Actually, there is no real limit on the number of applications that can link to a DLL at the same time. Windows keeps track of when the DLL needs to be loaded into memory, and when applications have finished with the DLL it can be unloaded from memory.

Some DLLs contain functions with fairly limited appeal. Others, such as Kernel32.dll, User32.dll and Gdi32.dll, are used by every Windows application to provide their basic operations: User32.dll provides the code that Windows provides for all aspects of interaction with the user interface; Gdi32.dll provides the code that is used for graphics rendering and interaction with other types of display device such as printers; and Kernel32.dll provides a host of routines for low-level system activities such as memory management and file i/o.

As a Windows application, our VBA code can also use the functions in these DLLs to achieve things that aren't otherwise supported in Access. There are literally hundreds of functions in these three DLLs, so we have plenty of scope! Of course, we can make use of functions in other DLLs as well and, if none provide the function we need, we can even build our own DLL if we have tools like Visual Basic or Visual C++ and know how to use them. They really do provide a useful way of extending the functionality of VBA without too much hard work.

So let's move on and see how we use DLLs in VBA.

Declaring a DLL in Code

Before we can use a procedure in a DLL, we must tell VBA where it is – both the name of the DLL itself, and which procedure in that DLL we want to use. VBA can then dynamically link to that routine, as required, while the application is running. VBA doesn't automatically check that the procedure exists, either when you compile or start the application. If it can't be accessed, you will only find this out when an error message appears as you make the call to the function.

One very useful DLL function we can use is `timeGetTime` which can be found in `Winmm.dll`. This function returns the number of milliseconds that have elapsed since Windows started. It is useful because we can execute this function twice, once before and once after executing a portion of code and, by subtracting one from another, we can determine how long the code took to execute. This is a typical example of using a procedure in a DLL to enhance standard Access or VBA functionality – the `Timer` function in Access is only accurate to a whole second. Another function, `GetTickCount` in `Kernel32.dll` can also be used to return the number of milliseconds that have elapsed since Windows started, but the accuracy of `GetTickCount` varies between different operating systems and processors.

> *The process of calling a procedure in a DLL is also referred to as 'making an API call'.* **API** *stands for* **Application Programming Interface** *– the published set of routines that a particular application or operating system provides for the programmer to use.*

In order to declare the `timeGetTime` function, we place the following statement in the `Declarations` section of a module:

```
Declare Function timeGetTime Lib "WINMM" () As Long
```

This indicates that the function is called `timeGetTime` and that it returns a `Long` type value. It is in the `WINMM` library (`Winmm.dll`) and it takes no parameters, hence the empty brackets towards the end of the function declaration.

> **Make sure that you type the function declaration exactly as it appears above. The names of functions and subprocedures in DLLs in 32-bit versions of Windows (i.e. Windows 95 and Windows NT) are case-sensitive. If you do not capitalize the name of the function or subprocedure correctly Access will generate an error message and the code will not execute correctly.**

Once a function has been declared in this manner, all we have to do is execute it. If you type the above declaration in a module, and then enter the following in the Immediate window:

```
?timeGetTime()
```

the number of milliseconds since Windows was started will be returned. We will return to this function later on when we look at optimizing VBA in Chapter 17.

Did you know that there is also an API call (i.e. DLL procedure) that can tell you whether or not the user has swapped the left and right mouse buttons around? To declare it, we place the following statement in the `declarations` section of a module:

```
Declare Function GetSystemMetrics Lib "user32" (ByVal nIndex As Long) As Long
```

The function is called `GetSystemMetrics` and is in the `User32.DLL` library. We haven't specified a path in front of the library name, so the following directories are searched in turn to find the DLL.

- ❑ The current directory.
- ❑ The Windows system directory.

❑ The Windows directory.

❑ The directories listed in the PATH environment variable.

If you want to use a DLL that resides anywhere else but these four locations, you need to qualify it with a full path.

The GetSystemMetrics function takes an argument nIndex of type Long and returns a Long. The function actually returns information about the layout of the user interface (e.g. the height of window title bars, the width of scroll bars) as well as other juicy tidbits such as whether the user has swapped the left and right mouse buttons (via the Control Panel). The argument nIndex is used to specify a constant indicating the type of information we want. In our case, we want to know whether the mouse buttons have been swapped. So we need to declare the following constant and pass it as an argument to the function:

```
Public Const SM_SWAPBUTTON = 23
```

In fact, you can try it out for yourself!

Try It Out – Using a Function in a DLL

1. Open the Chapter 11 Code module.

2. In the Declarations section, type the following function declaration:

```
Declare Function GetSystemMetrics Lib "user32" (ByVal nIndex As Long) As Long
```

3. Now declare the following constant, again in the Declarations section:

```
Public Const SM_SWAPBUTTON = 23
```

4. Create the ShowHands procedure by typing the following code into the module:

```
Sub ShowHands()

  If GetSystemMetrics(SM_SWAPBUTTON) = False Then
    MsgBox "Your mouse is right-handed!"
  Else
    MsgBox "Your mouse is left-handed!"
  End If

End Sub
```

5. Run the ShowHands procedure and a dialog box should appear which indicates whether your mouse is configured for right- or left-handed use.

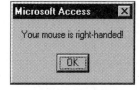

6. Now swap the left and right mouse buttons by altering the button configuration. You can do this by opening the Control Panel, selecting **Mouse** and changing the <u>B</u>utton configuration option on the **Buttons** tab of the dialog box that appears.

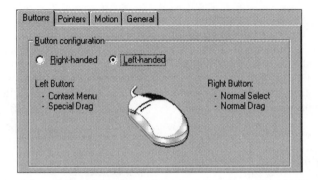

7. Hit the **OK** button to close the **Mouse Properties** dialog box and go back to the module that you have just created. You will probably notice at this stage that the mouse buttons have been swapped around.

8. Run the ShowHands procedure again. This time, the message box that appears should indicate that the mouse buttons have been swapped. Click the **OK** button to close the message box:

9. If you're still sitting there wondering why you can't seem to click the **OK** button, remember that you have swapped the mouse buttons round and you should be clicking the *other* button!

10. Finish up by changing the mouse buttons back to their original settings. (And then get even more annoyed on the way because you keep bringing up context-sensitive menus when you just want to click things!).

How It Works

As we explained just before the example, the GetSystemMetrics function returns information about the screen layout. The actual information that is returned depends on the argument we pass to the function. We passed it the SM_SWAPBUTTON constant. But how did we know that was the constant to use? And how did we know that this was the declaration for the constant?

```
Public Const SM_SWAPBUTTON = 23
```

Come to think of it, how did we even know about the GetSystemMetrics function?

Well, in the real world, the most popular libraries have good indexes, and it's the same in the programming world. For OLE libraries and Access library databases, such an index is provided by the Object Browser. However, for DLLs, we rely on the vendor's documentation for information about the functions within the DLL – what arguments they take, what values they return and so on.

Because User32.dll is such a vital and frequently used component of Windows, it is very well documented. The authoritative source of such information is the *Microsoft Platform SDK* (where SDK stands for Software Development Kit). You may find it easier to find the information by searching the Microsoft Developer Network or Microsoft TechNet CDs. This information is also available online from http://msdn.microsoft.com/developer. Alternatively, if you only want the function declaration and any constant or type declarations, you can use the Win32 API Viewer, which comes with Microsoft Office 2000 Developer Edition.

If you do look up the documentation, you will see that when GetSystemMetrics is called with the SM_SWAPBUTTON constant, it returns a non-zero value if the buttons have been swapped and False (i.e., zero) if they have not. It's as simple as that!

Enums

One cool new feature of VBA is the ability to create enumerated constants or **Enums**. An Enum is simply a list of constants that you can use to represent allowable integer values that can be passed to certain procedures. In the previous example we noted that 23 was an allowable value to pass as the nIndex argument to GetSystemMetrics and we declared a constant SM_SWAPBUTTON to represent this value. Let's see how we can make things even easier for the programmer by creating an Enum.

Try It Out – Creating an Enum

1. Open the Chapter 11 Code module.

2. In the Declarations section, delete the following line:

```
Public Const SM_SWAPBUTTON = 23
```

3. Now add the following lines to the Declarations section:

```
Public Enum SystemMetrics
    SM_MOUSEPRESENT = 19
    SM_SWAPBUTTON = 23
    SM_MOUSEWHEELPRESENT = 75
End Enum
```

4. Next, modify the GetSystemMetrics declaration so that it looks like this:

```
Declare Function GetSystemMetrics Lib "user32" (ByVal nIndex As SystemMetrics) As Long
```

5. Now, go to the Immediate window and type in the following line:

```
?GetSystemMetrics(
```

Note how, as you get to the part of the line where you should enter the argument to the `GetSystemMetrics` function, the **Auto List Members** feature of VBA presents you with a list of the three valid selections (There **are** three of them; one is hidden behind the tool-tip!).

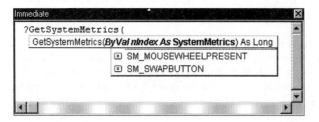

6. Select `SM_SWAPBUTTON`, close the parentheses and hit *Enter*. The result displayed should indicate whether you have configured your computer for left-handed use.

How It Works

This example should be fairly self-explanatory. First, we provide the definition of the `SystemMetrics` Enum

```
Public Enum SystemMetrics
    SM_MOUSEPRESENT = 19
    SM_SWAPBUTTON = 23
    SM_MOUSEWHEELPRESENT = 75
End Enum
```

As well as the value indicating whether the mouse buttons are swapped, we have also supplied another two values which, when passed to the `GetSystemMetrics` function indicate whether a mouse is present or whether a mouse wheel is present. These both return a non-zero value to indicate the presence of the relevant item and zero to indicate its absence.

Once we have specified the constituents of the Enum, we can use it as a way of limiting the values that can be supplied as an argument to certain functions.

```
Declare Function GetSystemMetrics Lib "user32" (ByVal nIndex As SystemMetrics) As Long
```

The great thing about using an Enum is that when we are writing our code, we are prompted with the acceptable values for a particular argument. It is one thing having the constant `SM_SWAPBUTTON` in place of the difficult to remember value `23`. But by creating an Enum and binding it to the argument `nIndex`, we can ensure that the programmer is prompted with that – and any other acceptable values – when using that function in code.

> Note that you will only be prompted with the contents of the Enum if the Enum if the **Auto List Members** option on the **Editor** tab of the **Tools/Options...** dialog is checked in the VBA IDE.

Aliases

Once you have declared your function, you can call it by name from within VBA, as if it were a native VBA function. However, there may be occasions when you want to change the name of the DLL function. For example, VBA has a `SetFocus` method that applies to forms and controls. Now there is also a `SetFocus` API call (i.e. there is a `SetFocus` function in the `User32.dll` library). If you were to declare it in the normal manner, it might cause confusion:

```
Declare Function SetFocus Lib "user32" (ByVal hwnd As Long) As Long
```

Now you would have both a `SetFocus` method and a `SetFocus` API call. To make things clearer, you could create an `Alias` for the API call. In other words, you could rename it. So, for example, you can declare the `SetFocus` API call, but rename it as `Win32SetFocus`:

```
Declare Function Win32SetFocus Lib "user32" Alias "SetFocus" _
  (ByVal hwnd As Long) As Long
```

The `Alias` keyword is also useful if the name of the DLL function isn't legal in VBA or Visual Basic. The API functions `_lopen`, `_lread` and `_lwrite` can't be declared directly because the use of an underscore at the beginning of a function name is illegal in VBA. However, they can be declared if they are aliased to a legal name such as `LOpen`.

You do not have to use aliases for your functions, but it is often a good idea, if only to avoid confusion. For example, you might want to give functions aliases which begin with the prefix api_, *such as* api_SetFocus. *This makes it easier for people reading your code to see when you are using native Access or VBA functions and when you are calling functions in other DLLs and this, in turn, can make the code easier to debug.*

Using the ByVal Keyword

We saw earlier that, by default, VBA passes arguments to a procedure by reference. In other words, Access passes a pointer to the memory address of the variable that is being passed, rather than the actual value of the variable. However, many functions in DLLs expect to receive the value of the variable, rather than a pointer to its memory address. If this is the case, you need to pass the argument by value by placing the `ByVal` keyword in front of the argument when you declare the function:

```
Declare Function GetSystemMetrics Lib "user32" (ByVal nIndex As Long) As Long
```

Passing Strings

The functions in most DLLs expect any strings which are passed to them to be **null-terminated** strings. A null-terminated string uses a null character (ASCII value 0) to indicate the end of the string. VBA, however, doesn't use null-terminated strings. Therefore, if you pass a string from VBA to a function in a DLL, you will need to convert it. This can also be done with the `ByVal` keyword.

When the `ByVal` keyword is used with a string argument, VBA converts the string variable into a null-terminated string and passes to the DLL function a pointer to the memory address of the null-terminated string (i.e. it passes the null-terminated string **by reference**).

Yes, this is the opposite of what we said earlier about using the `ByVal` keyword – but it only applies with VBA and VB strings.

Because the string is passed to the DLL function by reference, the DLL can modify it. This presents a problem. If the DLL attempts to modify the value of a null-terminated string and the new value is longer than the original one, the function doesn't increase the length of the string. Instead, it simply carries on writing the remainder of the string into the memory location adjacent to that of the null-terminated string. This is not good! In fact, if it happens, your application will probably crash.

To prevent this, you should make sure that the string you pass to the function is large enough to accept any value that the function may place in it. You do this by passing a **fixed-length** string of a suitably large size:

```
Dim strFilename As String * 255
```

You should consult the documentation for the DLL function to determine the maximum size, but 255 characters is usually sufficient.

Passing Arrays to a DLL

To pass an array of numeric values to a procedure in a DLL, you simply pass the first element of the array. You can do this because all the elements of a numeric array are laid out sequentially in contiguous memory space. After you have passed the first element of the array, the function is then able to retrieve the remaining elements by itself. However, you *can't* pass string arrays this way – attempting to do so may cause your application to crash!

Type Conversion

Because most DLLs are written in C or C++, the data types used by the arguments to the procedures within the DLL aren't identical to the data types used by VBA. However, it's not difficult to map the C data types to the Visual Basic data types if you consult the following table:

C Data type	Description	VBA Equivalent
BOOL	Boolean	ByVal b As Boolean
DWORD, LONG	Long Integer	ByVal l As Long
HWND	Handle	ByVal l As Long
INT, UINT, WORD	Integer	ByVal l As Long
LPDWORD	Pointer to a long integer	l As Long
LPINT, LPUINT	Pointer to an integer	l As Long
LPSTR	Pointer to a string	ByVal s As String
LPRECT (for example)	Pointer to a type	See below
NULL	Null	See below
VOID	Void	Use a subprocedure

User-defined Data Types

Often, procedures in DLLs use **structures** as their arguments. A structure is the C-language equivalent of a user-defined type in VBA, i.e. a type that you have defined yourself. If a procedure expects a structure, we can pass it a user-defined type so long as we pass it **by reference**.

> *User-defined types allow you to place several different data types together in one type, allowing you to group together related variables. For example, in an Accounting system you might wish to create a type for a Customer which includes the name, account number, credit limit, etc.*

One of the more frequently used structures in DLL functions is the RECT structure. This is a representation of a rectangular area and is composed of four elements representing the left, top, bottom and right coordinates of the rectangle.

The RECT structure can be represented by the following user-defined type in VBA:

```
Type RECT
    Left As Long
    Top As Long
    Right As Long
    Bottom As Long
End Type
```

It's typically used to represent a rectangular area on the screen. You can see from the diagram below that the coordinates for the four elements are measured from the top left corner of the screen:

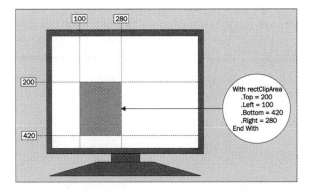

An example of a DLL procedure which uses this structure is the ClipCursor function. When this is passed a RECT structure, it confines the mouse pointer to a rectangular area on the screen defined by the coordinates of the structure.

```
Type RECT
    Left As Long
    Top As Long
    Right As Long
    Bottom As Long
End Type

Declare Function ClipCursor Lib "user32" (lpRect As RECT) As Long
```

```
Sub Foo()

    Dim rectClipArea As RECT
    Dim lngRetVal As Long

    With rectClipArea
        .Top = 200
        .Left = 100
        .Bottom = 420
        .Right = 280
    End With

    lngRetVal = ClipCursor(rectClipArea)

End Sub
```

Null Pointers

Sometimes a procedure in a DLL expects to be passed a **null pointer**. If you have confined the mouse pointer with the ClipCursor function, you can free it by passing a null pointer to the ClipCursor function. In VBA, the equivalent to a null pointer is just the value zero, usually written as:

```
ByVal 0&
```

The & is a type-declaration character which indicates that the pointer is a long (i.e. 32-bit pointer). Note that the null pointer *must* be passed by value. If the ByVal had been omitted, we would have found ourselves passing a pointer to 0& rather than a null pointer.

However, we told VBA in our function declaration that the argument is of type RECT, so it will generate its own error if we try and pass anything else – like a null pointer – to the function. The answer is to declare the argument with a type of Any:

```
Declare Function ClipCursor Lib "user32" (lpRect As Any) As Long
```

This turns off VBA's type checking and allows any data type to be passed to the function. So the call to free the mouse pointer would look like this:

```
lngRetVal = ClipCursor(ByVal 0&)
```

Let's try this out, just to prove that it works.

Try It Out – Clipping and Unclipping the Cursor

1. First, open the Chapter 11 Code module and add this type declaration and function declaration to the Declarations section (which, I do declare, is an excellent place to declare them).

```
Type RECT
    Left As Long
    Top As Long
    Right As Long
    Bottom As Long
End Type

Declare Function ClipCursor Lib "user32" (lpRect As Any) As Long
```

2. Create a new form and add two command buttons.

3. Rename the buttons cmdClip and cmdUnclip and change the captions on the button to read <u>C</u>lip and <u>U</u>nclip.

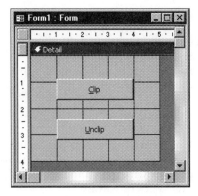

4. Place the code to clip the cursor in the event handler for the Click event of the <u>C</u>lip button:

```
Private Sub cmdClip_Click()

    Dim rectClipArea As RECT
    Dim lngRetVal As Long

    With rectClipArea
        .Top = 200
        .Left = 100
        .Bottom = 420
        .Right = 280
    End With

    lngRetVal = ClipCursor(rectClipArea)

End Sub
```

5. The second procedure simply passes the null value to turn off the clipping. Place this in the Click event of the <u>U</u>nclip button.

```
Private Sub cmdUnclip_Click()

    Dim lngRetVal As Long

    lngRetVal = ClipCursor(ByVal 0&)

End Sub
```

6. Now save the form as `frmClipCursor` and open it in form view. When you click on the <u>C</u>lip button the cursor will be restricted to the defined rectangle. Annoying, isn't it?

7. To cancel the clipping, click on the <u>U</u>nclip button. If you have placed the <u>U</u>nclip button outside the cursor area, don't panic! Just press *Tab* to move the button and then hit the *Spacebar* key. The `ClipCursor` function only affects the operation of the mouse, not the keyboard.

Admittedly, there is little chance of you having to use the `ClipCursor` function in your own application! But it was included here because it neatly illustrates four of the more advanced issues involved when using DLLs, which are: using null pointers, using user-defined types, using the `As Any` keywords and using aliases.

The Dangers of Using DLLs

Bear in mind when you use DLL functions that, as soon as execution passes into the DLL, you lose all the cozy protection that Visual Basic offers. Although Windows API functions themselves, and all good third-party DLLs, are designed to trap their own errors and exit gracefully, they will not always do this if you supply the wrong parameter types or values.

Each time your code calls *any* procedure – either another VBA routine or a DLL – the data type of each argument is checked against those declared in the procedure. If you try to pass a wrong data type to any function or subroutine you get a **Type Mismatch** error. When you declare a DLL procedure in VBA, you can take advantage of the built-in type checking that occurs. That way, if you pass a wrong data type, you'll get a friendly VBA error message rather than a system crash.

You could, of course, declare all the arguments as type `Any`, and VBA would allow you to pass any data type you wanted. Almost without exception, your next step would then be *Ctrl-Alt-Del* because the format of the arguments doesn't match those required by the DLL. It's not that the DLL has caused the error directly, but simply that it can't make head nor tail of what you've sent it!

So, to minimize errors, you should always place as tight a definition on your DLL data types as possible when you declare them. Of course, there are times, such as with the `ClipCursor` function you saw, that you can declare a function in two different ways. In this situation, one step you can take to make your declarations safer is to use an `Alias` to rename one or more of them:

```
Declare Function ClipCursorOn Lib "user32" Alias "ClipCursor" _
                                        (lpRect As RECT) As Long
```

```
Declare Function ClipCursorOff Lib "user32" Alias "ClipCursor" _
                                        (lpRect As Any) As Long
```

Both can coexist in your code together and you can call the correct forms of the function as you need them.

> When you use DLL or API functions you should *always* save your work regularly and back up any databases before you modify them. If you are using Windows 95 or 98, you should also ensure that no other applications (outside Access) have unsaved data in case you freeze Windows completely.

Well, that's three of our topics down and one to go. This final topic, like the one we have just covered, is also concerned with extending the functionality of Access. It's all about extending Data Access Objects by adding user-defined or custom properties.

Custom DAO Properties

As you know, a property is a characteristic attribute of an object. For example, all forms have a Caption property, which defines the text appearing in its title bar. This property can be read and written to, both at design time and at run-time. Reading the property allows its value to be stored in a variable. Writing to the property allows it to be changed.

Other properties are read-only. For example, the DBEngine object has a Version property which indicates the version number of the DAO interface. This can be inspected but not changed.

With other properties, whether you can read or write to them depends on whether the object is in Design view, or whether it is being run. For example, the AutoResize property of a form can be read or written to at design time, but is read-only at run-time.

A great deal of the time that you spend writing VBA will be spent modifying the in-built properties of Data Access Objects and other objects. But, even with all the versatility provided by these in-built properties, there are times when you would like that little bit more control. This is when you can take advantage of the custom properties which Access exposes.

The simplest way to create a custom property for a Data Access Object is to use the CreateProperty method. We are going to add a custom property to the tblResults table which we created in Chapter 8 and we are going to use the property to store the criteria which were used in the creation of the table.

Try It Out – Creating Custom DAO Properties

1. Open your IceCream.mdb database (if it's not open already) and open the code module behind the form frmCriteria.

2. Now find the BuildResultsTable procedure. This procedure builds a table of SalesIDs based on the selection made by the user on the form.

3. Add the following declaration to the list of variable declarations at the top of the `BuildResultsTable` procedure.

```
Dim prpCriteria As Property
Dim intWHEREPos As Integer
Dim tdf As TableDef
```

4. Now insert the following lines of code near the end of the procedure:

```
End Select
```

```
'Now add a custom property to the table to hold the criteria
db.TableDefs.Refresh
Set tdf = db.TableDefs(sTableName)
Set prpCriteria = tdf.CreateProperty("Criteria")
prpCriteria.Type = dbText
intWHEREPos = InStr(sSQL, " WHERE ")
If intWHEREPos = 0 Then
    prpCriteria.Value = "All Records"
Else
    prpCriteria.Value = Mid$(sSQL, intWHEREPos + 7)
End If

tdf.Properties.Append prpCriteria

BuildResultsTable = True
```

5. Now compile the code and close the form, saving the changes you have made.

6. Open the `frmCriteria` form and specify that you are looking for sales that meet the following criteria:

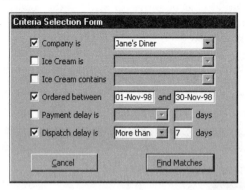

7. When a message box appears, asking you whether you want to see the results, hit the <u>N</u>o button.

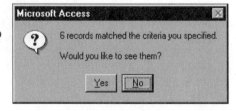

8. Now close the Criteria Selection form and switch to the Immediate window by hitting *Ctrl+G*. Then evaluate the following statement:

```
?currentdb.TableDefs("tblResults").Properties("Criteria")
```

9. The criteria you specified on the Criteria Selection form should now be displayed in the Immediate window (although you will probably notice that the Immediate window doesn't wrap the text for you):

```
s.fkCompanyID = 10 AND s.DateOrdered >= #11/01/98# AND s.DateOrdered <=
#11/30/98# AND (s.DateDispatched - s.DateOrdered) >7
```

How It Works

We created a new property called `Criteria` for the new table, and used it to store the criteria which was used to generate the table. Let's look at how we did it in a bit more detail.

First, we declare a variable having the data type `Property`.

```
Dim prpCriteria As Property
```

Next, we create a reference to the table we have just created.

```
Set tdf = db.TableDefs(sTableName)
```

Then we create a new property for that object. When we create the property, we need to give it a name. We have called it `Criteria`.

```
Set prpCriteria = tdf.CreateProperty("Criteria")
```

The next step is to specify the type of value that the property can hold. We want the new `Criteria` property to hold a textual value, so we specify the intrinsic constant `dbText` as the property's type.

```
prpCriteria.Type = dbText
```

Then, we assign a value to the property. If the SQL string contains no WHERE clause – because no criteria were entered – we set the value of the property to `"All Records"`, otherwise we set it to the WHERE clause of the SQL string that was passed in.

```
intWHEREPos = InStr(sSQL, " WHERE ")
If intWHEREPos = 0 Then
   prpCriteria.Value = "All Records"
Else
   prpCriteria.Value = Mid$(sSQL, intWHEREPos + 7)
End If
```

Finally, we need to make the property **persistent**. In other words, we need to save it to disk, so is preserved even when the application is closed. We do this by appending it to the `Properties` collection of the `TableDef` object for the table to which it belongs:

```
tdf.Properties.Append prpCriteria
```

The property can be inspected and set in the same way as any of the in-built properties, either in a procedure or in the Immediate window. So you can display the current value of the table's `Criteria` property by typing the following in the Immediate window:

```
?currentdb.TableDefs("tblResults").Properties("Criteria")
```

In the case where no criteria have been specified, `"All Records"` will be returned.

Database Properties

Of course, tables aren't the only Data Access Objects which can have custom properties. Some of the most useful applications of custom properties concern the `Database` object. To start with, let's have a look at how many properties a `Database` object has by default.

Try It Out – Custom Database Properties

1. Create a new Access database and call it `DBProperties.mdb`.

2. Create a new standard code module in the **new** database and then, in the References dialog (on the Tools menu in the VBE), make sure that there is a reference to Microsoft DAO 3.6 Object Library.

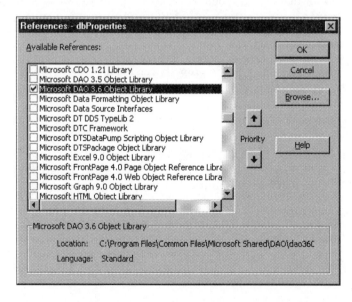

3. In the standard code module you have created, type in the following procedure:

```
Sub EnumDBProperties()

    Dim pty As Property
    Dim strTemp As String

    On Error Resume Next

    For Each pty In CurrentDb.Properties
        strTemp = pty.Name & ": "
        strTemp = strTemp & pty.Value
        Debug.Print strTemp
    Next

End Sub
```

4. Run the procedure. In the Immediate window, you should see a list of 13 properties, 9 of which have values displayed. Some of the values (such as the value of the Name property) might be different to the ones shown here, but you should still see 13 properties.

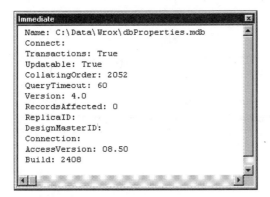

5. Now switch to the Database Window and open up the Start<u>u</u>p... dialog from the <u>T</u>ools menu. Give your application a name of 'My New Database' and hit the OK button.

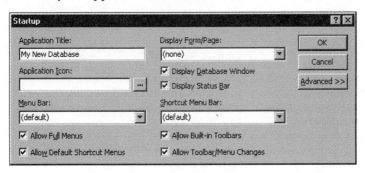

6. Now go back to the Immediate window and delete everything in it. Then run the `EnumDBProperties` procedure again. Things should look quite a bit different (we've highlighted the new properties that appear this time around).

How It Works

The `EnumDBProperties` procedure displays the properties of the current database. In fact, what we are doing here is looping through the `Properties` collection of the current `Database` object and for every `Property` object in that collection, we are displaying its `Name` and `Value`.

```
For Each pty In CurrentDb.Properties
    strTemp = pty.Name & ": "
    strTemp = strTemp & pty.Value
    Debug.Print strTemp
Next
```

You may have wondered why we put in the error handling line.

```
On Error Resume Next
```

The reason for this is that, whereas all `Property` objects have a `Name` property, not all have a `Value` property. Of the 13 standard properties of the `Database` object, one of them – the `Connection` property – does not have a `Value`. If we try to print the `Value` of a `Property` which doesn't have one, VBA would normally generate a run-time error. By inserting the statement `On Error Resume Next` we are telling VBA to ignore any statements that cause errors and simply resume execution on the next line.

But once we make a change in the Start<u>u</u>p... dialog from the <u>T</u>ools menu, we suddenly find that there are nine new properties. Where did these come from? The answer is that these are **application-defined properties**. In other words, they are not standard properties that exist in every new database, but are added by Access as needed.

You should also be aware that not all database properties can be accessed using the db.propertyname notation. So although we can do this in the Immediate window:

```
?Currentdb.Version
4.0
```

We can't do this:

```
?Currentdb.AppTitle
```

In order to determine the value of these non-standard properties, we have to get in through the Properties collection of the Database object. So to find the value of the AppTitle property, we would do this:

```
?Currentdb.Properties("AppTitle").Value
My New Database
```

This also means that we need to exercise a little care when setting the value of these properties. We need to check that the property exists before we set its value, and if it doesn't exist, we need to create it using the DAO hierarchy as we did earlier. So, if we wanted to programmatically prevent the user from bypassing the Autoexec macro or Start<u>u</u>p... dialog options, we would set the AllowBypassKey property of the database to False like this:

```
Sub KeepEmOut()

    Dim db As Database
    Dim pty As Property

    On Error GoTo KeepEmOut_Err

    Set db = CurrentDb
    db.Properties("AllowBypassKey").Value = False

KeepEmOut_Exit:
    Exit Sub

KeepEmOut_Err:
    If Err.Number = 3270 Then        'Error code for "Property not found"...
        'so we'll create it ourselves
        Set pty = db.CreateProperty("AllowBypassKey", dbBoolean, False)
        db.Properties.Append pty
    Else
        MsgBox Err.Description
        Resume KeepEmOut_Exit
    End If

End Sub
```

Summary

If you look back over this chapter, you'll see that we have covered a quite a few topics. We have looked at:

❑ Using functions to determine variables and arrays

❑ Multi-dimensional arrays

❑ Transferring recordsets into arrays using the GetRows method.

❑ Passing arguments by reference and by value, and the advantages of each method

❑ Enhancing the functionality of Access through use of DLLs

❑ User-defined and application-defined DAO properties

We are now getting to the stage where our code is getting a little complex. In one or two of the procedures in this chapter, we came into situations where the things we were trying to do might have caused errors to occur, so we had to put in some code to handle those situations. In fact, you will find out that even seemingly innocuous lines of code can sometimes cause errors to occur.

Now is probably the time to stop for a moment and spend some time looking at how we can make our VBA code more robust. That is why the next chapter will look at how we can ensure our code and applications work in the way they were intended to, by using sound debugging and error-handling techniques.

Exercises

1. Modify the frmCriteria form by giving it a custom property of type Long and called TimesOpened. Then you should try to write some code that increments the value of this new property whenever the form is opened.

2. The Kernel32 dynamic link library contains a function called GetWindowsDirectory which returns the path to the **Windows** directory. You can declare the function like this in VBA:

```
Private Declare Function GetWindowsDirectoryA Lib "kernel32" _
    (ByVal strBuffer As String, ByVal lngSize As Long) As Long
```

The first argument should be passed as a fixed-length string and will be populated by the function with a string representing the path to the Windows directory. You should populate the second variable (lngSize) with the length of strBuffer before you call the GetWindowsDirectory function. The GetWindowsDirectoryA function returns a long integer denoting the length (max. 255) of the value it has placed in strBuffer.

Use this function to create a VBA procedure called GetWinDir that accepts no arguments and simply returns the path to the Windows directory.

Error Handling and Debugging

So far in this book, we've talked a lot about programming, code, recordsets, and so on – all the things that can make your applications great. However, one important concept is that of errors. You've probably had several already, and that's perfectly understandable. So what you need to know is how to stop those errors occurring, and how to find problems when they do occur.

One point to remember is that there is no such thing as bug-free software. I'd love to believe it's possible, but programs get more and more complex every year, and that means more people working on them and more lines of code. The law of averages dictates that there must be some errors somewhere. Humans are fallible, so their software probably is too, and that includes both beginners and seasoned professionals.

Therefore, in this chapter we are going to look at:

- ❑ How to prevent errors from occurring
- ❑ The different types of error that you might face
- ❑ How to handle those errors when they occur
- ❑ How to use the error events to control errors

Planning for Errors

Despite the fact that I've said that errors will occur, it is possible to plan for errors. Someone once said that it's impossible to make anything foolproof because fools are so ingenious. Scott Adams (the Dilbert creator - see www.dilbert.com) says that everyone is an idiot, and he includes himself. We all make mistakes. We all do things that were unplanned. How many times have programmers thought "I don't need to add error code for this – the user will never do it", only to be proved wrong.

So, errors don't just mean mistakes, or things you didn't think of, but things the user does that you as a developer haven't accounted for. Perhaps they are using the application in a way that you just didn't think they would. Users don't really care about your code - they only see the visible portion of the application. So part of planning for errors is also planning for the way the application will be used, and planning for change, because applications do change over time.

The Design

If you've just said 'Design, what design?' then you're starting out on the wrong foot, and you're probably not alone. Remember back in chapter 2 how much we talked about design. The design is the most fundamental part of your application, and in some cases can actually take longer to produce than the application itself. The importance of design cannot be overstated, because it's at this point that you should work out what the application is supposed to do. That might seem an obvious point, but how many times have you created a small application only to realize once it was finished that you'd missed something out. Or you suddenly think of something extra to add that would really help.

One of the most common causes of errors is change. Every change you do gives the potential for errors, not only in the new code you are adding, but the possibility of upsetting existing code. Therefore, if you can avoid change, you reduce the possibility of errors. And one of the ways to reduce change is to plan ahead.

User Analysis

Another obvious point, but working out what the users want is pretty important. One simple way to do this is to just sit and watch them work. See what they do and how they do it. There's no point creating a wonderful application if they have to completely change the way they work. This isn't the most time effective approach, but it can be instructive. Surveys and questionnaires also work well as user requirements analysis tools.

Tables

I've said this before, but plan ahead. Try to think of the fields that might be required, rather than the fields that are required. If you collect sales figures for example, do you just collect the address of the purchaser? What if you want to analyze by region (East, Central, West, etc.) as well as by state? Make sure you add these future fields, even if you don't use them at the moment. It's a lot easier to combine fields together than it is to split them apart.

Queries

In previous versions of Access it was a good idea to create a query for every table, and then base your forms upon the query. This allowed you to change the table without having to change the forms, because you could just change the query. Any field changes could easily be coped with by aliasing the fields. Access 2000 has a really cool feature that can automatically rename all occurrences of an object. You can turn this on from the General tab on the Options dialog, accessible from the Tools menu:

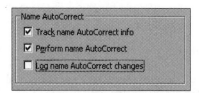

Selecting the first option allows Access to keep track of all of the objects and where they are used (except in code modules). The second option, if ticked, will automatically change all uses of an object name. If you don't want these changes automatically done, then leave this blank.

If tracking is on, Access will track the changes to objects; if auto correct is on, then Access will be able to find all occurrences of this object and change them accordingly. The third option allows a table called Name AutoCorrect Log to be created with details of all changes that Access makes.

> One thing to be aware of is that name tracking doesn't extend to modules. So any object names will remain as they are.

Forms and Reports

The key to creating maintainable reports is to keep it simple. I strongly believe in the 80/20 rule, which states that 80% of the people use 20% of the functionality. Your aim is to deliver an application that gives 100/100. You might find that the whole application doesn't achieve this, but that's normal. Not everyone uses all of the application, but try and target your forms accordingly.

With forms it's easy to try and fit everything onto one screen, so that it's there for the user, but do they really need it? And if they do, does the cluttered screen make it harder to navigate? Would a second screen, or even a Tab Control, make things easier?

Modules

Using modules sensibly can ease maintenance. The principle idea is to put all of your functions that are related into a single module. So put all of your string handling functions into one place. This makes them easier to find later, and naturally keeps related items together.

If you have global variables then consider a separate module just for their declaration. After all, if they are used everywhere it doesn't matter which module they are declared in, but it means that you can always go directly to the declaration if you need to. This works well for public constants and enumerated types too.

It's a fairly obvious solution, but one that works well.

Data Driven Design

This is another of those 'plan ahead' ideas. Think about information which is fairly static, but may one day change. Sales tax, for example. This may be fixed at the moment, but it could change. One way to solve this is to use a constant, so that you only have to change it in one place. An even better way is to store information like this in a table. When the application starts you can read your configuration information and it's then available to the code. If any of the values do change you've only got to edit a field. No messing about with code and recompiling, and so on. One small change and the next time your users log into the application it's done.

Another great advantage of using data driven design is that it's easier to accommodate historical data. Consider a sales system and the use of Sales tax. If you have a table storing your sales you might need to work out the total cost of an order, including the sales tax. If last year sales tax was 8% but it was changed to 9% this year you will have to store the date that it changed, otherwise when you look at past orders you might use the wrong sales tax.

Object Oriented Techniques

We're not really going to talk much about these techniques since they are covered in the next chapter, but it's worth pointing out that object orientation isn't something to be scared of. You've already done some object oriented programming in this book, even though you might not have been aware of it.

All that needs to be said here is that object oriented techniques can produce better applications, and reduce maintenance. The idea of an object that is completely self-contained means that all other programs see of the object is what you want them to see. You are free to change the inside in any way you feel fit, as long as the outside view stays the same.

If you think forward you might be able to create objects that will be usable in future projects. This saves not only the time taken to create future applications, but reduces the maintenance because pre-built objects should be error free.

Option Explicit

This has already been mentioned a couple of times so far, but it's worth mentioning again. You should ensure that this is the default for all modules in the VBE. It's available on the Options dialog from the Tools menu:

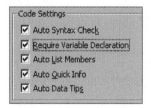

This option means that you cannot use a variable unless is has previously been declared, and thus allows VBA to pick up things such as typing mistakes, and incorrectly used variables. For example, consider the following:

```
Public Function Circumference(dblRadius As Double)

    Circumfrence = 2 * 3.1414926 * dblRadius

End Function
```

I'm sure you've all made similar mistakes – did you spot this one? The function name has been typed incorrectly when returning the function value. A simple example, but imagine a longer function, with many variables. You can see how it would be harder to track down. With Option Explicit set at the top of the module, VBA would warn you about undeclared variables.

Syntax Checking

The same set of options shown above also allows VBA to perform syntax checking on your code, as you type. This means checking for mismatched parenthesis and other stuff like that. It allows you to catch the errors as you type, rather than waiting until later. You may find this frustrating (I know I do), but the benefits outweigh any disadvantages.

Comments

This always causes contention among programmers, even Rob and me. I tend to put comments in as I go along, partly because I've got a bad memory. Rob has a memory like a sponge and tends to remember everything, so often codes furiously, and then adds comments later. There are some people who put in no comments whatsoever ('If it was hard to write, it should be hard to read'), and there are others who go overboard, commenting every line.

Effective comments are those that are used judiciously. You have to find your own happy medium, but here are some tips:

❑ You could put a comment at the top of each procedure describing what it does, what arguments it takes, etc. For example:

```
Public Function Circumference(dblRadius As Double)
'
' Purpose:      To calculate the circumference of a circle
' Arguments:    dblRadius    The circle radius
' Returns:      The circumference
' Author:       David Sussman
' Date:         15 December 1998
' Modification History:
' Who      When        Why
' DMS      15 Dec 98   Corrected spelling of return value

    Circumference = 2 * 3.1414926 * dblRadius

End Function
```

This gives a very clear picture of what the procedure is supposed to do, and what changes have been made to it. The procedure shown above only has one line of code, but for larger procedures you can see this would be useful.

❑ Comment variables, preferably on the same line, describing what they will be used for. For example:

```
Dim objRecSales As Recordset          ' recordset to hold sales figures
```

❑ Place comments on their own line, above the block of code to which they refer. For example: use comments for blocks of code, and describe functionality, rather than line by line.

❑ Do not comment the obvious. If the statement is self-describing then comment why you are doing it. For example, the OpenRecordset command is obvious – it opens a recordset, but you may want to comment why you need the recordset in the first place.

❑ Keep your comments up to date. If you change the code, comment it. This is especially true in projects with multiple authors.

❑ Debug code, not the comments. Don't always rely on the comments, as they may not be accurate.

The most important thing is to be consistent. You may feel the code header shown earlier is a bit too unwieldy, but that's fine. Pick something that you feel happy with, and use it. Everywhere.

Compiling

Always remember to compile your project before delivering it. Not only does a compiled application run faster, but you'll also be able to get rid of any funny compilation errors you may have forgotten about.

Testing

Many large organizations have departments devoted to testing. Others let their customers do it (that's what beta products are for). In many cases, though, it's you, the developer, who often ends up testing products. This is a good thing. As a programmer you have to take responsibility for your code, and producing bug-free code is not only a matter of pride, but a time saver too. You'll be the one who has to fix the error, and you can guarantee that it will take longer to fix once you've forgotten what the procedure does. Putting the effort in at development time is nearly always quicker than waiting until the users find the errors.

Testing can take several forms, and if possible you should build time for these into your project plan.

Functional Testing

Functional testing can involve checking that the whole application, or just a part of it, does what it is supposed to do. There are three ways to achieve this and they should be used in the correct order:

❑ Test it yourself, as you understand how it is supposed to work.

❑ Give it to the users. After all, they are the ones who know what it should do.

❑ Give it to a third party, along with the specification. If they know nothing about it, apart from what is written, they will not make any assumptions. They also will not worry about upsetting you if it does not come up to scratch.

When testing the functionality of the application you not only have to test individual items, such as procedures, forms, queries, etc., but how they fit together. Just because a query runs doesn't mean to say that the code that uses it works – in the code you may use a field that isn't in the query. You need to test the individual items, and then how they work together.

Usability Testing

Usability testing really applies to the visible portions of the application. You need to know whether it is easy to use. Does it confuse the users? Does it follow the usual conventions? After all, if the users don't like the application, it doesn't matter how well it meets their requirements. You may have your own ideas about what is good but, at the end of the day, you must supply something that the user will be happy with.

You may also wish to include the time it takes to accomplish a task as 'usability'. You may have to re-design your code if a particular function takes longer than acceptable to execute.

You should involve your users in the process of testing usability as soon as possible, preferably at the design stage - after all, what the application looks like and how it works are both part of the design. In some cases you can create dummy forms just to show users what the application will look like.

Destructive Testing

This is a fun stage. Give it to someone and ask him or her to break it. Tell them to try the unconventional. Search for that unplanned problem. If you are testing a form, then let someone who does not use forms, or even computers, play around. If you are testing some code, then give it to another programmer. They will love the chance to break your code. And you can be sure that once they have found a few glaring bugs to gloat over, you'll soon start to tighten up your own checking. It may hurt your pride initially, but in the long run you'll become a better programmer! (And you'll always get a chance for revenge when they ask you to test their code...)

Maintenance

It is said that 60% of a programmer's time is spent maintaining old programs (it's also said that 85% of statistics are made up, but that's another story). When making changes to code, whether it is an old program or a new one, there are some important things to consider:

- ❑ Will the change you are making impact on anyone else? If it is a library routine then check with other people who are using your routine before making any changes. If there is an error in the code, other people might have coded around the error, so if you correct your code, theirs might stop working.

- ❑ Keep focused on correcting the problem you are looking for. Don't get sidetracked if you find something else wrong.

- ❑ Only make one change at a time. Imagine correcting what you think are several problems, but when you run the code you get new errors. Which one of your changes caused this? If you track down problems one at a time, and test them one at a time, your overall maintenance time could be reduced.

- ❑ Comment your changes. Make sure that you add details of the change to the procedure header to show what you've done. You should also make sure that existing comments don't conflict with your changes - if they do, then change the comments to reflect the new functionality.

- ❑ Don't get distracted into 'tidying up' or improving code, unless that's the explicit reason you are modifying it. Remember that old axiom – If it ain't broke, don't fix it.

The above are really common sense, but you'd be surprised how often common sense flies out of the window when we have our heads stuck into code.

Types of Errors

However well you have designed and tested your application, there are bound to be errors. It's a fact of life. The important thing is to learn from them, fix them quickly, and never make the same error again.

At this stage it's important to distinguish between errors and bugs, although the two terms are often used interchangeably. A bug is generally something unforeseen, unexpected, a coding error. An error can be the same, but it can also be something expected, but something that we have realized might happen and we've catered for it in our code.

Syntax Errors

This is the simplest form of error, usually cause by typing mistakes. If you've graduated beyond the two-finger touch typing school, then you might find fewer typing errors, but the easiest way to handle these is to let VBA do it for you. Ensuring that variable declarations and syntax checking are on will save you the trouble of hunting these errors out.

You might also find times when you get a little confused between the various statements, but VBA will spot this too:

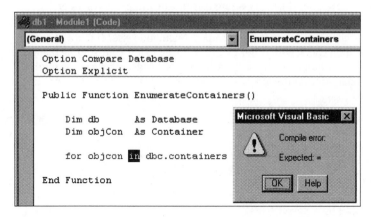

In this example the Each has been missed out from the For...Each statement, so VBA assumes it's a standard For...Next loop, and is expecting the equals sign. If you give this a try you'll find that the error message pops up when you press *Return* or *Enter* at the end of the line, and the line with the error turns red. You can click the OK button to cancel the error, and either fix the problem now or come back to it later.

Compile Errors

Another type of problem often encountered cannot be found immediately. For example:

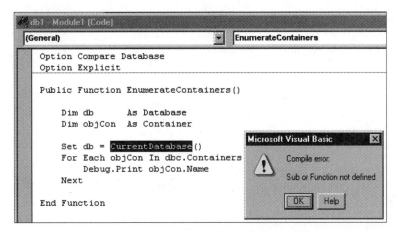

Notice that the `CurrentDatabase` function is highlighted, because VBA cannot find this function. This could either be because you meant to use the `CurrentDb` function, or that `CurrentDatabase` is a function of your own, but isn't visible. Perhaps it's not written yet, or maybe it's in another module and has been declared as `Private` instead of `Public`.

This type of error is called a compile error because the syntax of the above example is correct, but it cannot be compiled. Once the program is compiled, you know that the syntax is correct, and all functions that you've used have been found. However, there could be plenty of other errors lurking around.

Another error that is often confusing is the 'Expected variable or procedure, not module' compilation error. For example, consider the screenshot above. Let's assume we've fixed the compilation error shown and have saved the module. If we saved this module as `EnumerateContainers` and then tried to run the procedure, we'd get the following error:

This is telling us that the name of the procedure we are trying to run is also the name of a module.

Run-Time Errors

As the name suggests, run-time errors are only found once the program is running. In these cases the language is syntactically correct, and can be compiled, but something happens to cause the program to halt. The introduction of the Auto Tips in Access 97 eased a few of the run-time error problems, because it meant that you could see the order of parameters to as you are typing. This has meant (hopefully) the end of passing in parameters in the wrong order.

Another run-time error that often crops up is the Type Mismatch error, which can be very confusing to beginners. If you remember way back to chapter 4 we talked about variable types, and a type mismatch is where you assign a value of one type to a variable of another. You'll see this message if you do:

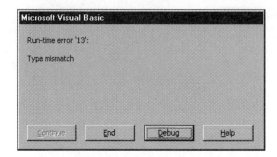

Clicking the Debug button will highlight the offending line:

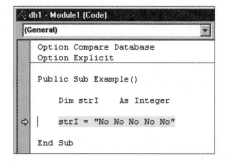

Here an integer variable is being assigned to a string. Notice that although the variable is an `Integer`, its naming convention is wrong - it should be `intI`. This has probably caused the error in the first place, and shows the importance of a naming standard. It's possible that someone changed the variable type without changing its name.

Semantic Errors

Semantic errors are the hardest to find, because they represent errors in the logic of the program. This means that the code you've written is correct VBA code, but it's not doing what it's supposed to do. Sometimes these produce errors and other times there are no errors, but certain procedures in your application don't work as expected. If errors do occur then you'll get an error dialog, and the opportunity to debug the program. However, this is just the line where the error manifested itself, and may not actually be where the real problem lies.

Imagine a function using a variable that has been passed in as an argument. If the variable has the wrong value, then it's not the procedure that is using it that is wrong, but the calling routine. This sort of situation can leave you several layers deep, with functions calling other functions, so you often need to work backwards to find the root of it all. We'll show you how to track backwards later in the chapter.

Finding semantic errors is also a test on you. As a programmer, probably the one who wrote the code, you tend to test what you think the code should be doing, rather than what it actually is doing. This is not as odd as it seems, because we do tend to assume certain things. Don't get into the habit of skipping sections of code because you think you know what they do. When testing and debugging you should throw away your perceptions of the problem and start from scratch. Never think, "That can't be happening." It can, and does. Not always, but if you take this approach, you'll be better for it.

Let's take a look at an example of some errors, and start to see how to track them down. We're going to create an example just to show you how lucky you really have to be to win the UK lottery. This uses 49 numbers from which you have to pick 6, in any order. The calculation for this is:

$$\frac{\left(\dfrac{NumberInPool!}{NumberRequired!} \right)}{(NumberInPool - NumberRequired)!}$$

Let's give this a go.

Try It Out – Run-time and Semantic Errors

1. Create a new form, and set the Scroll Bars property to Neither, and the Record Selectors, Navigation Buttons and Dividing Lines properties to No.

2. Put three text boxes and a command button on it, so it looks like this:

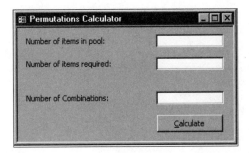

3. Name the text boxes `txtPool`, `txtRequired` and `txtCombinations`. Call the command button `cmdCalculate`, and then save the form as `frmCombinations`.

4. Press the Code button on the toolbar to switch to the code editor and create a code module for this form.

Remember that pressing Alt+F11 will also switch to the VBA IDE, but in this case the code module will not be created automatically.

5. Enter the following function:

```
Private Function Factorial (intNumber As Integer) As Double

    If intNumber < 0 Then
        Factorial = 0
    ElseIf intNumber = 0 Then
        Factorial = 1
    Else
        Factorial = intNumber * Factorial(intNumber - 1)
    End If

End Function
```

6. Now add the next function:

```
Private Function Combinations (intPool As Integer, _
    intRequired As Integer) As Double

    Combinations = Factorial(intPool) / _
        Factorial(intRequired) / _
        Factorial(intPool - intRequired)

End Function
```

7. Now in the `Click` event for the command button, add the following code:

```
txtCombinations = Combinations(txtPool, txtRequired)
```

8. Back in Access, switch the form back to form view and try the following numbers. Press <u>C</u>alculate to see what chance we in the UK have of winning our lottery.

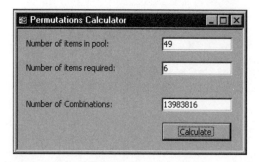

Yes, that's right. 14 million to 1! Not very favorable odds, but it shows the functions work OK. You might like to try the numbers from your local lottery.

9. Now change the number of items in the pool from 49 to 0 and try again.

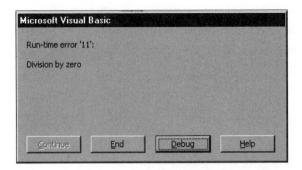

You're dumped rather nastily back into the VBE with a division by zero error.

10. Press the Debug button to get taken to the line where the error was generated.

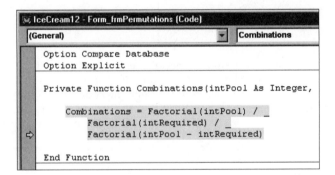

We know what the problem is, a division by 0, but where is it being generated and why? If you look at the above function and think about the arguments: `intPool` is `0`, and `intRequired` is `6`. This means that the final division here is the problem, as we're trying to get the factorial of a negative number, and our factorial program returns 0 if you try this.

Now for those of you with a math background, you might be starting to think about some problems we've got here. What do we correct? Should the Factorial function be corrected, because the factorial of a negative number isn't 0, it's infinity. So we've already introduced some error protection, but is it correct? Strictly speaking, no it's not, but what we've done is protect this function from raising errors that the user probably doesn't want to know about. The Factorial function could raise an error indicating a division by 0 but then we'd have to trap this error and act upon it (and we'll do this later in the chapter). For the moment a return value of 0 is fine. The division by 0 isn't, though.

11. Press the Reset button on the toolbar (or select Reset from the Run menu) to stop the program running.

12. Change the code in the Combinations function to the following:

```
If intRequired = 0 Or (intPool - intRequired) < 0 Then
    Combinations = -1
Else
    Combinations = Factorial(intPool) / _
            Factorial(intRequired) / _
            Factorial(intPool - intRequired)
End If
```

13. Back in Access try the same numbers again:

This is much better (although -1 isn't the correct answer) because for combinations to work the number of items in the pool can't be 0 - it must be larger than the number of items required. All we've done is move the problem somewhere else. We could change the code for the command button so that it checks the number of combinations, and if it is -1 it displays a more informative error, but for the moment we'll leave it as it is. We'll be coming back to this problem a little later.

Locating Errors

One thing to remember when tracking down errors is that Access is event driven. That means code runs in response to events, so you might find that code corresponding to certain events is being run without you being aware of it. Consider opening a form. You've already seen that there's a Load event, generated when the form is loaded, but there are in fact four other events generated as well, in this order:

Open → Load → Resize → Activate → Current

Closing a form generates

Unload → Deactivate → Close

So if opening the form appears to be a problem, don't forget to check the other events. You can see which events have code behind them because the events appear in bold in the event combo box in the code window:

Another good way not to miss code is to make sure you have the code window set to Full Module View – this can be set from the buttons at the bottom left of the code window:

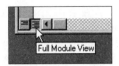

This shows all of the modules together in the code window, with a line to separate them, and makes seeing all of the code much easier.

Other Errors

There are occasions when other types of errors crop up, but with a bit of advanced planning you can probably circumvent them. There are times however, when you've no choice but to delve into the code line by line. Of course, the number of errors that occur is always in proportion to the importance of the application, and in inverse proportion to the time you have to fix them!

The cause of these other errors is almost limitless, but can include Dynamic Link Libraries (DLLs) and ActiveX controls. If the programmers who wrote these did a good job in testing them you shouldn't see any problems, but as I've already said – writing bug-free software is very hard. Other problems, such as lack of memory, network problems or registry problems, can cause some very odd things to happen.

Sometimes there is nothing you can do in these situations, but if you're stuck try the following steps:

❑ Check your code thoroughly, line by line, without any assumptions. Write down the state of variables as you go through to see what's changing.

❑ Try running the application on another machine. If it works, you could have a memory problem, or maybe an old version of a DLL or ActiveX control.

❑ Get someone else to check it for you. Even sitting down with someone else, with the code, trying to explain what it is doing can lead that light bulb above your head to flicker on, as you realize what the problem is.

❑ Buy a hat, fake glasses and beard, and get those tickets to a technology-free sunny island!

The last of these shouldn't really be an option, however tempting it sounds. (Well, not the hat, glasses and beard, but the sunny island sounds good!). If you are really stuck, then the Internet is wide and responsive, and the chances are that someone has either had a similar problem, or will be willing to help. One great place to look is the Microsoft Developer Network, which can be found at http://msdn.microsoft.com/developer/default.htm. The newsgroups are also a great place, full of helpful people. The Access ones are named microsoft.public.access.*, and most ISP's support them.

Debugging

So far in this chapter we've spent quite a lot of time discussing the different types of errors, and how to prevent them. Now you need to know how to track them down, and as you become more experienced, you'll find you get quite good at tracking down errors. In fact, you could say that making mistakes is a required part of the learning process, since it gives you first hand knowledge of the debugging process.

Program Execution

VBA provides a number of ways to help you navigate through your code while it's running. When tracking down errors, this allows you to start the debugging process at a place where you know the code works. You can then gradually narrow down the areas that need checking, until you find the error.

All of the useful debugging facilities are stored in two places within the Visual Basic Environment. The first is the Debug toolbar:

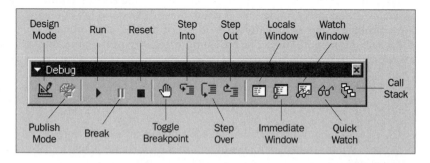

If this toolbar isn't visible you can make it so by the <u>T</u>oolbars option on the <u>V</u>iew menu.

The second set of facilities, which duplicates some of the debug toolbar, are available from the Debug menu:

You can customize the toolbars and menus, but these are the default settings, and allow you a great deal of control over how you debug your program. Let's look at these facilities in more detail before we start using them.

Breakpoints

Breakpoints are the heart of debugging, as they allow you to mark lines where you would like to suspend the program. This allows you to temporarily stop the program, perhaps to check some variables, or to start stepping through the code line by line. You can set breakpoints on a line in several ways:

❑ Clicking the Toggle Breakpoint button.

❑ Selecting the Toggle Breakpoint option from the Debug menu.

❑ Pressing F9.

❑ Clicking in the border at the left of the module window.

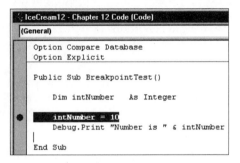

All of these methods act as a toggle, so if there is already a breakpoint on the line it will remove the breakpoint. There is no limit to the number of breakpoints you can have. You cannot set breakpoints on variable declarations, but you can set them on the start and end lines of procedures.

While the program is running and a line with a breakpoint is encountered, the program will halt and the breakpoint line will be highlighted. You can also halt the program by pressing *Ctrl-Break* whilst the program is running, which generates the following dialog:

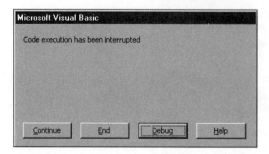

At this point you can continue with the program, end the program, or switch into debug mode, which stops the program after the line that is currently being executed.

Assertions

An assertion is something you use to test the value of an expression. When using the `Debug.Print` statement you probably saw Assert in the quick tips for Debug, allowing you to do `Debug.Assert`.

Assertions in VBA allow you to place expressions into your code that will be ignored if they are true, but will cause a breakpoint if they are false. For example, consider the following procedure:

```
Public Sub TestAssertion(intNumber As Integer)

    Debug.Assert intNumber = 10

End Sub
```

The expression we are testing for is if `intNumber` is `10`. If it is, nothing happens, but if it isn't, a breakpoint is generated on the line. This allows us to have conditional breakpoints, and can be quite useful if you only want to halt execution under certain conditions.

The Stop Statement

As well as breakpoints and assertions you can use the `Stop` statement anywhere in your code to force VBA to suspend execution. This is exactly like putting a breakpoint on the line, and is quite useful as it allows you to clear all breakpoints from a program, but still make sure a program halts at a selected place. For example:

```
Private Sub Foo()

    Dim intI As Integer

    Stop
```

```
      For intI = 1 To 1000
          . . .
      Next

End Sub
```

This would ensure that the code is halted on the `Stop` line, just before the loop.

Don't forget to remove any Stop statements before you release your product.

Continuing Execution ▶

You can use the `Continue` button to continue execution of a halted program. Execution will continue from the current line until user input is required, or a breakpoint is reached.

Stopping Execution ■

You can use the Reset button at any time to halt the execution of a running program. This doesn't place the program in debug mode, but stops all executions and resets all global and static variables.

Stepping Through Code

Stopping at a breakpoint is all very well, but you really need to look at lines of code as they are executed. Being able to move through the code one line at a time is a great way to examine variables, see what's happening, and generally understand how the program is working. This allows you to see exactly where problems lie. There are several ways of stepping through code:

Symbol	Shortcut	Description
⬆≣	*F8*	The **Step Into** button runs only the line that is currently highlighted, that is, the current line. If that line happens to be a procedure call, then it will step into the procedure, and continue single stepping through the code within the procedure.
⬇≣	*Shift+F8*	The **Step Over** button runs only the line that is currently highlighted, that is, the current line. If that line is a procedure, then the procedure is executed, but single stepping of the procedure does not occur. The next line to be single stepped will be the line after the procedure call.

Table Continued on Following Page

Symbol	Shortcut	Description
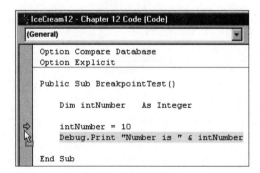	*Ctrl+Shift+F8*	The **Step Out** button continues execution of a procedure until the line after the calling procedure. So if Procedure A calls Procedure B and you accidentally step into Procedure B, when you really meant to step over it, you can Step Out, which will place you back in Procedure A, and the line after the call to Procedure B.
	Ctrl+F8	**Run To Cursor** continues execution from the current line and halts on the line that contains the cursor. It's a bit like setting a temporary breakpoint. This button isn't shown on the Debug toolbar by default, but can easily be added, or accessed through the shortcut or from the <u>D</u>ebug menu.

The advantage of the Step Into method is that you can check every line in every procedure that is used. However, if you have a large number of procedures, then this is also a disadvantage as it's much slower to step through more lines of code, especially if the procedures contain loops. For example, with a loop counting from 1 to 5000 you would have to step through the loop 5000 times. **Step Over** allows you to run a procedure quickly, and is especially useful if you know the procedure works. This allows you to concentrate on debugging the procedures that you are unsure of. Using **Run To Cursor** is really useful for loops, since it allows you to continue execution until the line after the loop.

Rerunning Lines of Code

When you start debugging programs, and are single stepping through code, you might find lines of code that are wrong. If you are in debug mode, then you can change lines of code while the program is running, and re-run the line. This allows you to fix problems without having to stop the program and start again, which is a real boon if you've got a complex procedure. There are some changes that will force the program to stop, such as deleting variables, but for many cases you can edit as you go.

To re-run a line of code you can just grab the arrow in the code window border that indicates the current line and drag it to the new line:

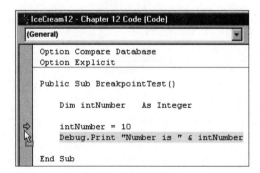

When the cursor is in the left margin the cursor changes to an arrow and you can press the left mouse button, and without releasing the mouse button, drag it to the new line. Once on the new line release the mouse button, and the new line is highlighted as being the next line to be run.

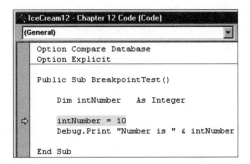

Now if you continue running the program it will run from the new line. This technique is also good for skipping lines of code.

Skipping Lines of Code

As you've seen in the previous example, you can re-run lines of code, but the same technique can be used to move the current line forward in a program. You can also place the cursor on the new line and press Ctrl+F9.

You should always be careful when skipping lines of code, especially if they contain procedures. Remember that this isn't like the Run To Cursor option where the code in between is run. Setting the next line forward in a program means that any lines you skip are not run, so if you are dependent upon what they do your code might not work in the way it is supposed to.

Changing Code

VBA allows you to change code whilst the program is stopped, so you can correct any errors as they occur. What you can't do is change variables whilst a procedure is running, since this impacts the way that VBA stored the variables. If you need to change variables, but don't want to reset your program and start from the beginning then you can only do this in procedures which are not currently being executed. So, you could finish the current procedure, step out of it, change the variables, and then step back into it again.

Changing code is not just limited to a single line. You can create whole chunks of code, use code structures and loops, and move the current line around as you see fit.

If you try to change variables, or make another change that might cause the program structure to change (such as adding or deleting procedures), then you'll get a warning message:

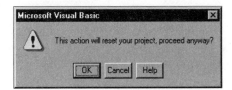

If you click the OK button your program will be stopped, just as if you'd pressed the Stop button. Pressing Cancel will undo the change you've just done that caused this error.

Commenting Out Lines

Another way to skip lines of code is just to comment them out by putting a comment character at the front of the line. If you comment out the currently active line, then VBA sets the next line as the active line. Uncomment the line again, and VBA moves the current line back – it's clever enough to realize that the line hasn't been run.

Bulk Commenting

This is a trick that doesn't work while you're in debug mode, as it causes the program to halt, but it's pretty useful if you need to comment out a whole section of code. The normal way to do this would be to put a comment character at the beginning of each line, which is quite tedious. However, there's a much quicker way, using block commenting. This is a feature of the VBA editor that puts a comment at the beginning of a whole block of code. This doesn't appear on any menus by default so you will have to customize a menu to add this feature.

If you press the right mouse button when the cursor is over a toolbar or menu you can select the Customize... option. Select the Commands tab, and then select Edit from the Categories list box. If you now scroll the Commands list a little you'll see two items - Comment Block and Uncomment Block. Just drag these and drop them onto a menu or toolbar of your choice - the Edit menu is a good place.

Once these are on the menu you can highlight a whole section of code and then select Comment Block from the menu. All of the selected code will have a comment character placed at the beginning of the line.

The Call Stack

The Call Stack is a list of procedures that you are in the middle of executing. You might think it's obvious which procedure is being executed, but if you have highly-structured code, with several procedures, you might lose track of where you are. This is especially true if you have some generic procedures that are called from several places.

You can view the call stack by pressing the Call Stack button, which shows a list of currently active procedures:

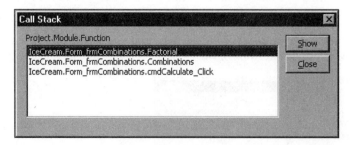

This shows what happens when we put a breakpoint in our Factorial routine. This is the current procedure so it is shown at the top. The first procedure called is shown at the bottom - in our case this is the Click event procedure for the cmdCalculate button. Any other procedures are shown in the order in which they were called, from the bottom upwards.

When this window is shown you can double click (or select the procedure and click Show) on any procedure to be taken to the code for that procedure. For example, if we show the code for the command button:

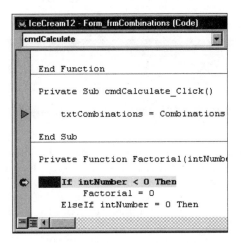

Here you can see that the first line in Factorial is highlighted, showing it is the current line, but that an arrow points to the line in the click event that caused Factorial to be called. You can see this is a call to Combinations, which in turn calls Factorial.

The Immediate Window

You've already seen and used the Immediate window, but since you'll be using it a lot more we ought to just examine the things that are possible in it. Quite simply it allows you to examine variables, change variables, and even run procedures.

If you want to output information to the Immediate window you use the Debug.Print statement, followed by the details you want printed. Within the window you've seen that the use of the question mark allows you print out the value of a variable or expression. In fact you can use Debug.Print, Print, or ? to see a value.

In Access 97 this window was called the Debug window, although in previous versions it was the Immediate window.

The Locals Window

The Locals window contains all of the variables, and values, that are within the current scope. So that is all variables local to the current procedure, as well as global variables. For example, when our code was at a breakpoint in the Factorial function, the Locals window looks like this:

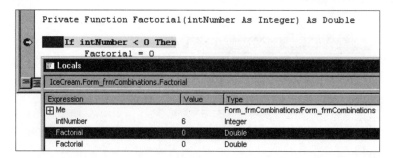

You can see there are three local variables, along with their values and data types. One, intNumber, is the function argument, and there are two local variables for the function name. Don't worry about this, as there are always two copies when using functions. At the top you can see Me, with a small plus sign next to it. As you know, Me corresponds to the current form, so clicking on the plus sign will expand Me to show you all of the properties for the form.

As you step through the program the values of the variables change, so you can see exactly what's happening.

The Watch Window

The watch window is similar to the Locals window, but is used only for variables you choose. In fact, it's very similar to a window for assertions, since you can specify variables and conditions, and specify whether a break point is to occur when those conditions are met. You can also set breakpoints for when a variable changes, which can be extremely useful if a variable is being changed, but you're not sure where. You might not think this could be a problem, but with a large program and lots of variables, it's easy to lose track. This does slow down execution of the program though, but this is generally not a problem when you are debugging.

Instant Watches

Instant watches are just a quick way to view the contents of a variable. When the cursor placed on a variable, or an expression is highlighted, you can press the Instant Watch button, or Shift+F9 to see the value of the variable or the result of the expression. Since expressions don't appear in the Locals window, you have to add a permanent watch, or use Instant Watches to view these.

Hovering

This is the trick of holding the mouse over a variable when the program is paused to see the contents:

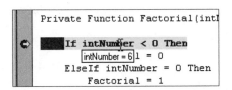

This is great for quickly finding out the value of variables.

In this example, we're going to be looking at two procedures. The first, ShowIces, will print all of the ice cream names to the Immediate window. The second, ShowIngredients, prints the ingredients for each ice cream. If you don't want to type this code in you can find it in the IceCream12.mdb database, in the **Chapter 12 Code** module.

1. Create a new module, and add a global variable.

```
Private m_db As Database
```

2. Now create the first procedure:

```
Public Sub ShowIces(blnQuantity As Boolean)

    Dim recIces As Recordset

    Set m_db = CurrentDb()
    Set recIces = m_db.OpenRecordset("tblIceCream")

    While Not recIces.EOF
        Debug.Print recIces("IceCream")
        ShowIngredients recIces("IceCreamID"), blnQuantity
        recIces.MoveNext
    Wend

    recIces.Close
    Set recIces = Nothing

End Sub
```

3. Now the second procedure:

```
Private Sub ShowIngredients(lngIceID As Long, blnShowQuantity As Boolean)

    Dim recIngredients As Recordset
    Dim strSQL As String
```

```
    strSQL = "SELECT tblIceCreamIngredient.Quantity, tblIngredient.Name "
& _
    "FROM tblIngredient INNER JOIN tblIceCreamIngredient " & _
    "ON tblIngredient.IngredientID=tblIceCreamIngredient.fkIngredientID"
& _
    " WHERE tblIceCreamIngredient.fkIceCreamID = " & lngIceID

  Set recIngredients = m_db.OpenRecordset(strSQL)

  While Not recIngredients.EOF
     Debug.Print vbTab; recIngredients("Name");
     If blnShowQuantity Then
        Debug.Print vbTab; recIngredients("Quantity");
     End If
     Debug.Print
     recIngredients.MoveNext
  Wend

  recIngredients.Close
  Set recIngredients = Nothing
End Sub
```

4. Now put a breakpoint on the first executable line in the first procedure. That's the one with `CurrentDb()` on it:

```
Set m_db = CurrentDb()
```

5. View the Immediate window and run our first function by typing in:

```
ShowIces True
```

6. When the code has stopped at the first line, view the Locals window:

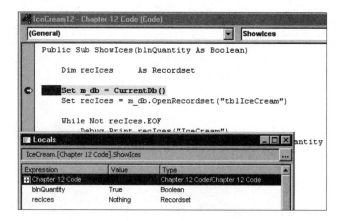

7. Press *F8* to step through the first line, and click on the plus sign next to Chapter 12 Code in the Locals window:

Expression	Value	Type
⊟ Chapter 12 Code		Chapter 12 Code/Chapter 12 Code
└⊞ m_db		Database/Database
blnQuantity	True	Boolean
recIces	Nothing	Recordset

Notice that this has expanded to show all of the global variables in the module – in this case there's only one. You can see that recIces is a Recordset, and that because it hasn't been assigned yet is has the value of Nothing.

8. Press *F8* again to step through the next line of code. This opens the recordset on the ice creams table. Keep an eye on the Locals window:

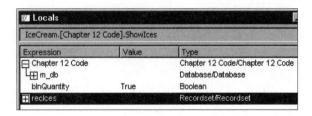

9. Notice that recIces is no longer set to Nothing. If you expand recIces, you'll see all of the recordset information. You can also verify this from the Immediate window. Try typing this:

```
?recIces("IceCream")
```

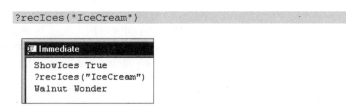

This prints out the value of the IceCream field for the current record.

10. Press *F8* again, and hold the cursor over recIces:

```
        While Not recIces.EOF
⇨ |         Debug.Print recIces("IceCream")
            Shot recIces("IceCream") = "Walnut Wonder" CreamID"), blnQuantity
            recIces.MoveNext
        Wend
```

This is a really quick way of getting to see what's in a variable.

11. Make sure the Debug toolbar is visible (just right-mouse click over an existing toolbar and select Debug from the pop up menu).

12. Press the Step Over button, or press *Shift+F8* to step over the Debug.Print line. For a line that is not a procedure call it doesn't actually matter whether you Step Over or Step Into. If you look at the Immediate window, you'll see that the ice cream name has been printed out.

13. Now you are on a procedure line. Let's first step over, so you can see what happens, so press *Shift+F8* again. Have a look at the Immediate window:

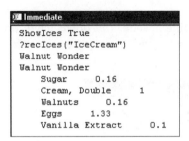

```
Immediate
ShowIces True
?recIces("IceCream")
Walnut Wonder
Walnut Wonder
    Sugar        0.16
    Cream, Double      1
    Walnuts      0.16
    Eggs      1.33
    Vanilla Extract       0.1
```

Notice that the ShowIngredients procedure has run, but that you didn't have to single step through it.

14. Press Step Into or Step Over four more times, so that you are back on the call to ShowIngredients. Now press Step Into to step into the procedure. See how you are now on the first line of the new procedure.

15. Press Step Into three times, until you are on the While statement. Keep an eye on the Locals window, just so you can see the values of the variables changing. Now click on the Wend statement and select Run To Cursor (either from the Debug menu, or by right-mouse clicking for a pop-up menu). Notice how one set of ingredients has been printed to the Immediate window.

16. Select Step Out from the toolbar. This will run the rest of this procedure, and place us back in the calling procedure:

```
Set m_db = CurrentDb()
Set recIces = m_db.OpenRecordset("tblIceCream")

While Not recIces.EOF
    Debug.Print recIces("IceCream")
    ShowIngredients recIces("IceCreamID"), blnQuantity
    recIces.MoveNext
Wend
```

17. Press *F8* three times, until you are back on the Debug.Print line. Highlight recIces("IceCream") and press the **Quick Watch** button, or *Shift+F9*:

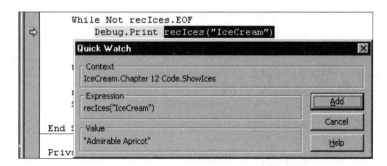

Notice how this shows another way of viewing the variable details. Press the **Cancel** button to close this dialog.

18. Switch into the Immediate window and type the following:

```
blnQuantity=False
```

This sets the value of the variable blnQuantity to False. Did you notice how the quick tips worked in the Immediate window, showing you the possible values for blnQuantity? That's because VBA knows this is a Boolean variable and that it can only have one of two values – True or False.

19. Press **Step Over** twice and look at the Immediate window again:

```
Admirable Apricot
     Milk, Full Fat
     Sugar
     Cream, Double
     Eggs
     Dried Apricots
```

Notice how the quantities are no longer shown. That's because we've changed the value of the Boolean variable that tells the ShowIngredients procedure whether the quantity should be printed.

20. Keep pressing **Step Into** until you are back in the ShowIngredients procedure. You want to be on the While statement.

Ok, let's take a little breather here, and recap what we've done so far. Don't press any other keys or stop the program yet - we'll be continuing in a little while.

What we've done so far is use the stepping facilities to step over lines of code and step into procedures. Remember that **Step Over** doesn't mean the line isn't executed - it just means that if the line is a procedure call we don't step through the lines of that procedure.

You've also seen that the **Locals** window has a lot of information in it. Object variables, such as recIces, appear with a plus sign against them, a bit like the Windows explorer. You can use this plus sign to drill down into the properties, examining the object in more detail.

You've also seen that you can use the **Immediate** window to not only view variables, but to change them as well. This allows you to perhaps correct variables that have the wrong values.

The process of stepping through each line and examining variables is time intensive, and often not a productive way to trap errors. For the next stage in the debugging process, we'll use watches, which allow us to run the program as normal, but watch individual variables, performing some action when these variables change. This allows us to target our debugging much more narrowly, and frees us from the drudgery of stepping through the code one line at a time.

Try It Out – Debugging Code (continued)

1. Highlight recIngredients.EOF and press the Quick Watch button. This shows the value of the EOF property is False, which is correct since we've only just opened the recordset, and we know there are some records in there.

2. Cancel the **Quick Watch** and highlight Not recIngredients.EOF, and press the **Quick Watch** button again.

3. Now the value shows as True. Again, this is correct because we are watching a different expression, this time one that gives the opposite of the EOF flag. This shows that you can include more than single variables in a watch expression.

4. Press the **A**dd button to make this watch permanent.

5. Don't step any more yet, but highlight recIngredients("Name") on the following line and press the Quick Watch button. When the watch appears press **A**dd to add this watch.

6. Now have a look at the Watches window. You can view this by pressing the Watch window on the toolbar, or selecting the same options from the View menu:

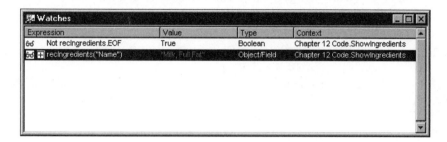

This is a little like the Locals window, but you can only see variables that you have added.

7. Press **Step Over**, going round the loop a few times, and notice how the value of the ingredient in the Watches window changes.

If you accidentally loop through too many times, you can position the yellow arrow to the While Not recIngredients.EOF *line at the start of the loop. Before you can continue looping again, you will need to type* recIngredients.MoveFirst *in the Immediate window.*

8. Highlight recIngredients("Name") watch in the Watches window, and from the Debug menu select Edit Watch...:

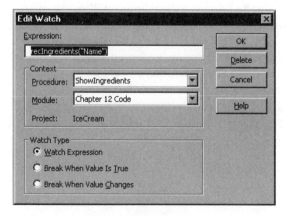

This allows you to edit the watch details. Notice that there are three Watch Types:

❑ **Watch Expression**, which is the type you've seen so far. This just shows the value in the watch window.

> ❑ **Break When Value Is <u>T</u>rue**, watches the expression, but if the value of the expression is True, the program halts and enters debug mode.
>
> ❑ **Break When Value <u>C</u>hanges**, watches the expression, but if the value changes, the program halts and enters debug mode.

9. Click the last of these (**Break When Value Changes**).

10. Change the Expression so that it says `recIngredients("Name").Value,` and then click the **OK** button.

11. Press *F5* to continue running the program. Notice that the program halts on the `Wend` statement. This is the line after the `MoveNext`, which changes the record in the recordset, so the break is working.

But why did we have to add the `.Value` to the end of the expression? Well, `Value` is the default property, so in general use you can omit it, but when you need to break in a Watch expression, you have to add it in.

12. Select this watch in the Watches window, and from the **<u>D</u>ebug** window select **<u>E</u>dit Watch...** (or use Ctrl+W for a quicker method).

13. Change the watch expression to `recIngredients("Quantity") > 1` and press **OK**.

14. Press *F5* to continue and see where it stops next. If you hover the cursor over `recIngredients("Quantity")` on the `Debug.Print` line you'll see the quantity is 1.33. So not only can you break on values, but on expressions too.

15. Press the **Stop** button. Notice how the **Locals** window is cleared, because there are now no active statements. The watch window also changes to show **<Out of Context>** for the watches, because there is no active code.

16. From the **<u>D</u>ebug** menu, select **<u>C</u>lear All Breakpoints**. This will clear all breakpoints, but not the breaks in the Watches window.

17. In the **Immediate** window run the procedure again, by typing:

```
ShowIces True
```

This will run the program until the Watch causes a break – remember that it is looking for a change in the Boolean value of `RecIngredients("Quantity") > 1`.

18. Press the Call Stack button on the Debug toolbar:

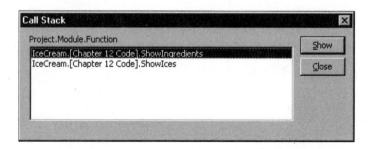

19. This shows that we are in the `ShowIngredients` procedure, but this was called from the `ShowIces` procedure. Select **ShowIces** and click the **Show** button:

```
        While Not recIces.EOF
            Debug.Print recIces("IceCream")
            ShowIngredients recIces("IceCreamID"), blnQuantity
            recIces.MoveNext
        Wend
```

Here you can see the arrow indicating the line in the `ShowIces` procedure that called `ShowIngredients`. The current executable line, however, hasn't changed, so pressing any of the Step buttons, or continuing, will not continue from the arrow in the diagram above, but from the current line.

20. Press F8 to step and you're now switched back to `ShowIngredients`.

21. Place the cursor on the `recIngredients.Close` line and from the **Debug** menu select **Set Next Statement**. Notice how the highlight moves to that line. All of the code in the loop has been skipped.

22. Press the **Stop** button to halt the code.

Hopefully you can see that being able to step through the code in a variety of methods is extremely flexible. You can examine variables in several ways, monitor them closely, and even change them. As you use VBA, you'll become more familiar to using the various windows in the VBE.

Error Handling

Now that you know how to prevent mistakes, and how to use debugging to find the ones you did not prevent, you really need to know how to handle errors gracefully. We've all seen those odd error messages with obscure numbers, but you should really try to prevent these in a more user-friendly manner. So the errors that we are going to look at now are the run-time errors that you can foresee.

For example, consider the situation of dealing with external data, perhaps linking an external text file. What happens if the text file is missing, or if it is stored on a network drive and the network has died? You need to be able to inform the user of the problem in a clear and concise way.

The Err Object

When an error is generated in VBA, the details are stored in the Err object. This has several properties and methods that we can use to customize our error handling:

Property	Description
Number	The unique error number.
Description	Some descriptive text explaining what the error is.
Source	The name of the object or application that generated the error.
LastDLLError	A system error code returned from a Dynamic Link Library.
HelpContext	The context ID for the help topic in the help file.
HelpFile	The name of the help file.

There are two methods:

Method	Description
Clear	Clears all of the property settings of the Err object.
Raise	Generates a run-time error.

The most useful properties are Number and Description, although when generating your own error messages you might well set Source. Let's look at how we handle errors in code.

Visual Basic Errors

You've already seen some examples of error handling code. Remember back in Chapter 6 when we first started looking at the objects in Access, and we were changing the font on forms? We used error handling there to ignore a certain error. If you use the Control Wizard to add controls to forms, some of the code they create also contains some default error handling.

Before you can deal with errors in VBA you need to announce your intention to handle them. For this you use the On Error statement and **labels**. A label is a marker in the code, a bit like a bookmark, that allows us to jump to certain places when an error occurs. You use On Error in one of three ways:

❑ On Error Goto 0, which disables any enabled error handler in the procedure.

❑ On Error Goto Label_Name, which, when an error is generated, causes execution to continue from the label named Label_Name.

❑   On Error Resume Next, which, when an error is generated, cause
     execution to continue on the line after the one that generated the error.

A Label name follows the same naming rules as a variable, except that it ends with a colon. The
general rule is to call the label after the name of the procedure and append _Err to the end of it.
For example:

```
Public Sub Foo()

    On Error Goto Foo_Err

    ' some code goes here

Foo_Err:
    ' Error handling code goes here

End Sub
```

However, this isn't a correct solution, because the label isn't a terminator of any sort, just a marker.
So if no errors occurred, the code would just drop through the label and continue to run the error
handling code, which could give some unusual results. There are two ways to get around this:

```
Public Sub Foo()

    On Error Goto Foo_Err

    ' some code goes here

    Exit Sub

Foo_Err:
    ' Error handling code goes here

End Sub
```

There is now an Exit Sub just before the error label, which forces the subroutine to exit
immediately, without erroneously running the error code. Another solution, which is better, is:

```
Public Sub Foo()

    On Error Goto Foo_Err

    ' some code goes here

Foo_Exit:
    ' clean up code goes here
    Exit Sub

Foo_Err:
    ' Error handling code goes here
    Resume Foo_Exit

End Sub
```

This introduces a new label, Foo_Exit, which indicates the exit point of the procedure. Now we can use a new statement, Resume Foo_Exit, in the error handling code to say that once the error has been handled, Resume processing at the label indicated. This means that there is only one exit point in the procedure, which makes it easier if you need to do any tidying up, such as closing recordsets, clearing variables, etc.

There are three ways in which Resume can be used in error handling code:

❑ You can use Resume on its own, which tells VBA to try the statement that caused the error again. This allows you to handle an error, perhaps fixing the problem, and then try again. You should use this option with care, as you don't want to keep generating the error, as this would leave you stuck in a loop.

❑ You can use Resume Next, which is the same as when used in the On Error statement, telling VBA to continue at the line after the line that generated the error. This means that you can handle an error and then continue, as if nothing happened.

❑ You can use Resume Label_Name to jump to a label, where processing will continue.

OK, now that you've seen how the error handler will work, it's time to give it a go.

Try It Out – Creating an Error Handler

1. Create a new procedure, called ErrorHandling:

```
Public Sub ErrorHandling()

    Dim dblResult As Double

    dblResult = 10 / InputBox("Enter a number:")

    MsgBox "The result is " & dblResult

End Sub
```

2. Run this procedure from the Immediate window, or by pressing *F5* when the cursor is in the procedure, enter a number and press **OK**. This simply divides a number by 10. Not very exciting, but it will allow us to generate some errors.

3. Run the procedure again and enter 0:

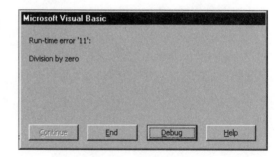

The good old divide by zero error.

4. Press the <u>E</u>nd button, and run the code once more. This time don't enter anything but just press OK straight away:

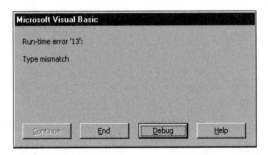

Press <u>E</u>nd once more. These are the two errors that we are going to trap.

5. Amend the code so that it looks like this:

```
Public Sub ErrorHandling()

    On Error GoTo ErrorHandling_Err

    Dim dblResult As Double

    dblResult = 10 / InputBox("Enter a number:")

    MsgBox "The result is " & dblResult

ErrorHandling_Exit:
    Exit Sub

ErrorHandling_Err:
    MsgBox "Oops: " & Err.Description & " - " & Err.Number
    Resume ErrorHandling_Exit

End Sub
```

6. Run the procedure again twice, re-creating the two errors - first entering 0 to get a division by zero, and then pressing OK without entering anything:

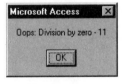
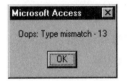

Notice that although the error details are the default ones, we've added a bit of our own code. There's also no option to debug – pressing OK just ends the procedure. Let's customize the error handling, checking for these errors.

7. Modify the code again, changing the error handling procedure to this:

```
ErrorHandling_Err:
    Select Case Err.Number
    Case 13          ' Type mismatch - empty entry
        Resume
    Case 11          ' Division by 0
        dblResult = 0
        Resume Next
    Case Else
        MsgBox "Oops: " & Err.Description & " - " & Err.Number
        Resume ErrorHandling_Exit
    End Select

Exit Sub
```

8. Now try to recreate the errors, and notice what happens. Entering 0 gives a result of 0, and a blank entry doesn't do anything – you're prompted again for a number.

How it Works

Instead of VBA just displaying a default error message, we are checking the error Number:

```
Select Case Err.Number
```

From our previous examples we know the numbers of the two errors we need to trap. The first is for a Type Mismatch:

```
Case 13
    Resume
```

What we want to do here is just try again. A type mismatch indicates an incompatibility between variable types. In this case trying to divide a number by an empty string, which is what is returned if nothing is entered in an InputBox. In this case we just want the input box re-displayed, so using Resume does this, because this resumes on the line that caused the error. This sort of error is one reason why the results of an InputBox statement shouldn't be used directly in expressions.

For a Division By 0, we also know the error number:

```
Case 11
    dblNumber = 0
    Resume Next
```

Here we just set the result of the division to 0 and the resume at the next line, which is the MsgBox statement.

For any other error we want to display the error details:

```
Case Else
    MsgBox "Oops: " & Err.Description & " - " & Err.Number
    Resume ErrorHandling_Exit
```

This uses a standard message box to display the error details, and then resumes execution and the procedure exit point. Since we don't know what the error is, it's safest just to end the procedure.

If you are handling errors you should always include an `Else` clause like this, to cater for unexpected situations.

Form Errors

The above examples have mentioned VBA errors, but in Access there are errors associated with forms. If an error occurs during processing in a form, the `Form_Error` event is generated. This is just a normal event procedure, giving you the details of the error and allowing you to decide whether you want to handle the error, or whether you want Access to handle it:

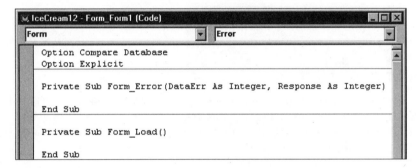

The first argument, `DataErr`, is the error number, and can be used in the same way as the `Err.Number` shown earlier.

The second argument, `Response`, is an output argument, so you set this in the procedure to tell Access what to do about the error. You can set it to `acDataErrContinue` and Access will ignore the error and continue with your code, allowing you to use your own error messages instead of the default ones. If you set it to `acDataErrDisplay`, which is the default, then Access displays its error message. Let's look at an example of this.

Try It Out – The Form_Error Event

1. In the main database window select tables, and open tblIceCreamIngredient.

2. From the toolbar select the AutoForm button:

This creates a new form for you.

3. On the new form, add a new record (use the navigation buttons or Ne<u>w</u> Record from the <u>I</u>nsert menu).

4. Select Apples for the Ingredient ID and leave the Ice Cream ID blank.

5. Navigate to the previous record, and you'll see the following error:

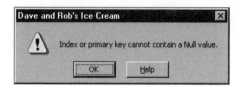

A pretty scary error message, and certainly not one we would like a user to see. The problem is that both of the ID fields are part of a unique primary key, which means that they both have to be filled in. We left one field blank, which is not allowed. We need to replace the default Access error message with one of our own.

6. Press OK to get back to the form and then press *Escape* to clear the record.

7. Switch the form into design view and click the Code button on the toolbar to create a code module for this form.

8. In the form's `Error` event, add the following code:

```
If DataErr = 3058 Then
    MsgBox "You must supply values for Ice Cream and Ingredient"
    Response = acDataErrContinue
End If
```

9. Back in Access, switch the form back into Form view and try the same procedure again – selecting only one of the ID values and then navigating away from the record. This time you get a more sensible message:

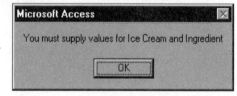

When you close the form, save it as frmErrorHandling.

> *Notice that when you save the form, the default name you are prompted to save it as is actually "tblIceCreamIngredient". This is purely down to the fact that you created the form (using AutoForm) based upon this table.*

How it Works

We know that the error number we need to trap is 3058. How do we know? Well there are two easy ways. The first is just to do what I did – create the same code as above, this time using an error number of 1, and put a breakpoint on the line. Then create the error, and when the breakpoint is triggered just see what the value of DataErr is, and then change the 1 to the correct number. The second method is to look up the error number, either in the help or in the error numbers table, as described in the next section.

Once we know what the error number is we can just output our own message, and set Response to tell Access that we are handling the error and it shouldn't display its own message. It's as simple as that.

You can use this technique for all sorts of errors that might violate the database, such as index errors or data integrity errors.

Access and VBA Errors

If you want to know what the standard Access and VBA error numbers are, it's quite simple. There are two procedures in the help files for this, under **Microsoft Access Visual Basic Reference: Error Codes**. Both of these procedures are in the **Chapter 12 Code** in IceCream12.mdb. You should note that these procedures use ADO and ADO Extensions, so if you want to use them in your own databases you need to go to the References option in the Tools menu when in the VBE. Select both **Microsoft ActiveX Data Objects 2.1 Library** and **Microsoft ADO Ext. 2.1 for DDL and Security**. The database IceCream12.mdb has both of these selected for you, and running these procedures create tables with the error numbers and descriptions in them.

Data Access Errors

So far we've talked about VBA errors, but there are plenty of occasions when errors are generated in response to data access, when using databases, recordsets, etc., and in this case you need a way to access the error details. Remember how we said that the Err object relates to VBA errors? That means there must be another method for handling data access errors.

Data Access Objects

When using DAO, there is an Errors collection, which contains Error objects. Each Error object contains a single piece of information about an error. When using DAO methods, the Errors collection is cleared automatically, so it will only contain details of a single data access error. The reason it is a collection is that a single data access error might result in more than one piece of error information. This is especially true of ODBC databases.

This means that there are two places you must check for errors – the `Err` object and the `Errors` collection. If a DAO error occurs then `Err` is set to indicate this, as well as the `Errors` collection being filled. However, the reverse isn't true – a VBA run-time error only ever fills `Err`.

Try It Out – The Errors Collection

1. Create a new procedure called `ShowErrors` and add the following code:

```
Public Sub ShowErrors()

    Dim db   As Database
    Dim recT As Recordset
    Dim errE As Error

    On Error GoTo ShowErrors_Err

    Set db = CurrentDb()
    Set recT = db.OpenRecordset("NonExistantTable")
    recT.Close

ShowErrors_Exit:
    Exit Sub

ShowErrors_Err:
    Debug.Print "Err = " & Err.Number & ": " & Err.Description
    Debug.Print

    For Each errE In DBEngine.Errors
        Debug.Print "Errors: " & errE.Number & ": " & errE.Description
    Next
    Resume ShowErrors_Exit

End Sub
```

2. Run the procedure from the Immediate window. You'll see two copies of the same error are printed:

```
Immediate
ShowErrors
Err = 3078: The Microsoft Jet database engine cannot find

Errors: 3078: The Microsoft Jet database engine cannot fin
```

3. Now add the following line of code, directly before the `OpenRecordset` line:

```
Forms!frmCompany.Caption = "A new caption"
```

4. Run the procedure again:

```
Immediate
ShowErrors
Err = 2450: Dave and Rob's Ice Cream can't find the form 'frmCompany'

Errors: 3078: The Microsoft Jet database engine cannot find the input
```

How It Works

The first time the procedure is run we try to open a recordset on a table that doesn't exist, so this generates an error. We jump down to the error routine, which prints out the contents of both the `Err` object and the `Errors` collection. Since this was a DAO error, both of these are the same. This shows that when the DAO error is generated, the details are put into the `Err` object as well as the `Errors` collection.

The second time around though, the first error is that we try to set the property of a form that isn't open. This is a VBA run-time error – 2450. As soon as this is generated, the procedure jumps to the error routine, prints the error details and exits. That means that the `OpenRecordset` hasn't been called. So why does the `Errors` collection still show an error? Remember how we said that a DAO method call clears the `Errors` collection – well we haven't yet done a DAO method call, so the `Errors` collection still holds the details of the previous errors.

This shows that the `Err` object and the `Errors` collection can hold different things, and that they both should be checked. The `Err` object always contains the details of the error, whether it is a VBA or a DAO error. You should compare the error number held in the `Err` object with that held in the `Errors` collection and if the numbers are different, then it is a VBA error. If the numbers are the same, you might want to loop through the `Errors` collection, in case there are any further DAO errors. In the example above the DAO error only generated one error, but ODBC errors nearly always generate more. Have a look at this screen shot:

```
Immediate
ODBCErr
Err = 3146: ODBC--call failed.

Errors: 547: [Microsoft][ODBC SQL Server Driver][SQL Server]INSERT statement c
Errors: 3621: [Microsoft][ODBC SQL Server Driver][SQL Server]Command has been
Errors: 3146: ODBC--call failed.
```

This shows the result of trying to add a record to a table linked with ODBC from a SQL Server database. The details we tried to add were incorrect and violated some SQL Server rules, so an ODBC error was generated. Notice that `Err` shows that this is an ODBC error, and this error matches the last error in the `Errors` collection. There are two other error messages that SQL Server has generated, and these have been added to the collection first. This means, that to have a proper error routine you should really check `Err` against the last `Error` object in the `Errors` collection. Something like this:

```
Dim errE As Error

    '  '  '

    If Err.Number = DBEngine.Errors(DBEngine.Errors.Count - 1).Number Then
        Debug.Print "Data Access Error"
        For Each errE In DBEngine.Errors
            Debug.Print "Errors: " & errE.Number & ": " & errE.Description
        Next
    Else
        Debug.Print "VBA run-time Error"
        Debug.Print "Err = " & Err.Number & ": " & Err.Description
    End If
```

This uses the Count property of the Errors collection to see how many errors there are. We subtract one from it because the Errors collection is zero based, and this gives us the last object in the collection. We can then compare this against the Err object to see whether it is a VBA error or a DAO error.

ActiveX Data Objects

Although we are concentrating on DAO in this book, we need to briefly cover the same sort of things in ADO. Luckily there's not too much difference, as ADO has an Errors collection too, with similar properties, so you can use similar code.

With DAO the Errors collection belongs to the DBEngine object, but in ADO it belongs to the Connection object. So our code might look something like this:

```
Dim db As New ADODB.Connection
Dim recT As New ADODB.Recordset
Dim errE As ADODB.Error

On Error GoTo ShowErrors_Err

db.Open "DSN=pubs", "sa", ""
recT.Open " NonExistantTable ", db, adOpenKeyset, _
    adLockOptimistic, adCmdTable
recT.Close

ShowErrors_Exit:
    Exit Sub

ShowErrors_Err:
    Debug.Print "Err = " & Err.Number & ": " & Err.Description
    Debug.Print

    For Each errE In db.Errors
        Debug.Print "Errors: " & errE.Number & ": " & errE.Description
    Next
    Resume ShowErrors_Exit
```

This example uses an ODBC DSN to connect to a SQL Server database, and the ODBC driver has good error reporting (ODBC DSN's are explained in Appendix H). The native OLEDB Providers seem to return less error information. For multiple errors ADO also returns the error details in the opposite order to DAO, so you should compare the first member in the collection against Err, rather than the last.

User Defined Errors

Much has been said about Access errors, but you can also define your own errors. This is very useful because it allows you to create a specific error in your procedure if something happens, then handle it in the same way as built-in errors. It also allows you to trigger the default error routines yourself without actually having an error occur.

Using the Raise method of the Err object generates user-defined errors. All this does is cause the object to report an error in the normal way. The difference is that you must supply an error number. This can be a VBA standard error number, such as 13 for Type Mismatch, or one of your own that is outside the range VBA uses. The highest number is 65535, but VBA doesn't itself use anything above 31999 so you have plenty to choose from.

1. Open the `ErrorHandling` procedure that you were looking at earlier and modify the code to read as follows:

```
Public Sub ErrorHandling()

    Dim dblResult As Double
    Dim VarNumber As Variant

    On Error GoTo ErrorHandling_Err

    VarNumber = InputBox("Enter a number:")
    If Not IsNumeric(VarNumber) Then
        Err.Raise 32000
    End If
    dblResult = 10 / VarNumber
    MsgBox "The result is "& str$(dblResult)

ErrorHandling_Exit:
    Exit Sub

ErrorHandling_Err:
    Select Case Err.Number
    Case 13 ' Type mismatch - empty entry
        Resume
    Case 11 ' Divide by zero
        dblResult = 0
        Resume Next
    Case Else
        MsgBox Err.Description & " - " & Err.Number
        Resume ErrorHandling_Exit
    End Select

End Sub
```

Now, if the entry is not numeric, the error routine is called with an error number of 32000. However to prevent conflicts with Access, make sure that you always use numbers 32000 and above for your code.

If you don't explicitly handle your user-defined errors, but simply use a message box to display the standard error text, you'll get the message **Application-defined or object-defined error**.

```
MsgBox Err.Description & " - " & Err.Number
```

For example, this would display the message **Application-defined or object-defined error - 32000**, if used in the previous procedure.

2. Now modify the error handling routine so that it has an extra selection:

```
Case 32000
    MsgBox "Must be a number"
    Resume ErrorHandling_Exit
```

3. Run the procedure and enter a letter. The new error handler processes the error number 32000 in exactly the same way as other errors. So now the function displays our own message.

The Error Stack

Because Access is event-driven, it is constantly running small pieces of code which correspond to events. As each procedure is entered, the error handler is reset and so any error is treated as the only error. Access does not keep a list of errors, but responds to them as they occur. This is fairly sensible, but you need to understand where Access looks for the error-handling code.

When an error occurs, Access backtracks through its currently active procedures looking for an error-handling routine and executes the first one it finds. If it does not find one, the default error handler routine is called.

For example, let's imagine that you have three procedures, A, B and C. A calls B, and B in turn calls C. If C generates an error, Access will backtrack through B to A looking for an error routine. If it does not find one in B or A, it calls the default routine.

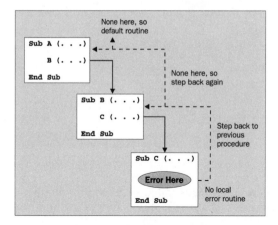

Note that this does not affect the flow of control in the program, as procedure C is still currently active. The backward arrows just show what Access does when searching for an error routine.

Now suppose that you need to add a little more meaning to this default error routine so you decide to create your own. Do you put a routine in each of A, B and C, or do you make use of the backtracking feature and just put it in A? Clearly, if you are dealing with similar errors, it makes sense to have one error routine and, because of the backtracking, it is also sensible to put it at the highest level.

Now imagine that you have the following error-handling code in procedure A, and none in the other procedure:

```
A_Err:
    Select Case Err.Number
    Case w ' Dangerous, so quit
```

```
    Resume A_Exit
Case x ' Safe to carry on to next line
    Resume Next
Case y ' Retry again
    Resume
Case z ' A default error, let Access 2000 handle it
    Err.Raise q
End Select
```

This seems straightforward but there is one serious drawback. This can change the program flow. Neither `Resume` nor `Resume Next` continues execution in procedure C as you would think, but at the current line in the procedure that handles the error (see diagram below).

So `Resume` will resume execution at the line that called procedure B – this is the current line in procedure A.

Likewise, `Resume Next` will continue on the line after the call to procedure B. Notice that neither method will return execution to procedure C. Have a look at this diagram to see what happens:

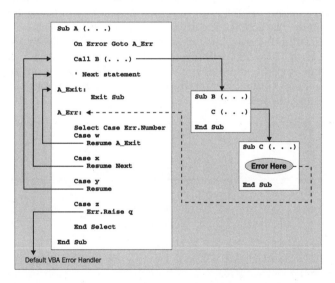

This clearly shows the danger of using a single routine for errors. However, it can also be useful – the thing to do is to be aware of this and plan accordingly. You can, for example, have a single error routine in A, and then another in C. The one in C would handle errors generated there, allowing continuation in non-fatal circumstances, whereas the one in A could be used to cope with errors from A and B. You could also use `Err.Raise` in C to force Access to move the error handler up to the next level. For example, look at the following code:

```
Sub C()

    On Error GoTo c_Err

    Dim intOne As Integer
```

```
    intOne = 123456789
    intOne = "wrong"

C_Exit:
    Exit Sub

C_Err:
    Select Case Err.Number
    Case 13
        MsgBox "C: Error " & Err.Number & ": " & Err.Description
    Case Else
        Err.Raise Err.Number, "C", Err.Description
    End Select
    Resume C_Exit

End Sub
```

This procedure has an error handler that checks the error number. If it is error 13 (Type Mismatch), then the error is displayed here, but any other error is handled by sending the error back up to the calling procedure. This is done by using the `Raise` method of the `Err` object, which in effect fires the error off again. The three arguments are the error number, the source (in this case the procedure 'C'), and the description. The actual code of the procedure only consists of two lines, both of which generate errors. The first sets an integer variable to a very large value, which will cause an overflow – this is not error 13, and so will raise the error again. The second line is error 13, and so would be handled here. In this example, you would have to comment out setting the variable to the large value before you could generate this error though, as they can't both happen. Let's look at a procedure that calls this one:

```
Sub B()

    Dim intI As Integer

    Debug.Print "In B"

    Call C

    Debug.Print "In B: setting intI to 123456789"

    intI = 123456789

End Sub
```

This procedure just calls procedure C and then generates its own error – an overflow. It has no error handling of its own, so Access will search back through the call tree to find an error handler, and in this example it's in procedure A:

```
Sub A()

    On Error GoTo A_Err

    Debug.Print "In A"

    Call B

    Debug.Print "In A: 2 / 0 = " & 2 / 0
```

```
A_Exit:
    Exit Sub

A_Err:
    MsgBox "A (" & Err.Source & "): Error " & Err.Number & _
        ": " & Err.Description
    Resume A_Exit

End Sub
```

This does have an error handler, which displays the source of the error, the number and the description. Let's review the procedures:

❑   A calls B, which calls C.

❑   C has its own error handler, but this only handles error 13 – all others are sent back to B.

❑   B does not have its own error handler, so it sends the error back to A.

❑   The handler in A displays the error message.

This shows you can handle some errors locally, but still have a general error handler to cope with the others. The Source property of the Err object allows you to identify where the error was generated.

Debugging your Debugging Code

There may be times when you have added some error-handling routines but these themselves have errors in them. What you do in these circumstances is go to the Tools menu, pick Options, and then select the Advanced pane. Among the Coding Options group is Break on All Errors:

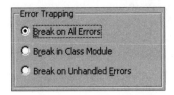

If you turn on this option, Access will ignore your error-handling routines and always use the default. This allows you to code error routines as you create your application, but have the option to turn your error routines off for debugging purposes.

Summary

If you've been reading between the lines, you may have realized that the underlying message in this chapter is **planning**. A huge amount of effort goes into tracking down problems in software, and even a little forethought would reduce this wasted, and expensive, time. It always pays off in the end.

Part of this planning process is pre-empting the user. Try to think of the things that they do, so that your program is easy to use. Try not to get into the position where an error message leads them into thinking they've done something wrong – I call this rude software. It's just plain nasty popping up horrible error messages telling them they've done something wrong. If you can write your program in a way that doesn't allow them to do wrong things, then you've got less of a problem trying to handle those unforeseen errors.

So, in this chapter we've looked at:

- ❏ What errors are, and how you should design your program to minimize them.
- ❏ The type of testing you should use.
- ❏ How to debug your application if you do find errors.
- ❏ How to write error-handling code.

It would be great if you never had to reference this chapter again. Not because you've remembered what was in it, but because you don't need to. However you probably will have to do some debugging at one stage or another, so learning what to do and how to prevent it can only make your life easier. Another method of preventing errors is using object orientation, and that's the topic of the next chapter.

Exercises

1. Examine the forms in the sample database. Do you think that any error routines could be removed and a global error routine used instead? What would be the disadvantage of this?

2. Having thought about a central error routine, create one. Give it two arguments: strProc, which should be the name of the procedure that calls the routine, and optionally, strDesc, for a general description. The routine should check to see if the error was a VBA error or a Data Access error, and display any messages in a message box, along with the procedure that called the routine, and the additional text.

Using Classes

Back in Chapters 6 and 7, we introduced the concept of object-oriented programming. We looked at the Access object model and the Data Access Object hierarchy and how working with these different types of objects is really at the heart of programming in VBA. In this chapter, we are going to look at how we can create our own objects and how we can extend the functionality of Access and VBA.

For many people, the idea of object-orientation seems a bit scary. There are all those long words like **instantiation**, **encapsulation**, **inheritance** and (my favorite) **polymorphism**. And don't you need to know all about **callback functions** and **inproc servers** and all that? Well, not really. The implementation of class modules and user-defined objects in Access 2000 is actually fairly simple. It may not give you the flexibility of tools such as Visual C++, but what that means in turn is that it is very easy to pick up. Hopefully, this chapter will show you just how easy it is, and by the time you finish you should have added a very powerful tool to your programming armory.

We'll be looking at the following topics in this chapter:

- ❑ What objects are
- ❑ The benefits of object-based programming
- ❑ Building and instantiating custom objects
- ❑ Building object hierarchies through collections
- ❑ Custom properties and methods for forms
- ❑ Creating multiple instances of a form

Class Modules and Custom Objects

If you can remember that far back, in Chapters 6 and 7 we looked at the two primary groups of objects that we work with in Access. The Access objects themselves – including Form, Report and Module objects – allow us to manipulate the composition of an Access application whereas the Data Access Object hierarchy – including TableDef, QueryDef and Recordset objects – allows us to access and modify the data in tables programmatically. We are going to spend a little time now reviewing the basics in a little more detail, before we examine how Access provides developers with the capability to create their own custom objects through the use of class modules.

What Are Objects?

Object-oriented development has been a hot topic for quite a few years now, but for many people the topic is one still shrouded in mystery. It often involves obscure jargon and seemingly acrobatic mental leaps and many of the tools that are provided to implement object-oriented development have a steep learning curve. The end result is that many regard it as a black art to be practiced only by the brave, which is a shame, because the principles behind object-orientation are really fairly straightforward, once you get beyond the jargon.

So let's start with the basics and find out what objects really are. There are many definitions of what an object is, but we'll use a simple one to start with and say this:

> An **object** is a self-contained entity that is characterized by a recognizable set of attributes and behaviors.

For example, think of a dog as an object. Dogs are certainly recognizable by their characteristics and their behavior. If we were to put some of these down on paper we might come up with a list like this:

Characteristics	Behaviors
They are hairy	They bark
They have four legs	They bite mailmen
They have a tail	They sniff things

Now, if you were to ask anyone what is hairy, has four legs and a tail and barks, bites and sniffs things, there aren't many people who wouldn't instantly know that you were talking about a dog – you would have described to them quite succinctly the characteristics and behavior of a dog.

In fact, what you would be describing was not any single dog. Rather, you were describing the characteristics and behavior of all dogs. In one sense, what makes a dog a dog is that it is like all other dogs. Sure, there are some minor differences, in size, color (and smell), but all dogs have a certain dogginess. Now, before you start to think that you are reading a book on canine philosophy, let's apply that to the world of software. An object-oriented programmer would have summarized those last couple of paragraphs like this:

- ❑ There exists a **class** called Dog

- ❑ **Instances** of this Dog **class** have the following **properties**: Hairiness, Four-Leggedness, Tailedness, Size, Color, Smelliness

- ❑ **Instances** of this Dog class expose the following **methods**: Bark, Bite, Sniff

OK, so let's look at some of that jargon. First of all – **classes**. A **class** is a type of blueprint or mold. In the case of animals that blueprint is genetic. If the object we were talking about were candles, the blueprint would be the mold into which the wax is poured.

Individual dogs and candles are **instances** of their particular class, and as such they inherit the characteristics of the class to which they belong. Dogs bark because that is a characteristic of the Dog class. So we can now define a class.

> A **class** is a blueprint or template that defines the methods and properties of a particular type of object.

Now, let's have a look at an object in the Data Access Object hierarchy with which we are already familiar – the Recordset object – and see how it fits into our model. First of all we can say that all Recordset objects have the same properties and methods. The properties include things like the RecordCount property, which is the number of records in the Recordset object, and the Updatable property, which indicates whether the Recordset object can be updated. The methods include the GetRows method, which takes a given number of records and places them into an array. All Recordset objects possess the same built-in methods and properties, because they are all derived from the same class. As Access developers we cannot see the class itself – all we see are the objects that are instantiated from that class. The class itself (CDaoRecordset) was defined by Microsoft developers using the language C. What we see in VBA are instances of that class.

Why Use Objects?

Now we are getting a feel for what objects and classes are, we can start to think about some of the benefits of using them. Hopefully, this section will blow away some of the mystique that surrounds the long words that plague object orientation. The major benefits of using classes to create custom objects in Access originate from the principles of abstraction, encapsulation and polymorphism. We'll have a look at what those mean right now...

Abstraction

One of the more important advantages of using classes is gained through something called **abstraction**. What that means is simply that users of the object shouldn't have to know the nitty-gritty of how the object does what it does. In other words, the developer doesn't need to worry about technicalities. It is a bit like turning an electric light on. People don't need to know anything about voltage, current and resistance. All they need to know is how to flick a switch. They are removed from the physics that results in the bulb lighting and the room getting brighter.

We can see how this works with built-in DAO objects such as the Recordset object. All we need to do is to use the Requery method and somehow the Recordset object is repopulated with a more recent set of data. How does it do it? Who cares! All we need to know is that it works. And that is cool, because it means that we can spend more time developing our application rather than worrying about the low-level details of things like cursor functionality.

We can do the same with the custom objects that we build using class modules. In fact one of our goals when creating objects using class modules should be to keep the interface as simple as possible, irrespective of how complicated the implementation might be.

> Abstraction means we can use objects without having to know the software details of how the object does what it does. This makes them easy to use and is one of the key advantages of using classes to define custom objects in Access.

Encapsulation

Closely related to abstraction is the idea of **encapsulation**. Objects should encapsulate within them everything they need to allow them to do what they do. That means that they should contain their own methods, properties and data – and it means that they don't need to rely on other objects to allow them to exist or to perform their own actions.

As we saw in Chapter 6, Forms and Reports are types of objects. They illustrate encapsulation quite well – if you use VBA for your event procedures you can import a form into another database and all the controls on the form and the code in its module go over with it. It's all encapsulated in the form.

Another good example of encapsulation is an ActiveX control such as the Calendar control. The Calendar control carries with it – or encapsulates – its own methods and properties, which are immediately accessible to you when you place it on a form. You could even think of this as a kind of software Plug and Play technology for developers: one programmer writes a component – and that component can simply be plugged into another program and function properly.

> Encapsulation makes it easy to reuse classes. This can, not only speed up subsequent development projects that use these objects, but it also makes group development much easier. This reusability is a key benefit of building our own custom objects in Access – if we do it right!

Polymorphism

What a great word! The concept is pretty cool – it just means that you can have a whole load of disparate objects, but you can tell them all to do the same thing and they'll all know how to do it. Put another way, it means that objects can share the same methods and properties, but have different content behind the methods and properties to implement their behavior. For example, controls, forms and pages in Access all have a SetFocus method. In all these cases, invoking the method shifts focus to the selected object, but the way they do it 'under the hood' is different in each case.

We can implement polymorphism in the custom objects we build in Access using class modules in two ways: through early binding and through late binding. We will look at both of these techniques later in this chapter.

> The advantage of polymorphism is that we can present a familiar, consistent interface to the users of our custom objects, whilst hiding the differences in implementation.

Inheritance

Inheritance is mentioned here, as it is a fairly key concept of object-oriented design. What it means is that you can use a class to create a subclass that inherits all of the class's methods and properties. In the analogy we have been using, we could say that the Dog class is a subclass of the Mammal class. It therefore inherits the properties and methods of that class. Properties such as hairiness and methods such as suckling are inherited from the Mammal class.

Inheritance makes it easier to create new classes, as you are often able to simply sub-class an existing class and then add some specialization. However, there is no opportunity for this when using custom objects in Access, as VBA does not support it.

The MyRectangle Class

That's enough of the theory. What we'll do now is to build a fairly simple class so that we can analyze how Access implements the four features of abstraction, encapsulation, polymorphism and inheritance.

In fact, we will be creating a simple method of determining the area of a rectangle given its height and width. The formula that we use to calculate the area is quite straightforward:

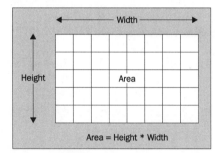

However, we would like our programmers to be able to derive the area without having to remember even this bit of mathematics.

This is, of course, a deliberately simple example. Later in the chapter, once we have got to grips with how class modules work, we will look at a more realistic example of using an object to hide the technicalities of some of the business rules used by the Ice Cream Shop.

Try It Out – Creating the MyRectangle Class

1. Open up the `IceCream.mdb` database and switch to the VBA IDE by hitting *ALT+F11*.

2. Insert a new class module. You can do this either by selecting **C**lass Module from the **I**nsert menu or by hitting the Insert Class Module button on the toolbar.

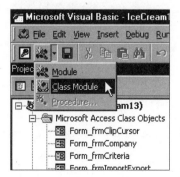

3. A new class called `Class1` should now appear in the Project Explorer window. If the Properties window is not visible, make it so by hitting *F4* and then change the name of the class to `MyRectangle`.

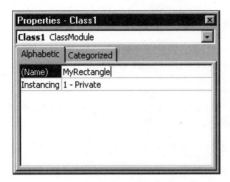

4. Now, in the code window, add the following declarations to the `Declarations` section of the class module.

```
Option Compare Database
Option Explicit

Private dblHeight As Double
Private dblWidth As Double
```

5. Next add the following two `Property Let` procedures making sure that you declare them with `Public` scope. Don't worry about the strange syntax; we will look at how they work in just a moment.

```
Public Property Let Height(dblParam As Double)

    dblHeight = dblParam

End Property
```

```
Public Property Let Width(dblParam As Double)

    dblWidth = dblParam

End Property
```

6. Now you want to add the following three `Property Get` procedures as they appear below. Again, we will look at how they work later on.

```
Public Property Get Height() As Double

    Height = dblHeight

End Property
```

```
Public Property Get Width() As Double

    Width = dblWidth

End Property
```

```
Public Property Get Area() As Double

    Area = dblHeight * dblWidth

End Property
```

7. That is our class completed, so save the module as `MyRectangle` by hitting *CTRL+S*.

8. Now create a new standard code module and call it `Chapter 13 Code`. Add the following procedure to the new module.

```
Sub ClassDemo()

Dim objRect As MyRectangle

Set objRect = New MyRectangle

objRect.Height = 5
objRect.Width = 8

Debug.Print "The area of a rectangle measuring " & objRect.Height & _
            " x " & objRect.Width & " is " & objRect.Area

Set objRect = Nothing

End Sub
```

9. Now run the `ClassDemo` procedure by typing its name in the Immediate window and hitting *Enter*. If you have typed everything in correctly, you should see the following result.

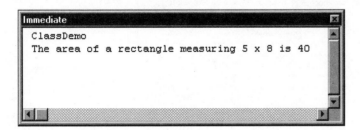

So there we have a fully functioning class that we can use to determine a rectangle's area whenever we want to!

How It Works

In this exercise we created a `MyRectangle` class. This has three properties: `Height`, `Width` and `Area`.

The first thing that we did was to create a new class by inserting a new class module into our project, a simple enough process. We then declared two private variables that would be used to store the dimensions of the height and width of the rectangle:

```
Private dblHeight As Double
Private dblWidth As Double
```

It is important to notice that these variables all have `Private` scope. That is to say that although available for use anywhere within the class module, they cannot be accessed from outside the class module. These are part of the implementation of the class; they are not part of its interface and their values can only be viewed or changed by code within the class module itself.

> *The interface is that part of an object that is exposed on the outside to users of the object; it defines how we are allowed to interact with the object. The implementation is the code, internal to the class and invisible from the outside, which is responsible for defining how the object does what it does. If the lighting in your house was implemented as an object, the interface would consist of the light switches and lamps, and the implementation would consist of the electrical wiring.*

So how do developers specify the dimensions of the rectangle? The answer is that they set the object's `Height` and `Width` properties. We expose properties by using two special types of procedure. A `Property Let` procedure is used to expose a writeable property and a `Property Get` procedure is used to expose a readable property. In other words, we use a `Property Let` if we want developers to be able to let the object's property equal some value; and we use a `Property Get` if we want developers to be able to get (i.e. read) the value of the property. If a property is to be readable and writeable then we use both a `Property Get` and a `Property Let` procedure.

We'll have a look first at one of the writeable properties:

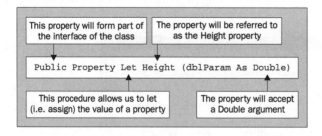

Once the object has been created, a developer can set the value of the `Height` property like this:

```
objRect.Height = 5
```

When this happens, the value (5) is automatically passed into the Property Let procedure as the argument dblParam. The single line of code in the Property Let procedure places this value in the module-level Private variable dblHeight that we declared earlier.

```
dblHeight = dblParam
```

The Area property is exposed as a read-only property. That means that we do not need a Property Let procedure, but use a Property Get procedure instead.

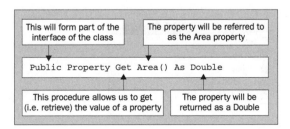

The value returned by the Area property is the result of multiplying the rectangle's height by its width.

```
Area = dblHeight * dblWidth
```

The Height and Width properties are readable and writeable because they each have a Property Get and a Property Let procedure. By contrast, the Area property is read-only because it has a Property Get procedure but no Property Let procedure.

Less commonly we may encounter write-only properties (that is properties whose values we can set but cannot inspect). The Password property of the User object in the DAO hierarchy is a write-only property. If we wanted to implement a write-only property in one of our class modules, we would do so by exposing the property via a Property Let procedure with no associated Property Get procedure.

> The point of this example is to show how you can hide a piece of logic behind a simple interface. In this case, the logic (working out the area of the rectangle) is very straightforward, but in many situations the logic stored within the implementation of object can be quite complex. In fact the more complex the logic, the more benefit can be realized by wrapping it up in an object with a simple interface.

That is really all there is to defining our class. What we end up with is a class that can be used to create MyRectangle objects. It has two read/write properties (Height and Width) and a read-only Area property.

When we want to use one of these MyRectangle objects, we create it using this syntax.

```
Dim objRect As MyRectangle

Set objRect = New MyRectangle
```

The first line creates a variable `objRect` designed to hold a pointer to the `MyRectangle` object. Note that at this stage the object has not been created, there is just a variable ready to reference the object once it is created. The second line is the one that actually creates an instance of a `MyRectangle` object and returns a reference to it as `objRect`.

You might have noticed as we were typing in the first line of code that the `MyRectangle` class actually appeared within the list of available object types.

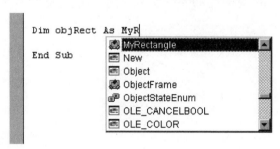

The next step is to create an instance of a `MyRectangle` and we do this by using the `New` keyword.

```
Set objRect = New MyRectangle
```

This is a key moment in the whole process. It is the programming equivalent of Dr. Frankenstein throwing the big switch on the wall and looking on in amazement as his creation comes to life. Whereas before we just had a lifeless class, we now have a living, breathing object... A `MyRectangle` object has been created and a reference to it is returned in the `objRect` variable. Oh, the rapture...

A little more prosaically, once the new `MyRectangle` object has been created, we can then set its `Height` and `Width` properties:

```
objRect.Height = 5
objRect.Width = 8
```

And then, we can inspect the object's `Height`, `Width` and `Area` properties.

```
Debug.Print "The area of a rectangle measuring " & objRect.Height & _
            " x " & objRect.Width & " is " & objRect.Area
```

Again, notice that as we type in the lines above, we are prompted with the names of the properties that we created because they form part of the object's public interface.

Finally, once we have finished with our monster (sorry, object) we destroy it by setting it to `Nothing`, so releasing any resources that it was using up.

```
Set clsRect = Nothing
```

So, that's how easy it is to implement an object with readable and writeable properties. But what about methods? Well, we'll see just how easy that is now by implementing a new method for our MyRectangle object. The new DoubleSides method will double the height and width of the rectangle that we create.

Try It Out – Extending the MyRectangle Class

1. Open up the MyRectangle class module which we created in the previous exercise and add the following procedure definition:

```
Public Sub DoubleSides()

    dblHeight = dblHeight * 2
    dblWidth = dblWidth * 2

End Sub
```

2. Now open the Chapter 13 Code module, locate the ClassDemo procedure and add the following lines of code to it:

```
Debug.Print "The area of a rectangle measuring " & objRect.Height & _
            " x " & objRect.Width & " is " & objRect.Area
```

```
objRect.DoubleSides

Debug.Print "The area of a rectangle measuring " & objRect.Height & _
            " x " & objRect.Width & " is " & objRect.Area
```

```
Set objRect = Nothing
```

3. Now save the changes you have made and run the ClassDemo procedure in the Immediate window. This time the result you see should look like this:

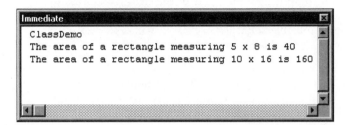

```
ClassDemo
The area of a rectangle measuring 5 x 8 is 40
The area of a rectangle measuring 10 x 16 is 160
```

As you can see, the DoubleSides method has doubled the rectangle's height and width (and the area has therefore increased four-fold).

How It Works

To implement a method in our custom object, we simply need to add a public procedure to the class module. The procedure needs to be Public, because it forms part of the MyRectangle object's interface.

This procedure can then be invoked as a method of the MyRectangle object. And as we would expect, it appears in the Auto List Members popup when we refer to our object in code:

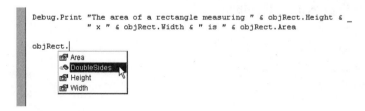

It really is as simple as that!

Before we look in more detail at creating methods and properties, let's revisit those four concepts that we discussed earlier in relation to classes (abstraction, encapsulation, polymorphism and inheritance) and see how they apply in this situation.

Abstraction

The principle behind abstraction is producing a simple interface and hiding the complexity of the implementation. It's a bit like watching a swan gliding across the water. It looks so graceful you would think that there was nothing to it, but if you look underwater you will see that its legs are pumping away like there is no tomorrow! That's what we should aim for with our classes, a simple interface irrespective of the complexity of the implementation.

To be fair, the MyRectangle class does not contain any excessively complex logic. The calculation of the area is fairly straightforward. But that's because this is a deliberately simple example to show you how to build classes. In practice the logic implemented by a class's methods and properties might be exceedingly obscure and complicated. But users of the class won't need to worry about what is going on under the hood. They simply set or inspect the properties or invoke the methods and all the hard work is done by the object. Easy!

Encapsulation

This is a strong point of the MyRectangle class. It is completely self-contained and doesn't rely on the existence of any other objects in order to allow it to operate properly. We could export this class into another database and it would function just as well there.

The other thing to notice is that the two key variables that hold the sizes of the height and width of the rectangle (dblHeight, dblWidth) are owned by the object itself (i.e. they are Private) and cannot be manipulated directly by external code. The only way that developers can interact with our MyRectangle object is through the interface we have defined, while the rest of the implementation is hidden away.

So our MyRectangle class scores highly for encapsulation.

Polymorphism

This is a slightly tougher one. If you remember, polymorphism means that different objects can share the same methods and properties, but can have different content behind the methods and properties to implement their behavior. On its own the MyRectangle doesn't exhibit polymorphism, but we can see how we can introduce it if we define a new MyKite class.

A kite is a two-dimensional object whose area can be calculated by multiplying its height by its width and dividing by two.

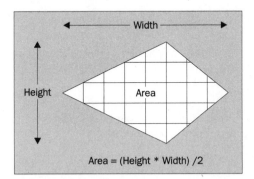

So we can create a MyKite class to return an Area property like this:

```
Option Compare Database
Option Explicit

Private dblHeight As Double
Private dblWidth As Double

Public Property Let Height(dblParam As Double)

    dblHeight = dblParam

End Property

Public Property Let Width(dblParam As Double)

    dblWidth = dblParam

End Property

Public Property Get Height() As Double

    Height = dblHeight

End Property

Public Property Get Width() As Double

    Width = dblWidth

End Property
```

```
Public Property Get Area() As Double

    Area = (dblHeight * dblWidth) / 2

End Property
```

```
Public Sub DoubleSides()

    dblHeight = dblHeight * 2
    dblWidth = dblWidth * 2

End Sub
```

> *You might find this section easier to follow if you build the* MyKite *class by using the code laid out in this section. Alternatively, you can find all of this code in the* IceCream13.mdb *database.*

Now if we wanted to determine the area of a kite, we could use our MyKite class to do this by writing a procedure such as this in a standard code module:

```
Sub ClassDemo2()

Dim objKite As MyKite

Set objKite = New MyKite

objKite.Height = 5
objKite.Width = 8

Debug.Print "The area of a kite measuring " & objKite.Height & _
            " x " & objKite.Width & " is " & objKite.Area

objKite.DoubleSides

Debug.Print "The area of a kite measuring " & objKite.Height & _
            " x " & objKite.Width & " is " & objKite.Area

Set objKite = Nothing

End Sub
```

If you run this code, you should see this in the Immediate window:

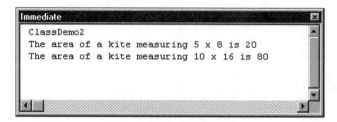

This should look fairly familiar! Both the MyRectangle class and the MyKite class share two read-write properties (Height and Width), a read-only Area property and a DoubleSides method. We have implemented a form of polymorphism across our objects. So what good is that?

Well, for one thing it makes it easier for the developer to learn how to use the objects, as there is just one interface to learn. We define the dimensions of the MyRectangle and MyKite objects with just the same syntax, and we can find their areas by inspecting the same property

It also means that we can write a procedure that treats both MyRectangle and MyKite objects the same like this:

```
Function GetObjectArea(obj As Object, _
                       dblHeight As Double, _
                       dblWidth As Double) As Double


obj.Height = dblHeight
obj.Width = dblWidth
GetObjectArea = obj.Area

End Function
```

If we wanted to, we could pass a MyRectangle object to the GetObjectArea function:

```
Sub ClassDemo3()

Dim objRectangle As MyRectangle
Set objRectangle = New MyRectangle

Debug.Print "The rectangle's area is " & GetObjectArea(objRectangle, 5, 8)

Set objRectangle = Nothing

End Sub
```

Or we could pass a MyKite object in, just as easily:

```
Sub ClassDemo3a()

Dim objKite As MyKite
Set objKite = New MyKite

Debug.Print "The kite's area is " & GetObjectArea(objKite, 5, 8)

Set objKite = Nothing

End Sub
```

And in both situations, the GetObjectArea function is able to use the object's Height, Width and Area properties, irrespective of whether the object passed in is a MyRectangle object or a MyKite object.

```
obj.Height = dblHeight
obj.Width = dblWidth
GetObjectArea = obj.Area
```

The problem with this technique is that we have to use a generic object variable (i.e. the variable obj uses the Object data type). Because of this, VBA does not know what type of object will be stored in the variable and, as a result, we are not prompted with the names of the properties when we use the dot operator after the variable obj.

More importantly, if we mis-spell the name of one of the properties, VBA will not pick up this error when we compile our code. Instead, the first time we will know that we have got the property name wrong is when we try to run our code. So a line like this will not cause a compile-time error:

```
obj.Heigjt = dblHeight
```

But when we try to run the ClassDemo3 procedure, VBA will generate a run-time error.

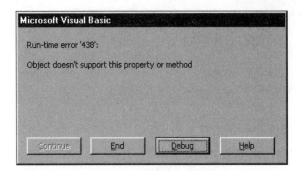

This is because VBA is using a technique known as **late binding**. Not only does late binding make it harder to ensure our code is error-free at design-time; it also makes our code run slower. Fortunately, there is a better way to implement polymorphism.

We will look at the performance implications of late binding later on in Chapter 17.

Polymorphism through Early Binding

Thus far the MyRectangle and MyKite objects share the same interface because we happened to give them both the same properties and methods. However, in VBA it is now possible to implement polymorphism through the use of the Implements keyword. We'll try this out for ourselves, and then investigate how it works and what its implications are.

Try It Out – Using the Implements keyword

1. In the IceCream.mdb database insert a new class module and call it Shape.

2. Add the following code in the code window of the Shape class:

```
Option Compare Database
Option Explicit
```

```
Public Property Let Height(dblParam As Double)
End Property
```

```
Public Property Get Height() As Double
End Property
```

```
Public Property Let Width(dblParam As Double)
End Property
Public Property Get Width() As Double
End Property
```

```
Public Property Get Area() As Double
End Property
```

```
Public Sub DoubleSides()
End Sub
```

3. Now insert a new class module and call it `MyShapelyRectangle`.

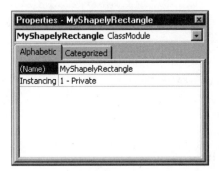

4. At the top of this new class module, add the following statement:

```
Option Compare Database
Option Explicit
```

```
Implements Shape

Private dblHeight As Double
Private dblWidth As Double
```

5. If you look in the object box at the top of the module window, you should see that there is now a reference to `Shape` object.

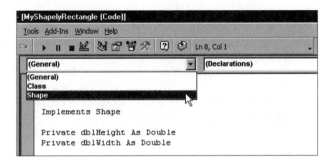

6. Select the Shape object and you should then be able to see the names of the available properties and methods in the procedure combo. Start by selecting the Height property:

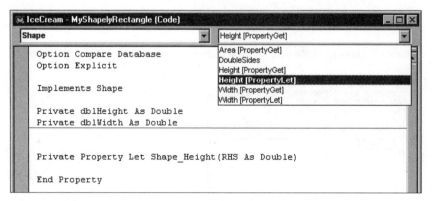

7. Add the following code to the Shape_Height property Let procedure and the Shape_Height property Get procedure:

```
Private Property Let Shape_Height(RHS As Double)

    dblHeight = RHS

End Property

Private Property Get Shape_Height() As Double

    Shape_Height = dblHeight

End Property
```

8. Now add the code for the remaining two properties and for the DoubleSides method. The completed module should now look like this:

```
Option Compare Database
Option Explicit

Implements Shape

Private dblHeight As Double
Private dblWidth As Double

Private Property Get Shape_Area() As Double

    Shape_Area = dblWidth * dblHeight

End Property

Private Sub Shape_DoubleSides()

    dblWidth = dblWidth * 2
    dblHeight = dblHeight * 2

End Sub
```

```
Private Property Let Shape_Height(RHS As Double)

    dblHeight = RHS

End Property

Private Property Get Shape_Height() As Double

    Shape_Height = dblHeight

End Property

Private Property Let Shape_Width(RHS As Double)

    dblWidth = RHS

End Property

Private Property Get Shape_Width() As Double

    Shape_Width = dblWidth

End Property
```

9. Next, create a new `MyShapelyKite` class and repeat steps 4 to 8. However, this time, make sure to define the `Shape_Area` property so that it returns half of the width multiplied by the height. The resultant `MyShapelyKite` module should look like this:

```
Option Compare Database
Option Explicit

Implements Shape

Private dblHeight As Double
Private dblWidth As Double

Private Property Get Shape_Area() As Double

    Shape_Area = (dblWidth * dblHeight) / 2

End Property

Private Sub Shape_DoubleSides()

    dblWidth = dblWidth * 2
    dblHeight = dblHeight * 2

End Sub

Private Property Let Shape_Height(RHS As Double)

    dblHeight = RHS

End Property
```

```
Private Property Get Shape_Height() As Double

    Shape_Height = dblHeight

End Property
```

```
Private Property Let Shape_Width(RHS As Double)

    dblWidth = RHS

End Property
```

```
Private Property Get Shape_Width() As Double

    Shape_Width = dblWidth

End Property
```

10. Now open the code module Chapter 13 Code which you created earlier in this chapter and add the following three procedures:

```
Function GetShapeArea(shp As Shape, _
                      dblHeight As Double, _
                      dblWidth As Double) As Double


shp.Height = dblHeight
shp.Width = dblWidth
GetShapeArea = shp.Area

End Function
```

```
Sub ClassDemo4()

Dim shpRectangle As Shape
Set shpRectangle = New MyShapelyRectangle

Debug.Print "The rectangle's area is " & GetShapeArea(shpRectangle, 5, 8)

Set shpRectangle = Nothing

End Sub
```

```
Sub ClassDemo4a()

Dim shpKite As Shape
Set shpKite = New MyShapelyKite

Debug.Print "The kite's area is " & GetShapeArea(shpKite, 5, 8)

Set shpKite = Nothing

End Sub
```

11. Finally, run the ClassDemo4 and ClassDemo4a subprocedures in the Immediate window. You should see the correct results:

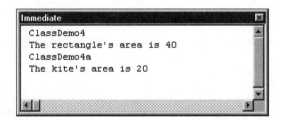

So now we have two separate objects, the MyShapelyKite and the MyShapelyRectangle objects, sharing a single common interface define by the Shape class module. "So what?" you might say! Well, just like in the previous example, we can treat these two objects the same (that is they can both be passed in to the GetShapeArea procedure). The key difference, however is that this time we are using **early-binding**. That means that not only will our code execute more quickly at run-time, but also we are much less likely to make mistakes when we write our code in the first place. Let's look at how it works.

How It Works

The first thing that we do in this exercise is to create a dummy interface class called Shape. The purpose of this class is purely to provide a common interface that other classes can then use to provide their own interface services.

As you can see, the only thing that this class contains is the definitions for the methods and properties that will appear in the interface.

```
Option Compare Database
Option Explicit

Public Property Let Height(dblParam As Double)
End Property

Public Property Get Height() As Double
End Property

Public Property Let Width(dblParam As Double)
End Property

Public Property Get Width() As Double
End Property

Public Property Get Area() As Double
End Property

Public Sub DoubleSides()
End Sub
```

As in the previous examples, the interface for this class will contain a read-write Height and Width property, both of which accept a Double value and one read-only Area property, which returns a Double. There is also a DoubleSides method.

Note how the `Shape` class contains only the definitions for the methods and properties. There is no code to explain how these methods and properties will be implemented. So the interface is now totally separate from the implementation (Object Nirvana!).

The next step is to instruct VBA that the `MyShapelyRectangle` and `MyShapelyKite` classes will use the `Shape` class to provide their interface. We do that by using the `Implements` keyword in the `Declarations` section of the `MyShapelyRectangle` and `MyShapelyKite` class modules.

```
Implements Shape
```

When you insert an `Implements` statement into a class module, VBA then causes the interface elements (that is, the method and property declarations) to be inherited by the class in which the `Implements` keyword is placed. This means that both the `MyShapelyRectangle` and `MyShapelyKite` classes inherit the `Height`, `Width` and `Area` properties and the `DoubleSides` method defined in the `Shape` class. That is why this method of sharing interfaces is sometimes referred to as **interface inheritance**.

We need to be careful when using interface inheritance to make sure that the class inheriting the interface provides handlers for every element of the interface defined in the dummy interface class. In our example, that means that the `MyShapelyRectangle` and `MyShapelyKite` methods must provide handlers for the `Height`, `Width` and `Area` properties and the `DoubleSides` method defined in the `Shape` class.

In order to implement a handler for the inherited interface element, we simply provide a `Private` procedure with the name of the procedure modified to indicate that it represents an inherited element. So whereas our `MyRectangle` class originally implemented its own native `Height` property like this:

```
Public Property Let Height(dblParam As Double)
```

the new `MyShapelyRectangle` now implements the `Height` property that it has inherited from the `Shape` dummy interface class like this:

```
Private Property Let Shape_Height(RHS As Double)
```

As you can see, the first difference is that the name of the procedure is prefixed with the name of the class from which the interface element has been inherited. More interestingly, the property is now declared with the `Private` keyword. So, why is it private? The answer is that the `MyShapelyRectangle` object is now all implementation and no interface. We only want developers to manipulate the object via the `Shape` interface, so that is why the `Shape` class is the only module that will contain public procedures.

> *If you are wondering why VBA gives the parameter the somewhat obscure variable name RHS, it is because the parameter represents the value on the Right Hand Side of the equals sign in the property assignment, i.e.* `shpKite.Height = 8`.

One of the key advantages of interface inheritance is that it allows early binding. Because both `MyShapelyRectangle` and `MyShapelyKite` objects share the same `Shape` interface, we can define a variable as a `Shape` and then use it store references to both `MyShapelyRectangle` and `MyShapelyKite` objects.

So, whereas before we had to pass the generic object like this:

```
GetObjectArea (obj As Object, ...
```

We can now pass it like this:

```
GetShapeArea (shp As Shape, ...
```

The advantage of this technique is that, because VBA knows that we will be dealing with objects that use the Shape interface, it can prompt us with the names of the objects' methods and properties as we are typing code in the GetShapeArea procedure.

```
Function GetShapeArea(shp As Shape, _
                      dblHeight As Double, _
                      dblWidth As Double) As Double


shp.Height = dblHeight
shp.
     📷 Area
     ➡️ DoubleSides
     📷 Height
     📷 Width
```

In fact, we can use the very same variable within the same subroutine to contain a reference first to MyShapelyRectangle object, and then to a MyShapelyKite object, as shown in the code sample below:

```
Sub ClassDemo4b()

Dim shp As Shape

'First we use shp to refer to a MyShapelyKite object
Set shp = New MyShapelyKite

shp.Height = 8
shp.Width = 5
Debug.Print "The kite's area is " & shp.Area

Set shp = Nothing

'And then we use it to refer to a MyShapelyRectangle object
Set shp = New MyShapelyRectangle

shp.Height = 8
shp.Width = 5
Debug.Print "The rectangle's area is " & shp.Area

Set shp = Nothing

End Sub
```

In this example, we would again be prompted with the names of the methods and properties because we are using a Shape object variable:

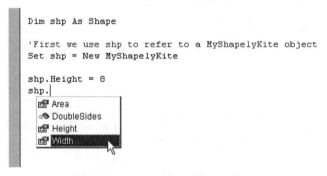

```
Dim shp As Shape

'First we use shp to refer to a MyShapelyKite object
Set shp = New MyShapelyKite

shp.Height = 8
shp.|
```

That shows that VBA is now using **early binding**, which means that not only will it prove easier for us to write error-free code at design-time but also that our code will execute more quickly at run-time.

Inheritance

The fourth and final feature which we noted earlier was characteristic of object-oriented development was inheritance. Unfortunately the current version of VBA does not support inheritance in the traditional sense. True inheritance allows us to take an existing class and derive a subclass from it which inherits both interface and implementation details from the original class. Although VBA allows us to implement interface inheritance through the use of the Implements keyword, there is no easy way to inherit functionality from another class.

The PaymentStats Class

So far we have covered what might seem like a lot of new ground to many of you. If this is your first experience with object-oriented programming, then you might find the wealth of new terminology somewhat overwhelming. So what we'll do now is to look at how we can implement a class in the Ice Cream database. Hopefully, this will help to reinforce some of the concepts that we have covered earlier, while allowing us to look at some more of the features of class-based development in VBA.

The Business Need

As you know, the database that we are using throughout this book is the IceCream.mdb, a database that contains stock and sales information for an ice-cream making company. Anyone who has been involved in running a company will know that one of the most important internal functions within a company is collecting payments. Invoicing clients on a timely basis is fine, but, as the saying goes, "Cash is King!" If clients don't pay their bills in a timely fashion, then a company can very soon find itself facing cash-flow problems.

For this reason, the Dave and Rob's Ice Cream Company employ a credit collection agency, "Harry, Grabbit and Scarper", to collect payment on their outstanding invoices. The Finance Director at Dave and Rob's know that they will be OK if they can ensure that 90% of their invoices are paid within 40 days of the order being received. So Dave and Rob's have a service level agreement in place which states that every month, if Harry, Grabbit and Scarper fail to collect 90% of invoices within 40 days, then they will be fined $1,000 for every percentage point of invoices not collected within that period.

For example, if Harry, Grabbit and Scarper only collect 84% of invoices issued in September within 40 days, then they will have to pay a fine of (90 – 84) * $1,000.00 = $6,000.00

The Finance Director would therefore like to be provided with the following information on a monthly basis for presenting to Board meetings:

❑ What percentage of invoices, for orders placed within that month, were collected within 40 days?

❑ Did Harry, Grabbit and Scarper hit the targets in the service level agreement and, if not, what fine do they owe us?

The Finance Director would also like to know:

❑ What is the shortest delay between a client placing an order in that month and paying for it?

❑ What is the longest delay?

❑ What is the average delay?

The Object Model

To help us to answer these questions, we will build a custom object. This object, which we will call PaymentStats, will contain a month's payment information and will expose a number of simple properties, which allow us to determine the information requested by the Finance Director.

The following table details the properties that our PaymentStats object will need to expose:

Property	Data Type	Read/Write	Comments
MeanDelay	Double	Read Only	Stores the average delay (in days) between invoicing (i.e. DateOrdered) and payment (DatePaid)
MinimumDelay	Integer	Read Only	Stores the minimum delay (in days) between invoicing and payment
MaximumDelay	Integer	Read Only	Stores the maximum delay (in days) between invoicing and payment

The PaymentStats object will also need to return the percentage of invoices paid within 40 days and the fine payable by Harry, Grabbit and Scarper. But these will be implemented as methods.

Method	Arguments	Return Data Type	Comments
Percentile	Days (Integer)	Single	Returns the percentage of invoices paid within the number of days specified by the Days argument
Fine Payable	Days (Integer) Percent (Single) UnitFine (Currency)	Currency	Returns the size of the fine payable calculated according to the following formula: [UnitFine] times ([Percent] minus percent of invoices paid within [Days] days)

The reason that these two methods are exposed as methods, rather than properties, is that by being implemented as methods, we can pass parameters to them. We could have implemented a Percentile property to return the percentage of invoices paid within 40 days. However, that is fairly inflexible. If we changed the service level agreement to say that 90% of invoices had to be paid within 35 days, we would need to re-write the way that the Percentile property was implemented. By implementing Percentile as a method, we can still return a value, but we can parameterize the method to allow us to specify the delay for which we want the percentile returned.

The same argument applies for the FinePayable method. By implementing it as a method rather than a property we can vary the number of days, the percentage cut-off and the unit fine per percentage point by which the credit collection company missed its target.

If we are concerned about the fact that developers will have to remember extra arguments when calling these methods, we can implement them as optional arguments with default values. In other words, for Percentile method, we can make the Delay optional (that is, the programmer can choose to feed it a value or not) but set the default to 40. That way, if there is no argument provided, 40 will be used. This reduces the chances for error but still allows the programmer to change the delay if needed.

Finally, we will need a method for loading the payment data into the PaymentStats object before we perform the various calculations.

Method	Arguments	Return Data Type	Comments
LoadData	Month (Integer) Year (Integer)	N/A	Loads payment data for the specified Month of the specified Year.

Building The Interface

The first step is to create the interface for the new `PaymentStats` object. Once we have done that we can add the implementation.

1. Open up the `IceCream.mdb` database and switch to the VBA IDE by hitting *ALT+F11*.

2. Insert a new class module. You can do this either by selecting <u>C</u>lass Module from the <u>I</u>nsert menu or by hitting the Insert Class Module button on the toolbar.

3. In the Properties window, rename the class `PaymentStats`.

4. Add the following code to create the declarations for the three properties:

```
Option Compare Database
Option Explicit
```

```
Public Property Get MeanDelay() As Double
End Property

Public Property Get MinimumDelay() As Integer
End Property

Public Property Get MaximumDelay() As Integer
End Property
```

5. Now add the declarations for the three methods:

```
Public Sub LoadData(Month As Integer, Year As Integer)
End Sub

Public Function Percentile(Optional Days As Integer = 40) As Single
End Function

Public Function FinePayable(Optional Days As Integer = 40, _
                            Optional Percent As Single = 90, _
                            Optional UnitFine As Currency = 1000) As Currency
End Function
```

6. Save the changes you have made to this class module and then open up the standard code module `Chapter 13 Code`.

7. Add the following procedure that we will use to create an instance of the `PaymentStats` class, load it with data and then retrieve the information we want.

```
Sub ShowPaymentStats(intMonth As Integer, intYear As Integer)

Dim objPayStats As PaymentStats
Set objPayStats = New PaymentStats

objPayStats.LoadData intMonth, intYear

Debug.Print "  Min Delay: "; objPayStats.MinimumDelay
Debug.Print "  Max Delay: "; objPayStats.MaximumDelay
Debug.Print " Mean Delay: "; objPayStats.MeanDelay
Debug.Print " 40 day %ile: "; objPayStats.Percentile
Debug.Print "Fine Payable: "; objPayStats.FinePayable

End Sub
```

8. Next compile the project by selecting **Compile Ice Cream** from the **Debug** window.

9. Finally, run the `ShowPaymentStats` procedure by typing the following in the Immediate window and hitting *Enter*.

```
ShowPaymentStats 12, 1998
```

You should see the results shown below.

How It Works

Ok, so there is not a lot of functionality here at the moment, but at least we have got the interface sorted out. The `ShowPaymentStats` procedure accepts two arguments, `intMonth` and `intYear`, which between them denote the month whose data is to be analyzed.

The first two lines of the `ShowPaymentStats` procedure create a new instance of the `PaymentStats` class.

```
Dim objPayStats As PaymentStats
Set objPayStats = New PaymentStats
```

We then invoke the `LoadData` method, which will load the appropriate month's data into the object.

```
objPayStats.LoadData intMonth, intYear
```

Next, we inspect the three properties of the `PaymentStats` object.

```
Debug.Print "   Min Delay: "; objPayStats.MinimumDelay
Debug.Print "   Max Delay: "; objPayStats.MaximumDelay
Debug.Print "  Mean Delay: "; objPayStats.MeanDelay
```

And finally we invoke the two methods that return values.

```
Debug.Print " 40 day %ile: "; objPayStats.Percentile
Debug.Print "Fine Payable: "; objPayStats.FinePayable
```

Notice that we are not supplying arguments to these two methods. That is because the arguments have been declared as `Optional` and have default values. This means that the two lines above are equivalent to these:

```
Debug.Print " 40 day %ile: "; objPayStats.Percentile 40
Debug.Print "Fine Payable: "; objPayStats.FinePayable 40, 90, 1000
```

Implementing the Logic

Now that we have implemented the interface for the `PaymentStats` class, we can set about implementing its functionality. That's what we will do in this next exercise.

Try It Out – Implementing the PaymentStats logic

1. Open up the code window for the `PaymentStats` class module and add the following private variable declarations at the top of the class module.

```
Option Compare Database
Option Explicit
```

```
Private varSalesArray As Variant
Private lngTotalRecords As Long
Private lngTotalDelay As Long
Private dblMeanDelay As Double
Private intMinDelay As Integer
Private intMaxDelay As Integer
Private sngPercentile As Single
```

2. Now add the following code to the procedure which defines the `LoadData` method:

```
Dim rec As Recordset
Dim strSQL As String
```

```
strSQL = "SELECT DatePaid - DateOrdered AS PaymentDelay " & _
        "FROM tblSales " & _
        "WHERE Month(DateOrdered) = " & Month & " " & _
        "AND Year(DateOrdered) = " & Year & " " & _
        "AND Not IsNull(DatePaid) " & _
        "ORDER BY DatePaid - DateOrdered"
Set rec = CurrentDb.OpenRecordset(strSQL, dbOpenSnapshot)
If rec.RecordCount Then
    rec.MoveLast
    rec.MoveFirst
    varSalesArray = rec.GetRows(rec.RecordCount)
End If
rec.Close

If VarType(varSalesArray) And vbArray Then
    CalcStats
End If
```

3. Next add the `CalcStats` procedure to the class module, making sure to define it as a `Private` subprocedure:

```
Private Sub CalcStats()

Dim i As Integer

'Determine total records
lngTotalRecords = UBound(varSalesArray, 2) + 1

'Determine total dispatch delay
lngTotalDelay = 0
For i = 0 To lngTotalRecords - 1
    lngTotalDelay = lngTotalDelay + varSalesArray(0, i)
Next

'Determine mean payment delay
dblMeanDelay = lngTotalDelay / lngTotalRecords

'Determine minimum and maximum delays
intMinDelay = varSalesArray(0, 0)
intMaxDelay = varSalesArray(0, lngTotalRecords - 1)

End Sub
```

4. Now we need to put in the code which will return values from the three properties:

```
Public Property Get MeanDelay() As Double

MeanDelay = dblMeanDelay

End Property
```

```
Public Property Get MinimumDelay() As Integer

MinimumDelay = intMinDelay

End Property
```

```
Public Property Get MaximumDelay() As Integer

MaximumDelay = intMaxDelay

End Property
```

5. Finally, we need to implement the logic to return values from the `Percentile` and `FinePayable` methods. To do this, modify these two procedures so that they look like this:

```
Public Function Percentile(Optional Days As Integer = 40) As Single

Dim i As Integer

If VarType(varSalesArray) And vbArray Then
    Percentile = 100
    For i = 0 To lngTotalRecords - 1
        If (varSalesArray(0, i)) > Days Then
            Percentile = 100 * i / lngTotalRecords
            Exit Function
        End If
    Next
End If

End Function
```

```
Public Function FinePayable(Optional Days As Integer = 40, _
                            Optional Percent As Single = 90, _
                            Optional UnitFine As Currency = 1000) As Currency

Dim sngPercentActual As Single

If VarType(varSalesArray) And vbArray Then
    sngPercentActual = Percentile(Days)
    If sngPercentActual < Percent Then
        FinePayable = (Percent - sngPercentActual) * UnitFine
    End If
End If

End Function
```

That is the class completed! All that remains is to test it out by re-running the `ShowPaymentStats` procedure and inspecting the results for December 1998. You can do this by typing `ShowPaymentStats 12, 1998` in the Immediate window. You should see the following results.

465

How It Works

Now there is quite a lot of material to cover here, but most of it uses techniques that we have already encountered.

```
Private varSalesArray As Variant
Private lngTotalRecords As Long
Private lngTotalDelay As Long
Private dblMeanDelay As Double
Private intMinDelay As Integer
Private intMaxDelay As Integer
Private sngPercentile As Single
```

First up, we declare the variables that we will be using within this class. Note that these are all declared privately. That means that the variables can only be viewed within the class module and are not viewable from outside it. Remember, we don't want to expose any of the details of the implementation; all we want to expose is the interface we defined earlier.

The next step is to build the `LoadData` method for loading the sales data into our object. We do this by creating a `Recordset` object, which extracts the payment delay for all orders that were placed in the month specified by the programmer. (For purposes of simplicity we have chosen to exclude orders that have not been paid for yet).

```
strSQL = "SELECT DatePaid - DateOrdered AS PaymentDelay " & _
        "FROM tblSales " & _
        "WHERE Month(DateOrdered) = " & Month & " " & _
        "AND Year(DateOrdered) = " & Year & " " & _
        "AND Not IsNull(DatePaid) " & _
        "ORDER BY DatePaid - DateOrdered"
```

Note that we are retrieving the records ordered in such a way that the orders with the smallest payment delay are retrieved first and the orders with the greatest payment delay last.

We retrieve the records using a read-only cursor. However, we have to be alive to the possibility that there might be no records for the particular month that we have selected. That is why we test the `Recordset` object's `RecordCount` property before we attempt to extract the records into a variable.

```
Set rec = CurrentDb.OpenRecordset(strSQL, dbOpenSnapshot)
If rec.RecordCount Then
    rec.MoveLast
    rec.MoveFirst
    varSalesAray = rec.GetRows(rec.RecordCount)
End If
```

If you can remember that far back, we saw in Chapter 7 that – even though not all of the records might have been returned immediately – the `RecordCount` will always give you an indication of whether at least one record has been returned. That is because, when the `OpenRecordset` method is invoked, VBA will always wait until at least the first record in a non-empty recordset is returned before it passes control to the next line of code. So, the `RecordCount` property of the query will only be 0 if there will definitely be no records in the recordset.

If the query does return records, we need to retrieve them into a variable. However for this operation, we need to make sure that all of the records have finished being retrieved and the easiest way to ensure this is to use the MoveLast method of the Recordset object. Now that is all well and good, but the GetRows method – which is what we will use to copy the records from the Recordset object into the variable – copies rows from the current record onwards. That is why we then need to invoke the MoveFirst method to move back to the beginning of the Recordset object before we invoke the GetRows method.

So, by this stage we have retrieved details of the payment delays for orders placed in the specified month and we have copied them into the variant varSalesArray. Now that we have done that we can perform some the calculations in the CalcStats procedure.

```
If VarType(varSalesArray) And vbArray Then
    CalcStats
End If
```

Of course, we only want to perform these calculations if we were successful in retrieving any records. That is why we use the VarType function to determine what type of variable varSalesArray is. The varSalesArray variable was originally declared as a variant and would have had a VarType of 0 – the default empty data type for uninitialized variables. However, once a value is assigned to varSalesArray, the VarType changes to match the data type of the value held by the variable. Now we saw in Chapter 11 that when an array is placed in a variant variable, the number representing the variable's VarType is incremented by 8192, which is represented by the intrinsic constant vbArray. So, the expression VarType(varSalesArray) And vbArray will return 0 (False) if varSalesArraydoes not contain an array and it will contain a non-zero value if it does contain an array.

> *For more information on using logical operators with the VarType function, have a look back at Chapter 11. If you are still not sure how this works, don't worry. You can achieve a similar effect by replacing the expression VarType(varSalesArray) And vbArray with VarType(varSalesArray) >= vbArray.*

So, if varSalesArray contains an array, we run the CalcStats procedure. This is a fairly straightforward procedure.

```
lngTotalRecords = UBound(varSalesArray, 2) + 1
```

The first step is to determine the total number of records that we have copied into our varSalesArray array. The GetRows method creates a two dimensional array, the first dimension of which represents the number of fields in the original Recordset object and the second representing the number of rows. The array created by GetRows is zero-based, so although the expression UBound(varSalesArray, 2) will return the index of the last element of the array in the dimension representing the rows, we need to add 1 to this to determine the number of elements and therefore the number of rows returned.

Having determined the total number of records, we then loop through the array to determine the total of all of the payment delays added together.

```
lngTotalDelay = 0
For i = 0 To lngTotalRecords - 1
    lngTotalDelay = lngTotalDelay + varSalesArray(0, i)
Next
```

This value is stored in the variable `lngTotalDelay`. It is then very easy to determine the average payment delay:

```
dblMeanDelay = lngTotalDelay / lngTotalRecords
```

The next step is to determine the minimum and maximum payment delays.

```
intMinDelay = varSalesArray(0, 0)
intMaxDelay = varSalesArray (0, lngTotalRecords - 1)
```

These values will be located in the first and last elements of the array because our query returned the records ordered by the magnitude of the payment delay.

So, let's take stock of where we are at the moment. If the `LoadData` method is invoked, the payment delays for the specified period are returned and the values loaded into an array. From this we determine the mean delay, the minimum delay and the average delay. These are calculated in the `CalcStats` function (called by the `LoadData` method after the data has been loaded into the object) and are stored in three private variables (`dblMeanDelay`, `intMinDelay` and `intMaxDelay`). If we want to expose these to the outside world, we need to return them as the values of the relevant properties of the `PaymentStats` object.

```
Public Property Get MeanDelay() As Double
    MeanDelay = dblMeanDelay
End Property

Public Property Get MinimumDelay() As Integer
    MinimumDelay = intMinDelay
End Property

Public Property Get MaximumDelay() As Integer
    MaximumDelay = intMaxDelay
End Property
```

Now that is most of the functionality of the class implemented. All we need to do now is to return the percentage of payments made within a certain number of days and any fine that is due. The `Percentile` method returns the percentage of payments made and relies on the fact that our array is ordered by the magnitude of payment delay.

Because this calculation is carried out every time this method is invoked, we need to check again that the `varSalesArray` variable contains an array.

```
If VarType(varSalesArray) And vbArray Then
  .
  .
  .
End If
```

If it does, then we loop through the array until we find the first element with a payment delay greater than the payment delay specified as an argument to this method:

```
For i = 0 To lngTotalRecords - 1
    If (varSalesArray(0, i)) > Days Then
    .
    .
    .
    End If
Next
```

As soon as we find one, we know that this and all future elements will have a payment delay greater than the one specified. So we can say that the percentage of elements with a payment delay of less than or equal to the specified payment delay is 100 times the current index of the array (i) divided by the total number of elements in the array (lngTotalRecords).

```
Percentile = 100 * i / lngTotalRecords
```

Of course, if a payment delay is specified which is greater than all of those in the array, this line of code will never be reached. That is why we started by initializing the value of Percentile to 100 (i.e. 100%).

```
Percentile = 100
```

The final stage is to calculate the fine payable. To do this, we must again check that there are elements in the array. After all, there is nothing to stop someone invoking the FinePayable method prior to invoking the LoadData method.

Then we find percentage of payments made within the specified period represented by the argument Days (which defaults to 40 days):

```
sngPercentActual = Percentile(Days)
```

And finally we take the difference between the percentage specified by the user (which defaults to 90) and the percentage of payments actually made. If fewer payments than the specified percentage have been made then we multiply the difference by the UnitFine (which defaults to $1000).

```
If sngPercentActual < Percent Then
    FinePayable = (Percent - sngPercentActual) * UnitFine
End If
```

That is the class finished. So we test it out by loading it with data and inspecting its properties.If we have typed all of our code in correctly, we should see the right results!

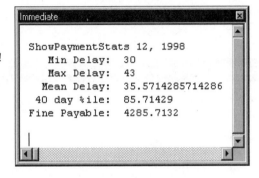

You should be able to see that we could use the same class to give us a listing of all of the fines payable by our credit collection agency in 1998, simply by running the following procedure:

```
Sub ShowFines(intYear As Integer)

Dim i As Integer
Dim objStats As New PaymentStats

For i = 1 To 12
    objStats.LoadData i, intYear
    Debug.Print MonthName(i, True) & _
    " Fine Payable: "; FormatCurrency(objStats.FinePayable, 2, , , vbTrue), _
    objStats.Percentile(40)
Next

End Sub
```

If you run this in the Immediate window, you should see these results.

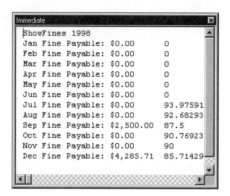

Finishing Touches

So far, we have seen how to create objects with custom methods by using either public functions or public subprocedures. Public subprocedures are used for methods that simply perform an action (for example PaymentStats.LoadData), whereas public functions are used for methods that return a value, such as PaymentStats.FinePayable.

We have also looked at how to expose properties by using Property Get and Property Let procedures. We will use that knowledge to implement an Accuracy property that will allow us to specify the number of decimal places that will be used when returning values from the PaymentStats object.

Try It Out – Adding a Writeable Property

1. Add the following variable declaration to the Declarations section of the PaymentStats object we just created.

```
Private intMaxDelay As Integer
Private sngPercentile As Single
Private intAccuracy As Integer
```

2. Now add the following procedure, which will allow us to inspect the value of the Accuracy property

```
Public Property Get Accuracy() As Integer

Accuracy = intAccuracy

End Property
```

3. Next we will add a procedure to allow us to assign a value to the Accuracy property of the PaymentStats object.

```
Public Property Let Accuracy(DecimalPlaces As Integer)

If DecimalPlaces < 0 Or DecimalPlaces > 9 Then DecimalPlaces = 3
intAccuracy = DecimalPlaces

End Property
```

4. The next step is to use the Accuracy property to modify the way that properties are returned. So we will modify the line in the Percentile property that returns the value so that it now looks like this:

```
If (varSalesArray(0, i)) > Days Then
    Percentile = Round(100 * i / lngTotalRecords, intAccuracy)
    Exit Function
```

5. Then modify the MeanDelay property so that it looks like this:

```
Public Property Get MeanDelay() As Double

MeanDelay = Round(dblMeanDelay, intAccuracy)

End Property
```

6. Save the changes to the PaymentStats object and switch to the Chapter 13 Code module.

7. Finally, modify the ShowPaymentStats subprocedure to include a line to specify the number of decimal places that will be used in returning values from the PaymentStats object.

```
Sub ShowPaymentStats(intMonth As Integer, _
                     intYear As Integer, _
                     Optional intDecimalPlaces As Integer)

Dim objPayStats As PaymentStats
Set objPayStats = New PaymentStats

objPayStats.Accuracy = intDecimalPlaces
objPayStats.LoadData intMonth, intYear
```

```
Debug.Print "   Min Delay: "; objPayStats.MinimumDelay
Debug.Print "   Max Delay: "; objPayStats.MaximumDelay
Debug.Print "  Mean Delay: "; objPayStats.MeanDelay
Debug.Print " 40 day %ile: "; objPayStats.Percentile
Debug.Print "Fine Payable: "; objPayStats.FinePayable

End Sub
```

8. Now, when you run the `ShowPaymentStats` procedure in the Immediate window, it should return the `MeanDelay` property and `Percentile` method to the specified number of decimal places.

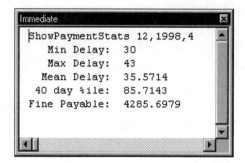

You may find it odd that the accuracy of the fine payable is to 4 decimal places rather than 2 – after all it is a currency value we wish to display. We've left that for you to change as an exercise at the end of this chapter.

How It Works

A value is passed in via the `DecimalPlaces` argument and is stored in the `intAccuracy` variable.

```
intAccuracy = DecimalPlaces
```

It is later used as an argument to the `Round` function when modifying the result of the `MeanDelay` property procedure and the `Percentile` method.

Because the `FinePayable` method uses the `Percentile` method in its calculations, the value it returns is also affected by the use of the `Accuracy` property.

The only thing we need to check is that an appropriate value is passed in as the `Accuracy` argument. If the value is too high or too low, we simply choose to use 3 decimal places instead.

```
If DecimalPlaces < 0 Or DecimalPlaces > 9 Then DecimalPlaces = 3
```

Once the `Accuracy` argument has been added to the interface of the `PaymentStats` object, we can use it in the `ShowPaymentStats` procedure.

```
objPayStats.Accuracy = intAccuracy
```

If we then want to inspect the value of `intAccuracy`, we can do so through the `Public Property Get Accuracy()` procedure which makes the `Accuracy` property readable.

Of course, now that we are using the private `intAccuracy` variable – exposed as the `Accuracy` property – to regulate the number of decimal places in answers returned by the `MeanDelay` property and `Percentile` method, we need to consider what will happen if we do not assign a value to this property. For example, if we ran the `ShowPaymentStats` procedure without assigning a value to the `Accuracy` property, we would get these results:

```
    Min Delay:   30
    Max Delay:   43
   Mean Delay:   36
 40 day %ile:   86
Fine Payable:   4000
```

That is because the `intAccuracy` variable, like all integer variables, is initialized to 0 if no one explicitly assigns a value to it. So, by exposing the `Accuracy` property, we have made the default accuracy for the `PaymentStats` to be zero decimal places. We will look in a few moments at how we can keep the `Accuracy` property readable and writeable, but allow it to default to a different value.

Benefits of an Object-Oriented Approach

But at this stage it is worth looking at the benefits that this approach offers the developer when compared to alternative techniques. If we had not decided to use an object-oriented approach to solving this problem, how could we have done it?

The most likely approach is that we would have used a series of functions, so that our code would have looked something like this:

```
Debug.Print "    Min Delay: "; GetMinimumDelay(intYear, intMonth)
Debug.Print "    Max Delay: "; GetMaximumDelay(intYear, intMonth)
Debug.Print "   Mean Delay: "; GetMeanDelay(intYear, intMonth)
Debug.Print " 40 day %ile: "; GetPercentile(intYear, intMonth)
Debug.Print "Fine Payable: "; GetFinePayable(intYear, intMonth)
```

In this case, each of the five functions would accept a year and month as an argument and return the requested statistic relating to the sales data for that period. Each of these five functions would need to fetch the required subset of data from the sales table and analyze it to determine the correct value of the required statistic. That's five potentially expensive queries to be executed compared to the single one required by our object-based approach.

If we had wanted to minimize the number of times we fetched data from the database, we could incur the one database hit up front like this:

```
Dim varMonthlyDataArray As Variant

varMonthlyDataArray = GetMonthlyData(intYear, intMonth)

Debug.Print "    Min Delay: "; GetMinimumDelay(varMonthlyDataArray)
Debug.Print "    Max Delay: "; GetMaximumDelay(varMonthlyDataArray)
Debug.Print "   Mean Delay: "; GetMeanDelay(varMonthlyDataArray)
Debug.Print " 40 day %ile: "; GetPercentile(varMonthlyDataArray)
Debug.Print "Fine Payable: "; GetFinePayable(varMonthlyDataArray)
```

In this situation, the initial `GetMonthlyData` function would return an array containing the month's sales data and the five subsequent functions would each return the required statistic from that data. Although more efficient from a data access point of view, there is still a major drawback compared to the object-oriented approach.

The drawback is this: if we want to use this functionality in another database, with the procedural approach shown above, we have to copy all six procedures into our new database; with the object-based approach we only have to copy one class module. Because the class encapsulates within itself everything it needs in order to function properly, it provides a significantly more manageable way of building applications than the procedural approach. Now, the `PaymentStats` class is only a very simple business object and the benefits that this encapsulation offers over the procedural approach, although noticeable, are not necessarily compelling. But the more complex the object becomes (and, therefore, the more discrete procedures that can be replaced by a single object) the more convincing the argument for an object-oriented approach becomes.

Another key benefit of the object-oriented approach is the way that it makes programming more intuitive in the VBA programming environment. The ability of VBA to expose an object's properties and methods to a developer via the **Auto List Members** feature (those funny pop-up thingies) means that the object-oriented approach is likely to yield fewer design-time errors and so lead to faster development than the procedural approach. And again, the more complex the object becomes, the more noticeable will be the benefits that this approach offers over the traditional procedural approach.

Using class modules will inevitably involve a slight development overhead compared to the traditional procedural approach, especially if you are new to the concepts of object orientation. For very simple processes, this overhead may not be worth entertaining, but for more complex processes the use of an object-oriented approach will make subsequent programming more intuitive, will increase the possibilities for code reuse and will make code maintenance significantly easier. How can you say no to that?

Class Events

We have seen so far that class modules resemble standard modules, in that they contain a `Declarations` section and can contain `Public` and `Private` procedures. In class modules, `Private` procedures are used to construct the implementation of the class and `Public` procedures are used to expose methods in the interface of the class.

Unlike standard code modules, however, class modules can contain `Public Property` procedures, which are used to expose properties in the interface of the class. `Public Property Get` procedures are used to make properties readable and `Public Property Let` procedures are used to make properties writeable.

> *In fact, there is also a third type of* `Public Property` *procedure, the* `Public Property Set` *procedure, which is used to make properties writeable in situations where the property returns a reference to an object.*

However, there is another, more fundamental way in which standard modules and class modules differ. Standard modules are in scope for the duration of the VBA project to which they belong.

That means that if a variable, constant or procedure is declared with `Public` visibility in a standard code module, then that variable, constant or procedure will remain publicly visible for the whole of the time that the Access database in which that code module is located remains open. Standard code modules do not need to be explicitly loaded or instantiated; they are always there and always accessible.

By way of contrast, class modules provide templates for objects, rather than being objects in their own right. That means that we need to explicitly create an instance of an object based on a class before we can access any of the public procedures (i.e. methods) or properties in the object's interface.

The process of creating a new instance of an object from a class is called instantiation, and we have already seen this in action several times already. For example, we created an instance of the `PaymentStats` class. First, we declared a variable to hold a reference to the new `PaymentStats` object once it was created:

```
Dim objPayStats As PaymentStats
```

And then we actually created an instance of the object and place a reference to it in the `objPayStats` variable:

```
Set objPayStats = New PaymentStats
```

It is worth remembering that it is the second of these lines that actually causes the object to come into existence. You might sometimes see this alternative method of instantiating objects being used:

```
Dim objPayStats As New PaymentStats
```

However, it is recommended that you avoid using this technique for a number of reasons. When you use the `Dim... As New...` syntax, VBA creates a variable to hold a reference to the new object, but it does not actually create an instance of the object until the object is next referenced in code. In fact, when you use this syntax, every time that you subsequently refer to the `objPayStats` variable, VBA checks to see whether the object has been instantiated. If it has, VBA uses the existing object; if not, VBA creates a new instance. The overhead of checking for the existence of this object every time it is referenced means that this method is noticeably slower than specifically instantiating the object straight away using the `Set... = New...` syntax.

The other disadvantage of the `Dim... As New...` syntax is that it is sometimes difficult to keep track of when the object is actually instantiated as this only happens the next time that the object is referenced after the `Dim... As New...` statement.

The Class Initialize and Terminate Events

The more perceptive of you will have noticed that class modules contain a couple of events that do not appear in standard code modules. These are the `Initialize` and the `Terminate` events of the `Class` object. You can see these if you look in the object and procedure combo boxes for the code window of a class module.

The Class_Initialize event fires whenever an object is instantiated from a class module and the Class_Terminate event is fired whenever the object is destroyed.

> Objects can be destroyed either explicitly (by setting the object variable to Nothing) or implicitly when the variable containing the object goes out of scope. Bear in mind that if an object has several variables all containing a reference to it, the object will only be destroyed when all of the variables containing a reference to it go out of scope. We will examine this in more detail later when we look at how to create multiple instances of a form.

A frequent use of the Class_Initialize event is to initialize the value of variables within the new object. For example, we could use the Class_Initialize event of the PaymentStats object to ensure that the initial value of the Accuracy property is something other than 0. To do this, we would add the following code to the Class_Initialize event of the PaymentStats object.

```
Private Sub Class_Initialize()

intAccuracy = 3

End Sub
```

Now, whenever a new instance of the PaymentStats object is created, a value of 3 is instantly assigned to the Private variable intAccuracy. This is exposed as the Accuracy property, and is used to limit the number of decimal places that will be used when returning values via the MeanDelay property and the Percentile method.

Forms as Class Modules

We mentioned earlier in the book that all forms and reports are able to have class modules associated with them. In fact, forms and reports do not have associated class modules by default. The class module is only created when you first attempt to view or enter code in the form's class module. You can actually tell whether a form or report has an associated module by inspecting its HasModule property. This returns True or False to indicate whether the object has an associated class module. This property is read-only at run-time but can be written to at design time.

You can also tell whether a form or report has an associated class module by looking in the Project Explorer window in VBA. If the form or report has a class module it will be listed as a Microsoft Access Class Object.

Creating Custom Properties for Forms

We create custom properties for forms and reports in just the same manner as we do for other classes. The easiest way to see this is to try it out for yourself – so let's do it! In the following example, we will create a Maximized property for the form frmSales and define what happens when the property is set.

Try It Out – Creating a Custom Form Property

1. Open the Chapter 13 Code module that we have been using in this chapter and type the following declaration in the Declarations section of the form's module:

```
Public Declare Function IsZoomed Lib "User32" (ByVal hWnd As Long) As Integer
```

2. Now open the code module for the form frmSales and type in the two new procedures listed below:

```
Public Property Get Maximized() As Boolean

    If IsZoomed(Me.hWnd) Then
        Maximized = True
    Else
        Maximized = False
    End If

End Property

Public Property Let Maximized(blnMax As Boolean)

    If blnMax Then
        Me.SetFocus
```

```
        DoCmd.Maximize
    Else
        Me.SetFocus
        DoCmd.Restore
    End If

End Property
```

3. Close `frmSales`, saving the changes that you have made. Then open it up in Form view. Make sure it isn't maximized and it should look something like this:

4. The important thing to notice on this form is that the control buttons in the top right corner indicate that the form is not maximized.

5. Now switch to the Immediate window by hitting *Ctrl+G*.

6. Inspect the form's `Maximized` property by typing the following in the Immediate window and hitting the *Enter* key.

```
?forms("frmSales").Maximized
```

7. It should return `False`, indicating that the form is not maximized.

8. Now switch back to Access and maximize `frmSales`. Then inspect its `Maximized` property again in the Immediate window. This time it should return `True`, indicating that the form is maximized.

9. Finally set the form's `Maximized` property to `False` in the Immediate window with the following statement.

```
forms("frmSales").Maximized=False
```

10. If you switch back to Access, you should see the form has returned to its normal non-maximized state.

How Does It Work?

In order to create a custom form property, we use the now-familiar `Property Let` and `Property Get` procedures. The `Property Let` procedure allows us to set the property's value and the `Property Get` procedure allows us to interrogate its value. The first procedure we wrote was the `Property Get` procedure.

```
Public Property Get Maximized() As Boolean
```

The procedure creates a property called `Maximized`, which can be either `True` or `False`, and which is `Public`, i.e. visible to all procedures.

```
If IsZoomed(Me.hWnd) Then
    Maximized = True
Else
    Maximized = False
End If
```

These next lines are responsible for determining the value returned to anyone interrogating the value of the `Maximized` property. If `IsZoomed(Me.hWnd)` returns a non-zero value, then the `Maximized` property is returned as `True`, otherwise it is returned as `False`.

`IsZoomed()` is simply an API function, a procedure in an external DLL. The DLL, `User32`, contains procedures that handle interaction of Windows programs with user interfaces, and so is responsible for tasks such as window management.

The `IsZoomed()` procedure takes the handle of a Window as an argument. It returns `False` if the window is not maximized and a non-zero value if it is maximized. A handle is simply a unique long integer identifier generated by Windows and used to allow it to keep track of individual windows and controls. We get the handle of the form's window by using the form's hWnd property. You probably won't come across this property very much, and when you do it will almost invariably be when you want to pass the handle to an API function.

To set the property we use the `Property Let` statement.

```
Public Property Let Maximized(blnMax As Boolean)
```

Again, we can see from the opening line of this procedure that the property's name is `Maximized` and that it has a `Boolean` datatype.

As for the rest of the procedure, it is fairly straightforward.

```
If blnMax Then
    Me.SetFocus
    DoCmd.Maximize
Else
    Me.SetFocus
    DoCmd.Restore
End If
```

If the value to which `Maximized` is being set is non-zero, we need to maximize the form. If the value is being set to `False`, we need to restore the form.

As you can see, creating custom form properties is just the same as creating properties for other class modules and is a fairly simple task once you have got your mind around the syntax of the `Property Let` and `Property Get` statements.

Custom Form Methods

As well as custom form and report properties, you can also create custom form and report methods. To create a custom method, you simply write a procedure within the form (or report) module and expose it outside the form by making it `Public`.

So, to create a `Maximize` method that increases the size of the form in the manner described above, simply type this code into the form module of `frmSales`:

```
Public Sub Maximize()

    Me.Maximized = True

End Sub
```

Because this procedure has been made `Public`, it can be invoked from outside the form in the following manner.

```
forms("frmSales").Maximize
```

And there you have a custom form method! Now that wasn't too hard, was it?

Creating Multiple Instances of Objects

Now we'll move on to another feature that is exposed to us through the object-oriented nature of Access and VBA – the ability to create multiple instances of a single form. When you open a form, you are creating an **instance** of that form. The first instance is called the **default instance**. Most of the time, that is the only instance you will need, but there may be occasions when you want to have multiple instances of the same form open at the same time.

Typically, you will create multiple instances of forms when you want to view two records alongside each other. We will try that out now by creating a popup form to give details of the ingredients of ice creams that appear in the `frmSales` form.

1. In the `IceCream.mdb` database, make a copy of the `frmsubIceCreamIngredients` form, call it `frmIceCreamPopup` and open it up in design view.

2. Open the Properties window and change the form's Pop Up and Has Module properties to Yes.

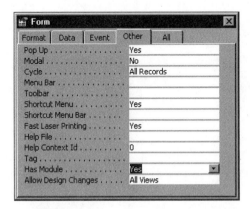

3. Next change the form's RecordSource property to the following SQL string.

```
SELECT *
FROM tblIceCreamIngredient
WHERE fkIceCreamID=[forms]![frmSales]![fkIceCreamID]
```

4. Now close the form, saving changes when prompted to do so.

5. Next, switch to VBA by hitting *ALT+F11* and open `Form_frmSales`, the class module for the `frmSales` form.

6. Add the following code to the `Declarations` section of the class module.

```
Private colForms As New Collection
```

7. Now add the following code to the `DblClick` event handler for the `fkIceCreamID` control.

```
Private Sub fkIceCreamID_DblClick(Cancel As Integer)

Dim frmPopup As Form_frmIceCreamPopup

Set frmPopup = New Form_frmIceCreamPopup

frmPopup.Caption = fkIceCreamID.Column(1)
frmPopup.Visible = True
```

```
colForms.Add frmPopup

End Sub
```

8. Now switch to Access and close the `frmSales` form, saving changes when prompted to do so.

9. Next, open the `frmSales` form and double-click on the combo box containing the name of an ice cream for one of the sales records. This should cause a form to appear detailing the ingredients of that ice cream.

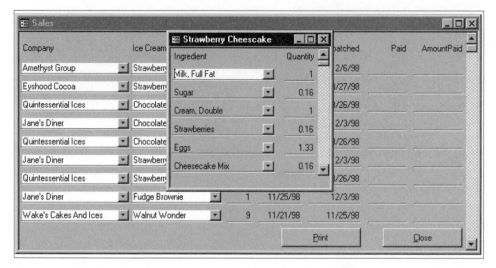

10. Move the pop-up form to one side and double-click on the name of a different ice cream on the `frmSales` form. This should cause a second pop-up form to appear.

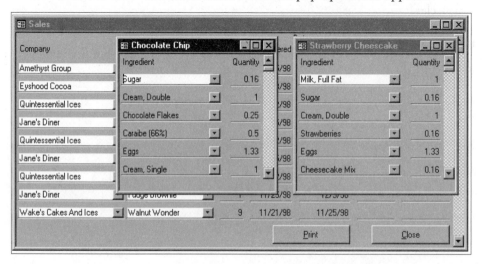

11. Now close the `frmSales` form. This should automatically close both of the pop-up forms as well.

How It Works

This is not as confusing as it might look at first glance. After creating the `frmIcecreamPopup` form, the first thing we have to do is to make sure that the new form has a class module. The reason for that is that we can only create instances of (as opposed to simply open) forms with a class module behind them. That is why we set the form's `HasModule` property to `True`. We also change the form's `Popup` property to `True` to ensure that the form will always remain topmost on the screen.

We then modify the pop-up form's `RecordSource` property to ensure that it will only display details of the selected ice cream.

Next, we add the code to the `frmSales` form to create a new instance of the pop-up form every time the ice cream combo box is double-clicked. Most of this code should seem straightforward. The only unusual line is the one in which we add the variable referring to the pop-up form to a collection declared at the form level.

```
Private Sub fkIceCreamID_DblClick(Cancel As Integer)

Dim frmPopup As Form_frmIceCreamPopup

Set frmPopup = New Form_frmIceCreamPopup

frmPopup.Caption = fkIceCreamID.Column(1)
frmPopup.Visible = True

colForms.Add frmPopup

End Sub
```

Form instances perish when the variables referencing them go out of scope. The variable `frmPopup` was declared at the procedure level, and so will go out of scope when the procedure exits. In other words, the `fkIceCreamID_DblClick` procedure creates a form instance that dies immediately as the procedure ends.

In order to prolong the lifetime of the form instance, we add it to a collection that was declared at the form level (i.e. in the `Declarations` section of the form module for `frmSales`).

```
Option Compare Database
Option Explicit

Dim colForms As New Collection
```

We can then add the form instance to the collection.

```
colForms.Add frmPopup
```

This variable will only go out of scope when the form `frmSales` is closed. Any form instances that are added to the collection survive beyond the end of the procedure that created them, but perish when `frmSales` is closed because, at that point, the collection variable `colForms` goes out of scope.

This is one example where it makes sense to use the `Dim... As New...` *syntax. Remember, when you use the* `New` *keyword in the variable declaration, it is not the declaration of the object (in this case a* `Collection` *object) that causes it to be created. Rather, the object is only instantiated when it is first referenced thereafter. So, in our procedure the* `Collection` *object is created when we try to add the first* `frmPopup` *object to it.*

Collections – Creating a Hierarchy

In fact, collections have another use in object-oriented programming in VBA. You can use collections to create an object hierarchy, just like the Data Access Object hierarchy. For example, if you cast your mind back to the `MyRectangle` class that we created earlier in this chapter, we could have created a `Sides` collection to contain a `Side` object for each of the four sides of the rectangle.

To do this, we would first need to create a public collection in the `Declarations` section of the `MyRectangle` class to contain the child objects.

```
Public Sides As New Collection
```

Next we would need to create a new `Side` class, with the appropriate methods and properties. For example, we could create a `Side` class with a `Length` property – corresponding to the length of the side in centimeters – and an `ImperialLength` property corresponding to the length of the side in inches.

Finally, we would need to add a new instance of the `Side` class to the `Sides` collection of the `MyRectangle` object for each of the four sides of the rectangle when the object was instantiated.

It is left to you as an exercise to implement this `Sides` *collection, but if you want to see how it works you can see it implemented in the final version of the* `MyRectangle` *object in the Solutions database.*

Getting the Most from Class Modules

To finish with, here are five closing thoughts to help you on your way when using objects and collections. It really is worthwhile getting to grips with class modules as they are a key part of Microsoft's programming strategy across all their development products.

Hide Your Data

Make sure that you declare everything privately unless you really want to expose it as a method or property of the class. Public variables act like properties, in that they can be inspected or set from outside the module. However, unlike properties – which have clearly defined `Property Let` and `Property Get` statements – there is no way of detecting when a public property is being set or inspected. So, if you want to expose something, use a property or a method to do so.

If you accidentally expose something you shouldn't, then one of three things could happen:

- ❑ Code outside your object might accidentally alter data within your object.

  This could cause your object to behave in a way other than it should and can be a beast of a bug to track down.

- ❑ Procedures that use your objects may rely on those wrongly-exposed properties for their functionality.

  This makes maintenance a nightmare. You expect to have to check procedures that access your object when you modify your class's interface, but you don't want to have to check that they will still work whenever you modify the implementation as well.

- ❑ Variable names within your objects may clash with variable names in procedures that use your objects.

  This kind of thing doesn't make you too popular…

Don't Overdo It

Although objects are useful in some situations, that's no reason for using them everywhere. Creating an instance of an object and invoking a method of that object not only consumes more memory than calling the function in a standard module, but is also more time-consuming. So use class modules judiciously.

Avoid Get and Set Methods

It is not good practice to create objects with lots of methods whose names begin with `Get` and `Set`. For example, we could have implemented a `GetAccuracy` and `SetAccuracy` method to allow developers to inspect and set the value of the accuracy to be used in the `PaymentStats` object. But if you want users of your objects to 'get' some form of information about of your object, then you should formally expose that information as a property. And if you want users to alter properties of your object, you should make those properties writeable.

Get the Object Model Right

It is easy to just wade in and create models without thinking through exactly what your object model should look like. But the same warning applies to designing objects that applies to designing databases: design time is the best time to design! If you have to redesign your object model halfway through the build process, the chances are that you will then have to change all the code that uses those objects. That's seldom cheap and it's never, ever fun.

Make it Look Easy

We mentioned earlier that one great advantage of using objects is that they offer the possibility of abstraction. In other words, the code inside the object might be quite complex, but the interface the object presents to users is very straightforward. Although it required knowledge of geometry to design the implementation of the `Area` property of the `MyRectangle` class, no such knowledge is required to use the property. The implementation might be complex, but the interface is easy. What's more, implementing polymorphism, through the use of the `Shape` interface class, meant that the `MyShapelyRectangle` and `MyShapelyKite` objects exposed identical properties and methods and so were easier to use. If you knew how to use one, you knew how to use the other.

Summary

That's pretty good going! In just over fifty pages you've got to grips with object-oriented programming! Obviously this chapter doesn't cover everything to do with OOP in Access, but we have covered a good deal of material and certainly enough to get you started.

If you are coming to this from a traditional programming background, you might find it takes a little time to feel totally comfortable with the way it works. But don't worry, just read the chapter again, try out the code and don't be afraid to experiment. After all it's often only when you get down to cutting code for yourself that you really understand how it all fits together.

Exercises

1. In `PaymentStats` class you added a write-only property, `Accuracy`. Make sure that the accuracy is applied to the `FinePayable` method.

2. Try to modify the `MyRectangle` class so that it contains a `Sides` collection. This collection should contain a `Side` object for each of the four sides of the rectangle. The `MyRectangle` should create these when it is created.

   Each of these `Side` objects should have a `Length` property (the length of the side in centimeters which is specified when the `Height` and `Width` properties of the `MyRectangle` are set) and a read-only `ImperialLength` property, which specifies the length of the side in inches (1 inch = 2.54 cm). When you have made these modifications, you should be able to use this procedure to print the area of the rectangle and the lengths of the four sides.

```
Sub ClassDemo5()

Dim objRect As MyRectangle
Dim sd As Side

Set objRect = New MyRectangle

objRect.Height = 5
objRect.Width = 8
```

```
Debug.Print "Area:"; objRect.Area; "cm"

For Each sd In objRect.Sides
    Debug.Print sd.Length; "cm", sd.ImperialLength; "inches"
Next

Set objRect = Nothing

End Sub
```

This should yield the following results:

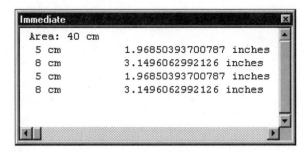

For an indication of the steps you will need to follow to implement this solution, have another look at the section on creating hierarchies using collections towards the end of this chapter.

Libraries and Add-Ins

This chapter is all about code libraries. We're all familiar with libraries of books, and the concept of code libraries is similar. A book library is a public place, and after a quick registration process you can borrow books. You can join many different libraries, giving you a wider range of books to select from. The books are generally arranged according to subject (Fiction, Reference, etc.) and there is usually a full index allowing you to quickly find what you are looking for.

A code library is much the same. It will contain code, forms, tables, etc., and after registering it, you can use the items in the library as though they were in your current database. This means you can use other people's code as well as your own. You've already seen the advantages to code re-use, so this just takes it one step further.

In this chapter we'll be looking at the following:

- ❑ Creating a library database
- ❑ Referencing library databases
- ❑ Creating class libraries
- ❑ Using Add-Ins
- ❑ Creating your own Add-Ins

Library Databases

All of the code (as well as the forms) we have written so far only works in the database in which it was written. There is nothing wrong with this, since in most cases it's exactly what is required, but given the advantages of code reuse, wouldn't it be good to share your hard work amongst other databases of yours, or even allow others to use it?

A library database is just a repository of these fragments of code, forms, etc., which you would like to use elsewhere. It allows you to write normal VBA code, in a normal Access database, and then allow it to be used in any other Access database.

Creating a Library Database

One of the first things I do when starting a new Access project is to create some error logging routines. Instead of just flashing up a message telling the user what the problem is, they also log the error to a table. There are two really good reasons for this:

❑ It's a great development tool. If errors occur during your development and testing they will be logged into a table, so you don't have to keep writing them down (and invariably losing the bit of paper).

❑ It's a great feature during run-time. Very often users fall into the habit of just clicking on an error message and trying again, or phoning you to tell you something is wrong, but not writing down the error message. With this sort of logging you don't have to worry because the details will all be stored for you.

Since this feature is pretty useful, let's create a library database to do this. If your fingers are feeling a little tired there's a ready-made database called `ErrorLogging.mdb` for you.

Try It Out – Creating a Library Database

1. Start Access and create a new database. This should be a standard, blank database. Call the database `ErrorLogging`.

2. Create a new code module and save it, calling it `ErrorLoggingRoutines`. From the **Tools** menu, select **References**. Unselect the **Microsoft ActiveX Data Objects 2.1 Library**, scroll down a little, and select **Microsoft DAO 3.6 Object Library**. Click the **OK** button to close the dialog.

3. Add the following globals to the module:

```
Private Const m_ERROR_TABLE As String = "tblErrorLog"

Private m_UserDb As Database
Private m_recErrLog As Recordset
```

4. Write this procedure which creates a table to hold the error details:

```
Private Sub CreateErrorTable()

  On Error GoTo CreateErrorTable_Err

  Dim tblE As TableDef
  Dim strSQL As String

  Set m_UserDb = CurrentDb

  Set tblE = m_UserDb.TableDefs(m_ERROR_TABLE)
  Set tblE = Nothing
```

```
CreateErrorTable_Exit:
   Exit Sub

CreateErrorTable_Err:
   If Err.Number = 3265 Then
      strSQL = "CREATE TABLE " & m_ERROR_TABLE & " (" & _
         "ErrorID      AUTOINCREMENT, " & _
         "UserName     TEXT(50), " & _
         "ErrDate      DATETIME, " & _
         "ErrNumber    INTEGER, " & _
         "Description  TEXT(255), " & _
         "Source       TEXT(50))"
      m_UserDb.Execute strSQL
   Else
      Err.Raise Err.Number, "ErrorLogging:CreateErrorTable", _
         Err.Description
   End If


   Resume CreateErrorTable_Exit

End Sub
```

5. Now create a new procedure, to log the errors, with the following code:

```
Public Sub ErrorLog()

   Dim lngNum As Long
   Dim strDesc As String
   Dim strSource As String
   Dim errE As Error

   lngNum = Err.Number
   strDesc = Err.Description
   strSource = Err.Source

   CreateErrorTable

   Set m_recErrLog = m_UserDb.OpenRecordset(m_ERROR_TABLE)

   If lngNum = DBEngine.Errors(DBEngine.Errors.Count - 1).Number Then
      For Each errE In DBEngine.Errors
         WriteError errE.Number, errE.Description, errE.Source
      Next
   Else
      WriteError lngNum, strDesc, strSource
   End If

   m_recErrLog.Close

End Sub
```

6. Next, create another procedure, to actually write the errors to the error table:

```
Private Sub WriteError(lngNum As Long, strDesc As String, strSource As String)

    With m_recErrLog
        .AddNew
        !UserName = Trim$(CurrentUser())
        !ErrDate = Now()
        !ErrNumber = lngNum
        !Description = Trim$(strDesc)
        !Source = Trim$(strSource)
        .Update
    End With

End Sub
```

7. Save the module, and from the Debug menu select Compile ErrorLogging.

8. Close the database and open IceCream.mdb. Create a new module and add the following code. You should recognize this from our debugging code earlier in the book:

```
Sub TestErrorLogging()

    Dim db   As Database
    Dim recT As Recordset
    Dim errE   As Error

    On Error GoTo TestErrorLogging_Err

    Set db = CurrentDb()
    Forms!frmCompany.Caption = "A new caption"
    Set recT = db.OpenRecordset("NonExistentTable")
    recT.Close

TestErrorLogging_Exit:
    Exit Sub

TestErrorLogging_Err:
    ErrorLog

End Sub
```

9. From the Tools menu select References. Select the Browse button and change the Files of type drop down to Microsoft Access Databases (*.mdb).

10. Pick `ErrorLogging` from this dialog:

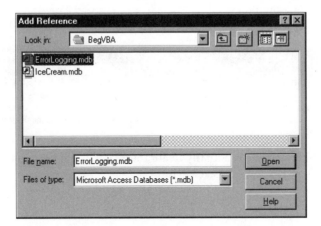

11. Click the **Open** button, and you'll be returned to the **References** dialog showing the `ErrorLogging` database selected:

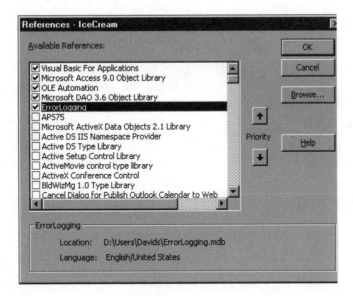

12. Press the **OK** button to close this dialog. From the Immediate window, run the procedure. Nothing visible will happen.

13. Now comment out the line (by placing a single apostrophe at the start of the line) that sets the `Caption`, and run the procedure again.

14. Switch back to Access and you should notice a new table – `tblErrorLog`. If it's not there, press F5 to refresh the window.

ErrorID	UserName	ErrDate	ErrNumber	Description	Source
1	Admin	12/30/98 6:42:02 PM	2450	Dave and Rob's Ice Cream can't find the form	MSAccess
2	Admin	12/30/98 6:42:05 PM	3078	The Microsoft Jet database engine cannot find the input	DAO.Database

tblErrorLog : Table

15. Notice that although the code is actually in another database, it has created a table in the local database and added rows for each error.

How it Works

Let's look at the global variables first, and then the `CreateErrorTable` routine, since this is what actually creates the table in the database:

For the globals, we define a constant, which defines the name of the error logging table. Using a constant means we can easily change the name if required. Then there are two global variables. The first will point to the database that the user currently has open, and the second will be a recordset, pointing to the error logging table, that we will use to add records to the error logging table.

```
Private Const m_ERROR_TABLE As String = "tblErrorLog"

Private m_UserDb As Database
Private m_recErrLog As Recordset
```

In the `CreateErrorTable` procedure, the first thing to do is to set some error handling. This is because we need to see if the error log table already exists, and the simplest way to do that is to just set a variable to point to it. If it doesn't exist, and an error is generated, and we can trap that error:

```
On Error GoTo CreateErrorTable_Err
```

Once the error handling is active, we define a couple of variables. The first will point to the error table, and the second will hold the SQL string that creates the table.

```
Dim tblE As TableDef
Dim strSQL As String
```

Now we need to open the database. Notice that we use the `CurrentDb` function here, as `CurrentDb` points to the database currently open in the database window in Access. So, even though this code is in a different database, we still use the active database. If we wanted to access tables, etc., in the database where the code is we could use the `CodeDB` function.

```
Set m_UserDb = CurrentDb
```

Now we need to see if the table exists. The `TableDefs` collection holds all of the existing tables, so we simply set out variable to point to the error logging table. If it exists then we can clear the reference, and exit:

```
   Set tblE = m_UserDb.TableDefs(m_ERROR_TABLE)
   Set tblE = Nothing

CreateErrorTable_Exit:
   Exit Sub
```

If the table doesn't exist, then the error handling comes into place. We check for error number 3265, which means that the object we were looking for (`tblErrorLog`) wasn't found in the collection (the `TableDefs` collection).

```
CreateErrorTable_Err:
   If Err.Number = 3265 Then
```

If the table wasn't found we need to create it, so we construct a SQL statement to do this, and then `Execute` the SQL statement. We used the `CREATE TABLE` method here because it's quite simple - some other methods for creating tables were discussed in chapter 8.

```
      strSQL = "CREATE TABLE " & m_ERROR_TABLE & " (" & _
         "ErrorID      AUTOINCREMENT, " & _
         "UserName     TEXT(50), " & _
         "ErrDate      DATETIME, " & _
         "ErrNumber    INTEGER, " & _
         "Description  TEXT(255), " & _
         "Source       TEXT(50))"
      m_UserDb.Execute strSQL
   Else
```

If any other type of error is found then we use the default VBA error handler.

```
      Err.Raise Err.Number, "ErrorLogging:CreateErrorTable", _
         Err.Description
   End If

   Resume CreateErrorTable_Exit
```

Now that you've seen how the table is created, lets look at the error logging routine itself, `ErrorLog`:

The first three variables will hold the error details, from the `Err` object. We need to save them because as you've just seen, the table creation routine uses error handling and using `On Error` clears `Err`. The last variable will hold the error details if the error is a data access error.

```
Dim lngNum As Long
Dim strDesc As String
Dim strSource As String
Dim errE As Error
```

The first thing to do is to store the error details, and then call the routine that creates the error table.

```
lngNum = Err.Number
strDesc = Err.Description
strSource = Err.Source

CreateErrorTable
```

Now we know that the error table exists we can open it.

```
Set m_recErrLog = m_UserDb.OpenRecordset(m_ERROR_TABLE)
```

And now we can use the same routine you saw in the debugging chapter, where we check to see if the error number matches the last error in the Errors collection. If it does, then this is a data access error, so we loop through the collection, calling the WriteError routine for each error. If it isn't a data access error we just call the WriteError routine with the details from Err.

```
If lngNum = DBEngine.Errors(DBEngine.Errors.Count - 1).Number Then
    For Each errE In DBEngine.Errors
        WriteError errE.Number, errE.Description, errE.Source
    Next
Else
    WriteError lngNum, strDesc, strSource
End If

m_recErrLog.Close
```

The routine that actually writes the error details to the table is quite simple:

```
Private Sub WriteError(lngNum As Long, strDesc As String, strSource As String)

    With m_recErrLog
```

Since we are adding a new record we use the AddNew method – this creates a blank record for us to add the details to.

```
        .AddNew
```

We then set the user details. The CurrentUser function returns the name of the current user. If you're not using security then this will always be Admin, but if security is set up this will be the name of the user that logged into Access. For more details on this, see chapter 16.

```
        !UserName = Trim$(CurrentUser())
```

Next we set the date and time using the Now function:

```
        !ErrDate = Now()
```

And now the actual details of the error:

```
        !ErrNumber = lngNum
        !Description = Trim$(strDesc)
        !Source = Trim$(strSource)
```

Finally, we can update the record with the new details.

```
      .Update
   End With

End Sub
```

So that's it. Let's just summarize the concept:

- ❑ A library database is a normal Access database.

- ❑ Any procedures in the library database that you want other databases to use should be `Public` procedures. All other procedures should be `Private`.

- ❑ To use a library database you create a Reference to it, from the Tools menu in the VBE.

Considerations

One thing to beware of when using library databases is name clashes. It's quite possible that you might have a public function in your library database that has the same name as a function in a database that is using the library database. If this happens then Access uses the local procedure, and not the procedure in the library database.

There are two ways to get around this problem. The first is to qualify the procedure name when you use it. So, assume that `ErrorLog` existed in both the local database and the library database. Calling `ErrorLog` like this:

```
ErrorLog
```

would use the local procedure. But calling it like this:

```
[ErrorLogging].ErrorLog
```

would call the one in the library database, because we have put the module name in front of the procedure call.

The second method is to make sure your procedures won't clash, by uniquely naming them. For example:

```
Public Sub logErrorLogging()
```

This puts a unique identifier in front of each public procedure. If you make sure that each library database you create has a unique identifier then you should never get clashes.

Class Libraries

In the previous chapter we extolled the virtues of object orientation, and how classes can promote not only good programming, but also good code reuse as well. Since we've shown that using library databases is just another way of promoting code reuse, it seems sensible that that we should use classes within a library database. The unfortunate fact is, though, that although classes can be used outside of the database within which they reside, they cannot actually be instantiated. However, there is a way around this, because we know that normal procedures can be used outside of their own database, so we can provide a wrapper function in the library database that just instantiates the object, and passes it back to the calling object.

So, what we can't do is this:

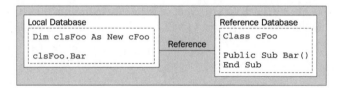

But what we can do is this:

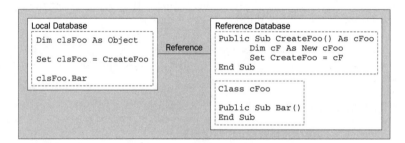

The class is exactly the same, but there is now a public function, in a normal module, that instantiates the class object. The disadvantage of this method is that you can't use early binding, since Access has no knowledge of what the class is. Despite this, though, it's a very good way of using classes in multiple databases.

An ADO Class Library

Although we're concentrating on DAO in this book, there are some things that ADO can do easily that DAO can't, and one of these is the User Roster. This allows us to see which users are logged into a database – extremely useful if you need to make changes or shut down a server. A set of support libraries were shipped with older versions of Access, but the ADO way is much simpler.

If you want to use ADO you know that you need to have the ActiveX Data Objects reference set in the VBE, and the same applies with DAO, where you need the Data Access Objects reference set. Having the two set together isn't a problem, but can lead to some confusion. For example, consider the following line of code:

```
Dim recIces As Recordset
```

Does this refer to a DAO recordset or an ADO recordset? In fact, if you don't specify the data access method, then DAO is the default. To clarify which method you want to use, you can prefix the object with its type:

```
Dim recIces As DAO.Recordset
Dim recIces As ADODB.Recordset
```

This makes it very clear, but it looks a little ugly. If all we are using ADO for is the user roster, then it seems sensible to put this into a class library. That way the class library can have the reference to ADO, so we don't need this reference in our database, which makes things simpler.

Try It Out – Creating a Class Library

1. Create a new database called `MiniADO`.

2. Create a new class module (from the Insert menu), and add the following code:

```
Private Const JET_SCHEMA_USERROSTER = "{947bb102-5d43-11d1-bdbf-00c04fb92675}"

Public Sub GetUserRoster(vUserList As Variant, lReturnType As ReturnType)

   Dim conADO As ADODB.Connection
   Dim recADO As ADODB.Recordset

   Set conADO = CurrentProject.Connection

   Set recADO = conADO.OpenSchema(adSchemaProviderSpecific, , _
      JET_SCHEMA_USERROSTER)

   If lReturnType = RETURN_ARRAY Then
      vUserList = recADO.GetRows
   Else
      vUserList = recADO.GetString(adClipString, , ",", vbCrLf)
   End If

   recADO.Close
   conADO.Close

End Sub
```

3. In the properties window set the class **Name** to `clsADO` and the **Instancing** to `2 - PublicNotCreatable`.

4. Save this module as `clsADO`.

5. Create a normal module and add the following code:

```
Public Enum ReturnType
    RETURN_ARRAY
    RETURN_STRING
End Enum

Public Function CreateMiniADO() As clsADO

    Dim cADO As New clsADO

    Set CreateMiniADO = cADO

End Function
```

6. Save this module as `MiniADOEntryPoints`.

7. Close this database and open `IceCream.mdb`.

8. Add a reference to `MiniADO.mdb` as before.

9. In the code module for this chapter add a new procedure:

```
Public Sub WhosIn()

    Dim objMiniADO As Object
    Dim varUsers As Variant

    Set objMiniADO = CreateMiniADO

    objMiniADO.GetUserRoster varUsers, RETURN_STRING

    Debug.Print varUsers

End Sub
```

10. From the Immediate window run this procedure:

This shows only one user logged in. The columns (separated by commas) are: `Computer Name`, `Login Name`, `Connected`, and `Suspect State`.

11. Now open another copy of the same database and run the procedure again:

```
▣ Immediate
  WhosIn
  OFFICE2000        ,Admin         ,-1,

  WhosIn
  OFFICE2000        ,Admin         ,-1,
  PIGLET            ,Admin         ,-1,
```

The above diagram shows two machines accessing the database – the first machine is called OFFICE2000 and the second machine is called PIGLET. At this stage you might not think this is too useful, since both users are Admin. However, that's only because we haven't set up security. Once you look at chapter 16 on multi-user issues, you'll see how to set up security to allow users to log into an Access database under user names. When no security is involved, all users are Admin, although the machine name shows up correctly. So, even if you aren't using security, you can still get a good form of user list if you name your machines correctly.

How it Works

Let's look at the class first. At the top of the class we define a constant, which is the special key, called a GUID. A GUID (**G**lobally **U**nique **ID**entifier) is a special number that is unique across the whole world, and this is used by the operating system to identify objects, components, libraries, etc. Generally you don't need to know about them as most objects have a proper name, but this user roster doesn't have a name - just a GUID.

```
Private Const JET_SCHEMA_USERROSTER = "{947bb102-5d43-11d1-bdbf-00c04fb92675}"
```

Next comes the definition of the method, taking two arguments. The first is a variant, which will hold the user details, and will either be returned containing a string or an array. The second argument identifies whether a string or an array of the user details is to be returned.

```
Public Sub GetUserRoster(vUserList As Variant, lReturnType As ReturnType)
```

Now we have two ADO objects – one for the connection to the database, and one for the recordset of connected users.

```
Dim conADO As ADODB.Connection
Dim recADO As ADODB.Recordset
```

Next, we connect to the current database. The `CurrentProject` object is an Access object that points to the currently open database – not the library database. The `Connection` property of this object contains the ADO connection details.

```
Set conADO = CurrentProject.Connection
```

Now that we are connected to the database we need to get the users, and for that we use the OpenSchema method. Schemas are really just collections of like objects, and most databases have schemas for tables, queries, users, and so on – they describe what the data is and how it is stored. ADO has provided this method to access these details, and it also allows the data provider (in this case the JET database engine) to specify its own schemas as well as the default ones. This is done using adSchemaProviderSpecific as the first argument of the OpenSchema method. The second argument allows us to filter the results – we've left this empty because we want all of the users returned. The third argument is the special key that tells the data provider (JET) what to return.

```
Set recADO = conADO.OpenSchema(adSchemaProviderSpecific, , _
    JET_SCHEMA_USERROSTER)
```

At this stage recADO contains a recordset of the user details. We can't just return this recordset because the whole purpose of this class is to encapsulate ADO, allowing it to be used from another database without setting ADO references. So we want to return the recordset as a comma-separated string, or as an array. That's where the second argument to the GetUserRoster procedure comes in – you'll see where the values are defined in a minute.

If the return type is to be an array, then we call the GetRows method of the recordset. This is exactly the same as the GetRows method of the DAO recordset, and converts a recordset into an array. We assign the result of the GetRows method to the variant parameter passed into the GetUserRoster procedure – remember that this is a Variant, and variants can hold different variable types.

```
If lReturnType = RETURN_ARRAY Then
    vUserList = recADO.GetRows
```

If the return type isn't to be an array, then it must be a string. In this case we use the GetString method of the recordset, which converts a recordset into a string. The two important arguments to this method are the last two. The first of these identifies the separator between the fields, in this case a comma, and the latter identifies the separator between the rows, in this case a carriage return and new line.

```
Else
    vUserList = recADO.GetString(adClipString, , ",", vbCrLf)
End If
```

The last thing to do is close both the recordset and the connection.

```
recADO.Close
conADO.Close

End Sub
```

That's it for the class – it has just one method. One thing to notice is the setting for the Instancing property of the class – we set this to 2 - PublicNotCreatable. This defines the class as Public, meaning it can be used outside of the database in which it is defined, but that it cannot be created in another database. Unfortunately Access doesn't allow Public Creatable classes, where they can be instantiated and used outside of their own database. It's for this reason that we have to have a normal module with a public procedure to create the object.

Let's now look at the normal module associated with the class. Firstly there's an Enum statement, to define the two possible return types for the list of users.

```
Public Enum ReturnType
    RETURN_ARRAY
    RETURN_STRING
End Enum
```

Now we have a Public function, which returns a type of the MiniADO class. In this function we simply instantiate a new object of that class type, and then return this object.

```
Public Function CreateMiniADO() As clsADO

    Dim cADO  As New clsADO

    Set CreateMiniADO = cADO

End Function
```

So, at this stage we have finished the class library. We have a class with one method, and a function that creates the class for us. Let's look at how it's used now, in the WhosIn procedure.

Firstly there are two variables. The first is a generic object, which will hold the MiniADO class. Remember that we can't define this as clsADO because the class can't be seen outside of its own database, and it's in the library database. The second variable is a variant that will hold the user details.

```
Dim objMiniADO As Object
Dim varUsers As Variant
```

To instantiate the class we have to call the public function in the library database. This creates the class object and returns it to us.

```
Set objMiniADO = CreateMiniADO
```

Then we call the GetUserRoster method of the class.

```
objMiniADO.GetUserRoster varUsers, RETURN_STRING
```

And finally, we can print out the user details.

```
Debug.Print varUsers
```

If you wanted to return an array of the user details all you have to do is change RETURN_STRING for RETURN_ARRAY, and after the GetUserRoster method is called varUsers will hold an array of the details. In this case you would use the normal array indexing methods to access the details:

```
Debug.Print varUsers(0,0)
```

This would print out the machine name of the first user. Remember that this array is like a recordset, so the first array index is the rows, and the second index the columns.

As you can see, creating class libraries is fairly simple. The only downside is the instancing problem, but using a function to create the class object can circumvent this. We used this method here to encapsulate some ADO functionality, and another good area is API functions, or general programming libraries.

Add-Ins

Add-Ins are another form of library, and although they contain objects such as code, tables and forms, they are generally complete tools, rather than collections of code. Library databases are generally for the developer to use, but Add-Ins are usually for the end-user. They generally provide features, which while being useful to some users, are not really required as a central part of Access. By building these features into an Add-In you get the benefit of extra functionality combined with the ability to load it at will.

There are different types of add-ins, and which you use depends upon the task you need to accomplish. If you are creating objects, the add-in will probably be a wizard or a builder, such as the controls wizards, form creation wizard, or the color builder. If you need to do more than this, or something that is completely separate from other objects, then creating an Add-In is probably the way to go. From here on, we're going to take an in-depth look at an example Add-In. We'll see how we can put it together and then use it in any database we want.

The Language Converter Add-In

Let's imagine that you've just spent six months building your new application, and it's finally finished. The users have done their own testing and are really happy with it, and so is your manager. In fact, with a surprising amount of common sense, your manager has agreed that this application will be used in all of the company's offices around the world. "Great," you think, "at last, recognition for all of that hard work." So you start writing up installation instructions and all, only to be told that the application has to work in the native language of the company office. Oh boy. How do you manage that? All of the forms and reports will have to be translated, and your foreign language ability is well, shall we say, slightly lacking. Also, how do you manage the various copies of the application? Will you have to keep a copy for each language? But then what happens if you need to make a change? It's not looking good, is it?

Fear not, because this can all be done automatically (apart from the translation, of course). We can write an add-in that allows the users to add new languages, edit the language details, and change all of the application's details. But how?

Remember how we looped through the controls on a form and changed the `Font` property? Well, the `Caption` is just another property, so this can be changed too. Here's how it's going to work.

- [ ] We create a language table in the database, with the following columns: `FormName`, `ControlName`, `ControlType`, `DateUpdated`. These are the basic columns that hold the details of each control on each form.

- [ ] Then, for each language, we add another column.

❑   We loop through all of the forms and controls, and add a row into our table or each control that has a `Caption` property, setting the language field to the actual caption.

At this stage we have a table that looks something like this:

FormName	ControlName	ControlType	DateUpdated	English	French	German
frmSwitchboard	cmdExit	Command button	1/4/99 8:18:37 PM			
frmSwitchboard	cmdIceCreams	Command button	1/4/99 8:18:37 PM			
frmSwitchboard	cmdIngredients	Command button	1/4/99 8:18:37 PM			
frmSwitchboard	cmdMaintenance	Command button	1/4/99 8:18:37 PM			
frmSwitchboard	cmdReports	Command button	1/4/99 8:18:37 PM			
frmSwitchboard	cmdSuppliers	Command button	1/4/99 8:18:37 PM			
frmSwitchboard	frmSwitchboard	Form	1/4/99 8:18:37 PM	Dave and Rob's Ice Cream		
frmSwitchboard	lblExit	Label	1/4/99 8:18:37 PM	E&xit Database		
frmSwitchboard	lblIceCreams	Label	1/4/99 8:18:37 PM	Ice Cream &Details		
frmSwitchboard	lblIngredients	Label	1/4/99 8:18:37 PM	&Ingredients		
frmSwitchboard	lblMaintenance	Label	1/4/99 8:18:37 PM	Database &Maintenance		
frmSwitchboard	lblReports	Label	1/4/99 8:18:37 PM	&Reports		
frmSwitchboard	lblSuppliers	Label	1/4/99 8:18:37 PM	&Supplier Lists		

We can now add text for the other language columns. To change the language, we can open the form in design mode, loop through the controls, and set the Caption property of the control to the value in the table.

This may sound rather complex, but it's quite easy. Let's give it a go.

If you don't feel like typing all of these procedures in, then have a look in the Lang.mda database on the CD – they are all in there.

Try It Out – The Language Converter Add-In

1.   Create a new database called `Lang.mda`. Notice that this is an `mda` file and not an `mdb`. There is no physical difference between an `mdb` and an `mda` file, but add-ins are generally given the `mda` suffix to differentiate them from standard Access databases. You can make sure you create the correct type by making sure you select **All Files (*.*)** in the **Save as type** field on the new database dialog. If you don't do this you'll get a database called `Lang.mda.mdb`.

2. Create a new table with the following fields:

Field Name	Type	Length
FormName	Text	30
ControlName	Text	30
ControlType	Text	20
DateUpdated	Date/Time	
English	Text	255
French	Text	255

3. Set the primary key to be both FormName and ControlName. You can do this by highlighting these two fields and the pressing the **Primary Key** button:

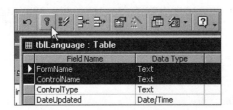

4. Once set, the fields show the key symbol against them:

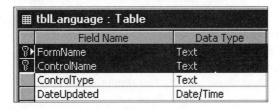

5. Set the Allow Zero Length property for the English and French columns to Yes:

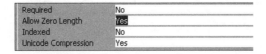

6. Save this table as tblLanguage, and close it.

7. Create a new module, and from the Tools menu pick References. Clear the box against Microsoft ActiveX Data Objects 2.1 Library, scroll down, and tick the box against Microsoft DAO 3.6 Object Library. Click OK to close the References dialog.

8. In the empty module, add the following constant:

```
Private Const wcs_LANGUAGE_TABLE As String = "tblLanguage"
```

9. Add the following procedure, which will loop through all of the forms:

```
Public Sub LangEnumerateForms(bolExtract As Boolean, strLang As String)

    Dim db As Database
    Dim recLang As Recordset
    Dim objAO As AccessObject
    Dim objCP As Object

    ' open the database and language recordset
    Set db = CurrentDb()
    Set recLang = db.OpenRecordset (wcs_LANGUAGE_TABLE)
    recLang.Index = "PrimaryKey"

    ' enumerate the forms
    Set objCP = Application.CurrentProject
    If bolExtract Then
        For Each objAO In objCP.AllForms
            LangExtractControls recLang, strLang, objAO.Name
        Next objAO
    Else
        For Each objAO In objCP.AllForms
            LangSetControls recLang, strLang, objAO.Name
        Next objAO
    End If

    ' close up
    recLang.Close

End Sub
```

10. And now another procedure, this time to loop through the controls on a form, extracting the caption into our language table:

```
Private Sub LangExtractControls(recLang As Recordset, strLang As String, strFormName
As String)
    Dim frmF As Form
    Dim ctlC As Control
    Dim strControlName As String
    Dim datNow As Date
    Dim intControlType As Integer
        ' open the form, hidden, in design view
    DoCmd.OpenForm strFormName, acDesign, , , , acHidden
    datNow = Now()
```

```
' add the form caption
Set frmF = Forms(strFormName)
With recLang
    .Seek "=", strFormName, strFormName

    ' Add or update the form in the language table
    If .NoMatch Then
        .AddNew
    Else
        .Edit
    End If

    ' set the details
    !FormName = strFormName
    !ControlName = strFormName
    !ControlType = "Form"
    !DateUpdated = datNow
    .Fields(strLang) = frmF.Caption
    .Update

    ' now loop through the controls
    For Each ctlC In frmF.Controls

        ' we are only interested in the controls
        ' with a Caption property
        intControlType = ctlC.ControlType
        If ControlHasCaption(intControlType) Then

            ' find the control in the language table
            strControlName = ctlC.Name
            .Seek "=", strFormName, strControlName

            ' Add or update the control in the language table
            If .NoMatch Then
                .AddNew
            Else
                .Edit
            End If

            ' set the details
            !FormName = strFormName
            !ControlName = strControlName
            !ControlType = ControlTypeName(intControlType)
            !DateUpdated = datNow
            .Fields(strLang) = ctlC.Caption
            .Update
        End If
    Next
End With

' close the form and save it
DoCmd.Close acForm, strFormName, acSaveYes

End Sub
```

11. Now the opposite function, to loop through the controls setting the `Caption` property with the text in our languages table:

```
Private Sub LangSetControls(recLang As Recordset, _
         strLang As String, strFormName As String)

    Dim frmF As Form
    Dim ctlC As Control
    Dim strControlName As String
    Dim intControlType As Integer

    ' open the form, hidden, in design view
    DoCmd.OpenForm strFormName, acDesign, , , , acHidden

    ' add the form caption
    Set frmF = Forms(strFormName)
    With recLang
        .Seek "=", strFormName, strFormName

        ' Add or update the form in the language table
        If .NoMatch Or IsNull(.Fields(strLang)) Then
            frmF.Caption = ""
        Else
            frmF.Caption = .Fields(strLang)
        End If

        ' now loop through the controls
        For Each ctlC In frmF.Controls

            ' we are only interested in the controls
            ' with a Caption property
            intControlType = ctlC.ControlType
            If ControlHasCaption(intControlType) = True Then
                ' find the control in the language table
                strControlName = ctlC.Name
                .Seek "=", strFormName, strControlName

                ' Add or update the control in the language table
                If .NoMatch Or IsNull(.Fields(strLang)) Then
                ctlC.Caption = ""
                Else
                    ctlC.Caption = .Fields(strLang)
                End If
            End If
        Next
    End With

    ' close the form and save it
    DoCmd.Close acForm, strFormName, acSaveYes

End Sub
```

12. Now a function to determine if the control has a `Caption` property or not:

```
Private Function ControlHasCaption(intCtlType As Integer) As Boolean

    Select Case intCtlType
       Case acCommandButton, acLabel, acToggleButton
          ControlHasCaption = True
       Case Else
          ControlHasCaption = False
    End Select

End Function
```

13. And finally, a function to return the type name of controls with a `Caption` property.

```
Private Function ControlTypeName(intCtlType As Integer) As String

    Select Case intCtlType
       Case acLabel
          ControlTypeName = "Label"
       Case acCommandButton
          ControlTypeName = "Command button"
       Case acToggleButton
          ControlTypeName = "Toggle button"
    End Select

End Function
```

At this stage the add-in is functionally complete, so compile the code and make sure you save it – call it Language Handling. There are some things we need to do, though, before we can use it as an add-in, so let's give it a test before turning it loose on another database.

14. Create a new form in this database, adding the following controls:

- ❑   A text box
- ❑   A list box
- ❑   A combo box
- ❑   A label
- ❑   A Command Button
- ❑   A Toggle button

It doesn't matter what's in these controls. I made mine look like this:

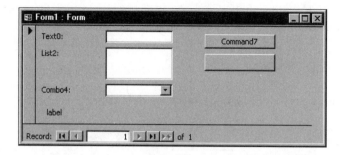

15. Save the form as `Form1`. Then switch back to the VBA IDE, and from the Immediate window run your new code, by typing:

```
LangEnumerateForms True, "English"
```

16. The code will run quite quickly, and when it's done switch back to Access and open the languages table:

FormName	ControlName	ControlType	DateUpdated	English	French
Form1	Command7	Command button	1/5/99 1:56:01 PM	Command7	
Form1	Form1	Form	1/5/99 1:56:01 PM		
Form1	Label1	Label	1/5/99 1:56:01 PM	Text0:	
Form1	Label3	Label	1/5/99 1:56:01 PM	List2:	
Form1	Label5	Label	1/5/99 1:56:01 PM	Combo4:	
Form1	Label6	Label	1/5/99 1:56:01 PM	label	
Form1	Toggle8	Toggle button	1/5/99 1:56:01 PM		

17. Add some values into the French column. If your language ability is like mine (I once got 7% in a French exam!) then you can do something like this:

English	Frenc
Command7	le comma
	le form
Text0:	le text
List2:	le list
Combo4:	le combo
label	le label
	le toggle

And please. No feedback from linguistic experts (or French people, come to think of it). This is just for testing. If you can speak French (and as you can see, I can't!) you might like to add some proper translations.

18. Close the language table and switch back to the Immediate window. Now run the language converter in its other mode – setting the language for the forms:

```
LangEnumerateForms False, "French"
```

19. When this has run, switch back to Access and view the form:

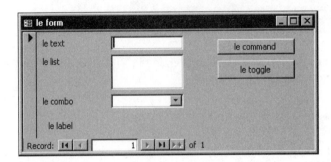

There you have it – easy conversion. You can add languages to the language table, and all you have to do is add the new details in the new language column. The great beauty of this method is that you can create multi-lingual applications even if you can't speak the language the application needs translating into. All you need is someone who can speak the language to add the correct translations.

Let's have a quick look at how this works before we convert it into an Add-In.

How It Works – Converting Languages

Although it looks a little complex, it's actually quite simple. All it does is this:

Mode 1 – extracting the existing captions for the form and controls

❑ Pull out the caption for the form, and store it in the appropriate column in the languages table. Set the other details for the form (control name, type, and modification date). If no previous record exists for the form, a new one is created.

❑ Similarly, loop through all the controls on the form, checking for any that have captions (by calling another function). A record is created (or edited) for each control that has a caption. Set the details as above (calling a function to determine the control type).

Mode 2 – changing the language of the captions on the form and controls

❑ Change the caption of the form to that specified in the form's record, in the relevant language column.

❑ Loop through the controls, checking for any that have captions (as above). For each of these, find the right control in the language table, and change its caption as specified in the correct language column.

Some of the techniques we've used have been explained before, so they shouldn't need too much detail.

Let's start with the `LangEnumerateForms` procedure. Depending on the argument passed to this procedure, we're either in extract mode (mode 1) or set mode (mode 2). The first thing we do here is to open both the database and the language table. Then we set the current index to be the primary index – that's because we will be using the `Seek` method later on.

```
Set db = CurrentDb()
Set recLang = db.OpenRecordset("tblLanguage")
recLang.Index = "PrimaryKey"
```

Now we need to loop through all of the forms using the `AllForms` collection, calling the correct procedure for each one, depending on our mode. If the `bolExtract` argument is `True`, we're in mode 1, so we call `LangExtractControls`; but if `bolExtract` is `False`, then we're in mode 2, so we call `LangSetControls`.

```
Set objCP = Application.CurrentProject
If bolExtract Then
   For Each objAO In objCP.AllForms
      LangExtractControls recLang, strLang, objAO.Name
   Next objAO
Else
   For Each objAO In objCP.AllForms
      LangSetControls recLang, strLang, objAO.Name
   Next objAO
End If

' close up
recLang.Close
```

Mode 1

Let's now look at `LangExtractControls`. The first thing to do is to open the form, hidden, in design view. We also set a variable to hold the current date and time – this will allow us to see when the form details were last extracted.

```
DoCmd.OpenForm strFormName, acDesign, , , , acHidden
datNow = Now()
```

Next we set a form variable to point to the newly opened form. We then use the `With` statement on the language recordset. Both of these are for speed and clarity, as they are not only quicker, but they also make the code easier to read. Remember that the `With` statement allows us to just use the property or method name, in this case of the recordset, without repeating the recordset name.

```
Set frmF = Forms(strFormName)
With recLang
```

Now we look for the form name in the languages table. Forms have a `Caption` property, so we want to extract this:

```
.Seek "=", strFormName, strFormName
```

The `Seek` method sets the `NoMatch` property to `True` if the item sought wasn't found. So, if we don't find an existing record, we'll want to add a new one. Otherwise, we just want to edit the existing record.

```
If .NoMatch Then
    .AddNew
Else
    .Edit
End If
```

We are now on the correct record (either a new one or an existing one), so we want to set the details. We set the `FormName` and `ControlName` to the name of the form (remember this is the form's `Caption` property), the `ControlType` and the `DateUpdated`.

```
!FormName = strFormName
!ControlName = strFormName
!ControlType = "Form"
!DateUpdated = datNow
```

We then need to set the value for the correct language, so we use the `Fields` collection of the recordset, using `strLang` as the index to this collection – `strLang` contains the name of the language, and was passed into this procedure as an argument.

```
.Fields(strLang) = frmF.Caption
```

Finally, for the form, we update the record.

```
.Update
```

At this stage all we have done is added, or updated, a single record in the languages table (the one for the form), so we now need to loop through the controls:

```
For Each ctlC In frmF.Controls
```

We are only interested in controls that have a caption, so we call the `ControlHasCaption` function – this returns `True` if the control has a `Caption` property. We'll look at this function in a little while.

```
intControlType = ctlC.ControlType
If ControlHasCaption(intControlType) = True Then
```

Now, in a similar way to the form, we use `Seek` to find the record in the languages table for this control, and we either add a new record, or update an existing record, depending upon whether it was found or not:

```
strControlName = ctlC.Name
.Seek "=", strFormName, strControlName

If .NoMatch Then
    .AddNew
Else
    .Edit
End If
```

Once on the correct record, the details need updating. The `FormName` and `ControlName` are pretty obvious, as is the date. For the `ControlType` we call a separate function, `ControlTypeName`, to identify the type of control – again, we'll look at that function in a while.

```
        !FormName = strFormName
        !ControlName = strControlName
        !ControlType = ControlTypeName(intControlType)
        !DateUpdated = datNow
```

Then, as with the form, we set the field for the correct language:

```
        .Fields(strLang) = ctlC.Caption
```

And then we update this record, and move onto the next control.

```
            .Update
        End If
    Next
End With
```

Finally, we close the form, saving the changes.

```
DoCmd.Close acForm, strFormName, acSaveYes
```

It's really only a few steps. Let's see how the opposite function, `LangSetControls`, works.

Mode 2

As with the previous function, we open the form in design mode.

```
DoCmd.OpenForm strFormName, acDesign, , , , acHidden
```

The next thing to do is get the text from the language table and set the `Caption` property of the form. As before, we use `Seek` to find the correct record.

```
Set frmF = Forms(strFormName)
With recLang
    .Seek "=", strFormName, strFormName
```

If no record was found (`NoMatch` is `True`), or if the entry for this language is empty, then we set the caption to an empty string, otherwise we set the caption to the value of the language field.

```
    If .NoMatch Or IsNull(.Fields(strLang)) Then
        frmF.Caption = ""
    Else
        frmF.Caption = .Fields(strLang)
    End If
```

Now we need to loop through the controls, again only checking the ones that have a caption.

```
    For Each ctlC In frmF.Controls
        intControlType = ctlC.ControlType
        If ControlHasCaption(intControlType) = True Then
```

Like the form, we use Seek to find the record, and set the caption to the value of the field in the language table, or to a blank string if the control wasn't found in the language table:

```
            strControlName = ctlC.Name
            .Seek "=", strFormName, strControlName

            If .NoMatch Or IsNull(.Fields(strLang)) Then
                ctlC.Caption = ""
            Else
                ctlC.Caption = .Fields(strLang)
            End If
        End If
    Next
End With
```

And finally, we close and save the form.

```
    DoCmd.Close acForm, strFormName, acSaveYes

End Sub
```

The Supporting Functions

The only things left now are the two supporting functions. The first just identifies those controls that have a Caption property. Note that we define these ourselves.

```
Private Function ControlHasCaption(intCtlType As Integer) As Boolean

    Select Case intCtlType
    Case acCommandButton, acLabel, acToggleButton
        ControlHasCaption = True
    Case Else
        ControlHasCaption = False
    End Select

End Function
```

The second returns a string for the control type. This isn't really required, but it makes it easier to see in the language table what type a control is.

```
Private Function ControlTypeName(intCtlType As Integer)

    Select Case intCtlType
    Case acLabel
        ControlTypeName = "Label"
    Case acCommandButton
        ControlTypeName = "Command button"
    Case acToggleButton
        ControlTypeName = "Toggle button"
    End Select

End Function
```

That's all there is to this basic add-in. There are still two things to do, however. The first is to give our add-in a form of its own, so that other people can use it without resorting to the code windows. The second is to add some Access bits and pieces that will allow this database to be used as an Add-In.

Creating the Add-In

1. Delete the test form and any records in the languages table.

2. Create a new form, making it look like this:

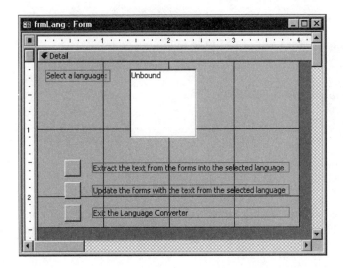

3. Name the list box `lstLang`, set its Row Source Type to Value List and its Row Source to English;French:

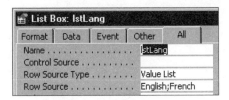

4. Name the three command buttons `cmdExtract`, `cmdSet`, and `cmdExit`, in order of top to bottom.

5. In the form design view, press the `Code` button to create a code module for this form, and switch to the VBE.

6. In the click event for `cmdExit`, add the following line of code:

```
DoCmd.Close
```

7. In the click event for cmdExtract, add the following code:

```
If lstLang.ListIndex = -1 Then
    MsgBox "Please select a language"
Else
    LangEnumerateForms True, lstLang
End If
```

8. In the click event for cmdSet, add the following code:

```
If lstLang.ListIndex = -1 Then
    MsgBox "Please select a language"
Else
    LangEnumerateForms False, lstLang
End If
```

9. Save the form as frmLang.

10. That's all we need for the user form. It allows the user to pick a language and then either extract, or set, the caption details. Now we need a public function to open this form, so create a new module, and add the following code:

```
Public Function wrox_Lang()

    DoCmd.OpenForm "frmLang"

End Function
```

11. Save this module as Language Entry Point.

12. And finally, let's set the database properties, so that the Add-In shows up nicely in the Add-In Manager. So, back in Access, select **Database Properties** from the File menu, and make them look like this:

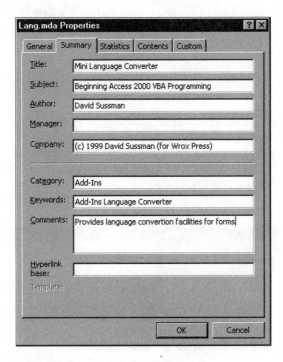

You can change the author and company if you like.

Now on to the final piece of the Add-In.

Try It Out – Creating the USysRegInfo Table

To use a database as an Add-In you need to create a special table, called USysRegInfo. This is a system table, so is not normally seen, and it needs to contain four columns and three rows. Rather than create this table yourself, it's a lot easier to just import it from the supplied language converter, Lang.mda, from the CD. You don't really need to know much about this table, except it's this table that Access uses to store some of the details for the Add-In.

1. In Access, from the Tools menu, select Options.

2. From the View tab, make sure the System Objects check box is selected. This allows us to see system objects, which are normally invisible.

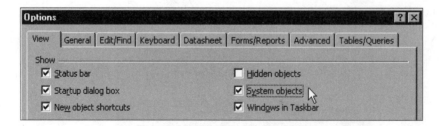

3. From the File menu, select Get External Data, and then Import.

4. From the File dialog, find and select Lang.mda on the CD, and press the Import button.

5. From the Import Objects dialog, on the Tables tab, select USysRegInfo, and press the OK button.

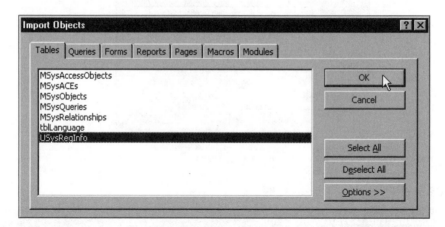

6. Open up the newly imported table:

This table must contain these details for an Add-In to work, as the Add-In Manager uses these values to update the registry. The Subkey column shows the name of the Add-In – in this case we've called in Language Converter – the ampersand identifies the hot key, so the C will be underlined.

You can ignore the Type and ValNames columns, as long as the values you enter are the same as shown.

The `Value` column, for the bottom two rows, contains the important details. The first, for the expression, identifies the entry point of the Add-In. This is the function that Access will call when the Add-In is run. It must be a `Public Function`. The second value, for the library, identifies the directory and database name of the Add-In. The name is `Lang.mda`, and `|ACCDIR\` means that the Add-In will be copied into the Access add-ins directory. We'll see this happening a little later.

The Language Converter Add-In is now complete, so let's give it a go.

Try It Out - Using the Language Converter

1. Close the add-in, and open up a database. Any one with forms will do. You might like to copy a database you've already got; that way your changes won't be permanent.

2. From the **Tools** menu, select **Add-Ins**, and then **Add-In Manager**. The list of installed Add-Ins will probably be blank, unless you've already used some.

3. Press the **Add New...** button, and from the file dialog select the `Lang.mda` you've just created, and press the **Open** button.

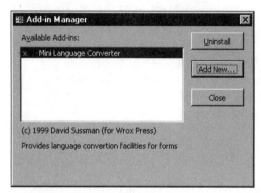

4. The Add-In is now installed. Notice the details at the bottom of this dialog – these come from the database properties that we set in the Add-In.

5. Press the **Close** button.

6. Before the Add-In can be used, you'll need a language table in this database, so from the **File** menu, select **Get External Data**, and then **Import**.

7. From the file dialog, find `Lang.mda`, and press the **Open** button.

8. From the **Import Objects** dialog, select **tblLanguage** from the **Tables** tab, and press the **OK** button. This imports the language table into the local database.

9. From the **Tools** menu, select **Add-Ins**, and then **Mini Language Converter**. The main screen pops up just as it did when testing.

10. Select English and press the Extract button. This will extract all of the captions from the forms.

11. Open the language table to have a look at what it's done.

12. Add some text to the French column, and then try setting the captions to French.

So, there you have it. Some code which is fairly simple, in a stand-alone database, which can be shipped to any office, in any country, and works with any database. Your boss will be very impressed, so go for that pay rise!

The Complete Language Converter Add-In

There are a number of small faults with the language converter as it stands:

❑ You have to manually create, or import, the language table into any database in which you wish to use the converter. The table should really be created automatically for you.

❑ To add new languages you have to edit the table. This should also be automatic, removing what could be a complex task for a user.

❑ To edit the details you have to open the table manually. A nice form to allow editing would be better.

Although not major faults, these could be considered bad programming, since they give the user tasks to perform which could either be eliminated or smoothed. There are two ways around this problem:

❑ As an exercise, add these facilities to the converter you've just created.

❑ Use the Language.mda converter, supplied on the CD. This is a fully completed version, which looks like this:

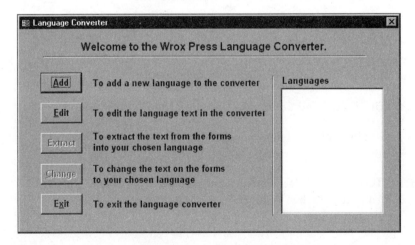

The code is only slightly different from the converter you've just created, and it has a few extra facilities. But you're well on the way to creating this yourself, so why not give it a try?

The Color Schemes Add-In

Another Add-In that's quite useful is the Color Schemes one. Do you like the way Windows allows you to select the Appearance of various screen items? So do I, so I thought a similar facility for Access forms might be a good idea.

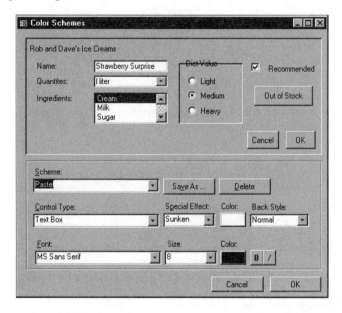

This uses a very similar technique to the language converter, looping through the controls on a form and setting the various properties. In fact, the above form is more complex than the code that applies the scheme.

We're not going to look at the code here, but you might like to browse through it. You can find it on the CD-ROM, called `Schemes.mda`.

Creating Add-Ins Summary

Although creating Add-Ins is quite simple, it's worth re-iterating a few points.

- ❑ You must have a `USysRegInfo` file in the Add-In. The Add-In Manager requires this to be able to load your Add-In. You can copy this table from any other Add-In and just modify the values.

- ❑ The entry function pointed to in `USysRegInfo` should be a Public Function.

- ❑ Make all of your procedures Private, unless you want them exposed to calling databases.

❑ If your Add-In takes several steps, then display your forms as dialog boxes (set the `WindowMode` argument to `acDialog`). This prevents the user from continuing until your form has finished.

❑ Bound objects are bound to the data in the Add-In. So a form based on a table shows the records in the table in the Add-In. If you need to use bound forms you can link user tables into the Add-In database for the duration of processing. The Color Schemes Add-In does this.

❑ If you are creating recordsets then remember that `CurrentDB()` points to the user database, and `CodeDB()` points to the Add-In database. You can also use the new Access objects **CurrentData** and **CurrentProject** to point to the user database, and **CodeData** and **CodeProject** to point to the Add-In database.

❑ Don't let your add-in change the state of the user database. This doesn't apply to add-ins that change forms, but to Access options. If you need to change any global options, keep a copy of what they are so they can be reset when your Add-In finishes.

❑ Create error-handling code. Your Add-In is meant to make the user's life easier, so don't dump them out to horrible error messages.

If you stick to these few basic rules you should be OK.

Updating your Add-In

There's one thing to watch during the development of Add-Ins, and that's the location of the Add-In that's running. Office 2000 is a very user-based application, so when you install an add-in it copies it into its own directory. Under Windows 98 this is:

```
\Windows\Application Data\Microsoft\Addins
```

Under Windows NT, this is:

```
\WinNT\Profiles\username\Application Data\Microsoft\AddIns\
```

This means that once installed, there are two copies of the Add-In. One in the original directory, and one in the AddIns directory, so any changes you do must be done in the right place.

There's no problem with leaving the Add-In installed and editing the mda file directly in the AddIns directory, but you must close down any instances of Access that have been using the Add-In. That's right – close Access. Just closing the database doesn't free the lock.

These aren't major problems, but can be a bit of a pain. Just bear them in mind while you are developing your Add-Ins.

Summary

In this chapter we've looked at ways to extend the functionality of Access, both from a programmers point of view, by using library databases, and from a users point of view, by using Add-Ins. Both of these use standard Access databases, so there's no major difference between what you do in these databases to what you do in normal databases.

What we've concentrated on are:

❑ Using library databases to provide common functionality to many databases. This allows you to provide routines to other Access programmers, and is especially useful for supplying routines to power users, who are good at using Access, but haven't mastered VBA yet.

❑ Using object oriented features, by providing class libraries. These extend the benefits of classes, putting them in a more distributable format.

❑ Using Add-Ins to extend the functionality of Access, providing users with a richer working environment.

As you've seen, there's not a great deal of complexity involved in using libraries and Add-Ins, just a few points to follow and a few points to watch out for.

Now it's time to look at extended the functionality of Access by using other applications, such as Word and Excel.

Exercises

1. Think about how you could use the language converter so that the language is changed as the form is opened, rather than a permanent change. If used with security, you could store a table of user names, along with their preferred language, and as each form is opened run a procedure that changes the controls. You've already seen how quick this is, so there will be no apparent slow down from the users point of view.

2. Add a facility to allow message boxes to have language facilities. This is fairly easy to do, as you could just add records into the language table, using a unique name for each message box. Then instead of calling MsgBox with a direct string, you could replace the string with a call to a function that looked up the language string in the table.

Automation

Life, it seems, is getting more and more hectic for everyone. Every business needs a competitive advantage and that generally revolves around its business processes. The more efficient you can make them, the quicker, and therefore cheaper, they are to perform. One way to achieve this is to automate and re-use existing processes. That's really what a lot of programming is anyway: the automation of complex or monotonous processes.

In this chapter we are going to see how object orientation can be used at a much higher level than you've seen so far. We've talked about code and object re-use, but here we are going to look at application re-use. All of the Microsoft Office applications have the ability to be used as objects from within VBA, so that we can use things that Microsoft has written for us.

What we're going to look at here is:

- ❑ What exactly automation is.
- ❑ Understanding how to use other applications.
- ❑ How to use Outlook for mail and appointments.
- ❑ How to use charts.
- ❑ How to use Word for reporting.

What Is Automation?

Even though you may not realize it, you've already seen automation in action, as using any stand-alone object is a form of automation. Remember when you went into the References and selected the DAO Library and then defined a variable as type Recordset? Well, that's just using an existing object.

So, in VBA and programming terms, automation is just the use of other objects. At the application level that means using such things as Outlook to send mail messages, or perhaps embedding an Excel chart on an Access form. What these do is just use some existing functionality, but instead of this functionality coming from a class, or a small object, it comes from an application. So you must get into the habit of thinking of everything as an object, even applications.

There are two descriptions that you might hear about when dealing with automation, and they are **Automation Server** and **Automation Client**.

Automation used to be called OLE Automation, so you might hear of OLE Servers and OLE Clients, but these days it's generally just referred to as Automation.

An Automation Server is the object you are using (it has nothing to do with physical machines), and an Automation Client is the one using the object. So, if you have some VBA code in an Access module, and that code uses Microsoft Excel, then Access is the Client, and Excel is the Server.

Interfaces and Object Models

Objects have **Interfaces**, and these define what parts of the object the programmer can see – this usually means the methods, properties and events. Remember when we looked at classes the Public procedures became methods and the Property procedures became properties? That's the interface – the view the user of the object has. All of the Private procedures and Private variables are part of the object, but they are not part of the interface, because they cannot be seen outside of the object.

An Object Model is just another way of saying Interface, and is usually a diagram showing the objects and collections. For example, a portion of the DAO object model is shown below:

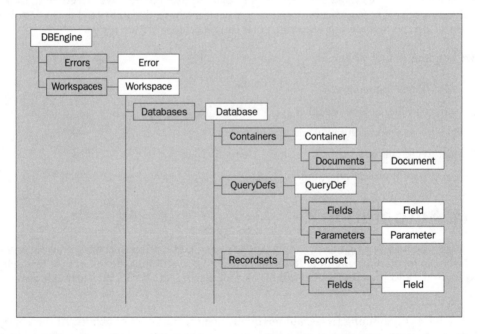

The `Objects` are shown shaded and the `Collections` are in white. This sort of diagram allows us to clearly see the hierarchy of objects, and makes it easier to find our way around the objects. For example if we have a `Recordset` object we know it has a `Fields` collection. This means we can instantly know that code like this will work:

```
For Each objField in objRec.Fields
Next
```

Understanding the object model is paramount to using automation. All of the Office applications have an object model, but we won't be including them in the book, as they are far too large. They are well covered in the Office documentation (make sure you install the VBA help for all of the applications), and we've also included them on the CD. Wrox also have a range of Office VBA books – check out www.wrox.com for more details.

Object References

Before you can use an Automation Object you need to create a reference to the appropriate object library. An **Object Library** is usually a DLL or OCX file that contains the code for the object. You can see which objects are installed on your machine by switching to the VBA IDE and selecting References... from the Tools menu:

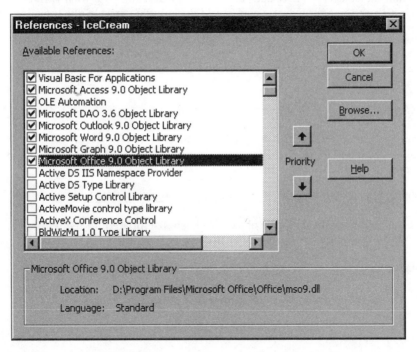

In the example above, the database has 8 references set – these are the ones with check marks against them. You can easily set a reference by just checking an item, and unchecking an item removes the reference – it doesn't remove the object library, just the reference. You saw in the previous chapter that you can use the Browse... button to browse for other objects that are not already registered – such as an Access Add-In.

> To complete the exercises in this chapter you should ensure that you have the references for Outlook, Word, Graph and Office set, just like the picture above. You can scroll down through the list to find the libraries that you need.

Creating Automation Objects

Because automation objects are just objects, you can create them in the same way as you've created other objects. For example, to create a recordset object variable you use this:

```
Dim objRec As Recordset
```

Similarly, to create an instance of an application object, you generally use this format:

```
Dim objApp As application_name.Application
```

Here, `application_name` would be Word, Outlook, or Excel. Using this just creates a variable to hold an object of the appropriate type, and doesn't actually create the object. This method is generally used when the object already exists, and you are just using your own variable. For example, consider a Field in a recordset – you would declare the variable like this:

```
Dim objFld As Field
```

This doesn't create a new Field object, but just creates a variable to hold an existing Field. This means that you cannot do this:

```
objFld.Name = "NewField"
```

If you try this you will get an error (Error 91 – Object variable or With block variable not set). That's because objFld is not an object, just an object variable – it hasn't been instantiated. If you want to create a new object then you use the New keyword. For example:

```
Dim objFld As New Field
```

You can then set the field name because the object has been instantiated. In reality the object is instantiated when you access the first property or method of the object.

So, the rules are:

- ❑ If you are going to point to an object that already exists, just use the normal syntax.
- ❑ If you are creating a new object, then you must use the New keyword.

Microsoft Outlook

You saw in Chapter 9 how easily mail can be sent from within Access, using DoCmd.SendObject, but this is rather restrictive. It doesn't allow you to set options on the message, or do anything complex – it's really just designed for sending objects. To achieve a greater degree of control over the mail procedure you can use the Outlook object model to send messages.

To use Outlook there are only a few objects you need to know about:

Object	Description
Outlook.Application	The main Outlook application.
MailItem	A mail message.
AppointmentItem	A diary appointment.
NoteItem	A note.

In fact, most of the folders in Outlook have an associated Item object.

Using Outlook programmatically means that we can build sending mail into existing processes. Consider the ingredients table, which has the UnitsInStock and ReOrderPoint fields. Every time an order is placed the UnitsInStock field should be decreased, and if it drops below the ReOrderPoint, then an order could be mailed automatically. This would prevent the ingredients from ever running out. Or you could run this as a weekly procedure, so that you don't send lots of small orders to the same supplier. That's what we'll do here. We'll create a query that shows us which items are below the re-order point, and then well create a mail message to our supplier requesting these items.

If you are an AOL user, then you won't be able to use Microsoft Outlook to send a mail message. AOL uses a proprietary mail system. You can still run through the exercise, but you won't actually be able to send mail.

Try It Out – Using Automation for Email

1. Create a new query, adding tblIngredient and tblSupplierList. Add fkCompanyID from tblSupplierList, and Name and ReOrderPoint from tblIngredient.

2. In the **Criteria** field for ReOrderPoint add the following:

```
> [UnitsInStock]
```

The query should now look like this:

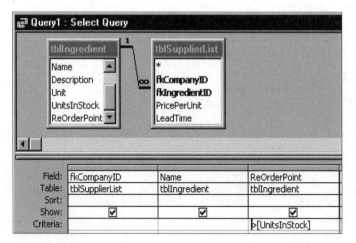

3. Close the query, saving it as `qryReOrder`. Now create a new query, adding `tblCompany`, `tblSupplierList` and `tblIngredient`.

4. Add `CompanyID`, `CompanyName`, `ContactName` and `Email` from `tblCompany`, and `ReOrderPoint` from `tblIngredient`.

5. For the **Criteria** for `ReOrderPoint` add the following:

```
> [UnitsInStock]
```

The query should now look like this:

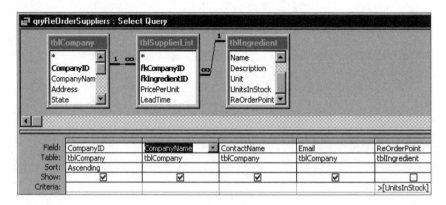

6. View the properties of the query. You can do this by the **Properties** button on the toolbar, or by selecting <u>P</u>roperties from the <u>V</u>iew menu, or <u>P</u>roperties from the context-menu (right mouse button).

7. Change the Unique Records property to Yes. Now close the query, saving it as qryReOrderSuppliers.

8. Create a new module. From the Tools menu, select References, check Microsoft Outlook 9.0 Object Library, and press OK to close the dialog.

9. Create a new procedure called ReOrder in the empty module. Add the following code:

```
Public Sub ReOrder()

Dim db As Database

Dim recReOrder As Recordset

Dim recSupps As Recordset
Dim objOutlook As New Outlook.Application
Dim objMessage As MailItem
Dim strSQL As String
Dim strOrder As String
Dim strItems As String

Set db = CurrentDb()

Set recSupps = db.OpenRecordset("qryReOrderSuppliers")

While Not recSupps.EOF
    strSQL = "SELECT * FROM qryReOrder " & _
        "WHERE fkCompanyID = " & recSupps("CompanyID")
    Set recReOrder = db.OpenRecordset(strSQL)

    strItems = "Item" & vbTab & "   Quantity"
    While Not recReOrder.EOF
        strItems = strItems & vbCrLf & recReOrder("Name") & _
            vbTab & recReOrder("ReOrderPoint")
        recReOrder.MoveNext
    Wend
    recReOrder.Close

    strOrder = "Dear " & recSupps("ContactName") & _
        vbCrLf & vbCrLf & _
        "Once again we are running short of the following items:" & _
        vbCrLf & vbCrLf & _
        strItems & _
        vbCrLf & vbCrLf & _
        "I'd be grateful if you could deliver " & _
        "these as soon as possible." & _
        vbCrLf & vbCrLf & _
        "Many Thanks" & _
        vbCrLf & vbCrLf & _
        "Dave"
```

```
    If Not IsNull(recSupps("Email")) Then
        Set objMessage = objOutlook.CreateItem(olMailItem)
        With objMessage
            .To = recSupps("Email")
            .Subject = "New Order"
            .Body = strOrder
            .Send
        End With
    End If

    recSupps.MoveNext
Wend

recSupps.Close
Set recSupps = Nothing
Set recReOrder = Nothing
Set objOutlook = Nothing
Set objMessage = Nothing

End Sub
```

10. Save the module as `Email`. Now switch to the Immediate window and try the procedure out, by typing `ReOrder`.

11. When the procedure has finished, open Outlook and have a look in either your **Outbox** or your **Sent Items** folder. You should have a mail message there somewhere The procedure sends one mail message to each supplier with an email address (here, there's only one supplier). Where the message appears depends on whether you've got a connection set up.

Admittedly the order details could be formatted a little nicer, but that's not a great deal of trouble. We're really concentrating on sending the message here.

How It Works

Let's first look at the queries we created. The first, qryReOrder, shows the ingredients that need reordering. We've included the ReOrderPoint in this query because we are going to order the same number of items that the ReOrderPoint contains. The second query, qryReOrderSuppliers, shows the supplier details – contact name and email address. Setting the Unique Records property to Yes ensures that we only see one record for each supplier. If this value was No then we would see a row for each supplier, for each product that needed reordering. We want one entry for each supplier because we are going to send a single mail message to each supplier with all of the order details on it.

Now on to the procedure. The first thing it does is declare all of the variables. The first three you've seen before – a database object and two recordsets. We need a recordset for the suppliers and one for the order items. Next comes the two Outlook objects – the main Outlook application, and a mail message item. Finally there are three strings – to hold a SQL query, the full order text and the order details.

```
Dim db As Database
Dim recReOrder As Recordset
Dim recSupps As Recordset
Dim objOutlook As New Outlook.Application
Dim objMessage As MailItem

Dim strSQL As String
Dim strOrder As String
Dim strItems As String
```

Once the variables are declared, we can open the database and create the recordset of suppliers.

```
Set db = CurrentDb()
Set recSupps = db.OpenRecordset("qryReOrderSuppliers")
```

We now need to loop through each supplier.

```
While Not recSupps.EOF
```

We need to create a list of order items for this supplier, so we create a SQL string, based on qryReOrder. Once the SQL string is set we create a recordset from it.

```
    strSQL = "SELECT * FROM qryReOrder " & _
        "WHERE fkCompanyID = " & recSupps("CompanyID")
    Set recReOrder = db.OpenRecordset(strSQL)
```

Now we have a recordset containing ingredients for a particular supplier, and we want a list of these in our mail message, so we create a string containing the item to be ordered and the quantity to order. We simply loop through the recordset adding these details to a string. We use the intrinsic constants vbCrLf and vbTab to provide new lines and tabs in the string. Once the loop is finished we can close the recordset, because all of the details we need are now in the string. (The While… Wend loop behaves in a similar way to the Do While… Loop).

```
strItems = "Item" & vbTab & "    Quantity"
While Not recReOrder.EOF
    strItems = strItems & vbCrLf & recReOrder("Name") & _
        vbTab & recReOrder("ReOrderPoint")
    recReOrder.MoveNext
Wend
recReOrder.Close
```

We can't just send a message with a list of the ingredients, so we add the contact name as some more text, again using intrinsic constants to format this text. We use a separate string for the items and for the full order details, because we'll be using the items later in the chapter.

```
strOrder = "Dear " & recSupps("ContactName") & _
    vbCrLf & vbCrLf & _
    "Once again we are running short of the following items:" & _
    vbCrLf & vbCrLf & _
    strItems & _
    vbCrLf & vbCrLf & _
    "I'd be grateful if you could deliver " & _
    "these as soon as possible." & _
    vbCrLf & vbCrLf & _
    "Many Thanks" & _
    vbCrLf & vbCrLf & _
    "Dave"
```

If the Email address field in the database is empty, then obviously we can't send an email order. We didn't omit records that have no email address in the query because we are going to modify this procedure later on, and we want to make sure it copes with all suppliers, and not just those that have email addresses.

```
If Not IsNull(recSupps("Email")) Then
```

The string is now complete, so the mail message can be created. The variable objOutlook is an instance of the outlook application. One of the methods this has is CreateItem, which creates an item of a specific type – in this case we use an intrinsic constant to specify a mail item.

```
Set objMessage = objOutlook.CreateItem(olMailItem)
```

We now have a mail message item, so we can set some properties. The To property is the email address of the recipient, and the Subject property is the subject line. The Body property is the actual body of the message, so we set this to the string we have created. We then use the Send method to send the message.

```
With objMessage
    .To = recSupps("Email")
    .Subject = "New Order"
    .Body = strOrder
    .Send
End With
End If
```

That's the end of one supplier, so we move onto the next.

```
    recSupps.MoveNext
Wend
```

And that's the end of the suppliers, so we close the recordset and clean up any object references, to free the memory they use.

```
recSupps.Close
Set recSupps = Nothing
Set recReOrder = Nothing
Set objOutlook = Nothing
Set objMessage = Nothing
```

Pretty easy, huh? In fact the section of code that actually sends the message is far simpler than the code that creates the message body.

Another way of achieving the aim of ordering by email would be to create a file, perhaps a saved report or a Word document, containing the order details, and then attach that to the mail message. We'll look at that method in a little while, when we look at Word.

Next we'll look at how to create appointments in Outlook, which will hopefully cure you of some of those horrible yellow notes you've got stuck all around your monitor! What we'll do is add a reminder to our Outlook diary, reminding us when the orders we've just placed are due – they are usually expected within three days.

Try It Out – Using Automation for Appointments

1. Open the Email module you've just created.

2. Create a new Private procedure, as follows:

```
Private Sub MakeAppointment(objOApp As Outlook.Application, _
    strCompany As String, strBody As String)

    Dim objAppt As AppointmentItem

    Set objAppt = objOApp.CreateItem(olAppointmentItem)
    With objAppt
        .Subject = "Order due from " & strCompany
        .Body = strBody
        .Start = Date + 3 & " 8:00"
        .End = Date + 3 & " 8:00"
        .ReminderSet = True
        .Save
    End With

End Sub
```

3. Add a new line to the `ReOrder` procedure, after the mail message has been sent, just before moving to the next supplier:

```
    End With
  End If
```

```
MakeAppointment objOutlook, recSupps("CompanyName"), strItems
```

```
  recSupps.MoveNext
Wend
```

4. Save the module, and run it again from the Immediate window.

5. Open Outlook and have a look at the calendar, for three days from now:

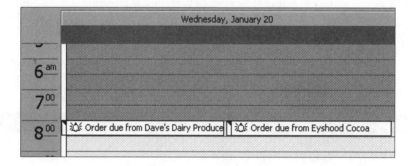

6. Open one of the appointments to look at it in detail:

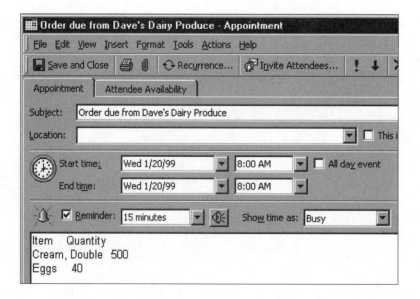

Notice how the start and end times are the same, and that the body of the appointment mirrors the details from the order.

How it Works

Let's first look at the `MakeAppointment` procedure, which takes three arguments. The first is the Outlook application object. This could have been declared as a global variable, but since it's only going to be used in two procedures, it seems sensible to pass it as an argument. The second argument is the company name, and the third the body of the apppointment.

```
Private Sub MakeAppointment(objOApp As Outlook.Application, _
   strCompany As String, strBody As String)
```

The first thing to do in the procedure is create an appointment item. This is the same method as we used to create a mail item – all we do is use a different constant.

```
Dim objAppt As AppointmentItem
Set objAppt = objOApp.CreateItem(olAppointmentItem)
```

Now we can set the appointment details. The `Subject` of the appointment is a note that the order is due from the company, and the `Body` contains the details passed in as the third argument. We'll see what these are in a minute.

```
With objAppt
   .Subject = "Order due from " & strCompany
   .Body = strBody
```

We set the `Start` and `End` times of the appointment to be today's date, as returned by the `Date` function, with three days added to it (remember from our early chapters on data types that adding a number to a date adds that number of days). We also append the time to this string, since without an explicit time, the appointment defaults to midnight.

```
   .Start = Date + 3 & " 8:00"
   .End = Date + 3 & " 8:00"
```

We then ensure that a reminder flag is set, and save the appointment.

```
   .ReminderSet = True
   .Save
End With

End Sub
```

To create the appointment, we simply call this function:

```
MakeAppointment objOutlook, recSupps("CompanyName"), strItems
```

We pass in the Outlook application object, the company name, and the list of ingredients.

Once again you can see that using automation to use the facilities of Outlook is extremely simple. With only a few extra lines of code we now have an automatic reminder system. You could also use this sort of thing for adding payment reminders when you send out orders to customers.

Microsoft Word

Using Automation to drive Microsoft Word is more complex than Outlook, because it has such a large object model. There are literally hundreds of options that you can use, and it's often very confusing for the beginner. This is not really surprising considering the large number of things that you can do in Word – format text, insert tables, etc. In some respects, because Word is such a visual tool, you wonder whether it's really worth delving into the object model.

The answer to that conundrum is obviously going to be yes, otherwise there wouldn't be anything about it in this chapter, but there are two ways to combine the use of Word and Access. The first, using Mail Merge, has Word as the master, requesting data from Access. You get the option to put Access fields in document templates, and then merge these into a document. However, this has always been rather restrictive. You can produce form letters, where the data from each row in the data source is inserted somewhere among the letter text. This is pretty much the way all that junk mail you receive works. You can also create a Catalog, where each row of data is shown after the previous one – exactly like a catalog. What's more difficult, however, is the combination of these two methods. Think about what we've just done with Outlook. We had a parent record (the supplier) and some child records (the order items). This isn't so easy to set up using a mail merge.

So a good way to achieve this is using the second way of combining Access and Word. Using automation from Access to push the data into Word documents. This involves starting Word, in much the same way as we started Outlook, creating documents, and adding text to them. This is perfect to fill the gap in our re-ordering setup. At the moment orders are only placed for those suppliers who have email addresses, so for those that don't have email we need some form of paper order. What we'll do is create a Word document containing the order details, and print this out. This can then be faxed or sent to the supplier.

Let's give it a go. The following example uses the Word template `Order.dot`, which is on the accompanying CD. We use a template just to give us the basic layout of the report. This should be copied into the directory where you have placed the other samples. The example also saves documents in this directory as well as printing them out.

If you have installed your samples in another location then you should change `C:\BegVBA` to the appropriate directory.

Try It Out – Creating a Word Document

1. Modify the query `qryReOrderSuppliers`, and add the `Address`, `State`, `City`, `PostCode`, and `Country` fields.

2. Now create a new module.

3. Add the following global variables:

```
Private Const m_strDIR As String = " C:\BegVBA\"
Private Const m_strTEMPLATE As String = " Order.dot"

Private m_objWord As Word.Application
Private m_objDoc As Word.Document
```

4. Now the main procedure, to create the order letter:

```
Public Sub CreateOrderLetter(recSupp As Recordset, recItems As Recordset)

    Set m_objWord = New Word.Application
    Set m_objDoc = m_objWord.Documents.Add(m_strDIR & m_strTEMPLATE)

    InsertTextAtBookMark "ContactName", recSupp("ContactName")
    InsertTextAtBookMark "CompanyName", recSupp("CompanyName")
    InsertTextAtBookMark "Address", recSupp("Address")
    InsertTextAtBookMark "City", recSupp("City")
    InsertTextAtBookMark "State", recSupp("State")
    InsertTextAtBookMark "PostCode", recSupp("PostCode")
    InsertTextAtBookMark "Country", recSupp("Country")

    InsertItemsTable recItems

    m_objWord.PrintOut Background:=False

    m_objDoc.SaveAs FileName:= m_strDIR & recSupp("CompanyName") & _
        " - " & FormatDateTime(Date, vbLongDate) & ".DOC"
    m_objDoc.Close
    m_objWord.Quit

    Set m_objDoc = Nothing
    Set m_objWord = Nothing

End Sub
```

5. Next comes a function to insert some text at a specific point:

```
Private Sub InsertTextAtBookMark(strBkmk As String, varText As Variant)

    m_objDoc.Bookmarks(strBkmk).Select
    m_objWord.Selection.Text = varText & ""

End Sub
```

6. And now a procedure to insert a table:

```
Private Sub InsertItemsTable(recR As Recordset)

    Dim strTable As String
    Dim objTable As Word.Table

    strTable = "Item" & vbTab & "Quantity" & vbCr
    recR.MoveFirst
    While Not recR.EOF
        strTable = strTable & recR("Name") & vbTab & _
            recR("ReOrderPoint") & vbCr
        recR.MoveNext
    Wend
```

```
    InsertTextAtBookMark "Items", strTable
    Set objTable = m_objWord.Selection.ConvertToTable(Separator:=vbTab)
    objTable.AutoFormat Format:=wdTableFormatClassic3, AutoFit:=True, _
        ApplyShading:=False

    Set objTable = Nothing

End Sub
```

7. The code for Word is now finished, so we just need to call the main function when we run our ReOrder procedure. Don't forget to save this module – call it Word Functions.

8. Open the Email module that you created earlier.

9. In the ReOrder procedure, add the following highlighted line. It should go after the string of items has been created, but before the recordset of items is closed:

```
    While Not recReOrder.EOF
        strItems = strItems & vbCrLf & recReOrder("Name") & _
            vbTab & recReOrder("ReOrderPoint")
        recReOrder.MoveNext
    Wend

    CreateOrderLetter recSupps, recReOrder

    recReOrder.Close
```

10. Save this module and run it from the Immediate window. It should take a little longer this time, and you might see a printing window, indicating that the order letter is being printed out.

11. When the procedure is finished have a look in C:\BegVBA (or wherever you installed your samples) for two new documents, which you can view in Word

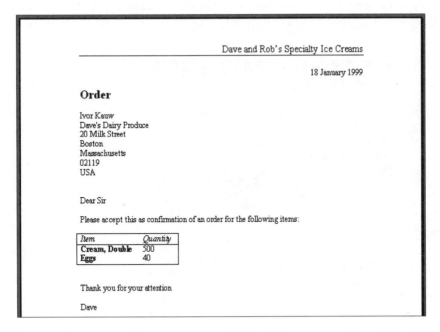

You can see that we now have a pretty good Word document, with a table of the orders.

How it Works

The first thing to do is look at the Word template.

What you'll notice here is the large I symbols – these represent bookmarks. If you don't see the bookmarks, then from the <u>T</u>ools menu select <u>O</u>ptions, and on the View tab select Boo<u>k</u>marks in the Show section:

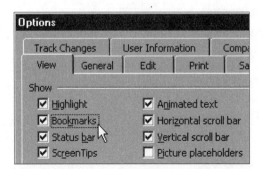

If you select Boo<u>k</u>marks from the <u>I</u>nsert menu you'll see a list of them:

Bookmarks in Word documents are just the same as bookmarks you place in books – that shopping receipt or envelope you tuck into a book to remind you where you are. This is the same – they allow you to jump to specified places in the document. Using automation we can jump to these bookmarks and insert text. Notice there's only one for the list of items. Although there are many items, what we'll be doing is inserting a table, so we only need one bookmark.

OK, let's take a look at the code, starting with the global variables. Firstly there are constants, defining the directory and the Word template to be used. Using a constant means that if we change the directory we don't have to crawl through the code looking for where we've used it.

```
Private Const m_strDIR As String = " C:\BegVBA\"
Private Const m_strTEMPLATE As String = " Order.dot"
```

Next come two Word object variables. The first is the main Word application, and the second will be the Word document. These correspond to the main Word window, and to an individual document within Word. We've used global variables here because they will be used in several procedures.

```
Private m_objWord As Word.Application
Private m_objDoc As Word.Document
```

Now let's look at the main procedure, which takes two arguments, both recordsets. The first is the recordset of the suppliers, and the second the items to be ordered for the supplier.

```
Public Sub CreateOrderLetter(recSupp As Recordset, recItems As Recordset)
```

Once in the procedure, the first thing we do is create an instance of Word – this actually starts Word, but hides it from view so you can't see it. After starting Word we use the Documents collection, and Add a new document. The argument we pass into the Add method is the name of the template that we want our new document to be based on.

```
Set m_objWord = New Word.Application
Set m_objDoc = m_objWord.Documents.Add(m_strDIR & m_strTEMPLATE)
```

The Documents collection just contains a list of all documents currently open, just like the Access Forms collection, which contains a list of all open forms.

At this stage we now have a new document based upon our template. That means that it has the default text from the template, but has empty spaces where the bookmarks are, so that's what we do next. Insert some text into the bookmarks. We call another function to do this, and we'll look at that in a moment, but you can see we are inserting the details from the supplier recordset into specific bookmarks.

```
InsertTextAtBookMark "ContactName", recSupp("ContactName")
InsertTextAtBookMark "CompanyName", recSupp("CompanyName")
InsertTextAtBookMark "Address", recSupp("Address")
InsertTextAtBookMark "State", recSupp("State")
InsertTextAtBookMark "PostCode", recSupp("PostCode")
InsertTextAtBookMark "Country", recSupp("Country")
```

Next is another function call, this time to insert the order items as a table. We'll look at that in a moment too.

```
InsertItemsTable recItems
```

At this stage all of the text has been inserted, so we print out a copy of the order, setting the Background argument to False. This ensures that we wait for Word to finish printing before we continue. This is important, as the next thing we do is save the document and quit Word, and you can't quit if the document is still being printed. We've used Background as a named argument as it makes it much clearer what we are doing.

```
m_objWord.PrintOut Background:=False
```

Once the document is printed it needs to be saved. The file name we use is the company name plus the current date. In real life you'd probably have an order number in there somewhere.

```
m_objDoc.SaveAs FileName:= m_strDIR & recSupp("CompanyName") & _
    " - " & FormatDateTime(Date, vbLongDate) & ".DOC"
```

Once saved we can close the document, quit Word, and clear any object references.

```
m_objDoc.Close
m_objWord.Quit

Set m_objDoc = Nothing
Set m_objWord = Nothing

End Sub
```

So that's it. We open a new document based upon a template, add some text at specified positions, print the document and then save it. Let's see how the text is actually inserted.

To use the bookmarks in the document we use the `Bookmarks` collection. This is just like the `Controls` collection on a form, and for a document, contains one entry for each bookmark in the document. We use the name of the bookmark to index into the collection, and use the `Select` method to make the bookmark the current selection. This would be the equivalent of just clicking on the bookmark in the Word document.

```
Private Sub InsertTextAtBookMark(strBkmk As String, varText As Variant)

    m_objDoc.Bookmarks(strBkmk).Select
```

Once this is done the `Selection` object is activated, containing the currently selected items. When typing documents the selection is visible as a highlight, for example when you select a word or sentence. The `Selection` object has a property called `Text`, which contains the text in the selection. We then set the text of the selection to the text we want to insert. We've appended an empty string onto the text because the text comes from the database, and might contain a null value. Adding this empty string just prevents any errors about null values.

```
    m_objWord.Selection.Text = varText & ""

End Sub
```

So that's how to add text at a bookmark. Let's see how to insert a table. This procedure takes a recordset of the order items, which we will use to create a table. The method we are going to use to create the table is similar to the way you might do it in Word, by just typing in the items, separated by tab characters, and then selecting the **Convert Text to Table** option from the **Table** menu. We use this method because it's actually simpler than creating a table, and then moving around the cells inserting the data.

```
Private Sub InsertItemsTable(recR As Recordset)
```

We have two variables. The first is a string, into which we will build up the table, separating the table columns by tab characters, and the table rows by carriage return characters. We've actually already done this procedure once, when we added these details to the mail message, but we're doing it again here to emphasize the method used to create tables.

```
Dim strTable As String
```

The second variable is another word object – a `Table`, which represents, unsurprisingly, a Word table.

```
Dim objTable As Word.Table
```

Now we create the string containing the table details, by looping through the recordset adding the ingredient name and the number of items to reorder.

```
strTable = "Item" & vbTab & "Quantity" & vbCr
recR.MoveFirst
While Not recR.EOF
    strTable = strTable & recR("Name") & vbTab & _
        recR("ReOrderPoint") & vbCr
    recR.MoveNext
Wend
```

Then we insert this string into the position marked by the `Items` bookmark.

```
InsertTextAtBookMark "Items", strTable
```

At this stage the document looks like this:

```
Dear·Sir¶
¶
Please·accept·this·as·confirmation·of·an·order·for·the·following·items:¶
¶
Item → Quantity¶
Cream,·Double    →    500¶
Eggs→40¶
¶
¶
Thank·you·for·your·attention¶
```

The inserted text is highlighted, so we now need to convert it into a table. To do this we use another method of the `Selection` object, `ConvertToTable`, using the `Separator` argument to tell the method what character is to be used as the column separator.

```
Set objTable = m_objWord.Selection.ConvertToTable(Separator:=vbTab)
```

Now the document looks like this:

```
Dear·Sir¶
¶
Please·accept·this·as·confirmation·of·an·order·for·the·following·items:¶
¶
Item¤                          Quantity¤                    ¤
Cream,·Double¤                 500¤                         ¤
Eggs¤                          40¤                          ¤
¶
¶
Thank·you·for·your·attention¶
```

The text has been converted into a table, but it's not a particularly nice table, so it needs a little formatting. We use the `AutoFormat` method of the table, supplying three arguments. The first, `Format`, identifies the auto format style to use, in this case the Classic 3 style. The second argument, `AutoFit`, is a Boolean, and indicates whether the columns of the table should be automatically sized to fit their contents. The third argument, `ApplyShading`, is another Boolean, identifying whether or not shading is to be used on the table.

```
objTable.AutoFormat Format:=wdTableFormatClassic3, AutoFit:=True, _
    ApplyShading:=False
```

The table is nicely formatted, so we've really finished our work. All that's left to do is tidy up the object reference.

```
    Set objTable = Nothing

End Sub
```

That's all there is to it. The final piece is to call all of this code from within our email procedure:

```
CreateOrderLetter recSupps, recReOrder
```

Here we simply call the procedure passing in the recordsets of the suppliers and order items.

Word Summary

As mentioned at the beginning of the section, using automation with Word can be complex, but we've only used a few features here, and managed to get quite a degree of flexibility. Using bookmarks as place markers for text insertion allows the Word document to change without affecting your code. As long as the bookmarks are in the document, then your code will still work.

This is actually quite a powerful concept, because you could use it to create a very flexible report writer. Often, one of the complaints of users is that the reports you've written don't quite do what they want. You could easily create a set of queries and some code that allows users to create their reports using Word. Just give them a list of queries and fields in each query, and they can add bookmarks to Word that match those fields. Your report writer code could search through the bookmarks in the document, and if it finds one that matches a field, could insert the text from the field.

Microsoft Excel

Microsoft Excel, again because of its complexity, has a large object model, so we're only going to look at one specific area – charts. Getting data into Excel is extremely simple from within Excel itself, and you can link data much more easily than you can with Word, so that's why we're not going to look at it here. However, if you're building an application, you generally have to provide some form of reporting, for all those managers and accountants. They like that sort of thing.

One of the great things about Access is that you can use objects from other applications on your forms. This is particularly useful for adding charts to your applications. So in this example, we're going to do our automation a little differently. Instead of creating an instance of an application, we're going to put the instance on a form, as a visible object.

Try It Out – A Chart on a Form

1. Create a new query without any tables or queries on it. From the Query menu, select SQL Specific, and then Union.

2. Type the following SQL statement into the blank window:

```
SELECT -1 As CompanyID, "<All>" As CompanyName
FROM tblCompany
UNION
SELECT CompanyID, CompanyName
FROM tblCompany
ORDER BY CompanyName
```

3. Close the query, saving it as qryuCompanyLookup. Create another new query, adding tblCompany and tblSales.

4. Add the CompanyName and Quantity fields, then into the next empty field add the following:

```
MonthName: Format([DateOrdered], "mmmm")
```

5. From the Query toolbar select Crosstab Query.

6. In the CompanyName column, set the Total entry to Group By and the Crosstab entry to Row Heading. Then, in the MonthName column set the Total entry to Group By and the Crosstab entry to Column Heading. Finally, in the Quantity column set the Total entry to Sum and the Crosstab entry to Value.

7. Your query should now look like this:

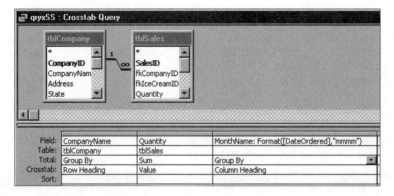

8. From the <u>V</u>iew menu select <u>P</u>roperties, and add the following into the Column Headings field:

```
January;February;March;April;May;June;July;August;September;October;November;December
```

Note: This should all be on the same line when you type it in.

9. Close the query, saving it as qryxSS.

10. Create another query, based upon qryxSS. Add all of the fields to the query, and change each of the month fields so that the name is the abbreviated month name, and they use the Nz function to return 0 if the field is null. This might be easier to do in SQL view, where the query will look like this:

```
SELECT qryxSS.CompanyName,
Nz(January,0) AS Jan, Nz(February,0) AS Feb, Nz(March,0) AS Mar,
Nz(April,0) AS Apr, Nz(May,0) AS May, Nz(June,0) AS Jun,
Nz(July,0) AS Jul, Nz(August,0) AS Aug, Nz(September,0) AS Sep,
Nz(October,0) AS Oct, Nz(November,0) AS Nov, Nz(December,0) AS [Dec]
FROM qryxSS;
```

11. Close the query, saving it as qryxSalesSummary. Now create a new form and add a combo box at the top. Name the combo box cboCompany, and change the label accordingly.

12. Set the Row Source Type to Table/Query and the Row Source to qryuCompanyLookup. Then set the Column Count to 2 and Columns Widths to 0.

13. Put a check box next to the combo box. Call it chkLegend and change the label to Show Legend.

14. From the toolbox select Unbound Object Frame and draw a large frame on the form, underneath the other two controls. From the Insert Object dialog, make sure that Create New is selected, and pick Microsoft Graph 2000 Object, before pressing the OK button. Your form will now look something like this:

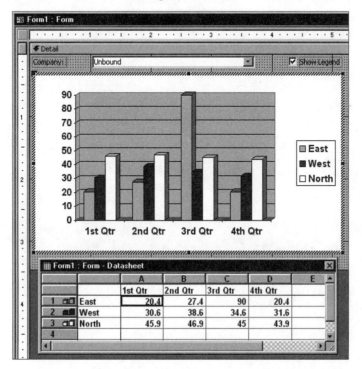

Don't worry about what the data is or what the graph looks like. We'll be changing that later.

15. Click on the form background, to the side of the new object, and the graph deactivates. Now view the properties for the graph object. Set the Name to ctlChart, the Row Source Type to Value List and the Column Heads to Yes. Then save the form as frmSalesFigures.

16. Press the Code button to create a code module, and from the Tools menu select References. Make sure the Microsoft Graph 9.0 Object Library is checked, before pressing the OK button. Now add the following module level variable to the new module:

```
Private m_objChart As Graph.Chart
```

17. In the Click event for chkLegend add this code:

```
m_objChart.HasLegend = chkLegend
```

18. In the `Load` event for the `Form` add the following:

```
Set m_objChart = ctlChart.Object
```

19. In the `Unload` event for the `Form` add the following – this will clear the memory used by the object variable:

```
Set m_objChart = Nothing
```

20. In the `Change` event for `cboCompany` add the following:

```
Private Sub cboCompany_Change()

   On Error Goto cboCompany_Change_Err

   Dim strSQL As String

   If cboCompany = -1 Then
      strSQL = "qryxSalesSummary"
   Else
      strSQL = "SELECT * FROM qryxSalesSummary WHERE CompanyName=""" & _
         cboCompany.Column(1) & """"
   End If

   ctlChart.RowSource = strSQL
   ctlChart.RowSourceType = "Table/Query"

   With m_objChart
      .ChartArea.Font.Size = 8
      .HasLegend = chkLegend

      If cboCompany = -1 Then
         .ChartType = xl3DColumn
         .Refresh
         .Axes(xlSeriesAxis).HasTitle = False
      Else
         .ChartType = xl3DColumnStacked
         .Refresh
      End If

      With .Axes(xlCategory)
         .HasTitle = True
         .AxisTitle.Caption = "Month"
      End With

      With .Axes(xlValue)
         .HasTitle = True
         .AxisTitle.Caption = "Total Sales"
      End With

   End With

cboCompany_Change_Exit:
   Exit Sub
```

```
cboCompany_Change_Err:
   If Err.Number = 1004 Then
      m_objChart.Refresh
   Else
      Err.Raise Err.Number, Err.Source, Err.Description, _
         Err.HelpFile, Err.HelpContext
   End If

End Sub
```

21. Save the code and switch back to Access. Now switch the form into form view. The Company combo box will be empty, so select Amethyst Group:

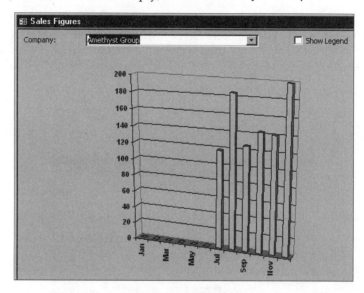

Pretty cool, huh? A chart of all sales for this company. Now select <All> from the combo box:

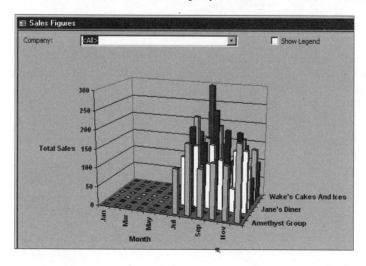

Even cooler. Clicking the show legend check box shows the legend for the various companies – they aren't all shown because there isn't room to show them all – this also happens with the month names.

How it Works

Let's first start with the queries, starting with `qryuCompanyLookup`. This is a `UNION` query, which joins two sets of data together. Why do we want to do this? Well, what we want on the form is a way for the user to choose either a single company or all the companies. You could have a combo box of companies and a check box for all companies, but this just seems a bit confusing. What's better is a single combo that shows <All> as the first record, and then the companies underneath that. So that's what this query does.

The first `SELECT` statement is used to produce the <All>, and shows a feature of SQL that you might not have seen before – you don't actually have to select data from a table. Here we are selecting two values of our choosing. Notice that we've used column aliases, giving our two values proper column names. That's because the columns in the two select statements must match.

```
SELECT -1 As CompanyID, "<All>" As CompanyName
FROM tblCompany
```

On its own this gives:

CompanyID	CompanyName
-1	<All>
-1	<All>
-1	<All>
-1	<All>
-1	<All>
-1	<All>
-1	<All>
-1	<All>
-1	<All>
-1	<All>

This is because we are selecting from a table but not selecting columns from that table, so we get a row in the output for each row in the table. But, because we are supplying our own values for the columns, all of the rows are the same.

*This in fact points to a bug in JET SQL, because you should be able to do **SELECT -1 As CompanyID, "<All>" As CompanyName** without the **FROM** clause. However, JET reports this as an error.*

Next we use the `UNION` statement to say that we want to join the first query with the second.

```
UNION
```

The second query is a normal `SELECT` statement.

```
SELECT CompanyID, CompanyName
FROM tblCompany
ORDER BY CompanyName
```

Having looked at the diagram above you might think that our combo box would show several rows of <All>, but by default a `UNION` query only shows unique records, so all of the duplicate values are stripped out.

This `UNION` technique is a great way to allow users to select one or all values from a table. One thing to note about `UNION` queries is that both of the queries must contain the same number of columns, otherwise errors will be generated.

OK, let's look at the crosstab query now. Crosstab queries allow us to make a row value become a column. So if we look at a non crosstab version of this query:

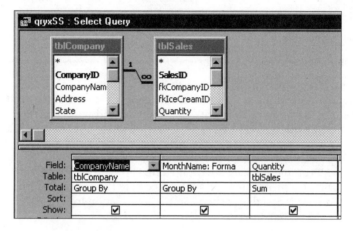

This gives a result of:

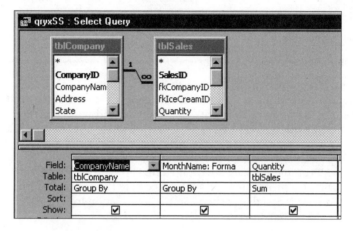

What we want is one row for each company, with the month names as columns. So a crosstab query allows us to specify three things:

❑ Row Heading, which will be `CompanyName`.

❑ Column Heading, which will be `MonthName`.

❑ Value, which will be `SumOfQuantity`.

However, on its own this just gives us:

Company Name	August	December	July
Amethyst Group	185	199	118
Eyshood Cocoa	11		
Flavors Of The World	163	162	131
Jane's Diner	100	109	148
Lloyds Luscious Lollie	153	71	193
Quintessential Ices	159	139	215
Wake's Cakes And Ic	295	95	165

What about all of the rest of the months, for which there is no data? They don't appear for that very reason – there is no data. A column is only created if there is a `MonthName` for it. To get column names for all of the months we have to specify the columns, and we do this by setting the `Column Headings` property of the query. This makes sure that we get a column for each month, even if there is no data.

This, however, still isn't complete, as cells with no data show up as empty, rather than 0. This isn't a problem here, but will be a problem when we try to create the graph. So, what we do is create another query based on our crosstab query, using the `Nz` function to return 0 if the column is null. Only now do we have the correct query.

Let's move onto the form now. The combo box just takes its values from the union query, and the check box is straightforward too. The Object Frame might be a new control to you though. You already know what objects are, so this is just a way to embed one of these objects on a form. In this case our object frame is used to contain a graph. If you've ever used graphs in Excel, then this isn't really any different, because the graph is a separate object. When you create a graph in Excel you are embedding a graph object in your spreadsheet.

Like many other controls the graph control on the form can be bound to a data source. To stop the graph trying to display data when it first loads we set the `Row Source Type` property to `Value List`. We also set the `Column Heads` property to `Yes` – for some reason this is required for the data to display correctly, but the reason is not documented.

Now let's move onto the code, starting with the global variables. To save lots of unnecessary referencing, we have a variable that will point to the chart.

```
Private m_objChart    As Graph.Chart
```

So when the form loads we can do this:

```
Set m_objChart = ctlChart.Object
```

This points to the chart object. This is an important point because you have to differentiate from the chart control and the chart object. The chart control is the visible control on the form, which is what Access controls. This includes things such as the height, width, border, etc, and is really how we, as the user, see the control. The chart object is the underlying chart, and is what controls the chart itself.

For the checkbox we only have one line of code – to change whether the chart has a legend or not, using the `HasLegend` property.

```
m_objChart.HasLegend = chkLegend
```

Now comes the real guts, as this is the code for the `Change` event of the combo box. Firstly we set some error handling – I'll explain why later.

```
Private Sub cboCompany_Change()

    On Error Goto cboCompany_Change_Err
```

Next we declare a string, which will hold the SQL statement – this is what we are going to use as the source of the chart data.

```
    Dim strSQL   As String
```

Now we need to set this SQL statement. Remember how our union query has –1 as the `CompanyID` for the `<All>` value – this allows us to identify in code whether `<All>` has been selected. If it has, we want to use all of the data from the crosstab query – remember that this contains data for every company.

```
    If cboCompany = -1 Then
        strSQL = "qryxSalesSummary"
```

If a company has been selected we only want to show values for that company, so we build a SQL string just picking out the correct values.

```
    Else
        strSQL = "SELECT * FROM qryxSalesSummary WHERE CompanyName=""'" & _
            cboCompany.Column(1) & """'"
    End If
```

We now set the source of the data for the chart, also setting the type of data to be a table or a query. We couldn't do this at design time because the source of the data wasn't known and an error would have occurred. Now we know the source of the data, it's safe to set it here.

```
    ctlChart.RowSource = strSQL
    ctlChart.RowSourceType = "Table/Query"
```

Now we need to set some properties of the chart.

```
   With m_objChart
```

We start with the font size. The `ChartArea` property applies to the whole chart, so allows us to set the font size for all aspects of the chart.

```
      .ChartArea.Font.Size = 8
```

Then we set the legend property.

```
      .HasLegend = chkLegend
```

If the user selects all companies, then we need to show a multi-dimensional graph. So we set the `ChartType` property to be a `3D Column`.

```
      If cboCompany = -1 Then
         .ChartType = xl3DColumn
```

Next we `Refresh` the chart, because we want to set some properties that are dependent upon the chart type. One of those is setting a title for one of the axis. When you have a 2D graph you only have the X and Y axes, but a 3D graph has a Z axis as well. This axis doesn't exist if the chart is 2D, but does if 3D, so we use `Refresh` to ensure that all axes are visible. We then turn off the `Title` for this axis.

```
         .Refresh
         .Axes(xlSeriesAxis).HasTitle = False
```

For a single company, we want a two-dimensional graph, so we use a different `ChartType`.

```
      Else
         .ChartType = xl3DColumnStacked
         .Refresh
      End If
```

Now we can deal with the X- and Y-axes, making sure that the title is visible, and the caption for the axis is set appropriately.

```
      With .Axes(xlCategory)
         .HasTitle = True
         .AxisTitle.Caption = "Month"
      End With

      With .Axes(xlValue)
         .HasTitle = True
         .AxisTitle.Caption = "Total Sales"
      End With
   End With
```

That's it, so we can simply exit.

```
cboCompany_Change_Exit:
   Exit Sub
```

The error handling here is a bit of a kludge, and is purely included to get around a timing problem. We've already mention that we use `Refresh` to ensure that properties are updated. There are occasionally times when trying to set a property occurs before that property is available, and an error is generated. So, we check the error number to see if it means that the property isn't available, and just `Refresh` to ensure it is. Any other error is sent back to the default error handler.

```
cboCompany_Change_Err:
   If Err.Number = 1004 Then
      m_objChart.Refresh
   Else
      Err.Raise Err.Number, Err.Source, Err.Description, _
         Err.HelpFile, Err.HelpContext
   End If

End Sub
```

The final thing to do is to clean up the object reference when the form is closed.

```
Set m_objChart = Nothing
```

That's all there is to it. Although it may look complex, we are really only dealing with a few properties. If you create a chart in Excel and use the dialog boxes and toolbars to modify the properties, you'll see a similar kind of result.

Graph Summary

The main properties we've looked at have been:

- ❑ `ChartType` identifies what type of chart you want to see.
- ❑ `HasLegend` identifies whether or not a legend is shown on the chart.
- ❑ `Axes(xlCategory)` identifies the X axis.
- ❑ `Axes(xlValue)` identifies the Y axis.
- ❑ `Axes(xlSeriesAxis)` identifies the Z axis, if it exists.

`Axes` is a collection containing objects of type `Axis`, so these have their own properties too.

Office Assistant

Since we're near the end of the book, and the rest of this chapter has been pretty sensible, let's just have a quick look at the Office Assistant to lighten the load a little. You need to make sure that the Office Assistant is installed for this example.

To save yourself a lot of unnecessary typing, import the form `frmAssistant` from IceCream15.mdb. Switch to the code module, and from the **Tools** menu pick **References**, making sure you check the **Microsoft Office 9.0 Object Library** before pressing the **OK** button. Now switch back to Access and open the form in form mode. Use the combo box to select the action for your assistant. Pretty fun, eh? You can look at the code here in more detail if you like, to see how you can use the Office Assistant yourself.

Summary

There is quite a lot of important code in this chapter, building on some of the techniques you've learned earlier in the book. In previous chapters we've looked at classes and building your own objects, but this chapter focuses on using objects that have been built by other people – in this case Microsoft. We know that using classes is a great way to promote code re-use and provide ready made functionality to other programmers, and using Automation just takes this one step further.

In this chapter we've looked at the following topics:

- ❑ What Automation is and how it works.
- ❑ How you can use the functionality of existing applications.
- ❑ Using Outlook to send email messages and make appointments.
- ❑ Using Word as a basic report writer.
- ❑ Combining Excel Charts with Access to provide graphs on forms.

The important thing about using automation is the Object Model. Once you have a basic understanding of the object model of the application you are using, then almost anything is possible.

Now it's time to turn our sights back towards Access, and see how it handles multiple users, and the security of those users.

Exercise

1. For the Sales Figures Chart form (`frmSalesFigures`) add four buttons to allow the user to rotate the chart. The buttons should rotate the chart left, right, up and down.

    Hint: The chart has properties called `Rotation` and `Elevation` – make sure you check the help files for their acceptable values.

Multi-User

In this chapter we will be looking at a number of different issues that face developers as they develop applications for a multi-user environment. The most obvious of these is the issue of record locking; what happens when two users want to update the same record at the same time? We will look at how we can programmatically control shared access to data and how we can gracefully handle errors that arise when two users attempt to access the same data at the same time.

Then we will go on to look at the whole issue of security. Broadly speaking, security is implemented within database applications for two reasons. It allows us, as developers, to restrict unauthorised access to areas of the database that we wish to remain off-bounds and it allows the application to identify users so that it can both personalise their interaction with the database and audit their use of application and database resources.

Finally, we will look at another related issue – compilation. This is the process of wrapping up or packaging an application before it is developed so that it runs more efficiently and is less susceptible to accidental design changes than it would be if it were in an uncompiled state.

Multi-Developer Issues

In this chapter, we are going to tackle the question of how Access functions in a multi-user environment. But we'll just take a moment to look at the other side of the coin – how does Access work as a **multi-developer** product? So far, we have concentrated on the functionality that Access, DAO and VBA provide for the user and developer but we have been considering these from quite an isolated viewpoint. To a large degree that is inevitable. After all, developing applications does tend to be a fairly personal experience. Sure, we may work in project teams and, yes, we may have weekly design meetings where we collaborate on various aspects of the design and development of the product we are working on, but when it comes down to the nitty-gritty of cutting code – most of us tend to work on our own.

I am not suggesting that the cubicle culture – familiar to anyone who reads Dilbert cartoons – is the ideal way to work, but a lot of the design and development process is a fairly cerebral process and lends itself to isolated, concentrated effort rather than a more communal approach.

To a large degree this has been exacerbated by the limited support that Access has traditionally offered for team development. Previous versions of Access allowed multiple developers to make design changes to Access objects and code in the same open database but implemented it through a complex procedure behind the scenes which fooled Access into thinking that only one developer at a time was making those changes. In Access 97, multi-developer support was greatly enhanced by the addition of source code control via a component which shipped with the Microsoft Office 97 Developer Edition Tools (ODE Tools) and which integrated with Microsoft Visual SourceSafe. In Access 2000, use of the source code add-ins that ship with the Developer Edition will be essential for anyone wanting to develop in a team environment. That is because the Access 2000 – in line with the other Office 2000 applications – no longer allows multiple developers to make native design changes to Access objects and code in the same open database. So, if you want to develop in teams, you are going to need the Developer Edition.

The upshot of this approach is that many developers tend only to consider the multi-user aspects of their applications towards the end of the development and testing cycle. Even if they design their applications in teams, many developers build their code alone, and do their system testing alone and it is only when user acceptance testing starts and two or three people use the database at the same time that odd problems start to occur. And then, the application is rolled out in production to thirty users and it comes to a grinding halt. The developer says out loud "That's odd!", while he is really thinking "Oh <expletive deleted>!" and it is back to the drawing board, do not pass "Go" and do not collect $200...

Record Locking in Access 2000

The most significant change to the whole issue of record locking in JET 4.0 is the introduction of record-level locking. Let's start by looking at what that means.

Page Locking vs. Record Locking

If you have used Microsoft Access before, you might have noticed that the Advanced page of the Tools/Options... dialog box now contains a checkbox that was not present in previous versions.

We can now decide whether we want use record-level locking or page-level locking when we open databases.

In previous versions of Access, Microsoft employed a **page-level locking** strategy. That is to say that instead of placing locks on individual records, Access placed locks on the underlying data page on which the record resided. Data pages were 2Kb in length and could contain multiple records. What that means is that the act of placing a lock on a data page could lock a great many records apart from those which were actually being edited.

By contrast, **record-level locking** – introduced in Access 2000 – places locks on individual records. So, if one record is locked, other users can still access all other records in the base table including the records on the same page as the locked record. To many people this will seem like an overwhelmingly obvious approach. Why did previous versions of Access not employ record-level locking in the first place?

Well, page-level locking does have some advantages. The process of obtaining and releasing locks is an expensive process in terms of both the CPU activity and the memory overhead required to maintain the lock structure. Because page-level locking locked multiple records it meant that fewer locks were typically required than if record-level locking had been implemented. Fewer locks means less work for the processor and less memory overhead. However, it also means less concurrency (the ability for multiple users to access the same data at the same time). Microsoft believed that page-locking offered the best solution to this problem.

Several things have changed since the days of page-level locking in Access 1.0. The dramatic improvements in processor performance, coupled with reductions in memory prices mean that for most modern PCs the overhead incurred by locking is less onerous than it once was. Record-level locking is a relatively less expensive option than it was back in November 1992.

Coupled to the improvement in PC performance is the fact that Access 2000 now offers full Unicode support. That means that Access 2000 can now support the characters that appear in a variety of international languages rather than simply supporting the 256 commonly used characters of the ANSI character set. The downside to this, however, is that Access 2000 now uses 2 bytes rather than 1 for each character. In order to support this, the size of data pages has grown from 2 Kb to 4 Kb. Now if locking a 2 Kb page full of records when only one record is being updated is a controversial move, then just think of the effect of locking a 4Kb page. In a table with relatively short records – say, an average of 20 bytes in length – then a 4 Kb page would contain approaching 200 records.

Another important factor behind the decision to introduce record-level locking in Access 2000 was compatibility with Microsoft SQL Server, which, from version 7.0 onwards, supports record-level locking. The introduction of this feature in Access 2000 therefore allows developers to migrate applications from Access to SQL Server without having to worry about changes in locking strategies.

Record Level Locking

So Microsoft have finally relented and have offered users the option to use either page-level or record-level locking in Access 2000. You can make this choice by checking or unchecking the **Open databases using record-level locking** checkbox on the **Advanced** page of the <u>T</u>ools/<u>O</u>ptions... dialog box in Access.

Not surprisingly, if the checkbox is checked, Access will attempt to open future databases with a record-level locking mechanism. In contrast, if it is unchecked Access will try to use page-level locking.

Which should you select? For most people, the new default – record-level locking – will be the preferred choice because of the benefits it offers in terms of concurrency. Actually, if a database has been opened in record-level locking mode, JET will still use page locks in those situations where it is more appropriate to do so.

Specifically, if you perform set-based operations such as UPDATE, INSERT or DELETE queries, then JET will temporarily switch to a page-locking mechanism in order to perform the query more effectively. If, however, you are performing a cursor-based operation (such as looping through all of the records in a recordset and updating records individually) then JET will use record-level locking.

However, there are a couple of caveats. Firstly, you will only be able to realise the concurrency benefits of record-level locking in code if you place your data modification statements inside transactions.

> A **transaction** is a method of programmatically grouping together a number of data modification statements into a single unit. They are normally used to promote database consistency, by ensuring that either all of the statements in the transaction are executed successfully, or none of them are. A discussion of transaction usage is a little beyond the scope of this chapter, but if you want to know more about transactions, you should take a look at the topic "*BeginTrans, CommitTrans, Rollback Methods*" in the Visual Basic help file.

Secondly, and potentially more confusingly, in a multi-user environment, the decision as to whether a database will be opened with page or row locking is determined by the first person that opens the database. So if the first person to open a database has record-level locking specified as an option, then the database will be opened with record-level locking and this option will apply to all other users who then access the database while it is open, irrespective of the locking level that they might have specified as an option. After the last person closes this database, the level of locking selected the next time the database is opened will be decided again by the person who opens the database first.

> **What this means is that in a multi-user environment there is no easy way of determining whether a database that you have opened in is in row-level or page-level mode!**

To change the granularity of locking (i.e. record-level or page-level) programmatically simply use the SetOption method of the Application object like this:

```
Application.SetOption "Use Row Level Locking", True
```

> *This has exactly the same effect as checking the **Open databases using record-level locking** checkbox on the **Advanced** page of the **Tools/Options...** dialog box in Access.*

So, now that we have looked at the way that Access provides a method of altering the granularity of locking, let's have a look at when JET places and releases locks.

Optimistic and Pessimistic Locking

Access 2000, just like previous versions of Access, employs two methods of locking records – optimistic and pessimistic locking:

❑ With **pessimistic** locking, Access locks a record (or the page the record is on) whenever someone starts to change the contents of that record

❑ With **optimistic** locking, Access only tries to place the lock when someone tries to save the changes that they have made

Let's look at an example to clarify the difference between the two. Suppose John and Mary are both using the same database and are editing records in the same table. If John decides just to view record #30 then, irrespective of the type of locking strategy involved, Mary will still also be able to look at the contents of that record.

However, suppose John now decides to edit the contents of that record by typing a new value in one of the fields on his form. If pessimistic locking is being employed, Access will now lock that record so that only John can change it.

> Pessimistic locking implies that when a user edits a record, Access pessimistically assumes that someone else will also want to edit that same record and so needs to lock it.

Mary will now see the 'record locked' indicator on her form, which tells her that she can't edit the record. In fact, she will not be able to edit that record until John has finished with record #30 and has saved his changes.

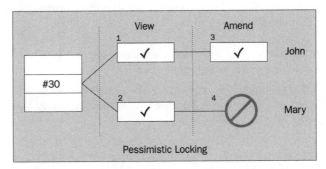

However, if an optimistic locking strategy were being used, Mary would have been able to make changes to record #30, even while John was editing it.

> Optimistic locking implies that, when a user edits a record, Access optimistically assumes that no-one else will want to edit the same record, and so it doesn't lock it.

This can be a very dangerous scenario. Assume that both John and Mary are now editing the same record – what happens when John tries to save the record? Nothing out of the ordinary... he is able to save the record as if nothing had happened. But what happens when Mary tries to save the record?

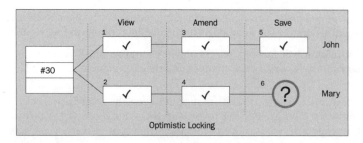

The answer is that when she tries to save a record that has changed since she opened it, she is presented with this dialog box:

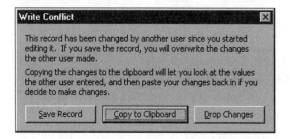

Sometimes, when a dialog box pops up you instantly know what is wrong and what you need to do. But this one carries a rather complicated message. You really need to think twice about how to respond to it and for those seeing it for the first time, it can be quite confusing. Essentially, the dialog box is telling Mary that she has three choices:

❑ She can save her record. This will overwrite the changes that John has just made without John being aware of the fact.

❑ She can copy her changes to the clipboard. She will then be able to see the changes that John has made and decide whether she still wants to make her changes.

❑ Or she can just call it a day and drop the changes she has just made. In this case, John's amended record will remain in the table but the changes that she has made will be lost.

Choosing a Locking Strategy

So which locking strategy should you choose? Optimistic or pessimistic? There is no simple answer, but in general:

- ❑ If it is unlikely that any two users will want to amend the same record simultaneously, use optimistic locking.

- ❑ If it is likely that two or more users may want to amend the same record simultaneously, choose pessimistic locking.

You are probably getting fed up with us saying this again, but developing Access applications involves a large degree of compromise. When choosing a locking strategy, the compromise is one of concurrency versus complexity.

	Optimistic Locking	Pessimistic Locking
For	Locks are only in place for a short time, increasing concurrency.	If you are have started to modify a record, you know that you will be able to save those changes.
Against	You cannot guarantee that you will be able to save a record once you have started to modify it. This leads to complex decision-making to decide which changes will receive priority and be committed.	Locks are in place for a long time (i.e. from when a user **starts** to edit a record until the changes are saved or cancelled). This means concurrency is reduced and users may have to wait longer before they can access data.

> The introduction of record-level locking in Access 2000 makes pessimistic locking a significantly less expensive strategy in terms of concurrency than it was in previous versions of Access.

Setting the Default Record Locking Mechanism

To choose a particular locking strategy for your Access environment, you should select the appropriate option from the Advanced page of the Tools/Options... dialog box:

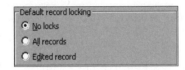

No Locks invokes **optimistic locking**. A record is locked only when it is actually being saved.

All Records (exclusive locking) causes the entire table or tables, which form the recordsource of the object, to be locked when any record is edited. This is fairly extreme and generally should only be used by the administrator, when performing maintenance.

Edited Record invokes **pessimistic locking**. A record will be locked as soon as someone starts to edit it.

Try It Out – Changing the Default Locking Mechanism

1. Open up IceCream.mdb and make sure the Default Record Locking option on the Advanced page of the Tools/Options... dialog box is set to No Locks. Click the OK button.

2. Create a new module called Chapter 16 Code and type the following procedure into it:

```
Sub SetLocking ()

    Application.SetOption "Default Record Locking", 2

End Sub
```

3. Run this procedure by typing SetLocking in the Immediate window.

4. Now open the Advanced page of the Tools/Options... dialog box again. The Default Record Locking option should now be Edited Record:

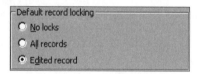

How It Works

There are three different settings for the Default Record Locking option in Access. The table below shows the different options and the VBA statement that is used to set each of those options. As with all multi-select options, the value used in the SetOption method corresponds to the zero-based order in which the option appears on the Tools/Options... dialog box.

This option...	...is also known as...	...and is set like this
No Locks	Optimistic Locking	Application.SetOption "Default Record Locking", 0
All Records	Exclusive Locking	Application.SetOption "Default Record Locking", 1
Edited Records	Pessimistic Locking	Application.SetOption "Default Record Locking", 2

In order to determine what the current locking option is, you can use the `GetOption` method. Here's a procedure you can write to allow you to set and then read the Default Record Locking option:

```
Sub SetAndGetLocking(strLockType As String)

    Dim intLockIndex As Integer
    Dim strLockDesc As String

    'Convert the string argument into a option index
    Select Case strLockType
        Case "Optimistic"
            intLockIndex = 0
        Case "Exclusive"
            intLockIndex = 1
        Case "Pessimistic"
            intLockIndex = 2
        Case Else
            intLockIndex = -1
    End Select

    'Set default record locking option
    If intLockIndex <> -1 Then
        Application.SetOption "Default Record Locking", intLockIndex
    End If

    'Now determine and display default record locking option
    Select Case Application.GetOption("Default Record Locking")
        Case 0
            MsgBox "The default locking method is optimistic."
        Case 1
            MsgBox "The default locking method is exclusive."
        Case 2
            MsgBox "The default locking method is pessimistic."
    End Select

End Sub
```

If you run this procedure by typing the following in the Immediate window,

```
SetAndGetLocking "Exclusive"
```

the default locking option will be set to Exclusive (All Records) and you will see this dialog box:

Implementing Record Locking on Forms

So far, we have only really considered the record-locking mechanism that applies to the tables and queries in your database. But you can also specify the locking method used by individual forms and reports. You do this by setting the RecordLocks property of the object concerned. For example, look at this code:

```
Dim frm As Form

DoCmd.OpenForm "frmCompany"
Set frm = Forms!frmCompany
frm.RecordLocks = 2
```

This will set pessimistic locking (**Edited Records**) for the frmCompany form. In other words, as soon as someone edits a record using frmCompany, Access will attempt to lock that record (or the data page that the record is on if page-level locking is implemented). This will prevent anyone else from editing that record (or page), whether from frmCompany or any other forms, or with a query or directly within the table where that record exists.

The RecordLocks property uses the same three arguments as the Application.SetOption method. They are described below:

This option...	...is set like this...	...and has this effect
No Locks	.RecordLocks = 0	Tries to obtain a lock on the underlying data only when a user attempts to save an amended record.
All Records	.RecordLocks = 1	Tries to lock all records in the underlying table(s) whenever someone has the form open.
Edited Records	.RecordLocks = 2	Tries to obtain a lock whenever someone starts to amend a record on the form. The lock stays in place until the user finishes editing the record.

If you don't explicitly set the RecordLocks property for a form, report or query, the object inherits the default record locking option that was in place when the object was created.

Recordsets and Record Locking

Earlier in the book we looked at how we could create Recordset objects. The basic syntax for creating a Recordset object is as follows:

```
Set rs = db.OpenRecordset(source, type, option, lockedits)
```

The source argument simply defines where the records will come from that will populate the recordset. This can be the name of a table or query, or an SQL string. You should be familiar with this by now, but what of the other arguments? Well, let's take a more detailed look now at the other arguments that we can supply to the OpenRecordset method and, in particular, how these arguments affect the way that locking is handled.

The Type Argument

In Chapter 7 we said that there were four different types of recordset that JET provides. To specify the type of recordset we wish to open, we use the appropriate `type` argument with the `OpenRecordset` method. The following four intrinsic constants can be used for that type argument to create JET `Recordset` objects:

- ❑ dbOpenTable
- ❑ dbOpenDynaset
- ❑ dbOpenSnapshot
- ❑ dbOpenForwardOnly

You should be familiar with these arguments by now. We looked at these in detail in Chapter 7. If you feel a little unsure of the differences between these types of `Recordset` objects, you should run through that chapter again. As far as we are concerned right now, however, the major difference is that you cannot edit the records in a snapshot or forward-only `Recordset` object.

The Option Argument

The third argument affects the updateability of the recordset is as a whole. Valid choices for this argument, together with their meanings, are shown below:

This option	...has this effect
dbDenyWrite	No one else can modify or add records while we have the recordset open.
dbDenyRead	No one else can read data in the table while we have the recordset open.
dbSeeChanges	If one person tries to save changes to a record that another user has modified since the first user started editing it, Access generates a run-time error.
dbAppendOnly	We can only add records to the recordset and cannot view or amend existing ones. We can only use this option with dynaset-type recordsets.
dbInconsistent	We can modify columns on both sides of the join in a dynaset built from multiple tables. This can leave the recordset in an inconsistent state.
dbConsistent	We can only modify columns that leave the dynaset consistent. So we can't alter the joined field on the 'many' side of a one-to-many join to a value that doesn't appear on the 'one' side.

If you need to, you can combine two or more of these options in a single statement like this:

```
Set rs = db.OpenRecordset(strSQL, dbOpenDynaset, dbConsistent + dbDenyRead)
```

There are a few other valid constants you can supply as the option argument, but they are either for use with non-Access databases or are present only for backwards compatibility.

The LockEdits Argument

The final argument is used to specify the type of record locking that will be used when we – or other users – try to edit records that appear in the recordset.

This argument	...has this effect
dbReadOnly	No one else can amend records that appear in our recordset so long as we have the recordset open.
dbPessimistic	A pessimistic locking strategy is applied (see earlier).
	No one else can amend records that appear in our recordset if we are in the process of editing them. Similarly, we can't edit a record in our recordset if someone else is already editing it.
dbOptimistic	An optimistic locking strategy is applied (see earlier).
	Two or more users can try concurrently to amend a record that appears in our recordset. However, only the first person to save his or her changes will be successful. When other users try to save a record that the first user has changed, Access generates a run-time error.

Again, there are another couple of arguments as well, but they are only for use with ODBCDirect, so we don't need to worry about them.

So, if we wanted to create a dynaset-type recordset based on the table tblSales that would allow us to add and edit records to the table, but didn't allow anyone else to view the records in tblSales while the recordset was open, we would use the following code:

```
Dim db As Database
Dim rec As Recordset

Set db = CurrentDB()

Set rec = db.OpenRecordset("tblSales", dbOpenDynaset, dbDenyRead)
.
.
.
rec.Close

db.Close
```

The LockEdits Property

Once a recordset is open, we can also change its locking behavior by setting its LockEdits property. To change the locking behavior for a recordset to optimistic locking, we set the LockEdits property of the recordset to False. To apply a pessimistic locking strategy, we set the LockEdits property of the recordset to True.

For example, the following piece of code opens a recordset and changes the locking behavior of the recordset to optimistic:

```
'This opens a recordset with pessimistic locking (default)
Set rec = db.OpenRecordset("Country", dbOpenDynaset)

'This line sets the locking behavior to optimistic locking
rec.LockEdits = False

...'Do something with the records

rec.Close        'Close the recordset
```

Although the LockEdits argument of the OpenRecordset method and the LockEdits property of a Recordset object do the same thing, the difference is when they are used. The LockEdits argument of the OpenRecordset method can only be used when you open a recordset, whereas you can set the LockEdits property of a recordset any time after the recordset has been opened, until the recordset is closed.

> Some recordsets, such as those based on tables in ODBC data sources, do not support pessimistic locking. Attempting to set the LockEdits property of such a recordset to True will cause Access to generate a run-time error.

Handling Record Locking Errors

It is all very well to say that, when a recordset is opened with the dbDenyWrite option, no one else can add or edit records in the underlying table(s), but what actually happens when a procedure attempts to open an exclusively locked table? The answer is that a run-time error occurs and, if we don't have any error handling, our application will stop. It is important, therefore, to know the types of record-locking errors that can occur at run-time, and how our error-handling code should deal with them.

Optimistic Locking Errors

With optimistic locking we should not encounter any errors when attempting to edit a record – only when we try to update or add one.

Likely Errors

If we are using optimistic locking, the three most common error codes we will experience are 3186, 3197 and 3260.

Error 3186 Could not save; currently locked by user <xxx> on machine <xxx>

This error only occurs when optimistic locking is being used. It indicates that we are trying to save a record that is locked.

Error 3197 The Microsoft Jet database engine stopped the process because you and another user are attempting to change the same data at the same time.

This error occurs when we try to use the Update method but another user has changed the data that we are trying to update. The other user will have changed the data between the time we used the Edit method and the Update method. This is the same situation that led to the **Write Conflict** dialog box that we saw at the start of this chapter.

Error 3260 **Couldn't update; currently locked by user <xxx> on machine <xxx>**

This error will occur if we use the Update method to try to update a record we have added or changed, but where another user has since locked that record.

If page-level locking is in place, this error may also occur when we use the AddNew method to add a record to a recordset where the page on which the new record resides is locked.

> *You might have noticed that errors 3186 and 3260 have similar causes. In fact, although they can occur at subtly different times, as far as we are concerned we should handle them in exactly the same way.*

How to Deal with Optimistic Locking Errors

For error codes 3186 and 3260, we should wait a short period of time and then attempt to save the record again. If we still can't save the record after several attempts, we should cancel the operation, inform the user of what has happened and let him or her do something else.

For error code 3197, we should requery the database to see what the new value of the record is, display it to the user and ask him or her if they want to overwrite the record with their own changes.

The following sample of code illustrates how we can gracefully handle the type of errors that occur when we are using optimistic locking:

```
Function OptErrors() As Boolean

    Dim db As Database
    Dim rec As Recordset
    Dim intLockRetry As Integer
    Dim i As Integer
    Dim intRetVal As Integer
    Dim recClone As Recordset

    Const LOCK_RETRY_MAX = 5
    Const LOCK_ERROR$ = "Could not save this record. " & _
                        "Do you want to try again?"
    Const SAVE_QUESTION$ = "Do you want to save YOUR changes?"

    On Error GoTo OptErrors_Err

    Set db = CurrentDb()
    Set rec = db.OpenRecordset("tblCountry", dbOpenDynaset, ,dbOptmistic)

    '
    ' This is the main body of your code
    '

OptErrors = True

OptErrors_Exit:
    Exit Function
```

```
OptErrors_Failed:
    OptErrors = False

    'This is where you put code to handle what
    'should happen if you cannot obtain a lock

    GoTo OptErrors_Exit

OptErrors_Err:
    Select Case Err
        Case 3197                       'Data has changed

            'Make a copy of the recordset
            Set recClone = rec.OpenRecordset()

            'Move to amended record
            '...

            'Display amended record
            '...

            'Ask user what to do
            intRetVal = MsgBox(SAVE_QUESTION$, vbExclamation + vbYesNo)

            'If the user wants to save their changes
            If intRetVal = vbYes Then
                'Try to update again
                Resume
            Else
                'Else just call it a day
                Resume OptErrors_Failed
            End If
        Case 3186, 3260

            'Record is locked so add 1 to counter
            'indicating how many times this happened
            intLockRetry = intLockRetry + 1

            'Have you already retried too many times?
            If intLockRetry < LOCK_RETRY_MAX Then

                'If you haven't, then wait for a short period
                For i = 0 To intLockRetry * 1000
                Next

                'Now try again
                Resume

            Else

                'But if you have already tried 5 times
                'ask if user wants to retry.
                'If they say yes then...
                If MsgBox(LOCK_ERROR$, vbExclamation + vbYesNo) = vbYes Then

                    intLockRetry = 0   '...set counter to 0
                    Resume             'and do it over
```

```
        Else        'But if they have had enough
                    'just call it a day

                Resume OptErrors_Failed

            End If

        End If
    Case Else           'Catch all other errors
        MsgBox ("Error " & Err & ": " & Error)
        Resume OptErrors_Failed
    End Select

End Function
```

Pessimistic Locking Errors

If we are using pessimistic locking, we can normally guarantee that we will be able to save any record that we have opened with the Edit method. For this reason, we shouldn't encounter error 3186. However, we may come across the other two errors.

Likely Errors

Error 3197   The Microsoft Jet database engine stopped the process because you and another user are attempting to change the same data at the same time.

When using pessimistic locking, this error occurs if we try to use the Edit method on a record but the data in the record has changed since it was last accessed. This may happen, for example, if someone has changed or deleted the record since we opened the recordset.

Error 3260   Couldn't update; currently locked by user <xxx> on machine <xxx>

Don't be misled by the word 'update' in the message. If we are using pessimistic locking, this error will occur if we try to use the Edit or AddNew methods on a record where the record (or page) is already locked by someone else.

How to Deal with Pessimistic Locking Errors

For error code 3260, we should wait a short period of time and then attempt to edit the record again. If we still can't edit the record after several attempts, we should give the user the choice of continuing to attempt to edit the record or canceling the operation.

For error code 3197, we should requery the database to see what the new value of the record is and try the Edit method again. If the record had only been changed, we should be able to edit it now. If it was deleted though, we will encounter error code 3167 (Record is deleted).

The function below contains an error handling routine that should take care of these errors:

```
Function PessErrors() As Integer

    Dim db As Database
    Dim rec As Recordset
    Dim intLockRetry As Integer
    Dim i As Integer
```

```
    Const LOCK_RETRY_MAX = 5
    Const LOCK_ERROR$ = "Could not save this record. " & _
                        "Do you want to try again?"

    On Error GoTo PessErrors_Err

    Set db = CurrentDb()
    Set rec = db.OpenRecordset("tblCountry", dbOpenDynaset)

    '
    ' This is the main body of your code
    '

PessErrors = True

PessErrors_Exit:
    Exit Function

PessErrors_Failed:
    PessErrors = False
    'This is where you put code to handle what should
    'happen if you cannot obtain a lock after many attempts

    GoTo PessErrors_Exit

PessErrors_Err:
    Select Case Err
        Case 3197          'If data has changed, then
            rec.Requery    'simply refresh the recordset
            Resume         'and try again.
        Case 3167
            'You have not got much choice
            'if someone else has deleted this record
            MsgBox "Someone else has deleted this record"
            Resume PessErrors_Failed
        Case 3260
            'But if the record is locked, add 1 to counter
            'indicating how many times you have retried
            intLockRetry = intLockRetry + 1

            'Have you already retried 5 times?
            If intLockRetry < LOCK_RETRY_MAX Then

                'If not then wait for a short period
                For i = 0 To intLockRetry * 1000
                Next

                'Now try again
                Resume

            Else
                'If you have already tried 5 times
                'ask the user if they want to retry
                'If they hit the yes button then...
                If MsgBox(LOCK_ERROR$, 'vbExclamation + vbYesNo) = vbYes Then

                    'Set counter to 0 and do it over again
                    intLockRetry = 0
                    Resume
```

```
            Else
                  'But if they have had enough
                  'just call it a day
                  Resume PessErrors_Failed

            End If

         End If
      Case Else
         MsgBox ("Error " & Err & ": " & Error)
         Resume PessErrors_Failed
   End Select

End Function
```

Well, that's about all we are going to say about record locking. I hope you have managed to keep track! In practice, managing locking is not too tricky provided that you take the time to think before you start building the database about how users are going to be interacting with it. Predicting usage patterns is as vital a part of the analysis process as any. If you take the time to do it properly, then you will be able to produce a more appropriate database (and code) design and you will end up – all things being equal – with happier customers.

Security

So far in this chapter, then, we have looked at the way in which Access handles record locking, when multiple users are attempting to use the database at the same time. We will now take a look at another key issue that raises its head in a multi-user scenario – how Access enforces security.

Why Security?

The first question that needs to be answered is "Do I need to secure my database?" This is a question that you should ask when designing any database. Implementing a security mechanism adds a maintenance overhead – so does your application merit it? Quite often the answer will be that it doesn't. The ease with which database applications can be created with Access means that they are now frequently used for fairly trivial functions, which don't always require security. However, if you are concerned about any of the following issues, you should consider implementing some method of securing your application:

❑   Your database contains confidential information that you don't want unauthorized personnel to view.

Frequently, databases are used to store confidential information about personal or financial details. Such data needs to be protected from accidental or deliberate access by people who aren't authorized to view it.

❑ You want to protect your database objects from accidental change.

It may have taken you a lot of time to create your database application. The last thing you want is for one of the users of the application to modify the design of a form or query so that the application no longer works.

❑ You want some of your users to be able to use certain functionality within your application but don't want this to be generally available.

Often, your application will contain functionality that is only appropriate to a subset of users. For example, you may wish only Grade 3 managers to be able to use the application to approve expense checks.

❑ You want to implement an audit trail to monitor who has been doing what in your application.

As well as building an audit trail specifically for security purposes, you may find it useful to build one for use during the application's testing cycle or initial roll-out, so you can log how people have been using the application.

Security can be defined as a method of restricting the access that users have to a database and the objects within that database. You are probably already familiar with the methods of securing an Access database using the menu commands and standard Access dialogs. The main two ways of securing a database in this way involve:

❑ Creating a password for the database

❑ Establishing user-level security

Over 90% of the time you will perform these tasks through the user interface. These two options can be reached from the Security option on the Tools menu:

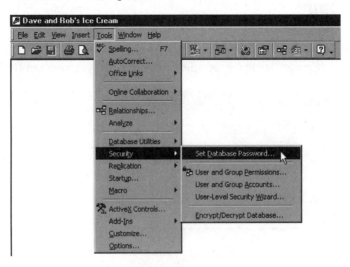

However, there may be occasions when it is preferable to administer these tasks from within VBA code. For example, you might wish to provide the users of your application with the ability to change the database password for themselves. Instead of expecting users to set the database password via the toolbar, you might wish to provide a simple password form that would allow users to enter the new database password. You could then add a procedure that programmatically changed the database password when the user hit the OK button on the form.

We will start by looking at the code that we would use to set a database password programmatically, and after that we'll examine the security model that Access employs and how it can be manipulated in VBA code.

Setting a Database Password from VBA

To set a database password from VBA, we simply apply the NewPassword method to a Database object representing the database. This method takes the existing password and the new password as its arguments.

```
Set db = CurrentDB()
db.NewPassword "", "Valerie"
```

The code above would add a password (Valerie) to a database that previously didn't have one. To change this password, we would use this syntax.

```
Set db = CurrentDB()
db.NewPassword "Valerie", "Smith"
```

And to clear the password, we would specify an empty string for the new password:

```
Set db = CurrentDB()
db.NewPassword "Smith", ""
```

Protecting Your Code

Access 2000 also provides us with the capability to protect the code in the VBA project associated with our database. To set the VBA project password, select the Protection tab from the dialog that appears when you choose <ProjectName> Properties from the Tools... menu in the VBE.

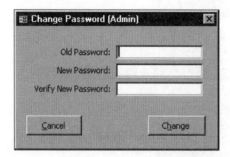

If you select the **Lock project for vie**wing checkbox and enter a password, subsequent users of the database will not be allowed to view the VBA code for the database unless they enter the specified password.

If, instead, you enter a password but leave the **Lock project for vie**wing checkbox unchecked, users will be able to view and amend the VBA code for the database, but will not be able to display the <ProjectName> Prop**e**rties dialog.

> *This behavior is new to Access 2000. In previous versions of Access, code could be protected by assigning user-level permissions (see later) to individual code modules and class modules. In Access 2000 it is not possible to assign permissions to individual modules.*

The Access Security Model

So let's have a look now at how we can use user-level security to assign permissions to users and groups on individual database objects.

The Access security model consists of two elements:

- ❑ The workgroup information file
- ❑ User and group permissions

The workgroup information file contains:

- ❑ The names of all users in the workgroup
- ❑ The names of all groups in the workgroup
- ❑ Information about which users belong to which groups
- ❑ Each user's password (in encrypted form)
- ❑ A unique SID (Security ID) for each user and group (in a non-readable binary format)

The location of the workgroup information file is specified by using the MS Access Workgroup Administrator (WRKGADM.EXE). If you have accepted the default installation options when installing Access 2000, a shortcut to this file will be located in C:\Program Files\Microsoft Office\Office.

Permissions for using individual data objects within a database are stored in the database that contains the objects. We'll look at how you modify these permissions a little later. First, we are going to look at how to modify the user and group information in the workgroup information file through VBA.

Manipulating Users and Groups

The Data Access Object hierarchy, which we have already noted to be central to VBA coding, contains the following security objects:

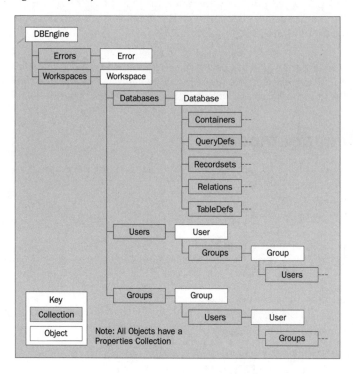

The most striking feature of this hierarchy is its seemingly recursive structure. A User object contains a Groups collection and a Group object contains a Users collection. The hierarchy is implemented in this way to allow for the many-to-many relationship between Users and Groups. A user can belong to one or more groups, each of which can contain many users.

Notice also that the Users and Groups collections belong to the Workspace object, rather than the Database object. Although the properties for individual objects are contained within each database, users and groups are defined within the workgroup information file and are available to all databases which are opened in the security context (i.e. Workspace) defined by that workgroup information file. So we can think of the Workspace as being the object which is primarily responsible for access to user and group maintenance in VBA.

So, let's have a look at how we can use these data access objects to perform the following tasks:

❑ Create new users and groups

❑ Add users to groups

❑ Change a user's password

> Note that for the following examples to work, you must be logged in with the correct permissions for being able to create and modify users. The same rules apply for creating and modifying users and groups in VBA as they do when you use the **Security** menu options. Normally it is only members of the Admins group who should modify security options.

Enumerating Users and Groups

To enumerate all of the users and groups in the current Workspace, we simply need to loop through the Users and Groups collections.

```
Sub EnumGroupsAndUsers()

Dim grp As Group
Dim usr As User

For Each usr In DBEngine(0).Users
    Debug.Print usr.Name
    For Each grp In usr.Groups
        Debug.Print vbTab; grp.Name
    Next
Next

End Sub
```

Note how we can use DBEngine(0) to refer to the default workspace. We can do that because Workspaces is the default collection of the DBEngine object, so that line of code is equivalent to:

```
For Each usr In DBEngine.Workspaces(0).Users
```

If we were to run this procedure in a database while using the default system.mdw workgroup information file that is installed with Access, we would see the following in the Immediate window:

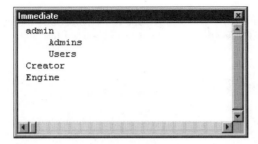

As expected, we see the admin user. By default, Access will attempt to log on all users with a user name of admin with a blank password. If you want Access to display the logon dialog in order to allow users to log on with a different user name, you should first change the password of the admin user. This will cause the default login mechanism to fail and the login dialog box will be displayed.

As you can see, the admin user is a member of the two built-in groups, Admins and Users. We can verify this much if we switch to Access and display the **User and Group Accounts...** dialog from the Tools/Security... menu.

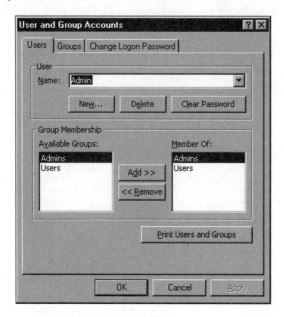

But what of the two other users whose names we saw in the Immediate window? Creator and Engine are actually a couple of internal system accounts. They are used by JET and are not accessible to users and so do not appear when viewing and setting users and groups through the graphical interface. They are mentioned here not because we will use them at all, but simply to alert you of their presence. So, leaving aside the Creator and Engine user accounts we have one built-in user (admin) and two built-in groups (Admins and Users). Let's see how we programmatically add new users and groups.

Creating a New User

Creating a new user is very straightforward – you simply use the CreateUser method against the Workspace object. For example, the following piece of code can be used to create a user called Mark Fenton:

```
Sub UserAdd()

    Dim wks As Workspace
    Dim usrMark As User
    Dim strUsersPID As String

    Set wks = DBEngine(0)
    strUsersPID = "1234abcd"

    'Start by creating a new User account
    Set usrMark = wks.CreateUser("Mark Fenton")

    'Now set the User's properties
    usrMark.Password = "Doctor"
    usrMark.PID = strUsersPID
```

```
     'Append User to the Users collection of this workspace
     wks.Users.Append usrMark

End Sub
```

As you can see, the first step is to create a new user object. We do this by applying the `CreateUser` method to the workspace object and supplying the name of the new user:

```
Set usrMark = wks.CreateUser("Mark Fenton")
```

The next step is to set the properties of the new `User` object. The properties you can set are the `Password` property, the `PID` property and the `Name` property. Note that we set the `Name` property of the user object when we created it with the `CreateUser` method.

The `PID` property is a string of between four and twenty characters which is used to uniquely identify a user:

```
usrMark.PID = strUsersPID
```

The `Password` property, a string of up to fourteen characters, corresponds to the password that the new user will need to enter. This is simply an additional way of verifying the user's identity and is *not* the same as the database password.

```
usrMark.Password = "Doctor"
```

After you have set these three properties, you are ready to append the `User` object to the collection of `Users` already defined in the current workspace. This will save the user, and its properties, in the workgroup information file.

```
wks.Users.Append usrMark
```

If you type the procedure into a new module and then run it, you can check the existence of the new user by going to the User and Group Accounts... section of the Security submenu on the Tools menu:

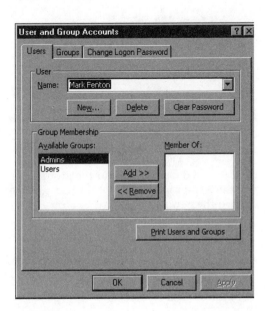

Notice, however, that the new user has not been added to any groups. That's not really surprising, as we never added the user to any groups in our code! We'll see next how we can create a new group and then add a user to that group.

Creating a New Group

A group is used to collect together users to whom you wish to assign the same permissions. For example, you may have thirty different registrars who will use your database, each of whom you want to define as a user in an Access workgroup. It would be very tiresome if you then had to assign permissions on every single database object to each of the thirty users. So, instead, you can create a group called Registrars, add the thirty users to it, and then assign database object permissions just to that group.

> Wherever possible, you should assign permissions to groups rather than to individual users.

Creating a group is a very similar process to the one we employed above for creating new users:

```
Sub GroupAdd()

    Dim wks As Workspace
    Dim grpRegistrars As Group
    Dim strGroupPID As String

    Set wks = DBEngine(0)
    strGroupPID = "5678"

    'Start by creating a new Group account
    Set grpRegistrars = wks.CreateGroup("Registrars")

    'Now set the Group's properties
    grpRegistrars.PID = strGroupPID

    'Append Group to the Groups collection of this workspace
    wks.Groups.Append grpRegistrars

End Sub
```

First we create a group object within the current workspace:

```
Set grpRegistrars = wks.CreateGroup("Registrars")
```

Next we set the properties for the group. The only two properties of a group are the Name property and the PID property. We set the Name property when we create the group, just as we did when we created the new user.

```
grpRegistrars.PID = strGroupPID
```

And finally we save the group by appending it to the Groups collection in the current workspace:

```
wks.Groups.Append grpRegistrars
```

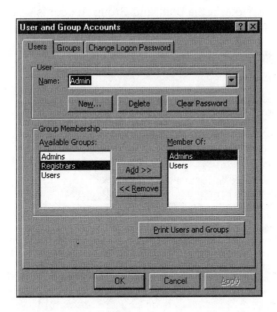

Adding a User to a Group

Once we have created the Registrars group, we want to add our new user to it. The following piece of code will achieve this:

```
Sub AddUserToGroup()

    Dim wks As WorkSpace
    Dim usrMark As User

    Set wks = DBEngine(0)
    Set usrMark = wks.CreateUser("Mark Fenton")

    wks.Groups("Registrars").Users.Append usrMark

End Sub
```

First, we declare an object variable of type User and use it to reference the user object that we want to add to the Registrars group:

```
Set usrMark = wks.CreateUser("Mark Fenton")
```

All of the details concerning the user object Mark Fenton were set in the procedure UserAdd, so now it's just a case of appending the user object to the Users collection, which belongs to the Registrars group.

```
wks.Groups("Registrars").Users.Append usrMark
```

If you run the procedure and then look at the **User and Group Accounts** section again, you will see that Mark Fenton is now a member of the `Registrars` group.

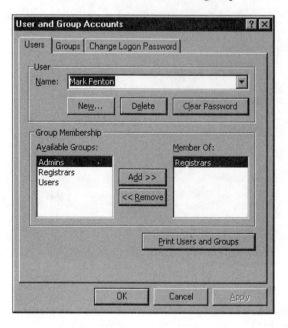

Also, if you refer back to the DAO hierarchy, you will realize that we could have achieved this the other way round:

```
Sub AddUserToGroup()

    Dim wks As WorkSpace
    Dim grpRegistrars As Group

    Set wks = DBEngine(0)
    Set grpRegistrars = wks.CreateGroup("Registrars")

    wks.Users("Mark Fenton").Groups.Append grpRegistrars

End Sub
```

In this example, we append the `Registrars` group object to the `Groups` collection, which belongs to the user called Mark Fenton.

Changing a Password

To change our user's password we simply use the `NewPassword` method of the user object:

```
Dim wks As WorkSpace
Set wks = DBEngine(0)

wks.Users("Mark Fenton").NewPassword "Doctor", "Nurse"
```

And to clear Mark Fenton's password, we supply an empty string as the new password:

```
Dim wks As WorkSpace
Set wks = DBEngine(0)

wks.Users("Mark Fenton").NewPassword "Doctor", ""
```

> To change a `User`'s password you must be logged on to that database either as
> that user or as a member of the `Admins` `Group`.

Now that we have got this far, we should be able to create a form that allows the users of our
database to change their password.

Try It Out – Creating a 'Change Password' Form

> I strongly recommend you read through this exercise thoroughly before entering
> any code, as you will be changing the Admin User's password – you wouldn't
> want to be locked out of your own database by mistake now would you?

1. In the `IceCream.mdb` database, create a new blank form in Design view and set the
following properties for it:

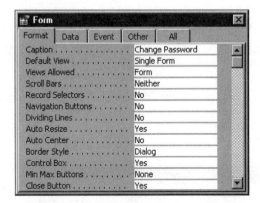

2. Add three text boxes. Call them `txtOldPwd`, `txtNewPwd` and `txtVerify` and change the
text of their labels to read **Old Password**, **New Password** and **Verify New Password**.

3. Now select the three text boxes (hold down shift as you click on each item) and change
them to password input boxes by changing their **Input Mask** property to **Password**.

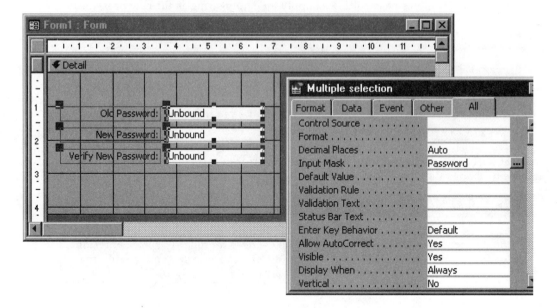

4. Add the following code to the form's Load event handler:

```
Private Sub Form_Load()

    Me.Caption = Me.Caption & " (" & CurrentUser & ")"

End Sub
```

5. Now add two command buttons. Call them cmdCancel and cmdChange and change their captions to Cancel and Change. Make sure that the Command Button Wizard isn't enabled when you create these buttons.

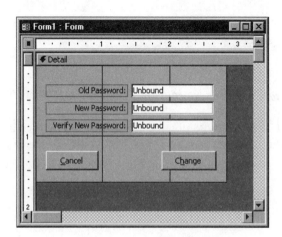

6. Next, add the following routines to the Click event handlers of each button. This code for the Cancel button:

```
Private Sub cmdCancel_Click()

    DoCmd.Close

End Sub
```

7. And this code for the Change button:

```
Private Sub cmdChange_Click()

Dim strOld As String
Dim strNew As String
Dim strVerify As String
Dim strMsg As String

strOld = Nz(txtOldPwd, "")
strNew = Nz(txtNewPwd, "")
strVerify = Nz(txtVerify, "")

If ChangePassword(strOld, strNew, strVerify) = True Then

    If strNew = "" Then
        strMsg = "Your password has been cleared"
    Else
        strMsg = "Your password has been changed"
    End If

    MsgBox strMsg, vbOKOnly

    txtOldPwd = Null
    txtNewPwd = Null
    txtVerify = Null


End If

End Sub
```

8. Next, write the code for the function that we referred to in the cmd_Change_Click procedure.

```
Function ChangePassword(strOld As String, _
                        strNew As String, _
                        strVerify As String) As Boolean

Dim wks As Workspace

On Error GoTo ChangePassword_Err

Set wks = DBEngine(0)
```

```
If strNew <> strVerify Then
    MsgBox "Your new password and the verification of your " & _
        "new password do not match." & _
        vbCrLf & vbCrLf & _
        "Please try again.", vbExclamation
End If

wks.Users(CurrentUser).NewPassword strOld, strNew

ChangePassword = True

ChangePassword_Exit:
    Exit Function

ChangePassword_Err:
    MsgBox "Cannot change this password.  Please ensure that " & _
        "you have typed the old password correctly.", _
        vbExclamation
    Resume ChangePassword_Exit

End Function
```

9. Close the form and save it as `frmPassword`.

10. Finally, open the form and try it out!

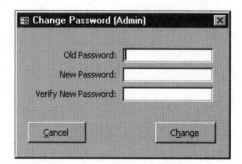

> Beware! If Access does not ask you for a password when you start it up, then
> Access will log you on as `Admin` with an empty password. Once you change the
> `Admin` password to something other than an empty password, Access will always
> ask for a login and password when it starts. So when you use the password form,
> if you are changing the password for the `Admin` user, make sure you write it down
> (remember that it's case-sensitive), because if you forget it you won't be able to
> get back in. To stop Access asking you for a login and password when it starts, set
> the password for `Admin` back to an empty string.

How It Works

If you followed the description of how to change passwords in the section above this example, you
should have no problem understanding how the code works. The form simply allows a user to
either enter a new password, change an existing one or clear the current password.

The code behind the `cmdCancel` button shouldn't need any explanation.

The `cmdChange` button is used to change the password of the user who is currently logged on. The user must enter their current password in `txtOldPwd` and new password in `txtNewPwd`. The user must also enter it again in the `txtVerify` box to ensure that no mistake has been made. When the `cmdChange` button is clicked, the procedure in the `Click` event of the button starts by converting any null strings into empty strings:

```
strOld = Nz(txtOldPwd, "")
strNew = Nz(txtNewPwd, "")
strVerify = Nz(txtVerify, "")
```

We do this because Access treats text boxes that contain no text as if they contained the value `Null`. Now that might be appropriate for forms that are used to enter values into a database, but it is not appropriate in this situation. The `NewPassword` method of the `User` object, which we will use to change the user's password can only accept string values and `Null` is not a valid string value. If we want the user to have a blank password, we need to use an empty string (`""`) instead.

The simplest way to convert `Null` values into any other value is to use the `Nz` (`Null`-to-zero) function. This function accepts two arguments and checks whether the first is `Null`. If it is not `Null`, the function returns that first argument as its return value; but if the first argument is `Null`, the function returns the value of the second argument.

For example, if the value of `txtNewPwd` is `Null`, then `Nz(txtOldPwd, "")` returns an empty string. But, if the value of `txtNewPwd` is not `Null`, then `Nz(txtOldPwd, "")` returns `txtNewPwd`.

Once we have converted any `Null` values into empty strings, we call the `ChangePassword` function and determine whether it returns `True` or `False`.

```
If ChangePassword(strOld, strNew, strVerify) = True Then
```

If it returns `True` then we know that the password has been successfully changed, so we can display a message to the user stating that the password has either been changed or cleared (i.e. changed to a blank password).

```
If strNew = "" Then
    strMsg = "Your password has been cleared"
Else
    strMsg = "Your password has been changed"
End If

MsgBox strMsg, vbOKOnly
```

And lastly we clear the values from the three text boxes on the form.

```
txtOldPwd = Null
txtNewPwd = Null
txtVerify = Null
```

Now that is simple enough, but how does the `ChangePassword` function work? Well, again it is fairly straightforward. The first task is to get hold of a reference to the current `Workspace` object.

```
Set wks = DBEngine(0)
```

Remember that the `Workspace` object is the object that gives us access to the `Users` collection and we need to use a `User` object if we are to change the current user's password.

We then perform a check to ensure that the new password and the confirmation of the new password have been entered correctly. If they are different, we display a warning message and exit the `ChangePassword` function.

```
If strNew <> strVerify Then
    MsgBox "Your new password and the verification of your " & _
        "new password do not match." & _
        vbCrLf & vbCrLf & _
        "Please try again.", vbExclamation
End If
```

Once we have performed that check, we can try to change the password

```
wks.Users(CurrentUser).NewPassword txtOldPwd, txtNewPwd
```

If the attempt is successful the function returns `True`:

```
ChangePassword = True

ChangePassword_Exit:
    Exit Function
```

However, if an error occurs, it is trapped in the error handler. An error here will almost certainly be caused by the user supplying an incorrect current password, so we display an appropriate message:

```
ChangePassword_Err:
    MsgBox "Cannot change this password.  Please ensure that " & _
        "you have typed the old password correctly.", _
        vbExclamation
    Resume ChangePassword_Exit
```

> Notice that the `ChangePassword` function only returns `True` if the password has been successfully changed. That is because the value of the `ChangePassword` function is only set to `True` once the password has been changed. If the function exits before this point (either because the new password and confirmation are different or because of some other error) the function will return `False`. That is because the function returns a `Boolean` value and the initial value of all `Boolean` variables is `False`.

This form is still only very rudimentary in many ways, but it does illustrate how you can very quickly provide a simple interface to allow users to maintain their own passwords.

Setting Object Permissions with Visual Basic

Now that we have created users and groups and have learned how to assign them passwords, we shall take a look at how to give those users and groups permissions on objects. We said earlier that permissions for using specific objects within a database are held within each individual database. But how do we find out what those permissions are and how do we set them?

The keys to retrieving and setting permissions are Documents and Containers. As you may know, a Document is an object which contains information about a specific object in the database. A Container is an object which contains information about a collection of objects in the database. You will not be surprised to know that some of the information held by Document objects and Container objects is information about permissions.

Try It Out – Retrieving Permissions

1. In the IceCream.mdb database, add the following procedure to the Chapter 16 Code module:

```
Sub ShowPerms()

    Dim objContainer As Container
    Dim objDoc As Document

    For Each objContainer In CurrentDb.Containers
        Debug.Print "--> Container: " & objContainer.Name
        For Each objDoc In objContainer.Documents
            Debug.Print "Document: " & objDoc.Name & "   ";
            objDoc.UserName = "Admin"
            Debug.Print "Perms: " & objDoc.AllPermissions
        Next
    Next

    Debug.Print "Done"

End Sub
```

2. Run the procedure from the Immediate window. You will get a large output similar to the following:

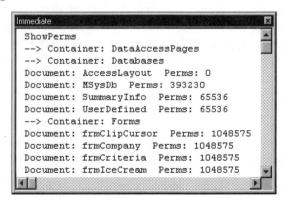

How It Works

The procedure loops through all the Container objects within the database and assigns a reference to each of them in turn to the variable objContainer. It then prints the Name of the Container object.

```
For Each objContainer In CurrentDb.Containers
    Debug.Print "--> Container: " & objContainer.Name
```

It then loops through all of the Document objects within the Container object referenced by objContainer and assigns them in turn to the variable objDoc.

```
For Each objDoc In objContainer.Documents
```

It then displays the name of the Document object and the permissions in that Document object for the Admin user:

```
Debug.Print "Document: " & objDoc.Name & "   ";
objDoc.UserName = "Admin"
Debug.Print "Perms: " & objDoc.AllPermissions
```

To display the permissions for a specific user you must first set the UserName property of the Document object you are inspecting to the user's name. The semicolon at the end of the first Debug.Print statement tells Access not to move onto a new line for the next Debug.Print statement.

Note that we inspect the AllPermissions *property of the document. The* Permissions *property only reflects the permissions that are explicitly and separately assigned to a user. The* AllPermissions *property reflects those permissions explicitly assigned to the user and those the user inherits from the group to which it belongs.*

Analyzing the Output

Don't panic if you're a bit confused by the output you get in the Immediate window. We'll go through this now.

Containers and Documents

Containers are not the same as collections. For example, the Forms **collection** contains references to those forms that are currently open, and it contains information about the design and properties of those forms. The Forms **container**, by contrast, has a Document for every saved form in the database – whether it is loaded or not – and this Document contains information about the form's owner and permissions.

Each database will have within it the following nine containers: DataAccessPages, Databases, Forms, Modules, Relationships, Reports, Scripts, SysRel, Tables.

Of these, three (Databases, Tables and Relations) are defined by JET, whereas the other six (DataAccessPages, Forms, Modules, Reports, Scripts, SysRel) are defined by the Access application.

Now the contents of most of these containers are fairly obvious but you might be confused by the `Relationships` and `SysRel` containers. Well, the `Relationships` container holds information about all the relationships that have been defined between the tables in the current database, while the other container object, `SysRel`, is used internally by Access to store information about the layout of the System Relationships window. We need not concern ourselves with that here. You should also note that there is no separate container for queries. Instead, these appear within the `Tables` container.

So much for containers, but what about the documents? If you look at the names of these `Document` objects, you will recognize most of them as saved objects within the database. There are a few oddities, however, such as `AccessLayout`, `SummaryInfo` and `UserDefined`. These are all in the `Databases` container that refers to the current database.

The `SummaryInfo` Document has a `Properties` collection which contains the properties on the **Summary** page of the **Database Properties...** dialog box, found on the **File** menu. Similarly, the `UserDefined` Document has a `Properties` collection containing the user-defined properties, found on the **Custom** page of the same dialog box. Finally, the `AccessLayout` Document is a system document used internally by Access.

So that explains the unfamiliar documents and containers. The rest of them apply to familiar objects and collections within the database.

Permissions

The next thing we must explain is the permission values. What does a `Permissions` property of `1048575` for `frmCompany` mean? To find out, we must use some intrinsic constants. Have a look at the following intrinsic constants which represent user permissions:

This constant	...equals	...and means that
dbSecNoAccess	0	The user can't access the object at all.
dbSecDelete	65536	The user is able to delete the object.
dbSecReadSec	131072	The user can read the security information about the object.
dbSecWriteSec	262144	The user is able to alter access permissions for the object.
dbSecWriteOwner	524288	The user can change the `Owner` property setting of the object.
dbSecFullAccess	1048575	The user has full access to the object.

You will no doubt have spotted that `1048575` is represented by the constant `dbSecFullAccess`, indicating that, in our previous example, `Admin` has full permissions for the form we created earlier, `frmCriteria`.

So, if we wanted, we could now alter our function so that it only shows whether or not a user has permission to, say, delete documents. In this case, it would read like this:

```
Sub ShowNoDelPerms()
```

```
      Dim objContainer As Container
      Dim objDoc As Document

  For Each objContainer In CurrentDb.Containers
      Debug.Print "--> Container: " & objContainer.Name
      For Each objDoc In objContainer.Documents
          If (objDoc.AllPermissions And dbSecDelete) = dbSecDelete Then
              Debug.Print "Can Delete Document: " & _
                            objDoc.Name & "   ";
              objDoc.UserName = "Admin"
              Debug.Print "Perms: " & objDoc.AllPermissions
          Else
              Debug.Print "Cannot Delete Document: " & _
                            objDoc.Name & "   ";
              objDoc.UserName = "Admin"
              Debug.Print "Perms: " & objDoc.AllPermissions
          End If
      Next
  Next

  Debug.Print "Done"

End Sub
```

To check whether the user has permission to delete the object associated with a document, we compare the document's AllPermissions property with the constant dbSecDelete using the And operator:

```
 If (objDoc.AllPermissions And dbSecDelete) = dbSecDelete Then
```

If the result of this expression is True, the user has permission to delete the document.

If you are a bit confused by that last statement, then don't worry too much. It is not that important that you understand how these logical operators work at a low level. What is important is that you know how to use these operators to determine permission values.

To determine if a user has permissions represented by one of the security constants on a certain object we use the And operator. So the following expression will return True if the user **does** have the permission represented by the security constant and will return False if the user **does not** have that permission:

```
(objDoc.AllPermissions And <security constant>) = <security constant>
```

Setting Permissions

We can also set permissions as well as retrieve them. Suppose we want to make sure that one of our users, Mark Fenton, doesn't accidentally delete frmPassword that we so carefully created earlier on. To do this, we can modify the Permissions property of the document for frmPassword. This is what the following procedure does:

```
Sub ProtectItFromMark()

    Dim db As Database
    Dim Doc As Document

    Set db = CurrentDb()
    Set Doc = db.Containers("Forms").Documents("frmPassword")
```

```
      Doc.UserName = "Mark Fenton"
      Doc.Permissions = dbSecFullAccess And Not dbSecDelete

End Sub
```

The first thing to notice about this piece of code is the way in which we select the document whose permissions we wish to alter. In the previous example, we simply looped through the container and document collections in turn. But if you want to, you can select a specific document or container by name. In this example, we are selecting the document for the object called frmPassword. Because this is a form, its document will be located in the container called Forms, hence the line:

```
Set Doc = db.Containers("Forms").Documents("frmPassword")
```

We then need to specify the user to whom these permissions should apply:

```
Doc.Username = "Mark Fenton"
```

Finally, we specify the permissions we want to give Mark. Here we are saying that we want Mark to be able to do everything but delete the form:

```
Doc.Permissions = dbSecFullAccess And Not dbSecDelete
```

Again, you don't need to understand exactly why And Not removes permissions. What you need to remember is that it works. The following code fragments show how to add and remove permissions to objects.

To replace all permissions on an object with a new single permission, use this:

```
Set Doc.Permission = <security constant>
```

To replace all permissions on an object with a new set of permissions, use this:

```
Set Doc.Permission = <security constant> Or <security constant>
```

To add a new single permission while retaining the existing permissions, use this:

```
Set Doc.Permission = Doc.Permission Or <security constant>
```

To add a new set of permissions while retaining the existing permissions, use this:

```
Set Doc.Permission = Doc.Permission Or <security constant> Or _
                     <security constant>
```

To remove a single permission from the existing permissions, use this:

```
Set Doc.Permission = Doc.Permission And Not <security constant>
```

To remove a set of permissions from the existing permissions, use this:

```
Set Doc.Permission = Doc.Permission And Not (<security constant> Or _
                     <security constant>)
```

There are many ways you can manipulate object permissions through VBA. After all, there are 25 security constants! But the principle is the same whichever you use. The full range of security constants is shown below:

```
acSecMacExecute          dbSecDBAdmin          dbSecReadSec
acSecMacReadDef          dbSecDBCreate         dbSecReadDef
acSecMacWriteDef         dbSecDBExclusive      dbSecReplaceData
acSecFrmRptExecute       dbSecDBOpen           dbSecRetrieveData
acSecFrmRptReadDef       dbSecDelete           dbSecWriteSec
acSecFrmRptWriteDef      dbSecDeleteData       dbSecWriteDef
acSecModReadDef          dbSecFullAccess       dbSecWriteOwner
acSecModWriteDef         dbSecInsertData
dbSecCreate              dbSecNoAccess
```

Workspaces

Finally, a quick note about workspaces. Many of the code snippets in this last section have started with the following line:

```
Set wks = DBEngine(0)
```

This means that any code that follows which uses the wks workspace object will execute in the current workspace. In other words, it will run in the security context of the currently logged on user. There are times, however, when we might want to run some code in the security context of a different user. For example, our database may contain a function which lists the groups to which the user belongs. The problem is that we need to be logged on with administrative privileges to do this.

The way to impersonate another user in code is to create a new workspace, which we do like this:

```
Set wks = DBEngine.CreateWorkspace("MyWorkspace", "Admin", "Glenfarclas")
```

This has the effect of programmatically logging us on as the user called Admin with a password of Glenfarclas and creates a workspace called MyWorkspace. Any operations performed on users or groups within that workspace will be executed as if they were being performed by the user called Admin, irrespective of how the current user is currently logged on to Access.

In fact, if you want to try this out, you can have a go in one of the exercises at the end of this chapter!

Compiling

One of the final issues that we will discuss in this chapter is the ability to protect your source code by saving a database as an MDE file. An MDE file is, in essence, a pre-compiled version fo the database. But before we look at MDE files in more detail, let's just take a moment or two to see how Access projects are compiled.

We saw earlier in the book how compiling our code can alert us to any errors we may have made in our code. Some errors can be detected by Access as we are writing our code. For example, let's suppose we type the following line of code in a module:

```
DoCmd openform "frmSwitchboard"
```

As soon as we try to move off this line of code onto a new line, Access will alert us with a message box informing us that the line of code contains a syntax error.

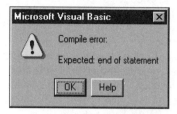

In this case, the error was generated because we omitted the period between the words DoCmd and OpenForm. Despite the misleading message box that Access displays, this isn't really a compile error; it is a **syntax** error. By default, Access will check the syntax of every line of code you enter and flag any errors it notices like the one above. If you want to, you can disable this automatic syntax checking by unchecking the **Auto Syntax Check** box on the **Module** tab of the **Tools/Options…** dialog.

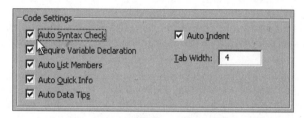

Be wary of disabling automatic syntax checking. There are occasions when it can be useful to disable it. For example, you might be pasting a large chunk of code from, let's say, Access Basic into the module window and you know it will need a fair bit of rework before it will work in VBA. In that case you won't want message boxes appearing every time you move from one line to another.

But in most other situations, you will want automatic syntax checking enabled. Most of the errors it determines are genuine mistakes and are much more easily corrected on the spot.

Whereas syntax errors are easily recognizable as soon as they occur, there are other types of errors that can creep into our code that cannot be detected until later on. For example, what if we create a Do...Loop structure and forget to put the Loop statement at the end? We certainly wouldn't want Access to flag the error when we move off the line containing the Do statement. So when should these errors be detected? The answer is that these are compile errors and are detected when VBA attempts to compile the project. We'll look now at what compilation actually involves and the implications of the different types of compilation afforded to us by VBA. Then we'll look at ways of compiling our code programmatically.

What is Compilation?

So what happens when a VBA project is compiled? Normally when programmers talk about compiling an application, they mean that the human-readable code is converted into native machine-readable code that can be executed directly. Access works slightly differently, in that the VBA code that we write is not converted directly into machine-readable code but is instead converted into an intermediate format called p-code. When the application is run, the p-code is interpreted (i.e. translated into machine-readable code) line-by-line by a run-time DLL.

Many developers regard p-code as an unnecessary evil and bemoan the performance degradation that results from VBA not being compiled into native machine code. In point of fact, although native code can be substantially faster than interpreted p-code for computationally-intensive operations, which rearrange lots of bits and bytes all over the place, most of the VBA code we write is no slower in p-code than native code. After all, the VBA functions we use already reside in a run-time library which is highly optimized, so there won't be too much overhead there. And, in any case, once you start calling subprocedures, DLLs or other objects, the overhead of setting up things like stack frames makes the difference between p-code and native code performance negligible. Add to that the fact that the average application spends less than 5% of the time running code and you will see that the p-code versus natively compiled argument doesn't hold that much water when it comes to VBA projects in Access. (With Visual Basic it's a different argument as you are more likely to write apps in Visual Basic that are computationally-intensive and would therefore benefit from native machine code compilation – and that is why from version 5.0 onwards Visual Basic Professional and Enterprise Editions have let you do just that.)

All the same, the process of compilation still causes the code we have written to be checked for syntax and integrity. And it's that stage of the process that is most noticeable to us. `If` structures without an `End If`, variables that haven't been declared, calls to procedures that don't exist – these are all the types of error that are detected and flagged to us when we compile our code. In fact, the whole process of checking the syntax and integrity of the code and then compiling it into p-code can be quite lengthy, especially where large amounts of code are involved.

If compiling code takes time and highlights errors in our code, the corollary is that trying to run uncompiled code will be just as slow (because the code will have to be compiled when it is run) and may contain bugs. So, get into the habit of regularly compiling your code and always compile it before you distribute a finished application.

How do we Compile Code?

Compiling a project is a simple enough process. The easiest way is to simply choose the Compile <ProjectName> item from the <u>D</u>ebug menu in the VBE.

This menu item is only available while the project is in an uncompiled state. If the project is already compiled, the Compile <ProjectName> item is disabled on the menu bar.

I am extremely lazy and find the effort of two clicks on the menu bar just a little bit too tiring, so I prefer to put a button on the toolbar that allows me to see whether my code is compiled and to compile it with just a single click. To do this, select <u>C</u>ustomize... from the <u>A</u>dd or Remove Buttons on the VBE toolbar.

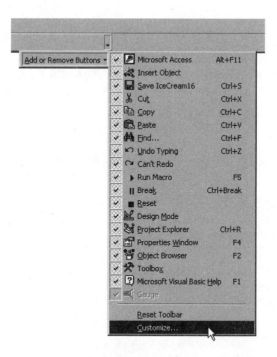

Then, simply locate the **Compile Project** button from the **Debug** category and drag it onto the toolbar.

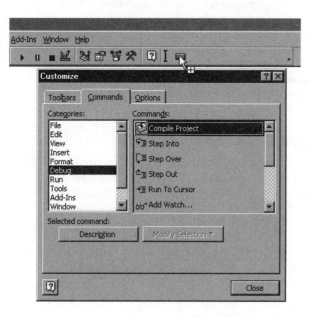

Lo and behold, you now have a toolbar button that allows you to compile your code at a simple click and – much more usefully – whose status indicates whether a project is compiled or not.

In previous versions of Access this button was on the toolbar by default. Its removal in the current version of Access is a consistency issue; because none of the other implementations of VBA (i.e. in Word, Excel etc.) have historically had this button on the toolbar it has been removed from VBA in Access. Frankly, I would prefer to have seen it added to the toolbar by default. After all, the first thing that all the developers I know do when they install Access is to add the button anyway!

Compile On Demand

You may have noticed two options - Compile On Demand and Background Compile – on the General tab of the Tools/Options… dialog in the VBE.

If VBA needs to execute a procedure and the procedure is in a module that is not compiled, it will automatically compile the module before it runs the procedure. It has to because VBA code is not machine-readable, so the VBA has to be converted into p-code that can then be interpreted into a machine-readable format.

If the Compile On Demand option is checked, then VBA will load and compile only those modules which contain procedures that are potentially called by the about-to-be-executed procedure.

However, if the Compile On Demand option is not checked, then VBA will load and compile all modules in the project. This can cause a notable performance hit, if your database contains a lot of uncompiled code, so you are advised to leave the Compile On Demand option checked at all times.

If on-demand compiling is enabled, you can also use the Background Compile checkbox to instruct VBA to use idle time to compile a project in the background, so reducing the number of times that you will need to compile your project explicitly.

When does Code Decompile?

By this stage, you might be wondering whether the Compile On Demand option really makes much difference. Surely if you compile your code before you ship your application you won't have any decompiled code, so you won't have to worry about how long it takes to compile. Most of the time that's fine. However, there are one or two things that your users can do that may cause code in your application to decompile. These include:

- ❑ Adding a form, report, control or module
- ❑ Modifying the code in a form, report, control or module
- ❑ Deleting a form, report, control or module
- ❑ Renaming a form, report, control or module
- ❑ Adding or removing a reference to an object library or database

If any of these occurs and the project needs to be recompiled, your users could experience a significant delay if they then have to wait for the entire project to be recompiled. In such a case, selecting the **Compile On Demand** option could make a big difference to perceived performance.

Using MDE files

A feature introduced in Access 97 was the ability to save a database as an MDE file. When you save a database as an MDE file, Access creates a new database, into which it places a copy of all the database objects from the source database except for the modules. It then compiles all of the modules in the source database and saves them in their compiled form in the target database, which it then compacts. The target database does not contain a copy of the source VBA code, only compiled p-code.

There are three main benefits to be gained from creating an MDE file from a database:

❑ The p-code is smaller than the source VBA code, so the MDE file will take up less space and therefore have a smaller memory footprint.

❑ The modules are already compiled, so performance of the database will be optimal.

❑ Users are unable to perform certain modifications to MDE files (see Restrictions on MDE Files). This presents excellent opportunities for tightening the security of your application.

Note, however, that an MDE is not an executable file. In other words, it cannot be run as a standalone application in the way that an .exe file can be.

Saving a Database as an MDE file

Saving a database as an MDE file couldn't be easier. But you must meet certain prerequisites before Access will allow you to do so. The prerequisites are as follows:

❑ You must use a workgroup information file that contains users defined to access the database

❑ You must be logged on as a user with Open and Open Exclusive permissions for the database

❑ You must be logged on as a user with Modify Design or Administer privileges for tables in the database (or you must own the tables in the database)

❑ You must be logged on as a user with Read Design permissions for all objects in the database

If you use the replication features of Access, you should also note that you cannot convert a replicated database to an MDE file until you have removed all of the replication system tables from the database.

If all these criteria are met, then you can save the database as an MDE file. The process of creating an MDE file requires that Access should be able to exclusively lock the database, so you should make sure that no one else is using the database as well.

Then you simply select the Make MDE File... option from the Database Utilities item on the Tools menu.

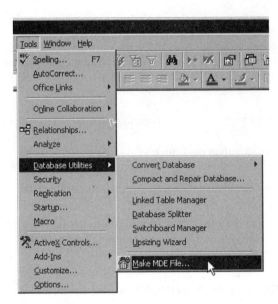

In the Save MDE As dialog which then appears, you should type the name and location that you want for the new MDE file. And that's it!

Restrictions on MDE Files

We noted earlier on that there are various actions that will cause code in a database to decompile. Because MDE files can only contain compiled code, those actions that cause code to decompile are not allowed in a database that has been saved as an MDE file. In other words, users cannot perform any of the following actions in databases saved as MDE files:

- ❑ Add a form, report, control or module
- ❑ Modify the code in a form, report, control or module
- ❑ Delete a form, report, control or module
- ❑ Rename a form, report, control or module
- ❑ Add or remove a reference to an object library or database
- ❑ Change the Project Name for the database in the Tools/Options... dialog

However, users are free to import or export tables, queries and macros to or from MDE or non-MDE databases.

When using MDE files, you should also note that future versions of Access may not be backward compatible with Access 2000 MDE files. In other words, if you create an MDE file with Access 2000, you may not be able to open it or run it in future versions of Access, nor may there be a way to convert it to newer versions of Access.

*These two limitations – the fact that you cannot modify forms, reports or modules, and that MDE files are not upgradeable – should make you realize the importance of hanging onto your source code. When you save a database as an MDE file, you should **always** make sure that you keep a copy of the original source database, because you will need it if you want to make any changes to the design of forms, reports or modules or if you want to use the database with future versions of Access.*

Using MDEs with Add-Ins and Libraries

A final consideration applies if the database that you are saving as an MDE file contains references to other databases as either add-ins or libraries. In short, before you save a database as an MDE file, you should save as an MDE file any databases to which the source database contains references, and then redirect the references to the MDE files rather than to the original add-ins or libraries. Only then can you save the original database as an MDE file. The example below should clarify the situation.

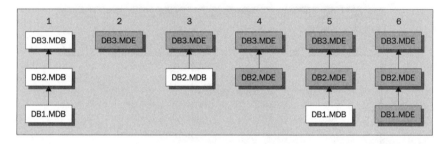

Let us suppose that we have a database DB1.MDB, which contains a reference to DB2.MDB, and that DB2.MDB in turn contains a reference to DB3.MDB (stage 1). The first step is to save DB3.MDB as an MDE file (stage 2) and then set a reference from DB2.MDB to the new compiled DB3.MDE (stage 3). Once you have set the reference, you can then save DB2.MDB as an MDE file (stage 4) and set a reference to it from DB1.MDB (stage 5). Only once you have done that, can you save DB1.MDB as an MDE file (stage 6).

Encrypting

There remains one final method of preventing unwanted access to the data in a database and that is to encrypt the database. Although methods such as protecting databases or projects with passwords and setting security on DAO objects are useful methods of limiting access to a database, there is nothing to prevent someone from simply opening up an Access database in an editor such as Notepad. In fact, you can get a lot of data out of an Access database just by looking at the raw data.

```
___€?_,€O_,€__,€o_,  ___ _   ÿþWake's Cakes And Icesÿþ72 High Street
BirminghamÿþB27 2AAU K ÿþ+44 121 789 4562ÿþKaren Waked × × × × F B 9 9 __
w__
    ÿþJane's Dinerÿþ1827 East 1st Avenue
DenverC O ÿþ80206ÿþUSAÿþ303 322-1070ÿþJane Donnelly_ P P P P B = 6 2 __
    □       ÿþQuintessential Icesÿþ14 Hambledon Road
GodalmingÿþSurreyÿþGU8 1AAU K ÿþ+44 1428 121212ÿþChris Quink ____ N J A ⁹
__ _
    □__ _   ÿþLloyds Luscious Lolliesÿþ18-20 Alverston RoadÿþLondonÿþE5 9JWU K
ÿþ+44 181 745 1322ÿþ+44 181 745 1765ÿþJanine Lloyd{ m m m [ I E = 5
```

In order to prevent this low-level access, you can encrypt a database. This is simple enough to do. Just close down the database that you want to encrypt and select Encrypt/Decrypt Database… from the Tools/Security menu in Access.

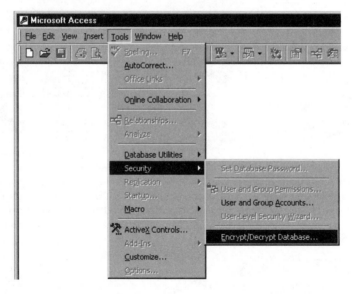

You will be prompted for the name of the database you want to encrypt and the name of the file you want to save the encrypted database as.

Encrypted databases can be used from within Access just like unencrypted databases but their contents are indecipherable when viewed as plain text. There is a slight overhead in terms of performance incurred when using a database in an encrypted state and you will need to bear this in mind if you decide to encrypt database applications for which execution speed is a priority.

Summary

Well then, in this chapter we have looked at the many problems that can arise when more than one person wants to use a database at the same time. In fact they aren't so much problems, as issues. They only become problems when you ignore or forget about them.

The key to producing an Access database that will function as happily with ten people using it as with one, is to plan ahead. If you bear in mind the issues we have looked at in this chapter, and apply them to your databases from the moment you start building them, you should have very few problems. On the other hand, if you wait until the last moment to add a veneer of multi-usability on top of your database, you will spend some very long days and nights trying to iron out problems which wouldn't have arisen if you had been a little more far-sighted in the beginning!

This chapter has covered:

❑ The difference between page-level and row-level locking

❑ The difference between optimistic and pessimistic locking

❑ How to apply locking

❑ The locking errors you are likely to encounter and how to deal with them

❑ How to use the user and group objects to secure a database

❑ How to set and change passwords

❑ Compiling projects

❑ Creating and using MDE files

❑ Encrypting databases

Exercises

1. Earlier in this chapter we looked at how it was possible to use the `CreateWorkspace` method to allow us to act in the security context of another user. One potential use of this is to allow us to create a procedure that lists all of the groups to which the current user belongs. The potential problem is that only members of the `Admins` group have permission to view this information. See if you can write a procedure that lists all of the groups to which the current user belongs, even if the user is not a member of the `Admins` group.

2. The password form we created in this chapter is still fairly rudimentary. You can probably think of many ways to improve it. For example, some security systems force you to change your password at monthly intervals and will not allow you to reuse any of your, say, five previous passwords. See if you can modify the password form so that it enforces these two rules.

Hint: If you decide to store users' passwords in a table you need to make sure that you will be able to read the table from code, but also that normal users won't be able to read the data in the table.

The Internet

There is no one who can deny the pervasive nature of the Internet, and whether you love it or loathe it, there's no doubt it will be with us for a long time to come. It's already proved to be an important tool for many businesses and there are a great many ways in which it can aid your work practices.

In chapter 15, you saw how email can be easily integrated into Access applications, easing communications and improving ordering. Now we need to look at the other features of Access that can integrate to the Internet.

In particular we are going to look at:

- How to use hyperlinks in your applications.
- How to publish data to the Internet.
- How to use a Web Browser within your application.

The Internet

I'm sure you know what the Internet is by now, but let's start with a few definitions so that we're all on common ground:

- **HyperText Markup Language (HTML)** is the format in which Internet documents are stored. It is a fairly simple language and is really just designed for the layout of documents (the Markup part), and the linking of documents to each other (the HyperText part).
- A **hyperlink** is what identifies the link between HTML documents.
- **Dynamic HyperText Markup Language (DHTML)** was created to overcome the rather static nature of HTML, where there is no ability for HTML pages to interact with the user. The Dynamic ability is provided by programming code embedded into the HTML page.
- A **web page** is a page of text formatted in HTML.

❑ A **browser**, or **web browser**, is a program that displays HTML pages. The two most popular are Microsoft Internet Explorer and Netscape Navigator.

❑ A **web server** is a system that stores HTML pages and sends them to a browser when the browser requests them.

❑ **Active Server Pages** (ASP) is Microsoft's technology for web servers which allows programming code to be run on the web server before the web page is sent to the browser.

❑ A **website** is a collection of web pages, usually related. The Wrox Press website, for example, can be found at http://www.wrox.com. Most web addresses are preceded by "www".

❑ A **Uniform Resource Locator (URL)**, or **web address**, is the name given to a website, or a page within it. For example, the URL for the books catalog page at the Wrox Press website is http://www.wrox.com/Store.

There are also a number of protocols that are used around the Internet. A protocol is simply the name given to the way that computers communicate with each other. For example:

❑ **HyperText Transfer Protocol (HTTP)** is the main protocol for transferring web pages between the web server and the web browser. That's why many URLs start with **http:**

❑ **File Transfer Protocol (FTP)** allows you to download, and upload, programs to web servers. FTP addresses start with **ftp:**

❑ **Mail**, which allows mail to be sent over the Internet. A URL that represents a mail address starts with **mailto:**

There are many other protocols, but they don't play as important a role for us when we're working with VBA.

The HyperLink Data Type

Access 2000 has a data type that allows us to use hyperlinks, either within tables or directly within code and on forms. Data formatted as a hyperlink holds a URL and can store three pieces of information:

❑ **Some displayed text**. Since a URL can be rather ugly to read, you can display some meaningful text for the user to read, and hide the complexities of the actual URL.

❑ **The URL address**, which points to the actual item to be linked to.

❑ **The URL sub-address**, which can be an item within the URL address, such as a named location within a file.

For a `Hyperlink` data type, these three parts are separated by a hash sign:

```
Display Text#Address#Sub Address
```

Let's look at some examples to see this more clearly:

URL	Display	Action taken
http://www.microsoft.com	http://www.microsoft.com	Jumps to the Microsoft home page.
Microsoft on the Web#www.microsoft.com	Microsoft on the Web	Jumps to the Microsoft home page.
Send us feedback#mailto:feedback@wrox.com	Send us feedback	Opens the mail program with `feedback@wrox.com` as the mail address
Hyperlinks#C:\BegVBA_Internet.doc#Hyperlinks	Hyperlinks	Opens the document C:\BegVBA\Internet.doc and jump to the Word bookmark Hyperlinks
Ice Creams#C:\BegVBA\IceCream.mdb#Form frmIceCream	Ice Creams	Opens the form `frmIceCream` in the database C:\BegVBA_IceCream.mdb
Ice Creams##Form frmIceCream	Ice Creams	Opens the form `frmIceCream` in the current database

Notice that the hyperlink data type does not restrict URLs to just HTML documents. You can also point to Word documents, Excel spreadsheets, Access forms, etc. which gives you a great deal of flexibility. With the ability to open forms, you can even replace the code behind buttons with that of a hyperlink address – this would open the form without any code or macros.

> And that's an important point, because that's all it does – open the form. No filtering, adding WHERE clauses, or error handling can be done if you use hyperlinks in this way.

How to use Hyperlinks

If you've looked at the Companies table then you've already seen a hyperlink field:

As you can see this one is designed to hold the web address of the companies and, because the field is a Hyperlink, clicking on the field will launch your web browser to point at this web site. However, notice that the mail address doesn't look like a hyperlink – that's because this is a plain text field. Let's convert this to a hyperlink and see how it behaves.

Try It Out – Using Hyperlink fields

1. Open tblCompany in design mode.

2. Change the **Data Type** property for the Email column from **Text** to **Hyperlink**. Make sure the **Allow Zero Length** property is set to **Yes**.

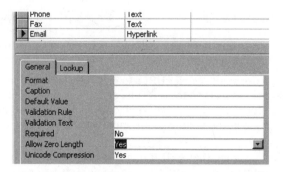

3. Save the changes and switch the table into datasheet view.

4. Find **Dave's Dairy Produce** and notice the Email and Web fields.

Although they look similar, we want one to behave like an email address, launching our email program when clicked, and one to behave like a web address, launching the web browser when it's clicked. Since there is nothing in the properties of the hyperlink field to identify this, we have to use the hyperlink itself, and that's where the protocols come in. The default protocol is http, so at the moment Access thinks the email address is a web address. That means you can't just click in the column to edit the field, as this tries to jump to the hyperlink.

5. To get around this, click in the Email column for either of the empty records either side of the Dave's Dairy record, and use the cursor keys to move to the Email column for Dave's Dairy.

6. Enter the following into the Email column:

```
mailto:sales@davesdairy.com
```

7. Click on the new mail hyperlink, and you'll see your mail program loaded.

So, you can see that the Hyperlink column type is extremely useful as it gives you, and your users, quick access to web pages and mail address. If you want to hide even more complexity from your users you can use the display part of the hyperlink to show different text. Rather than delete and re-type the hyperlink, let's edit it in a different way.

With your mouse over the email address column, click the right mouse button and select Hyperlink, and then Edit Hyperlink from the next menu. This brings up the Edit Hyperlink window:

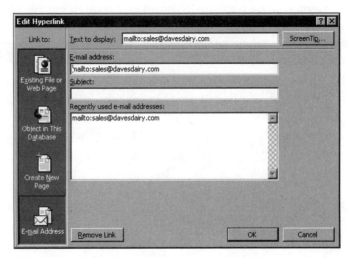

If you now change the Text to Display field and press the OK button you'll see that what's displayed in the column is now the text you typed in, rather than the email address.

Hyperlinks in VBA

You've seen how easy it is to use hyperlinks in tables, but you might be wondering how you can use them in your code. The Hyperlink data type is more like an object, with several properties and methods:

Item	Type	Description
Address	Property	The main hyperlink address.
EmailSubject	Property	The Subject line if the hyperlink is an email.
ScreenTip	Property	The Screen Tip or Tool Tip text to display for the hyperlink. This requires IE4 or later to work.
SubAddress	Property	The sub-address of the hyperlink.
TextToDisplay	Property	The visible text to show on the screen.
AddToFavorites	Method	Add the hyperlink to the favorites folder.
CreateNewDocument	Method	Creates a new document associated with the hyperlink.
Follow	Method	Follows the hyperlink, opening the program (browser, mail, etc) associated with the hyperlink.

Custom Hyperlink Form

You've seen the Edit Hyperlink dialog, which allows all of the values for a hyperlink to be edited, but you may not want your users using this form. After all, it looks fairly confusing and has more information than we really need, so you may want to provide something simpler. Let's make a more user-friendly form for editing hyperlinks.

Try It Out – Editing Hyperlinks

1. Open frmCompany in design view, and add two small buttons to the right of the Email and Web fields. You might need to widen the form a bit to get the buttons on:

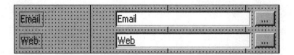

2. Name these buttons cmdEmail and cmdWeb. If you make these as small as the diagram then you might need to reduce the font size to make the dots show up – 7-point seems to work well.

3. In the Click event for cmdEmail add the following code (make sure you get the number of commas correct – there are five of them).

```
DoCmd.OpenForm "frmHyperlink", , , , , acDialog, "Email"
```

4. In the Click event for cmdWeb, add the following code:

```
DoCmd.OpenForm "frmHyperlink", , , , , acDialog, "Web"
```

5. Save and close this form. Now create a new form and add three text boxes and three text buttons:

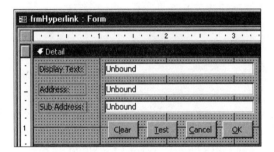

6. The text boxes should be named txtDisplay, txtAddress and txtSubAddress, and the command buttons cmdClear, cmdTest, cmdCancel and cmdOK.

7. Set the Record Selectors and Navigation Buttons properties for the form to No. Now save the form as frmHyperlink.

8. Create a code module for the form by pressing the code button, and add the following global variable:

```
Option Compare Database
Option Explicit

Dim m_ctlHyperlink As Control
```

9. Now we'll place code for each of our command buttons in their respective event procedures. First, in the Click event for cmdCancel, add the following:

```
Private Sub cmdCancel_Click()
    DoCmd.Close
End Sub
```

Next, in the Click event for cmdOK, add the following:

```
Private Sub cmdOK_Click()
    m_ctlHyperlink = txtDisplay & "#" & txtAddress & "#" & txtSubAddress
    DoCmd.Close
End Sub
```

Now add the following line to the `Click` event of the `cmdTest` button:

```
Private Sub cmdTest_Click()
    m_ctlHyperlink.Hyperlink.Follow
End Sub
```

Next, add this code to the `Click` event of the `cmdClear` button:

```
Private Sub cmdClear_Click()
    txtDisplay = ""
    txtAddress = ""
    txtSubAddress = ""
End Sub
```

10. To wrap up the procedure, add this code to the `Load` event for the `Form`:

```
Private Sub Form_Load()
    Set m_ctlHyperlink = Forms!frmCompany.Controls(OpenArgs)
    With m_ctlHyperlink.Hyperlink
        txtDisplay = .TextToDisplay
        txtAddress = .Address
        txtSubAddress = .SubAddress
    End With
End Sub
```

11. Save the module, switch back to Access, and save and close the form.

12. Now open `frmCompany` in form view, and view the record for **Dave's Dairy**.

13. Press the button alongside the Mail field, which will bring up the **Edit Hyperlink** form below:

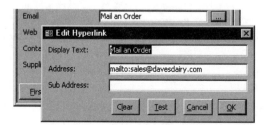

14. Just press the **T**est button to launch the mail program.

So with just a few lines of code, you've made a simpler form for editing hyperlinks.

How it Works

We've done two things here. The first has been to modify the company form, because that's where the hyperlinks are shown. The second has been to create a new form to allow editing of those hyperlinks. Let's first look at the new code in the company form, behind the two buttons that open the hyperlink form:

```
DoCmd.OpenForm "frmHyperlink", , , , , acDialog, "Email"
```

```
DoCmd.OpenForm "frmHyperlink", , , , , acDialog, "Web"
```

You've seen forms being opened before, but this format does require a little explanation. The last two arguments are the ones we're interested in. The first of these, acDialog, tells Access that the form is to be opened modally, as though it were a dialog form – that means that you have to close the form before you can continue. The last argument is a string that gets passed into the hyperlink form, and is used to identify which control we are editing the hyperlink for.

Let's now look at the code for the hyperlink form. Firstly there's a global variable, m_ctlHyperlink, which is a Control. This will point to the actual control on the calling form – this will be either the Email or Web address control.

Now for the Form_Load procedure. Firstly we set this global variable to point to the control on the previous form. We're using a special variable called OpenArgs here – this contains the value that was passed in as the last argument of the OpenForm command shown earlier. In this case it's the name of a control, so we can use this to index into the forms Controls collection:

```
Set m_ctlHyperlink = Forms!frmCompany.Controls(OpenArgs)
```

Now we want to display the various parts of the hyperlink on our form. For this we refer to the Hyperlink property of the control, which allows us to access the various hyperlink elements.

```
With m_ctlHyperlink.Hyperlink
    txtDisplay = .TextToDisplay
    txtAddress = .Address
    txtSubAddress = .SubAddress
End With
```

When the user presses the OK button we want to be able to update the hyperlink control. We can't use the Hyperlink property and its elements like we did when the form was opened because the individual elements are read-only, but we can combine the elements together, using the hash symbol to separate them.

```
m_ctlHyperlink = txtDisplay & "#" & txtAddress & "#" & txtSubAddress
DoCmd.Close
```

The Clear button simply clears the values from the form fields. This saves the user having to clear them individually.

The last piece of code is for the Test button, when we want to launch the application associated with the hyperlink. For this we use the Follow method of the Hyperlink property.

```
m_ctlHyperlink.Hyperlink.Follow
```

That's all there is to it! An easier form, with only a few lines of code. Although we've only shown this code working for the email address, it works the same way for Web addresses. Why not try adding some real Web URLs to see it in action?

Publishing Data to the Internet

Although not specifically a VBA topic, publishing data is one of the most common database/Internet-related activities, and so deserves a mention. If you want to publish data to the Internet then you need to consider one important point – how often do you want the data shown on the Web to change? Is the data static, does it change once a month, or how about daily? Should we be showing our Web visitors up-to-the-minute data?

If you are not worried too much about the data then you could use plain HTML files and update these on a regular basis, say once a month. If you need the very latest data, then there are two options – you can use ASP files to show the latest data every time the web page is viewed, or you can use Access Data Pages, which show a live view of the data. Both HTML and ASP files give the advantage that any browser can view the page, whereas Data Pages only work in Internet Explorer 5, which is supplied with Office 2000.

Let's give all of these methods a try – we'll create a web page to display our ice creams.

Try It Out – Creating HTML Files

1. In the database window select tblIceCream.

2. From the File menu select Export.

3. From the export dialog, change the Save as type to HTML Documents (*.html; *.htm).

4. Press the Save button to create the HTML file.

5. The new HTML file isn't automatically displayed, so switch to Windows Explorer and find the file, then double-click it to launch Internet Explorer.

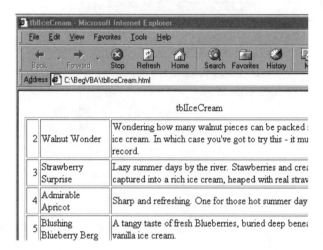

You now have a static HTML file, which will not change if the data changes.

Live Data

Publishing live data to the Internet means that every time the Web page is viewed, the data is fetched from the database. This has the advantage of the data always being up-to-date (and so requiring less upkeep) but with the downside of taking longer to set up and having a slightly longer loading time.

To use Active Server Pages (ASP) you will need either Microsoft Internet Information Server (IIS) for Windows NT 4.0 Server, or Microsoft Personal Web Server (PWS) for Windows NT 4.0 Workstation, Windows 95, or Windows 98. Both of these (including the Windows 9x versions) are available as part of the Windows NT 4.0 Option Pack, or alternatively, PWS is available on the Windows 98 CD.

The following example requires the use of an ODBC DSN and a PWS virtual directory. To keep this chapter focused we've included an appendix (Appendix H) detailing how to set up an ODBC Data Source Name (DSN) and how to set up a virtual directory in PWS.

Try It Out – Creating ASP Files

1. Follow steps 1 and 2 from the previous example.

2. From the export dialog, instead of HTML, change the Save as type: to Microsoft Active Server Pages (*.asp):

3. Press the <u>S</u>ave button to open the **ASP Options** dialog:

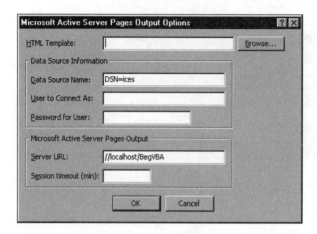

Since the data is updated every time the ASP page is loaded, you need to fill in some details:

Field	Description
HTML Template	If you've got an HTML template you can enter its name here. This can help give your ASP pages a consistent look.
Data Source Name	This can be an ODBC DSN (as shown) or an ADO connect string. This is how the ASP page connects to the Access database to get the data.
User name and password	If you have security set on your Access database you should enter a user name and password here, otherwise you can leave them blank.
Server URL	This allows you to enter the default URL of the web server that will host this page. Unlike HTML pages, which can be viewed directly by a browser, an ASP file must be processed by the web server before the browser can use it.

4. After entering these details you can view the web page:

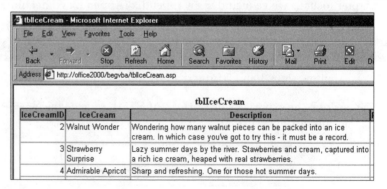

This looks pretty similar to the previous example, but this time the data will be fetched from the database every time the web page is viewed.

5. Switch back into Access, and open the Ice Cream table. Change the description for Walnut Wonder, adding in some text at the beginning.

6. Switch back to your browser, and press the Refresh button:

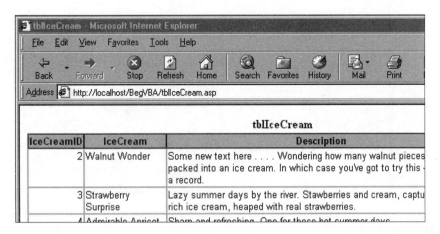

Notice how the new data is visible immediately. You don't have to export this again, because each time this web page is viewed, the data is fetched directly from the database.

Let's now look at another way of presenting current data on a web page: Data Access Pages.

Try It Out – Data Access Pages

Remember, to view Data Access Pages you require Internet Explorer 5.

1. In the database window select the Pages object.

2. Select Create data access page by using wizard – you can double click to set this off.

3. Follow the wizard through its steps. Select **tblIceCream** as the table, selecting all fields. You don't need to add any grouping or sorting. After the wizard has finished you'll see your Data Access Page in design view:

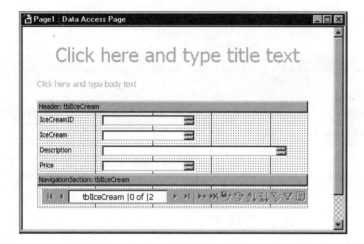

Notice how much this looks like the standard form and report designer, but in fact it's an HTML page, with embedded objects.

4. Save this page and view it:

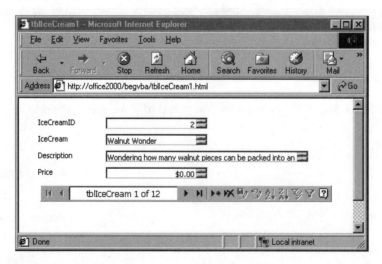

This looks very much like a normal Access form. It shows a single record at a time, and the navigation bar works the same as it does in Access.

Uploading Data

Being able to create HTML or ASP files is all very well, but what do you do about getting these files onto your web server? Well, if your web server is local to your network then you can just copy the files, but how about if your web server is hosted by an ISP? If this is the case you might have to use FTP to upload the files to the ISP's server. Under normal circumstances you could do this with an FTP program (there are plenty available), but if you've got the Office Developer Edition, then you can use the Internet Transfer Control. This is an ActiveX control that allows you to perform HTTP or FTP operations. You might also have this control if you've got Visual Basic.

If you've got access to an FTP Server on your network you can give this a try.

Try It Out – Using the Internet Transfer Control

1. Create a new form. Add three text boxes to the form, naming them txtURL, txtUser and txtPassword.

2. Click the More Controls button on the toolbox:

From the list that appears, select Microsoft Internet Transfer Control, version 6.0.

3. Draw the control on your form. Don't worry about the size, as it's an invisible control and has a fixed size. Name the control ctlInternet.

4. Create a label on the form and call it lblState.

5. Create a command button on the form and call it cmdUpload. Your form should now look something like this:

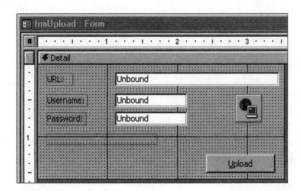

6. Press the Code button on the main toolbar to create a code window for this form.

7. In the Click event for cmdUpload, add the following code:

```
On Error GoTo cmdUpload_Err

DoCmd.TransferText acExportHTML, , "tblIceCream", _
   "C:\BegVBA\tblIceCream.html"

With ctlInternet
   .RequestTimeout = 30
   .AccessType = icDirect
   .Protocol = icFTP
   .URL = txtURL
   .UserName = txtUser
   .Password = txtPassword
   .Execute , "PUT C:\BegVBA\tblIceCream.html tblIceCream.html"
End With

cmdUpload_Err:
```

8. Select the Internet control in the Object drop-down list box, and select the StateChanged event from the procedure window:

9. Add the following code to this event procedure:

```
Dim strState As String

Select Case State
   Case icConnected
      strState = "Connected"
   Case icConnecting
      strState = "Connecting"
   Case icDisconnected
      strState = "Disconnected"
   Case icDisconnecting
      strState = "Disconnecting"
   Case icError
      strState = "Error: " & ctlInternet.ResponseInfo
   Case icHostResolved
      strState = "Host resolved"
   Case icReceivingResponse
      strState = "Receiving response"
   Case icRequesting
      strState = "Requesting"
   Case icRequestSent
      strState = "Request sent"
```

```
Case icResolvingHost
    strState = "Resolving host"
Case icResponseCompleted
    strState = "Response completed"
Case icResponseReceived
    strState = "Response received"
End Select

lblState.Caption = strState
```

10. Save all of your changes and switch the form into form mode.

11. Enter the name of your FTP server, and the user name and password you connect with:

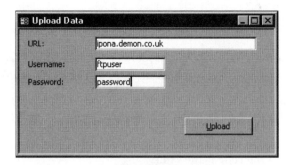

12. Press the upload button. The HTML file will be created locally, then uploaded to your server. Have a look on your FTP server to make sure it worked.

How it Works

Let's look at the code that performs the upload.

The first thing to do is turn on error handling, since it's possible to mistype the user name or password.

```
On Error GoTo cmdUpload_Err
```

Next we use the `TransferText` command to save the table as an HTML file.

```
DoCmd.TransferText acExportHTML, , "tblIceCream", _
    "C:\BegVBA\tblIceCream.html"
```

Now we can start using the transfer control. The first property setting sets the time-out to 30 seconds, meaning we don't have to wait too long to find out we've typed in the wrong password. The file we're uploading is small, so it will take a considerably shorter amount of time, but if we were using a table with a lot of records it would take longer.

```
With ctlInternet          ‹
    .RequestTimeout = 30
```

The next two properties set the connection type and protocol. Using `icDirect` ensures that the connection is direct to the FTP server (and does not go through a proxy server), and `icFTP` says we are using FTP (as opposed to HTTP).

```
.AccessType = icDirect
.Protocol = icFTP
.URL = txtURL
```

Next we set the user name and password to connect with:

```
.UserName = txtUser
.Password = txtPassword
```

And finally we can run the `Execute` method, using a `PUT` command. The `PUT` command takes two arguments – the name of the local file and the name of the remote file.

```
   .Execute , "PUT C:\BegVBA\tblIceCream.html tblIceCream.html"
End With
```

The last thing in this procedure is the empty error handler. We've left this empty because we do want to trap errors, but we don't want anything done about them. This is because the Internet control uses an event procedure to tell us its state, and this will identify errors.

```
cmdUpload_Err:
```

Let's look at the event procedure now. We'll skip some of the code here, since we only need to explain what's going on, and most of the code is the same.

The event procedure has an argument, `State`, which identifies the current state of the command. Since this can take many values we use the `Select Case` statement to check it against some predefined constants, setting a string to a description of the state. If an error is received we add on the `ResponseInfo`, which will contain the error string. (Note that this is just a piece of the code above, not the whole `Select Case` statement).

```
Select Case State
Case icConnected
   strState = "Connected"
Case icError
   strState = "Error: " & ctlInternet.ResponseInfo
Case icResponseReceived
   strState = "Response received"
End Select
```

That's all there is to it. A few lines of code and you have a fully functioning FTP client. Although this only performs one upload, it's quite easy to see how it could be modified to perform several in a row.

Summary

In this chapter we've looked at how Access can be used to interface to the Internet. The rise of the Internet in the last year has meant that more and more people are creating web sites and learning new technologies, such as HTML, ASP, and so on. To make a Web site dynamic it must be driven by data, and the ease of using Access has fueled the desire for people to know Access.

What we've covered are the major areas where Access can be used in this respect, notably:

❑ The user of hyperlinks within tables and forms, to allow users to jump directly to Web sites, or to send mail.

❑ The various types of Internet document that you can create when exporting data from Access.

❑ How you can automate the transfer of Web documents to your ISP, or to a Web server.

This really is only the tip of the iceberg as far as Internet and data go, but to delve further you'll need to study an Internet book. For now, though, we've almost come to the end of our journey. The last topic we're going to look at is how to optimize your code, and put those finishing touches to your database to make sure everything is as polished as possible.

Exercises

1. We want to publish a list of our ice creams to our Internet site, and we want to use plain HTML files. Add some code to the ice creams form, so that any time an ice cream entry is changed, a new HTML file is generated.

2. See if you can create a Web browser using an Access form. Hint – there's a control you can add to your form – when in form design mode, press the **More Controls** button on the **Toolbox** to see if you can find the right control.

Optimizing Your Application

Chambers 20th Century English Dictionary defines optimization as:

Preparing or revising a computer system or program so as to achieve the greatest possible efficiency.

That is the focus of this chapter. We shall be looking at the different methods available to you as a developer to ensure that your database application operates as efficiently as possible.

In particular, we will cover:

❑   What makes a piece of code efficient

❑   How to measure the speed of a program

❑   Some coding tips for creating faster programs

❑   What to bear in mind when writing networked applications

Efficiency

The Performance Analyzer (which you can access from the menu bar by clicking T̲ools/Analyze and then selecting P̲erformance) is a useful enough tool. It can help you to a large degree in identifying potential problems with database performance and it is always useful to run it against a poorly performing database application. However, the Performance Analyzer doesn't help you with several other factors that you should consider, one of these being optimization of your VBA code.

If our aim is to achieve maximum efficiency, the key question is, of course, "What constitutes efficiency?" This is a more complex question than it may at first appear. Listed below are four of the most frequently cited benchmarks for evaluating the efficiency of a database application:

❑   Real execution speed

❑   Apparent speed

❑   Memory footprint (i.e. size)

❑   Network traffic

It is nearly always possible to optimize your application with respect to one of these benchmarks, but how do you optimize with respect to them all? The simple answer is that you can't – and you shouldn't try to.

One of the key tasks at the start of a development project is to devise a list of coding priorities. Which of the factors listed above are most important for the successful implementation of the application? Which would it be nice to have? And which are irrelevant?

To the four factors listed above, you can add another five:

- ❑ Portability
- ❑ Robustness
- ❑ Scalability
- ❑ Maintainability
- ❑ Re-usability

And perhaps most important are scheduling factors. Although not optimal, poor performance might be an acceptable price to pay if only the application can be delivered within schedule.

Of course, none of these factors will necessarily help to increase the efficiency of the application – optimizing a piece of code for portability or robustness may well cause the code to run slower or consume more memory than before.

In fact, these various factors can all pull in separate directions. Consider these two bits of code:

```
If (bln1 = True And bln2 = True) Or (bln1 = False And bln2 = False) Then
    blnResult = False
Else
    blnResult = True
End If
```

```
blnResult = (bln1 Xor bln2)
```

Both of these examples produce the same result. However, the first can take approximately four times as long to execute as the second. If you were optimizing for speed, you would go for the latter.

On the other hand, many developers, especially inexperienced ones with no knowledge of bitwise comparisons, would find the first example easier to follow. If you were optimizing for maintainability, you would probably choose the first one (especially given that, on a typical machine, both examples execute in little more than a thousandth of a second).

This chapter, then, is not going to tell you the optimal way to write your code. That will depend on the coding priorities that you determine for your application. What this chapter will do is to highlight the impact, in terms of the four most frequently cited coding priorities, of various coding practices.

All of the code that is used in this chapter can be found in the `Performance.mdb` *database that accompanies this book.*

Reducing Memory Overhead

A modern desktop computer running Access will typically have between 24 and 128 Mb of memory (RAM). This is where all of your application's code is executed. The more memory your computer has, the more likely it will be that the data needed by an application will be available in memory and therefore the less frequently the application will need to read from and write to the disk. Reading and writing to disk is a relatively slow process and the less disk access is required, the faster the program will typically run.

As a general rule, more memory equals better performance. In the dim and distant past, computers were limited to around 32 or 64 **kilobytes** of memory. To put this in perspective, that is about 2000 times less than the amount in the machine that I am using to produce this chapter. Even if you had an operating system or program able to use 96 Mb of RAM in those days – and that is much more than was utilized in many mainframes – the sheer cost of the memory would have torn your scheme to shreds.

It's not surprising, therefore, that with such limited memory available, programmers spent a great deal of time shoe-horning their quart of code into the pint pot that was their computer. The key phrase was 'disciplined programming'; the language was typically assembler or machine code (almost impenetrable to the layman) and the results produced were a testimony to the ingenuity and patience of the programmers involved.

But these days we live on easy street... if a program is running slowly, just spend $100 on another 16 Mb of RAM for your machine! This isn't a completely heinous attitude – after all, it might cost $40,000 in man-days to re-code the program so that it runs as quickly on a computer with 24Mb of memory as the old version of the program did on a computer with 40 Mb of memory!

However, that is not to say that we should let this newfound freedom allow us to churn out sloppy code. Memory, although relatively cheap, is still precious. The less memory your program takes up, the faster it, and all the other programs running simultaneously, should perform.

Additionally, if you are writing an application that will be used by a thousand users, then every extra megabyte of memory required by your application equates to 1000 Mb of memory across all those machines.

In other words, for most projects, producing an application with a small memory footprint is still a very real coding priority.

You should, therefore, bear the following guidelines in mind when developing any application:

- ❑ Use the right data type
- ❑ Group procedures into modules
- ❑ Reclaim memory where possible
- ❑ Don't load unnecessary modules/libraries
- ❑ Save the database as an MDE file

Use the Right Data Type

Different types of variable take up different amounts of memory. The size of the memory taken up by each of the data types is shown in the table below:

Data type	Storage size	Range
Byte	1 byte	0 to 255
Boolean	2 bytes	True or False
Integer	2 bytes	-32,768 to 32,767
Long	4 bytes	-2,147,483,648 to 2,147,483,647.
Single	4 bytes	-3.403E38 to -1.401E-45; 0; 1.401E-45 to 3.403E38
Double	8 bytes	-1.798E308 to -4.941E-324; 0; 4.941E-324 to 1.798E308
Currency	8 bytes	-922,337,203,685,477.5808 to 922,337,203,685,477.5807.
Decimal	12 bytes	-7.923E28 to 7.923E28 (varies with number of decimal places in number stored)
Date	8 bytes	January 1, 100 to December 31, 9999
Object	4 bytes + the size of the object	A reference to any object
Fixed String	1 byte per character	Up to approx. 65,400 characters
Variable Length String	10 bytes + 1 byte per character	Up to approx. 2 billion characters
Variant (numeric)	16 bytes	As double
Variant (string)	22 bytes + 1 byte per character	As variable length string

As you can see, variables of type Long take up twice as much memory as variables of type Integer. But then again, optimization is a question of compromise – Long variables can hold a much wider range of values than Integer variables can.

The problem of memory usage becomes even more marked when dealing with arrays. This line:

```
ReDim adbl(9, 9) As Double
```

declares an array containing 100 elements and takes up around 800 bytes of memory, compared to the 200 or so bytes taken up by this one:

```
ReDim aint(9, 9) As Integer
```

> *For more detailed information on calculating the memory requirements of arrays, refer back to the Memory Considerations section in Chapter 11.*

As a rule, if memory footprint size is a coding priority – as it nearly always is – you should choose the smallest variable that can hold the values that you will be dealing with. To remind you to explicitly assign types to variables, you should tick the <u>R</u>equire Variable Declaration option on the Editor tab in the VBA <u>T</u>ools/<u>O</u>ptions... dialog.

And it has been said before – but I make no apology for saying it again – always, always be wary of the Variant data type. Although there are situations in which it is useful – and sometimes necessary – to use a Variant data type, you should bear in mind that not only does it take up significantly more memory than the other data types, but it can also lead to errors in your code going undetected. For example, I'll wager that no one reading this will be able to accurately predict what 10 values the following procedure will print in the Immediate window... Try it out and see how many you guessed correctly!

```
Sub AreYouSure()

Dim v1 As Variant
Dim v2 As Variant
Dim v3 As Variant

v1 = 1
v2 = "1"
v3 = "(1)"

Debug.Print v1 + v2
Debug.Print v1 + v3
Debug.Print v2 + v3
Debug.Print
Debug.Print v1 & v2
Debug.Print v1 & v3
Debug.Print v2 & v3
Debug.Print
Debug.Print v2 + v1 + v3
Debug.Print v2 & v1 + v3
Debug.Print (v1 & v2) + v3
Debug.Print v1 + (v1 & v2) + v3

End Sub
```

The answers are as follows:

```
v1 + v2                = 2
v1 + v3                = 0
v2 + v3                = 1(1)

v1 & v2                = 11
v1 & v3                = 1(1)
v2 & v3                = 1(1)

v2 + v1 + v3           = 1
v2 & v1 + v3           = 10
(v1 & v2) + v3         = 11(1)
v1 + (v1 & v2) + v3    = 11
```

Group Procedures into Modules

VBA only loads modules when a procedure in that module is called. This is called loading on demand. Therefore, if you have a routine that calls three procedures and they are all in separate modules, all three modules will be loaded into memory. By judiciously grouping related procedures into the same module, you can minimize the number of modules loaded into memory at any one time.

Reclaim Memory Where Possible

You can use the Erase statement to reclaim the memory used by a dynamic array. When you have finished with the array, using the Erase statement will discard the data in the array and free up the memory that it had been using.

The Erase statement doesn't reclaim space from static (fixed-size) arrays. However, it does re-initialize them. For more information on re-initializing arrays, refer back to Chapter 11.

You can also reclaim the memory used by object variables when you have finished with them. You do this by setting them to a special value called Nothing.

```
Set objExcel = Nothing
```

Remember, however, that the memory used by an object cannot be reclaimed if there is another reference to the object elsewhere in code. We used this to our advantage when we examined classes where we prevented an instance of a popup form from being destroyed by placing a reference to it in a collection declared at the module level of another form. This ensured that the popup form was not destroyed until the second form was closed and the collection went out of scope.

Don't Load Unnecessary Libraries

We saw earlier how library databases can be a useful way to store and re-use frequently needed procedures. They can also be used to house wizards and add-ins, such as the control and form-design wizards that ship with Access. However, each of these library databases needs to be loaded into memory when used and that can have a significant hit on the amount of memory that is being used. So, to reduce the memory footprint of your installation, you should use the Add-In Manager (available from the Tools/Add-Ins menu in Access) to unload any library databases or add-ins that are not essential.

Save as an MDE

In chapter 16, we looked at the final touches that you should apply to your application before you give it to the end users of the databases. One of those things is converting your database into an MDE file. This conversion compiles any modules within the database and then strips out the original source code. This in turn has the twin advantages of making your database more secure and reducing the memory footprint of your application.

Bear in mind that you cannot modify the design of MDE files and that you should always keep an original source version of your database in MDB format.

A Final Recommendation – Buy More Memory!

No, it's not cheating! It is recommended that you have 24 Mb or more of memory if you are running Access on Windows 95 or later, and if you are running it on Windows NT 4.0 or later, 40 Mb of memory is recommended.

If you are running on a network, or intend to use other Windows applications at the same time, you will find that the extra few dollars it will cost to buy another 16 or 32 Mb will be well worth it.

Increasing Execution Speed

Reducing the amount of memory that your Access database and its code occupy may result in both it and other Windows applications running faster. But, if fast execution is a real coding priority, there are other methods you can consider:

- ❑ Use constants
- ❑ Use specific object types (early binding)
- ❑ Use variables, not properties
- ❑ Avoid slow structures
- ❑ Beware of IIf
- ❑ Use integer arithmetic where possible

- ❏ Use in-line code
- ❏ Use DoEvents judiciously
- ❏ Use the Requery method not the Requery action
- ❏ Use Me
- ❏ Speed up database operations

We'll look at these in more detail and provide some code samples that prove the point. The code samples have been included so that you can gauge the impact of these techniques for yourself. After all, computers differ greatly in terms of the amount of RAM, processor speed, cache size, disk speed, etc... And these differences are reflected in the performance of VBA on those machines. Don't take my word for it; try out these examples for yourself!

Looking at the results below, you might be forgiven for wondering whether it is worth bothering with some of the improvements. After all, if it only takes three milliseconds to perform an operation, why bother going to the effort of optimizing your code so that it only takes one millisecond? After all, who's going to notice? Well, although it's fair to say that the difference may not be noticeable in a single line of code, it might be if that code is executed many times. For example, you may be looping through all the controls on a form to check for a certain condition. Or you might be looping through all the records in a recordset. Get into the habit of coding efficiently all the time – then it won't be a struggle to do it when it really matters.

Timing the Code Samples

The simplest method for timing how long a piece of code takes to execute is to use the Timer function. For example, we could use the following sample of code to time how long it takes for a For... Next... structure to loop through 100,000 values.

```
Sub TimeLoop()

Dim sngStart As Single
Dim sngEnd As Single
Dim lngLoop As Long

sngStart = Timer

For lngLoop = 0 To 100000
Next lngLoop

sngEnd = Timer

Debug.Print "It took " & Format$(sngEnd - sngStart, "0.000") & " secs."

End Sub
```

The `Timer` function returns a `Single` indicating the number of seconds elapsed since midnight. In the example above, we save the value of `Timer` in the variable `sngStart` before the loop commences:

```
sngStart = Timer
```

and then save the value of `Timer` in the variable `sngEnd` when the loop has finished:

```
sngEnd = Timer
```

By subtracting one from the other, we can determine how long it took for the loop to execute:

```
Debug.Print "It took " & Format$(sngEnd - sngStart, "0.000") & " secs."
```

Now you could include this code in all of the procedures that you want to time. However, if you will be doing a lot of code timings, you might want to set up a test harness like this...

Try It Out – Creating A Test Harness

1. Open a standard code module and type in the procedure `TestPerformance` listed below:

```
Sub TestPerformance(lngIterations As Long, intRuns As Integer)

Dim intLoop As Integer
Dim lngLoop As Long
Dim sngStart As Single
Dim sngCorrection As Single
Dim sngTime As Single
Dim sngTimeTotal As Single

sngStart = Timer
For lngLoop = 1 To lngIterations
    EmptyRoutine                '<--- This is an empty procedure
Next
sngCorrection = Timer - sngStart

For intLoop = 1 To intRuns
    sngStart = Timer
    For lngLoop = 1 To lngIterations
        TestProc                '<--- This is the procedure we are testing
    Next
    sngTime = Timer - sngStart - sngCorrection
    Debug.Print "Run " & intLoop & ": " & sngTime & " seconds"
    sngTimeTotal = sngTimeTotal + sngTime
Next

Debug.Print
Debug.Print "Correction : " & Round(sngCorrection, 3) & " seconds"
Debug.Print
Debug.Print "AverageTime: " & Round(sngTimeTotal / intRuns, 3) & " seconds"

End Sub
```

2. Also, create two procedures called `EmptyRoutine` and `TestProc`, looking like this:

```
Sub EmptyRoutine()

End Sub
```

```
Sub TestProc()

Dim sngTime As Single

sngTime = Timer

Do While sngTime + 5 > Timer
   DoEvents
Loop

End Sub
```

3. Now, open the Immediate window, type in the following code to run the `TestPerformance` procedure and hit *Enter*.

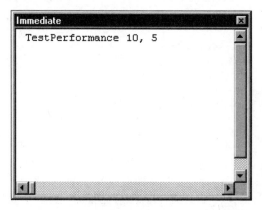

4. The results of running the `TestProc` procedure 10 times in 5 different test runs will (eventually) be shown in the Immediate window.

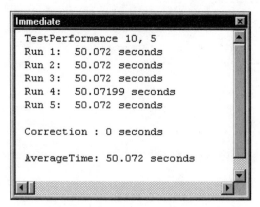

How It Works

The `TestPerformance` procedure accepts two arguments. The first of these is the number of times that the procedure we want to test (`TestProc`) will be executed in each run; the second argument indicates the number of runs that we want to time.

The important part of this procedure is a loop that runs the code to be tested a certain number of times:

```
For lngLoop = 1 To lngIterations
    TestProc
Next
```

In this case, `TestProc` is the name of the procedure that we wish to test. When you want to time a different procedure, simply substitute its name at this point of the `TestPerformance` procedure

The difference between the time at the start and end of this loop is then displayed. However, the loop itself has its own overhead. For this reason, we also use another loop to monitor the overhead that is incurred by executing the loop.

```
sngStart = Timer
For lngLoop = 1 To lngIterations
    EmptyRoutine
Next
sngCorrection = Timer - sngStart
```

The `EmptyRoutine` function is simply a procedure which contains no code.

The overhead that is recorded is then stored in a variable called `sngCorrection` and is used to correct the eventual timings that the function displays after each of the test runs:

```
sngTime = Timer - sngStart - sngCorrection
Debug.Print "Run " & intLoop & ":  " & sngTime & " seconds"
```

Don't forget, if you do not want to build this `TestProcedure` function, you can find the code for this – and everything else in this chapter – in the `Performance.mdb` database.

You will notice that the code we test is in a `For...Next` loop which iterates many times. We need to do this because, although the `Timer` function is very accurate, each function executes extremely quickly and so executing many iterations of the function increases the accuracy of our measurement.

The sample timings shown in this chapter were produced on a 300MHz Pentium machine with 2 x 1Gb IDE disks (10ms access) and 96Mb RAM. These timings can also be found in the `Performance.xls` spreadsheet accompanying this book.

> If you want to test these code samples for yourself, just substitute the name of the procedure that you want to time in place of **TestProc** in the **TestPerformance** procedure.

When testing the execution speed of your code, you should make the test conditions as realistic as possible. In other words, test the application on the same specification of computer that will be used in production, load up any other applications which the users will be running, use realistic volumes of data and (if possible) have realistic numbers of users accessing the shared data in the database. Also, run your tests three or four times to see if performance varies from run to run. You might find that the first run of the following examples will give varying results as the code and any data has to be loaded into memory before it can be run. On subsequent runs the code and data should already be in memory so the speed will improve and the results will be more consistent.

Anyway, that's enough about timing our code. Let's get on with looking at methods for improving our code's performance...

Use Constants

If you use values in your code that do not change, then you should consider assigning them to constants rather than to variables. As well as the overhead incurred by dimensioning the variable, whenever a variable is encountered in a line of VBA code, Access needs to access the memory location that contains the variable in order to determine the value of the variable. In contrast, the value of a constant is resolved and written into the code at compile time. As a result, reading values from constants generally works out slightly quicker than reading values from variables.

Like variables, constants can be declared at the procedure or at the module level and can have either Public *or* Private *scope.*

```
Sub ConstantsNotVariables()

Const sDummy = "This is a string which is saved as a constant " & _
               "rather than as a variable. This means that it is " & _
               "resolved and written into the code at compile time."

Const sDummy2 = "This is a string which is saved as a constant " & _
                "rather than as a variable. This means that it is " & _
                "resolved and written into the code at compile time."

If sDummy = sDummy2 Then
End If

End Sub
```

```
Sub VariablesNotConstants()

Dim sDummy As String
Dim sDummy2 As String

sDummy =  "This is a string which is saved as a variable " & _
          "rather than as a constant. This means that it has to be " & _
          "retrieved every time it needs to be used."

sDummy2 = "This is a string which is saved as a variable " & _
          "rather than as a constant. This means that it has to be " & _
          "retrieved every time it needs to be used."

If sDummy = sDummy2 Then
End If

End Sub
```

Procedure	Iterations	Elapsed Time	Improvement
VariablesNotConstants	30,000	755 ms	
ConstantsNotVariables	30,000	320 ms	2.36 times

Don't be vague!

Although the use of 'loose' data types such as Variant and Object can make it easier to write generic code, they are usually slower to use than more specific data types.

Use Specific Object Types (Early Binding)

In Chapter 13 we looked at the difference between using early and late binding. The two procedures that we looked at were GetObjectArea (which used late binding), and GetShapeArea (which used early binding).

```
Function GetObjectArea(obj As Object, _
                       Side1 As Double, _
                       Side2 As Double, _
                       Side3 As Double) As Double

    obj.Construct Side1, Side2, Side3
    GetObjectArea = obj.Area

End Function
```

Although this code will run, it is not very efficient. Because the object variable obj has been declared As Object, Access does not know what type of object it is. This in turn means that whenever we try to inspect or set a property value, or invoke a method against that object at run-time, Access must first check whether or not that property or method is appropriate for the object.

```
Function GetShapeArea(shp As Shape, _
                      Side1 As Double, _
                      Side2 As Double, _
                      Side3 As Double) As Double

    shp.Construct Side1, Side2, Side3
    GetShapeArea = shp.Area

End Function
```

The second procedure uses what is known as **early binding**. This time around, Access knows what type of object shp is. This means that it can determine at compile time which properties and methods are appropriate to it. Because Access only has to perform this check once, and it does it prior to run-time, the difference in execution speed at run time between code using the two methods can be very significant.

A secondary advantage of early binding is that because Access can determine which properties and methods are appropriate at compile time, any errors in your code which result from misspelling property or method names are caught at compile time rather than appearing as run-time errors. In addition, without early binding you won't see the auto-complete features of VBA such as Auto List Members and Auto Quick Info.

The procedures we use to test these two techniques are shown below:

```
Sub UseLateBinding()

Dim tri As Triangle
Set tri = New Triangle

GetObjectArea tri, 5, 6, 7

End Sub
```

```
Sub UseEarlyBinding()

Dim shp As shpTriangle
Set shp = New shpTriangle

GetShapeArea shp, 5, 6, 7

End Sub
```

Procedure	Iterations	Elapsed Time	Improvement
UseLateBinding	30,000	22033 ms	
UseEarlyBinding	30,000	5129 ms	4.3 times

Use Variables, Not Properties

You can realize similar performance benefits if you use variables to refer to forms, controls and properties. If you are going to refer to a form, report or control more than once in a procedure, you should create an object variable for the object and then refer to that instead of the object itself.

The following procedure opens the Switchboard form and determines whether the name of various command buttons on that form is "Blobby". If any of the buttons does have that name, then code execution will stop on the line which performs the comparison for that button.

The Assert method of the Debug object is useful for debugging and causes code execution to stop when a given expression (like frm.cmdExit.Name <> "Blobby") evaluates to False.

```
Sub UseFormVariables()

Dim frm As Form_frmSwitchboard
Set frm = Forms("frmSwitchboard")
```

```
Debug.Assert frm.cmdExit.Name <> "Blobby"
Debug.Assert frm.cmdIceCreams.Name <> "Blobby"
Debug.Assert frm.cmdIngredients.Name <> "Blobby"
Debug.Assert frm.cmdMaintenance.Name <> "Blobby"
Debug.Assert frm.cmdReports.Name <> "Blobby"
Debug.Assert frm.cmdSuppliers.Name <> "Blobby"

Set frm = Nothing

End Sub
```

Alternatively, we could have rewritten this code to take advantage of the With structure.

```
Sub UseFormVariablesAndWith()

Dim frm As Form_frmSwitchboard
Set frm = Forms("frmSwitchboard")

With frm
    Debug.Assert .cmdExit.Name <> "Blobby"
    Debug.Assert .cmdIceCreams.Name <> "Blobby"
    Debug.Assert .cmdIngredients.Name <> "Blobby"
    Debug.Assert .cmdMaintenance.Name <> "Blobby"
    Debug.Assert .cmdReports.Name <> "Blobby"
    Debug.Assert .cmdSuppliers.Name <> "Blobby"
End With

Set frm = Nothing

End Sub
```

Code written using either of these two syntaxes will execute considerably faster than code which uses the long-hand syntax.

```
Sub UseLongHandSyntax()

Debug.Assert Forms!frmSwitchboard!cmdExit.Name <> "Blobby"
Debug.Assert Forms!frmSwitchboard!cmdIceCreams.Name <> "Blobby"
Debug.Assert Forms!frmSwitchboard!cmdIngredients.Name <> "Blobby"
Debug.Assert Forms!frmSwitchboard!cmdMaintenance.Name <> "Blobby"
Debug.Assert Forms!frmSwitchboard!cmdReports.Name <> "Blobby"
Debug.Assert Forms!frmSwitchboard!cmdSuppliers.Name <> "Blobby"

End Sub
```

In this situation the With...End With syntax is only fractionally faster than the first method which simply uses object variables. This is because of the overhead involved in setting up the With structure. However, you would find that if you were to add more and more references to the specified object between the With and End With statements, then this structure would become even more efficient.

Procedure	Iterations	Elapsed Time	Improvement
UseLongHandSyntax	30,000	68675 ms	
UseFormVariables	30,000	48095 ms	1.43 times
UseFormVariablesAndWith	30,000	46465 ms	1.48 times

Avoid Slow Structures

Another way to make your VBA code run faster is to avoid using slow structures. What does this mean? Well, most languages offer the programmer several different methods of performing a single task. If real execution speed is a coding priority, you should test each of these different methods for speed and decide which to use accordingly. For example, in Chapter 13 we discovered that there are two methods of determining the area of a triangle, given the lengths of all three sides.

Method A: (Trigonometrical Method)

```
Function Area1(dblSide1 As Double, _
               dblSide2 As Double, _
               dblSide3 As Double) As Double

Dim dblAngle1 As Double

dblAngle1 = ((dblSide2 ^ 2) + (dblSide3 ^ 2) - (dblSide1 ^ 2)) _
        / (2 * dblSide2 * dblSide3)
dblAngle1 = Atn(-dblAngle1 / Sqr(-dblAngle1 * dblAngle1 + 1)) + 2 * Atn(1)

Area1 = dblSide2 * dblSide3 * Sin(dblAngle1) * 0.5

End Function
```

Method B: (Heron's Formula)

```
Function Area2(dblSide1 As Double, _
               dblSide2 As Double, _
               dblSide3 As Double) As Double

Dim dblSemiPerim As Double

dblSemiPerim = (dblSide1 + dblSide2 + dblSide3) / 2

Area2 = Sqr((dblSemiPerim) * _
        (dblSemiPerim - dblSide1) * _
        (dblSemiPerim - dblSide2) * _
        (dblSemiPerim - dblSide3))

End Function
```

Both functions return identical results, but the second of these executes noticeably faster. In this situation, there would seem to be little reason not to choose the second method. However, in other situations you might find that the faster method conflicts with another of the project's coding priorities, so you may have to compromise. Even if this is the case, though, the time spent timing the code will not have been wasted as you will be able to use this knowledge in future projects.

Procedure	Iterations	Elapsed Time	Improvement
Area1	30,000	386 ms.	
Area2	30,000	108 ms.	3.57 times

Other examples of potentially slow structures are now described.

Immediate If (IIf)

The Immediate If (IIf) function is often viewed as a quick and easy way to return one of two values depending on whether an expression evaluates to True. We looked at this function in Chapter 5. Its syntax is:

```
value = IIf(Expression, TruePart, FalsePart)
```

TruePart is returned if Expression is True and FalsePart is returned if Expression is False. This is the same as writing:

```
If Expression Then
    value = TruePart
Else
    value = FalsePart
EndIf
```

However, the key difference between the two formats is that the IIf function will always evaluate both TruePart and FalsePart, whereas the normal If structure will only evaluate the part which is returned. To see the implications of this, consider these two portions of code:

```
Function IIfTest(lngNumber As Long)

Dim lngRetVal As Long

lngRetVal = IIf(lngNumber = 5, 10, _
                DMin("Quantity", "tblSales", "AmountPaid > 180"))

End Function
```

```
Function IfTest(lngNumber As Long)

Dim lngRetVal As Long

If lngNumber = 5 Then
    lngRetVal = 10
Else
    lngRetVal = DMin("Quantity", "tblSales", "AmountPaid > 180")
End If

End Function
```

Both of these procedures do the same thing. They evaluate the variable lngNumber and if it is equal to 5, the procedure sets the value of lngRetVal to 10. If it isn't, the procedure sets the value of lngRetVal to a value that it looks up in the tblSales table.

The difference between the procedures is that the first one will always look up the record from tblSales whether it's required or not. So whenever these procedures are called with lngNumber equal to 5, the first one will be considerably slower.

Procedure	Iterations	Elapsed Time	Improvement
IIfTest (10)	3,000	48666 ms	
IfTest (10)	3,000	46271 ms	1.05 times
IIfTest (5)	3,000	48662 ms	
IfTest (5)	3,000	13 ms	3743.23 times

Use Integer Arithmetic Where Possible

The speed with which arithmetic calculations are performed depends on the data type of the variables concerned and the type of operation being performed.

In general, however, Integer and Long variables are faster than Single and Double variables. These, in turn, are faster than Currency variables. Variant variables are considerably slower, with most operations taking typically twice as long as with other data types.

Although the difference in execution times for a single operation is very small, it will become more noticeable for repeated operations (such as within large loops).

Use In-Line Code

Earlier on, we noted that variables could be passed as arguments to procedures by reference or by value. When a variable is passed by reference (the default), the procedure that is called is passed a pointer to the memory location of the variable being passed. In contrast, when a variable is passed by value, a copy of the variable is made and is passed to the procedure. Although passing variables by value has its uses, it is fractionally slower than passing by reference.

Both of these methods are slower, however, than placing the code in-line (within the body of the original procedure). The downside of in-line code is that it is more difficult to maintain if you have the same code appearing in-line in multiple procedures. In addition, having the same code appearing in-line in multiple procedures will increase the memory footprint of your code. But if your chief coding priority is execution speed, you should seriously consider using in-line code, particularly if this code is frequently called or within in a loop structure.

The following procedures can be used to illustrate the difference between the three methods described above:

```
Sub TestPassingByValue()

Dim dbl1 As Double
Dim dbl2 As Double

dbl1 = 1234

'Placing the argument in parentheses passes it by value
dbl2 = FourthPower((dbl1))

End Sub
```

```
Sub TestPassingByReference()

Dim dbl1 As Double
Dim dbl2 As Double

dbl1 = 1234

'Passing by reference
dbl2 = FourthPower(dbl1)

End Sub
```

```
Sub TestPassingInLine()

Dim dbl1 As Double
Dim dbl2 As Double

dbl1 = 1234

'Inline coding
dbl2 = dbl1 ^ 4

End Sub
```

```
Function FourthPower(dblVal As Double)

FourthPower = dblVal ^ 4

End Function
```

Procedure	Iterations	Elapsed Time	Improvement
TestPassingByValue	30,000	215 ms	
TestPassingByReference	30,000	207 ms	1.04 times
TestPassingInLine	30,000	61 ms	3.52 times

Use DoEvents Judiciously

When a VBA procedure is running, it will act very selfishly and hog the Access limelight unless you tell it otherwise. For example, if you were to run the following portion of code, you would find that Access was locked up until the code finished running.

```
Sub NoDoEvents

Dim lngCounter As Long
Dim i As Integer

For lngCounter = 1 to 1000000
    i = Rnd*12
Next lngCounter

End Sub
```

This routine takes approximately 1.7 seconds to execute on my computer. But it is considered good etiquette (and common sense) to yield control to Windows every so often. For example, while your routine is running you may wish to cancel it, pause it for a moment or do something else. If your routine ignored all your requests then you wouldn't be very happy. What you need is a way to allow other events to be processed while your routine runs.

This can be achieved with the DoEvents statement. This instructs Windows to process any messages or keystrokes that are currently queued. In the following portion of code, whenever the loop reaches the DoEvents statement, control passes to Windows which checks to see whether any other application has any messages or keystrokes waiting to be processed. It then passes control back to the procedure.

```
Sub AllDoEvents

Dim lngCounter As Long
Dim i As Integer

For lngCounter = 1 to 1000000
    i = Rnd*12
    DoEvents
Next lngCounter

End Sub
```

Although this is good practice, it does take up time. In fact, the routine, which checks for events every time the loop is passed through, takes *over 50 minutes* to run! If you want to use the DoEvents statement, do so sparingly. The portion of code shown above can be rewritten like this:

```
Sub SomeDoEvents

Dim lngCounter As Long
Dim i As Integer

For lngCounter = 1 to 1000000
    i = Rnd*12
    If lngCounter Mod 50000 = 0 Then DoEvents
Next lngCounter

End Sub
```

Now, control passes to Windows every 50,000 loops. This means 20 times in the 2.4 seconds or so that the loop now takes to finish, which leaves you with a well-behaved and yet fast bit of code. The DoEvents adds only 0.7 seconds to the execution time of this code.

Procedure	Iterations	Elapsed Time	Difference
NoDoEvents	1 x 1,000,000	1672 ms.	
AllDoEvents	1 x 1,000,000	3081340 ms.	+51.33 min.
SomeDoEvents	1 x 1,000,000	2416 ms.	+0.74 sec.

Obviously, the number of DoEvents statements that you actually use will vary depending on the degree of interactivity that the procedure demands. For example, a procedure that runs for 10 minutes at the dead of night when everyone is in their beds and while no other applications are running will typically require less interactivity (and thus fewer DoEvents statements) than a procedure which updates the screen to display real-time stock prices to a user.

*Whenever you yield control to the processor from within a procedure, you should always write your code in such a way that the procedure will not be executed again from a different part of your code before the first call returns. If it does (this is called **reentrancy**) your code will probably not work the way you intended it to and the application may either hang or crash.*

Use the Requery Method, not the Requery Action

Another method of speeding up your procedures is to avoid using the Requery action to display up-to-date values in a form or control. Use the Requery method instead. This is quicker as it simply re-runs the query behind the form or control instead of closing it, re-opening it and then re-running it, as the Requery action does.

```
DoCmd Requery ctlText.Name          'This is slow

ctlText.Requery                     'This is much quicker
```

Use Me

When you use the Me keyword to refer to a form within an event procedure, Access only searches in the local name space for the form. This means that the form is found more quickly than if the full reference to the form is specified.

```
Forms!frmFoo.BackColor = QBColor(9)     'This is slow

Me.BackColor = QBColor(9)               'This is quicker
```

Speed Up Database Operations

Whereas the optimizations you can realize through changing the syntax of your VBA are sometimes marginal, optimizing your database calls almost always leads to substantial performance benefits. The reason for that is simple. Database calls generally take longer to execute than normal VBA statements because they involve accessing the hard disk as opposed to changing the contents of the computer's memory, so a 10% improvement in performance in both will be more noticeable in the case of the database call. We'll look below at some of the ways you can improve the way that VBA code interacts with your database.

Creating Test Data

When you run your performance testing, you should replicate both the expected data volumes and the conditions of the production environment as closely as you can. It may not always be possible to obtain a copy of live data to perform your testing against, so you may need to generate test data.

There are two stages to producing a set of test data: creating the test table(s) and populating the test table(s). To see how easy it can be to build large volumes of test data, let's try it out for ourselves.

Try It Out – Creating Test Data

1. Create a new database in which to store the test data that we will create. Call the new database `PerformanceData.mdb`.

2. In the `PerformanceData.mdb` database, switch to VBA by hitting *ALT+F11*.

3. Display the References dialog by selecting References... from the Tools menu. When the dialog appears, uncheck the reference to **Microsoft ActiveX Data Objects 2.1 Library** and check the reference to the **Microsoft DAO 3.6 Object Library**. Then hit the OK button.

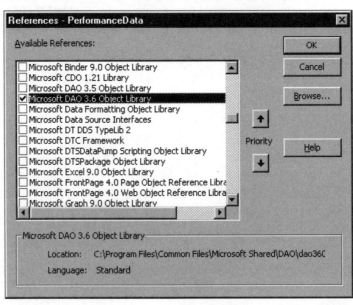

4. Next, create a new module by selecting Insert/Module from the toolbar.

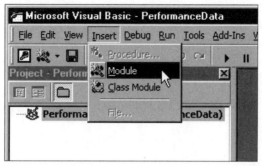

5. Add the following procedure to the new module. This will be used to create the test table.

```
Sub BuildPerformanceTable()

On Error GoTo BuildPerformanceTable_Error

Dim db As Database
Dim tdf As TableDef
Dim fld As Field
Dim idx As Index

Set db = CurrentDb()

'Try to delete the tblPerformance table
db.TableDefs.Delete ("tblPerformance")

'Create a new tabledef object
Set tdf = db.CreateTableDef("tblPerformance")

'Create and save an ID counter field
Set fld = tdf.CreateField("ID", dbLong)
fld.Attributes = fld.Attributes Or dbAutoIncrField
tdf.Fields.Append fld

'Create and save an unindexed 255-character text field
Set fld = tdf.CreateField("UnindexedText", dbText, 255)
tdf.Fields.Append fld

'Create and save an indexed 255-character text field
Set fld = tdf.CreateField("IndexedText", dbText, 255)
tdf.Fields.Append fld

Set idx = tdf.CreateIndex("TextIndex")
Set fld = idx.CreateField("IndexedText")
idx.Fields.Append fld
tdf.Indexes.Append idx

'Create and save an integer field
Set fld = tdf.CreateField("Num1in100", dbInteger)
tdf.Fields.Append fld
```

```
'Create and save another integer field
Set fld = tdf.CreateField("Num1in1000", dbInteger)
tdf.Fields.Append fld

'Create and save (yet) another integer field
Set fld = tdf.CreateField("Num1in10000", dbInteger)
tdf.Fields.Append fld

'Create and save a Yes/No field
Set fld = tdf.CreateField("YesNo", dbBoolean)
tdf.Fields.Append fld

'Save the tabledef into the database
db.TableDefs.Append tdf

BuildPerformanceTable_Exit:
  Exit Sub

BuildPerformanceTable_Error:
  Select Case Err
    Case 3265         'Item not found in this collection
      Resume Next
    Case Else
      MsgBox "The following unexpected error occurred:" & vbCrLf & _
          Err.Description & " (Error " & Err.Number & ")", vbCritical
      Resume BuildPerformanceTable_Exit
  End Select

End Sub
```

6. Next, add the following procedure to the new module. This will be used to insert the data into the newly created table:

```
Sub PopulatePerformanceTable(lngRecords As Long)

Dim lngRecordLoop As Long
Dim intLoop As Long
Dim recPerformance As Recordset
Dim strText As String

Set recPerformance = CurrentDb.OpenRecordset("tblPerformance", dbOpenDynaset, _
dbAppendOnly)

For lngRecordLoop = 1 To lngRecords

  'Prepare to add new record
  recPerformance.AddNew

  'Add string up to 5 chars long into [UnindexedText] field
  strText = ""
  For intLoop = 1 To (1 + Int(5 * Rnd))
    strText = strText & Chr$(65 + Int(26 * Rnd))
  Next intLoop
  recPerformance("UnindexedText") = strText
```

```
    'Add string up to 255 chars long into [IndexedText] field
    strText = ""
    For intLoop = 1 To (1 + Int(255 * Rnd))
        strText = strText & Chr$(65 + Int(24 * Rnd))
    Next intLoop
    recPerformance("IndexedText") = strText

    'Add integer between 1 and 100 into [Num1in100] field
    recPerformance("Num1in100") = 1 + Int(100 * Rnd)

    'Add integer between 1 and 1000 into [Num1in1000] field
    recPerformance("Num1in1000") = 1 + Int(1000 * Rnd)

    'Add integer between 1 and 10000 into [Num1in10000] field
    recPerformance("Num1in10000") = 1 + Int(10000 * Rnd)

    'Add True or False into [YesNo] field
    recPerformance("YesNo") = (Rnd < 0.5)

    'Save new record
    recPerformance.Update

Next

recPerformance.Close

MsgBox lngRecords & " rows were added to the tblPerformance table." & vbCrLf & _
    "It now has " & CurrentDb.TableDefs("tblPerformance").RecordCount & _
    " records."

End Sub
```

7. Check that there are no compilation errors in the code that you have just typed in by selecting Compile PerformanceData from the Debug menu.

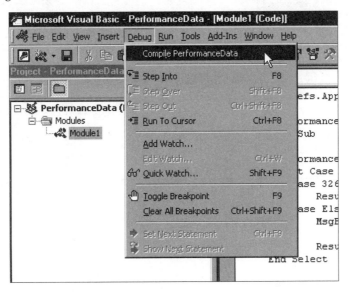

8. Now make sure that the Immediate window is visible by hitting *CTRL + G*. Run the procedure to create the test table by typing the following into the Immediate window and hitting *Enter*.

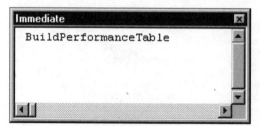

9. Check that the table has been created by switching back to Access. You can do this by hitting *ALT + F11*. The new table should appear in the database window. If it does not appear, you might have to refresh the database window by hitting *F5*:

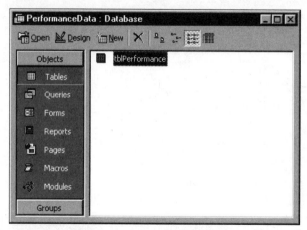

10. Now, switch back to VBA and populate the table with test data. To do this, type the following into the Immediate window and hit *Enter*.

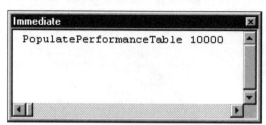

11. When the procedure has finished executing, a message box will inform you of the fact.

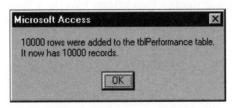

12. Switch back to Access and open the table. It should contain 10,000 records of random-looking data.

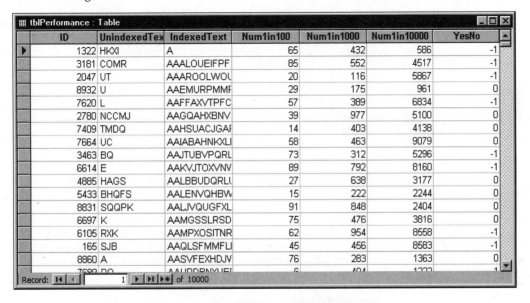

ID	UnindexedTex	IndexedText	Num1in100	Num1in1000	Num1in10000	YesNo
1322	HKXI	A	65	432	586	-1
3181	COMR	AAALOUEIFPF	85	552	4517	-1
2047	UT	AAAROOLWOL	20	116	5867	-1
8932	U	AAEMURPMMF	29	175	961	0
7620	L	AAFFAXVTPFC	57	389	6834	-1
2780	NCCMJ	AAGQAHXBNV	39	977	5100	0
7409	TMDQ	AAHSUACJGAF	14	403	4138	0
7664	UC	AAIABAHNKXLI	58	463	9079	0
3463	BQ	AAJTUBVPQRL	73	312	5296	-1
6614	E	AAKVJTOXVNV	89	792	8160	-1
4885	HAGS	AALBBUDQRLL	27	638	3177	0
5433	BHQFS	AALENVQHBW	15	222	2244	0
8831	SQQPK	AALJVQUGFXL	91	848	2404	0
6697	K	AAMGSSLRSD	75	476	3816	0
6105	RXK	AAMPXOSITNR	62	954	8558	-1
165	SJB	AAQLSFMMFLI	45	456	8583	-1
8860	A	AASVFEXHDJV	76	283	1363	0

Record: |◄ ◄| 1 |► ►| ►*| of 10000

13. Finally, save the module and take a look at the size of the database in Explorer. You should see that it is a little over 5 Mb. Not a bad amount of test data for five minutes' work!

How It Works

Don't be daunted by the length of the two procedures we use in this example. They are actually fairly straightforward. The first of these, the `BuildPerformanceTable` procedure, builds an empty table with the following structure:

Field	Datatype
ID	AutoNumber
UnindexedText	Text(5)
IndexedText	Text(255)
Num1in100	Integer
Num1in1000	Integer
Num1in10000	Integer
YesNo	Yes/No

It creates this table by using DAO, which is the reason that we replace the default reference to ADO with a reference to DAO in step 3.

The first task in the `BuildPerformanceTable` procedure is to delete any existing tables with the name `tblPerformance`. Although not necessary in the exercise above, this step is useful if you are going to execute this procedure more than once.

```
db.TableDefs.Delete ("tblPerformance")
```

However, it could be that there was no existing table with that name (such as when this procedure is run for the first time), in which case this line of code would normally cause a run-time error to occur.

That is why our error handler contains a test for that specific error code.

```
BuildPerformanceTable_Error:
    Select Case Err
        Case 3265        'Item not found in this collection
            Resume Next
        Case Else
            MsgBox "The following unexpected error occurred:" & vbCrLf & _
                Err.Description & " (Error " & Err.Number & ")", vbCritical
            Resume BuildPerformanceTable_Exit
    End Select
```

If the error does occur, we simply ignore the error and resume execution on the next line of code in the main body of the procedure. Any other errors that occur cause a generic message box to display the error code and description.

The next step is to create the table and append the seven fields to it. This is all fairly straightforward and should hold few surprises for you.

If you aren't quite sure how this table creation process works, it is described in much more detail in Chapter 8.

Once we have created the table, we need to populate it with random data. That is what the `PopulatePerformanceTable` procedure does.

If you have read the previous chapters in this book, then there should be little to surprise you in this procedure. The first step is to open the recordset that will be used to insert new records into:

```
Set recPerformance = CurrentDb.OpenRecordset("tblPerformance", dbOpenDynaset, _
dbAppendOnly)
```

The important feature to notice here is the fact that the `Recordset` has been opened with the `dbAppendOnly` flag. This indicates that an empty `Recordset` should be opened for the sole purpose of adding new records. This speeds up the opening of the `Recordset`, especially in situations where the underlying table contains a large number of records.

The next step is to prepare to insert the specified number of records. The basic structure for adding new records looks like this:

```
For lngRecordLoop = 1 To lngRecords

    'Prepare to add new record
    recPerformance.AddNew
    .
    .
    .
    'Save new record
    recPerformance.Update

Next
```

If you remember back as far as Chapter 7, you will recall that there are three steps to adding records to a recordset. First, a new record is placed into the copy buffer:

```
recPerformance.AddNew
```

Next, the fields in the copy buffer are amended. And finally, the contents of the copy buffer are appended to the table.

```
recPerformance.Update
```

That's straightforward enough, but how do we generate the random data that we will insert into the table? The key to it is the `Rnd` statement.

Generating Random Numbers

The Rnd statement generates a pseudo-random number which is greater than or equal to 0 and less than 1. We can take advantage of the Rnd function to define both a random length and a random value for data to be inserted. Inserting a random integer between 1 and, say, 100 is simple enough:

```
recPerformance("Num1in100") = 1 + Int(100 * Rnd)
```

The Int function truncates numbers rather than rounding them. So, if a number generated by the Rnd function satisfies this condition,

$$0 \leq r < 1$$

then (100*Rnd) yields this

$$0 \leq r < 100$$

and Int(100*Rnd) yields an integer such that

$$0 \leq r \leq 99$$

To yield an integer between 1 and 100, rather than between 0 and 99, we simply add 1.

```
1 + Int(100 * Rnd)
```

So adding random numbers poses no problems. But how do we add random text strings? The answer is to use to the Chr$ function. This returns a character based on its ANSI code. The American National Standards Institute (ANSI) character set used by Microsoft Windows contains 256 characters. The first 32 characters (from 0 to 31) represent special characters such as tab and backspace characters. The next 96 characters (from 32 to 127) correspond to the letters and symbols on a standard U.S. keyboard. The final 128 characters represent special characters, such as letters in international alphabets, accents, currency symbols, and fractions. Appendix G lists the ANSI character set:

If you look at the ANSI character set, you will notice that the letters A-Z have ANSI codes ranging from 65-90. So, if we want to generate a random letter between A and Z we need to generate an integer between 65 and 90 and pass that number to the Chr$ function. That is just what this line does:

```
strText = strText & Chr$(65 + Int(26 * Rnd))
```

If we want our string values to be of random length between 1 and 5 characters, we simply need to execute this line of code a random number of times between 1 and 5.

```
For intLoop = 1 To (1 + Int(5 * Rnd))
    strText = strText & Chr$(65 + Int(24 * Rnd))
Next intLoop
```

You can also determine a character's ANSI code by using the Asc function, e.g. Asc("A") returns 65.

In some situations you might want to be able to generate a reproducible series of random numbers. You can easily do this by resetting the Rnd function. We can do this by passing a negative number to the Rnd function. For example, the following procedure will always generate the same random numbers.

```
Sub PseudoRandom()

Dim i As Integer

Rnd (-2)
For i = 1 To 5
    Debug.Print Rnd
Next

End Sub
```

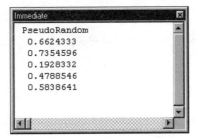

To generate a different series of reproducible random numbers, simply pass a different negative number to the Rnd function.

Of course, the numbers returned by Rnd – just like the numbers returned by any mathematical algorithm - are not truly random. They are pseudo-random. However, they are random enough for the purpose of generating test data!

Populating the Test Table

To fill the table with random data, we simply need to run the PopulatePerformanceTable procedure, passing to it as an argument the number of records that we wish to insert. When the procedure has finished executing, it displays a message box explaining the number of records it has added and the total number of records now in the table.

Be careful not to get carried away when running this procedure. On a PC with a 300 MHz Pentium processor and 64Mb of memory this procedure will add records at a rate of nearly 250 per second. Put another way, that means that the database will grow at a rate of around 10 Mb per minute!

Something else to be wary of is the fact that deleting and recreating tables can quickly lead to database bloat. That is a condition which arises when unused space is not reclaimed as objects are deleted and it manifests itself in ever increasing database sizes. To reduce database bloat, you should compact the database regularly, a task described in more detail later on in this chapter.

Fortunately, the new auto-compact feature in Access 2000 means that bloated databases will automatically be compacted when they are closed.

So now we have a relatively straightforward method for generating large volumes of test data at great speed. Now let's look at some ways that we can improve access to that data.

Use Indexes

Adding an index to a field can be an excellent way of improving the performance of searches on that field. Although adding indexes slows updates and increases locking contention, very often this overhead is more than offset by the performance benefits gained if the fields are frequently used for query searches.

The following procedure counts the number of records in which the IndexedText field begins with the letter X, using the set of 10,000 records which we created in the previous exercise:

```
Sub IndexedSQL()

Dim strSQL As String
Dim rec As Recordset

strSQL = "SELECT Count(*) FROM tblPerformance WHERE IndexedText LIKE 'X*'"
Set rec = CurrentDb.OpenRecordset(strSQL, dbOpenDynaset)
rec.Close

End Sub
```

Whereas this procedure runs the same query against the UnindexedText field.

```
Sub UnindexedSQL()

Dim strSQL As String
Dim rec As Recordset

strSQL = "SELECT Count(*) FROM tblPerformance WHERE UnindexedText LIKE 'X*'"
Set rec = CurrentDb.OpenRecordset(strSQL, dbOpenDynaset)
rec.Close

End Sub
```

On my computer the indexed search took one second the first time it was run and less than half a second for subsequent executions. By way of contrast, the unindexed search took over half a minute the first time and about 3 seconds subsequently.

Operation	Elapsed Time	Improvement
UnindexedSQL (1st run)	16760 ms	
IndexedSQL (1st run)	443 ms	37.83 times
UnindexedSQL (subsequent runs)	2979 ms	
IndexedSQL (subsequent runs)	381 ms	7.82 times

> The vast difference between the first and subsequent executions of these searches shows the impact of caching. The first time that these searches are performed, the data has to be physically read in from disk, whereas for subsequent searches the data only needs to be read in from memory – a substantially faster operation.

Use Appropriate Recordset Types

Another way of increasing the performance of data access in code is to use a more efficient type of `Recordset` object, a subject we have already looked at in Chapter 7.

```
Sub TestSnapshot()

Dim strSQL As String
Dim rec As Recordset

strSQL = "SELECT * FROM tblPerformance WHERE IndexedText > 'N*'"
Set rec = CurrentDb.OpenRecordset(strSQL, dbOpenSnapshot)
rec.MoveLast
rec.Close

End Sub
```

The procedure above returns all of the records from the `tblPerformance` table which have a value in the `IndexedText` field which begins with an `N` or any letter alphabetically after `N`.

Because dynaset-type `Recordset` objects only cache a copy of the key values of the result set, they will typically open more quickly than snapshot-type `Recordset` objects in situations where the result set is larger than, say, 500 records.

```
Sub TestDynaset()

Dim strSQL As String
Dim rec As Recordset

strSQL = "SELECT * FROM tblPerformance WHERE IndexedText > 'N*'"
Set rec = CurrentDb.OpenRecordset(strSQL, dbOpenDynaset)
rec.MoveLast
rec.Close

End Sub
```

Where the result set is extremely large, or where the base tables are located on the other side of a slow network, the difference can be quite significant.

The following table indicates the results of running these two procedures against a `tblPerformance` table with 30,000 rows (of which approximately half are returned by the query).

Procedure	Elapsed Time	Improvement
TestSnapshot (1ˢᵗ run)	34289 ms.	
TestDynaset (1ˢᵗ run)	13659 ms.	2.51 times
TestSnapshot (subsequent runs)	22078 ms.	
TestDynaset (subsequent runs)	72 ms	306.64 times

If you cannot use a dynaset-type `Recordset` object, you might find that you achieve slightly better performance if you use a forward-only `Recordset` object.

These only allow you to scroll downwards through a recordset and you cannot use certain methods (e.g. `MoveLast`) against recordsets created like this. Although this means that you cannot use forward-only recordsets in all situations, the fact that they do not need a complicated cursoring mechanism means that they will often outperform conventional recordsets.

In a multi-user environment, you might also see some small advantage from using read-only recordsets.

Still better performance gains, however, can be achieved by opening an append-only recordset. These recordsets are empty and can only be used to add new records, rather than for inspecting existing records. Because append-only recordsets do not require any records to be retrieved, they will typically open significantly faster than fully-populated recordsets, especially when the base table contains many records.

The performance of any of the `Recordset` types described in this section is highly dependent on the size of the base table, the restrictiveness of the criteria and which fields are indexed. In short, there is no substitute for performance testing on your own database.

Use Bookmarks

Each record in a recordset is automatically assigned a `Bookmark` when the recordset is opened. If you are in a recordset and know that you will want to move back to the record that you are currently on, you should save the record's `Bookmark` to a variable. By setting the `Bookmark` property of the `Recordset` object to the value you saved in the variable, you will be able to return to the record far more quickly than you would be able to if you used any of the `Find` or `Seek` methods.

Bookmarks are stored as arrays of byte data and so should be saved as byte arrays rather than strings. Although you can save a `Bookmark` to a string variable, comparing a record's `Bookmark` to a `Bookmark` stored in a string variable will not yield correct results, unless the comparison is performed as a binary comparison. For more information on using `Bookmarks` and performing binary comparison, refer to Chapter 7.

Increasing Apparent Speed

Although you may be able to do much to increase the real execution speed of your VBA code and your database calls, there is only so far you can go. So what happens if you have optimized your application for real execution speed and it still appears sluggish? One option is to increase the application's **apparent** speed. This is how fast the user *thinks* the application is, rather than how fast it really is.

> *Users of an application do not get upset when the application is slow. They get upset when they **notice** that it is slow! There is a big difference.*

Consider the following ways of making an application appear more quickly:

- ❑ Using a startup form
- ❑ Using gauges
- ❑ Removing code from form modules
- ❑ Pre-loading and hiding forms
- ❑ Caching data locally

Startup Forms and Splash Screens

One trusted method of distracting users from the fact that an application is taking a long time to perform some task is to distract them with some fancy graphics. After all, Microsoft do it all the time. What happens when you start up Access, Word or Excel? You see a startup form or **splash screen**:

"Gosh! That's pretty. I wish my application looked so professional!" you think to yourself. And by the time you have snapped out of your reverie, the application has loaded.

If there had been no splash screen you would have probably thought to yourself, "What on earth is happening! Why does it take so long for this application to start?" Splash screens really do work.

The good news is that it takes next to no effort to implement a splash screen in Access 2000. There are two techniques we can use. The first technique is to replace the Access splash screen with our own splash screen.

Try It Out – Creating A Custom Splash Screen

1. Create a new database and call it `splashy.mdb`. It doesn't matter where you create this database, so long as you keep a note of the directory it is in.

2. Now close the database and use Microsoft Paint or any other bitmap-editing tool to create a new bitmap file. (For the rest of this exercise, we will assume that Microsoft Paint is being used).

3. Change the size of the bitmap to an appropriate size for your target audience. If users will be viewing your database on screens with a resolution of 800 x 600 pixels, then a bitmap of 360 x 240 pixels will look good. At a resolution of 1024 x 768, a bitmap of 480 x 360 might look better. You can change the bitmap's size by selecting Attributes... from the Image menu and typing the new size into the Width and Height boxes in the dialog that subsequently appears.

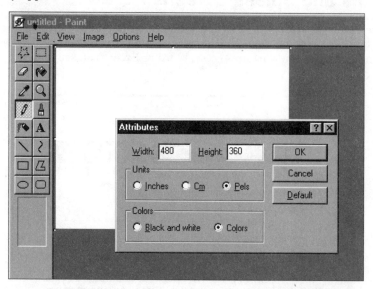

4. Now let your artistic talents roam free. Remember, this is the image that we will use to replace the default Access splash screen, so use your creative talents wisely!

5. When you have finished creating the image, close down Microsoft Paint and when prompted, save the bitmap as `splashy.bmp`. Place it in the same directory as the database that we created in step 1.

6. Now locate the database `splashy.mdb` in Explorer and double-click its icon to open it up. And look at that! Your artistic masterpiece is displayed in place of the normal Access splash screen! Doesn't that look good?

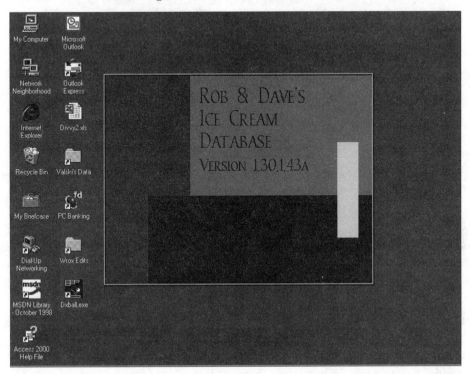

7. Well, maybe not!

As the exercise above shows, to create a custom splash screen for a particular database, simply create an appropriate bitmap with the same name as the database in the database's directory. You should note, however, that this custom splash screen will only be displayed when you open the database directly. In other words, if you start Access and then open the `splashy.mdb` database from within Access, the custom splash screen will not be shown.

Using a Start-Up Form

Once the database has opened, you can also configure a database form to be the **start-up form**. A start-up form is simply an Access form which is displayed as soon as a database is opened. To make a form the start-up form, simply specify its name in the Display Form/Page box on the Tools/Startup... dialog in Access.

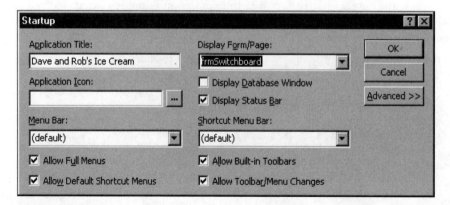

The example above will cause `frmSwitchboard` to be displayed as soon as Dave and Rob's Ice Cream database has been opened (but after the Access/custom splash screen and logon dialog box).

A word of warning – don't overload your startup form with too many controls or complex `Load` event code or else it will take too long for the form to appear, and you will have defeated the object of the exercise!

Use Gauges

Another way that you can distract users – and re-assure them that *something* is happening – is to show a meter displaying the progress of operations which are being performed. The `SysCmd` function provides a simple way of doing this. There are three steps involved in displaying a progress meter in the status bar of your application:

- ❑ Initialize the meter and specify its maximum value and text to be displayed
- ❑ Repeatedly update the meter to show progress
- ❑ Remove the meter

The following code illustrates one way of displaying a progress meter:

```
Sub ShowProgress()

Dim i As Integer
Dim j As Integer
Dim intRnd As Integer

'Initialise Progress Meter and set Maximum to 300
SysCmd acSysCmdInitMeter, "Testing...", 300

For i = 0 To 300
    'Perform some processing or other...
    For j = 0 To 10000          'Your real code
        intRnd = Rnd * 10 + 1   'would replace
    Next j                      'this test loop
```

```
    'Update Meter to Show Progress
    SysCmd acSysCmdUpdateMeter, i
    DoEvents
Next i

'Remove Meter from Status Bar
SysCmd acSysCmdRemoveMeter

End Sub
```

This procedure causes a gradually filling progress meter to be displayed with the text "Testing..."

The progress meter is displayed in the status bar of the main Access window, so you will have to switch from the VBA IDE to Access if you want to see it.

Of course, you do not need to set up a loop to update your progress meter. Instead you could structure your procedure like this:

```
Sub ShowProgress()

'Initialise Progress Meter and set Maximum to 30
SysCmd acSysCmdInitMeter, "Testing...", 30

'Perform some processing or other...
....
'Update Meter to Show Progress
SysCmd acSysCmdUpdateMeter, 5

'Perform more processing...
....
'Update Meter to Show Progress
SysCmd acSysCmdUpdateMeter, 10

'And yet more...
....
'Update Meter to Show Progress
SysCmd acSysCmdUpdateMeter, 15

.
.
.

'Remove Meter from Status Bar
SysCmd acSysCmdRemoveMeter

End Sub
```

The three constants `acSysCmdInitMeter`, `acSysCmdUpdateMeter` and `acSysCmdRemoveMeter`, which are used to initialize, update and remove the status bar, are intrinsic to Access. In other words, they are built into the Microsoft Access 9.0 Object Library. Since our project has a reference to that library, we do not need to declare these constants anywhere in our code.

Note also that the progress meter will only be shown if the status bar is visible in your database. To make it visible, select Startup from the Tools menu option (available when the database window is active) and tick the Display Status Bar option. You will have to reopen the database for this to take effect.

Remove Code from Form Modules

Users are likely to get irritated if they click a button to open a form and it then seems to take ages for the form to appear. This usually happens when a form has substantial amounts of code in its module which delays the form's loading. In this situation, you might consider removing the code from the form module and placing it in a standard code module. This will cause the form to load more quickly, as code will only be loaded on demand after the form has opened.

Pre-Load and Hide Forms

Alternatively, if you find that you use a form frequently and it takes a long time to load and unload, you might choose to load the form during the application's startup and then make it visible and invisible instead of loading and unloading it.

This technique will slow down the startup of your application but will appear to increase its subsequent performance. You can even delay the loading of the form until after the main form has already appeared. While the user is looking at the main form, the other form can be loading in the background.

This method works well if apparent speed is a coding priority, but it does increase the complexity of the application. You should also bear in mind that having several forms loaded concurrently will increase the application's memory usage.

Cache Data Locally

A **cache** is just an area of memory (or hard disk space) which is used to hold values that have been retrieved from somewhere else, ready to be used again. For example Windows 95 places the data that comes from your hard disk into a cache made up of an area of memory. Often a program uses the same data over and over again. This way it can just read it from the cache the next time instead of having to fetch it from the hard disk again. And of course reading from memory is much quicker and more efficient that reading from a hard disk.

So you can increase an application's performance by caching data in one form or another. In decreasing order of speed (in other words, fastest first), the three methods of data retrieval are:

- ❑ Reading data from memory (e.g. variables, arrays)
- ❑ Reading data from local tables
- ❑ Reading data from tables across the network

If you want to increase the perceived speed of your application, think about how you can cache data to 'move it up' a level.

If you keep frequently accessed, non-volatile data (in other words, data that doesn't change much) in a table on a network server, you might consider copying that data to the local client machine to make the application run faster. However, you will need to make sure that whenever data is updated on the server, it is also updated on all client machines as well (and vice versa).

Similarly, if you have data in a lookup table which you frequently access in VBA code, you could create an array to hold that data with the `GetRows` method. This could make retrieving the data substantially faster. However, it will also increase the memory usage of your application.

*Both these methods increase the **apparent** speed of your application. They may not increase the actual speed, because there will be a performance overhead involved in the process of caching the data in the first place. Remember that caching only works well if you need to read the data several times. If you only read it once, caching will slow your application down.*

Network Considerations

So far, we have concentrated on writing code that fits into as small an amount of memory, and can be executed as quickly as possible – or at least appears to do so. But that is only part of the story. One of the major reasons why Access database applications run slowly has nothing to do with memory footprints or code execution speed. Instead, the albatross around the neck of many applications is the vast amount of data which needs to be read from disk and passed across a network.

A network has two major drawbacks. Firstly, performance across a network – particularly a slow one – can be worse than performance against local tables. Secondly, you might find that your application generates a lot of network traffic. This will not make you popular with other users of the network, who find that their applications have slowed down considerably because of the log-jam. If either of these causes you a problem, consider:

- ❑ Searching on indexed fields in attached tables
- ❑ Putting non-table objects on the local machine
- ❑ Disabling `AutoExpand`

Search on Indexed Fields in Attached Tables

One method of minimizing the amount of data that an application has to read from disk is to ensure that fields used in the queries are indexed. If you run a query with a criterion against a field which is indexed, Access will be able to determine the exact data pages which contain the records it needs to retrieve in order to run the query. It will retrieve only the data pages that contain those records.

However, if you are running a query which uses a criterion against a field which is not indexed, Access will need to read into memory every single record in the underlying table, to see whether it meets the criterion. If the table is large and is on a network server, this will result in large amounts of network traffic and a very slow and frustrating query.

To look at an example of this in a little more detail, consider the following query:

```
SELECT *
FROM tblPerformance
WHERE ID=4000
```

If the ID field in tblPerformance is indexed, then the Jet engine knows that it will only need to retrieve the pages containing records with an ID of 4000 from the tblPerformance table.

However, if the ID field is not indexed, then Jet will have to read the whole of the tblPerformance table from disk and transfer it into the memory of the PC running the query. If the tblPerformance table is on a network server, this means that the whole table will need to be transferred across the network. Once it is in local memory, Jet can determine which records match the criterion by going through each record in turn and checking whether the ID field is equal to 4000. This is known as a table scan and is slow.

Imagine if the tblPerformance table contained half a million records, each approximately 260 bytes long. A table scan on an attached table would mean reading (500,000 x 260 bytes =) 130 Mb across the network and trying to fit them into local memory...

As a rule, therefore, always use indexes on fields which are involved in joins or which have criteria applied to them in queries.

Put Non-Table Objects on the Local Machine

Another way to minimize the amount of network traffic that a networked application generates is to place tables on the network server but to place other objects into a local copy of the database. Then the data in the tables can be shared by all users, but all other objects (queries, forms, reports, macros and modules) will reside on the local computer. Consequently, when that object is activated – say, when a form is opened – the computer only needs to read it into memory from its local disk. This will generally be quicker than loading it over the network and will also mean a noticeable reduction in network traffic.

The downside of this strategy is that you will have to distribute a new copy of the database to each user whenever you revise the code or any of the objects in it. Despite this, most applications benefit from this sort of segmentation.

Disable AutoExpand

The AutoExpand property of a combo box forces Access to fill it automatically with a value that matches the text you have typed. Although this is a neat feature and can make the process of filling in forms less of a chore, it comes at a price – the table that supplies the values has to be queried as the user types in text. If the table on which the combo box is based resides across the network the result may be a substantial increase in network traffic, especially if the combo box contains many values.

Finishing Touches

All of the tips so far have been aimed at specific coding priorities. Some increased real execution speed, others reduced network traffic, still others reduced the memory footprint of the database application.

In some cases, a single optimization may bring many benefits. For example, changing a variable's data type from variant to integer will reduce memory demands *and* may increase execution speed.

However, in other cases an optimization may have an antagonistic effect. It may bring a benefit *and* incur a cost. For example, loading forms and hiding them will increase the apparent execution speed of your application, but it will also increase your application's memory footprint. In that situation you must decide what your priorities are and act accordingly.

The final section of this chapter concentrates on the things that you can do which will always benefit your application – irrespective of your coding priorities. These include:

❑ Compacting the database

❑ Compiling all modules

❑ Opening databases exclusively .

Compact the Database

Over a period of time you may find that the performance of your database slowly degenerates. This may be because the database has become fragmented.

Fragmentation occurs when objects are deleted from a database, but the space used by those objects isn't reclaimed. The database becomes like a Swiss cheese – full of little holes. As pretty a simile as that may be, it also means that your database slows down. It's not damaged in any way, but performance suffers. This is because it is physically slower to read non-contiguous (fragmented) data from a disk than it is to read contiguous data.

Compacting a database removes any unused space (the holes in the cheese!) and makes all the data pages in the database contiguous. This has two benefits:

❑ Database performance improves

❑ The size of the database file is reduced

As well as allowing you to compact a database from the menu bar – just select Compact and Repair Database... from the Database Utilities submenu on the Tools menu – Access 2000 now provides you with the ability to compact databases automatically when they are closed. In order to turn on this feature, simply check the Compact on Close checkbox on the General tab of the Access Tools/Options... dialog box.

You can also compact a database from VBA, using the `CompactDatabase` method of the `DBEngine` object:

```
DBEngine.CompactDatabase "c:\myold.mdb","c:\mynew.mdb"
```

For optimal performance, you should occasionally use a disk defragmentation program (such as the Disk Defragmenter supplied with Windows 95) before compacting your database.

Compile All Modules

You have been working feverishly all weekend to get that database application finished for Monday's demonstration to the board. You tested the application last night – making sure you tested it in a production environment – and it was really zippy. There's an hour to go and you think you might as well run that little library routine of yours to add fancy headers to the procedures. It only takes a couple of minutes to run and you've done it so often you know that it's bug free.

The time comes, the board members sit down and you hit the icon to start your application...and wait...and wait...and wait...

"Whaaaaat!" you scream, inwardly of course, "What's happened to my speedy app???" It's suddenly performing like a three-legged dog... in a coma. Looks like you forgot to re-compile your application!

When you make any changes to code in a standard code module or a class module (including form and report modules), the module has to be re-compiled before it can be run. To compile the code in all the modules in your database, choose Compile <ProjectName> from the Debug menu in the VBA IDE.

If you don't explicitly compile your code in this manner, VBA compiles your code at run-time. This can cause a significant delay, especially if there is a lot of code in the module being compiled. This delay is reduced, however, if you have checked the Compile On Demand box on the Module page of the Tools/Options... dialog. In this case, VBA only compiles the parts of the code that are called by the procedure that is executing – the call tree – rather than all of it. So there is less delay. However, to be safe, you should always compile all your code before delivery. After all, compilation will also detect compile-time errors such as a `For...` statement without a corresponding `Next` statement.

You can increase performance further still by saving your database as an MDE file. We looked at MDE files – and the whole area of compilation – in more detail in chapter 16.

Open Databases Exclusively

If you are the only person who will be using the database at any one time, you should open the database **exclusively**. This means that your application will perform better because Access will not have to spend time monitoring whether other users want to lock records. You can ensure that databases are opened exclusively by default by selecting Exclusive as the Default Open Mode on the Advanced page of theAccess Tools/Options... dialog.

If you use a command line to start your application, you can use the /Excl switch to achieve the same result.

```
c:\access\msaccess.exe c:\abwrox\code\wrox.mdb /Excl
```

And if you are opening the database in VBA, set the Exclusive argument to True when using the OpenDatabase method:

```
Set db = DBEngine(0).OpenDatabase("c:\abwrox\code\wrox.mdb", True)
```

Summary

Producing an application is one thing. Producing an application that runs (or at the very least, appears to run) quickly and doesn't hog the whole of your computer's memory is quite another – but this is what will make or break your application. Users are impatient beings, and to them there is nothing worse than an inefficient program.

This chapter has covered several tips and tricks for improving the general speed of your code. Before you start to put your application together, you should decide what your coding priorities are, and then follow the guidelines drawn up here to achieve them. Remember that optimizing for one priority, such as maintainability, may adversely affect a secondary aim, such as the speed of your code – it is up to you to decide which is more important.

> *Remember, also, that you can spend forever tweaking your application to go a fraction faster, but will it be worth the amount of time you're putting in? Do you have a deadline to meet? Is it worth it?*

So, in this chapter have covered:

- ❑ How to reduce memory overhead by choosing the right data types, reclaiming memory and grouping procedures strategically

- ❑ Which coding techniques to employ to increase execution speed

- ❑ Tricks, such as using a startup screen and progress gauges, to distract the user and make it appear that an application is running quicker

- ❑ How to make a networked application more efficient

Exercises

1. We can write a procedure in a number of ways according to our coding priorities. Try to write a procedure that tells you the delivery day for corn syrup (the second Wednesday of every month) for a given year and month. Now re-write the procedure so that it is optimized for:

- ❑ Real execution speed

- ❑ Maintainability

- ❑ Re-usability

2. Create a form and place a button on it. Now write a procedure that prints to the debug window the number of fields and records in each table in the database when the button is clicked. Now add a gauge to the status bar to display the progress of this operation.

Exercise Solutions

This chapter contains the exercises and solutions for the book Beginning Access 2000 VBA Programming. Where appropriate the code for the solutions are shown here, and if not, they are contained in `solutions.mdb`. This is a copy of `IceCream.mdb` as complete at the end of the book, but with the addition of the exercises completed.

Chapter 1

There are no exercises for this chapter.

Chapter 2

1. With Office applications you have the **Customize** dialog (available from **Toolbars** on the **View** menu) to allow you to create custom menus, toolbars and shortcut menus – something that was only possible with macros in previous versions of Access. Make sure that you know how to take advantage of this powerful new dialog. Try adding a menu bar to the **Company Details** form (`frmCompany`) that allows the user to navigate through the records in the same way as the buttons in the form footer without using macros.

Solution

There's no real solution to this – it was thought of more as a process of discovery for you. We hope you managed to try out the Customize stuff, as it's really good. If you had a little trouble playing with this, then there are a few easy things to remember:

❑   A right-mouse click over any menubar/toolbar will give the **Customize…** option and dialog (unless it's disabled for that bar).

❑   Dragging items between the toolbar and the **Customize** dialog adds and removes them.

❑   To add submenus pick the **Commands** tab and the **New Menu** Category. Then drag the **New Menu** command onto your toolbar.

Exercise Solutions

When the **Customize** dialog is displayed you can right-mouse click over a toolbar item to customize it further, changing the text, button image, etc.

2. The Autokeys macro is used to associate macro actions with keyboard shortcuts. Try using the Autokeys macro to display the property window whenever you hit *F4.* When does this shortcut not work? What happens if you try to associate this action with *Alt+F4* and why?

For a hint, use the Access Help and search for Autokeys using the Answer Wizard.

Solution

The macro name should be {F4}. We use curly braces to tell Access this is a special key (look under Autokeys in the help for a full description of the other keys). The `Action` should be `RunCommand` and the `Command` should be `Properties`. There are several places when this doesn't work. One is the Macro design Window. Another is when running a form. We are sure you found others, just by pressing *F4* wherever you were. You cannot assign any action to *Alt+F4*, as this is the Windows command to end an application.

Chapter 3

1. One of the most important things to remember when working with events in VBA is the order in which events occur. For example, when you save a record on a form, several events occur, one after another. By looking at the list of events on the property sheet, try to work out the order in which they happen.

Solution

There's also a good way to see this in action yourself. Create a new form and put Debug messages in each event handler that you are interested in. Then when you open the form the messages are written to the Debug window and you can see the order in which they have been displayed. The solutions database has a copy of the company form called `frmEventOrder`, which prints all of the events to the debug window. You might like to experiment with this. Be careful though, as it's based upon the company data, so any records you change affect the other forms and queries using this data.

2. Take some time to read through the list of events and their uses. You will find that some events are more useful that others – in other words, you will find yourself writing custom event handlers for some events more often that for other events. Look at the list and try to think about which events you would most commonly handle with custom event handlers.

Solution

This was really just a mental exercise. The most common event procedures are probably:

❑ The `Click` event for command buttons. This is generally used to close the current form, open new forms etc.

❑ The `Open` event for forms. This is typically used to set some properties on the form, perhaps depending upon some value on another form.

Chapter 4

1. Create a function called `Power` with two integer arguments, the second of which is optional. The function should raise the first argument to the power of the second. If the second argument is omitted then raise the first number to the power of 2.

Solution

This is quite simple, and can be done in two ways. The first uses a `Variant` argument and the `IsMissing` function:

```
Public Function Power (intNumber As Integer, _
              Optional intPower As Variant) As Long

    If IsMissing(intPower) Then
        Power = intNumber ^ 2
    Else
        Power = intNumber ^ intPower
    End If

End Sub
```

The second method uses a default value:

```
Public Function Power (intNumber As Integer, _
              Optional intPower As Integer = 2) As Long

    Power = intNumber ^ intPower

End Sub
```

You can see that the second method is much neater.

2. Spend some time looking through the help file, especially the list of VBA functions. You can find these under **Visual Basic Language Reference, Functions**.

Solution

There's obviously no solution to this one. The reason we've included this as an exercise is that it's important to know what functions are available, so that you don't constrain yourself by thinking that something is too hard to do. It will also save you having a good idea for a function, spending hours trying to write it, and then finding out that there's already a built in version.

Chapter 5

1. Using a control structure, create a procedure to print a number out as a string, such as those used on checks. For example, 120 should be printed as ONE TWO ZERO. Hint-Convert the number to a string first.

Solution

```
Function NumberToString(lngNumber As Long) As String

    Dim strNumber   As String      ' will hold the string of numbers
    Dim intLoop     As Integer     ' loop counter
    Dim strRV       As String      ' return value - ie the string
    Dim strTemp     As String      ' temporary work string

    ' convert the number into a string
    strNumber = lngNumber

    ' loop through each character in the string
    ' this will be a signle digit of the number
    For intLoop = 1 To Len(strNumber)
        ' extract the digit from the string and convert it
        ' to a name of the number
        Select Case Mid$(strNumber, intLoop, 1)
        Case "0"
            strTemp = "Zero"
        Case "1"
            strTemp = "One"
        Case "2"
            strTemp = "Two"
        Case "3"
            strTemp = "Three"
        Case "4"
            strTemp = "Four"
        Case "5"
            strTemp = "Five"
        Case "6"
            strTemp = "Six"
        Case "7"
            StrTemp = "Seven"
        Case "8"
            strTemp = "Eight"
        Case "9"
            strTemp = "Nine"
        End Select

        ' add the single digit name onto the full string
        strRV = strRV & strTemp & " "
    Next

    ' and return the string
    NumberToString = strRV

End Function
```

I've called the function NumberToString and it takes one argument, the number to convert. I've made this a long, so I'm assuming whole numbers. The first thing I do is assign the number to a string – this automatically converts it into a string of numbers for us. Next I loop from 1 to the number of characters in the string, and then I extract the current character and compare it to strings of the characters, setting a temporary variable to the string equivalent of the number. Before the loop cycles again, I append this temporary string to a string containing all of the numbers so far. And lastly I return the value.

2. Convert the above function to use an array of strings for the words and replace one of the control structures. Now compare this version with the previous version and think about how this type of look-up can be used to improve the speed of functions within loops.

Solution

```
Function NumberToString(lngNumber As Long) As String

    Dim strNumber   As String    ' will hold the string of numbers
    Dim intLoop     As Integer   ' loop counter
    Dim strRV       As String    ' return value - ie the string
    Dim strTemp     As String    ' temporary work string
    Dim astrNumbers As Variant   ' array of digit names
    Dim iNumber     As Integer   ' digit number

    ' create an array of the digit names
    astrNumbers = Array("Zero", "One", "Two", "Three", "Four", _
                        "Five", "Six", "Seven", "Eight", "Nine")

    ' convert the number into a string
    strNumber = lngNumber

    ' loop through each character in the string
    ' this will be a signle digit of the number
    For intLoop = 1 To Len(strNumber)
        ' extract the digit from the string and convert it
        ' to a single digit for the number
        iNumber = Int(Mid$(strNumber, intLoop, 1))

        ' use that digit to index into the array of names
        ' and add it to the string
        strRV = strRV & astrNumbers(iNumber) & " "
    Next

    ' return the string
    NumberToString = strRV

End Function
```

The function declaration is the same. As well as the other variables you notice I now have a Variant too - this is one time where they are useful, as I can now use the Array function. This takes a list of arguments and converts it into an array – very simple. You could use a normal string array and assign the values individually, but this way is much easier to code. Inside the loop I turn the individual number from the string back into an integer, and then I use this to index into the array. It's not much different in execution speed from the first example, but it's easier to maintain.

3. Create a user logon form that asks for a user name and a password and only lets the user carry on if the correct details have been entered. Think of two ways that you can use to make the user name case insensitive (so it ignores case)

Solution

I won't go into detail here, but just put a text box on a form and set its **Input Mask** property to **Password**. This is a special mask that shows a * for every character you type. Put a button on the form too, and in the `Click` event for this button just check the text from the textbox against a password string. The text won't contain the *, this is just the visible character. To make the password case insensitive use either `LCase` or `UCase` on the string entered before comparing it with the password. Chapter 16 looks at password forms in a little more detail, in particular a form that allows you to change user passwords.

Chapter 6

1. For the `FormsFonts` procedure, think about how you could make the changes to the font permanent. Remember that the `Forms` collection only shows the open forms, so you would have to use the `AllForms` collection. You should also remember that changes to a form opened in form view are never saved, so the form should be opened in design view. Have a look at the `OpenForm` and `Close` methods of the `DoCmd` object.

Solution

```
Sub PermanentFormFonts (strFont As String)

    Dim objAO       As AccessObject    ' an Access object - ie a form
    Dim objCP       As Object          ' Current Access project
    Dim ctlControl  As Control         ' control on a form

    ' point to the current project
    Set objCP = Application.CurrentProject

    ' loop through the forms in the project
    For Each objAO In objCP.AllForms
        ' open the form in design view, and hidden
        DoCmd.OpenForm objAO.Name, acDesign, , , , acHidden

        ' loop through the controls setting the font
        For Each ctlControl In objAO.Controls
            ctlControl.FontName = strFont
        Next

        ' close the form, saving the changes
        DoCmd.Close acForm, objAO.Name
    Next

End Sub
```

2. The above routine doesn't take into account controls that don't have a `FontName` property. You might like to amend it so that it does, in a similar fashion to the Try It Out – Objects, Controls and Errors.

Solution

```
Sub PermanentFormFonts (strFont As String)

    On Error GoTo PermanentFormFonts_Err

    Dim objAO       As AccessObject    ' an Access object - ie a form
    Dim objCP       As Object          ' Current Access project
    Dim ctlControl  As Control         ' control on a form

    ' point to the current project
    Set objCP = Application.CurrentProject

    ' loop through the forms in the project
    For Each objAO In objCP.AllForms
        ' open the form in design view, and hidden
        DoCmd.OpenForm objAO.Name, acDesign, , , , acHidden

        ' loop through the controls setting the font
        For Each ctlControl In objAO.Controls
            ctlControl.FontName = strFont
        Next

        ' close the form, saving the changes
        DoCmd.Close acForm, objAO.Name, acSaveYes
    Next

PermanentFormFonts_Exit:
    Exit Sub

PermanentFormFonts_Err:
    If Err.Number = 438 Then
        Resume Next
    Else
        MsgBox Err.Description
        Resume PermanentFormFonts_Exit
    End If

End Sub
```

Chapter 7

1. Earlier in this chapter we looked at the `AbsolutePosition` property of the recordset. See if you can use this to create a record indicator on the Company form (`frmCompany`). What are the limitations of this record indicator?

Exercise Solutions

Solution

There are a couple of ways you could use `AbsolutePosition` on the form. One way would be to just put a label on the form to indicate the current record number. Then, in the `Form_Current` event, after you have synchronized the bookmarks, just set this label to show the position, as so...

```
recClone.Bookmark = Me.Bookmark
lblPosition.Caption = recClone.AbsolutePosition
```

You might also want to blank this label for a new record.

Another way would be to put some sort of gauge on the form, to show how far into the records you are – you could also use the `PercentPosition` for this.

The limitation of this property is that for certain recordsets it does not get updated. Personally, I don't think a user should ever need to know the position of a record – it doesn't really make much sense, since the data can be re-ordered.

2. We mentioned earlier on that the `Relations` collection contains a `Relation` object for every relation defined between tables in a database. See whether you can write a procedure to document these relations in the Immediate window like this:

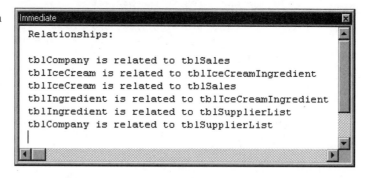

```
Relationships:

tblCompany is related to tblSales
tblIceCream is related to tblIceCreamIngredient
tblIceCream is related to tblSales
tblIngredient is related to tblIceCreamIngredient
tblIngredient is related to tblSupplierList
tblCompany is related to tblSupplierList
```

Solution

This is quite a simple procedure and relies upon the `Relations` collection:

```
Public Sub ShowRelations()

    Dim db          As Database     ' current database
    Dim relR        As Relation     ' an individual relation object
    Dim strDetail   As String       ' string of the relationship details

    ' point to the current database
    Set db = CurrentDb()

    Debug.Print "Relationshipts:"
    Debug.Print

    ' loop through the Relations collection
    For Each relR In db.Relations
        strDetail = relR.Table & " is related to " & relR.ForeignTable
        Debug.Print strDetail
    Next

End Sub
```

Chapter 8

1. You can use the Immediate window to inspect the properties of data access objects. What line would you have to type in the lower pane of the debug window to determine how many fields there are in the tblSales table?

Solution

There are two approaches you can use here:

```
?CurrentDb().TableDefs("tblSales").Fields.Count
```

or

```
?DBEngine.Workspaces(0).Databases(0).TableDefs("tblSales").Fields.Count
```

Although these produce the same result, there is a subtle difference. See the breakout box in Chapter 7, in the Database Object section for an explanation of this.

2. See if you can use the Immediate window to determine how many properties each of the fields in the tblSales table have. Why do some have more properties than others?

Solution

You can use a similar method to that shown above:

```
?CurrentDb().TableDefs("tblSales").Fields(0).Properties.Count
?CurrentDb().TableDefs("tblSales").Fields(1).Properties.Count
?CurrentDb().TableDefs("tblSales").Fields(2).Properties.Count
```

The difference between the number of properties is because of the different data types for the fields. Numeric fields, for example, have properties such as precision and number of decimal places etc., while text fields don't.

3. In this chapter, we used the BuildResultsTable procedure to build up the tblResults table from a given SQL string. We built the table by running a make-table query. See if you can rewrite the BuildResultsTable procedure to build the table using the Data Access Object hierarchy instead. Once the table has been built using DAO, the procedure should populate it with an append query, for example:

```
INSERT INTO tblResults SELECT SalesID FROM …
```

Exercise Solutions

Solution

This is really simple, and consists of only a few lines of code:

```
Dim db       As Database     ' current database
Dim tdfT     As TableDef     ' the new tabledef
Dim fldF     As Field        ' a new field

' point to the current database
Set db = CurrentDb()

' create a new tabledef - use strTableName as the name
Set tdfT = db.CreateTableDef(strTableName)

' create a new field
Set fldF = tdfT.CreateField("SalesID")

' set the field properties
fldF.Type = dbLong

' append the field to the Fields collection of the tabledef
tdfT.Fields.Append fldF

' append the tabledef to the TableDefs collection of the database
db.TableDefs.Append tdfT
```

The solutions database (solutions.mdb) has this code built into the BuildResultsTable function, in the code module for frmCriteria.

4. Next (if you are feeling really brave) see if you can modify the BuildResultsTable function so that it has more flexibility. Change the function so that the declaration looks like this:

```
Function BuildResultsTable(sSQL As String, _
                  sTableName As String, _
                  lRecordsAffected As Long, _
                  Optional vIndexed As Variant, _
                  Optional vMethod As Variant)
```

The function arguments we want you to use are described below:

This argument...	does this...
SSQL	supplies the SQL statement which was built up from the selections made on the criteria selection form.
sTableName	supplies the name for the table to be created.
lRecordsAffected	is used to return a long integer signifying the number of records placed into the new table.
vIndexed	is used to indicate whether the new table should be indexed on the SalesID field. If this argument is not supplied, the field will not be indexed.

This argument...	does this...
vMethod	is used to specify what method will be used to build the new table. If this argument is not supplied, the table will be created using a make-table query. The alternative is to use DAO which you should have completed in the previous exercise.

Solution

We won't go into the code here, as the solutions database (solutions.mdb) has this code built into the BuildResultsTable function, in the code module for the form frmCriteria.

5. Finally, see if you can modify the application so that it informs the user how many records met the criteria and asks whether the frmSales form should be displayed. Use this for the cmdFind_Click procedure on the criteria form and then put the required functionality into the DisplayResults procedure.

Solution

To do this you need to create a routine called DisplayResults:

```
Function DisplayResults(lRecords As Long) As Boolean

    Dim iReturn    As Integer    ' user response to question
    Dim sMsg    As String    ' string to display

    ' how many records were there
    Select Case lRecords
    Case 0
        sMsg = "No records matched the criteria you specified."
        MsgBox sMsg, vbExclamation, Application.Name
        DisplayResults = True
        Exit Function
    Case 1
        sMsg = "1 record matched the criteria you specified."
        sMsg = sMsg & vbCrLf & vbCrLf & "Would you like to see it?"
    Case Is > 1
        sMsg = lRecords & " records matched the criteria you specified."
        sMsg = sMsg & vbCrLf & vbCrLf & "Would you like to see them?"
    End Select

    ' ask the user if they want to see the results
    iReturn = MsgBox(sMsg, _
            vbQuestion + vbYesNo + vbDefaultButton1, _
            Application.Name)

    ' if yes, then show the sales form
    If iReturn = vbYes Then
        DoCmd.OpenForm "frmSales"
        DoCmd.Close acForm, Me.Name
    End If
```

```
        DisplayResults = True

End Function
```

This just accepts a single parameter to identify the number of records that matched the criteria. It then builds a string, which either tells the user that no records matched, or tells them how many matched and asks if they want to see the results. If they do wish to see the results the sales form is opened.

In the Click event for the Find button, instead of opening the form directly, we call the new procedure:

```
Private Sub cmdFind_Click()

Dim sSQL As String
Dim lRecordsAffected As Long

If Not EntriesValid Then Exit Sub

If Not BuildSQLString(sSQL) Then
    MsgBox "There was a problem building the SQL string"
    Exit Sub
End If

If Not BuildResultsTable(sSQL, "tblResults", lRecordsAffected, vMethod:="DAO",
vIndexed:=True) Then
    MsgBox "There was a problem building the results table"
    Exit Sub
End If

If Not DisplayResults(lRecordsAffected) Then
    MsgBox "There was a problem displaying the results"
    Exit Sub
End If

End Sub
```

Chapter 9

1. Use the Database Splitter to create a back-end and front-end database. Are there any changes you need to make to the front-end to make sure that it still works correctly?

Solution

The first part of this is just an experiment for you, just so you are familiar with how it works. There might be some changes to make, but it really depends upon how you've written your application. The main thing to look out for is use of the Seek method, as this is not valid against attached tables. Other than that you should find your application works as normal.

2. If you are connected to a mail system, create a form to allow users to fill in Bug Reports and Enhancement Requests, and use the SendObject method to let the user send them to you.

Solution

I won't put the form here, but it's in the solutions database, as `frmBugReport`.

I put on the form several fields:

- ❑ User Name
- ❑ Department
- ❑ Problem Description
- ❑ Severity (ie, "Can work around", "Fatal", etc)
- ❑ Date Occurred

Then I put a command button on the form, and in the **OnClick** event for the button I put this code:

```
DoCmd.SendObject acSendForm, "frmBugReport", acFormatTXT, _
     "Your Mail Name", , , "Bug Report", , False
```

This sends the text from the form as a mail attachment. You'll see other ways to do this later.

Chapter 10

1. For the filter form, how could you modify this so that instead of being fixed to the date ordered, you can pick any of the fields on the form?

Solution

It's fairly easy to do this, but there are limitations. Let's look at a solution that just allows you to pick fields from the detail section. Add a combo box (`cboField`) to the form and set its **Row Source Type** property to **Value List**. In the `Load` event for the filter form (`frmReportFilter`) you could have this code:

```
Dim ctlC        As Control    ' general control
Dim strField    As String     ' list of fields

' point to the open report
Set m_rptSales = Reports("Sales By Supplier By Month")

' loop through the controls in the detail section
For Each ctlC In m_rptSales.Section("Detail").Controls
    strField = strField & ctlC.Name & ";"
Next

' set the source of the combo to the string
cboField.RowSource = strField
```

This loops through the controls in the detail section and adds them to the combo box. You could equally loop through all controls on the Report, but this would show up all labels, lines, etc.

Exercise Solutions

In the Apply button, you then change the WHERE clause:

```
strWhere = "[" & cboField & "] " & _
    cboOperator & txtValue
```

So instead of using a fixed field name you use the name that's in the combo box.

The problem with this method is that the user has to add any field-specific bits – such as hash signs around the date or quotes around strings. The user will have to do this because you cannot find out what data type the control is. With a form, you have the Recordset property, which is the underlying set of records, and through this you can get the data type. Reports, however, don't have a Recordset property, so you can't get at the underlying data type. You could make a guess using the format of the field, but that's not guaranteed.

Chapter 11

1. Modify the frmCriteria form by giving it a custom property of type Long and called TimesOpened. Then you should try to write some code that increments the value of this new property whenever the form is opened.

Solution

The initial part of this is fairly easy, since it only involves creating a module level variable and a Property Get procedure:

```
Private m_lngTimesOpened As Long

Public Property Get TimesOpened() As Long

    TimesOpened = m_lngTimesOpened

End Property
```

That's the simple bit. What's harder is where to store this value on a permanent basis – remember that a private variable loses its value when it goes out of scope, and in this case that's when the form is closed. So, currently, this would only ever show a value of 0. The sensible place to store this is as a new property on the Document – remember how there are Containers (Tables, Queries, Forms, and so on) and each of these has a Documents collection? These collections store the saved form, and not just the active instance. So, for the Forms container, there is a Document named frmCriteria. If we create a property on this Document, then it's permanent.

One of the disadvantages of properties is that you can't check to see if the property exists or not. You have to access the property and then see if you get an error. Although this isn't complex, it makes your code a little less readable. One way around this is to create a couple of procedures, GetAccessProperty and SetAccessProperty, which will read and write the property details, creating the property if it doesn't exist.

To create properties you use the `CreateProperty` method. We won't go into the details of it here (it's well documented), and the `GetAccessProperty` and `SetAccessProperty` functions are in the `Solutions` database, in the `Chapter 11 Code` module. Using these functions is simple – we simply place them in the `Open` event for the form:

```
Dim db          As Database
Dim docForm     As Document

' point to the current document - this is the saved version of the form
Set db = DBEngine.Workspaces(0).Databases(0)
Set docForm = db.Containers("Forms").Documents(Me.Name)

' set the current property to the saved property + 1
m_lngTimesOpened = GetAccessProperty(docForm, "TimesOpened", dbInteger) + 1

' resave the property
SetAccessProperty docForm, "TimesOpened", dbInteger, m_lngTimesOpened
```

All that's left to do is show this value somewhere. So, create a text box on the form, call it `txtTimesOpened`, and add the following just after the call to `SetAccessProperty`:

```
' display it
txtTimesOpened = m_lngTimesOpened
```

That's it. Now when you open the form, a text box shows how many times the form has been opened.

2. The `Kernel32` dynamic link library contains a function called `GetWindowsDirectory` which returns the path to the **Windows** directory. You can declare the function like this in VBA:

```
Private Declare Function GetWindowsDirectoryA Lib "kernel32" _
(ByVal strBuffer As String, ByVal lngSize As Long) As Long
```

The first argument should be passed as a fixed-length string and will be populated by the function with a string representing the path to the `Windows` directory. You should populate the second variable (`lngSize`) with the length of `strBuffer` before you call the `GetWindowsDirectory` function. The `GetWindowsDirectoryA` function returns a long integer denoting the length (max. `255`) of the value it has placed in `strBuffer`.

Use this function to create a VBA procedure called `GetWinDir` that accepts no arguments and simply returns the path to the Windows directory.

Solution

Most of what you need is in the chapter, but there's one catch, which you might have found. Here's the code:

```
Public Function GetWinDir() As String

    Dim strBuffer    As String * 255    ' holds windows directory
    Dim lngRetVal    As Long            ' return value of API call
```

```
    lngRetVal = GetWindowsDirectoryA(strBuffer, Len(strBuffer))

    If lngRetVal > 0 Then
        GetWinDir = Left$(strBuffer, lngRetVal)
    Else
        GetWinDir = "Unknown"
    End If

End Function
```

Remember that strings for API calls are fixed length. Once the string has been filled, it is null terminated, and VBA doesn't recognize the null as the end of the string. So if you just print out the string directly after the API call, it will have lots of spaces at the end. So the trick is to use the return value of this API call, which identifies how many characters it used. We can then use this to just trim off the correct number of characters from the left hand side of the string.

Chapter 12

1. Examine the forms in the sample database. Do you think that any error routines could be removed and a global error routine used instead? What would be the disadvantage of this?

Solution

Yes you could quite easily remove much of the error handling to a single location. In fact, for those occasions that just report the error and exit, there's no reason not to do so. There's actually no real disadvantage if all you are doing is reporting errors. However, if you want to be more selective in your error handling, then you've just got to be sure that this central routine is able to process every type of error. This means that it could get quite large, with lots of little pieces of code handling specific errors. It's always a trade-off, so don't automatically create a central routine.

I like to create a central routine for the purpose of error logging (to a table), and that allows one very important thing. Easier support. How many times have you had a user complain about an error but they can't remember what it said on the screen? Or you can't reproduce it? Logging the error details means that they will always be available to you.

2. Having thought about a central error routine, create one. Give it two arguments: strProc, which should be the name of the procedure that calls the routine, and optionally, strDesc, for a general description. The routine should check to see if the error was a VBA error or a Data Access error, and display any messages in a message box, along with the procedure that called the routine, and the additional text.

Solution

Here's a little sample routine:

```
Public Sub ErrorHandler(ByVal strProc As String, _
                    Optional strDesc As String)
```

```
    Dim errE    As Error       ' Error object
    Dim strErr  As String      ' holds the error message

    ' what sort of an error is it?
    If Err.Number = DBEngine.Errors(DBEngine.Errors.Count - 1).Number Then
        ' add the procedure name and description
        strErr = "Data Access Error in " & strProc & _
            vbCr & vbCr & _
            strDesc & _
            vbCr & vbCr

        ' now loop through the errors
        For Each errE In DBEngine.Errors
            strErr = strErr & _
                "Error: " & errE.Number & ": " & _
                errE.Description & vbCr
        Next
    Else
        Debug.Print "VBA run-time Error in " & strProc & _
            vbCr & vbCr & _
            strDesc & _
            vbCr & vbCr _
            "Err = " & Err.Number & ": " & Err.Description
    End If

    MsgBox strErr, vbOKOnly, "Error"

End Sub
```

This is quite simple, and takes two arguments. The first is the procedure name, and the second, optionally, is a description. The routine builds a string of the error details and then displays it, much as we did in the chapter. It could be called like this:

```
ErrorHandler "Foo", "Something bad happened"
```

Chapter 13

1. In `PaymentStats` class you added a write-only property, `Accuracy`. Make sure that the accuracy is applied to the `FinePayable` method.

Solution

This simply involves using the `Round` function and the accuracy to ensure that the fine payable is shown correctly:

```
Public Function FinePayable(Optional Days As Integer = 40, _
                            Optional Percent As Single = 90, _
                            Optional UnitFine As Currency = 1000) As Currency

Dim i As Integer
Dim sngPercentActual As Single
```

```
If VarType(varSalesArray) And vbArray Then
   sngPercentActual = Percentile(Days)
   If sngPercentActual < Percent Then
      FinePayable = Round((Percent - sngPercentActual) * UnitFine, intAccuracy)
   End If
End If

End Function
```

2. Try to modify the `MyRectangle` class so that it contains a `Sides` collection. This collection should contain a `Side` object for each of the four sides of the rectangle. The `MyRectangle` should create these when it is created.

Each of these `Side` objects should have a `Length` property (the length of the side in centimeters which is specified when the `Height` and `Width` properties of the `MyRectangle` are set) and a read-only `ImperialLength` property which specifies the length of the side in inches (1 inch = 2.54 cm). When you have made these modifications, you should be able to use this procedure to print the area of the rectangle and the lengths of the four sides.

```
Sub ClassDemo5()

Dim objRect As MyRectangle
Dim sd As Side

Set objRect = New MyRectangle

objRect.Height = 5
objRect.Width = 8

Debug.Print "Area:"; objRect.Area; "cm"

For Each sd In objRect.Sides
    Debug.Print sd.Length; "cm", sd.ImperialLength; "inches"
Next

Set objRect = Nothing

End Sub
```

This should yield the following results:

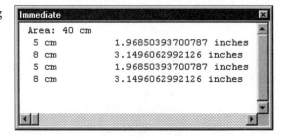

For an indication of the steps you will need to follow to implement this solution, have a look at the section on creating hierarchies using collections towards the end of Chapter 13.

Solution

This isn't as complex as it sounds, and doesn't involve much coding. The important thing is to think very carefully about what you need to do before you do it. Let's start with the `Side` object – here's the class:

```
Private dblLength As Double
```

```
Public Property Get Length() As Double

    Length = dblLength

End Sub
```

```
Public Property Get ImperialLength() As Double

    ImperialLength = dblLength / 2.54

End Sub
```

```
Public Property Let Length(dblParam As Double)

    dblLength = dblParam

End Sub
```

This simply declares a private variable to store the length of the side, and adds `Property Let` and `Get` routines to make this a property of the object. A property for the imperial length is also added, but as a read-only property.

To use this object you need to modify the rectangle class. You'll need a Collection to store the four instances of the `Side` object, and when the rectangle is constructed, you create a new `Side` object for each side of the rectangle and add it to the collection. To do this you need to add a new public variable to the rectangle class at the top of the class module, just under the variable declarations:

```
Public Sides As New Collection
```

Now you need to create a `Class_Initialize` event:

```
Dim sd As Side
Dim i  As integer

For i = 1 To 4
    Set sd = New Side
    Sides.Add sd
    Set sd = nothing
Next
```

This simply creates four objects of type `Side`, and adds each to the `Sides` collection.

Exercise Solutions

Next we need to remove these sides where the class is destroyed, so the following needs adding into the `Class_Terminate` event:

```
Dim i  As integer

For i = 1 To 4
    Sides.Remove 1
Next
```

Notice that we delete the `Side` object, which has an index of 1, four times over. We do this because when we delete `Side(1)`, `Side(2)` becomes `Side(1)`, `Side(3)` becomes `Side(2)` and `Side(4)` becomes `Side(3)` – **and so on each time we delete**. That's a bit sneaky!

Now all you have to do is set the length of these new `Side` objects, and this is done when we set the `Height` and `Width` of the rectangle:

```
Public Property Let Height(dblParam As Double)

    dblHeight = dblParam
    Sides(1).Length = dblParam
    Sides(3).Length = dblParam

End Property
```

```
Public Property Let Width(dblParam As Double)

    dblHeight = dblParam
    Sides(2).Length = dblParam
    Sides(4).Length = dblParam

End Property
```

That's it. Now when a rectangle is created, four new `Side` objects are added to the `Sides` collection. When the height and width of the rectangle are set, the sides take on these values.

Chapter 14

1. Think about how you could use the language converter so that the language is changed as the form is opened, rather than a permanent change. If used with security, you could store a table of user names, along with their preferred language, and as each form is opened run a procedure that changes the controls. You've already seen how quick this is, so there will be no apparent slow down from the users point of view.

Solution

We won't implement a full solution here, but there's a solution on the CD-ROM. Most of the solutions are in the solutions database (`solutions.mdb`), but for this exercise there is a directory, `Language Solutions`, containing two databases: `Language.mda` (a modified version of the standard `Language.mda` add-in), and `TestLanguages.mdb`, which is a copy of `IceCream18.mdb`, modified to use the new languages add-in. This version of `Language.mda` will work the same way as the one described in Chapter 14, but it has the additions for the dynamic setting of languages.

If you open the test database you need to use the **Add-Ins** option from the **Tools** menu to access the standard part of the add-in, and you'll also need to set a Reference to it (**References** from the **Tools** menu when in the VBA IDE).

Let's look at what I did:

The code that changes the text on the forms permanently is in the module for the form `frmLanguageConverter`, in a procedure called `LanguageFormControlsEnumerate`. This opens the form in design view, loops though the controls, sets the caption text, and then closes the form, saving the changes. For our new solution we need a procedure that just loops through the controls on a single form, setting the caption for each control. I created a new procedure in the `Language` module:

```
Public Sub wcs_SetLanguageText(frmF As Form)

    Dim ctlC        As Control      ' control to set caption for
    Dim recLang     As Recordset    ' language recordset
    Dim strLanguage As String       ' use language

    ' point to the user database
    Set wcs_dbUser = CurrentDb

    ' get the user language
    ' this would either use the CurrentUser() function to look up the
    ' language preference for the current user (if using Access security),
    ' or would, perhaps, use a global variable set when the user logged in
    ' if a simpler security scheme was in use.
    strLanguage = GetUserLanguage(CurrentUser())

    ' open the language table
    Set recLang = wcs_dbUser.OpenRecordset(wcs_LANGUAGE_TABLE)
    recLang.Index = "PrimaryKey"

    ' set the form caption
    frmF.Caption = GetLanguageText(recLang, strLanguage, _
                    frmF.Name, frmF.Name)

    ' now the controls
    For Each ctlC In frmF.Controls
        If LanguageControlHasCaption(ctlC.ControlType) = True Then
            ctlC.Caption = GetLanguageText(recLang, strLanguage, _
                    frmF.Name, ctlC.Name)
        End If
    Next

    ' close the language table
    recLang.Close
    Set recLang = Nothing

End Sub
```

This function does some very familiar things, such as looping through the controls on a form, setting their `Caption` property. It uses `CurrentUser()` to get the current user name. If you haven't got an Access security scheme in place, then this will always return `Admin` – I left it at this because this is something you will have to decide yourself.

Exercise Solutions

You can either use a security database, in which case you have to supply valid user credentials before you can access the database – in this case `CurrentUser()` will return the correct user name. Alternatively, you could just have a startup form that asks for a user name and password, and then store this user name in a global variable.

The `GetUserLanguage` function looks up the user's preferred language, using a table stored in the user database. This table just contains two columns: the user name and the user language.

```
Private Function GetUserLanguage(sUserName As String) As String

    Dim recUL        As Recordset     ' user language

    ' open the user language table
    Set recUL = wcs_dbUser.OpenRecordset(wcs_LANG_USR_TABLE)

    With recUL
        ' find the user
        .FindFirst "UserName = '" & sUserName & "'"

        ' return their language of choice (or English if no preference)
        If .NoMatch Then
            GetUserLanguage = "English"
        Else
            GetUserLanguage = recUL("UserLanguage")
        End If
    End With

    ' clean up
    recUL.Close
    Set recUL = Nothing

End Function
```

The `GetLanguageText` function looks up the text for a control on the language table:

```
Private Function GetLanguageText(recR As Recordset, _
        strLanguage As String, strFormName As String, _
        strControlName As String) As String

    recR.Seek "=", strFormName, strControlName

    If recR.NoMatch Then
        GetLanguageText = ""
    Else
        GetLanguageText = recR(strLanguage) & ""
    End If

End Function
```

Ok. That completes the changes to the add-in. In the database that uses this (`TestLanguages.mdb`), I added a table of the user names and language preferences. This only has one user (`Admin`) at the moment. I than added the following to the `Form_Open` event of the switchboard:

```
wcs_SetLanguageText Me
```

This just calls the new function in the add-in database, passing in the current form. Now whenever the form is opened, the language details are changed. Try changing the language in the `LanguageUser` table from `French` to `English` and back, opening the switchboard each time. See how the language changes depending upon the value in the table.

Obviously you must make sure that you run the extraction part of the add-in first, so that the languages table is created and filled. This is something that you'd do as the application is installed.

2. Add a facility to allow message boxes to have language facilities. This is fairly easy to do, as you could just add records into the language table, using a unique name for each message box. Then instead of calling `MsgBox` with a direct string, you could replace the string with a call to a function that looked up the language string in the table.

Solution

Unlike forms, it's quite difficult to extract the message box information. With forms and controls it's easy to extract the textual information, because you can just look at the `Caption` property. Message boxes, however, are more complex, because you have to cater with the various formats that `MsgBox` can take:

```
MsgBox "This is plain text"
MsgBox "This is plain text" & _
    " but on two lines"
MsgBox FunctionThatReturnsString()
If MsgBox("Are you sure?") = vbYes Then
```

You can see that it would be quite difficult to accurately automate this, without a lot of complex code. Considering the number of message boxes there usually are in code, I feel it's not too much of a hardship to manually change them.

The only change you need to make to the add-in is to create a new function to get the language text for the message box:

```
Public Function wcs_GetLanguageTextMsgBox (strForm As String,
            strMsgBox As String) As String

    Dim ctlC       As Control      ' control to set caption for
    Dim recLang    As Recordset    ' language recordset
    Dim strLanguage As String      ' use language

    ' point to the user database
    Set wcs_dbUser = CurrentDb

    ' get the user language
    ' this would either use the CurrentUser() function to look up the
    ' language preference for the current user (if using Access security),
    ' or would, perhaps, use a global variable set when the user logged in
    ' if a simpler security scheme was in use.
    strLanguage = GetUserLanguage(CurrentUser())

    ' open the language table
    Set recLang = wcs_dbUser.OpenRecordset(wcs_LANGUAGE_TABLE)
    recLang.Index = "PrimaryKey"
```

```
    ' get the text for the message box
    wcs_GetLanguageTextMsgBox = GetLanguageText (recLang, strLanguage,
            strForm, strMsgBox)

    ' clean up
    recLang.close
    Set recLang = Nothing

End Function
```

This is similar to earlier functions, but instead of looping through the controls on a form, it gets the language text for a single control. You can then use this function in any code module:

```
MsgBox wcs_GetLanguageTextMsgBox (module_name, msgbox_name)
```

For example, in a form you might do this:

```
MsgBox wcs_GetLanguageTextMsgBox (Me.Name, "MsgBox1")
```

Or, in a code module:

```
MsgBox wcs_GetLanguageTextMsgBox ("Solutions Module","MsgBox12")
```

The switchboard in the `TestLanguages` database has a message box that does this.

Because there is no automatic population of the languages table you'll have to add these entries yourself:

FormName	ControlName	ControlType	DateUpdated	English	French
frmSwitchboard	lblReports	Label	i/99 3:34:51 PM	&Reports	le reports
frmSwitchboard	lblSuppliers	Label	i/99 3:34:51 PM	&Supplier Lists	le suppliers
frmSwitchboard	MsgBox1	MsgBox	i/99 3:34:51 PM	Message box text in	le french text
frmUpload	cmdUpload	Command butto	i/99 3:34:51 PM	&Upload	

Chapter 15

1. For the Sales Figures Chart form (`frmSalesFigures`) add four buttons to allow the user to rotate the chart. The buttons should rotate the chart left, right, up and down.

Hint: The chart has properties called `Rotation` and `Elevation` – make sure you check the help files for their acceptable values.

Solution

This is actually quite easy, and looks really cool. I added four buttons like so:

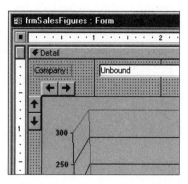

I named the buttons cmdRotateLeft, cmdRotateRight, cmdRotateUp, and cmdRotateDown, and added the following code:

```
Private Sub cmdRotateLeft_Click()

    If m_objChart.Rotation > 355 Then
        m_objChart.Rotation = 0
    Else
        m_objChart.Rotation = m_objChart.Rotation + 5
    End If

End Sub
```

```
Private Sub cmdRotateRight_Click()

    If m_objChart.Rotation < 5 Then
        m_objChart.Rotation = 360
    Else
        m_objChart.Rotation = m_objChart.Rotation - 5
    End If

End Sub
```

```
Private Sub cmdRotateUp_Click()

    If m_objChart.Elevation < 5 Then
        m_objChart.Elevation = 90
    Else
        m_objChart.Elevation = m_objChart.Elevation - 5
    End If

End Sub
```

```
Private Sub cmdRotateDown_Click()

    If m_objChart.Elevation > 85 Then
        m_objChart.Elevation = 0
    Else
        m_objChart.Elevation = m_objChart.Elevation + 5
    End If

End Sub
```

Exercise Solutions

These simply set the `Elevation` and `Rotation` properties of the chart object. We have to add a bit of checking into these routines because these properties have limits to their values, so we just make sure that we don't overstep them.

You might also like to try another solution to this, by adding two scroll bars instead of the buttons. Add a vertical scroll bar to control the elevation and a horizontal scroll bar to control the rotation. I think this looks much neater, so I've added it to the solutions database.

Chapter 16

1. Earlier in this chapter we looked at how it was possible to use the `CreateWorkspace` method to allow us to act in the security context of another user. One potential use of this is to allow us to create a procedure that lists all of the groups to which the current user belongs. The potential problem is that only members of the `Admins` group have permission to view this information. See if you can write a procedure that lists all of the groups to which the current user belongs, even if the user is not a member of the `Admins` group.

Solution

The tricky part of this is given in the chapter, and involves creating a new workspace, using the details of the Admin user. You can then use the `Users` and `Groups` collections to find each Group to which the current user belongs:

```
Public Sub ListGroupsForUser()

    Dim wksNew      As Workspace
    Dim grpUG       As Group        ' user group

    ' create a new workspace, using the Admin user
    Set wksNew = DBEngine.CreateWorkspace("AdminWorkspace", "Admin", "")

    ' loop through the groups for this user
    Debug.Print "Groups for user " & CurrentUser() & " are:"
    For Each grpUG In wksNew.Users(CurrentUser()).Groups
        Debug.Print vbTab; grpUG.Name
    Next

    wksNew.Close
    Set wksNew = Nothing
    Set grpUG = Nothing

End Sub
```

2. The password form we created in this chapter is still fairly rudimentary. You can probably think of many ways to improve it. For example, some security systems force you to change your password at monthly intervals and will not allow you to reuse any of your, say, five previous passwords. See if you can modify the password form so that it enforces these two rules.

Hint: If you decide to store users' passwords in a table you need to make sure that you will be able to read the table from code, but also that normal users won't be able to read the data in the table.

Solution

To implement this sort of password system you'll need two main pieces of information:

❑ The last time the user changed their password.

❑ A list of their last five passwords.

This obviously means a table to store this information in. A simple one will do, with the following fields:

Field	Type	Field Size
UserName	Text	20
LastPasswordChange	Date/Time	
Password1	Text	14
Password2	Text	14
Password3	Text	14
Password4	Text	14
Password5	Text	14

This simply stores the user name, the date they last changed their password, and their last five passwords. You don't need to worry about storing user passwords in the table, because you can set the permission on this table so that only the **Admin** user can view it. You then work in an Admin workspace, so that you have permissions to view it.

Now when the user changes their password from the password form (frmPassword), you need to find the user in the above table and check the five password fields to see if the new password has been used before. If it has you can display a warning and make the user pick another password, otherwise you can update their password, update the five password fields, and update the date it was last changed. Something like this:

```
Dim wksNew      As Workspace
Dim db          As Database
Dim recUser     As Recordset
Dim intPwd      As Integer

' create a new workspace, using the Admin user

Set wksNew = DBEngine.CreateWorkspace("AdminWorkspace", "Admin", "")

' open a database in the Admin workspace
Set db = wksNew.OpenDatabase("CurrentDb.Name)
```

```
' open the user/password table
Set recUser = db.OpenRecordset("tblPasswords", dbOpenDynaset)

' find the current user
recUser.Find "UserName = """ & CurrentUser() & """"

' change their password
wksNew.Users(CurrentUser()).NewPassword txtOldPwd, txtNewPwd

' update the passwords table
With recUser
    .Edit

    ' move the passwords 2 to 5, into positions 1 to 4
    For intPwd = 1 To 4
        .Fields("Password" & intPwd) = .Fields("Password" & intPwd + 1)
    Next

    ' update the current password
    .Fields("Password5") = txtNewPwd
    .Fields("LastPasswordChange") = Now()
    .Update
End With

' tidy up
recUser.Close
Set recUser = Nothing
db.Close
Set db = Nothing
wksNew.Close
Set wksNew = Nothing
```

If you want to force the user to change their password at regular intervals, then when the first form is shown you should look in the passwords table to check the date. If the password was last changed within the allowable limit, you can continue as normal, otherwise you should display the change password form.

In the solutions database we've created a class to encapsulate a lot of this functionality. The class is called cUser and has the following properties and methods:

Item	Type	Description
Name	Property	Sets the name of the current user, and fills the LastPasswordChange property.
PasswordChange	Method	Changes the user password. Takes three arguments: the old password, the new password, and a string to fill with the error details if the password cannot be changed.
LastPassword Change	Property	Identifies the last time the password was changed for this user. Read-only.
PasswordCheck	Property	Checks the supplied password against the latest password in the stored list.

Item	Type	Description
PasswordNeeds Changing	Property	Identifies whether the password has expired and needs changing

You can use the class like this:

```
Dim clsUser As New cUser

' set the user name - this reads in the current user
' password and last change date
cUser.Name = CurrentUser()

' see if the password needs changing
If cUser.PasswordNeedsChanging Then
    ' password has expired so force a password change
    DoCmd.OpenForm "frmPassword", . . .
End If

' change the password
If cUser.PasswordChange ("OldPassword", "NewPassword", strResult) = True Then
    MsgBox "Password change succeeded."
Else
    MsgBox strResult
End If
```

The reason for putting this functionality into a class is that it makes this code easy to use from different places. Remember that the password table will have security on it, and only the Admin user can read the table contents. So every time you need to access this table you have to create a workspace, open the database, open the table, etc., which gets quite tedious. Putting everything into a class means it's easy to use from anywhere. The password form has changed to use this, as has the switchboard form, which checks for password expiry before letting users into the database.

One thing to note about the class is that it doesn't actually change the real password, as stored in the User object in the Users collection – this line in the code is commented out. This is because most of you probably will not be using a security database, and we don't want you to accidentally change the Admin password, and then forget what it is.

Chapter 17

1. We want to publish a list of our ice creams to our Internet site, and we want to use plain HTML files. Add some code to the ice creams form, so that any time an ice cream entry is changed, a new HTML file is generated.

Exercise Solutions

Solution

This is a simple one, and is just a single line of code. In the `AfterUpdate` event for the form `frmIceCream`, add the following line of code:

```
DoCmd.TransferText acExportHTML, , "tblIceCream", _
    "C:\BegVBA\IceCreams.html"
```

2. See if you can create a Web browser using an Access form. Hint – there's a control you can add to your form – when in form design mode, press the **More Controls** button on the **Toolbox** to see if you can find the right control.

Solution

This is actually extremely easy, and can be achieved with a single line of code. The control you need is the **Microsoft Web Browser** control – just draw this onto a form. You might have to resize the browser control once it's been drawn – give it a name of `ctlBrowser`. Then add a text box to the top of the form, calling it `txtURL`. For the `Exit` event of the text box, add the following line of code:

```
ctlBrowser.Navigate txtURL
```

Save the form and give it a try. Yes, that's really all there is to it. There's a form (`frmBrowser`) in the `Solutions` database with just this in it.

Have a look in the help file for more details, and also use the Object Browser, once the control is drawn on the form. The browser control shows up as `sSHDocVw`.

Chapter 18

1. We can write a procedure in a number of ways according to our coding priorities. Try to write a procedure that tells you the delivery day for corn syrup (the second Wednesday of every month) for a given year and month. Now re-write the procedure so that it is optimized for:

   ❑ Real execution speed

   ❑ Maintainability

   ❑ Re-usability

Solution

In some respects, this is a subjective answer, since you may find one solution more maintainable or easier to understand than another. Before we tackle the solutions, let's look at some background to this problem. We rely on the fact that the second Wednesday in a given month can be no earlier than the 8th (that's the date the second week starts) and no later than the 14th (that's the date the second week ends). If the month starts on a Wednesday then the second Wednesday will be the 8th, and if the month starts on a Tuesday, then the second Wednesday will be the 9th.

This means that the second Wednesday can be defined as:

8th + (0 days if the 8th is a Wednesday)
8th + (1 day if the 8th is a Tuesday)
8th + (2 days if the 8th is a Monday)
8th + (3 days if the 8th is a Sunday)
8th + (4 days if the 8th is a Saturday)
8th + (5 days if the 8th is a Friday)
8th + (6 days if the 8th is a Thursday)

Knowing these details we can utilize two VBA functions. The first, DateSerial, returns a date given the three parts of: year, month and day. The second, WeekDay, returns the day number in the week for a given date.

OK, that's enough background, let's first tackle the maintainability issue – the code for this is shown below:

```
Public Function DeliveryDateMaint(intYear As Integer, intMonth As Integer)


    Dim datStart  As Date


    datStart = DateSerial(intYear, intMonth, 8)
    Select Case Weekday(datStart, vbSunday)
    Case vbSunday
        DeliveryDateMaint = datStart + 3
    Case vbMonday
        DeliveryDateMaint = datStart + 2
    Case vbTuesday
        DeliveryDateMaint = datStart + 1
    Case vbWednesday
        DeliveryDateMaint = datStart
    Case vbThursday
        DeliveryDateMaint = datStart + 6
    Case vbFriday
        DeliveryDateMaint = datStart + 5
    Case vbSaturday
        DeliveryDateMaint = datStart + 4
    End Select

End Function
```

The function accepts the year and month for which we need to find the second Wednesday – remember that this can be no earlier than the 8th – so we create a date variable containing the 8th of the month. We then use the Weekday function to find out the day number in the week that the 8th falls on. The argument vbSunday indicates that the week should start on a Sunday (so Sunday is day 1, Monday day 2, etc.). So, if the 8th is a Sunday we need to add 3 days to get to Wednesday. If the 8th is a Monday, then only 2 days need to be added, and so on.

Exercise Solutions

The above procedure is easy to read, understand, and maintain, but it's probably not the fastest. The solution below is optimized for speed:

```
Public Function DeliveryDateFast(intYear As Integer, intMonth As Integer)

    Dim datStart          As Date

    datStart = DateSerial(intYear, intMonth, 8)
    DeliveryDate = datStart + (7 - Weekday(datStart, vbThursday))

End Function
```

This solution shows the use of `Weekday` with another day as the start of the week. This allows us to find out the day number in the week, as though Thursday was the start of the week. In this case Thursday would be day 1, Friday would be day 2, and so on. So, subtracting this day number from 7 gives us the number of days after the 8th that the next Wednesday falls on.

To make this function more usable it would be good to be able to pick the nth day. Perhaps the 3rd Friday, or the 1st Saturday. Here's the code, based on the quicker solution:

```
Public Function DeliveryDateReuse(intYear As Integer, _
        intMonth As Integer, intDayRequired As vbDayOfWeek, _
        intNth As Integer)

    Dim datStart          As Date
    Dim varStartDay       As Variant

    varStartDay = Array(0, 1, 8, 15, 22, 29)

    datStart = DateSerial(intYear, intMonth, varStartDay(intNth))
    DeliveryDateReuse = datStart + _
            (7 - Weekday(datStart, intDayRequired + 1))

End Function
```

This version adds two new parameters. The first, `intDayRequired`, is the ordinal required – i.e. the 1st, 2nd, etc. The second, `intDayRequired`, is the day to find. Notice that `intDayRequired` is of the type `vbDayOfWeek`, which is the type that specifies the day numbers used in the `DateSerial` function.

To find the nth day we need to know the actual start day of the week – this is easy, since the month always starts on the 1st, the second week starts on the 8th, and so on. These day numbers are put into an array, and the day number from this array is used in the `DateSerial` function. The `WeekDay` function, instead of accepting a fixed constant for the day name, now takes the day we pass in as a parameter. We add one, because if we specify to find the 3rd Friday, we want `WeekDay` to use Saturday.

So that's three solutions for the same problem, but all coded with different aims in mind.

2. Create a form and place a button on it. Now write a procedure that prints to the debug window the number of fields and records in each table in the database when the button is clicked. Now add a gauge to the status bar to display the progress of this operation.

Solution

This code is in the form name `frmShowProgress`:

```
Dim db          As Database         ' current database
Dim tblT        As TableDef         ' current table
Dim intTable    As Integer          ' current table number

' point to the current database
Set db = CurrentDb

' initialize the meter
SysCmd acSysCmdInitMeter, "Working ...", db.TableDefs.Count

' loop through the tables
For Each tblT In db.TableDefs
    ' update the meter
    SysCmd acSysCmdUpdateMeter, intTable

    ' print the details
    Debug.Print tblT.Name & " contains " & _
                tblT.Fields.Count & " fields " & _
                tblT.RecordCount & " records"
    intTable = intTable + 1
Next

' clear the meter
SysCmd acSysCmdRemoveMeter

' clean up
Set tblT = Nothing
Set db = Nothing
```

It simply uses the `TableDefs` collection to loop through the tables. At the start of the procedure the meter is initialized, and updated each time we move onto a new table. The only trouble with this procedure is that it's quite quick, so if you blink you might miss the meter moving.

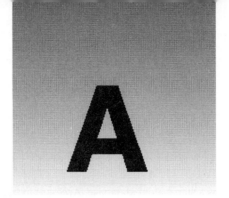

Choosing Between MSDE and Jet

As we explained briefly at the beginning of the book, there are great differences in the ways you can use Access. If you've used previous versions then you've still got the good old mdb file, but if you want to do some client/server work, then you're in a whole new ball game. Either way, you need to make some decisions:

- ❑ Which database should I use? Jet or MSDE?
- ❑ Which data access method should I use? DAO or ADO?

Although the MSDE is SQL Server, it's not the full version of SQL Server, and you still use Access as your development tool. You still have forms, reports, modules, and so on stored in an Access Project, but the data is now stored in the SQL Server database engine. So the discussion in this appendix is that of using Access as your development tool, but storing your data in either Access or SQL Server. It's a quick discussion just to explain a few reasons why you should chose one data store over the other.

The decision of which data store to use depends upon what you are trying to achieve, which can generally be categorized in one of several ways:

1. Only you will use the database.

2. The database will only be used by a small number of people, perhaps 10 or so.

3. The database will only be used by a small number of people, but might be used by a large number of people in the future.

4. Your database is extremely large.

5. A large number of people require simultaneous access to the database.

You can probably guess that choices 1 and 2 are best suited to Jet, and that 5 is best suited to MSDE, or even the full version of SQL Server. Option 4 is a fairly simple choice too, as Jet is best used in smaller databases (and by small, I really mean under 2Gb, preferably even smaller). Option 3 proves a little harder, since you could quite easily choose either database type, and the tools provided to convert from one to another are good. So, perhaps what you need is a list of the pros and cons of each database:

Access

Pros

- ❑ **Simplicity**. When used as a stand-alone database, Access is extremely easy to use, and is very similar to previous versions. No other knowledge is needed.

- ❑ **Portability**. The Access mdb file contains everything about the database, and this can therefore be transported easily.

Cons

- ❑ **Scalability**. Access is designed as a workgroup database, and is therefore best with fewer than 20 users. Access can cope with more users as long as the processing is not too intensive.

- ❑ **Database size**. Access can only be used with databases up to 2Gb.

- ❑ **Fault tolerance**. Access doesn't support logging of transactions, therefore should a failure occur within the database (such as a corrupt database), a previous version must be restored. Any changes made between the last backup and the failure point will be lost.

MSDE/SQL Server

Pros

- ❑ **Speed**. Under normal operating conditions, SQL Server should give a speed increase over Access.

- ❑ **Scalability**. SQL Server is designed to handle a larger number of users.

- ❑ **Database size**. SQL Server has a virtually unlimited database size.

- ❑ **Fault tolerance**. SQL Server is designed with fault-tolerance in mind, therefore problems with the database are rarely fatal, and data can usually be recovered.

Cons

- ❑ **Complexity**. SQL Server is more complex than Access. Although the use of Access as a front-end has simplified this, things like views, stored procedures and referential integrity are hidden less than when using an Access database.

❑ **Portability**. An Access project comprises two parts – the mdb file, containing the Access specific items (such as forms) and the SQL Server database containing the tables and data. This makes it harder to transfer.

Summary

You can probably see that the good things about one database are the bad things about the other, and it's this that can make your decision hard, since you understandably want the best of both worlds. The Access Project has undoubtedly made using SQL Server an easier process, but it's still more complex. SQL Server is always a good skill to learn, but don't take that to mean that you should stop using Access.

If you need a smallish database, with relatively few users, then an Access database will serve you well.

Choosing Between DAO and ADO

Like the previous appendix, we described this briefly at the beginning of the book, but it's worth repeating because it's an important topic, and it fits neatly with the discussion of Access and SQL Server.

The choice here is much easier to make:

- ❑ If you are using an Access mdb file, then use DAO. It provides much better integration with the Jet database.
- ❑ If you are using MSDE, then ADO is your best bet. Part of its design means it copes with SQL Server much better than DAO does, and performs better in a client/server situation.

That's an easy choice to make. The only other point you should consider is if you are using an Access mdb file and know that you will be upsizing this to SQL Server in the future. In this case you might prefer to use ADO so that you won't have to make any changes to your code during the upgrade process.

DAO and ADO Usage

Since ADO is a big topic, and it hasn't been covered in depth in this book, here are a few samples that show you the differences between DAO and ADO. We're not going to cover every usage of DAO and ADO, but just a few of the major ones that you'll use most. There are documents on the Microsoft website (see http://www.microsoft.com/data) that fully cover the topic of migrating from DAO to ADO, as well as provide a good set of examples. Wrox Press also have a pure ADO book, the ADO 2.1 Programmer's Reference - see http://www.wrox.com for more details.

Opening the current database

DAO

```
Dim db As DAO.Database

Set db = CurrentDB()
```

ADO

```
Dim objConn As ADODB.Connection

Set objConn = CurrentProject.Connection
```

Opening a new database

DAO

```
Dim db As DAO.Database

Set db = DBEngine.OpenDatabase ("C:\BegVBA\IceCream.mdb")
```

ADO

```
Dim objConn As New ADODB.Connection

objConn.Open "Provider=Microsoft.Jet.OLEDB.4.0; Data Source = C:\BegVBA\IceCream.mdb"
```

or

```
Dim objConn As New ADODB.Connection

objConn.Provider = "Provider=Microsoft.Jet.OLEDB.4.0"
objConn.Open "Data Source= C:\BegVBA\IceCream.mdb"
```

Opening a database as a User

DAO

```
Dim db As DAO.Database
Dim objWks As DAO.Workspace

DBEngine.SystemDB = "C:\BegVBA\IceUsers.mdw"
Set objWks = DBEngine.CreateWorkspace("", "user_name", "password")
Set db = objWks.OpenDatabase ("C:\BegVBA\IceCream.mdb")
```

ADO

```
Dim objConn As ADODB.Connection

objConn.Provider = "Provider=Microsoft.Jet.OLEDB.4.0"
objConn.Properties("Jet OLEDB:System database") = "C:\BegVBA\IceUsers.mdw"
objConn.Open "Data Source= C:\BegVBA\IceCream.mdb; User Id=user_name;
Password=password"
```

Recordset/Lock Types

The recordset/cursor type can be determined according to the table below:

DAO Recordset Type property	ADO CursorType property	ADO Options property
dbOpenDynaset	adOpenKeyset	none
dbOpenSnapshot	adOpenStatic	none
dbOpenForwardOnly	adOpenForwardOnly	
dbOpenTable	adOpenKeyset	adCmdTableDirect

The lock type can be determined according to the table below:

DAO LockEdits property	ADO LockType property
dbReadOnly	adLockReadOnly
dbPessimistic	adLockPessimistic
dbOptimistic	adLockOptimistic

Opening a recordset

These examples assume the database has already been opened.

DAO

```
Dim recR As DAO.Recordset

Set recR = db.OpenRecordset ("SELECT * FROM tblOrders", dbOpenForwardOnly)
```

ADO

```
Dim recR As New ADODB.Recordset

recR.Open "SELECT * FROM tblOrders", objConn, adOpenForwardOnly, adLockReadOnly
```

Editing Records

These examples assume the database has already been opened.

DAO

```
Dim recR As DAO.Recordset

Set recR = db.OpenRecordset ("SELECT * FROM tblOrders", dbOpenDynaset)

recR.Edit
recR.Fields("field_name").Value = "a new value"
recR.Update
```

ADO

```
Dim recR As New ADODB.Recordset

recR.Open "SELECT * FROM tblOrders", objConn, adOpenKeyset, adLockOptimistic

recR.Fields("field_name").Value = "a new value"
recR.Update
```

Finding records

DAO has four find methods, whereas ADO has only one method with arguments:

DAO	ADO **Find** method	
Method name	**SkipRows** argument	**SearchDirection** argument
FindFirst	0	adSearchForward
FindLast	0	adSearchBackward
FindNext	1	adSearchForward
FindPrevious	1	adSearchBackward

DAO

```
objRec.FindFirst

objRec.FindNext
```

ADO

```
objRec.Find 0, adSearchForward

objRec.Find 1, adSearchForward
```

ADO 2.1 Object Model

All properties are read/write unless otherwise stated.

Objects

Name	Description
Command	A Command object is a definition of a specific command that you intend to execute against a data source.
Connection	A Connection object represents an open connection to a data store.
Error	An Error object contains the details about data access errors pertaining to a single operation involving the provider.
Errors	The Errors collection contains all of the Error objects created in response to a single failure involving the provider.
Field	A Field object represents a column of data within a common data type.
Fields	A Fields collection contains all of the Field objects of a Recordset object.
Parameter	A Parameter object represents a parameter or argument associated with a Command object based on a parameterized query or stored procedure.
Parameters	A Parameters collection contains all the Parameter objects of a Command object.
Properties	A Properties collection contains all the Property objects for a specific instance of an object.
Property	A Property object represents a dynamic characteristic of an ADO object that is defined by the provider.
Recordset	A Recordset object represents the entire set of records from a base table or the results of an executed command. At any time, the Recordset object only refers to a single record within the set as the current record.

Command Object

Methods

Name	Returns	Description
Cancel		Cancels execution of a pending Execute or Open call.
CreateParameter	Parameter	Creates a new Parameter object.
Execute	Recordset	Executes the query, SQL statement, or stored procedure specified in the CommandText property.

Properties

Name	Returns	Description
ActiveConnection	Variant	Indicates to which Connection object the command currently belongs.
CommandText	String	Contains the text of a command to be issued against a data provider.
CommandTimeout	Long	Indicates how long to wait, in seconds, while executing a command before terminating the command and generating an error. Default is 30.
CommandType	CommandTypeEnum	Indicates the type of Command object.
Name	String	Indicates the name of the Command object.
Parameters	Parameters	Contains all of the Parameter objects for a Command object.
Prepared	Boolean	Indicates whether or not to save a compiled version of a command before execution.
Properties	Properties	Contains all of the Property objects for a Command object.
State	Long	Describes whether the Command object is open or closed. Read-only.

Connection Object

Methods

Name	Returns	Description
BeginTrans	Integer	Begins a new transaction.
Cancel		Cancels the execution of a pending, asynchronous `Execute` or `Open` operation.
Close		Closes an open connection and any dependent objects.
CommitTrans		Saves any changes and ends the current transaction.
Execute	Recordset	Executes the query, `SQL` statement, stored procedure, or provider-specific text.
Open		Opens a connection to a data source, so that commands can be executed against it.
OpenSchema	Recordset	Obtains database schema information from the provider.
RollbackTrans		Cancels any changes made during the current transaction and ends the transaction.

Properties

Name	Returns	Description
Attributes	Long	Indicates one or more characteristics of a `Connection` object. Default is 0.
Command Timeout	Long	Indicates how long, in seconds, to wait while executing a command before terminating the command and generating an error. Default is 30.
Connection String	String	Contains the information used to establish a connection to a data source.
Connection Timeout	Long	Indicates how long, in seconds, to wait while establishing a connection before terminating the attempt and generating an error. Default is 15.
Cursor Location	Cursor Location Enum	Sets or returns the location of the cursor engine.
Default Database	String	Indicates the default database for a `Connection` object.

Table Continued on Following Page

Name	Returns	Description
Errors	Errors	Contains all of the Error objects created in response to a single failure involving the provider.
Isolation Level	Isolation LevelEnum	Indicates the level of transaction isolation for a Connection object. Write only.
Mode	Connect ModeEnum	Indicates the available permissions for modifying data in a Connection.
Properties	Properties	Contains all of the Property objects for a Connection object.
Provider	String	Indicates the name of the provider for a Connection object.
State	Long	Describes whether the Connection object is open or closed. Read-only.
Version	String	Indicates the ADO version number. Read-only.

Events

Name	Description
BeginTransComplete	Fired after a BeginTrans operation finishes executing.
CommitTransComplete	Fired after a CommitTrans operation finishes executing.
ConnectComplete	Fired after a connection starts.
Disconnect	Fired after a connection ends.
ExecuteComplete	Fired after a command has finished executing.
InfoMessage	Fired whenever a ConnectionEvent operation completes successfully and additional information is returned by the provider.
RollbackTransComplete	Fired after a RollbackTrans operation finishes executing.
WillConnect	Fired before a connection starts.
WillExecute	Fired before a pending command executes on the connection.

Error Object

Properties

Name	Returns	Description
Description	String	A description string associated with the error. Read-only.
HelpContext	Integer	Indicates the ContextID in the help file for the associated error. Read-only.
HelpFile	String	Indicates the name of the help file. Read-only.
NativeError	Long	Indicates the provider-specific error code for the associated error. Read-only.
Number	Long	Indicates the number that uniquely identifies an Error object. Read-only.
Source	String	Indicates the name of the object or application that originally generated the error. Read-only.
SQLState	String	Indicates the SQL state for a given Error object. It is a five-character string that follows the ANSI SQL standard. Read-only.

Errors Collection

Methods

Name	Returns	Description
Clear		Removes all of the Error objects from the Errors collection.
Refresh		Updates the Error objects with information from the provider.

Properties

Name	Returns	Description
Count	Long	Indicates the number of Error objects in the Errors collection. Read-only.
Item	Error	Allows indexing into the Errors collection to reference a specific Error object. Read-only.

Field Object

Methods

Name	Returns	Description
AppendChunk		Appends data to a large or binary `Field` object.
GetChunk	Variant	Returns all or a portion of the contents of a large or binary `Field` object.

Properties

Name	Returns	Description
ActualSize	Long	Indicates the actual length of a field's value. Read-only.
Attributes	Long	Indicates one or more characteristics of a `Field` object.
DataFormat	Variant	Write only.
DefinedSize	Long	Indicates the defined size of the `Field` object. Write only.
Name	String	Indicates the name of the `Field` object.
Numeric Scale	Byte	Indicates the scale of numeric values for the `Field` object. Write only.
Original Value	Variant	Indicates the value of a `Field` object that existed in the record before any changes were made. Read-only.
Precision	Byte	Indicates the degree of precision for numeric values in the `Field` object. Read-only.
Properties	Properties	Contains all of the `Property` objects for a `Field` object.
Type	DataType Enum	Indicates the data type of the `Field` object.
Underlying Value	Variant	Indicates a `Field` object's current value in the database. Read-only.
Value	Variant	Indicates the value assigned to the `Field` object.

Fields Collection

Methods

Name	Returns	Description
Append		Appends a `Field` object to the `Fields` collection.

Name	Returns	Description
Delete		Deletes a `Field` object from the `Fields` collection.
Refresh		Updates the `Field` objects in the `Fields` collection.

Properties

Name	Returns	Description
Count	Long	Indicates the number of `Field` objects in the `Fields` collection. Read-only.
Item	Field	Allows indexing into the `Fields` collection to reference a specific `Field` object. Read-only.

Parameter Object

Methods

Name	Returns	Description
AppendChunk		Appends data to a large or binary `Parameter` object.

Properties

Name	Returns	Description
Attributes	Long	Indicates one or more characteristics of a `Parameter` object.
Direction	Parameter Direction Enum	Indicates whether the `Parameter` object represents an input parameter, an output parameter, or both, or if the parameter is a return value from a stored procedure.
Name	String	Indicates the name of the `Parameter` object.
NumericScale	Byte	Indicates the scale of numeric values for the `Parameter` object.
Precision	Byte	Indicates the degree of precision for numeric values in the `Parameter` object.
Properties	Properties	Contains all of the `Property` objects for a `Parameter` object.
Size	Long	Indicates the maximum size, in bytes or characters, of a `Parameter` object.

Table Continued on Following Page

Name	Returns	Description
Type	DataTypeEnum	Indicates the data type of the Parameter object.
Value	Variant	Indicates the value assigned to the Parameter object.

Parameters Collection

Methods

Name	Returns	Description
Append		Appends a Parameter object to the Parameters collection.
Delete		Deletes a Parameter object from the Parameters collection.
Refresh		Updates the Parameter objects in the Parameters collection.

Properties

Name	Returns	Description
Count	Long	Indicates the number of Parameter objects in the Parameters collection. Read-only.
Item	Parameter	Allows indexing into the Parameters collection to reference a specific Parameter object. Read-only.

Properties

Methods

Name	Returns	Description
Refresh		Updates the Property objects in the Properties collection with the details from the provider.

Properties

Name	Returns	Description
Count	Long	Indicates the number of Property objects in the Properties collection. Read-only.
Item	Property	Allows indexing into the Properties collection to reference a specific Property object. Read-only.

Property Object

Properties

Name	Returns	Description
Attributes	Long	Indicates one or more characteristics of a Property object.
Name	String	Indicates the name of the Property object. Read-only.
Type	DataTypeEnum	Indicates the data type of the Property object.
Value	Variant	Indicates the value assigned to the Property object.

Recordset Object

Methods

Name	Returns	Description
AddNew		Creates a new record for an updateable Recordset object.
Cancel		Cancels execution of a pending asynchronous Open operation.
CancelBatch		Cancels a pending batch update.
CancelUpdate		Cancels any changes made to the current record, or to a new record prior to calling the Update method.
Clone	Recordset	Creates a duplicate Recordset object from an existing Recordset object.
Close		Closes the Recordset object and any dependent objects.
Compare Bookmarks	Compare Enum	Compares two bookmarks and returns an indication of the relative values.
Delete		Deletes the current record or group of records.
Find		Searches the Recordset for a record that matches the specified criteria.
GetRows	Variant	Retrieves multiple records of a Recordset object into an array.
GetString	String	Returns a Recordset as a string.

Table Continued on Following Page

Name	Returns	Description
Move		Moves the position of the current record in a Recordset.
MoveFirst		Moves the position of the current record to the first record in the Recordset.
MoveLast		Moves the position of the current record to the last record in the Recordset.
MoveNext		Moves the position of the current record to the next record in the Recordset.
MovePrevious		Moves the position of the current record to the previous record in the Recordset.
NextRecordset	Recordset	Clears the current Recordset object and returns the next Recordset by advancing through a series of commands.
Open		Opens a Recordset.
Requery		Updates the data in a Recordset object by re-executing the query on which the object is based.
Resync		Refreshes the data in the current Recordset object from the underlying database.
Save		Saves the Recordset to a file.
Seek		Searches the Index of a Recordset to locate a row that matches a value, and changes the current row to the found row. This feature is new to ADO 2.1.
Supports	Boolean	Determines whether a specified Recordset object supports particular functionality.
Update		Saves any changes made to the current Recordset object.
UpdateBatch		Writes all pending batch updates to disk.

Properties

Name	Returns	Description
AbsolutePage	PositionEnum	Specifies in which page the current record resides.
AbsolutePosition	PositionEnum	Specifies the ordinal position of a Recordset object's current record.
ActiveCommand	Object	Indicates the Command object that created the associated Recordset object. Read-only.

Name	Returns	Description
ActiveConnection	Variant	Indicates to which Connection object the specified Recordset object currently belongs.
BOF	Boolean	Indicates whether the current record is before the first record in a Recordset object. Read-only.
Bookmark	Variant	Returns a bookmark that uniquely identifies the current record in a Recordset object, or sets the current record to the record identified by a valid bookmark.
CacheSize	Long	Indicates the number of records from a Recordset object that are cached locally in memory.
CursorLocation	CursorLocation Enum	Sets or returns the location of the cursor engine.
CursorType	CursorTypeEnum	Indicates the type of cursor used in a Recordset object.
DataMember	String	Specifies the name of the data member to retrieve from the object referenced by the DataSource property. Write-only.
DataSource	Object	Specifies an object containing data to be represented as a Recordset object. Write only.
EditMode	EditModeEnum	Indicates the editing status of the current record. Read-only.
EOF	Boolean	Indicates whether the current record is after the last record in a Recordset object. Read-only.
Fields	Fields	Contains all of the Field objects for the current Recordset object.
Filter	Variant	Indicates a filter for data in the Recordset.
Index	String	Indicates the name of the current Index for the Recordset. This property is new to ADO 2.1.
LockType	LockTypeEnum	Indicates the type of locks placed on records during editing.
MarshalOptions	MarshalOptions Enum	Indicates which records are to be marshaled back to the server.

Table Continued on Following Page

Name	Returns	Description
MaxRecords	Long	Indicates the maximum number of records to return to a Recordset object from a query. Default is zero (no limit).
PageCount	Long	Indicates how many pages of data the Recordset object contains. Read-only.
PageSize	Long	Indicates how many records constitute one page in the Recordset.
Properties	Properties	Contains all of the Property objects for the current Recordset object.
RecordCount	Long	Indicates the current number of records in the Recordset object. Read-only.
Sort	String	Specifies one or more field names the Recordset is sorted on, and the direction of the sort.
Source	String	Indicates the source for the data in a Recordset object.
State	Long	Indicates whether the recordset is open, closed, or whether it is executing an asynchronous operation. Read-only.
Status	Integer	Indicates the status of the current record with respect to match updates or other bulk operations. Read-only.
StayInSync	Boolean	Indicates, in a hierarchical Recordset object, whether the parent row should change when the set of underlying child records changes. Read-only.

Events

Name	Description
EndOfRecordset	Fired when there is an attempt to move to a row past the end of the Recordset.
FetchComplete	Fired after all the records in an asynchronous operation have been retrieved into the Recordset.
FetchProgress	Fired periodically during a length asynchronous operation, to report how many rows have currently been retrieved.
FieldChangeComplete	Fired after the value of one or more Field object has been changed.
MoveComplete	Fired after the current position in the Recordset changes.
RecordChangeComplete	Fired after one or more records change.

Name	Description
`RecordsetChangeComplete`	Fired after the `Recordset` has changed.
`WillChangeField`	Fired before a pending operation changes the value of one or more `Field` objects.
`WillChangeRecord`	Fired before one or more rows in the `Recordset` change.
`WillChangeRecordset`	Fired before a pending operation changes the `Recordset`.
`WillMove`	Fired before a pending operation changes the current position in the `Recordset`.

Constants

AffectEnum

Name	Value	Description
`adAffectAll`	3	Operation affects all records in the recordset.
`adAffectAll Chapters`	4	Operation affects all child (chapter) records.
`adAffectCurrent`	1	Operation affects only the current record.
`adAffectGroup`	2	Operation affects records that satisfy the current `Filter` property.

BookmarkEnum

Name	Value	Description
`adBookmarkCurrent`	0	Default. Start at the current record.
`adBookmarkFirst`	1	Start at the first record.
`adBookmarkLast`	2	Start at the last record.

CEResyncEnum

Name	Value	Description
`adResyncAll`	15	Only invoke the `Resync` for each row that has pending changes.

Table Continued on Following Page

Name	Value	Description
adResyncAuto Increment	1	Default. Only invoke Resync for all successfully inserted rows, including their AutoIncrement column values.
adResyncConflicts	2	Only invoke Resync for which the last Update or Delete failed due to a concurrency conflict.
adResyncInserts	8	Only invoke Resync for all successfully inserted rows, including their Identity column values.
adResyncNone	0	Do not invoke Resync.
adResyncUpdates	4	Only invoke Resync for all successfully updated rows.

CEResyncEnum is new to ADO 2.1.

CommandTypeEnum

Name	Value	Description
adCmdFile	256	Indicates that the provider should evaluate CommandText as a previously persisted file.
adCmdStoredProc	4	Indicates that the provider should evaluate CommandText as a stored procedure.
adCmdTable	2	Indicates that the provider should generate a SQL query to return all rows from the table named in CommandText.
adCmdTableDirect	512	Indicates that the provider should return all rows from the table named in CommandText.
adCmdText	1	Indicates that the provider should evaluate CommandText as textual definition of a command, such as a SQL statement.
adCmdUnknown	8	Indicates that the type of command in CommandText is unknown.

CompareEnum

Name	Value	Description
adCompareEqual	1	The bookmarks are equal.
adCompareGreaterThan	2	The first bookmark is after the second.
adCompareLessThan	0	The first bookmark is before the second.
adCompareNotComparable	4	The bookmarks cannot be compared.
adCompareNotEqual	3	The bookmarks are not equal and not ordered.

ConnectModeEnum

Name	Value	Description
adModeRead	1	Indicates read-only permissions.
adModeReadWrite	3	Indicates read/write permissions.
adModeShareDeny None	16	Prevents others from opening connection with any permissions.
adModeShareDeny Read	4	Prevents others from opening connection with read permissions.
adModeShareDeny Write	8	Prevents others from opening connection with write permissions.
adModeShare Exclusive	12	Prevents others from opening connection.
adModeUnknown	0	Default. Indicates that the permissions have not yet been set or cannot be determined.
adModeWrite	2	Indicates write-only permissions.

ConnectOptionEnum

Name	Value	Description
adAsyncConnect	16	Open the connection asynchronously.
adConnect Unspecified	-1	The connection mode is unspecified.

ConnectPromptEnum

Name	Value	Description
adPromptAlways	1	Always prompt for connection information.
adPromptComplete	2	Only prompt if not enough information was supplied.
adPromptComplete Required	3	Only prompt if not enough information was supplied, but disable any options not directly applicable to the connection.
adPromptNever	4	Default. Never prompt for connection information.

CursorLocationEnum

Name	Value	Description
adUseClient	3	Use client-side cursors supplied by the local cursor library.
adUseClientBatch	3	Use client-side cursors supplied by the local cursor library.
adUseNone	1	No cursor services are used.
adUseServer	2	Default. Uses data provider driver supplied cursors.

CursorOptionEnum

Name	Value	Description
adAddNew	16778240	You can use the AddNew method to add new records.
adApproxPosition	16384	You can read and set the AbsolutePosition and AbsolutePage properties.
adBookmark	8192	You can use the Bookmark property to access specific records.
adDelete	16779264	You can use the Delete method to delete records.
adFind	524288	You can use the Find method to find records.
adHoldRecords	256	You can retrieve more records or change the next retrieve position without committing all pending changes.
adIndex	8388608	You can use the Index property to name an index. This value is new to ADO 2.1.
adMovePrevious	512	You can use the ModeFirst, MovePrevious, Move and GetRows methods.
adNotify	262144	The recordset supports Notifications.
adResync	131072	You can update the cursor with the data visible in the underlying database with the Resync method.
adSeek	4194304	You can use the Seek method to find a row in a Recordset. This value is new to ADO 2.1.
adUpdate	16809984	You can use the Update method to modify existing records.
adUpdateBatch	65536	You can use the UpdateBatch or CancelBatch methods to transfer changes to the provider in groups.

CursorTypeEnum

Name	Value	Description
`adOpenDynamic`	2	Opens a dynamic type cursor.
`adOpenForwardOnly`	0	Default. Opens a forward-only type cursor
`adOpenKeyset`	1	Opens a keyset type cursor.
`adOpenStatic`	3	Opens a static type cursor.
`adOpenUnspecified`	-1	Indicates an unspecified value for cursor type.

DataTypeEnum

Name	Value	Description
`adBigInt`	20	An 8-byte signed integer.
`adBinary`	128	A binary value.
`adBoolean`	11	A `Boolean` value.
`adBSTR`	8	A null-terminated character string.
`adChapter`	136	A chapter type, indicating a child recordset.
`adChar`	129	A `String` value.
`adCurrency`	6	A currency value. An 8-byte signed integer scaled by 10,000, with 4 digits to the right of the decimal point.
`adDate`	7	A `Date` value. A `Double` where the whole part is the number of days since December 31 1899, and the fractional part is a fraction of the day.
`adDBDate`	133	A date value (yyyymmdd).
`adDBFileTime`	137	A database file time.
`adDBTime`	134	A time value (hhmmss).
`adDBTimeStamp`	135	A date-time stamp (yyyymmddhhmmss plus a fraction in billionths).
`adDecimal`	14	An exact numeric value with fixed precision and scale.
`adDouble`	5	A double-precision floating point value.
`adEmpty`	0	No value was specified.
`adError`	10	A 32-bit error code.

Table Continued on Following Page

Name	Value	Description
adFileTime	64	A DOS/Win32 file time. The number of 100 nanosecond intervals since Jan 1 1601.
adGUID	72	A globally unique identifier.
adIDispatch	9	A pointer to an IDispatch interface on an OLE object.
adInteger	3	A 4-byte signed integer.
adIUnknown	13	A pointer to an IUnknown interface on an OLE object.
adLongVarBinary	205	A long binary value.
adLongVarChar	201	A long String value.
adLongVarWChar	203	A long null-terminated string value.
adNumeric	131	An exact numeric value with a fixed precision and scale.
adPropVariant	138	A variant that is not equivalent to an Automation variant.
adSingle	4	A single-precision floating point value.
adSmallInt	2	A 2-byte signed integer.
adTinyInt	16	A 1-byte signed integer.
adUnsignedBigInt	21	An 8-byte unsigned integer.
adUnsignedInt	19	A 4-byte unsigned integer.
adUnsignedSmallInt	18	A 2-byte unsigned integer.
adUnsignedTinyInt	17	A 1-byte unsigned integer.
adUserDefined	132	A user-defined variable.
adVarBinary	204	A binary value.
adVarChar	200	A String value.
adVariant	12	An Automation Variant.
adVarNumeric	139	A variable width exact numeric, with a signed scale value.
adVarWChar	202	A null-terminated Unicode character string.
adWChar	130	A null-terminated Unicode character string.

EditModeEnum

Name	Value	Description
adEditAdd	2	Indicates that the AddNew method has been invoked and the current record in the buffer is a new record that hasn't been saved to the database.
adEditDelete	4	Indicates that the Delete method has been invoked.
adEditInProgress	1	Indicates that data in the current record has been modified but not saved.
adEditNone	0	Indicates that no editing is in progress.

ErrorValueEnum

Name	Value	Description
adErrBoundToCommand	3707	The application cannot change the ActiveConnection property of a Recordset object with a Command object as its source.
adErrDataConversion	3421	The application is using a value of the wrong type for the current application.
adErrFeatureNotAvailable	3251	The operation requested by the application is not supported by the provider.
adErrIllegalOperation	3219	The operation requested by the application is not allowed in this context.
adErrInTransaction	3246	The application cannot explicitly close a Connection object while in the middle of a transaction.
adErrInvalidArgument	3001	The application is using arguments that are the wrong type, are out of the acceptable range, or are in conflict with one another.
adErrInvalidConnection	3709	The application requested an operation on an object with a reference to a closed or invalid Connection object.
adErrInvalidParamInfo	3708	The application has improperly defined a Parameter object.
adErrItemNotFound	3265	ADO could not find the object in the collection.
adErrNoCurrentRecord	3021	Either BOF or EOF is True, or the current record has been deleted. The operation requested by the application requires a current record.

Table Continued on Following Page

Name	Value	Description
adErrNotExecuting	3715	The operation is not executing.
adErrNotReentrant	3710	The operation is not reentrant.
adErrObjectClosed	3704	The operation requested by the application is not allowed if the object is closed.
adErrObjectInCollection	3367	Can't append. Object already in collection.
adErrObjectNotSet	3420	The object referenced by the application no longer points to a valid object.
adErrObjectOpen	3705	The operation requested by the application is not allowed if the object is open.
adErrOperationCancelled	3712	The operation was cancelled.
adErrProviderNotFound	3706	ADO could not find the specified provider.
adErrStillConnecting	3713	The operation is still connecting.
adErrStillExecuting	3711	The operation is still executing.
adErrUnsafeOperation	3716	The operation is unsafe under these circumstances.

EventReasonEnum

Name	Value	Description
adRsnAddNew	1	A new record is to be added.
adRsnClose	9	The object is being closed.
adRsnDelete	2	The record is being deleted.
adRsnFirstChange	11	The record has been changed for the first time.
adRsnMove	10	A Move has been invoked and the current record pointer is being moved.
adRsnMoveFirst	12	A MoveFirst has been invoked and the current record pointer is being moved.
adRsnMoveLast	15	A MoveLast has been invoked and the current record pointer is being moved.
adRsnMoveNext	13	A MoveNext has been invoked and the current record pointer is being moved.
adRsnMovePrevious	14	A MovePrevious has been invoked and the current record pointer is being moved.
adRsnRequery	7	The recordset was requeried.

Name	Value	Description
`adRsnResynch`	8	The recordset was resynchronized.
`adRsnUndoAddNew`	5	The addition of a new record has been cancelled.
`adRsnUndoDelete`	6	The deletion of a record has been cancelled.
`adRsnUndoUpdate`	4	The update of a record has been cancelled.
`adRsnUpdate`	3	The record is being updated.

EventStatusEnum

Name	Value	Description
`adStatusCancel`	4	Request cancellation of the operation that is about to occur.
`adStatusCantDeny`	3	A `Will` event cannot request cancellation of the operation about to occur.
`adStatusErrors Occurred`	2	The operation completed unsuccessfully, or a `Will` event cancelled the operation.
`adStatusOK`	1	The operation completed successfully.
`adStatusUnwanted Event`	5	Events for this operation are no longer required.

ExecuteOptionEnum

Name	Value	Description
`adAsyncExecute`	16	The operation is executed asynchronously.
`adAsyncFetch`	32	The records are fetched asynchronously.
`adAsyncFetchNon Blocking`	64	The records are fetched asynchronously without blocking subsequent operations.
`adExecuteNo Records`	128	Indicates `CommandText` is a command or stored procedure that does not return rows. Always combined with `adCmdText` or `adCmdStoreProc`.

FieldAttributeEnum

Name	Value	Description
adFldCache Deferred	4096	Indicates that the provider caches field values and that subsequent reads are done from the cache.
adFldFixed	16	Indicates that the field contains fixed-length data.
adFldIsNullable	32	Indicates that the field accepts Null values.
adFldKeyColumn	32768	The field is part of a key column.
adFldLong	128	Indicates that the field is a long binary field, and that the AppendChunk and GetChunk methods can be used.
adFldMayBeNull	64	Indicates that you can read Null values from the field.
adFldMayDefer	2	Indicates that the field is deferred, that is, the field values are not retrieved from the data source with the whole record, but only when you access them.
adFldNegative Scale	16384	The field has a negative scale.
adFldRowID	256	Indicates that the field is some kind of record ID.
adFldRowVersion	512	Indicates that the field time or date stamp used to track updates.
adFldUnknown Updatable	8	Indicates that the provider cannot determine if you can write to the field.
adFldUpdatable	4	Indicates that you can write to the field.

FilterGroupEnum

Name	Value	Description
adFilterAffected Records	2	Allows you to view only records affected by the last Delete, Resync, UpdateBatch, or CancelBatch method.
adFilterConflicting Records	5	Allows you to view the records that failed the last batch update attempt.
adFilterFetched Records	3	Allows you to view records in the current cache.
adFilterNone	0	Removes the current filter and restores all records to view.

Name	Value	Description
`adFilterPending Records`	1	Allows you to view only the records that have changed but have not been sent to the server. Only applicable for batch update mode.
`adFilterPredicate`	4	Allows you to view records that failed the last batch update attempt.

GetRowsOptionEnum

Name	Value	Description
`adGetRowsRest`	-1	Retrieves the remainder of the rows in the recordset.

IsolationLevelEnum

Name	Value	Description
`adXactBrowse`	256	Indicates that from one transaction you can view uncommitted changes in other transactions.
`adXactChaos`	16	Default. Indicates that you cannot overwrite pending changes from more highly isolated transactions.
`adXactCursor Stability`	4096	Default. Indicates that from one transaction you can view changes in other transactions only after they have been committed.
`adXactIsolated`	1048576	Indicates that transactions are conducted in isolation of other transactions.
`adXactRead Committed`	4096	Same as `adXactCursorStability`.
`adXactRead Uncommitted`	256	Same as `adXactBrowse`.
`adXactRepeatable Read`	65536	Indicates that from one transaction you cannot see changes made in other transactions, but that requerying can bring new recordsets.
`adXactSerializable`	1048576	Same as `adXactIsolated`.
`adXactUnspecified`	-1	Indicates that the provider is using a different `IsolationLevel` than specified, but that the level cannot be identified.

LockTypeEnum

Name	Value	Description
adLockBatch Optimistic	4	Optimistic batch updates.
adLockOptimistic	3	Optimistic locking, record by record. The provider locks records when Update is called.
adLockPessimistic	2	Pessimistic locking, record by record. The provider locks the record immediately upon editing.
adLockReadOnly	1	Default. Read-only, data cannot be modified.
adLockUnspecified	-1	The clone is created with the same lock type as the original.

MarshalOptionsEnum

Name	Value	Description
adMarshalAll	0	Default. Indicates that all rows are returned to the server.
adMarshalModified Only	1	Indicates that only modified rows are returned to the server.

ObjectStateEnum

Name	Value	Description
adStateClosed	0	Default. Indicates that the object is closed.
adStateConnecting	2	Indicates that the object is connecting.
adStateExecuting	4	Indicates that the object is executing a command.
adStateFetching	8	Indicates that the rows of the recordset are being fetched.
adStateOpen	1	Indicates that the object is open.

ParameterAttributesEnum

Name	Value	Description
adParamLong	128	Indicates that the parameter accepts long binary data.
adParamNullable	64	Indicates that the parameter accepts Null values.
adParamSigned	16	Default. Indicates that the parameter accepts signed values.

ParameterDirectionEnum

Name	Value	Description
adParamInput	1	Default. Indicates an input parameter.
adParamInputOutput	3	Indicates both an input and output parameter.
adParamOutput	2	Indicates an output parameter.
adParamReturnValue	4	Indicates a return value.
adParamUnknown	0	Indicates parameter direction is unknown.

PersistFormatEnum

Name	Value	Description
adPersistADTG	0	Default. Persist data in Advanced Data Table Gram format.
adPersistXML	1	Persist data in XML format.

PositionEnum

Name	Value	Description
adPosBOF	-2	The current record pointer is at BOF.
adPosEOF	-3	The current record pointer is at EOF.
adPosUnknown	-1	The Recordset is empty, the current position is unknown, or the provider does not support the AbsolutePage property.

PropertyAttributesEnum

Name	Value	Description
adPropNotSupported	0	Indicates that the property is not supported by the provider.
adPropOptional	2	Indicates that the user does not need to specify a value for this property before the data source is initialized.
adPropRead	512	Indicates that the user can read the property.
adPropRequired	1	Indicates that the user must specify a value for this property before the data source is initialized.
adPropWrite	1024	Indicates that the user can set the property.

RecordStatusEnum

Name	Value	Description
adRecCanceled	256	The record was not saved because the operation was cancelled.
adRecCantRelease	1024	The new record was not saved because of existing record locks.
adRecConcurrency Violation	2048	The record was not saved because optimistic concurrency was in use.
adRecDBDeleted	262144	The record has already been deleted from the data source.
adRecDeleted	4	The record was deleted.
adRecIntegrity Violation	4096	The record was not saved because the user violated integrity constraints.
adRecInvalid	16	The record was not saved because its bookmark is invalid.
adRecMaxChanges Exceeded	8192	The record was not saved because there were too many pending changes.
adRecModified	2	The record was modified.
adRecMultiple Changes	64	The record was not saved because it would have affected multiple records.
adRecNew	1	The record is new.
adRecObjectOpen	16384	The record was not saved because of a conflict with an open storage object.
adRecOK	0	The record was successfully updated.
adRecOutOfMemory	32768	The record was not saved because the computer has run out of memory.
adRecPendingChanges	128	The record was not saved because it refers to a pending insert.
adRecPermission Denied	65536	The record was not saved because the user has insufficient permissions.
adRecSchema Violation	131072	The record was not saved because it violates the structure of the underlying database.
adRecUnmodified	8	The record was not modified.

ResyncEnum

Name	Value	Description
adResyncAllValues	2	Default. Data is overwritten and pending updates are cancelled.
adResyncUnderlyingValues	1	Data is not overwritten and pending updates are not cancelled.

SchemaEnum

Name	Value	Description
adSchemaAsserts	0	Request assert information.
adSchemaCatalogs	1	Request catalog information.
adSchemaCharacterSets	2	Request character set information.
adSchemaCheck Constraints	5	Request check constraint information.
adSchemaCollations	3	Request collation information.
adSchemaColumn Privileges	13	Request column privilege information.
adSchemaColumns	4	Request column information.
adSchemaColumnsDomain Usage	11	Request column domain usage information.
adSchemaConstraintColumn Usage	6	Request column constraint usage information.
adSchemaConstraintTable Usage	7	Request table constraint usage information.
adSchemaCubes	32	For multi-dimensional data, view the Cubes schema.
adSchemaDBInfoKeywords	30	Request the keywords from the provider.
adSchemaDBInfoLiterals	31	Request the literals from the provider.
adSchemaDimensions	33	For multi-dimensional data, view the Dimensions schema.
adSchemaForeignKeys	27	Request foreign key information.
adSchemaHierarchies	34	For multi-dimensional data, view the Hierarchies schema.

Table Continued on Following Page

Name	Value	Description
adSchemaIndexes	12	Request index information.
adSchemaKeyColumn Usage	8	Request key column usage information.
adSchemaLevels	35	For multi-dimensional data, view the Levels schema.
adSchemaMeasures	36	For multi-dimensional data, view the Measures schema.
adSchemaMembers	38	For multi-dimensional data, view the Members schema.
adSchemaPrimaryKeys	28	Request primary key information.
adSchemaProcedure Columns	29	Request stored procedure column information.
adSchemaProcedure Parameters	26	Request stored procedure parameter information.
adSchemaProcedures	16	Request stored procedure information.
adSchemaProperties	37	For multi-dimensional data, view the Properties schema.
adSchemaProvider Specific	-1	Request provider specific information.
adSchemaProvider Types	22	Request provider type information.
adSchemaReferential Contraints	9	Request referential constraint information.
adSchemaSchemata	17	Request schema information.
adSchemaSQLLanguages	18	Request SQL language support information.
adSchemaStatistics	19	Request statistics information.
adSchemaTable Constraints	10	Request table constraint information.
adSchemaTable Privileges	14	Request table privilege information.
adSchemaTables	20	Request information about the tables.
adSchemaTranslations	21	Request character set translation information.
adSchemaTrustees	39	Request trustee information. This value is new for ADO 2.1.
adSchemaUsage Privileges	15	Request user privilege information.

Name	Value	Description
adSchemaViewColumn Usage	24	Request column usage in views information.
adSchemaViews	23	Request view information.
adSchemaViewTable Usage	25	Request table usage in views information.

SearchDirection

Name	Value	Description
adSearchBackward	-1	Search backward from the current record.
adSearchForward	1	Search forward from the current record.

SearchDirectionEnum

Name	Value	Description
adSearchBackward	-1	Search backward from the current record.
adSearchForward	1	Search forward from the current record.

SeekEnum

Name	Value	Description
adSeekAfter	8	Seek the record after the match.
adSeekAfterEQ	4	Seek the record equal to the match, or if no match is found, the record after where the match would have been.
adSeekBefore	32	Seek the record before the match.
adSeekBeforeEQ	16	Seek the record equal to the match, or if no match is found, the record before where the match would have been.
adSeekFirstEQ	1	Seek the first record equal to the match.
adSeekLastEQ	2	Seek the last record equal to the match.

SeekEnum is new to ADO 2.1

StringFormatEnum

Name	Value	Description
`adClipString`	2	Rows are delimited by user defined values.

XactAttributeEnum

Name	Value	Description
`adXactAbortRetaining`	262144	The provider will automatically start a new transaction after a `RollbackTrans` method call.
`adXactAsyncPhaseOne`	524288	Perform an asynchronous commit.
`adXactCommitRetaining`	131072	The provider will automatically start a new transaction after a `CommitTrans` method call.
`adXactSyncPhaseOne`	1048576	Performs a synchronous commit.

Method Calls Quick Reference

Command

Command.Cancel
Parameter = *Command*.CreateParameter(*Name As String, Type As DataTypeEnum, _*
    Direction As ParameterDirectionEnum, Size As Integer, [Value As Variant])
Recordset = *Command*.Execute(*RecordsAffected As Variant, Parameters As Variant, _*
    Options As Integer)

Connection

Integer = *Connection*.BeginTrans
Connection.Cancel
Connection.Close
Connection.CommitTrans
Recordset = *Connection*.Execute(*CommandText As String, RecordsAffected As Variant, _*
    Options As Integer)
Connection.Open(*ConnectionString As String, UserID As String, Password As String, _*
    Options As Integer)
Recordset = *Connection*.OpenSchema(*Schema As SchemaEnum, [Restrictions As Variant], _*
    [SchemaID As Variant])
Connection.RollbackTrans

Errors

Errors.Clear
Errors.Refresh

Field

Field.AppendChunk(*Data As Variant*)
Variant = Field.GetChunk(*Length As Integer*)

Fields

Fields.Append(*Name As String, Type As DataTypeEnum, DefinedSize As Integer, _*
    Attrib As FieldAttributeEnum)
Fields.Delete(Index As Variant)
Fields.Refresh

Parameter

Parameter.AppendChunk(*Val As Variant*)

Parameters

Parameters.Append(*Object As Object*)
Parameters.Delete(*Index As Variant*)
Parameters.Refresh

Properties

Properties.Refresh

Recordset

Recordset.AddNew([*FieldList As Variant], [Values As Variant]*)
Recordset.Cancel
Recordset.CancelBatch(*AffectRecords As AffectEnum*)
Recordset.CancelUpdate
Recordset = Recordset.Clone(*LockType As LockTypeEnum*)
Recordset.Close
CompareEnum = Recordset.CompareBookmarks(*Bookmark1 As Variant, Bookmark2 As Variant*)
Recordset.Delete(*AffectRecords As AffectEnum*)
Recordset.Find(*Criteria As String, SkipRecords As Integer, _*
    SearchDirection As SearchDirectionEnum, [Start As Variant])
Variant = Recordset.GetRows(*Rows As Integer, [Start As Variant], [Fields As Variant]*)
String = Recordset.GetString(*StringFormat As StringFormatEnum, _*
    NumRows As Integer, ColumnDelimiter As String, RowDelimeter As String, _
    NullExpr As String)
Recordset.Move(*NumRecords As Integer, [Start As Variant]*)
Recordset.MoveFirst
Recordset.MoveLast
Recordset.MoveNext
Recordset.MovePrevious
Recordset = Recordset.NextRecordset([*RecordsAffected As Variant]*)
Recordset.Open(*Source As Variant, ActiveConnection As Variant, _*
    CursorType As CursorTypeEnum, LockType As LockTypeEnum, Options As Integer)
Recordset.Requery(*Options As Integer*)

Recordset.Resync(*AffectRecords As AffectEnum, ResyncValues As ResyncEnum*)
Recordset.Save(*FileName As String, PersistFormat As PersistFormatEnum*)
Recordset.Seek(*KeyValues As Variant, SeekOption As SeekEnum*)
Boolean = Recordset.Supports(*CursorOptions As CursorOptionEnum*)
Recordset.Update(*[Fields As Variant], [Values As Variant]*)
Recordset.UpdateBatch(*AffectRecords As AffectEnum*)

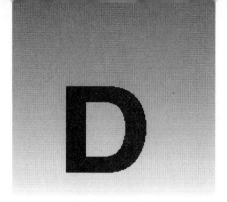

Access Object Model

The full Access object model is extremely large, so we've decided to give you a cut-down version, highlighting the most important objects. So, unlike the two data access object models, what you've got here are the main objects. One of the reasons why it's not feasible to print the whole object model is that each property, method and event would be shown. When designing a form, if you look at the properties for a control, you'll see how many there are for just that one control. Now add in every other object, and you've got a lot of properties, many repeated.

Below is a list of the objects. We've also added the method calls as these are really useful for a reference, but we've left out all of the methods, properties and events of the objects.

Objects

Name	Description
AccessObject	Refers to a particular Access object, such as a form or report.
AccessObject Property	A built-in or user defined property of an Access object.
AccessObject Properties	A collection of `AccessObjectProperty` objects.
AllDataAccess Pages	A collection of `AccessObject` objects for each data access page.
AllDatabase Diagrams	A collection of `AccessObject` objects for each database diagram in an Access Project.
AllForms	A collection of `AccessObject` objects for each form.
AllMacros	A collection of `AccessObject` objects for each macro.
AllModules	A collection of `AccessObject` objects for each module.
AllQueries	A collection of `AccessObject` objects for each query.
AllReports	A collection of `AccessObject` objects for each report.

Table Continued on Following Page

Name	Description
AllStored Procedures	A collection of AccessObject objects for each stored procedure in an Access Project.
AllTables	A collection of AccessObject objects for each table.
AllViews	A collection of AccessObject objects for each view in an Access Project.
Application	The main Access application.
BoundObject Frame	An OLE Object bound to a column in a table.
Checkbox	A Yes/No checkbox.
Combobox	A combo box.
CommandButton	A command button.
Control	A generic control on a form or report.
Controls	A collection of Control objects.
CurrentData	The current data database.
CurrentProject	The current code database.
DataAccessPage	A data access page.
DataAccess Pages	A collection of DataAccessPage objects.
DefaultWeb Options	Default options for saving web pages.
DoCmd	Allows running of actions.
Form	A form.
Forms	A collection of Form objects.
Format Condition	A conditional format for a combo box or text box on a form or report.
Format Conditions	A collection of FormatCondition objects.
GroupLevel	The group level used when sorting or grouping in a report.
Hyperlink	Represents an Internet hyperlink.
Image	An image control.
ItemsSelected	A collection of items selected in a multi-select list box.
Label	A label control.
Line	A line control.

Name	Description
ListBox	A list box control.
Module	A code module.
Modules	A collection of Module objects.
ObjectFrame	An OLE Object, or ActiveX component.
OptionButton	An option button control.
OptionGroup	An option group control.
Page	A page on a tab control.
Pages	A collection of Page objects.
PageBreak	A page break control on a form or report.
Property	An individual property of an object.
Properties	A collection of Property objects.
Recordset	A collection of records.
Rectangle	A rectangle object.
Reference	A reference set to an external objects (such as a type library).
References	A collection of Reference objects.
Report	A report.
Reports	A collection of Report objects.
Screen	The form, report or control that has the focus.
Section	A section of a form or report.
SubForm	A sub-form control.
SubReport	A sub-report control.
TabControl	A tab control.
Textbox	A text box control.
ToggleButton	A toggle button control.
WebOptions	The properties of a data access page.

Method Calls

AccessObjectProperties

AccessObjectProperties.Add(*PropertyName As String, Value As Variant*)
AccessObjectProperties.Remove(*Item As Variant*)

Application

Variant = Application.AccessError(*ErrorNumber As Variant*)
Application.AddAutoCorrect(*ChangeFrom As String, ChangeTo As String*)
Application.AddToFavorites
Variant = Application.AppLoadString(*id As Integer*)
Application.BeginUndoable(*Hwnd As Integer*)
String = Application.BuildCriteria(*Field As String, FieldType As SmallInt, _
    Expression As String*)
Variant = Application.BuilderString
Application.CloseCurrentDatabase
Application.CodeDb
Application.CreateAccessProject(*filepath As String, [Connect As Variant]*)
Control = Application.CreateControl(*FormName As String, ControlType As AcControlType, _
    Section As AcSection, [Parent As Variant], [ColumnName As Variant], _
    [Left As Variant], [Top As Variant], [Width As Variant], [Height As Variant]*)
Control = Application.CreateControlEx(*FormName As String, ControlType As AcControlType, _
    Section As AcSection, Parent As String, ControlSource As String, Left As Integer, _
    Top As Integer, Width As Integer, Height As Integer*)
DataAccessPage = Application.CreateDataAccessPage(*FileName As Variant, _
    CreateNewFile As Boolean*)
Form = Application.CreateForm(*[Database As Variant], [FormTemplate As Variant]*)
Integer = Application.CreateGroupLevel(*ReportName As String, Expression As String, _
    Header As SmallInt, Footer As SmallInt*)
Report = Application.CreateReport(*[Database As Variant], [ReportTemplate As Variant]*)
Control = Application.CreateReportControl(*ReportName As String, _
    ControlType As AcControlType, Section As AcSection, [Parent As Variant], _
    [ColumnName As Variant], [Left As Variant], [Top As Variant], [Width As Variant], _
    [Height As Variant]*)
Application.CurrentDb
String = Application.CurrentUser
Variant = Application.DAvg(*Expr As String, Domain As String, [Criteria As Variant]*)
Variant = Application.DCount(*Expr As String, Domain As String, [Criteria As Variant]*)
Application.DDEExecute(*ChanNum As Variant, Command As String*)
Variant = Application.DDEInitiate(*Application As String, Topic As String*)
Application.DDEPoke(*ChanNum As Variant, Item As String, Data As String*)
String = Application.DDERequest(*ChanNum As Variant, Item As String*)
Application.DDETerminate(*ChanNum As Variant*)
Application.DDETerminateAll
Application.DefaultWorkspaceClone

Application.DelAutoCorrect(*ChangeFrom As String*)

Application.DeleteControl(*FormName As String, ControlName As String*)

Application.DeleteReportControl(*ReportName As String, ControlName As String*)

Variant = Application.DFirst(*Expr As String, Domain As String, [Criteria As Variant]*)

Variant = Application.DLast(*Expr As String, Domain As String, [Criteria As Variant]*)

Variant = Application.DLookup(*Expr As String, Domain As String, [Criteria As Variant]*)

Variant = Application.DMax(*Expr As String, Domain As String, [Criteria As Variant]*)

Variant = Application.DMin(*Expr As String, Domain As String, [Criteria As Variant]*)

Variant = Application.DStDev(*Expr As String, Domain As String, [Criteria As Variant]*)

Variant = Application.DStDevP(*Expr As String, Domain As String, [Criteria As Variant]*)

Variant = Application.DSum(*Expr As String, Domain As String, [Criteria As Variant]*)

Variant = Application.DVar(*Expr As String, Domain As String, [Criteria As Variant]*)

Variant = Application.DVarP(*Expr As String, Domain As String, [Criteria As Variant]*)

Application.Echo(*EchoOn As SmallInt, bstrStatusBarText As String*)

Variant = Application.Eval(*StringExpr As String*)

Application.FollowHyperlink(*Address As String, SubAddress As String, _*
    NewWindow As Boolean, AddHistory As Boolean, ExtraInfo As Variant, _
    Method As _LabelEvents, HeaderInfo As String)

Boolean = Application.GetHiddenAttribute(*ObjectType As AcObjectType, ObjectName As String*)

Variant = Application.GetOption(*OptionName As String*)

Variant = Application.GUIDFromString(*String As Variant*)

String = Application.HyperlinkPart(*Hyperlink As Variant, Part As AcHyperlinkPart*)

Application.InsertText(*Text As String, ModuleName As String*)

Application.LoadFromText(*ObjectType As AcObjectType, ObjectName As String, _*
    FileName As String)

Set *Object = Application*.LoadPicture(*FileName As String*)

Application.NewAccessProject(*filepath As String, [Connect As Variant]*)

Application.NewCurrentDatabase(*filepath As String*)

Variant = Application.Nz(*Value As Variant, [ValueIfNull As Variant]*)

Application.OpenAccessProject(*filepath As String, Exclusive As Boolean*)

Application.OpenCurrentDatabase(*filepath As String, Exclusive As Boolean*)

Application.Quit(*Option As AcQuitOption*)

Application.RefreshDatabaseWindow

Application.RefreshTitleBar

Application.ReloadAddIns

Application.ReplaceModule(*objtyp As Integer, ModuleName As String, FileName As _*
String,token As Integer)

Variant = Application.Run(*Procedure As String, [Arg1 As Variant], [Arg2 As Variant], _*
    [Arg3 As Variant], [Arg4 As Variant], [Arg5 As Variant], [Arg6 As Variant], _
    [Arg7 As Variant], [Arg8 As Variant], [Arg9 As Variant], [Arg10 As Variant], _
    [Arg11 As Variant], [Arg12 As Variant], [Arg13 As Variant], [Arg14 As Variant], _
    [Arg15 As Variant], [Arg16 As Variant], [Arg17 As Variant], [Arg18 As Variant], _
    [Arg19 As Variant], [Arg20 As Variant], [Arg21 As Variant], [Arg22 As Variant], _
    [Arg23 As Variant], [Arg24 As Variant], [Arg25 As Variant], [Arg26 As Variant], _
    [Arg27 As Variant], [Arg28 As Variant], [Arg29 As Variant], [Arg30 As Variant])

Application.RunCommand(*Command As AcCommand*)

Application.SaveAsText(*ObjectType As AcObjectType, ObjectName As String, FileName As String*)

Application.SetHiddenAttribute(*ObjectType As AcObjectType, ObjectName As String, _*
    fHidden As Boolean)

Application.SetOption(*OptionName As String, Setting As Variant*)

Application.SetUndoRecording(*yesno As SmallInt*)
Variant = *Application*.StringFromGUID(*Guid As Variant*)
Variant = *Application*.SysCmd(*Action As AcSysCmdAction, [Argument2 As Variant], _*
    [Argument3 As Variant])

BoundObjectFrame

BoundObjectFrame.Requery
BoundObjectFrame.SetFocus
BoundObjectFrame.SizeToFit

Checkbox

Checkbox.Requery
Checkbox.SetFocus
Checkbox.SizeToFit
Checkbox.Undo

Combobox

Combobox.Dropdown
Combobox.Requery
Combobox.SetFocus
Combobox.SizeToFit
Combobox.Undo

CommandButton

CommandButton.Requery
CommandButton.SetFocus
CommandButton.SizeToFit

Control

Control.Dropdown
Control.Requery
Control.SetFocus
Control.SizeToFit
Control.Undo

CurrentProject

CurrentProject.CloseConnection
CurrentProject.OpenConnection(*[BaseConnectionString As Variant], [UserID As Variant], [Password As Variant]*)

DataAccessPage

DataAccessPage.ApplyTheme(*ThemeName As String*)

DoCmd

DoCmd.AddMenu(*MenuName As Variant, MenuMacroName As Variant, StatusBarText As Variant*)
DoCmd.ApplyFilter([*FilterName As Variant*], [*WhereCondition As Variant*])
DoCmd.Beep
DoCmd.CancelEvent
DoCmd.Close(*ObjectType As AcObjectType, ObjectName As Variant, Save As AcCloseSave*)
DoCmd.CopyObject(*DestinationDatabase As Variant, NewName As Variant, _*
    SourceObjectType As AcObjectType, [SourceObjectName As Variant])
DoCmd.DeleteObject(*ObjectType As AcObjectType, [ObjectName As Variant]*)
DoCmd.DoMenuItem(*MenuBar As Variant, MenuName As Variant, _*
    Command As Variant, [Subcommand As Variant], [Version As Variant])
DoCmd.Echo(*EchoOn As Variant, [StatusBarText As Variant]*)
DoCmd.FindNext
DoCmd.FindRecord(*FindWhat As Variant, Match As AcFindMatch, MatchCase As Variant, _*
    Search As AcSearchDirection, SearchAsFormatted As Variant, _
    OnlyCurrentField As AcFindField, [FindFirst As Variant])
DoCmd.GoToControl(*ControlName As Variant*)
DoCmd.GoToPage(*PageNumber As Variant, [Right As Variant], [Down As Variant]*)
DoCmd.GoToRecord(*ObjectType As AcDataObjectType, ObjectName As Variant, _*
    Record As AcRecord, [Offset As Variant])
DoCmd.Hourglass(*HourglassOn As Variant*)
DoCmd.Maximize
DoCmd.Minimize
DoCmd.MoveSize([*Right As Variant*], [*Down As Variant*], [*Width As Variant*], _
    [*Height As Variant*])
DoCmd.OpenDataAccessPage(*DataAccessPageName As Variant, View As AcDataAccessPageView*)
DoCmd.OpenDiagram(*DiagramName As Variant*)
DoCmd.OpenForm(*FormName As Variant, View As AcFormView, FilterName As Variant, _*
    WhereCondition As Variant, DataMode As AcFormOpenDataMode, _
    WindowMode As AcWindowMode, [OpenArgs As Variant])
DoCmd.OpenModule([*ModuleName As Variant*], [*ProcedureName As Variant*])
DoCmd.OpenQuery(*QueryName As Variant, View As AcView, DataMode As AcOpenDataMode*)
DoCmd.OpenReport(*ReportName As Variant, View As AcView, [FilterName As Variant], _*
    [*WhereCondition As Variant*])
DoCmd.OpenStoredProcedure(*ProcedureName As Variant, View As AcView, _*
    DataMode As AcOpenDataMode)
DoCmd.OpenTable(*TableName As Variant, View As AcView, DataMode As AcOpenDataMode*)
DoCmd.OpenView(*ViewName As Variant, View As AcView, DataMode As AcOpenDataMode*)
DoCmd.OutputTo(*ObjectType As AcOutputObjectType, [ObjectName As Variant], _*
    [*OutputFormat As Variant*], [*OutputFile As Variant*], [*AutoStart As Variant*], _
    [*TemplateFile As Variant*])
DoCmd.PrintOut(*PrintRange As AcPrintRange, PageFrom As Variant, PageTo As Variant, _*
    PrintQuality As AcPrintQuality, [Copies As Variant], [CollateCopies As Variant])
DoCmd.Quit(*Options As AcQuitOption*)

DoCmd.Rename(*NewName As Variant, ObjectType As AcObjectType, [OldName As Variant]*)
DoCmd.RepaintObject(*ObjectType As AcObjectType, [ObjectName As Variant]*)
DoCmd.Requery(*[ControlName As Variant]*)
DoCmd.Restore
DoCmd.RunCommand(*Command As AcCommand*)
DoCmd.RunMacro(*MacroName As Variant, [RepeatCount As Variant], [RepeatExpression As Variant]*)
DoCmd.RunSQL(*SQLStatement As Variant, [UseTransaction As Variant]*)
DoCmd.Save(*ObjectType As AcObjectType, [ObjectName As Variant]*)
DoCmd.SelectObject(*ObjectType As AcObjectType, [ObjectName As Variant]*, _
    [InDatabaseWindow As Variant])
DoCmd.SendObject(*ObjectType As AcSendObjectType, [ObjectName As Variant]*, _
    [OutputFormat As Variant], [To As Variant], [Cc As Variant], [Bcc As Variant], _
    [Subject As Variant], [MessageText As Variant], [EditMessage As Variant], _
    [TemplateFile As Variant])
DoCmd.SetMenuItem(*MenuIndex As Variant, [CommandIndex As Variant]*, _
    [SubcommandIndex As Variant], [Flag As Variant])
DoCmd.SetWarnings(*WarningsOn As Variant*)
DoCmd.ShowAllRecords
DoCmd.ShowToolbar(*ToolbarName As Variant, Show As AcShowToolbar*)
DoCmd.TransferDatabase(*TransferType As AcDataTransferType, DatabaseType As Variant*, _
    DatabaseName As Variant, ObjectType As AcObjectType, [Source As Variant], _
    [Destination As Variant], [StructureOnly As Variant], [StoreLogin As Variant])
DoCmd.TransferSpreadsheet(*TransferType As AcDataTransferType*, _
    SpreadsheetType As AcSpreadSheetType, [TableName As Variant], _
    [FileName As Variant], [HasFieldNames As Variant], [Range As Variant], [UseOA As Variant])
DoCmd.TransferText(*TransferType As AcTextTransferType, [SpecificationName As Variant], [TableName
As Variant], [FileName As Variant], [HasFieldNames As Variant]*, _
    [HTMLTableName As Variant], [CodePage As Variant])

Form

Form.GoToPage(*PageNumber As Integer, Right As Integer, Down As Integer*)
Form.Recalc
Form.Refresh
Form.Repaint
Form.Requery
Form.SetFocus
Form.Undo

FormatCondition

FormatCondition.Delete
FormatCondition.Modify(*Type As AcFormatConditionType*, _
    Operator As AcFormatConditionOperator, [Expression1 As Variant], _
    [Expression2 As Variant])

FormatConditions

FormatCondition = FormatConditions.Add(*Type As AcFormatConditionType,* _
    Operator As AcFormatConditionOperator, [Expression1 As Variant], _
    [Expression2 As Variant])
FormatConditions.Delete

Hyperlink

Hyperlink.AddToFavorites
Hyperlink.CreateNewDocument(*FileName As String, EditNow As Boolean, Overwrite As Boolean*)
Hyperlink.Follow(*NewWindow As Boolean, AddHistory As Boolean, ExtraInfo As Variant,* _
    Method As _LabelEvents, HeaderInfo As String)

Image

Image.Requery
Image.SetFocus
Image.SizeToFit

Label

Label.SizeToFit

Line

Line.SizeToFit

ListBox

ListBox.Requery
ListBox.SetFocus
ListBox.SizeToFit
ListBox.Undo

Module

Module.AddFromFile(*FileName As String*)
Module.AddFromString(*String As String*)
Integer = Module.CreateEventProc(*EventName As String, ObjectName As String*)
Module.DeleteLines(*StartLine As Integer, Count As Integer*)
Boolean = Module.Find(*Target As String, StartLine As Integer, StartColumn As Integer,* _
    EndLine As Integer, EndColumn As Integer, WholeWord As Boolean, _
    MatchCase As Boolean, PatternSearch As Boolean)
Module.InsertLines(*Line As Integer, String As String*)
Module.InsertText(*Text As String*)
Module.ReplaceLine(*Line As Integer, String As String*)

ObjectFrame

ObjectFrame.Requery
ObjectFrame.SetFocus
ObjectFrame.SizeToFit

OptionButton

OptionButton.Requery
OptionButton.SetFocus
OptionButton.SizeToFit

OptionGroup

OptionGroup.Requery
OptionGroup.SetFocus
OptionGroup.SizeToFit
OptionGroup.Undo

Page

Page.Requery
Page.SetFocus
Page.SizeToFit

PageBreak

PageBreak.SizeToFit

Pages

Page = *Pages*.Add(*[Before As Variant]*)
Pages.Remove(*[Item As Variant]*)

Rectangle

Rectangle.SizeToFit

References

Reference = *References*.AddFromFile(*FileName As String*)
Reference = *References*.AddFromGuid(*Guid As String, Major As Integer, Minor As Integer*)
Reference = *References*.Item(*var As Variant*)
References.Remove(*Reference As Reference*)

Report

Report.Circle(*flags As SmallInt, X As Single, Y As Single, radius As Single, color As* Integer, start As Single, end As Single, aspect As Single)
Report.Line(flags As SmallInt, x1 As Single, y1 As Single, x2 As Single, y2 As Single, color As Integer)
Report.Print(Expr As String)
Report.PSet(flags As SmallInt, X As Single, Y As Single, color As Integer)
Report.Scale(flags As SmallInt, x1 As Single, y1 As Single, x2 As Single, y2 As Single)
Single = Report.TextHeight(Expr As String)
Single = Report.TextWidth(Expr As String)

SubForm

SubForm.Requery
SubForm.SetFocus
SubForm.SizeToFit

TabControl

TabControl.SizeToFit

Textbox

Textbox.Requery
Textbox.SetFocus
Textbox.SizeToFit
Textbox.Undo

ToggleButton

ToggleButton.Requery
ToggleButton.SetFocus
ToggleButton.SizeToFit
ToggleButton.Undo

WebOptions

WebOptions.UseDefaultFolderSuffix

Microsoft DAO 3.6 Object Library Reference

Objects

Name	Description
Connection	A Connection object represents a connection to an ODBC data source.
Connections	Contains one or more Connection objects.
Container	Details about a predefined type of Access object, such as Reports or Forms.
Containers	Contains one or more Container objects.
Database	Represents an open database.
Databases	Contains one or more Database objects.
DBEngine	The Jet database engine.
Document	Details about a saved Access object, such as an individual Report or Form.
Documents	Contains one or more Document objects.
Error	Details of a single error that occurred during a data access method.
Errors	Contains one or more Error objects.
Field	Details of an individual field, or column, in a table, query, index, relation, or recordset.
Fields	Contains one or more Field objects.
Group	Details of a group of User accounts.
Groups	Contains one or more Group objects.

Table Continued on Following Page

Name	Description
Index	Details about the ordering of table values.
Indexes	Contains one or more Index objects.
Parameter	Details of a parameter in a parameter query.
Parameters	Contains one or more Parameter objects.
Property	Details of a user-defined or built-in property on an object.
Properties	Contains one or more Property objects.
QueryDef	Details of a saved query.
QueryDefs	Contains one or more QueryDef objects.
Recordset	The records in an open table or query.
Recordsets	Contains one or more Recordset objects.
Relation	Details the relationship between fields in tables and queries.
Relations	Contains one or more Relation objects.
TableDef	Details of a saved table.
TableDefs	Contains one or more TableDef objects.
User	Details of a user account.
Users	Contains one or more User objects.
Workspace	Details of a session of the Jet database engine.
Workspaces	Contains one or more Workspace objects.

Connection

Methods

Name	Returns	Description
Cancel		Cancels the execution of a pending ODBCDirect asynchronous call.
Close		Closes the active connection.
CreateQueryDef	QueryDef	Create a new QueryDef object.
Execute		Runs a SQL statement or an action query.
OpenRecordset	Recordset	Opens a new recordset.

Properties

Name	Returns	Description
Connect	String	Defines the source of an open connection. Read-only.
Database	Database	Defines the Database object for the current connection. Read-only.
Name	String	Identifies the name of the connection. If the Connection object is not yet appended to the Connections collection, this property is read-only.
QueryDefs	QueryDefs	Collection of QueryDef objects for this database. Read-only.
QueryTimeout	Integer	When connected to an ODBC data source, specifies the number of seconds to wait before an error is generated. The default is 60.
RecordsAffected	Long	Contains the number of records affected by the last Execute method. Read-only.
Recordsets	Recordsets	Collection of Recordset objects open in this connection. Read-only.
StillExecuting	Boolean	For an ODBCDirect connection, identifies whether or not an asynchronous command has finished. Read-only.
Transactions	Boolean	Indicates whether or not the connection supports transactions. Read-only.
Updatable	Boolean	Indicates whether or not data in the connected database can be changed. Read-only.

Connections

Methods

Name	Returns	Description
Refresh		Updates the objects in the collection.

Properties

Name	Returns	Description
Count	Integer	Indicates the number of Connection objects in the collection. Read-only.
Item	Connection	Allows indexing into the collection to reference a specific object. This is the default property and can therefore be omitted. Read-only.

Container

Properties

Name	Returns	Description
AllPermissions	Long	Indicates all the permissions that apply to the Container. It can be one or more of the PermissionEnum constants. Read-only.
Documents	Documents	Collection of Document objects for a specific type of object. Read-only.
Inherit	Boolean	Indicates whether or not new Document objects will inherit default permissions.
Name	String	Indicates the name of the Container. Read-only.
Owner	String	Indicates the owner of the Container. This will be the name of a User or Group object.
Permissions	Long	Indicates the user permissions that apply to the Container. It can be one or more of the PermissionEnum constants.
Properties	Properties	Collection of Property objects. Read-only.
UserName	String	Indicates the user name or group of user names used when manipulating permissions.

Containers

Methods

Name	Returns	Description
Refresh		Updates the objects in the collection.

Properties

Name	Returns	Description
Count	Integer	Indicates the number of Container objects in the collection. Read-only.
Item	Container	Allows indexing into the collection to reference a specific object. This is the default property and can therefore be omitted. Read-only.

Database

Methods

Name	Returns	Description
Close		Closes the database object.
CreateProperty	Property	Creates a new user-defined Property.
CreateQueryDef	QueryDef	Creates a new QueryDef object.
CreateRelation	Relation	Creates a new Relation object.
CreateTableDef	TableDef	Creates a new TableDef object.
Execute		Runs a SQL statement or an action query.
MakeReplica		Creates a new replica from an existing database replica.
NewPassword		Changes the password for a user.
OpenRecordset	Recordset	Opens a recordset.
PopulatePartial		Synchronizes the partial replica database with the full replica database, in a specific manner.
Synchronize		Fully synchronizes two replica databases.

Properties

Name	Returns	Description
CollatingOrder	Long	Specifies the sort order. Returns one of the dbSort constants. Read-only.
Connect	String	Defines the source of an open connection.
Connection	Connection	Identifies the Connection object corresponding to the open database. Read-only.
Containers	Containers	Collection of Container objects defined in a Database object. Read-only.
DesignMasterID	String	Specifies the unique GUID that identifies the Design Master in a set of replicated databases.
Name	String	Identifies the database name. Read-only.
Properties	Properties	Collection of Property objects. Read-only.
QueryDefs	QueryDefs	Collection of QueryDef objects in a Database object. Read-only.
QueryTimeout	Integer	Indicates how long, in seconds, to wait before an error occurs whilst executing a query. The default value is 60.
RecordsAffected	Long	Contains the number of records affected by the last Execute method. Read-only.
Recordsets	Recordsets	Collection of Recordset objects open in a Database object. Read-only.
Relations	Relations	Collection of Relation objects in a Database object. Read-only.
ReplicaID	String	Specifies the unique GUID that identifies the replica database in a set of replicated databases. Read-only.
TableDefs	TableDefs	Collection of TableDef objects in a Database object. Read-only.
Transactions	Boolean	Indicates whether or not the database supports transactions. Read-only.
Updatable	Boolean	Indicates whether or not data in the database can be changed. Read-only.
Version	String	Returns the version of the Jet database. Read-only.

Databases

Methods

Name	Returns	Description
Refresh		Updates the objects in the collection.

Properties

Name	Returns	Description
Count	Integer	Indicates the number of Container objects in the collection. Read-only.
Item	Database	Allows indexing into the collection to reference a specific object. This is the default property and can therefore be omitted. Read-only.

DBEngine

Methods

Name	Returns	Description
BeginTrans		Starts a new transaction.
CommitTrans		Commits an existing transaction.
CompactDatabase		Compacts the database.
CreateDatabase	Database	Creates a new database.
CreateWorkspace	Workspace	Creates a new Workspace.
Idle		Frees Access, to allow the Jet Database Engine to complete any pending tasks.
ISAMStats	Long	Allows viewing of Jet statistics. Note: This method exists but is hidden.
OpenConnection	Connection	Opens a new connection.
OpenDatabase	Database	Opens a new database.

Table Continued on Following Page

Name	Returns	Description
RegisterDatabase		Adds the ODBC connection information to the registry
RepairDatabase		Repairs a database. Note: This method exists but is hidden.
Rollback		Rolls back a transaction.
SetOption		Allows temporary overwriting of the database engine.

Properties

Name	Returns	Description
DefaultPassword	String	Sets the password to use when a new Workspace is created.
DefaultType	Long	Indicates the type of workspace (i.e. Jet or ODBCDirect) to use when a new one is created.
DefaultUser	String	Sets the user name to use when a new Workspace is created.
Errors	Errors	Collection of Error objects from the most recently failed DAO operation Read-only.
IniPath	String	Indicates the registry key containing information for the Jet database engine.
LoginTimeout	Integer	When logging in to an ODBC database, indicates the number of seconds to wait before an error is generated. The default value is 20.
Properties	Properties	Collection of Property objects. Read-only.
SystemDB	String	Indicates the path for the workgroup information file.
Version	String	Indicates the version of DAO in use. Read-only.
Workspaces	Workspaces	Collection of open Workspace objects. Read-only.

Document

Methods

Name	Returns	Description
CreateProperty	Property	Creates a user-defined property.

Properties

Name	Returns	Description
AllPermissions	Integer	Indicates all the permissions that apply to the container. It can be one or more of the PermissionEnum constants. Read-only.
Container	String	Indicates the name of the Container to which this Document belongs. Read-only.
DateCreated	Variant	The date the Document was created. Read-only.
LastUpdated	Variant	The date the Document was last updated. Read-only.
Name	String	The name of the Document. Read-only.
Owner	String	Indicates the owner of the Document. This will be the name of a User or Group object.
Permissions	Long	Indicates the user permissions that apply to the Document.
Properties	Properties	Collection of Property objects. Read-only.
UserName	String	Indicates the user name or group of user names used when manipulating permissions.

Documents

Methods

Name	Returns	Description
Refresh		Updates the objects in the collection.

Properties

Name	Returns	Description
Count	Integer	Indicates the number of Document objects in the collection. Read-only.
Item	Document	Allows indexing into the collection to reference a specific object. This is the default property and can therefore be omitted. Read-only.

Error

Properties

Name	Returns	Description
Description	String	The description of the error. Read-only.
HelpContext	Long	The reference of the help text in the help file, if more details are available. Read-only.
HelpFile	String	The help file containing further details. Read-only.
Number	Long	The error number. Read-only.
Source	String	The object that created the error. Read-only.

Errors

Methods

Name	Returns	Description
Refresh		Updates the objects in the collection.

Properties

Name	Returns	Description
Count	Integer	Indicates the number of Container objects in the collection. Read-only.
Item	Error	Allows indexing into the collection to reference a specific object. This is the default property and can therefore be omitted. Read-only.

Field

Methods

Name	Returns	Description
AppendChunk		Appends binary or textual data to the end of the field.
CreateProperty	Property	Creates a user-defined property.
GetChunk	Variant	Retrieves binary or textual data from the field.

Properties

Name	Returns	Description
AllowZeroLength	Boolean	Indicates whether or not the field can be zero length.
Attributes	Long	Indicates the characteristics of a Field. Can be one or more of the FieldAttributeEnum constants.
CollatingOrder	Long	Identifies the sort sequence for the field. Read-only.
DataUpdatable	Boolean	Indicates whether or not the field data can be updated. Read-only.
DefaultValue	Variant	Indicates the default value for the field.
FieldSize	Long	Indicates the size, in bytes, of the field. Read-only.
ForeignName	String	If the field participates in a relationship, this identifies the name of the field in the foreign table.
Name	String	The name of the field.

Table Continued on Following Page

Name	Returns	Description
OrdinalPosition	Integer	Indicates the relative position of the Field in the Fields collection.
OriginalValue	Variant	For ODBCDirect, indicates the value of the field before the last update was performed. Read-only.
Properties	Properties	Collection of Property objects. Read-only.
Required	Boolean	Indicates whether or not the field is compulsory.
Size	Integer	Indicates the maximum size, in bytes, of the field
SourceField	String	Indicates the name of the field that is the original source of the data. Read-only.
SourceTable	String	Indicates the name of the table that is the original source of the data. Read-only.
Type	Integer	Indicates the type of data the field holds.
ValidateOnSet	Boolean	Indicates whether or not validation takes place as soon as the value of the field is changed.
ValidationRule	String	An expression that is the rule for validation.
ValidationText	String	Text to display if validation fails.
Value	Variant	The current value of the field.
VisibleValue	Variant	For ODBCDirect, the value in the database, as opposed to a value that might not yet have been sent to the database. Read-only.

Fields

Methods

Name	Returns	Description
Append		Appends a new Field to the collection
Delete		Deletes a Field from the collection
Refresh		Updates the objects in the collection.

Properties

Name	Returns	Description
Count	Integer	Indicates the number of Field objects in the collection. Read-only.
Item	Field	Allows indexing into the collection to reference a specific object. This is the default property and can therefore be omitted. Read-only.

Group

Methods

Name	Returns	Description
CreateUser	User	Creates a new user in the group.

Properties

Name	Returns	Description
Name	String	The name of the group.
PID	String	The Personal Identifier of the group.
Properties	Properties	Collection of Property objects. Read-only.
Users	Users	Collection of User objects for a Workspace or Group object. Read-only.

Groups

Methods

Name	Returns	Description
Append		Appends a new Group to the collection
Delete		Deletes a Group from the collection
Refresh		Updates the objects in the collection.

Properties

Name	Returns	Description
Count	Integer	Indicates the number of Group objects in the collection. Read-only.
Item	Group	Allows indexing into the collection to reference a specific object. This is the default property and can therefore be omitted. Read-only.

Index

Methods

Name	Returns	Description
CreateField	Field	Create a new Field in the index.
CreateProperty	Property	Creates a user-defined property on the index.

Properties

Name	Returns	Description
Clustered	Boolean	Identifies whether or not the index is clustered.
DistinctCount	Long	Identifies the number of unique values for the Index that are in the underlying table. Read-only.
Fields	Variant	Collection of Field objects in an Index object.
Foreign	Boolean	Indicates whether or not the index is a foreign key. Read-only.
IgnoreNulls	Boolean	Indicates whether or not the index ignores null values.
Name	String	The name of the index.
Primary	Boolean	Indicates whether or not this is the primary index.
Properties	Properties	Collection of Property objects. Read-only.
Required	Boolean	Indicates whether or not the index entry must have a value.
Unique	Boolean	Indicates whether or not this is a unique index.

Indexes

Methods

Name	Returns	Description
Append		Appends a new Index to the collection.
Delete		Deletes a Index from the collection
Refresh		Updates the objects in the collection.

Properties

Name	Returns	Description
Count	Integer	Indicates the number of Index objects in the collection. Read-only.
Item	Index	Allows indexing into the collection to reference a specific object. This is the default property and can therefore be omitted. Read-only.

Parameter

Properties

Name	Returns	Description
Direction	Long	Indicates the direction of the parameter. Can be one of the following ParameterDirectionEnum constants.
Name	String	The name of the parameter. Read-only.
Properties	Properties	Collection of Property objects. Read-only.
Type	Integer	The data type of the parameter.
Value	Variant	The value of the parameter.

Parameters

Methods

Name	Returns	Description
Refresh		Updates the objects in the collection.

Properties

Name	Returns	Description
Count	Integer	Indicates the number of Parameter objects in the collection. Read-only.
Item	Parameter	Allows indexing into the collection to reference a specific object. This is the default property and can therefore be omitted. Read-only.

Properties

Methods

Name	Returns	Description
Append		Appends a new Property to the collection.
Delete		Deletes an Property from the collection.
Refresh		Updates the objects in the collection.

Properties

Name	Returns	Description
Count	Integer	Indicates the number of Property objects in the collection. Read-only.
Item	Property	Allows indexing into the collection to reference a specific object. This is the default property and can therefore be omitted. Read-only.

Property

Properties

Name	Returns	Description
Inherited	Boolean	Returns whether a property is inherited from an underlying object. Read-only.
Name	String	Returns the name of this object.
Properties	Properties	Collection of Property objects. Read-only.
Type	Integer	Returns the data type of an object.
Value	Variant	Sets or returns the value of an object.

QueryDef

Methods

Name	Returns	Description
Cancel		Cancels execution of an asynchronous OpenRecordset method.
Close		Closes an open DAO object.
CreateProperty	Property	Creates a new user-defined Property object.
Execute		Executes an action query.
OpenRecordset	Recordset	Creates a new Recordset object.

Properties

Name	Returns	Description
CacheSize	Long	Sets or returns the number of records to be locally cached from an ODBC data source.
Connect	String	Sets or returns a value providing information about a data source for a QueryDef.

Table Continued on Following Page

Name	Returns	Description
DateCreated	Variant	Returns the date and time when the QueryDef was created. Read-only.
Fields	Fields	Collection of Field objects in a QueryDef object. Read-only.
LastUpdated	Variant	Returns the date and time of the most recent change to an object. Read-only.
MaxRecords	Long	Indicates the maximum number of records to return from a query.
Name	String	Returns the name of this object.
ODBCTimeout	Integer	Sets or returns the number of seconds before a timeout occurs on an ODBC database.
Parameters	Parameters	Collection of Parameter objects available for a QueryDef object. Read-only.
Prepare	Variant	Indicates whether to prepare a temporary stored procedure from the query.
Properties	Properties	Collection of Property objects. Read-only.
RecordsAffected	Long	Returns the number of records affected by the last Execute method. Read-only.
ReturnsRecords	Boolean	Sets or returns a value indicating whether a SQL pass-through returns records.
SQL	String	Sets or returns the SQL statement that defines the query.
StillExecuting	Boolean	Indicates whether an asynchronous method call is still executing. Read-only.
Type	Integer	Sets or returns the data type of an object. Read-only.
Updatable	Boolean	Returns whether the query definition can be changed. Read-only.

QueryDefs

Methods

Name	Returns	Description
Append		Appends a new Index to the collection.
Delete		Deletes a QueryDef from the collection.
Refresh		Updates the objects in the collection.

Properties

Name	Returns	Description
Count	Integer	Indicates the number of QueryDef objects in the collection. Read-only.
Item	QueryDef	Allows indexing into the collection to reference a specific QueryDef. This is the default property and can therefore be omitted. Read-only.

Recordset

Methods

Name	Returns	Description
AddNew		Creates a new record in the Recordset.
Cancel		Cancels execution of an asynchronous Execute, OpenRecordset, or OpenConnection.
CancelUpdate		Cancels any pending Update statements.
Clone	Recordset	Creates a duplicate Recordset.
Close		Closes an open DAO object.
CopyQueryDef	QueryDef	Returns a copy of the QueryDef that created the Recordset.
Delete		Deletes a record from a Recordset.

Table Continued on Following Page

Name	Returns	Description
Edit		Prepares a row of a Recordset for editing.
FillCache		Fills the cache for an ODBC-derived Recordset.
FindFirst		Locates the first record that satisfies the criteria.
FindLast		Locates the last record that satisfies the criteria.
FindNext		Locates the next record that satisfies the criteria.
FindPrevious		Locates the previous record that satisfies the criteria.
GetRows	Variant	Retrieves multiple records of a Recordset into an array.
Move		Moves the position of the current record in a Recordset.
MoveFirst		Moves to the first record in the Recordset.
MoveLast		Moves to the last record in the Recordset.
MoveNext		Moves to the next record in the Recordset.
MovePrevious		Moves to the previous record in the Recordset.
NextRecordset	Boolean	Fetches next recordset in a multi-query Recordset
OpenRecordset	Recordset	Creates a new Recordset object.
Requery		Re-executes the query the Recordset is based on.
Seek		Locates a record in a table-type Recordset.
Update		Saves changes made with the Edit or AddNew methods.

Properties

Name	Returns	Description
AbsolutePosition	Long	Sets or returns the relative record number of the current record.
BatchCollisionCount	Long	Indicates how many rows had collisions in the last batch update. Read-only.
BatchCollisions	Variant	Indicates which rows had collisions in the last batch update. Read-only.
BatchSize	Long	Determines how many updates to include in a batch.

Name	Returns	Description
BOF	Boolean	Indicates whether the current record position is before the first record. Read-only.
Bookmark		Uniquely identifies a particular record in a Recordset.
Bookmarkable	Boolean	Indicates whether a Recordset supports bookmark. Read-only.
CacheSize	Long	Sets or returns the number of records to be locally cached from an ODBC data source.
CacheStart		Sets or returns the bookmark of the first record to be cached from an ODBC data source.
Connection	Connection	Indicates which Connection owns the Recordset.
DateCreated	Variant	Returns the date and time when the underlying base table was created. Read-only.
EditMode	Integer	Returns the state of editing for the current record. Read-only.
EOF	Boolean	Indicates whether the current record position is after the last record. Read-only.
Fields	Fields	Collection of Field objects in a Recordset object. Read-only.
Filter	String	Sets or returns a value indicating a filter to apply to a Recordset.
Index	String	Sets or returns the name of the current Index object (table-type Recordset only).
LastModified		Returns a bookmark indicating the most recently added or changed record. Read-only.
LastUpdated	Variant	Returns the date and time of the most recent change to an object. Read-only.
LockEdits	Boolean	Returns the type of locking in effect during editing.
Name	String	Returns the name of this object. Read-only.
NoMatch	Boolean	Indicates whether a record was found with the Seek or Find method. Read-only.

Table Continued on Following Page

Name	Returns	Description
PercentPosition	Single	Sets or returns the approximate location of the current record.
Properties	Properties	Collection of Property objects. Read-only.
RecordCount	Long	Returns the number of records accessed in a Recordset. Read-only.
RecordStatus	Integer	Indicating the batch-update status of the current record. Read-only.
Restartable	Boolean	Indicates whether a Recordset object supports the Requery method. Read-only.
Sort	String	Sets or returns the sort order for records in a Recordset.
StillExecuting	Boolean	Indicates whether an asynchronous method call is still executing. Read-only.
Transactions	Boolean	Indicates whether the Recordset object supports transaction. Read-only.
Type	Integer	Returns the data type of an object. Read-only.
Updatable	Boolean	Returns whether records in the Recordset can be updated. Read-only.
UpdateOptions	Long	Determines how a batch update query will be constructed.
ValidationRule	String	Sets or returns a value indicating whether a field contains valid data. Read-only.
ValidationText	String	Sets or returns a value indicating a message if an entered value is invalid. Read-only.

Recordsets

Methods

Name	Returns	Description
Refresh		Updates the objects in the collection.

Properties

Name	Returns	Description
Count	Integer	Indicates the number of Recordset objects in the collection. Read-only.
Item	Recordset	Allows indexing into the collection to reference a specific object. This is the default property and can therefore be omitted. Read-only.

Relation

Methods

Name	Returns	Description
CreateField	Field	Creates a new Field object.

Properties

Name	Returns	Description
Attributes	Long	Sets or returns a value indicating characteristics of an object.
Fields	Fields	Collection of Field objects in a Relation object. Read-only.
ForeignTable	String	Sets or returns the name of a foreign table.
Name	String	Returns the name of this object.
PartialReplica	Boolean	Indicates whether a relation provides a partial replica's synchronizing rules.
Properties	Properties	Collection of Property objects. Read-only.
Table	String	Sets or returns the name of a primary table.

Relations

Methods

Name	Returns	Description
Append		Appends a new Relation to the collection.
Delete		Deletes a Relation from the collection.
Refresh		Updates the objects in the collection.

Properties

Name	Returns	Description
Count	Integer	Indicates the number of Relation objects in the collection. Read-only.
Item	Relation	Allows indexing into the collection to reference a specific object. This is the default property and can therefore be omitted. Read-only.

TableDef

Methods

Name	Returns	Description
CreateField	Field	Creates a new Field object.
CreateIndex	Index	Creates a new Index object.
CreateProperty	Property	Creates a new user-defined Property object.
OpenRecordset	Recordset	Creates a new Recordset object.
RefreshLink		Updates the connection information for a linked table.

Properties

Name	Returns	Description
Attributes	Long	Sets or returns a value indicating characteristics of an object.
ConflictTable	String	Returns the table name that contains conflicts that occurred during synchronization. Read-only.
Connect	String	Sets or returns a value providing information about a data source for a TableDef.
DateCreated	Variant	Returns the date and time when the table was created. Read-only.
Fields	Fields	Collection of Field objects in a TableDef object. Read-only.
Indexes	Indexes	Collection of Index objects associated with a TableDef object. Read-only.
LastUpdated	Variant	Returns the date and time of the most recent change to an object. Read-only.
Name	String	Returns the name of this object.
Properties	Properties	Collection of Property object. Read-only.
RecordCount	Integer	Returns the number of records in the Recordset. Read-only.
ReplicaFilter	Variant	Indicates which records to include in a partial replica.
SourceTableName	String	Sets or returns the name of a linked table's original source table.
Updatable	Boolean	Returns whether the definition of the table can be changed. Read-only.
ValidationRule	String	Sets or returns a value indicating whether a field contains valid data.
ValidationText	String	Sets or returns a value indicating a message if an entered value is invalid.

TableDefs

Methods

Name	Returns	Description
Append		Appends a new `TableDef` to the collection.
Delete		Deletes a `Relation` from the collection.
Refresh		Updates the objects in the collection.

Properties

Name	Returns	Description
Count	Long	Indicates the number of `TableDef` objects in the collection. Read-only.
Item	TableDef	Allows indexing into the collection to reference a specific object. This is the default property and can therefore be omitted. Read-only.

User

Methods

Name	Returns	Description
CreateGroup	Group	Creates a new `Group` object.
NewPassword		Changes the password of an existing user account.

Properties

Name	Returns	Description
Groups	Groups	Collection of `Group` objects in a `Workspace` or `User` object. Read-only.
Name	String	Returns the name of this object.
Password	String	Sets the password for a user account.
PID	String	Sets the personal identifier (PID) for a group or user account.
Properties	Properties	Collection of `Property` object. Read-only.

Users

Methods

Name	Returns	Description
Append		Appends a new User to the collection.
Delete		Deletes a User from the collection.
Refresh		Updates the objects in the collection.

Properties

Name	Returns	Description
Count	Integer	Indicates the number of User objects in the collection. Read-only.
Item	User	Allows indexing into the collection to reference a specific object. This is the default property and can therefore be omitted. Read-only.

Workspace

Methods

Name	Returns	Description
BeginTrans		Begins a new transaction.
Close		Closes an open DAO object.
CommitTrans		Ends the transaction and saves the changes.
CreateDatabase	Database	Creates a new Microsoft Jet database (.mdb).
CreateGroup	Group	Creates a new Group object.
CreateUser	User	Creates a new User object.
OpenConnection	Connection	Opens a connection to a database
OpenDatabase	Database	Opens a specified database.
Rollback		Rolls back any changes since the last BeginTrans.

Properties

Name	Returns	Description
Connections	Connections	Collection of Connection object. Read-only.
Databases	Databases	Collection of open Database object. Read-only.
DefaultCursorDriver	Long	Selects the ODBC cursor library
Groups	Groups	Collection of Group objects in a Workspace or User object. Read-only.
IsolateODBCTrans	Integer	Sets or returns a value indicating whether multiple transactions are isolated.
LoginTimeout	Long	Number of seconds allowed for logging in to an ODBC database
Name	String	Returns the name of this object.
Properties	Properties	Collection of Property object. Read-only.
Type	Long	Type (Field, Parameter, Property.) Read-only.
UserName	String	Sets or returns a user or group. Read-only.
Users	Users	Collection of User objects for a Workspace or Group object. Read-only.

Workspaces

Methods

Name	Returns	Description
Append		Appends a new Workspace to the collection.
Delete		Deletes a Workspace from the collection.
Refresh		Updates the objects in the collection.

Properties

Name	Returns	Description
Count	Integer	Indicates the number of Property objects in the collection. Read-only.
Item	Workspace	Allows indexing into the collection to reference a specific object. This is the default property and can therefore be omitted. Read-only.

Constants

CommitTransOptionsEnum

Name	Value	Description
dbForceOSFlush	1	When used with CommitTrans forces all updates to be immediately flushed to the disk.

DatabaseTypeEnum

Name	Value	Description
dbDecrypt	4	The database is not encrypted.
dbEncrypt	2	The database is encrypted.
dbVersion10	1	The database is a version 1.0 database.
dbVersion11	8	The database is a version 1.1 database.
dbVersion20	16	The database is a version 2.0 database.
dbVersion30	32	The database is a version 3.0 database.
dbVersion40	64	The database is a version 4.0 database.

DataTypeEnum

Name	Value	Description
dbBigInt	16	A signed integer.
dbBinary	9	A binary value, with a maximum length of 255 bytes.

Table Continued on Following Page

Name	Value	Description
dbBoolean	1	A Boolean value.
dbByte	2	A single byte value, for integer values from 0 to 255.
dbChar	18	A String value, for fixed length strings.
dbCurrency	5	A currency value. A signed integer with 4 digits to the right of the decimal point.
dbDate	8	A Date value, holding dates between December 31 1899 and December 31 9999 inclusive, and times between 00:00:00 and 23:59:59.
dbDecimal	20	A signed, exact numeric value.
dbDouble	7	A double precision floating point number.
dbFloat	21	A signed, approximate numeric value.
dbGUID	15	A Globally Unique Identifier.
dbInteger	3	An Integer, for values between –32,768 and 32,767.
dbLong	4	A Long Integer, for values between –2,147,483,648 and 2,147,483,647.
dbLongBinary	11	A Long Binary object, such as an OLE Object.
dbMemo	12	Text data, up to 1.2Gb in length.
dbNumeric	19	A singed, exact numeric value.
dbSingle	6	A single precision floating point number.
dbText	10	Text data for values up to 255 characters.
dbTime	22	A time value.
dbTimeStamp	23	A unique time stamp.
dbVarBinary	17	Variable length binary data, up to 255 bytes in length.

DriverPromptEnum

Name	Value	Description
dbDriverComplete	0	Only prompt if not enough information was supplied.
dbDriverComplete Required	3	Only prompt if not enough information was supplied, but disable any options not directly applicable to the connection.

Name	Value	Description
dbDriverNoPrompt	1	Default. Never prompt for connection information.
dbDriverPrompt	2	Always prompt for connection information.

EditModeEnum

Name	Value	Description
dbEditAdd	2	Indicates that the AddNew method has been invoked and the current record in the buffer is a new record that hasn't been saved to the database.
dbEditInProgress	1	Indicates that data in the current record has been modified but not saved.
dbEditNone	0	Indicates that no editing is in progress.

FieldAttributeEnum

Name	Value	Description
dbAutoIncrField	16	The field is an auto-incrementing field, such as an AutoNumber.
dbDescending	1	The field is stored in descending order.
dbFixedField	1	The field is a fixed size.
dbHyperlinkField	32768	The field is a hyperlink field.
dbSystemField	8192	The field holds replication information.
dbUpdatableField	32	The field is updateable.
dbVariableField	2	The field size is variable.

IdleEnum

Name	Value	Description
dbFreeLocks	1	Frees any read locks.
dbRefreshCache	8	Refreshes the memory with the most current data from the database.

LockTypeEnum

Name	Value	Description
dbOptimistic	3	Optimistic locking, record-by-record. The provider locks records when Update is called.
dbOptimisticBatch	5	Optimistic batch updates, allowing more than one update to take place before the data source is updated.
dbPessimistic	2	Pessimistic locking, record-by-record. The provider locks the record immediately upon editing.

ParameterDirectionEnum

Name	Value	Description
dbParamInput	1	Indicates an input parameter.
dbParamInputOutput	3	Indicates both an input and output parameter.
dbParamOutput	2	Indicates an output parameter.
dbParamReturnValue	4	Indicates a return value.

PermissionEnum

Name	Value	Description
dbSecCreate	1	The user can create new documents.
dbSecDBAdmin	8	The user can replicate a database and change the database password.
dbSecDBCreate	1	The user can create new databases.
dbSecDBExclusive	4	The user has exclusive access to the database.
dbSecDBOpen	2	The user can open the database.
dbSecDelete	65536	The user can delete the object.
dbSecDeleteData	128	The user can delete records.
dbSecFullAccess	1048575	The user has full access to the objects.
dbSecInsertData	32	The user can add records.
dbSecNoAccess	0	The user has no access to the object.
dbSecReadDef	4	The user can read the table definition.

Table Continued on Following Page

Name	Value	Description
dbSecReadSec	131072	The user can read the object's security details.
dbSecReplaceData	64	The user can modify records.
dbSecRetrieveData	20	The user can retrieve data from the object.
dbSecWriteDef	65548	The user can update the table definition.
dbSecWriteOwner	524288	The user can change the Owner property.
dbSecWriteSec	262144	The user can update the object's security details.

QueryDefTypeEnum

Name	Value	Description
dbQAction	240	The query is an Action query.
dbQAppend	64	The query is an Append query.
dbQCompound	160	The query contains an Action query and a Select query.
dbQCrosstab	16	The query is a Crosstab query.
dbQDDL	96	The query is a Data Definition query.
dbQDelete	32	The query is a Delete query.
dbQMakeTable	80	The query is a Make Table query.
dbQProcedure	224	The query executes a stored procedure (ODBCDirect only)
dbQSelect	0	The query is a Select query.
dbQSetOperation	128	The query is a Union query.
dbQSPTBulk	144	The query is an ODBC pass through query that doesn't return records. Used in conjunction with dbQSQLPassThrough.
dbQSQLPassThrough	112	The query is an ODBC pass through query.
dbQUpdate	48	The query is an Update query.

RecordsetOptionEnum

Name	Value	Description
dbConsistent	32	Allow only consistent updates to the recordset. Most useful for multi-table joins.
dbDenyRead	2	Prevent other users from reading data in the table.
dbDenyWrite	1	Prevent other users from modifying or adding records.
dbExecDirect	2048	For ODBCDirect only, allows the query to be sent directly to the server without being prepared.
dbFailOnError	128	Terminate the opening of the recordset if an error occurs.
dbForwardOnly	256	Creates a forward-only recordset.
dbInconsistent	16	Allow inconsistent updates to the recordset. Most useful for multi-table joins.
dbReadOnly	4	Creates a read-only recordset.
dbRunAsync	1024	For ODBCDirect, opens the recordset asynchronously.
dbSeeChanges	512	Allows errors to be generated when an attempt is made to edit a record that is already being edited by another user.
dbSQLPassThrough	64	Passes the SQL directly to the ODBC data source.

RecordsetTypeEnum

Name	Value	Description
dbOpenDynamic	16	A dynamic recordset (dynamic cursor).
dbOpenDynaset	2	A dynaset recordset (keyset cursor).
dbOpenForwardOnly	8	A forward-only recordset.
dbOpenSnapshot	4	A snapshot recordset (static cursor)
dbOpenTable	1	A table-type recordset.

RecordStatusEnum

Name	Value	Description
dbRecordDBDeleted	4	The record has been deleted both in the recordset and in the database.
dbRecordDeleted	3	The record has been deleted from the recordset, but has yet to be deleted from the database.
dbRecordModified	1	The record has been modified in the recordset, but not in the database.
dbRecordNew	2	The record has been added into the recordset, but not yet added to the database.
dbRecordUnmodified	0	The record has not been modified, or has been successfully modified.

RelationAttributeEnum

Name	Value	Description
dbRelationDeleteCascade	4096	Deletions will cascade to related tables.
dbRelationDontEnforce	2	No referential integrity is in place, and relationships are not enforced.
dbRelationInherited	4	The relationship is between two tables that exist in another database.
dbRelationLeft	16777216	The relationship is a left outer join.
dbRelationRight	33554432	The relationship is a right outer join.
dbRelationUnique	1	The relationship is one to one.
dbRelationUpdateCascade	256	Updates will cascade to related tables.

ReplicaTypeEnum

Name	Value	Description
dbRepMakePartial	1	Create a partial replica.
dbRepMakeReadOnly	2	Create read-only replica, prohibiting changes to replicable objects.

SetOptionEnum

Name	Value	Description
dbExclusiveAsyncDelay	60	Sets the ExclusiveAsyncDelay registry key.
dbFlushTransactionTimeout	66	Sets the FlushTransactionTimeout registry key.
dbImplicitCommitSync	59	Sets the ImplicitCommitSync registry key.
dbLockDelay	63	Sets the LockDelay registry key.
dbLockRetry	57	Sets the LockRetry registry key.
dbMaxBufferSize	8	Sets the MaxBufferSize registry key.
dbMaxLocksPerFile	62	Sets the MaxLocksPerFile registry key.
dbPageTimeout	6	Sets the PageTimeout registry key.
dbRecycleLVs	65	Sets the RecycleLVs registry key.
dbSharedAsyncDelay	61	Sets the SharedAsyncDelay registry key.
dbUserCommitSync	58	Sets the UserCommitSync registry key.

SynchronizeTypeEnum

Name	Value	Description
dbRepExportChanges	1	Export database changes.
dbRepImpExpChanges	4	Import and export database changes.
dbRepImportChanges	2	Import database changes.
dbRepSyncInternet	16	Synchronize changes over the Internet.

TableDefAttributeEnum

Name	Value	Description
dbAttachedODBC	536870912	The table is a linked table from an ODBC data source.
dbAttachedTable	1073741824	The table is a linked table from a non-ODBC data source.
dbAttachExclusive	65536	The table is a linked table, for exclusive use only.
dbAttachSavePWD	131072	The table is a linked table, and the user and password details are saved with the connection.

Name	Value	Description
dbHiddenObject	1	The table is a hidden table.
dbSystemObject	-2147483646	The table is a system table.

UpdateCriteriaEnum

Name	Value	Description
dbCriteriaAllCols	4	Use all columns in the WHERE clause to identify the record being updated.
dbCriteriaDelete Insert	16	A set of DELETE and INSERT statements are created to modify the row.
dbCriteriaKey	1	Use just the key columns in the WHERE clause to identify the record being updated.
dbCriteriaMod Values	2	Use the key columns and changed columns in the WHERE clause to identify the record being updated.
dbCriteria Timestamp	8	Only use a timestamp field, if available.
dbCriteriaUpdate	32	Use an UPDATE statement for the changed row.

UpdateTypeEnum

Name	Value	Description
dbUpdateBatch	4	Write all pending changes to the disk.
dbUpdateCurrent Record	2	Only write the pending changes for the current record to the disk.
dbUpdateRegular	1	Write the pending changes immediately to the disk, and don't cache them. This is the default.

WorkspaceTypeEnum

Name	Value	Description
dbUseJet	2	The Workspace is connected to a Jet database.
dbUseODBC	1	The Workspace is connected to an ODBC data source.

Method Calls

Connection

Connection.Cancel
Connection.Close
QueryDef = *Connection*.CreateQueryDef(*[Name As Variant]*, _
    [SQLText As Variant])
Connection.Execute(*Query As String, [Options As Variant]*)
Recordset = *Connection*.OpenRecordset(*Name As String, [Type As Variant]*, _
    [Options As Variant], [LockEdit As Variant])

Connections

Connections.Refresh

Containers

Containers.Refresh

Database

Database.Close
Property = *Database*.CreateProperty(*[Name As Variant], [Type As Variant]*, _
    [Value As Variant], [DDL As Variant])
QueryDef = *Database*.CreateQueryDef(*[Name As Variant], [SQLText As Variant]*)
Relation = *Database*.CreateRelation(*[Name As Variant], [Table As Variant]*, _
    [ForeignTable As Variant], [Attributes As Variant])
TableDef = *Database*.CreateTableDef(*[Name As Variant]*, _
    [Attributes As Variant], [SourceTableName As Variant], [Connect As Variant])
Database.Execute(*Query As String, [Options As Variant]*)
Database.MakeReplica(*PathName As String, Description As String, [Options As Variant]*)
Database.NewPassword(*bstrOld As String, bstrNew As String*)
Recordset = *Database*.OpenRecordset(*Name As String, [Type As Variant]*, _
    [Options As Variant], [LockEdit As Variant])
Database.PopulatePartial(*DbPathName As String*)
Database.Synchronize(*DbPathName As String, [ExchangeType As Variant]*)

Databases

Databases.Refresh

DBEngine

DBEngine.BeginTrans
DBEngine.CommitTrans(*Option As Integer*)
DBEngine.CompactDatabase(*SrcName As String, DstName As String,* _
    [DstLocale As Variant], [Options As Variant], [SrcLocale As Variant])
Database = DBEngine.CreateDatabase(*Name As String, Locale As String, [Option As Variant]*)
Workspace = DBEngine.CreateWorkspace(*Name As String, UserName As String,* _
    Password As String, [UseType As Variant])
DBEngine.Idle(*[Action As Variant]*)
Integer = DBEngine.ISAMStats(*StatNum As Integer, [Reset As Variant]*)
Connection = DBEngine.OpenConnection(*Name As String, [Options As Variant],* _
    [ReadOnly As Variant], [Connect As Variant])
Database = DBEngine.OpenDatabase(*Name As String, [Options As Variant],* _
    [ReadOnly As Variant], [Connect As Variant])
DBEngine.RegisterDatabase(*Dsn As String, Driver As String, Silent As Boolean,* _
    Attributes As String)
DBEngine.RepairDatabase(*Name As String*)
DBEngine.Rollback
DBEngine.SetOption(*Option As Integer, Value As Variant*)

Document

Property = Document.CreateProperty(*[Name As Variant], [Type As Variant],* _
    [Value As Variant], [DDL As Variant])

Documents

Documents.Refresh

DynaCollection

DynaCollection.Append(*Object As Object*)
DynaCollection.Delete(*Name As String*)
DynaCollection.Refresh

Errors

Errors.Refresh

Field

Field.AppendChunk(*Val As Variant*)
Property = Field.CreateProperty(*[Name As Variant], [Type As Variant],* _
    [Value As Variant], [DDL As Variant])
Variant = Field.GetChunk(*Offset As Integer, Bytes As Integer*)

Fields

Fields.Append(*Object As Object*)
Fields.Delete(*Name As String*)
Fields.Refresh

Group

User = Group.CreateUser(*[Name As Variant], [PID As Variant], [Password As Variant]*)

Groups

Groups.Append(*Object As Object*)
Groups.Delete(*Name As String*)
Groups.Refresh

Index

Field = Index.CreateField(*[Name As Variant], [Type As Variant], [Size As Variant]*)
Property = Index.CreateProperty(*[Name As Variant], [Type As Variant], _*
   [Value As Variant], [DDL As Variant])

Indexes

Indexes.Append(*Object As Object*)
Indexes.Delete(*Name As String*)
Indexes.Refresh

IndexFields

IndexFields.Append(*Object As Object*)
IndexFields.Delete(*Name As String*)
IndexFields.Refresh

Parameters

Parameters.Refresh

Properties

Properties.Append(*Object As Object*)
Properties.Delete(*Name As String*)
Properties.Refresh

QueryDef

QueryDef.Cancel
QueryDef.Close
Property = QueryDef.CreateProperty(*[Name As Variant], [Type As Variant], _*
    [Value As Variant], [DDL As Variant])
QueryDef.Execute(*[Options As Variant]*)
Recordset = QueryDef.OpenRecordset(*[Type As Variant], [Options As Variant], _*
    [LockEdit As Variant])

QueryDefs

QueryDefs.Append(*Object As Object*)
QueryDefs.Delete(*Name As String*)
QueryDefs.Refresh

Recordset

Recordset.AddNew
Recordset.Cancel
Recordset.CancelUpdate(*UpdateType As Integer*)
Recordset = Recordset.Clone
Recordset.Close
QueryDef = Recordset.CopyQueryDef
Recordset.Delete
Recordset.Edit
Recordset.FillCache(*[Rows As Variant], [StartBookmark As Variant]*)
Recordset.FindFirst(*Criteria As String*)
Recordset.FindLast(*Criteria As String*)
Recordset.FindNext(*Criteria As String*)
Recordset.FindPrevious(*Criteria As String*)
Variant = Recordset.GetRows(*[NumRows As Variant]*)
Recordset.Move(*Rows As Integer, [StartBookmark As Variant]*)
Recordset.MoveFirst
Recordset.MoveLast(*Options As Integer*)
Recordset.MoveNext
Recordset.MovePrevious
Boolean = Recordset.NextRecordset
Recordset = Recordset.OpenRecordset(*[Type As Variant], [Options As Variant]*)
Recordset.Requery(*[NewQueryDef As Variant]*)
Recordset.Seek(*Comparison As String, Key1 As Variant, [Key2 As Variant], _*
    [Key3 As Variant], [Key4 As Variant], [Key5 As Variant], [Key6 As Variant], _
    [Key7 As Variant], [Key8 As Variant], [Key9 As Variant], [Key10 As Variant], _
    [Key11 As Variant], [Key12 As Variant], [Key13 As Variant])
Recordset.Update(*UpdateType As Integer, Force As Boolean*)

Recordsets

Recordsets.Refresh

Relation

Field = Relation.CreateField(*[Name As Variant], [Type As Variant], [Size As Variant]*)

Relations

Relations.Append(*Object As Object*)
Relations.Delete(*Name As String*)
Relations.Refresh

TableDef

Field = TableDef.CreateField(*[Name As Variant], [Type As Variant], [Size As Variant]*)
Index = TableDef.CreateIndex(*[Name As Variant]*)
Property = TableDef.CreateProperty(*[Name As Variant], [Type As Variant], _*
    [Value As Variant], [DDL As Variant])
Recordset = TableDef.OpenRecordset(*[Type As Variant], [Options As Variant]*)
TableDef.RefreshLink

TableDefs

TableDefs.Append(*Object As Object*)
TableDefs.Delete(*Name As String*)
TableDefs.Refresh

User

Group = User.CreateGroup(*[Name As Variant], [PID As Variant]*)
User.NewPassword(*bstrOld As String, bstrNew As String*)

Users

Users.Append(*Object As Object*)
Users.Delete(*Name As String*)
Users.Refresh

Workspace

Workspace.BeginTrans
Workspace.Close
Workspace.CommitTrans(*Options As Integer*)
Database = *Workspace*.CreateDatabase(*Name As String, Connect As String, _
    [Option As Variant]*)
Group = *Workspace*.CreateGroup(*[Name As Variant], [PID As Variant]*)
User = *Workspace*.CreateUser(*[Name As Variant], [PID As Variant], [Password As Variant]*)
Connection = *Workspace*.OpenConnection(*Name As String, [Options As Variant], _
    [ReadOnly As Variant], [Connect As Variant]*)
Database = *Workspace*.OpenDatabase(*Name As String, [Options As Variant], _
    [ReadOnly As Variant], [Connect As Variant]*)
Workspace.Rollback

Workspaces

Workspaces.Append(*Object As Object*)
Workspaces.Delete(*Name As String*)
Workspaces.Refresh

Access Events

This section is a list of all events that occur in Access 2000, and should give you an idea of how much you can achieve.

Events new to Access 2000 are shown in **bold**. (Actually, there's only one – the **Dirty** event).

Event Property	Belongs to...	Occurs...	Can be used for (for example)...
After Del Confirm	Forms	after the user has confirmed deletion of records or after the Before Del Confirm event is canceled.	determining how the user reacted to confirmation of the deletion of records.
After Insert	Forms	after the new record has been added.	requerying a form's recordset to show up-to-date data.
After Update	Forms; controls on a form	after the changed data in a control or record has been saved.	requerying a form's recordset to show up-to-date data.
Apply Filter	Forms	after the user has chosen to apply or remove a filter, but before the filter is applied.	changing the appearance of the form, depending on the filter criteria selected.
Before Del Confirm	Forms	after the user has deleted records, but before Access 200 has asked for confirmation.	creating your own messages asking the user for confirmation of records.
Before Insert	Forms	after the user types the first character in a record, but before the record is actually created.	allowing the developer to populate hidden ID fields in subforms
Before Update	Forms; controls on a form	before the changed data in a control or record is saved.	validating data before it is saved.

Table Continued on Following Page

Event Property	Belongs to...	Occurs...	Can be used for (for example)...
Dirty	Form; Combo box; Tab control	when the contents of a form, the text of a combo box changes, or when the page changes on a tab control.	to identify when the details on a form have changed, so that they can be saved before closing the form.
Initialize	Class	when a new instance of a class is created.	set default properties.
ItemAdded	Reference	when a reference is added to the project from Visual Basic.	to add extra references where dependencies occur.
Item_ Removed	Reference	when a reference is removed from the project with Visual Basic.	to clean up anything done when the reference was added.
On Activate	Forms; reports	when a form or report becomes the active window and gets focus.	triggering the display of custom toolbars.
On Change	Controls on a form	after the contents of a control change (e.g. by typing a character).	triggering the update of related controls on the form.
On Click	Forms; controls and sections on a form	when the user clicks the mouse button over a form or control; when the user takes some action which results in the same effect as clicking would (for example pressing the spacebar to check a checkbox).	just about anything - this is one of the most used of all events and is about the only event used with command buttons.
On Close	Forms; reports	after a form or report has been closed and removed from the screen.	triggering the opening of the next form.
On Current	Forms	when the form is opened or requeried; after the focus moves to a different record, but before the new record is displayed.	implementing intelligent navigation buttons (see example below).
On Dbl Click	Forms; controls and sections on a form	when the user depresses and releases the left mouse button twice over the same object.	implementing drill-down functionality in EIS applications.
On Deactivate	Forms; reports	when a form loses focus within Access 2000.	triggering the concealment of custom toolbars.
On Delete	Forms	when the user attempts to delete a record.	preventing the user from deleting records.
On Enter	Controls on a form	before the control receives focus from another control on the same form.	similar to **On Got Focus**.

Event Property	Belongs to...	Occurs...	Can be used for (for example)...
On Error	Forms; reports	when a run-time database engine error occurs (but not a Visual Basic error).	intercepting errors and displaying your own custom error messages.
On Exit	Controls on a form	before the control loses focus to another control on the same form.	similar to On Lost Focus.
On Filter	Forms	after the user clicks the Advanced Filter/Sort or Filter By Form buttons.	entering default filter criteria for the user, or even displaying your own custom filter window.
On Format	Report sections	after Access 2000 determines which data belongs in each section of a report, but before the section is formatted for printing.	displaying information on a report which is dependent on the value of other data on that report.
On Got Focus	Forms; controls on a form	after a form or control has received the focus.	highlighting areas of the form which you wish to draw to the attention of the user when editing that control.
On Key Down	Forms; controls on a form	when the user presses a key over a form or control which has the focus.	writing keyboard handlers for applications which need to respond to users pressing and releasing keys.
On Key Press	Forms; controls on a form	when the user presses and releases a key or key combination.	testing the validity of keystrokes as they are entered into a control.
On Key Up	Forms; controls on a form	when the user releases a key over a form or control which has the focus.	see On Key Down.
On Load	Forms	after a form has been opened and the records displayed.	specifying default values for controls on a form.
On Lost Focus	Forms; controls on a form	after a form or control has lost the focus.	validating data entered into a control.
On Mouse Down	Forms; controls and sections on a form	when the user presses a mouse button.	triggering the display of custom pop-up shortcut menus.

Table Continued on Following Page

Appendix F

Event Property	Belongs to...	Occurs...	Can be used for (for example)...
On Mouse Move	Forms; controls and sections on a form	when the mouse pointer moves over objects.	displaying X and Y coordinates of the mouse pointer.
On Mouse Up	Forms; controls and sections on a form	when the user releases a mouse button.	triggering the concealment of custom pop-up shortcut menus.
On No Data	Forms; reports	after a report with no data has been formatted, but before it is printed.	suppressing the printing of reports which contain no data.
On Not In List	Controls on a form	when the user attempts to add a new item to a combo box.	creating a method for adding the item to the table which supplies values for the combo box.
On Open	Forms; reports	when a form or report is opened but before the first record is displayed.	setting focus on the form to a particular control.
On Page	Reports	after a page has been formatted for printing, but before it is printing.	drawing boxes, lines etc. on the page using various graphics methods.
On Print	Report sections	after a section has been formatted for printing, but before it is actually printed.	determining if a record is split across two pages.
On Resize	Forms	when a form is opened or resized.	preventing the user from reducing the size of a form beyond certain limits.
On Retreat	Report sections	during formatting when Access 2000 retreats to a previous section of a report.	undoing actions you may have already instigated in the Format event handler.
On Timer	Forms	every time the period of time specified as the TimerInterval property has elapsed.	causing controls to 'flash'.
On Unload	Forms	after a form has been closed but before it is removed from the screen.	displaying a message box asking the user for confirmation that the form should be closed.

Event Property	Belongs to...	Occurs...	Can be used for (for example)...
On Updated	Controls on a form	after an OLE objects data has been modified.	determining if the data in a bound control needs to be saved.
Terminate	Module	when the instance of the class module is destroyed	to clean up any actions that occurred when the class was instantiated.

ANSI Character Set

	0	32	64	96	128	160	192	224
0		Space	@	`	•		À	à
1		!	A	a		¡	Á	á
2		"	B	b	‚	¢	Â	â
3		#	C	c	ƒ	£	Ã	ã
4		$	D	d	„	¤	Ä	ä
5		%	E	e	…	¥	Å	å
6		&	F	f	†	¦	Æ	æ
7		'	G	g	‡	§	Ç	ç
8		(	H	h	ˆ	¨	È	è
9	Tab	)	I	i	‰	©	É	é
10		*	J	j	Š	ª	Ê	ê
11	LF	+	K	k	‹	«	Ë	ë
12	CR	,	L	l	Œ	¬	Ì	ì
13		-	M	m			Í	í
14		.	N	n	•	®	Î	î
15		/	O	o		¯	Ï	ï
16		0	P	p		°	Ð	ð
17		1	Q	q	'	±	Ñ	ñ
18		2	R	r	'	²	Ò	ò
19		3	S	s	"	³	Ó	ó

Table Continued on Following Page

	0	32	64	96	128	160	192	224
20		4	T	t	″	´	Ô	ô
21		5	U	u	•	µ	Õ	õ
22		6	V	v	–	¶	Ö	ö
23		7	W	w	—	·	×	÷
24		8	X	x	˜	¸	Ø	ø
25		9	Y	y	™	¹	Ù	ù
26		:	Z	z	š	º	Ú	ú
27		;	[	{	›	»	Û	û
28		<	\	|	œ	¼	Ü	ü
29		=	]	}		½	Ý	ý
30	-	>	^	~	•	¾	Þ	þ
31		?	_		Ÿ	¿	ß	ÿ

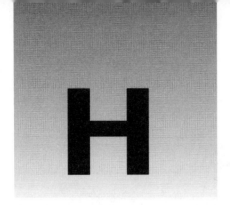

ODBC and PWS

This appendix covers the details required to set up an ODBC Data Source Name, and how to create virtual directories in Personal Web Server (PWS).

ODBC Data Source Names

As mentioned in the first chapter, Open DataBase Connectivity was the precursor to OLEDB and ADO, and still plays a large part in development issues. A Data Source Name (DSN) is simply a pointer to a particular source of data, and allows us to reference this data source just by a name, rather than by the physical location. This allows the location of the data to change without any changes to the code, because the code points to the DSN.

There are three types of DSN:

❑ **User DSN**, which is only visible to a single user. Other users on the machine cannot use this DSN.

❑ **System DSN**, which is visible to all users who use the machine, including the operating system.

❑ **File DSN**, which is a DSN stored in a file, and is visible to all users.

For Active Server Pages you only need to concern yourself with a System DSN.

To create a DSN you use the ODBC Data Sources applet in the Control Panel. Opening this gives the Administrator dialog:

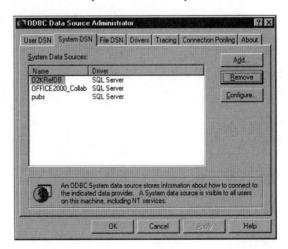

Appendix H

This shows a list of existing data sources. To create a new DSN click the A**dd**... button, where you will see a list of data stores drivers that you can connect to:

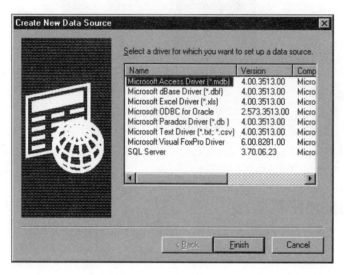

*A **driver** is what ODBC uses to connect us to the actual source of the data. There is a driver for each type of data that ODBC can handle.*

You'll need an Access DSN, so make sure the correct driver is selected, then press the F**inish** button to take you to the Access DSN setup dialog:

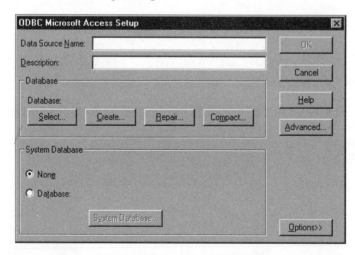

This is where you get a chance to enter the name and description of the data source. These can be anything, so it's best to make them fairly descriptive. You should use the Select... button to pick the Access database you wish to use as the source of the data – this will show the standard file dialogs, allowing you to browse the file system and find the correct mdb file.

Once you've found your database, the dialog box will look something like this:

Now you can press the OK button to add this DSN to the list you saw earlier.

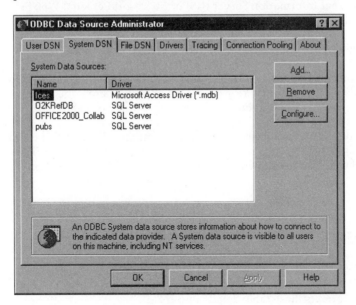

Creation of the DSN is now complete, so you can now close this dialog by pressing the OK button.

Networking

The use of some local internet facilities, such as PWS, requires that networking be installed on your machine. If you have a network of your own (in an office or at home) then you won't need to do anything special. If you are not connected to a network but have a network card, then you only need to install the network card drivers and the networking protocols – you should consult your documentation for this.

If you don't have a network card, there is a network protocol called the Microsoft Loopback Adaptor, which provides the ability to use the networking facilities without having a network present. This means that even a home machine can use networking. For more details on the Loopback driver should should consult the networking documentation for your operating system, or check an online reference such as http://msdn.microsoft.com.

Personal Web Server

To use Active Server Pages (ASP) files you need a Web server that supports ASP. For most people that will be Microsoft Internet Information Server (IIS) or Microsoft Personal Web Server (PWS), and it's the latter we shall look at quickly here.

You might be wondering why we are talking about a web server, as Internet Explorer can open Web files directly from the Windows Explorer. The trouble is that ASP files don't work if opened this way. Why is that? Well, a standard HTML file just contains text and HTML tags to tell the browser what the text should look like. There's an important point there – the HTML is interpreted by the browser. So the browser needs nothing else to be able to display a standard HTML page.

An ASP file however, is different, because not only does it contain HTML, it also contains scripting code. This is code, much like VBA, that is run by the Web server, before the ASP file is sent to the browser. In the case of the ASP pages shown in Chapter 17, here's what happens:

❑ The user requests the ASP page.

❑ The Web server finds the page and looks at the script in it.

❑ The script connects to the database and extracts the table details.

❑ The script then formats these table details into HTML.

❑ The Web server sends the HTML back to the user.

So the user only receives HTML, but to get that HTML the page has to be processed by a Web server. That's why we just can't open an ASP page directly in the browser – it has to go via the Web server.

Obtaining IIS and PWS

If you have Windows 98 (and possibly late versions of Windows 95) then PWS is included on the CD. It's not installed by default, but contains a simple installation program.

If you haven't got a copy on CD you can obtain PWS from the NT 4.0 Option Pack (you can get this from http://www.microsoft.com/ntserver/nts/downloads/recommended/NT4OptPk/ - just follow the download instructions). This contains versions for both NT and Windows 9x. The Option Pack contains several other programs (such as MTS), but they aren't required for PWS to run.

Virtual Directories

You know what a URL is, but what's virtual directory? Let's look at some of the Wrox Press Web Developer URLs:

```
http://webdev.wrox.co.uk
```

This is the top level (or root) URL. Physically this points to the main directory where PWS is installed – the default is C:\inetpub\wwwroot. To look at the books you could use this URL:

```
http://webdev.wrox.co.uk/books
```

Now you might think that if the top level URL points to C:\inetpub\wwwroot, then since the books URL is directly under the main URL, its directory would be C:\inetpub\wwwroot\books. This isn't always practical, since we might want to arrange our disks and directories in a more organized manner, so we created books as a Virtual Directory. That means that it doesn't really exist in the default directory, but points to somewhere else.

Creating Virtual Directories

You create a virtual directory from the Personal Web Manager, the administration interface for PWS, which itself is a set of web pages. Under Windows 95 and 98 this usually appears as a Tray Icon (once PWS has been installed). On Windows NT it can be found under the Windows NT 4.0 Option Pack folder. Once started you are greeted with the main page:

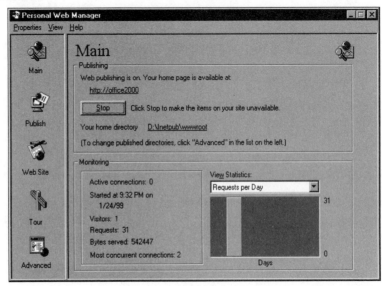

Here you can see the main URL for my machine, and the default directory. To create a virtual directory you need to select the **Advanced** option from the bottom left of the screen:

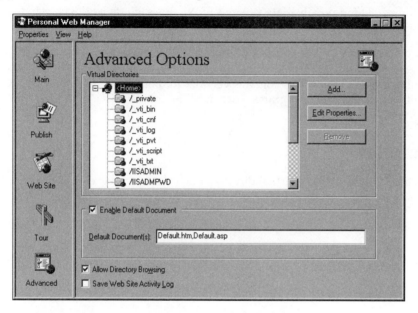

To add a new virtual directory you simply press the **Add...** button. Make sure you have the <Home> directory selected first, so that the new directory is created under it.

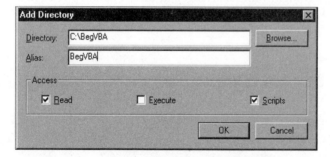

Here you can enter the physical directory, and the alias by which that directory will be know. Pressing OK here creates the virtual directory for you. You can now reference files in the virtual directory by adding the alias on to the end of the main URL for the site.

Default Documents and Directory Browsing

On the screen for the main options you may have noticed two options:

❑ **Enable Default Document.** If you don't explicitly state a document on the URL, then this option allows you to display a default document. If no default document is found, then an error is returned.

❑ Allow Directory Browsing. If no explicit document is requested, and there is no default document in the directory, then a listing of the directory is returned, much like a listing of files in Windows Explorer.

Directory browsing is extremely useful when testing as it allows you to quickly select files in the browser without having to explicitly type them in the URL. However, you should be wary of using directory browsing on live machines since it gives a complete list of every file in the virtual directory.

Localhost

Most URL's you see start with www, but if you are using your own machine you might not have all of these complex URL bits set up (it's part of networking). To get around this problem you can contact your local machine by the following:

```
http://localhost
```

This replaces the root part of the URL, and you can then add your virtual directories onto the end of this:

```
http://localhost/BegVBA
```

If you've got directory browsing enabled, and there's no default document, then this will show you a directory listing. Or, you can specify a document:

```
http://localhost/BegVBA/tblIceCream.asp
```

This tells the web server to fetch the specified ASP file.

Index

Index

Index

Index

Index

Index

Index

Index

Index